The JavaScript Workshop

A New, Interactive Approach
to Learning JavaScript

Joseph Labrecque, Jahred Love, Daniel Rosenbaum,
Nick Turner, Gaurav Mehla, Alonzo L. Hosford, Florian Sloot,
and Philip Kirkbride

The JavaScript Workshop

Authors: Joseph Labrecque, Jahred Love, Daniel Rosenbaum, Nick Turner, Gaurav Mehla, Alonzo L. Hosford, Florian Sloot, and Philip Kirkbride.

Reviewers: Andrew Artajos, Lior Avital, Archit Goyal, Christer Johansson, Peter Kehl, Gavin Orland, David Parker, Shubham Shrivatava, and Weijie (Kenvi) Zhu

Managing Editor: Vrushti Ajmera

Acquisitions Editor: Sarah Lawton

Production Editor: Shantanu Zagade

Editorial Board: Shubhopriya Banerjee, Bharat Botle, Ewan Buckingham, Megan Carlisle, Mahesh Dhyani, Manasa Kumar, Alex Mazonowicz, Bridget Neale, Dominic Pereira, Shiny Poojary, Abhishek Rane, Erol Staveley, Ankita Thakur, Nitesh Thakur, and Jonathan Wray

First published: November 2019

Production reference: 4040220

ISBN 978-1-83864-191-7

Published by Packt Publishing Ltd.

Livery Place, 35 Livery Street

Birmingham B3 2PB, UK

Experience the Workshop Online

Thank you for purchasing the print edition of *The JavaScript Workshop*. Every physical print copy includes free online access to the premium interactive edition. There are no extra costs or hidden charges.

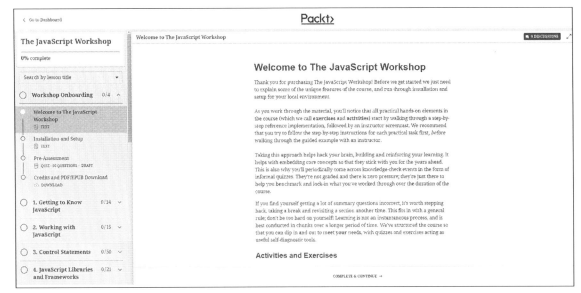

With the interactive edition you'll unlock:

- **Screencasts and Quizzes.** Supercharge your progress with screencasts of all exercises and activities. Take optional quizzes to help embed your new understanding.

- **Built-In Discussions.** Engage in discussions where you can ask questions, share notes and interact. Tap straight into insight from expert instructors and editorial teams.

- **Skill Verification.** Complete the course online to earn a Packt credential that is easy to share and unique to you. All authenticated on the public Bitcoin blockchain.

- **Download PDF and EPUB.** Download a digital version of the course to read offline. Available as PDF or EPUB, and always DRM-free.

To redeem your free digital copy of *The JavaScript Workshop* you'll need to follow these simple steps:

1. Visit us at https://courses.packtpub.com/pages/redeem.

2. Login with your Packt account, or register as a new Packt user.

3. Select your course from the list, making a note of the three page numbers for your product. Your unique redemption code needs to match the order of the pages specified.

4. Open up your print copy and find the codes at the bottom of the pages specified. They'll always be in the same place:

> Parameters can be optional, otherwise the wrong data can be passed. So, functions often have code that validates the parameter or provides a default value. In this example, the argument of the JavaScript built-in function known as **parseInt** is used to convert the argument into an integer. Its results are tested using the **isNaN** built-in function, which returns **true** or **false** if the number is not a number or the number is less than **1**. If any of that is true, the argument value is set to **1**. If not, the supplied number is passed through:

```
function getDiceRoll(numberOfDice){
  numberOfDice = (isNaN(parseInt(numberOfDice)) || numberOfDice< 1) ?1 :numberOfDice;
  var rollValue = 0;
  for (let i = 1; i<= numberOfDice; i++){
    rollValue += Math.floor(Math.random() * 6) + 1;
```

A B 2 1 C

5. Merge the codes together (without any spaces), ensuring they are in the correct order.

6. At checkout, click **Have a redemption code?** and enter your unique product string. Click **Apply**, and the price should be free!

Finally, we'd like to thank you for purchasing the print edition of *The JavaScript Workshop*! We hope that you finish the course feeling capable of tackling challenges in the real world. Remember that we're here to help if you ever feel like you're not making progress.

If you run into issues during redemption (or have any other feedback) you can reach us at workshops@packt.com.

Table of Contents

Chapter 2: Working with JavaScript   31

Chapter 8: Browser APIs   369

Preface

About

This section briefly introduces the coverage of this book, the technical skills you'll need to get started, and the hardware and software requirements required to complete all of the included activities and exercises.

About the Book

You already know you want to learn JavaScript, and a smarter way to learn JavaScript is to learn by doing. *The JavaScript Workshop* focuses on building up your practical skills so that you can develop cutting-edge applications for web, mobile, and desktop users. Alongside knowledge of HTML and CSS, JavaScript is a key skill for those looking to enter professional web development. You'll learn from real examples that lead to real results.

Throughout *The JavaScript Workshop*, you'll take an engaging step-by-step approach to understanding JavaScript code. You won't have to sit through any unnecessary theory. If you're short on time, you can jump into a single exercise each day or spend an entire weekend learning about functional programming. It's your choice. Learning on your terms, you'll build up and reinforce key skills in a way that feels rewarding.

Every physical copy of *The JavaScript Workshop* unlocks access to the interactive edition. With videos detailing all exercises and activities, you'll always have a guided solution. You can also benchmark yourself against assessments, track your progress, and receive content updates. You'll even earn a secure credential that you can share and verify online upon completion. It's a premium learning experience that's included with your printed copy. To redeem it, follow the instructions located at the start of your JavaScript book.

Fast-paced and direct, *The JavaScript Workshop* is the ideal companion for JavaScript beginners. You'll build and iterate on your JavaScript coding skills like a real software developer, learning along the way. This process means that you'll find that your new skills stick, embedded as best practice – a solid foundation for the years ahead.

About the Chapters

Chapter 1, Getting to Know JavaScript, introduces a foundational background of JavaScript in order to move forward and achieve competency. This chapter introduces you to JavaScript, through its history through to modern implementations, with additional information on various uses of the language to provide a proper context for what comes next.

Chapter 2, Working with JavaScript, covers some hands-on work with the language. We'll provide an overview of some popular tools for writing JavaScript and the various available runtimes for executing their code. We'll pay particular attention to the primary target for most JavaScript and a great tool in itself, the modern web browser.

Chapter 3, Programming Fundamentals, serves as an introduction to the fundamental concepts and structures involved when working in JavaScript and programming in general. We'll cover all the basics, from object types to conditionals and looping structures, how to go about writing and invoking functions, and even commenting and debugging their code.

Chapter 4, JavaScript Libraries and Frameworks, focuses on plain-old vanilla JavaScript, along with various frameworks and libraries that exist today. The primary focus of this chapter is to provide an understanding that while extensions to the core language can be great, sometimes, core JavaScript is really all you need.

Chapter 5, Beyond the Fundamentals, explains that data is represented differently in different languages and runtimes. JavaScript is based on the ECMAScript specification and has definitive rules for how data is represented. This chapter discusses data in JavaScript, how to convert between types, and how types are passed around within a script.

Chapter 6, Understanding Core Concepts, utilizes an HTML page using JavaScript in this book, as well as being the first to explain the abstract nature of the event messaging system. Understanding these concepts is very valuable when building a useful web application in JavaScript. Throughout this chapter, you will explore the various nuances of event message bubbling and capturing, along with how it can best be used to control the flow of information within an application. You will also see how to halt these events in their tracks and to create your own custom events. This chapter will give you a foundational arsenal at your disposal to tackle applications of any size or complexity.

Chapter 7, Popping the Hood, clarifies how the thing many people think of as 'just JavaScript' can actually be broken down into separate components: the JavaScript engine, consisting of the call stack, memory heap, and the garbage collector; and the JavaScript runtime environment, such as a browser, or Node.js, which contains the JavaScript engine, and gives the engine access to additional functions and interfaces, such as `setTimeout()` or a filesystem interface. We will also look at how JavaScript manages memory allocation and deallocation, and how even though it is managed automatically, it's important for developers to bear in mind the processes involved, in order to write code that enables the garbage collector to work correctly.

Chapter 8, Browser APIs, introduces a few of the most useful and interesting browser APIs that open up wide-ranging functionality that we can make use of in our JavaScript application. We'll see that while these APIs are most commonly accessed through JavaScript, they are not a part of the ECMAScript specification to which the JavaScript engines are programmed and are not part of JavaScript core functionality.

Chapter 9, Working with Node.js, guides us in unifying the entire web application development around a single programming language, as opposed to learning different languages and building different projects for server-side and client-side. In this chapter, you will go through how the node is working in the background and how it is processing requests asynchronously. Furthermore, you will study different types of modules and how to use them. You will also do a lot of important exercises to gain practical exposure.

Chapter 10, Accessing External Resources, explores the fact that web pages are static and of limited use without fresh data. This chapter covers various approaches to using Ajax to obtain data, primarily from RESTful services.

Chapter 11, Creating Clean and Maintainable Code, introduces you to best practices for clean and maintainable coding. You will learn that refactored code that uses clean coding techniques results in code that is much longer than before. But you will see that the code is much cleaner and easier to understand and test compared to the original. The value of this programming style really shows itself more in complex real-world applications, and it is good practice to work this way. Developers and tech leads need to decide what standards and clean coding practices make sense for their particular project.

Chapter 12, Using Next-Generation JavaScript, looks at the various tools available in the market for advanced development in JavaScript. We will learn how to use the latest JavaScript syntax in older browsers and identify the different options for the development of JavaScript applications in other languages. We will also explore various package managers, such as npm and Yarn, that are compatible with JavaScript, along with several different frameworks, such as AngularJS, React, and Vue.js. Finally, we will look at some server-side libraries, such as Express, Request, and Socket.IO.

Chapter 13, JavaScript Programming Paradigms, teaches you that JavaScript is a multi-paradigm programming language. We can use it to write code in procedural, object-oriented, and functional design patterns. During the learning phase of any programming language, people usually code in a procedural way where, instead of planning, they put most of their focus on the execution and understanding the concepts of that particular programming language. But when it comes to practical execution in real life, the **object-oriented programming** paradigm, or **OOP,** is a scalable option.

Chapter 14, Understanding Functional Programming, discusses how functional programming is quite different from other programming paradigms such as imperative and object-oriented approaches, and it takes some getting used to. But, properly applied, it is a very powerful way of structuring programs to be more declarative, correct, and testable with fewer errors. Even if you don't use pure functional programming in your projects, there are many useful techniques that can be used on their own. This is especially true for the `map`, `reduce`, and `filter` array methods, which can have many applications. The topics covered in this chapter will help you bolster the skills you need to pursue a programming project in the functional style.

Chapter 15, Asynchronous Tasks, discusses how asynchronous tasks allow the execution of the main thread of a program to proceed even while waiting for data, an event, or the result of another process, and achieve snappier UIs and some forms of multitasking. Recent enhancements to the language, such as promises and the `async/await` keywords, simplify such development and make it easier to write clean and maintainable asynchronous code.

> **Note**
>
> You can avail the bonus chapters on https://courses.packtpub.com/

Conventions

Code words in text, database table names, folder names, filenames, file extensions, pathnames, dummy URLs, user input, and Twitter handles are shown as follows:

"The `if`, `else if`, and `else` statements give you four structures for selecting or skipping blocks of code."

Words that you see on the screen, for example, in menus or dialog boxes, also appear in the text like this: "Press the F12 key to launch the debugger or select **More Tools | Developer Tools** from the menu."

A block of code is set as follows:

```
function logAndReturn( value ) {
  console.log("logAndReturn:" +value );
  return value;
}
if ( logAndReturn (true) || logAndReturn (false)) {
  console.log("|| operator returned truthy.");
}
```

New terms and important words are shown like this: "**Timer events** provide forced asynchronous functionality within your applications. They allow you to invoke a function after a period of time; either once or repeatedly."

Long code snippets are truncated and the corresponding names of the code files on GitHub are placed at the top of the truncated code. The permalinks to the entire code are placed below the code snippet. It should appear as follows:

`activity.html`

```
1  <!doctype html>
2  <html lang="en">
3  <head>
4      <meta charset="utf-8">
5      <title>To-Do List</title>
6      <link href=https://fonts.googleapis.com/
         css?family=Architects+Daughter|Bowlby+One+SC rel="stylesheet">
7      <style>
8          body {
9              background-color:rgb(37, 37, 37);
10             color:aliceblue;
11             padding:2rem;
12             margin:0;
13             font-family:'Architects Daughter', cursive;
14             font-size: 12px;
15         }
```

The full code is available at: https://packt.live/2Xc9Y4o

Before You Begin

Each great journey begins with a humble step. Our upcoming adventure with JavaScript programming is no exception. Before we can do awesome things using JavaScript, we need to be prepared with a productive environment. In this short note, we will see how to do that. If you have any issues or questions about installation please email us at **workshops@packt.com**.

Installing Visual Studio Code

Here are the steps to install Visual Studio Code (VSCode):

1. Download the latest VSCode from https://packt.live/2BIlniA:

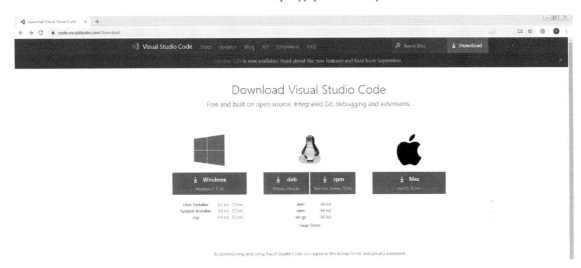

Figure 0.1: Downloading VSCode

2. Open the downloaded file, follow the installation steps, and complete the installation process.

Installing the "Open in Default Browser" Extension

1. Open your VSCode, click on the **Extensions** icon, and type in **Open In Default Browser** in the search bar, as shown in the following screenshot:

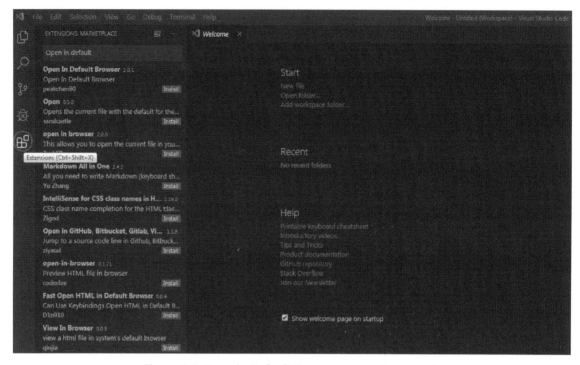

Figure 0.2: Open in Default Browser extension search

2. Click on **Install** to complete the installation process, as shown in the following screenshot:

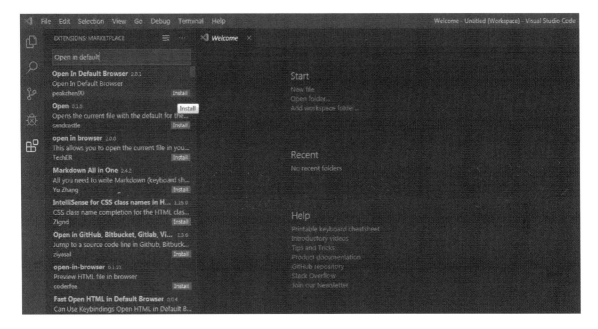

Figure 0.3: Installing the extension

Downloading Node.js

Node.js is open source and you can download it from its official website https://nodejs. org/en/download/ for all platforms. It supports all three major platforms: Windows, Linux, and macOS.

Windows

Visit their official website and download the latest stable .MSI installer. The process is very simple. Just execute the **.MSI** file and follow the instructions to install it on the system. There will be some prompts about accepting license agreements. You have to accept those and then click on **Finish**. That's it.

Mac

You have to download the .pkg file from the official website and execute it. Then, follow the instructions. You may have to accept the license agreement. After that, follow the prompts to finish the installation process.

Linux

In order to install Node.js on Linux, execute the following commands as root in the same order they are mentioned:

- `$ cd /tmp`

- `$ wget http://nodejs.org/dist/v8.11.2/node-v8.11.2-linux-x64.tar.gz`

- `$ tar xvfz node-v8.11.2-linux-x64.tar.gz`

- `$ mkdir -p /usr/local/nodejs`

- `$ mv node-v8.11.2-linux-x64./* /usr/local/nodejs`

Here, you first change the current active directory to the temporary directory (**tmp**) of the system. Second, you download the **tar** package of the **node** from their official distribution directory. Third, you extract the **tar** package to the **tmp** directory. This directory contains all the compiled and executable files. Fourth, you create a directory in the system for **Node.js**. In the last command, you are moving all the complied and executable files of the package to that directory.

Verifying the Installation

After the installation process, you can verify whether it is installed properly in the system by executing the following command in the directory of Node.js:

```
$ node -v && npm -v
```

It will output the current installed version of Node.js and npm:

Figure 0.4: Installed version of Node.js and npm

Here, it is showing that the 8.11.2 version of Node.js is installed on the system, as is the 5.6.0 version of npm.

Installing the Code Bundle

Download the code and relevant files from GitHub at https://github.com/PacktWorkshops/The-JavaScript-Workshop and place them in a new folder called C:\Code on your local system. Refer to these code files for the complete code bundle.

Getting to Know JavaScript

Overview

By the end of this chapter, you will be able to locate JavaScript elements along with other code elements in a web browser; identify different versions of JavaScript supported by various web browsers; construct simple JavaScript commands; discuss the range of modern approaches to JavaScript; describe JavaScript's capabilities and create an alert box popup in a web browser.

This chapter describes the foundational background of JavaScript so that we can move forward and achieve competency with this widely used programming language.

Introduction

JavaScript is a language with had interesting beginnings. In its early days, it was not taken very seriously—the only widely accepted, functionally correct use for the language was to perform client-side validation of form data. Many developers only copied and pasted simple code snippets that performed a single action on a website they were building. All these code snippets did were very simple actions such as reveal an alert to the user or provide a date countdown—simple logic.

Today, JavaScript is a whole different beast—and one with the power to literally build out entire HTML documents, revise CSS styling on the fly, and securely transport and interpret data from various remote sources. Whereas in times past, HTML was the primary technology on the web, in the present era, JavaScript is king.

Any introduction to JavaScript requires a foundational background of the history and origins of the language in order to move forward and achieve competency. This chapter introduces us to JavaScript, from its history to modern implementations. It also provides us with additional information on various uses of the language so that we can provide a proper context for what comes next.

What Is JavaScript and How Is It Used?

JavaScript is a weakly-typed, multi-paradigm, event-driven, object-oriented programming language. It includes the ability to work with strings, dates, arrays, objects, and more. It is generally used on the client-side within web browser environments but can also be used in other environments such as servers and desktop applications. The runtime environment is very important for JavaScript—especially since it, by itself, does not include any networking, file, graphics, or storage capabilities on its own.

JavaScript versus Other Languages

If you are approaching JavaScript with experience in other languages such as Java or Python, things might seem a bit odd. While many languages (such as Java) must be compiled to run, JavaScript is run exactly as-is and does not require this additional step.

Though the language is used within many environments and for many purposes, JavaScript is fundamentally one of the three languages that are native to the web. The other two languages are the HTML semantic markup language and the CSS styling and layout language. All three are very different from one another in purpose and function, but they are all meant to work together in a single environment. Let's go over them:

- **Hypertext Markup Language (HTML)**: This is the most fundamental of these three languages as it defines the elements that compose an HTML page and defines the flow of basic information that's presented to the user.

- **Cascading Style Sheets (CSS)**: This is used to define a set of stylistic layout rules, which adds visual flourish and advanced layout to defined HTML elements.

- **JavaScript(JS)**: This works to enable interactivity in web pages and is what will be the focus of this book.

With all three of these languages, there is a basic understanding of the separation of concerns, that is, HTML provides the content and structure, CSS provides the styling and layout, and JavaScript provides the interactivity. While this understanding still holds sway, many frameworks do not exactly abide by this separation and mix these various languages together in some shape or form. Some developers are okay with this, while others are not. It's definitely an issue to be aware of when getting into this field, but it is ultimately up to you which stance you take, based on your particular needs. In my opinion, there is no hard and fast answer to a question like this.

Exercise 1.01: Languages Discovery

Let's go ahead and examine a website to see whether we can spot how HTML, JavaScript, and CSS are all represented. You can choose any website you like for this exercise.

> **Note**
>
> All the examples and screenshots in this book will use Google Chrome as the web browser of choice. You can use the browser you prefer, though some of the steps that are shown may differ between various browsers.

Let's get started:

1. Within your web browser, enter a URL in the address bar and press *Enter/Return* to load the chosen resource. For this example, let's use https://angular.io/–the Angular website. Of course, you can choose any website that you'd like to explore.

2. Now, right-click anywhere within the browser viewport to summon a contextual menu. Select the option that allows you to view the source code of the page. In Chrome, this is labeled `View Page Source`.

3. The source code for the page will then appear in a new tab. You can examine how the page is structured and pick out the various HTML, CSS, and JavaScript elements from the bare source code:

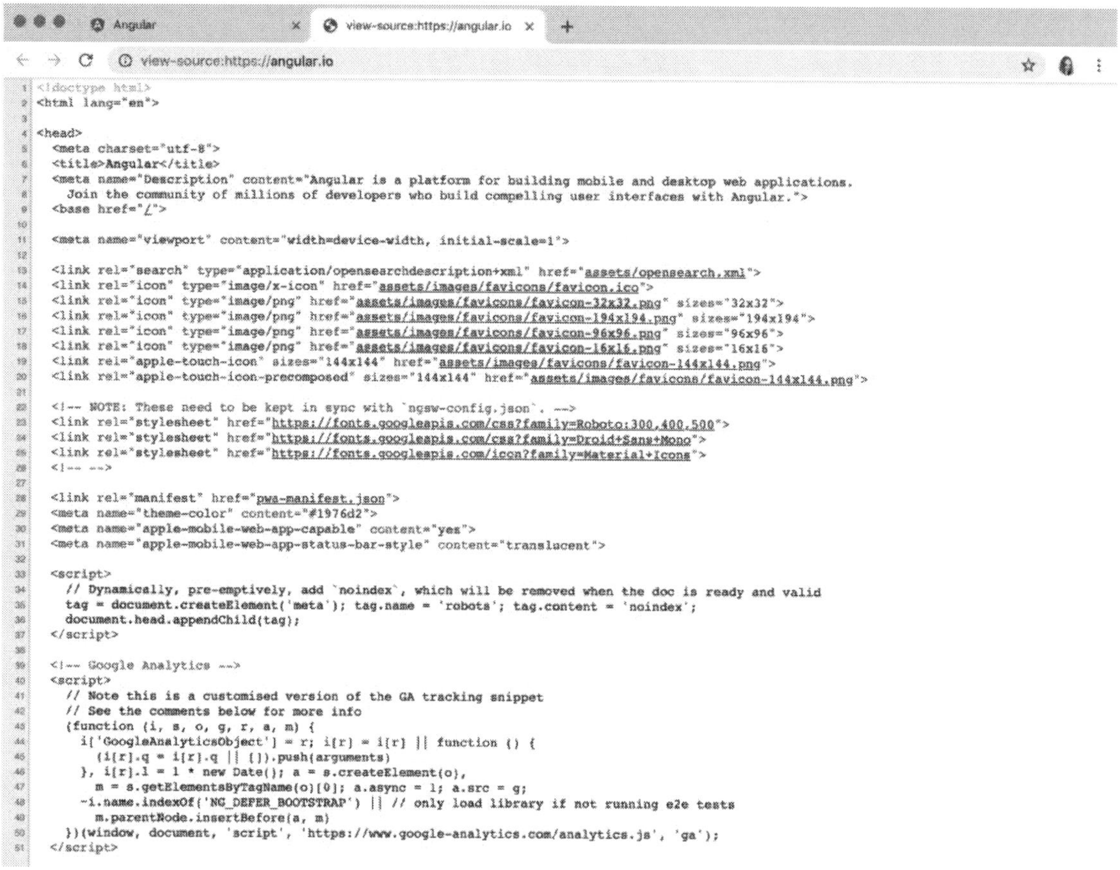

Figure 1.1: Much can be learned from examining the bare source code

4. With the source code exposed, scroll down and identify the various HTML elements within the page structure. You'll likely find a **\<head\>**tag and a **\<body\>**tag (which are mandatory), along with various **\<p\>** and **\<h1\>** to **\<h6\>** tags within the page.

Here is an example of some basic HTML content (not actually from the Angular website):

```
<body>
<h1>Welcome!</h1>
<p>Angular is a framework used to build web applications.</p>
<p>Create high-performing and accessible applications using Angular.</p>
</body>
```

5. Now, try and locate either embedded CSS rules within a **<style>** element, or even a linked CSS file. Here is an example of some embedded CSS:

```
<style>
color: red;
margin-top: 40px;
position: relative;
text-align center;
</style>
```

And here is a linked CSS file:

```
<link rel="stylesheet"href="styles.css">
```

6. Finally, we'll locate some JavaScript. Much like CSS, JavaScript can be found embedded within a page using the **<script>** tag, or entire JavaScript files can be linked though a similar mechanism. Here, we are locating some embedded JavaScript:

```
<script>
function writeMessage() {
document.getElementById("message").innerHTML = "Hello From
JavaScript!";
}
</script>
```

Here is a linked JavaScript file:

```
<script src="main.js"></script>
```

Choosing to view the source code of public web pages like this was once a common way to learn about web technologies.

> **Note**
>
> In various websites and examples, you may see a **type** attribute included with the **<script>** tag specifying **type="text/javascript"**. In HTML5, this is not necessary and is the default attribute. If you must target previous versions of HTML, you will need to specify it.

So far, we have introduced the JavaScript programming language and examined its primary runtime environment (the web browser). We also had a brief look at JavaScript's relationship to HTML and CSS as one of the three native web technologies.

In the next section, we'll take a look at the history of JavaScript and how it has evolved over the years.

A Brief History of the JavaScript Language

We've seen how JavaScript is often integrated within a web environment, but how did this language come about? We need to go back to the early 1990s and understand what the web looked like in those days before we begin talking about JavaScript itself.

The story really begins with Netscape and the web browser they created named **Netscape Navigator**. This new browser was based on the successful Mosaic web browser with the intent to commercialize it. During that time, and depending on who you speak to, Netscape Navigator was the web browser of choice to develop for. Around the middle of the decade, Microsoft released its **Internet Explorer** browser, which ignited the first browser wars.

Netscape Mocha and LiveScript

Around this same time, Netscape hired Brendan Eich to develop a programming language for Netscape's web browser. Eich took inspiration from Scheme (Lisp), Self, and most importantly, Java. The work on this language, then called **Mocha**, was initially (and infamously) completed in the time span of only 10 days. With the initial version completed, Netscape changed their name and began calling it **LiveScript**.

It turned out that LiveScript, as a language name, was just as temporary as Mocha until Netscape partnered with a certain other large company to advance the idea of a two-pronged approach to web development.

Sun Microsystems and Java

The popular Java language came into play with a partnership between Netscape and Sun Microsystems. Sun was looking at the web as the next step for Java, and Netscape was looking for allies in the coming war against Microsoft, so an allegiance was formed. The language being developed by Eich was from then on named **JavaScript** as it was meant to work alongside Java in the web browser as a more approachable way to add interactivity to that environment.

This would mean that the Java language would be what *serious* developers used to write interactive content for the web, while JavaScript would provide similar interactive capabilities but was geared more toward *hobbyists* and those who wanted to tinker.

> **Note**
>
> What happened, of course, was quite different. JavaScript was integrated into the browser well before Java was, and, once Java came on board, it was only through the use of applets. With Java applets falling out of popularity quite some time ago, we are left with JavaScript alone today and not the two languages that were initially envisioned, though the *JavaScript* name has stuck.

Ecma International and ECMAScript

Ecma adopted and standardized the specification and renamed the language itself to ECMAScript, with JavaScript becoming the commercial implementation of that specification. Ecma International remains the organization that develops and publishes the ECMAScript specification and all the new versions of it, which eventually influence the JavaScript language.

In this section, we read about how JavaScript came to be and performed a quick exercise that showed how it can be examined live within the web browser itself. At this point, you should have a pretty good idea of exactly what JavaScript is, where it came from, and how it operates.

In the next section, we'll look at some more history behind this language by examining the version history of JavaScript beyond ECMA standardization.

Versions of ECMAScript (and JavaScript)

With JavaScript now granted Ecma International standardization and the ECMAScript specification, it also needed to follow standard versioning practices. For the first few iterations of the language, this didn't mean much to developers. However, as you will see, as needs grew and the language evolved, major changes would be coming to ECMAScript. They would, in some cases, flow on to JavaScript, and in other cases die altogether.

ECMAScript 1 (1997)

The first version to undergo standardization codified its features more or less from LiveScript. This version is sometimes referred to as **ECMAScript First Edition**.

It generally corresponds to JavaScript version 1.3.

ECMAScript 2 (1998)

This release saw few changes aside from edits to better conform with established standards. It should probably have been labeled version 1.1.

It also generally corresponds to JavaScript version 1.3.

ECMAScript 3 (1999)

This version of ECMAScript added some fundamental, yet expected (necessary), language enhancements. One of the most important of these is the use of **regular expressions (regex)**, which allows complex pattern matching within text data. The `try`... `catch` conditional structure was also introduced, providing an alternative to the more basic `if`...`else` statement, allowing more sophisticated error handling. The `in` operator was also introduced. This generally corresponds to JavaScript version 1.5.

ECMAScript 4 (unreleased)

This release included real classes, modules, generators, static typing, and many language features that were added to the specification many years later.

> **Note**
>
> Eventually, due to committee and corporate infighting, ECMAScript 4 was completely abandoned. Instead, it was replaced with incremental improvements to ECMAScript 3, also known as ECMAScript 3.1.

At this time, Adobe decided to base a complete revision of the ActionScript language (ActionScript 3.0 on this new ECMAScript version. It was an attempt to closely align the language behind the Flash Player and the browsers that commonly hosted it. Here is an example of a basic ActionScript 3.0 class—note that it's quite different from previous versions of ECMAScript:

```
package com.josephlabrecque {

import flash.display.MovieClip;

public class Main extends MovieClip {

public function Main() {
// constructor code
}

}

}
```

ECMAScript 5 (2009)

This version is, in actuality, ECMAScript 3.1, with version 4 completely abandoned. This was more of a politically motived release than anything of substance, though certain bug fixes from ECMAScript 4 were included, along with strict mode, JSON support, and a number of additional methods for working with arrays.

This generally corresponds to JavaScript version 1.8.5 and is the version of JavaScript that conforms to most browsers today.

ECMAScript 6 (2015)

Features including arrow functions, maps, typed-arrays, promises, and many more were introduced with this version of ECMAScript, and many of them form the basis for modern development with JavaScript today. This specification also allows for the writing of classes and modules—finally. The following table explains the browser support for ES6:

Browser Support for ES6 (ECMAScript 2015)

Browser	Version	Date
Chrome	58	Apr 2017
Firefox	54	Jun 2017
Edge	14	Aug 2016
Safari	10	Sep 2016
Opera	55	Aug 2017

Internet Explorer does not support ECMAScript 2015.

Figure 1.2: Browser support table for ECMAScript 2015 via w3schools.com

This version of JavaScript is generally SVG supported by modern web browsers and is a major functional release.

ECMAScript 7 (2016), ECMAScript 8 (2017), and ECMAScript 9 (2018)

All versions post2015 have been incremental, with yearly modifications to what was established in ECMAScript 6. This has happened for a number of reasons:

- It establishes that this is a stable, mature language without the need for major disruption.

- It allows developers and browser vendors to easily keep up with the changes and enhancements that are adopted.

- It provides a stable release cycle for new versions of the specification:

Browser Support for ES7 (ECMAScript 2016)

Browser	Version	Date
Chrome	68	May 2018
Opera	47	Jul 2018

Figure 1.3: Browser support table for ECMAScript 2016 via w3schools.com

When writing in ECMAScript 2015 (or "ES6") and later, you will likely need to transpile your JavaScript down to a previous version so that it can be understood by the JavaScript engines within the current web browsers. While this is an additional step, the tooling to process tasks such as this has become more approachable in recent years.

Exercise 1.02: Can I Use This Feature?

There is no easy way to tell which versions of JavaScript are supported by which browsers—a more reliable approach is to test whether features you wish to use are supported by the engine currently running the code. Let's take a look at the **Can I Use** table:

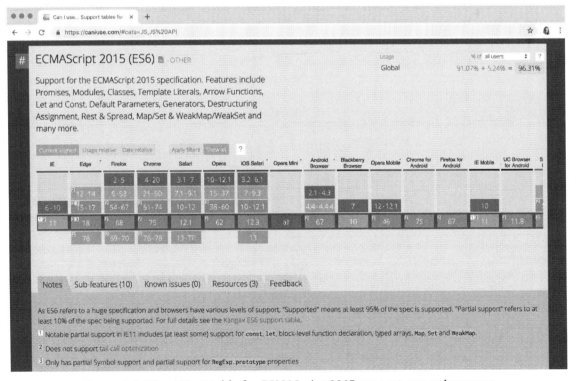

Figure 1.4: "Can I Use" table for ECMAScript 2015 support across browsers

To help us do this, there are a number of resources and services on the web that keep track of JavaScript features and the level of support within each browser. Probably, the most popular of these is the **Can I Use** table, which includes an abundance of support information around CSS, JavaScript, SVG, HTML5, and more.

Let's go ahead and check out the support for **Promise.prototype.finally**, which was first implemented in ECMAScript 2018:

1. Open a web browser and instruct it to load https://caniuse.com/. Notice that you have immediate access to the latest and most searched features directly from the home page, without even searching:

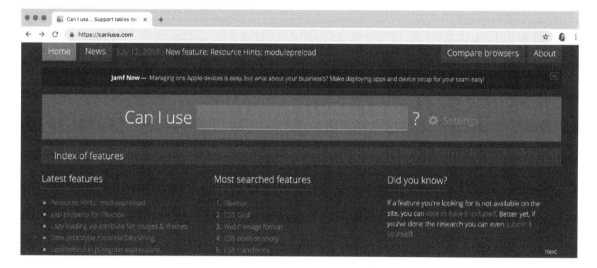

Figure 1.5: The Can I Use website

2. We are looking for something specific, though. Locate the search area toward the top, which reads **Can I use** _ _ _ _ _ _ _ _ _ _ _?,and type in `finally`, since we want to see which browsers support `Promise.prototype.finally`. The results for our search will be displayed automatically within a colored grid:

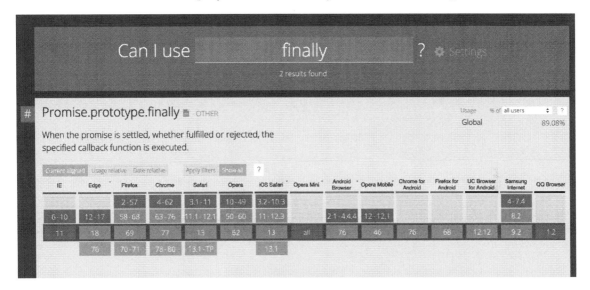

Figure 1.6: The grid of browser support for Promise.prototype.finally

Note that certain blocks are red, while others are green. A red color indicates that the feature is unsupported, and green indicates that the feature is supported. You may also see a yellow color, indicating partial support.

3. If you want to see the specifics pertaining to a certain browser version, hover your cursor over the indicated version or version range and a small overlay will appear with additional information such as the date of version release and even usage statistics for that version:

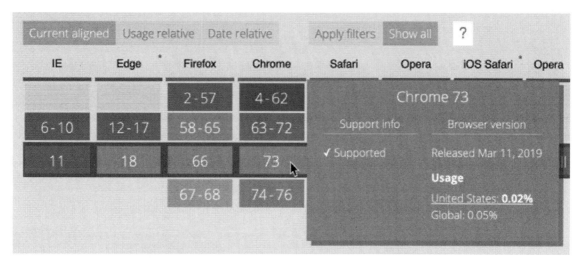

Figure 1.7: Specific support information for Chrome 73

Go ahead and search for additional options within the interface—there is a lot to explore.

In this section, we reviewed the different versions of ECMAScript and looked at how the features of JavaScript, which originated from those particular specifications, are supported within web browsers today.

In the next section, we'll look at how to access the web browser developer tools in order to get a better view of what JavaScript is doing—and even write JavaScript live in the browser.

Accessing Web Browser Developer Tools

Our understanding of JavaScript's relationship with the web browser is becoming clearer with each topic that we discuss. In the previous exercise, we saw how to dig in and discover the different levels of JavaScript feature support across different web browsers. That leads us directly to have a look at the various browsers themselves, as well as the tools that are available within each for inspecting and even writing JavaScript code.

Browsers are built to abide by standards such as HTML and CSS. However, there are many differences in both the interpretation of these standards and in the tooling available with each major web browser. When writing JavaScript for the web browser, it is important to know how to access and use the browser developer tools—*especially* the JavaScript console tab.

Google Chrome

Chrome is the most popular web browser at the time of this writing—this fact holds true for both general users and developers. Chrome was initially released in September 2008 and is now available on multiple desktops and mobile operating systems.

> **Note**
>
> You can download Google Chrome from https://www.google.com/chrome/browser/.

To access developer tools and the JavaScript console within Chrome, you can right-click anywhere in the viewport and choose **Inspect** from the menu that appears. Alternatively, press **F12**. Once the developer tools are open, click on the **Console** tab to inspect and write JavaScript code within Chrome itself:

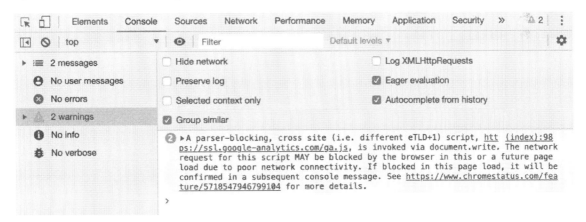

Figure 1.8: Google Chrome Developer Tools

Using the Chrome developer tools, you can filter the sort of things that show errors, warnings, or even just information such as that returned by **console.log()**. You can even write JavaScript within the browser using the **Console** tab view, as you'll see shortly. There is also a **Sources** tab, which allows for modifying and debugging of code.

Microsoft Edge

Having once reigned as the most used web browser in the world, Internet Explorer reached its final version with IE11. This doesn't mean that Microsoft is finished with web browsers though, as, with the release of Windows 10, the newly created Edge browser was made available to users as a replacement in July 2015.

> **Note**
>
> Microsoft Edge comes installed with Windows 10 (https://www.microsoft.com/windows).

To access the developer tools and the JavaScript console within Edge, you can right-click anywhere in the viewport and choose **Inspect Element** from the menu that appears. Alternatively, press **F12**:

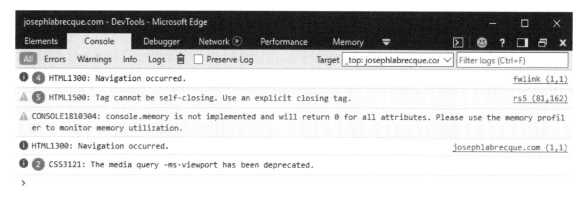

Figure 1.9: Microsoft Edge Developer Tools

The developer tools in Microsoft Edge are pretty ugly, aren't they? Much like other browsers, Edge's developer tools include a **Console** and a JavaScript **Debugger** view. Similar to Chrome, you can also filter the types of output present in the **Console** itself as your code executes.

> **Note**
>
> As of this writing, Microsoft Edge is being rewritten based on a Chromium base. This will mean that Chrome, Opera, Safari, and Edge will eventually make use of the exact same browser technologies under the hood.

Apple Safari

On Apple macOS and iOS operating systems, Safari is the default web browser and is tightly integrated into the user experience on those machines. Similar to Windows and Internet Explorer/Edge, many users will never deviate from the browser that is preinstalled on their machine.

Safari was once even available on Windows, but development ceased with the final Windows version in 2012.

> **Note**
>
> Apple Safari comes installed with Apple macOS (https://www.apple.com/macos/).

To access the developer tools and the JavaScript console within Safari, you must first tweak some of the preferences within the browser itself. Let's get started:

1. First, access the preferences dialog by choosing **Safari | Preferences** through the **Application** menu.

2. Within the **Preferences** dialog, click on the tab called **Advanced**.

3. Once the contents of the **Advanced** tab has appeared, look to the bottom and enable the **Show Develop menu in menu bar** option:

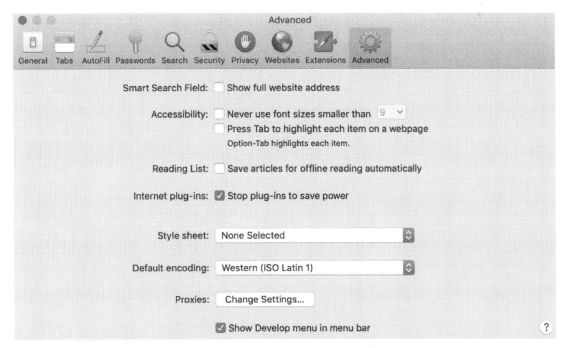

Figure 1.10: Apple Safari Advanced Preferences

4. With that option enabled, close the **Preferences** dialog.

5. Now, choose the newly enabled **Develop** option from the **Application** menu and select **Show JavaScript Console** to display the developer tools. You can also right-click and choose **Inspect Element** as well.

The good news is that once the **Develop** menu is enabled, it will remain so between sessions. You'll only need to open the developer tools to access these features:

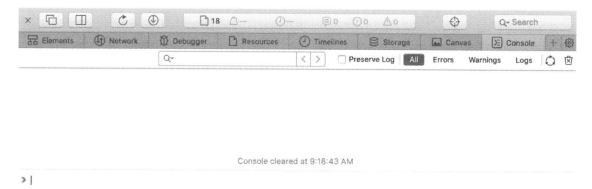

Figure 1.11: Apple Safari Developer Tools

Today, Safari does seem to lag behind most other browsers in adopting certain features, but you will find Apple's version of the **Console** and **Debugger** views in the developer tools all the same.

An Introduction to Variables

In almost any language, JavaScript included, the first step to programming is to understand the common variable. A variable can be thought of as an identifier for a certain piece of data. To declare a variable in JavaScript, we use the reserved word **var**:

```
var name;
```

In the preceding example, we declare a variable with the **name** identifier. Our variable does not have any data associated with it yet. For that, we must use an assignment operator:

```
name = "Joseph";
```

Since the variable name has already been declared, we no longer need to use **var** to declare it in this second step. We simply address the variable by its **name** and then follow that with an assignment operator of = and then a value, in this case, **"Joseph"**. Of course, you will likely want to use your own name here.

We terminate each line of code with a ; for convention and readability. Note that we can also perform the variable declaration and assignment in a single line of code:

```
var name = "Joseph";
```

You now know the foundations of how to declare and assign data values to a variable.

Exercise 1.03: Programming First Steps

Let's go ahead and step through a few bits of JavaScript code within the developer tools console before moving on. If you have your browser developer tools still open from the preceding section. If not, refer to the *Accessing Web Browser Developer Tools* section of this chapter to access the console.

With the console now available within the web browser, we'll step through a few basic JavaScript declarations:

1. Within the console, type in the following code and hit *Enter*:

    ```
    var myCity= "London";
    ```

    This declares a variable with the identifying name of **myCity**. This will allow you to invoke this variable later on.

2. Since this variable is now defined in memory, we can address it whenever we like. Type the following within the console and hit *Enter*:

    ```
    alert("Welcome to " + myCity + "!");
    ```

An alert will pop up over the browser viewport stating, **"Welcome to London!"**. To achieve the full greeting, we will also add additional string information to the variable using concatenation with the **+** operator. This allows us to mix variable values and plain text data together in our output.

Now, you know how to write values to a named variable and how to read those values out by using the variable name.

Activity 1.01: Creating an Alert Box Popup in the Web Browser

In this activity, you will call JavaScript and witness its tight relationship to the web browser. You will learn how to execute an alert within the web browser environment using the browser developer tools.

> **Note**
>
> We'll be using Google Chrome for the following instructions and output images. Other browsers will differ slightly.

Steps:

1. Press F12 to open the developer tools. Alternatively, a right-click may expose a menu from which you can select **Inspect**.

2. Activate the **Console** tab. The developer tools may default to this view. If not, there is likely a **Console** tab you can click on to activate it.

3. Within the console, write the JavaScript command.

4. Hit *Return/Enter* to execute the code.

Expected output:

The output should be similar to this:

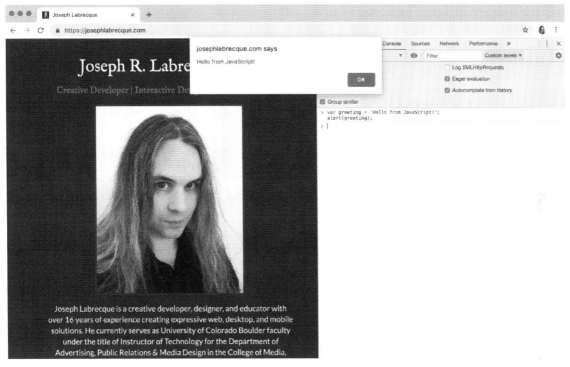

Figure 1.12: An alert appears with our message

> **Note**
>
> The solution to this activity can be found on page 710.

In this section, we had a look at how to access the web browser developer tools across a variety of popular browsers and had a look at some of the different views that can be accessed within.

In the next section, we'll get an overview of exactly what JavaScript is used for and take a general look at the capabilities of the language.

Overview of JavaScript Capabilities

Without JavaScript, the web would be a fairly bland and non-interactive experience. As one of the core technologies used to build the web alongside HTML and CSS, JavaScript is immensely important for anyone working with these technologies today. JavaScript allows us to perform complex interactions, ferry data into your application, and display restructured values within web views. It even has the ability to build, destroy, and otherwise modify an entire HTML document.

Client-Side Form Validation

Forms are everywhere on the web—and the HTML specification includes a wide variety of inputs, checkboxes, radio groups, text areas, and more. Often, even before this data hits the server, you'll want to have some logic that looks for certain formatting peculiarities or other aberrations that are present that have been entered by the user. You can trigger initial client-side validation once the **Submit** button has been clicked, or even as each input loses focus:

Figure 1.13: Form validation on a login

This is likely one of the most common uses for JavaScript on the web: you can provide basic feedback letting the user know they've done something in error—in this case, invalid login credentials.

JavaScript Widgets or Components

Whether using JavaScript snippets supplied by a component library such as **Bootstrap** or **jQuery UI**, or code supplied by specific vendors and services, people have been using JavaScript to include functional widgets and components for over two decades now. It truly is one of the most common uses for JavaScript on the web.

Normally, you are supplied a bit of code that often consists of both HTML and JavaScript. When it is run on the page, there is often either an embedded JavaScript library from which it can call functions, or a remote one, which then transforms the blank slate snippet into a fully functional piece of content for a specific purpose:

Figure 1.14: Embeddable Twitter widget

One of the best examples of a JavaScript-based component, or widget, is that of the Twitter timeline embed. You'll find similar embed types for Instagram and other social networks. Nearly all of them use JavaScript to insert dynamic content into a document.

> **Note**
>
> This is different from an **<iframe>** embed, in that with an **<iframe>** element, you are simply pulling in content from a remote resource and not building it on the fly.

XML HTTP Requests (XHR)

This technology was born from the concept of **Rich Internet Applications (RIA)**, which has been dominated by technologies such as Adobe Flash Player and Microsoft Silverlight around the turn of the century. What made RIAs great is that you no longer had to refresh the browser view in its entirety in order to see changes in data presented in the browser DOM. Using something such as Flash Player as a visual interactive layer, ActionScript could be used within the application to perform all the tasks related to retrieving data in the background, with the user interface then changes based on the data retrieved. In this way, the user was presented with a much better experience as the entire document wouldn't have to load and reload with every server interaction.

As developers began searching for ways to accomplish this same thing without the use of additional technologies, **XMLHttpRequest(XHR)** was introduced as part of Microsoft Internet Explorer in 1999 as **XMLHTTP**. Other browser makers, recognizing the obvious benefits of this implementation, went on to standardize it across their interpretations as **XMLHttpRequest**.

> **Note**
>
> Previous to this more modern naming, XHR was commonly referred to as Asynchronous JavaScript and XML, abbreviated as AJAX. When people refer to AJAX, they are referring to the XHR API.

Press F12 and navigate to **Network** | **Preview** to view the XHR network preview in your browser:

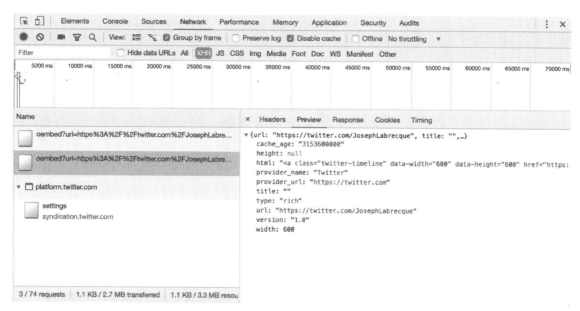

Figure 1.15: XHR network preview in Chrome

Browser developer tools all have a way of inspecting the files and data that are being transferred to and from the browser pertaining to the current website. For XHR, you can view raw header information, a formatted preview, and more.

Storing Local Data

Web browsers have been able to store local data for quite some time in the form of **cookies**. These are generally simple `data:value` pairs that allow some sort of session memory on the client-side of an application. Eventually, the need arose for much more complex ways of storing local data within the browser as applications grew in complexity.

We now have the **LocalStorage** API, which was introduced with HTML5, as a more performant, more secure, and more expansive way of storing local website data. You can think of `LocalStorage` as a better version of cookies all around, yet it still lacks the capabilities of a true database.

If you do need access to a real, client-side database for your web application, you'll want to explore the **Indexed Database (IndexedDB)** API. IndexedDB is a true client-side database and allows for complex data structures, relationships, and everything you'd expect from a database.

> **Note**
>
> Some web browsers also have access to a Web SQL database as well—but this is no longer considered appropriate by web standards bodies and should generally be avoided.

You can always check the local storage for any website you visit by digging into the developer tools. In Google Chrome, you will find local storage under the `Application` view:

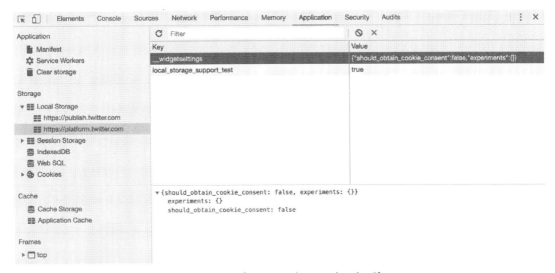

Figure 1.16: Local storage inspection in Chrome

DOM Manipulation

JavaScript can modify, create, and destroy elements and attributes within the **Document Object Model (DOM)**. This is a very powerful aspect of JavaScript and nearly all modern development frameworks leverage this capability in some way. Similar to XHR, the browser's page doesn't need to be refreshed for us to perform these client-side amendments using JavaScript.

We'll see a particular project based on this in the next chapter, where you'll get some first-hand experience with this very task.

Animations and Effects

Looking back at the web in its infancy, everything was a very static experience. Pages were served up in the browser and consisted of text and hyperlinks. Depending on the year, we usually saw black serif type against a white background with the occasional blue/purple hyperlink.

Eventually, images and different visual stylistic attributes were available, but things really changed with the advent of various extensions such as **Macromedia Shockwave** and **Flash Player**. All of a sudden, rich experiences such as interactive video, animation, gaming, audio playback, special effects, and more were all available.

The web standards bodies rightly recognized that all of these capabilities should not be locked behind different browser plugins, but rather be part of the native web experience using core web technologies. Of course, primary among these was JavaScript, though JavaScript often relied on a close relationship with HTML and CSS to make things work. The following screenshot shows an interactive animation created using the `CreateJS` library:

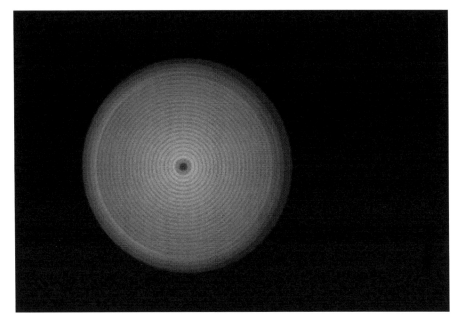

Figure 1.17: Interactive animation using the CreateJS JavaScript library

Today, we have rich implementations of the types of content creation that were previously only available with third-party plugins. Libraries such as **CreateJS** allow for a huge variety of effects, gaming applications, interactions, animations, and beyond and use native JavaScript.

> **Note**
>
> For a number of examples of what is possible in this area of development, have a look at the Google Doodles archive at https://www.google.com/doodles.

In this section, we looked at some of the common capabilities of JavaScript that are used on the web today. In the chapters that follow, we'll be exploring some of these capabilities in much greater detail.

Summary

In this chapter, we took some time to build a foundation of knowledge that will frame the rest of this book. We began with a historical overview and then examined the relationship between ECMAScript and JavaScript. We then moved on and explored JavaScript by accessing the developer tools of various browsers. Following a hands-on activity and writing a bit of JavaScript with the browser developer tools, we ended this chapter with an overview of JavaScript capabilities. This included DOM manipulation, local data storage, form validation, and other examples to get us into the right mindset when it comes to thinking about the possibilities of working in JavaScript.

In the next chapter, we will explore how to work with JavaScript in much greater detail by using an **integrated development environment** (**IDE**) and how to examine the syntax rules of JavaScript. We'll look much more deeply into the web browser as one of a variety of JavaScript runtimes. We'll also explore the use of browser development tools in more detail and get hands on with manipulating both browser elements and additional attributes associated with them.

Working with JavaScript

Overview

By the end of this chapter, you will be able to operate a modern **integrated development environment (IDE)**; identify and describe basic JavaScript structures; describe different JavaScript environments; recognize the major views and their uses within the popular web browser developer tools and construct HTML elements and modify their various attributes.

In this chapter, you will get an overview of some popular tools for writing JavaScript and the various available runtimes for executing code with a modern web browser and beyond.

Introduction

In the previous chapter, we explored a historical overview of JavaScript and examined the language's relationship with the Standard ECMAScript. We then explored JavaScript by accessing the developer tools of various browsers to provide a basic introduction to how JavaScript can be accessed.

Now that we are familiar with JavaScript in a more cerebral way, it's time for some hands-on work with the language. First, we'll provide an overview of some popular tools for writing JavaScript and of the various runtimes available for executing code. With those installed, we can begin writing some JavaScript in order to gain some familiarity with the language's syntax and structure—how to write code in a meaningful way and how to include it in a web environment.

Within this chapter, we will pay particular attention to the primary target for most JavaScript environments and a great tool in itself—the modern web browser. In the previous chapter, we looked at an overview of how to access developer tools in various web browsers. In this chapter, we will further explore how these tools can be used in JavaScript development.

Finally, we'll dig more deeply into web browser interactions and look at how we can control both the style and content of elements within the web browser with the use of common JavaScript functions. All the code in this chapter will be written using the editor that we are about to introduce.

Integrated Development Environments (IDE)

JavaScript is a language that is interpreted at runtime as there is no need for us to compile it beforehand. There are other ways of writing JavaScript in a non-direct way, such as through transpilation or compilation, but we'll review those later. Before we get too far into working with JavaScript and writing code, we should examine the benefits of using a dedicated development environment to write and manage our JavaScript code.

Using an IDE aligned with the platform and languages you work with provides a number of benefits over a simple text editor. For example, IDEs usually include the following features:

- Linting, formatting, and other cleanup utilities

- Integrated **Terminal** and command-line access

- Programming language **debugging tools**

- Robust code completion and hinting as you type

- Snippets and preformed code content

- Built-in compilers (depending on the language and platform)

- Potential **emulation features**–especially when dealing with mobile development

GitHub's Atom

A free and open-source editor, Atom is maintained by GitHub and is available for Microsoft Windows, Apple macOS, and various Linux distributions. Since this editor was created by GitHub, one of its main features is tight integration along with the other services they provide within the editor:

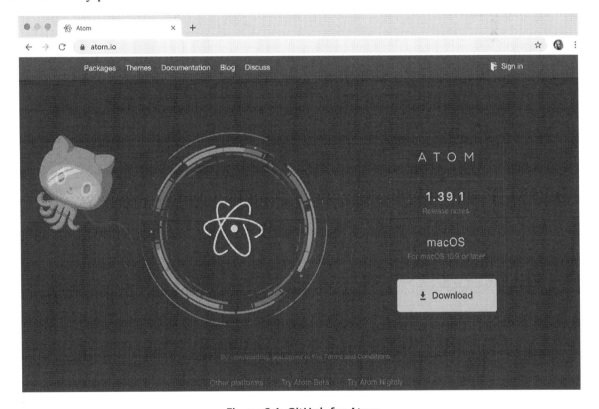

Figure 2.1: GitHub for Atom

The editor features a plugin system that allows users to add support for various languages and themes. Atom can be downloaded and installed for free from https:// atom.io/.

Sublime Text

Though a very popular editor some years back, it's still worth noting here as many developers use this IDE for JavaScript and more. Sublime Text supports Microsoft Windows, Apple macOS, and various Linux distributions. The latest version was released in 2019:

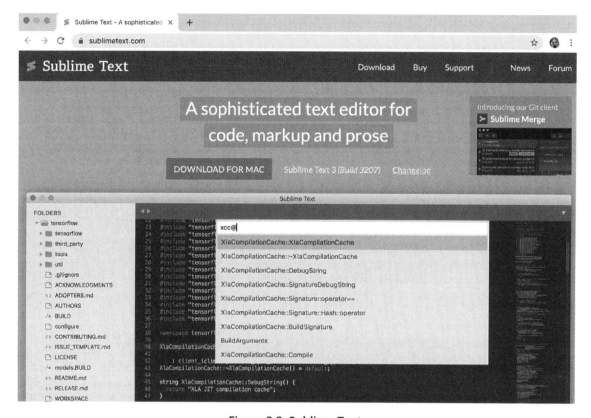

Figure 2.2: Sublime Text

Sublime Text can be downloaded and installed from https://www.sublimetext.com/ as a free evaluation tool; however, it requires you to purchase it for long-time use.

Adobe Dreamweaver

Previously the property of Macromedia, Adobe acquired that company and ceased the development of their existing web editing product, Adobe GoLive, and instead strengthened the support for Dreamweaver. In the years since then, the application has gone through several rewrites and adjustments, but the focus has always been split between a visual editing view and one targeted at developers in the form of bare code. The code editor within Dreamweaver is based on Adobe's open-source Brackets (https://packt.live/2WWMUH6) project:

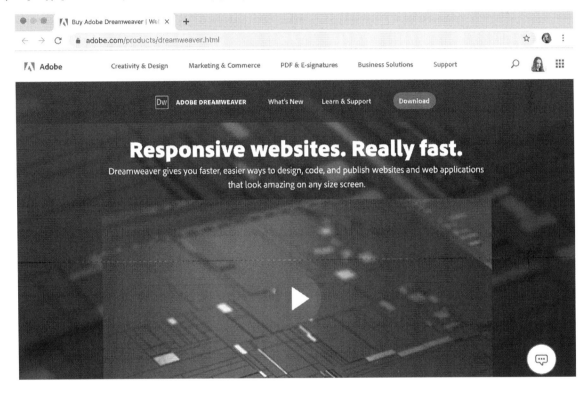

Figure 2.3: Adobe Dreamweaver

Dreamweaver can be downloaded and installed from https://www.adobe.com/products/dreamweaver.html as a trial but must be purchased for continued use.

JetBrains WebStorm

A variety of editors and other tools are available from JetBrains. Many of these build upon one another in terms of complexity and functionality. When looking primarily for a web editor for authoring JavaScript, HTML, and CSS, JetBrains WebStorm is a good choice, but it does have a bit of a learning curve in the way that it handles the management of projects and associated files:

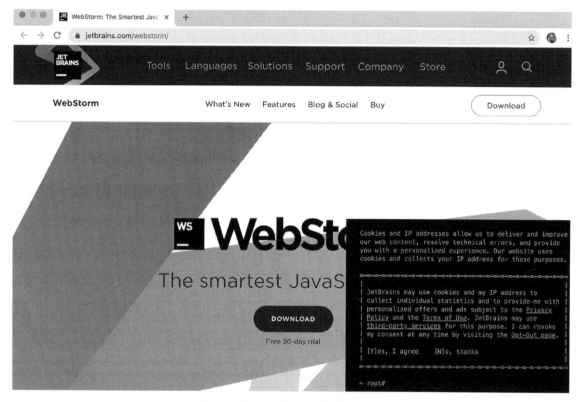

Figure 2.4: JetBrains WebStorm

WebStorm can be downloaded and installed from https://www.jetbrains.com/webstorm/ as a free trial, with various purchase options available afterward. Those affiliated with educational institutions can apply for a free license with yearly renewal.

Microsoft Visual Studio Code

For this module, we'll be using the Visual Studio Code as our IDE. This software application is a free, cross-platform IDE from Microsoft that is updated every month. It allows you to work with native web technologies in a very capable way—but also has the ability to support other languages and features through extensions. Visual Studio Code is very popular with developers of all sorts:

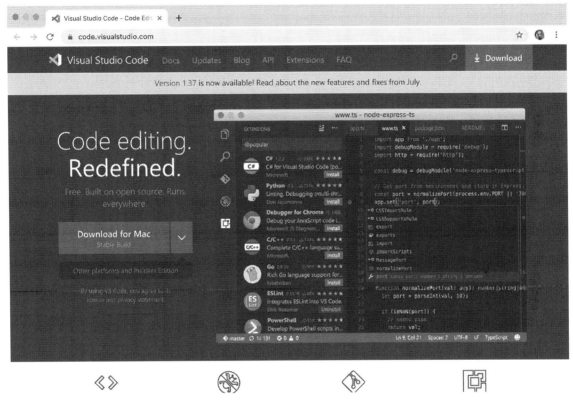

Figure 2.5: Microsoft Visual Studio Code

Visual Studio Code can be downloaded and installed for free from https://code.visualstudio.com/.

> **Note**
>
> The process of downloading and installing an IDE can be found in the *Preface* of this book.

JavaScript Project and File Management

Now that we have our development environment installed, we need to consider some best practices in terms of where we should store projects on our local machine, and how we should organize folders and files within each project. We'll also walk through a small exercise that will demonstrate how to load a project (including all associated files) into Visual Studio Code.

Project Folders and Files

It is advisable to set aside a directory on your local machine where you will place all the projects that you may be working on. For instance, you could create a directory called **Projects** on your local disk and then create specific project folders within it—one for each distinct project. This way, you can be sure of where all your projects are located. You can even create a shortcut to your **Projects** folder to get at it easily whenever you like:

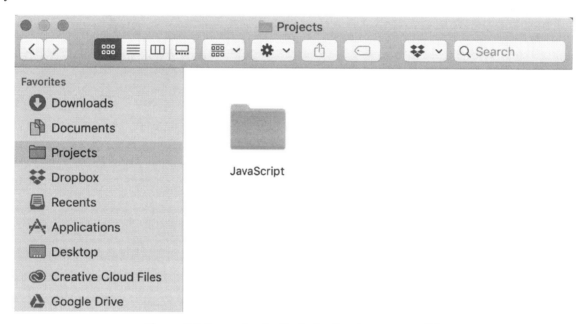

Figure 2.6: Example of a Projects directory on macOS

Individual projects will exist in specific folders within your main **Projects** directory. Depending on how many projects you work on, you may have to create many subfolders. Each project should be clearly named for ease of identification.

Exercise 2.01: Creating a Working Project Directory

Let's look at how to create a directory so that we can contain our working project and all its associated files and subfolders:

1. In your **filesystem**, locate a place that is easily accessible and to which your account has full read/write rights, as you'll be writing files at this location. If you already have a preexisting **Projects** directory, this is likely to be an ideal location.

2. Within this folder, create a new folder and name it **JavaScript**, or another name of your choice, like so:

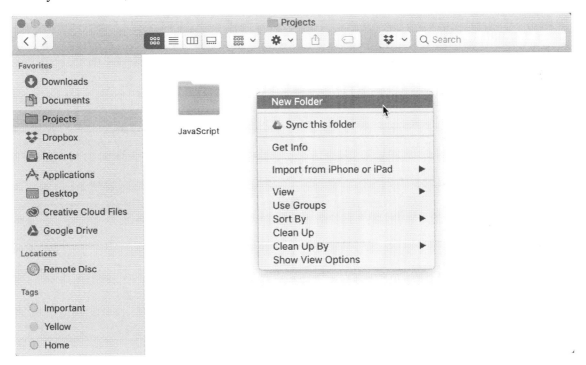

Figure 2.7: Creating a new folder on macOS

3. With your new project folder created, navigate to its parent directory. You may be there already or may need to go up one level in the **filesystem**. This all depends on your operating system and how you've created the folder.

4. Using your mouse, stylus, or touchpad, drag the working project folder from the file explorer into the Visual Studio Code application window:

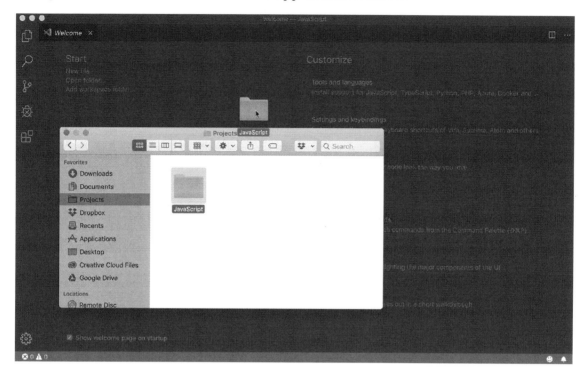

Figure 2.8: Loading the project into Visual Studio Code

5. The current tab's content within Visual Studio Code will become obscured, indicating that you can release the folder onto it. Go ahead and do this.

6. This will effectively set the folder you dragged onto the Visual Studio Code interface as your working project folder. Look to the left-hand pane and navigate the files and folders in it:

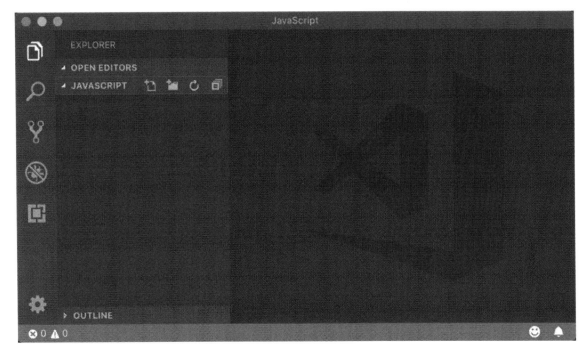

Figure 2.9: The declared working project folder

The newly created folder is now the working project folder within Visual Studio Code. Normally, you'd see a list of files and folders in the leftmost sidebar. We haven't created any files or folders yet, so there is nothing there.

> **Note**
>
> You can also declare the working project folder by choosing **File** | **Open** from the application menu and browsing for the folder.

Visual Studio Code, like many other editors, will remember projects you've opened within it and present a list of them when you next open the application.

In this section, you learned about the importance of having an organized folder structure on your local machine for managing all your projects. We also saw how to create a new working folder for a project and then opened it within our code editor.

In the next section, we'll use the project we just created to start writing and examining JavaScript syntax and common structural elements.

JavaScript Syntax and Structure

Now that we've installed an IDE and established how to manage a working project folder within our code editor, it's time to look at how JavaScript code is written and ordered within such an environment. The first thing we need to do is create a set of files within the **Project** folder because we will write our JavaScript instructions in these. We will create a set of files within the working project folder and then bind them to one another.

Exercise 2.02: Creating Project Boilerplate

The most common environment where JavaScript runs is inside a web browser. For JavaScript to run within this environment, it must be included within a host HTML file in some way. Let's create a basic HTML file and a JavaScript file and instruct the web browser to load our JavaScript file within the HTML at runtime. Let's get started:

1. Open the working project folder you created previously within your IDE (Visual Studio Code). No files will be listed in the leftmost pane since we haven't created any yet:

Figure 2.10: The current project contains no files

2. If you hover your mouse cursor over this leftmost area, you will notice a number of icons appear to the right of the project name. The leftmost of these icons allows for the creation of new files. The one next to it allows the creation of new folders. Click the **New File** icon:

Figure 2.11: Clicking the New File icon

A new file is immediately created and is available for us to name. You should immediately provide a name and file extension. The name should be something that tells you why the file exists, and the extension lets Visual Studio Code and other applications and services understand how to manage and run the file. Type in **index.html** for the name of the extension of the newly created file. The name **index** tells us that this file is the *root* or *index* HTML file for our project. The **.html** extension informs both us and the computer as to the nature of this file:

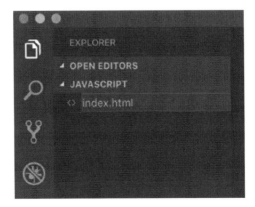

Figure 2.12: Naming the file index.html

3. Once complete, hit *Enter/Return* on your keyboard to commit the change. The file will immediately open in the editing pane of your editor. As you can see, it is completely blank:

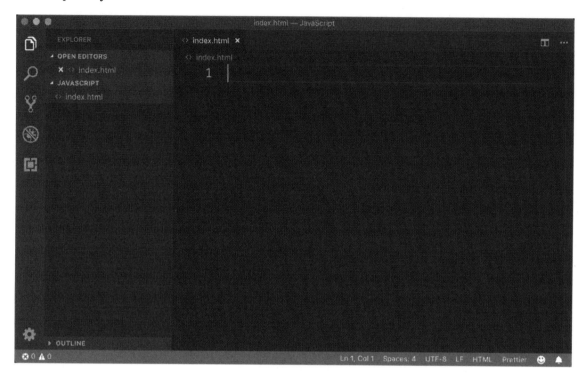

Figure 2.13: The file exists and is open, but it is empty

4. Type in the following boilerplate HTML code to set up the file's structure:

```html
<!DOCTYPE html>
<html lang="en">
  <head>
    <meta charset="utf-8">
    <title>JavaScript Project</title>
  </head>
  <body>
    <h1>Just an HTML page...</h1>
  </body>
</html>
```

5. We declare the file as HTML and establish a **<head>** tag and a **<body>** tag. The head of an HTML document includes invisible data such as declaring the character set and title. The body of an HTML document contains visible elements such as text and images. Notice that you must save the file using **File | Save** or by using *Command/Ctrl* + S:

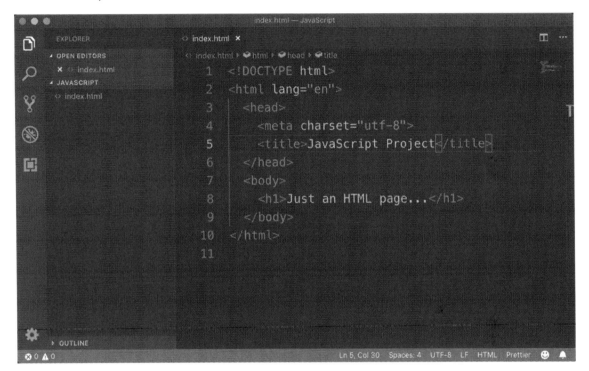

Figure 2.14: Our initial HTML markup structure

6. Create a new file once again, this time naming it **app.js**. This will signify that this is the main JavaScript file for the application. The **.js** file extension indicates an external JavaScript file.

7. The new JavaScript file will open just like the HTML file did. As you can see, it is also initially empty. Type in the following JavaScript code:

```
console.log("app.js JavaScript Included!");
```

8. Ensure that you save the JavaScript file again by navigating to **File** | **Save** from the application menu or by using the keyboard shortcut **Command/Ctrl** + **S**:

Figure 2.15: You should now have both a JavaScript file and an HTML file

9. In order to bind the newly created JavaScript file to our HTML so that it can run in the web browser, we must reference it within the HTML file itself. Switch to the HTML file titled **index.html** from earlier. Place the following code directly following the **<title>** tag and before the closing tag of the **<head>** element:

```
<script src="app.js"></script>
```

10. The **<script>** tag is used to either include an external **.js** file, as we are doing here, or it can be used to denote a block of JavaScript code directly within HTML. The full HTML file code should now appear as follows:

```
<!DOCTYPE html>
<html lang="en">
  <head>
    <meta charset="utf-8">
    <title>JavaScript Project</title>
    <script src="app.js"></script>
  </head>
  <body>
    <h1>Just an HTML page...</h1>
  </body>
</html>
```

11. With the new line of code added to the HTML, save the file once again. In Visual Studio Code, a file with unsaved changes is signified with a small, filled disc in the **File** tab within the project explorer:

Figure 2.16: A file with unsaved changes

12. Run the **index.html** file within a web browser. Open **developer tools** and activate the **Console** view. If all goes well, you will see the message we instructed JavaScript to output:

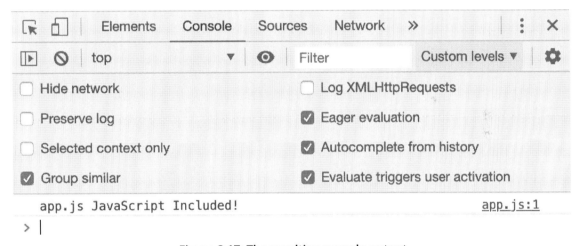

Figure 2.17: The resulting console output

We now know that our project boilerplate has been configured correctly since the HTML is running and has effectively called code from within the JavaScript file. We now have the beginnings of a web application—complete with structure (HTML) and logic (JavaScript) components.

Basic JavaScript Syntax

It is important to know the basic syntax of any programming language in order to write it correctly. To begin writing JavaScript, you'll need to know how to declare variables, assign data to variables, and terminate commands properly.

A variable in JavaScript is an **identifier** whose value can be retrieved or set and is normally defined with the **var** keyword. Here is an example of a variable declaration:

```
var myName;
```

To actually assign a value to this variable and give it something useful to do, we must use the assignment operator, =. Here is the same statement with a value assigned to the variable:

```
var myName = "Joseph";
```

> **Note**
>
> In this instance, we are assigning a string value to the variable. There are many different *types* of values, or data, that we can assign to variables, and we'll learn more about these in the next chapter.

You will note that we also place a **semicolon** after each variable declaration, whether we assign a value to it or not. While it is not absolutely necessary to do this, the use of a semicolon in this manner terminates a command. Multiple commands should, however, be placed across multiple lines, as demonstrated here:

```
var firstName = "Joseph";
var lastName = "Labrecque";
console.log("Hello, " + firstName + " " + lastName);
```

We assign string values to both a **firstName** and **lastName** variable, and then employ the **console.log()** method along with some string concatenation using the **+** operator to form a message and output it to the browser console. When executed in the browser, it appears like this:

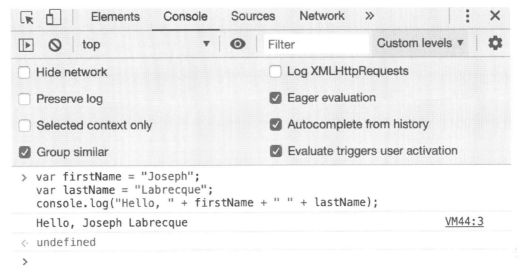

Figure 2.18: The resulting output message

> **Note**
>
> The term **concatenation** simply refers to joining plain strings and string variable values together, as we've done here.

That's about all you need to know regarding syntax to get started. Don't worry–there will be much more information around syntax when you reach *Chapter 5, Beyond the Fundamentals.*

JavaScript Execution Order

This section hearkens back to an example from the previous chapter in terms of the various ways JavaScript can be included within a web document. There are two choices here: either include an external JavaScript file somewhere within the **<head>** tag or the **<body>** tag of your HTML document or embed the code directly within the document itself, again at either location.

No matter how you include JavaScript within your HTML document, the web browser will always execute from top to bottom. Any JavaScript within the **<head>** tag of a document will execute before anything within the **<body>** tag of the document. Of course, you can compartmentalize blocks of JavaScript code within functions to execute when invoked as well, which effectively gets around this rule in some ways.

Exercise 2.03: Verifying an Execution Order

Let's conduct a small exercise to see whether, for any JavaScript, the **<head>** of a document will execute before anything with the **<body>** tag of the document. Let's get started:

1. In the exercise files for this chapter, you will find a document named **order.html**. Open this within Visual Studio Code to inspect it. You will see the following HTML code:

```
<!doctype html>
<html lang="en">
<head>
    <meta charset="utf-8">
    <title>JavaScript Execution Order</title>
</head>
<body>
    <h1>JavaScript Execution Order</h1>
    <p>View the browser console to see the effective order of
execution.</p>
</body>
</html>
```

2. You'll notice there is no JavaScript just yet, so let's insert some bits of code in various places for this demonstration. Add the following code beneath the **<title>** element within the document's **<head>** tag:

```
<script>console.log('Within the HEAD');</script>
```

3. Now, add this snippet directly above the **<h1>** element within the **<body>** tag of our document:

```
<script>console.log('Within the BODY');</script>
```

4. Finally, we'll add another line of code just before the **<body>** tag closes:

```
<script>console.log('At the very END');</script>
```

The document should now appear as follows:

```
<!doctype html>
<html lang="en">
<head>
    <meta charset="utf-8">
    <title>JavaScript Execution Order</title>
    <script>console.log('Within the HEAD');</script>
</head>
```

```
<body>
    <script>console.log('Within the BODY');</script>
    <h1>JavaScript Execution Order</h1>
    <p>View the browser console to see the effective order of
      execution.</p>
    <script>console.log('At the very END');</script>
</body>
</html>
```

5. Run this document within your web browser with the developer tools Console view open. You will be able to verify that yes—the code is certainly processed from top to bottom, as we explained:

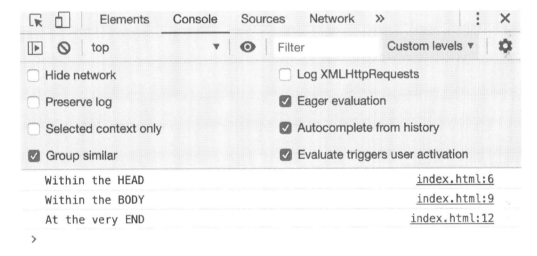

Figure 2.19: Verification of the execution order

The `console.log()` command in JavaScript will write any data within parentheses to the console. This is the simplest way of debugging JavaScript, though this will be explored further in the next chapter.

In this section, we've learned about several important fundamentals regarding the structure and syntax of JavaScript—particularly when it comes to the web browser environment.

In the next section, we'll explore other environments in which JavaScript can run.

Overview of JavaScript Environments

So far in our journey, we've only been exposed to the modern web browser as a JavaScript runtime, but even within browsers, there are a variety of JavaScript engines that serve as different runtimes for JavaScript. For instance, Chrome has the **V8 engine**, while Firefox runs JavaScript through **SpiderMonkey**. Just about every browser has its own distinct engine.

There are also other runtimes aside from those that are browser-based. We'll have a look at the variety of runtimes available to us now.

Browser-Based JavaScript

By far, the most common environment for using JavaScript throughout its entire history as a language is within the web browser. We've already spoken of this particular runtime quite a lot, so we will not spend time going over all of this again:

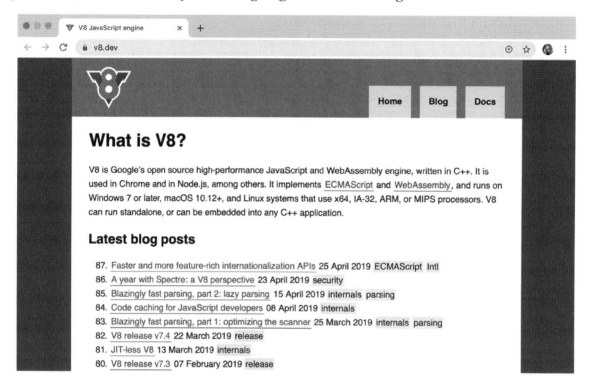

Figure 2.20: V8—JavaScript in the web browser

Some of the benefits of using the web browser as a JavaScript runtime are as follows:

- Web browsers are one of the most distributed software platforms in the world.
- Browsers include a set of built-in developer tools for debugging and monitoring JavaScript.
- Browsers are the absolute primary runtime for JavaScript and all others follow it.

You can learn more about each browser runtime at their respective websites. To learn more about V8, the runtime engine powering Chrome, visit https://v8.dev/.

Server-Based JavaScript

With the improvement in the performance of JavaScript engines in the web browser, people began wondering whether there may be other applications for the language and specific runtimes—particularly in terms of a server-based environment. In 2009, this became a reality with the creation of **Node.js**. A year before this, Google had open-sourced its powerful V8 JavaScript engine. This allowed developers to implement V8, along with specific operating system bindings, to produce the first version of Node.js:

Figure 2.21: Node.js—JavaScript on the server

The benefits of using a server-based JavaScript runtime include the following:

- Threadless execution of code.
- Events are completely non-blocking.
- Efficiency and performance are separated from the client.

You can learn more about Node.js at https://nodejs.org/.

Desktop JavaScript

While not exactly a new environment for JavaScript to run with, desktop applications are a segment that ripe for growth as additional runtimes and libraries mature. The most popular solution for building desktop applications is Electron. Like similar frameworks, when developing applications for Electron, you will be using native web technologies that end up being wrapped in a native-focused container for any target desktop operating system.

Electron apps can target Apple macOS, Microsoft Windows, or Linux, and are all built-in JavaScript:

Figure 2.22: Electron—JavaScript on the desktop

The benefits of using a desktop-focused JavaScript runtime include the following:

- The ability to use native web technologies to write desktop applications.

- Most functionality is platform-agnostic, so, often, no specific operating system commands are needed.

You can learn more about Electron at https://electronjs.org/.

Mobile JavaScript

Mobile devices have been huge since iPhone and Android first made their debuts nearly a decade ago. Of course, developers want to tap into this segment of the market and, thankfully, there have been a lot of pretty good solutions over the years that make use of JavaScript. For quite some time, Apache Cordova and Adobe PhoneGap were the primary frameworks that were used to translate web technologies into functional mobile applications. More recently, technologies such as **Ionic** have become incredibly popular for those using common JavaScript-based frameworks such as Angular, React, and Vue. With many of these tools, you can also use plain vanilla JavaScript as well:

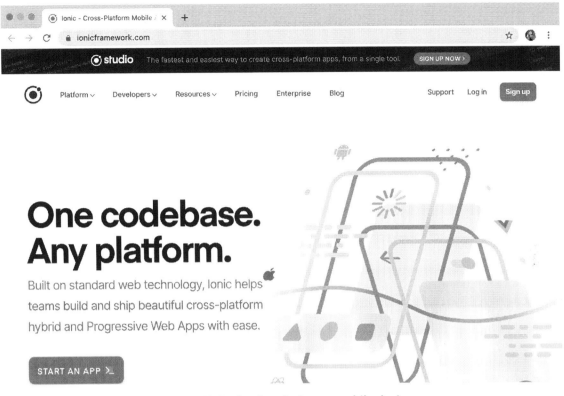

Figure 2.23: Ionic—JavaScript on mobile devices

The benefits of using a mobile-focused JavaScript runtime include the following:

- The ability to use native web technologies to write iOS and Android applications.

- Most functionality is platform-agnostic, so, often, no specific mobile operating system commands are needed.

You can learn more about Ionic at https://ionicframework.com/.

So far, we've had a brief overview of the various primary runtime environments for modern JavaScript.

In the next section, we'll focus once more on the web browsers that we introduced in the first chapter while paying more attention to the specific functions of some of the more useful views within their tools.

A Closer Look at Web Browser Developer Tools

In the previous chapter, we had a brief introduction to working with browser developer tools. We'll expand on our exploration of browser developer tools and examine a sample of the most used views when it comes to working with JavaScript in the web browser.

Of course, there are many other views and options than what will be mentioned here and, while we are examining these from within Google Chrome, they will differ in both overall look and functional use from browser to browser. This should give you a good idea of what is possible, though, no matter what your preferred browser is.

> **Note**
>
> To access Developer Tools in Google Chrome, press the **F12** key.

The Elements View

The primary view that you'll be presented with when exploring browser developer tools for the first time will most likely be the Elements view. This view is super useful as it presents all the elements of a web document and the associated content and attributes in a very structured way. You will also notice that the various styles and event listeners will be available for you to explore within this view. Selecting an element will display both the CSS rules and any associated event listeners:

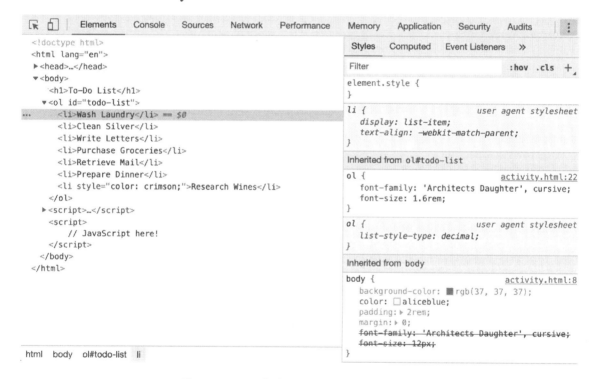

Figure 2.24: Web document Elements view

While you may think that there is no useful content being displayed in this view in terms of JavaScript, you actually have access to the entire **DOM** structure here and can monitor this structure and the associated attributes to verify and explore changes you are making via code.

The Console View

This is the developer tools view that we've had the most interaction with thus far and is likely to be the most important view when writing and testing JavaScript code. Any errors and warnings will be displayed within this view and you can also get the output on whatever data you wish as your code executes within the document. Using a JavaScript method such as `console.log()` will display output of all sorts of useful data for you to explore within the Console view, and you can even customize exactly the sort of data that is shown through various options associated with the view itself:

Figure 2.25: Browser console output

Every web browser has a Console view and even though specific use of this view may differ between browsers, the fundamental usage remains the same.

The Sources View

When it comes to any sort of programming, the ability to set breakpoints to effectively pause code execution and debug your program at a certain state is critical. Using the source view, we can do this effectively, right within the web browser itself.

This view provides a way for us to choose to view the source code for any HTML or JavaScript files that are currently running and set breakpoints at specific lines in order to cause the runtime to pause when the breakpoint is encountered. Once paused, we can then use additional tools within the source's view to examine our code in certain ways:

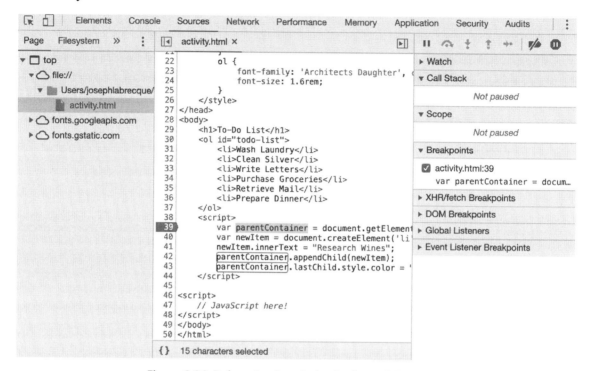

Figure 2.26: Debugging JavaScript in the web browser

In the preceding screenshot, we have set a breakpoint at line 39 of our HTML file, which includes embedded JavaScript code. With the code execution paused at this specific line, we can examine the state of our program in a very detailed way.

The Network View

The final developer tools view that we'll look at before moving on is the Network view. This allows you to keep tabs on everything being transferred as part of your application. HTML documents, JavaScript files, CSS files, and even invisible content such as **XMLHttpRequests (XHR)** and other behind the scenes data transmissions are all logged and measured here for you to inspect. If you want to see a specific type of network activity and hide all the others, there is even a handy filter along the top:

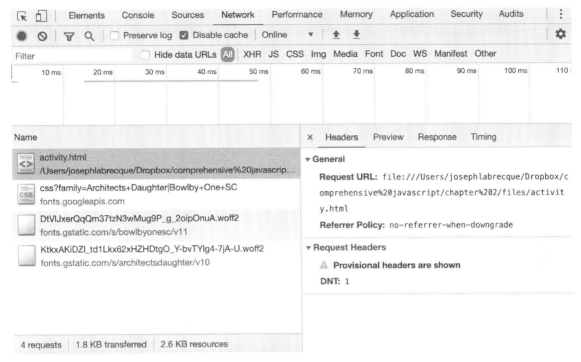

Figure 2.27: Viewing network activity in the web browser

One of the important aspects of the **Network** view that you'll want to note is that **Disable cache** is a tool option. Disabling the browser cache is an especially good idea if you are making many changes to externally loaded **.js** files while testing your program as it will prevent these files from being cached by the browser while testing.

In this section, we spent some more time getting familiar with some of the helpful views within web browser developer tools.

In the next section, we'll look at a hands-on activity that allows for the direct manipulation of HTML elements and their attributes through JavaScript code.

HTML Element Manipulation with JavaScript

We have alluded to the ability of JavaScript to directly manipulate elements within an HTML document a number of times. We'll now go ahead and see firsthand exactly how the language can be leveraged to perform this sort of manipulation.

Before moving on to the activity, there are a couple of concepts to understand so that you know how HTML elements function. As you've seen through example, elements in HTML generally consist of an opening and closing tag, within which there is often text data. If you think of a **<p>** tag or paragraph element in HTML, the text within that element, between the opening and closing tags, is the text displayed to the user.

If we need to address a specific HTML element to manipulate, the best way to do so is with the **getElementById()** JavaScript method. Of course, the element in question must contain an ID attribute for this to function as expected.

For example, maybe we have a simple HTML unordered list that contains a set of three list items:

```
<ul id="frameworks">
    <li>Angular</li>
    <li>Vue</li>
    <li>React</li>
</ul>
```

What if we wanted to manipulate this list through code? We can do so with some simple JavaScript. First, we have to store a reference to our list itself. Since the list element has an **id** attribute with a value of **frameworks**, we can store a reference to this element using the following code:

```
var frameworksList = document.getElementById('frameworks');
```

With a reference created, we can now easily create and add a new child element:

```
var newFramework = document.createElement('li');
newFramework.innerText = "Apache Royale";
frameworksList.appendChild(newFramework);
```

We can even adjust the style properties of our newly added element:

```
frameworksList.lastChild.style.color = "crimson";
```

getElementById() is a JavaScript function that returns an element that has been granted a certain ID attribute and is an exact match for the specific string. An HTML element ID attribute must be unique.

Once we have a reference to any element in JavaScript through the use of **getElementById()**, we can then get a reference to its child elements through the **children.length** child attribute and finally get a count of how many child elements exist by invoking the length property.

Additionally, any attributes that are defined as part of these elements can also be manipulated with JavaScript code. In this activity, we'll make adjustments to the **style** attribute—effectively modifying the visual appearance of the specific element content.

In this section, we've seen how to directly manipulate HTML elements and associated attributes using pure JavaScript code. You should now have a good idea of what this language is capable of.

Activity 2.01: Adding and Modifying an Item to/in the To-Do List

In this activity, we will be examining the beginnings of a small web-based view that is meant to list a set of to-do items. You need to create some boilerplate for the following code, which is currently static HTML and CSS with a placeholder **<script>** tag. You then need to add an item, **Research Wines**, to the to-do list and change the font color of the newly added item to crimson. Lastly, you need to verify the order that this code will be executed in.

This activity will help cement the relationship that exists between HTML, CSS, and JavaScript. The following code shows how JavaScript can impact the visual display styles and even the elemental content of HTML nodes:

`activity.html`

```
1  <!doctype html>
2  <html lang="en">
3  <head>
4      <meta charset="utf-8">
5      <title>To-Do List</title>
6      <link href=https://fonts.googleapis.com/
         css?family=Architects+Daughter|Bowlby+One+SC rel="stylesheet">
7      <style>
8          body {
9              background-color:rgb(37, 37, 37);
10             color:aliceblue;
11             padding:2rem;
12             margin:0;
13             font-family: 'Architects Daughter', cursive;
14             font-size: 12px;
15         }
```

The full code is available at: https://packt.live/2Xc9Y4o

The steps for this activity are as follows:

1. You will create the HTML file yourself and paste in the preceding boilerplate HTML code to get started. This file conforms to a standard HTML document targeting the HTML5 specification. It is structured with a **<head>** tag and a **<body>** tag, and nested within the **<body>** tag exists the visual elements and the data a user would be able to see within their web browser. Additionally, within this file, you will see a set of CSS style rules within the **<style>** tags, which provide visual HTML elements with some additional specific colors, fonts, and sizes. The CSS refers to additional stylistic font information being loaded from remote Google Fonts (https://fonts.google.com/) services.

2. Assign an ID to our list in order to identify it via code.

3. Create a new variable and use the ID to address this element directly by the use of the **getElementById()** method.

4. Create a new HTML list item element.

5. Populate the list item with a data value.

6. Add it to the visual document by appending it to a chosen parent container that already exists.

7. Change the color of the existing element.

8. Verify the execution order of our commands by counting the initial number of list items.

9. Then, count the final number of list items after code execution.

10. Refresh the browser view and watch the console.

> **Note**
>
> The solution to this activity can be found on page 712.

Summary

In this chapter, we had a look at different popular IDEs for writing and maintaining JavaScript code and chose Visual Studio Code as our primary editor for this portion of this book. We then used this editor to examine JavaScript file structures, syntax, and project management tasks. Following that, we had a brief overview of different JavaScript runtime environments—from the browser to the desktop, remote servers, and mobile devices. Finally, we had a better look at the various web browser developer tools available to us and performed an activity that allowed for the manipulation of HTML elements and their various attributes.

In the next chapter, we will explore fundamental concepts and structures that are involved when we're working in JavaScript, cover the basics from object types to conditionals and looping structures, how to go about writing and invoking functions, and even commenting out and debugging code.

3

Programming Fundamentals

Overview

By the end of this chapter, you'll be able to demonstrate JavaScript syntax and structure; write comments and debugging code; implement conditional logic and looping; write functions and invoke them in the code; and construct events that react to user input and update the DOM.

This chapter serves as an introduction to the fundamental concepts and structures that are involved when working in JavaScript and really, programming in general.

Introduction

In the previous chapter, you were introduced to some popular JavaScript tools and the various available runtimes for executing code with the modern web browser. We also explored web browser interactions and saw how we can control both the style and content of elements within the web browser with the use of common JavaScript functions in the **Integrated Development Environment (IDE)**.

You have already seen large chunks of JavaScript code; however, understanding what each function works for is a key skill for any good developer. This chapter serves as an introduction to the fundamental concepts and structures involved in writing programs in JavaScript. We'll cover all the basics, from object types to conditionals and looping structures, how to go about writing and invoking functions, and even commenting and debugging their code.

From using variables to store and calculate data to using `if/else` statements to apply conditions to different variables, this chapter will be one of the most important stepping stones in your JavaScript learning path. A detailed understanding of Booleans, strings, objects, arrays, functions, arguments, and so on will improve your development skills.

Data Types

Programming is all about manipulating data. Data can represent values such as people's names, temperature, image dimensions, the amount of disk storage, and total likes on a discussion group post.

All the data in a program has a data type. The data types that you usually learn to use first in JavaScript are number, string, boolean, object, array, and function. The number, string, and Boolean data types represent a single value. Objects represent more complex data. Functions are for writing programs.

Some common JavaScript data types with their uses and descriptions are as follows:

- **number**: Any positive or negative value whole numbers, usually called integers and floating-point numbers, that can be used in mathematical operations. It is used in product prices, checkout totals, the number of likes on a post, the geometry value of Pi, and can be used as a random number.

- **string**: Any set of valid characters that cannot be, or are not intended to be, used in computational operations. They are used to comment on a discussion post which can be a company name, a street address, name of a place, an account number, a telephone number, or a postal number.

- **boolean**: Any value representing true and false. It is used to check whether a form can be submitted, whether a password meets its required characters, whether an order balance qualifies for free shipping, and whether a button can be clicked.

- **object**: An unordered collection of values, called properties, and code, called methods, that are intended to work together. It is used for real-world objects such as an order, stopwatch, clock, date, or microwave. They can be used for software objects such as a web page document, an HTML element on a web page, a CSS style rule, or an HTTP request.

- **function**: A specialized object data type that represents a block of code. The code can use optional input data and optionally return data. They can be used for the conversion of data such as temperature, finding a value in a list, updating the style of an HTML element, sending data to a web server, revealing a message on the screen, or checking for valid data entry formats such as an email address.

Representation of Data

Data is represented in programs using expressions. If you've ever worked with a spreadsheet program, then expressions are analogous to cell formulas. Expressions can be resolved to a value representing a specific data type.

Expressions can be broken down into smaller parts, as follows:

- Literal values
- Operators
- Variables
- Functions that return data
- Object properties
- Object methods that return data

A good place to start learning about expressions is with literal values, operators, and variables. Functions and objects are covered separately, later in this chapter, and we will revisit them through their use in expressions.

Literal Values

Literal values are written into the programming code. Literal values are static. This means that they have the same value every time the line of code is executed, and they cannot be changed.

Literal data needs to be formatted according to the rules for its data type. Number, string, and Boolean values are a good place to start so that we can understand the formatting of literal values. Functions and object literals are covered in their own topics later. Here is a list of some of their types and their rules and an example of each valid and invalid case:

- **Number**: Numbers can appear in expressions. They cannot include formatting punctuation, such as currency symbols, comma separators, and spaces. Negative numbers are preceded with the minus symbol. Some valid examples include `1000000`, `101`, `9.876`, and `-0.1234`. Invalid examples include `1,000,000`, `$1000000`, and `1 000 000`.

- **String**: String data is encased in delimiters. The delimiters are either single or double quotes. Single quotes can appear within a double-quote delimited string, and double quotes can appear within a single-quote delimited string. Also, the escape character, \, is a delimiter that needs to appear as part of a string; for example, "ABC Company". Valid examples include `'ABC Company'`, `"Earth's Moon"`, `"She yelled \"duck\"!"`, `'She yelled "duck"!'`, and so on. Invalid examples include `ABC Company`, and `"She yelled "duck"!"`.

- **Boolean**: There are two keywords: true and false. They are lowercase. `true` and `false` are valid examples, whereas invalid examples include `True`, `TRUE`, `FALSE`, and `False`.

Using Operators in Expressions

Operators are used to performing arithmetic, combine text, make logical comparisons, and assign values to variables and properties.

The operators we look at can be grouped as follows:

- Arithmetic
- String
- Grouping
- Comparison
- Logical
- typeof

For math computations, we use arithmetic operators. The string operator allows us to combine parts of an expression into a string value. The following table describes certain arithmetic operators and some examples:

Operator	Description	Examples	Results
**	Exponentiation	2 ** 3	8
/	Division	200 / 5	40
		12 / 5	2.4
%	Remainder	200 % 5	0
		12 % 5	2
*	Multiplication	12.5 * 10	125
		1000 / 3	333.3333333333333
+	Addition	100 + 100	200
-	Subtraction	1000 - 2500	-1500

Figure 3.1: Arithmetic operators

Let's say we could use **+**, which is concatenation. It converts non-string data types into strings. The following code shows three separate examples:

```
"Blue" + "Moon"
"Blue" + " " + "Moon"
"$" + 100 * .10 + " discount"
```

The output for each would be as follows:

```
"BlueMoon"
"Blue Moon"
"$10 discount"
```

Expressions are not evaluated left to right. Instead, they are evaluated based on a preset operator order, which is called the operator precedence. For example, the multiplication operator has higher precedence than the addition operator does. You can override the operator's precedence using the grouping operator. It forces the evaluation of the expression contained within it before the rest of the expression is evaluated.

For example, the **()** operator controls the precedence of expression evaluation:

```
1 + 2 * 3
(1 + 2) * 3
10 + 10 * 5 + 5
(10 + 10) * (5 + 5)
```

The output for each of the preceding examples would be as follows:

```
7
9
65
100
```

Comparing data is an important part of programming. The resulting value of comparing data is either true or false. A portion of an expression can be compared to another portion using the comparison operators, which are sometimes called relational operators. The following table describes certain comparison operators, along with examples:

Operator	Description	Examples	Results
==	Equality	1 == 1	true
		1 == '1'	true
		1 == 2	false
===	Equality before any automatic data conversion	1 === 1	true
		1 === '1'	false
!=	Inequality	1 != 1	false
		1 != '2'	true
		1 != 2	true
!==	Inequality before any automatic data conversion	1 !== '1'	true
		1 !== '2'	true
		1 !== 2	true
>	Greater than	100 > 101	true
		101 > 100	false
<	Less than	100 < 101	false
		101 < 100	true
>=	Greater than or equals	100 >= 100	true
		100 >= 99	true
		100 >= 101	false
<=	Less than or equals	100 <= 100	true
		100 <= 99	false
		100 <= 101	true

Figure 3.2: Comparison operators

Multiple parts of an expression can be compared using logical operators. These are sometimes called Boolean operators. Some Boolean operators, along with a description of them and examples, are as follows:

Operator	Description	Examples	Results
&&	Logical AND. True if left side and right side are both true	3 > 0 && -3 < 0 3 < 0 && -3 < 0 3 > 0 && -3 > 0	true false false
||	Logical OR. True if either the left side or right side are true.	3 > 0 || -3 < 0 3 < 0 || -3 < 0 3 > 0 || -3 > 0 3 < 0 || -3 > 0	true true true false
!	Logical NOT. False if right side can be evaluated as true.	! (3 < 0) ! (3 > 0)	true false

Figure 3.3: Logical operators

Not all operators are symbols. A very helpful operator is **typeof**. It shows the data type as a string. The operator is all lowercase letters. Use the group operator to get the type of an expression using other operators.

For example, the **typeof** operator controls the precedence of expression evaluation:

```
typeof 100
TypeOf 100
typeof "100"
typeof true
typeof (1 > 2)
typeof (2 + " dozen eggs")
```

The output for each of the preceding examples would be as follows:

```
number
Uncaught SyntaxError: …
boolean
boolean
string
string
```

> **Note**
>
> It's good practice to surround operators with a space. Exceptions are to not use spaces before or after the grouping operator **( )** and before the logical not **!** operator.

Exercise 3.01: Implementing Expressions and Operators

In this exercise, you will interactively enter number, string, and comparison expressions into a web browser console window and review the results. Let's get started. Open the **data-expressions.html** document in your web browser:

1. Open the web developer console window using your web browser.

    In the next couple of steps, we will implement a few expressions using number data and arithmetic operators. Type the items on the lines beginning with the **>** symbol. The console window will show a response on the lines beginning with the **<** symbol.

2. Write the following code to add two literal whole numbers:

```
> 200 + 200
\\output
< 400
```

3. Write the following code to divide the literal whole numbers:

```
> 1000 / 4
\\Output
< 250
```

4. Now, write the following code to divide a real number by a whole number:

```
> 150.75 / 3
\\Output
< 50.25
```

5. Multiplication has a higher order of operator precedence, which is demonstrated with the following code:

```
> 100 + 100 * 2
\\Output
< 300
```

6. We can use parentheses to change the order of operational precedence, as shown here:

```
> (100 + 100) * 2
\\Output
< 400
```

7. To show the data type of a real number, we can use **typeof**, as shown here:

```
>typeof 987.123
\\Output
< "number"
```

8. Let's try the following command:

```
> 123 456 789
\\Output
< Uncaught SyntaxError: Unexpected number
```

The output is a syntax error because you cannot have a number in this format with spaces (**123 456 789** is not recognized as a number, but **123456789** is).

9. We can compare two whole numbers using the **>** operator, as shown here:

```
> 100 > 200
\\Output
< false
```

10. Similarly, we can compare two whole numbers using the **<** operator:

```
> 100 < 200
\\Output
< true
```

11. Now, we can switch over and work with string data. Let's have a look at the output when we enter a literal string using double quotes as a delimiter:

```
> "Albert Einstein"
\\Output
< "Albert Einstein"
```

The next couple of snippets will show different examples of using literal strings.

12. Using a literal string without delimiters would result in an error since JavaScript would not recognize such an input:

```
> Albert Einstein
\\Output
< Uncaught SyntaxError: Unexpected identifier
```

13. You can use a literal string using double-quotes. Suppose you want to return the statement in double-quotes. You can place the double quotes in between a single quote:

```
> 'The quote "The only source of knowledge is experience" is
attributed to Albert Einstein'
\\Output
< The quote "The only source of knowledge is experience" is attributed
to Albert Einstein
```

14. Use the **** escape character to use a delimiter. This turns special characters into string characters:

```
> "The quote \"The only source of knowledge is experience\" is
attributed to Albert Einstein"

\\Output. Notice the escape character is removed.

< The quote "The only source of knowledge is experience" is attributed
to Albert Einstein
```

15. A non-mathematic number such as a phone number without delimiters will be converted into a number:

```
> 123-456-7890
\\Output. Expression converted to number
< -8223
```

16. A non-mathematic number such as a phone number will appear as follows because we are using "":

```
> "123-456-7890"
\\Output
< "123-456-7890"
```

17. We can also combine numbers and a literal string, as shown here:

```
> 100 - 10 + " Main Street"

\\Output.

< "90 Main Street"
When string is in expression JavaScript attempts to convert all other
elements to a string.
```

18. We can use the == operator to compare two strings with the same case:

```
> "Albert Einstein" == "Albert Einstein"
\\Output
< true
```

19. Now, let's try comparing two strings with a different case:

```
> "Albert Einstein" == "ALBERT EINSTEIN"
\\Output
< false
```

20. When we compare a number with a string with the same numeric value using the == operator, data type conversion takes place. This is shown in the following snippet:

```
> 100 == "100"
\\Output. Data type conversion takes place
< true
```

21. If we want data type conversion to not take place before the comparison is made, we need to use the **===** operator, as shown here:

```
> 100 === "100"
\\Output. No data type conversion
< false
```

We used several operators and expressions in the preceding exercise. Real-world use cases of these operators and expressions would vary, depending on the type of applications being developed. However, the preceding exercise is a good starting point with regard to using these in actual programs. Note that, so far, the examples we used were using literal values. However, this may not always be the case in a real-world application. Often, values change dynamically while a program executes, and the use of variables in expressions becomes inevitable in such cases. The next section teaches you how you can use variables and constants in expressions.

Using Variables and Constants in Expressions

Variables and constants are symbolic names that are assigned to values. The value of a variable can be changed after it is assigned. The value that's assigned to a constant cannot be changed. Variables and constants involve the following items:

- Declaration keyword
- Name
- Assignment operator
- Expressions
- Data type

Variables and constants need to be **declared** before we can use them. For variables, there are two declaration keywords: **var** and **let**. For constants, the declaration keyword is **const**.

Variables and constants require a **name**. The JavaScript naming rules and conventions will be covered further in the chapter. The **assignment operator** is the single equals sign, **=**. The variable's data type is dynamic and is the same as the expression.

Variables do not need to be assigned a value when declared. A constant must be assigned a value when declared.

Have a look at the following examples of declaring a variable without assigning a value:

```
var firstName
var totalLikes
var errorMessage
var isSold
```

Variables that are not assigned a value still have a data type. That data type is named **undefined**. The `typeof` operator detects undefined data types.

Here are some examples of declaring a variable and assigning a value:

```
var firstName = "Albert"
var totalLikes = 50
var errorMessage = "Something terrible happened"
var isSold = false
```

Some examples of assigning a value to a variable that's been previously declared are as follows:

```
firstName = "Marie"
totalLikes = 50
errorMessage = "Something terrible happened"
isSold = false
```

Exercise 3.02: Working with Variables Using the Web Browser Console

In this exercise, you will use the web browser console window to work with variables. You will practice declaring variables, assigning values, and checking their data types. Let's get started:

1. Use the **variables.html** file from https://packt.live/370myse in your web browser.

2. Open the web developer console window using your web browser.

3. Type the items onto the lines beginning with the > symbol. The console window will show a response on the lines beginning with the < symbol.

4. Declare a variable named **firstName**:

```
> var firstName
\\Value is expressed as undefined
< undefined
```

5. Write the data type of the variable:

```
>typeoffirstName
\\Output
< "undefined"
This is expected as we have not defined our variable with any value.
```

6. Assign the string value **Albert** to the **firstName** variable:

```
>firstName = "Albert"
\\Output
< "Albert"
```

7. To find out what data type our input is, use the **typeof** keyword, as shown here:

```
>typeoffirstName
\\Output
< "string"
As expected, our input is correctly identified as beginning a string.
```

8. To find out what value our **firstName** variable is holding, we simply need to write the following code:

```
>firstName
\\Output
< "Albert"
Until now, we have used strings. In the next step, we will define a new
variable and store a number value in it.
```

9. Declare a variable and assign it to a number expression:

```
> var totalLikes = 50
\\Output. Console may express value when declared but before assigned
< undefined
```

10. Write the value of **totalLikes**:

```
>totalLikes
\\Output
< 50
```

11. To ascertain the data type, we will once again use **typeof**, as shown here:

```
>typeoftotalLikes

< "number"
```

So far, we haven't changed the values our variables are holding. We shall do this in the next step.

12. Here is the code for changing the value held by **totalLikes**:

```
>totalLikes = totalLikes + 1
\\Output. New value is expressed
< 51
```

We can use the comparison operator, **>**, to compare the value our variable is holding with a reference value. This is done in the next step.

13. Compare the value of **totalLikes** using the following code:

```
>totalLikes> 100

< false
```

The result is obviously false as the current value of **totalLikes** is **51**.

Now, let's define a new variable and use Boolean expressions.

14. Declare a variable and assign it to a Boolean expression:

```
> var isSold = false
\\Output. Console may express undefined data type when declared but
before assigned.
< undefined
```

15. Write the data type, like so:

```
>typeofisSold

< "boolean"
```

You have now interactively worked with declaring variables, assigned them values, and used them in expressions. We defined variables with different inputs such as strings, numbers, and Boolean values. You also used the **typeof** operator to reveal the data type of a variable. Now, we will progress to another important topic – functions.

Functions That Return Values

Functions may be written to return a value. In that case, we can use them in expressions. When we use a function, it is also called invoking the function.

To use a function in an expression, you need to include the function name, followed by parentheses. If the function requires input, it is placed inside the parentheses as valid expressions. These are called arguments. If more than one argument is needed, they are separated with commas.

These examples assume that the function will return a value.

Have a look at this example on expressing functions that do not require an argument:

```
getTotal()
isLoggedIn()
```

This example shows us expressing a function that has one argument expressed as a number literal:

```
getCelsiusFromFahrenheit(32)
```

This example shows us expressing a function that has multiple arguments using literal values:

```
getSearchResults("Pet Names", 25)
```

Finally, this example shows us expressing a function that has multiple arguments using variables:

```
var amount = 100000
var decimals = 2
var decimalSeparator = "."
var thousandsSeparator = ","
formatCurrency(amount, decimals, decimalSeparator, thousandsSeparator)
```

When you see a function in an expression, think of it as representing a value.

Exercise 3.03: Using Functions in Expressions

In this exercise, we will use a predefined function and then use it in expressions. This exercise will show how you can invoke, check, and return the data type, and use functions in expressions. For the purpose of this exercise, we will use a function defined as **getDiceRoll**. Let's get started:

1. Open the **use-functions.html** document in your web browser.

2. Open the web developer, **console window**, using your web browser.

    The web page has a function named **getDiceRoll**. It returns the value of one rolled dice. It has one argument. The argument allows you to supply the number of dice to roll. Type the items on the lines beginning with the **>** symbol. The console window will show a response on the lines beginning with the **< ·** symbol.

3. Express the data type. Note that a function name without parentheses is used:

```
>typeofgetDiceRoll
\\Expressed as a function type. It also assures us that there is a
function.
< ·function
```

4. Express the return value data type. Note that a function name with parentheses is used:

```
>typeofgetDiceRoll()
\\Function return value is a number. We do not see the actual value.
< ."number"
```

5. Invoke the function using the following code:

```
>getDiceRoll()
\\Your value will be 1 to 6. Repeat a few times.
< .3
```

We can also invoke functions in math expressions.

6. Invoke the function in a math expression:

```
> 100 * getDiceRoll()
\\Your value will be 100 to 600 Repeat a few times.
< .300
```

We can also invoke functions in a comparison expression.

7. Invoke the function in a comparison expression:

```
>getDiceRoll() == 4
\\You may need to repeat a few times to get a true result.
< .true
```

So far, we haven't passed any arguments for our functions. However, remember that we do have the option to do so as our function is defined to accept a single argument. This argument defines the number of dices that will be rolled. Let's try passing an argument in the next step.

8. Invoke and supply the argument for the number of dice to roll as 2:

```
>getDiceRoll(2)
\\You will receive values from 2 to 12.
< .11
```

Functions are critical to JavaScript programming. To get you started, we have only shown how you can use predefined functions. You will learn to write your own functions later in this chapter. However, you may come across scenarios in which you may have to use functions that have already been created. This exercise was a good starting point in showing you how this can be done.

The Object Data Type

JavaScript is designed around object data, thus making it important to understand. There are JavaScript objects that have been ready-made for us to use and you, as a programmer, will create objects. In either case, JavaScript objects are composed of **properties** and **methods**:

Property: A value that has an assigned named. Together, they are often called a name/value pair. Values can be any type, that is, data, a number, a string, a Boolean, or an object. Property values can be changed dynamically.

Method: A function that performs an action.

Ready-Made Objects

JavaScript has ready-made objects that we can use to help us begin to learn how to program. There are many useful objects built into JavaScript. Web browsers provide a collection of objects called the Document Object Model (DOM).

Some examples of ready-made objects are as follows:

- `window` is an object in DOM. It has access to the web browser's open window. Often considered a top-level DOM object containing other web browser-created objects as its properties, it has methods for setting timer events and printing.

- `console` is an object in DOM. It provides the ability to output to the web browser console window. It is also a property of the window object.

- `document` is an object in DOM. It has access to a web page's HTML elements, styles, and content. It is also a property of the window object.

- `location` is an object in DOM. It has information about the current URL. It is a property of the window object.

- `Math` is a built-in object. It consists of math constants such as Pi, and functions such as rounding.

- `Date` is a built-in object. It provides calendar date and time operations.

Exercise 3.04: Working with Ready-Made Objects

In this exercise, we will experiment with the properties and methods of ready-made objects that are available to JavaScript in the web browser. We will use the random, round, ceil, and floor methods to invoke a math object from a pre-defined object. Let's get started:

1. Open the **objects-ready-made.html** document in your web browser.

2. Open the web developer console window using your web browser.

3. First, we will start with the web browser document object. Type the items on the lines beginning with the **>** symbol. The console window will show a response on the lines beginning with the **<·** symbol.

4. Display the document object title property:

```
>document.title
\\Output
<< "JavaScript Data and Expression Practice | Packt Publishing"
```

5. Now, display the document object **doctype** property:

```
>document.doctype
\\Output
<<!doctype html>
```

6. Display the document object **lastModified** property:

```
>document.lastModified
\\Your output may have a different time and date value.
< "09/09/2019 21:58:25"
```

7. Declare a variable and assign it to the **HTMLElement** object variable using the document object **getElementById** method:

```
> var pageHeadEle = document.getElementById('page-heading')
\\Console may express undefined data type when declared but before
assigned.
< ·undefined
```

8. Display the **pageHeadEleHTMLElement** object:

```
>pageHeadEle
\\Output
<<div id="page-heading" class="heading-section">
<h1 class="center-text">JavaScript Data and Expression Practice</h1>
</div>
```

9. Write the **pageHeadEle object innerHTML** property:

```
>pageHeadEle.innerHTML
\\Output
<·"
<h1 class="center-text">JavaScript Data and Expression Practice</h1>
  "
```

10. Now, let's look at the JavaScript built-in **Math** object. Write the Math object PI property:

```
>Math.PI
\\Output
< 3.141592653589793
```

11. Invoke the **random** method for the Math object:

```
>Math.random()
< 0.9857480203668554
```

The **Math.random()** method returns a random number from the range **0** and **1**, both inclusive. It returns a different value with every call.

12. Invoke the **random** method for the Math object:

```
>Math.random()
<·0.3588305599787365
```

13. Invoke the **random** method for the Math object:

```
>Math.random()
<·0.45663802022566413
```

14. Use the Math object's **round** method:

```
>Math.round(10.5)
<·11
```

15. Use the Math object's **round** method:

```
>Math.round(10.4)
<·10
```

The **Math.round()** method returns the number after rounding it off to its nearest integer.

16. Use the Math object's `ceil` method:

```
>Math.ceil(10.5)
<·11
```

The `Match.ceil()` method returns the next smallest integer value that is greater than, or equal to, the given argument.

17. Use the Math object's `ceil` method:

```
>Math.ceil(10.4)
<·11
```

18. Use the Math object's `floor` method:

```
>Math.floor(10.4)
<·10
```

The `Math.floor()` method returns the previous largest integer value that is less than, or equal to, the given argument.

19. Use the Math object's `floor` method:

```
>Math.floor(10.6)
<·10
```

20. This is the expression we use to get a random dice value. The floor method argument is an expression, that is, `Math.random() * 6`. Its result is added to 1:

```
>Math.floor(Math.random() * 6) + 1
\\Output
< 1
```

There are many ready-made objects available in JavaScript. They are used just like other functions and variables, except we call the functions as methods and the variables as properties.

Self-Made Objects

You often have to create objects when developing real-world applications. They help you organize a set of data and functions that work together. Think about what properties and methods you may use for a stopwatch object.

You can see that we named the properties and methods as follows:

- **elapsedTime** is a property with a data type number. It displays the seconds that have elapsed since timing started.

- **resultsHistory** is a property data type object. It displays a list of previous timings.

- **isTiming** is a property data type Boolean. It displays the state of its timing.

- **isPaused** is a property data type Boolean. It displays the state if paused.

- **start** is a method data type function. It starts timing and sets **elapsedTime** to 0.

- **pause** is a method data type function. It pauses the timing.

- **resume** is a method data type function. It resumes the timing.

- **stop** is a method data type function. It stops timing and adds the result to **resultsHistory**.

Object Dot Notation

To reference object properties and methods, you use dot notation. This is the object name, followed by a period, and then the name of the property or method. Let's use the **stopWatch** object as an example:

```
stopWatch.elapsedTime
stopWatch.start()
stopWatch.start()
stopWatch.stop()
```

Methods require parentheses after the name. If the method requires data input, the data is placed inside the parentheses.

The Array Object

Arrays are objects that represent a list of values. Each item in the list is called an element. To initialize an array, you can set it to an array literal. An array literal is a comma-separated list of expressions enclosed in square brackets, like so:

```
["Saab", "Ford", "BMW", "GM"]
```

Elements in arrays can be different data types. Often, all the elements are the same data type:

```
["Milk", false, 123, document, "Gold", -.9876]
```

Elements in a literal array can be expressions, but they are evaluated and only the expression values are stored:

```
[price - cost, Math.random(), document.title, someVariable / 2]
```

Variables and object properties can contain arrays:

```
let todoList = [
  "Wash Laundry",
  "Clean Silver",
  "Write Letters",
  "Purchase Groceries",
  "Retrieve Mail",
  "Prepare Dinner"
]
game.scores = [120, 175, 145, 200]
```

Array elements can be arrays:

```
notes = [
  [
    "Wash Laundry",
    "Clean Silver",
    "Write Letters"
  ], 123, "999-999-9999"
]
```

The array objects with useful properties and methods are as follows:

- **length** is a property with a number data-type that displays the number of items in the array.

- **push** is a method with a number data-type that appends an element and returns the new length.

- **unshift** is a method with a number data-type that prepends an element and returns the new length.

- **shift** is a method with a mixed data-type that removes the first element and returns the removed element's value.

- **pop** is a method with a mixed data-type that removes the last element to return the removed element's value.

- **concat** is a method with a function data-type that merges two or more arrays to return a new array.

Using the Console Object

The **console** object has a method called **log** that we can use to test expressions in a JavaScript program. It takes an unlimited number of expressions separated by commas. All the expressions we enter into the console window would work with the **console. log** method. It evaluates the expressions and returns their results in the console. Multiple expressions are separated by a space.

The **console.log** method will be used in the upcoming exercises. Let's have a look at its syntax:

```
console.log(expression 1[, expression 2][, expression n])
```

Here are some examples of the **console.log** method:

```
console.log("Odd number count started!");
console.log("Iteration:", i);
console.log("Number:", number);
console.log(oddsCount + " odd numbers found!");
console.log(document);
```

Syntax

Programs follow a set of rules that define keywords, symbols, and structure. This is called the syntax. We have already learned about many of the syntax rules in JavaScript for expressing data, variables, and expressions. You will be required to name objects, properties, methods, variables, and functions.

The following is a basic set of rules and conventions. Conventions are another term for best practices. Although not following a convention will not cause issues in your coding, they can make your code less easy to follow and not palatable to other programmers, for example, who may be interviewing you for a job and ask to see your code samples.

The naming rules and conventions for functions and variables are as follows:

- 26 upper and lowercase letters (**A-Z, a-z**).

- Any character but the first character can be one of 10 digits (**0-9**).

- No spaces, dashes, or commas. The underscore (**_**) character is acceptable.

- Capitalization follows camelCase. This means that all characters are lowercase, except for the first letters of words and except for the first word in compound worded names.

- No JavaScript reserved words; for example, you cannot use **typeof**, **var**, **let**, and **const**.

Semicolon at the End of Code Statements

Some programming languages require a semicolon ; at the end of every executable code statement. JavaScript does not have this requirement, except when you have more than one executable code statement on the same line of a JavaScript file.

Requiring a semicolon ; at the end of every executable code statement is more of a personal or development team choice. Since the semicolon character ; is used in other languages, often, programmers prefer to use them in JavaScript so that they get into the habit of using them and so that they spend less time dealing with syntax errors. If you choose to use the semicolon character ;, then do it consistently.

Lines of Code versus Statements

Each line in a JavaScript source file does not need to be a single line of executable code. You can break a single line of executable code into multiple source file lines, or put multiple lines of executable code on a single source file line. This flexibility allows you to format the code so that it is easier to follow and edit.

The following is a single line of executable code using a single source file line:

```
let todoList = ["Laundry", "Letters", "Groceries", "Mail", "Dinner"]
```

However, it may be more desirable to use multiple source file lines, like so:

```
let todoList = [
  "Laundry",
  "Letters",
  "Groceries",
  "Mail",
  "Dinner"
]
```

You can have more than one line of code on the same line if you use ; after the previous code line:

```
var bid = 10; checkBid(bid)1
```

You will learn that, when JavaScript files are prepared for publishing, you can optionally use an optimizer program to compress all the lines in a source file into one line. In this way, the invisible end of a line character is removed to make the file smaller.

Comments

You can add a comment to your code since they are ignored when the program is executed. Comments can help us remember what the code does at a future date and inform other programmers who may need to use or work with your code.

Commenting is a useful tool to keep a line of code from executing in testing. For example, let's say you have one or more lines of code that are not working as expected and you want to try alternative code. You can comment on the code in question while you try the alternatives.

JavaScript has inline commenting, also known as single-line commenting. This uses the double forward slash, **//**. All the text following the double slash up to the end of the line is ignored when the program is executed.

Let's have a look at some examples of inline comments. The following comment explains the next line of code:

```
// Hide all result message elements
matchedMsgEle.style.display = 'none';
```

The comment at the end of the line is explaining the code:

```
let numberGuessed = parseInt(guessInputEle.value); // NaN or integer
```

JavaScript has block commenting, also known as multi-line commenting. This uses the combined forward slash asterisk characters to mark the beginning of the comment, and the reverse of a combined asterisk forward-slash to mark the end of the comment. All the text between **/*** and ***/** is ignored when the program is executed. Let's have a look at the various block comments.

The following is a multiple-line block comment that contains code. This code snippet would not be executed:

```
/* This is a block comment.
It can span multiple lines in the file.
Code in a comment is ignored such as the next line.
var profit = revenue - cost;
 */
```

A block comment can be a single line in the file:

```
/* This is a block comment. */
```

The following is an example of using **JDoc** block comments for a function:

```
/**
 * Shuffles array elements
 * @param {array} sourceArray - Array to be shuffled.
 * @returns {array} - New array with shuffled items
 */
function getNewShuffledArray(sourceArray){
    // Statements for function
}
```

There are also tools that use syntax to produce documentation of your code from comments (for example, JDoc). These tools read your source code and produce a documentation guide of your code. Comments increase the bandwidth for web pages, so they are often not seen in the source code when you inspect a web page. This is because, often, the original JavaScript file is not published, but rather a compressed version. The tools that compress the JavaScript file will remove comments by default. Comments are helpful for learning. You are encouraged to write comments in your code that explain what the code does.

Conditional and Loop Flow

Statements in JavaScript are processed sequentially in the order they're loaded. That order can be changed with conditional and loop code statements. The different parts of a control statement are as follows:

- Code blocks {...}

- Conditional flow statements, such as `if...else`, `switch`, `try catch finally`

- Loop statements, such as `for`, `do...while`, `while`, `for...in`, and `for...of`

- Other control statements, such as `labeled`, `break`, and `continue`

We will describe each of these in detail in the next section.

Code Blocks

Code blocks are statements that are placed between an open and close curly bracket. The syntax is as follows:

```
//Code block
{
    //Statement
    //Statement
    //Statement
}
```

Code blocks by themselves do not offer any statement flow advantage until you combine them with conditional or loop statements.

Conditional Flow Statements

Conditional statements use logic expressions to choose from among a set of statements to process.

if...else Statement

The **if**, **else...if**, and **else** statements give you four structures for selecting or skipping blocks of code.

if Statement

Code in an **if** statement is processed if the expression evaluates to **true** and is skipped if the expression evaluates to **false**. The syntax is as follows:

```
if(boolean expression){
    //Statement
    //Statement
    //Statement
}
if(boolean expression)
    //Single statement
```

This shows the flow of the **if** statement. If the Boolean expression is **true**, the code is processed. If **false**, the code is skipped:

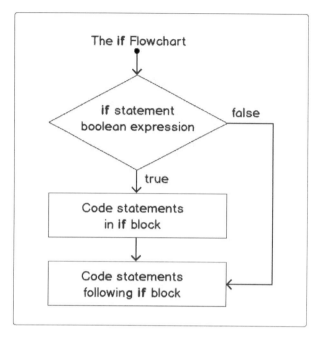

Figure 3.4: The if flowchart

Exercise 3.05: Writing an if statement

In this exercise, you will use the **if** statement to test for an even number between 1 and 6 and test the results in your web browser console window. Let's get started:

1. Open the **if-statement.html** document in your web browser.

2. Open the web developer console window using your web browser.

3. Open the **if-statement.js** document in your code editor, replace all of its content with the following code, and then save it:

```
var diceValue = Math.floor(Math.random() * 6) + 1;
console.log("Dice value:", diceValue);
if(diceValue % 2 != 0){
console.log("Is an odd number.");
}
```

4. The **Math.random()** function randomly creates a whole number from **1** to **6** and displays it in the console. Here, the **if** statement states that if the remainder of the number, divided by two, is not zero, that is, **diceValue % 2 != 0**, then the **if** expression is true and the **console.log()** message is displayed in the console.

5. Reload the **if-statement.html** web page in your web browser with the console window open. Repeat until you see a version of the two examples:

```
// Example of output if the number is odd.
  Dice value: 3
  Is an odd number.
// Example of output if the number is even.
  Dice value: 4
```

6. Edit the **if-statement.js** document using bolded lines and then save it:

```
var diceValue = Math.floor(Math.random() * 10) + 1;
console.log("Dice value:", diceValue);
console.log("Is an odd number.");
}
```

Because there is only one line of code in the **if** statement, the block brackets are not required.

7. Reload the **if-statement.html** web page in your web browser with the console window open. You should expect the same results.

8. Edit the **if-statement.js** document and add the highlighted line to **console.log()** and save it:

```
var diceValue = Math.floor(Math.random() * 6) + 1;
console.log("Dice value:", diceValue);
if(diceValue % 2 != 0)
console.log("Is an odd number.");
console.log('"You have to be odd to be number one", Dr. Seuss');
```

9. Reload the **if-statement.html** web page in your web browser with the console window open:

```
// Example of output if the number is odd.
  Dice value: 3
  Is an odd number.
  "You have to be odd to be number one", Dr. Seuss

// Example of output if the number is even.
  Dice value: 2
"You have to be odd to be number one", Dr. Seuss
```

The Dr. Seuss quote is shown regardless of whether the number is even or odd.

10. Edit the **if-statement.js** document lines in bold and save it. We added the block delimiters here:

```
console.log("Is an odd number.");
console.log('"You have to be odd to be number one", Dr. Seuss');
}
```

11. Reload the **if-statement.html** web page in your web browser with the console window open:

```
// Example of output if the number is odd. The Dr. Seuss quote is
included when the value is an odd number.
  Dice value: 3

Is an odd number.
"You have to be odd to be number one", Dr. Seuss


// Example of output if the number is even. The Dr. Seuss quote is
skipped when the value is an even number.
  Dice value: 2
```

You can see different outcomes depending on the logical expression of the **if** statement.

if Statement and else Statement

You can combine an **if** statement with an **else** statement. If the expression evaluates to **true**, the code in the **if** statement is processed and the code in the **else** statement is skipped. If the expression is false, the reverse happens; that is, the code in the **if** statement is skipped and the code in the **else** statement is processed. The syntax is as follows:

```
if(boolean expression){
    //Statement
    //Statement
    //Statement
}else{
    //Statement
    //Statement
    //Statement
```

```
}

if(boolean expression)
    //Single statement
else
    //Single statement
```

The **if...else** working is visible from the following flowchart:

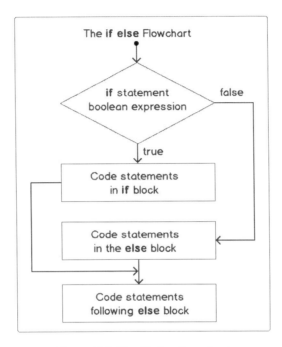

Figure 3.5: The if else flowchart

Exercise 3.06: Writing an if...else Statement

In this exercise, a random number is being used for a coin toss. A random value equal to .5 or greater is heads and less than .5 is tails. We will assume that multiple statement lines are required for each case. Let's get started:

1. Open the **if-else-statements.html** document in your web browser.

2. Open the web developer console window using your web browser.

3. Open the **if-else-statements.js** document in your code editor, replace all of its content with the following code, and then save it:

```
    var tossValue = Math.random();
console.log("Random toss value:", tossValue);
if(tossValue>= .5){
   console.log("Heads");
}
```

The **tossValue** variable is a value from 0 to 1, not including 1. For now, just an **else** statement is used for a head toss.

4. Reload the **if-else-statements.html** web page in your web browser with the console window open. Repeat until you see a version of the two examples:

```
// Example of output if the number is .5 or greater.
Random toss value: 0.8210720135035767
Heads
// Example of output if the number is less than .5.
Random toss value: 0.4565522878478414
//random()gives out a different value each time
```

> **Note**
>
> The numbers that you obtain are likely to be different to the ones presented here.

5. Edit the **if-else-statements.js** document, add the following bolded code, and then save it:

```
if(tossValue>= .5){
   console.log("Heads");
}else{
   console.log("Tails");
}
```

If the **if** statement expression is **true**, the statements in its block are processed and the **else** block statements are skipped. If the **if** block expression is **false**, only the statements in the **else** block are processed.

6. Reload the `if-else-statements.html` web page in your web browser with the console window open:

```
// Example of output if the number is .5 or greater.
Random toss value: 0.9519471939452648
Heads
// Example of output if the number is less than .5.
Random toss value: 0.07600044264786021
Tails
```

Again, you will see different outcomes depending on the logical expression of the `if` statement. Consider how an `if` statement may handle toggling a like icon on the screen.

if Statements with Multiple else...if Statements

You can have one or more `else...if` statements in addition to the `if` statement. The `if` statement and each `else...if` statement has its own expression. If the code in the first statement has an expression evaluated as **true**, it is processed and the code in all the other statements is skipped. If none of the expressions evaluate to **true**, all the code statements are skipped. The syntax is as follows:

```
if(boolean expression){
    //Statement
    //Statement
    //Statement
}else if(boolean expression){
    //Statement
    //Statement
    //Statement
}else if(boolean expression){
    //Statement
    //Statement
    //Statement
}

if(boolean expression)
    //Single statement
else if(boolean expression)
    //Single statement
else if(boolean expression)
    //Single statement
```

The following flowchart illustrates one or more **else...if** statements in addition to the **if** statement. Each of the Boolean expressions is evaluated in the order they're encountered. The code is processed if the first expression is **true**, and the code processing procedure skips to the code following the last **else...if** statement:

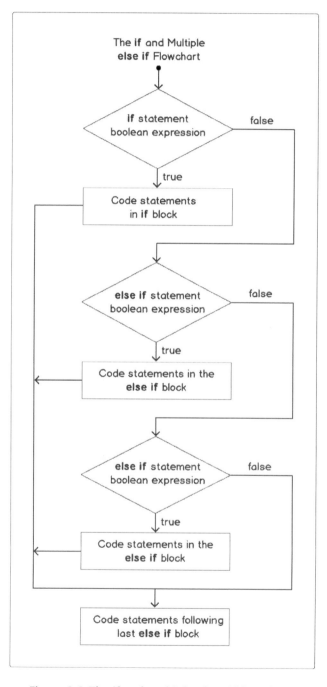

Figure 3.6: The if and multiple else...if flowchart

if Statement, Multiple else…if statements, and the else Statement

You can have one **else** statement follow the last **else...if** statement. If the code in the first statement has an expression evaluated to **true**, is it processed and the code in all other statements is skipped. If none of the expressions evaluate to **true**, then the code in the **else** statement is processed. The syntax is as follows:

```
if(boolean expression){
    //Statement
    //Statement
    //Statement
}else if(boolean expression){
    //Statement
    //Statement
    //Statement
}else if(boolean expression){
    //Statement
    //Statement
    //Statement
}else{
    //Statement
}

if(boolean expression)
    //Single statement
else if(boolean expression)
    //Single statement
else if(boolean expression)
    //Single statement
else
    //Single statement
```

The following flowchart the illustrates inclusion of the **else** statement, along with **else if** statements and the **if** statement. If all the Boolean expressions are false, then the code in the **else** block is processed:

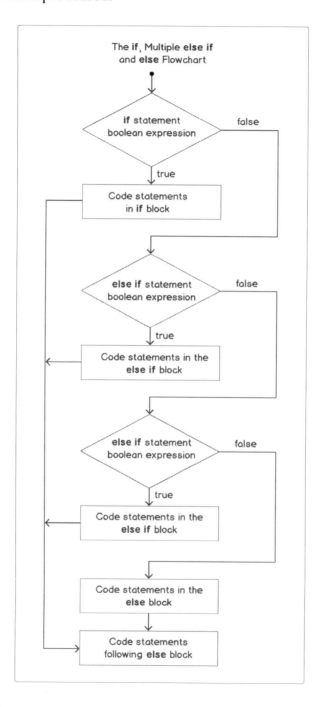

Figure 3.7: The **else** statement, along with **else...if** statements and the **if** statement

Exercise 3.07: Writing an if Statement with Multiple if else Statements and the else Statement

In this exercise, we will build a simple game that generates four random game numbers from 1 to 21 inclusive. One is the player's score, one is the target score, one is a lucky score, and the last is an unlucky score. The player gets a wallet of 20 times the player's score. There are five possible outcomes, with each assigning different wins or losses to the player's wallet:

- The player's score matches the lucky score, and the lucky score and the unlucky score are different. The wallet is increased by the lucky value plus the player's score times **10**.

- The player's score equals the unlucky score, and the lucky score and the unlucky score are different. The wallet is reduced to zero.

- The player's score equals the target score. The wallet is increased by the difference between **21** and the target score times **10**.

- The player's score beats the target score. The wallet is increased by the difference between the player's score and the target score times **10**.

- The target score beats the player's score. The wallet is decreased by the difference between the target score and the player's score times **10**.

    The steps for completion are as follows:

1. Open the **if-else-if-else-statements.html** document in your web browser.

2. Open the web developer **console window** using your web browser.

3. Open the **if-else-if-else-statements.js** document in your code editor, replace all of its content with the following code, and then save it:

```
var target = Math.floor(Math.random() * 21) + 1;
var player = Math.floor(Math.random() * 21) + 1;
console.log("Target score:", target);
console.log("Player score:", player);
if (player >= target){
  console.log("Player wins: beats target by " + (player - target));
}else{
  console.log("Player loses: misses target by " + (target - player));
}
```

We will start by matching the target or exceeding it using the **if** statement block, **if (player >= target)**. The **else** statement block stating "Player loses: misses target by" covers being below the target.

4. Reload the **if-else-if-else-statements.html** web page in your web browser with the console window open. Repeat until you see a version for each of these three examples.

    An example of the player's score exceeding the target is as follows:

    ```
    Target score: 5
    Player score: 13
    Player wins: beats target by 8
    ```

    The following is an example of the player's score matching the target. In this case, the message is not supporting the logic:

    ```
    Target score: 14
    Player score: 14
    Player wins: beats target by 0
    ```

    An example of the target exceeding the player's score is as follows:

    ```
    Target score: 19
    Player score: 1
    Player loses: misses target by 18
    ```

    Now, we can add a code some handle the player matching the target.

5. Edit the **if-else-if-else-statements.js** document, add the following bolded code, and then remove the strikethrough code and save it:

    ```
    console.log("Player score:", player);
    if (player == target){
     console.log("Player wins: ties target " + target);
    }else if (player > target){
     console.log("Player wins: beats target by " + (player - target);
    }else{
    ```

    A new **if** statement block is added to handle the condition when the player ties with the target. The original **if** statement block is replaced with an **else...if** statement block that only tests for conditions when the player's value exceeds the target.

6. Reload the **if-else-if-else-statements.html** web page in your web browser with the console window open. Repeat this until you see a version for each of these three examples.

An example of a player's score exceeding the target is as follows:

```
Target score: 7
Player score: 14
Player wins: beats target by 7
```

The following is an example of a player matching the target. In this case, the message is not supporting the logic:

```
Target score: 3
Player score: 3
Player wins: ties target 3
```

An example of the target exceeding the player's score is as follows:

```
Target score: 10
Player score: 5
Player loses: misses target by 5
```

7. Edit the **if-else-if-else-statements.js** document, update it using the following bolded code, and then save it.

A variable for the lucky and unlucky number are added and are output to the console so that we can observe them:

```
var target = Math.floor(Math.random() * 21) + 1;
var player = Math.floor(Math.random() * 21) + 1;
var lucky = Math.floor(Math.random() * 21) + 1;
var unlucky = Math.floor(Math.random() * 21) + 1;
console.log("Target score:", target);
console.log("Player score:", player);
console.log("Lucky score:", lucky);
console.log("Unlucky score:", unlucky);
```

8. Next, we add an **if** statement block when the lucky value does not match the unlucky value and the player value matches the lucky value. The use of the logical **&&** operator handles the two required tests, both of which need to be true.

This condition preempts the other winning and losing condition **if** statements, so it needs to precede them. Add the following bolded code and remove the strikethrough code:

```
if (lucky != unlucky && player == lucky){
  console.log("Player wins: matches lucky score.");
}else if (player == target){
  console.log("Player wins: ties target " + target);
}
```

9. We also want a condition when the lucky value does not match the unlucky value, and the player value matches the unlucky value. Again, the use of the logical **&&** operator handles the two required tests, both of which need to be true.

    This condition preempts the other winning and losing condition **if** statements, so it needs to precede them. Insert the following bolded code:

```
if (lucky != unlucky && player == lucky){
  console.log("Player wins: matches lucky score.");
}else if (lucky != unlucky && player == unlucky){
  console.log("Player loses: matches unlucky score.");
}else if (player == target){
```

10. Reload the **if-else-if-else-statements.html** web page in your web browser with the console window open. Repeat this until you see a version for each of these two examples.

    The following is an example of a player matching the lucky number, but not the unlucky number:

```
Target score: 7
Player score: 14
Lucky score: 16
Unlucky score: 20
Player wins: matches lucky score
```

The following is an example of a player matching the unlucky number, but not the lucky number:

```
Target score: 4
Player score: 9
Lucky score: 3
Unlucky score: 9
Player loses: matches unlucky score.
```

11. Edit the `if-else-if-else-statements.js` document, update it with the following bolded code, and then save it.

The initial wallet value is **10** times the player's score. It is displayed along with the other game data:

```
var unlucky = Math.floor(Math.random() * 21) + 1;
var wallet = player * 20;
console.log("Target score:", target);
console.log("Unlucky score:", unlucky);
console.log("Player initial wallet:", wallet);
```

If there is a match with the lucky number, the wallet is increased by the player's score and the lucky score times **10**.

```
if (lucky != unlucky && player == lucky){
  console.log("Player wins: matches lucky score.");
  wallet += (lucky + player) * 10;
```

If there is a match with the unlucky number, the wallet is decreased to zero:

```
}else if (lucky != unlucky && player == unlucky){
  console.log("Player loses: matches unlucky score.");
  wallet = 0;
```

If the player's score matches the target, the wallet is increased by the difference between **21** and the target:

```
}else if (player == target){
  console.log("Player wins: ties target " + target);
  wallet += (21 - target) * 10;
```

If the player's score exceeds the target, the wallet is increased by the difference times **10**:

```
}else if (player > target){
  console.log("Player wins: beats target by " + (player - target));
  wallet += (player - target) * 10;
```

The **else** statement block reduces the wallet by the difference between the target and the player. It ties **10**, but not below zero.

After the `if`, `if else`, and `else` block statements, the player's final wallet is displayed:

```
}else{
  console.log("Player loses: misses target by " + (target - player));
  wallet = Math.max(0, wallet - (target - player) * 10);
}
console.log("Player final wallet:", wallet);
```

12. Reload the **if-else-if-else-statements.html** web page in your web browser with the console window open. Repeat this until you see a version for each of these examples.

The following is an example of the target exceeding the player's score and the amount being deducted from the wallet exceeding the wallet balance. In this case, the wallet is reduced to zero:

```
Target score: 4
8 Player score: 1
Lucky score: 6
Unlucky score: 4
Player initial wallet: 20
Player loses: misses target by 3
Players final wallet: 0
```

The following is an example of the player's score exceeding the target score. The wallet increased by **10** times the difference exceeded:

```
Target score: 10
Player score: 18
Lucky score: 21
Unlucky score: 10
Player initial wallet: 360
Player wins: beats target by 8
Players final wallet: 440
```

The following is an example of the player's score matching the target score. The wallet increased by **10** times the difference of **21** and the target:

```
Target score: 19
Player score: 19
Lucky score: 4
Unlucky score: 7
Player initial wallet: 380
Player wins: ties target 19
Players final wallet: 400
```

The following is an example of the player matching the lucky number, but not the unlucky number. The wallet is increased by the player and the target times **10**:

```
Target score: 19
Player score: 1
Lucky score: 1
Unlucky score: 7
Player initial wallet: 20
Player wins: matches lucky score.
Players final wallet: 40
```

The following is an example of the player matching the unlucky number, but not the lucky number. The wallet is reduced to **0**:

```
Target score: 8
Player score: 13
Lucky score: 10
Unlucky score: 13
Player initial wallet: 260
Player loses: matches unlucky score.
Players final wallet: 0
```

This was a much longer exercise. It showed you how multiple **if** statements with different logic expressions can work together to produce one outcome. You will have noticed that the order of the logical expressions can make a difference because in this case, the lucky and unlucky values needed to be resolved before the target value expressions. Changing the order would produce a whole set of different outcomes.

The break Statement

The **break** statement is used within blocks for **loop** statements and the **switch** statements. When the **break** statement is encountered inside **loop** statement and **switch** statement blocks, program flow continues on the next line following the block. The syntax is as follows:

```
break
break label
```

The second syntax form is required when it's used within a labeled statement block. You will find out more about labeled statements later in this chapter. The upcoming exercises will make use of the **break** statement.

switch Statement

The **switch** statement defines a block of code divided up by **case** statements and an optional **default** statement. The **case** statements are followed by a possible value for the **switch** statement expression and then a colon, :. Optionally, the code will follow a **case** statement. The **default** statement is just followed by a colon, :.

How does it work? The **switch** statement's expression is evaluated and the code following the first **case** statement that has a value that matches the **switch** statement's expression value is processed until a **break** statement is reached. Then, any remaining code is skipped. If none of the **case** statement values match and there is a **default** statement, then the code following the **default** statement is processed. Otherwise, no code is processed. The syntax is as follows:

```
switch(expression){
    case expression_value:
        //Optional statement(s)
        break; //optional
    case expression_value:
        //Optional statement(s)
        break; //optional
    default:
        //Statement(s)
}
```

The following is a flowchart illustrating the **switch** statement:

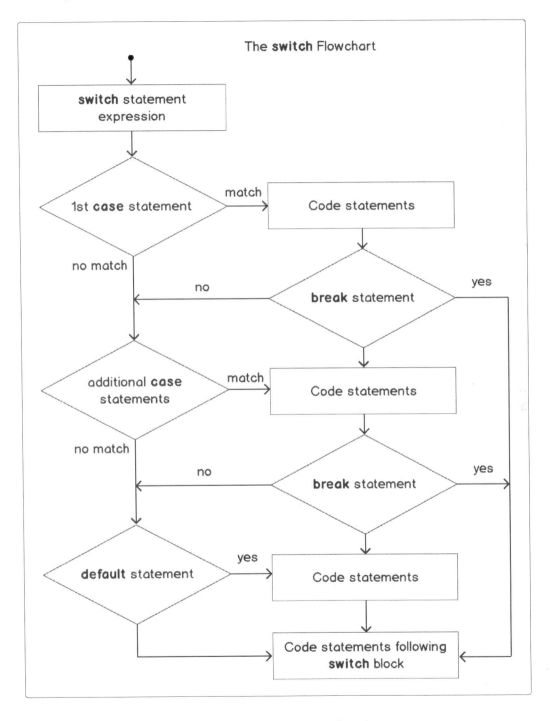

Figure 3.8: Switch statement flowchart

Exercise 3.08: Writing a switch Statement and Testing It

We are going to use the **switch** statement by simulating a game where the player can move their playing pieces using their keyboard. They can move left with the **A** key, right with the **S** key, up with the **W** key, and down with the **Z** key. To simulate a random selection of the keys, in either uppercase or lowercase, from the **keyNames** string, a variable will be used. Let's get started:

1. Open the **switch-statement.html** document in your web browser.

2. Open the web developer console window using your web browser.

3. Open the **switch-statement.js** document in your code editor, replace all of its content with the following code, and then save it:

```
var keyNames = "WASDwasd";
var keyName = keyNames.charAt(Math.floor(Math.random() * keyNames.
length));
console.log("keyName:", keyName);
```

The **Math.floor(Math.random() * keys.length)** expression is selecting a number from **0** to **7** that is then used by **charAt** to select the character from the **keyNames** string variable.

4. Run a few tests by reloading the **switch-statement.html** web page in your web browser with the console window open. Your results will show selections from the **ADWSadws** characters. Here are some examples of the console output:

```
keyName: a
keyName: S
```

5. Edit the **switch-statement.js** document so that it includes the following bolded lines and then save it.

The **switch** statement expression is as follows:

```
console.log("keyName:", keyName);
switch (keyName.toLowerCase()){
```

The **switch** statement expression converts the character into lowercase so that each case statement can check for one value. Here, we are checking whether the case value is equal to the switch term:

```
case "a":
  console.log("move left"); //This block will execute when break; //
keyName is a
case "d":
  console.log("move right");//This block will execute when break; //
keyName is d
```

```
  case "w":
    console.log("move up");//This block will execute when break; //
  keyName is w
  case "s":
    console.log("move down");//This block will execute when break; //
  keyName is s


}
```

The **switch** statement uses one expression and then determines the lines of code to process based on matching the result with the case statements. It is important to note that without a **break** statement, all the code to the end of the **switch** statement is processed once one case statement matches the expression value. This can be an advantage when more than one case statement uses the same code. The default statement allows for code that is being processed when none of the case statements match the expression value. However, remember that a default statement is not required. In this example, if the user pressed a wrong key, nothing would happen, which is often the case with game consoles.

6. Reload the **switch-statement.html** web page in your web browser with the console window open. The following are some sample results:

```
keyName: S
move down


keyName: d
move right
```

Let's use the **IJKL** keys to perform the same tasks. We'll use the **I** key for up, the **J** key for left, the **K** key for right, and the **M** key for down.

Edit the **switch-statement.js** document, include the following bolded lines and save it.

First, add the new key letters:

```
var keyNames = "WASDwasdIJKMijkm";
```

Next, add the case statements for each:

```
case "a":
case "j":
 console.log("move left");
 break;
case "d":
case "k":
 console.log("move right");
 break;
case "w":
case "i":
 console.log("move up");
 break;
case "s":
case "m":
 console.log("move down");
 break;
}
```

When case statements are not followed by a break, the next case statement's code is also processed.

7. Reload the **switch-statement.html** web page in your web browser with the console window open. The following are some sample results:

```
keyName: J
move left

keyName: w
move up
```

The simulated code does not generate any keys that are not matched by the **case** statements. If there were, the entire **switch** statement is skipped. The **switch** statement can handle other cases by using the **default** statement.

8. Edit the **switch-statement.js** document, include the following bolded lines, and then save it. First, let's add a few test characters:

```
var keyNames = "WASDwasdIJKMijkmRTXPrtxp";
```

Next, let's add the **default** statement:

```
case "m":
  console.log("move down");
  break;
default:
  console.log("invalid key");
  break;
}
```

9. Reload the **switch-statement.html** web page in your web browser with the console window open. Repeat this until you see a result indicating an invalid key:

```
keyName: R
invalid key
```

In this exercise, if the user pressed a wrong key, nothing would happen, which is often the case with game consoles.

Loop Statements

Loop code blocks are also called iterative blocks. They are designed to continue processing the code in their blocks until the **loop** statement expression becomes false. Iteration is a term that's used to indicate one time through the loop.

> **Note**
>
> A loop that does not terminate is called an infinite loop. A web browser may display a dialog with the option to terminate long-running loops.

for Statement

The **for** statement repeats the code until the repeat expression becomes **false**. The syntax is as follows:

```
for(initialize statement; repeat expression; post expression){
    //Statement
    //Statement
}
```

The following flowchart depicts how the **for** statement works:

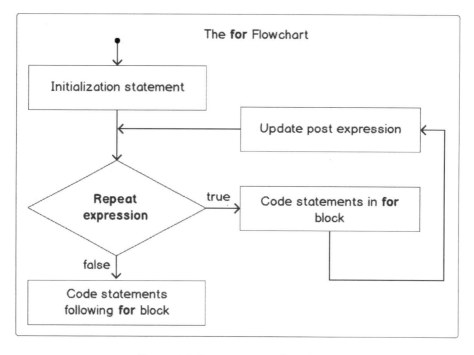

Figure 3.9: for statement flowchart

The first time the **for** statement is reached, the **initialize** statement is processed. It normally sets a variable that is used in the repeat expression. The post expression changes a value in the repeat expression. After the last line of code in the loop is processed, the post expression is processed and then the repeat expression is processed. If the repeat expression remains true, the first statement in the loop block is processed again. The post expression often makes use of the arithmetic operators called increment and decrement and the assignment addition and subtraction operators. Some examples of more arithmetic operators are as follows:

Operator	Description	Examples	Results
++	Increment	var i = 1	i = 1
		i++	i = 2
--	Decrement	var i = 10	i = 10
		i--	i = 9
+=	Addition	var i = 1	i = 1
		i += 4	i = 5
-=	Subtraction	var i = 10	i = 10
		i -= 4	i = 6
*=	Multiplication	var i = 2	i = 2
		i *= 5	i = 10
/=	Division	var i = 9	i = 9
		i /= 3	i = 3

Figure 3.10: More arithmetic operators

Exercise 3.09: Writing a for Loop and Testing It

This exercise demonstrates using the **for** statement to create an increasing counter and decreasing counter. Let's get started:

1. Open the **for-statement.html** document in your web browser.

2. Open the web developer console window using your web browser.

3. Open the **for-statement.js** document in your code editor, replace all of its content with the following code, and then save it:

```
for(var i = 1; i<= 5; i++){
  console.log(i);
}
```

This example is an incrementing counter loop. The **initialize** statement declares the **i** variable and assigns it a value of **1**. This is the value it has on the first iteration of the loop. At the end of the loop, the repeat expression is evaluated and, if true, the line following the loop is processed. The post expression uses the increment operator to increase the **i** 1 variable at the end of each loop.

4. Reload the **for-statement.html** web page in your web browser with the **console window** open. The following are the results:

```
1
2
3
4
5
```

5. Edit the **for-statement.js** document using the following bolded lines and then save it:

```
for(var i = 5; i>= 1; i--){
  console.log(i);
}
```

This example illustrates a decreasing counter loop. In this example, the post expression uses the decrement operator. The repeat expression is changed to be true until the **i** variable values are **1** or less. The **initialize** statement declares the **i** variable and sets it to **5**.

6. Reload the **for-statement.html** web page in your web browser with the console window open. The following are the results:

```
5
4
3
2
1
```

7. Edit the **for-statement.js** document using the following bolded lines and then save it:

```
for(var i = 2; i<= 10; i+=2){
  console.log(i);
}
```

This example features the addition assignment operator is used to create a counter loop that increments by **2**, starting with **2** and ending with **10**.

8. Reload the **for-statement.html** web page in your web browser with the console window open. The following are the results:

```
2
4
6
8
10
```

The **for** loop is the workhorse for repeating code for a counted number of iterations. You will find greater use for it by iterating through arrays.

do...while Statement

The **do...while** statement is a loop that executes code until the repeat expression value becomes false. The repeat expression is evaluated aftcr all the statements have been processed, resulting in the guarantee that they are processed once. The syntax is as follows:

```
do{
    //Statement
    //Statement
} while(repeat expression

do
    //Single statement
while(repeat expression)
```

A semicolon needs to be at the end of the **while** line if you are using it elsewhere.

Here is the flowchart for the **do...while** statement:

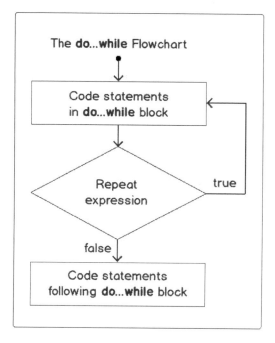

Figure 3.11: do...while statement flowchart

Exercise 3.10: Writing a do...while Loop and Testing It

In this exercise, you will use the **do...while** loop to simulate iterating the roll of two dice until they have the same value. Let's get started:

1. Open the **do-while-statements.html** document in your web browser.

2. Open the web developer console window using your web browser.

3. Open the **do-while-statements.js** document in your code editor, replace all of its content with the following code, and then save it:

```
do{
  var die1 = Math.floor(Math.random() * 6) + 1;
  var die2 = Math.floor(Math.random() * 6) + 1;
  console.log("Die 1:", die1, "Die 2:", die2);
}while(die1 != die2);
```

The second and third lines each compute a random number from **1** to **6** and store it in a variable. Those variables are displayed on the third line. These lines are always executed once. The **while** condition is true if the values of the **die1** and **die2** variables are not equal. If the values are equal, the expression is false and the loop repeats. If the values are not equal, any statements that follow the **do...while** loop are processed.

4. Run a few tests by reloading the **do-while-statements.html** web page in your web browser with the **console window** open. Your results will differ due to the random values.

The following is an example result of more than one iteration:

```
Die 1: 1 Die 2: 3
Die 1: 2 Die 2: 3
Die 1: 3 Die 2: 4
Die 1: 4 Die 2: 5
Die 1: 3 Die 2: 3
```

The following example shows the results of a single iteration. **do...while** loop statements are always processed one at a time:

```
Die 1: 5 Die 2: 5
```

5. Edit the **do-while-statements.js** document so that it includes the following bolded lines and then save it:

```
let iterations = 0;
do{
  iterations++;
  var die1 = Math.floor(Math.random() * 6) + 1;
  var die2 = Math.floor(Math.random() * 6) + 1;
  console.log("Die 1:", die1, "Die 2:", die2);

}while(die1 != die2);
console.log("The matched value is: ", die1);
console.log("Number of iterations: ", iterations);
```

The first line, **let iterations**, is declaring a variable named iterations and assigning it to **0**. Then, in the **do...while** loop, the iterations variable, **iterations++**, is incremented by **1**. After the loop, the matched value and the iterations are displayed.

6. Run a few tests by reloading the **do-while-statements.html** web page in your web browser with the console window open. Your results will differ due to the random values.

The following example is the result of more than one iteration:

```
Die 1: 1 Die 2: 3
Die 1: 2 Die 2: 3
Die 1: 5 Die 2: 4
Die 1: 3 Die 2: 1
Die 1: 4 Die 2: 4
The matched value is:   4
Number of iterations:   5
```

The following example is the result of a single iteration:

```
Die 1: 4 Die 2: 4
The matched value is:   4
Number of iterations:   1
```

while Statement

The **while** statement is a loop that executes code if the repeat expression is **true/false**. The repeat expression is evaluated before any code is executed, so there is the possibility that no code is processed if it is **false** the first time round. The syntax is as follows:

```
while(repeat expression){
    //Statement
    //Statement
}

while (repeat expression)
    //Single statement
```

The **while** statement flow is illustrated as follows:

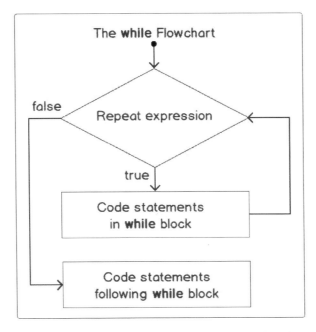

Figure 3.12: Code statements in the while block

Exercise 3.11: Writing a while Loop and Testing It

In this exercise, we will use the **while** loop to simulate how many dice rolls it takes to roll an even number. Let's get started:

1. Open the **while-statement.html** document in your web browser.

2. Open the web developer console window using your web browser.

3. Open the **while-statement.js** document in your code editor, replace all of its content with the following code, and then save it:

```
let iterations = 0;
while (iterations <10){
  console.log("iterations:", iterations);
  iterations ++;
}
```

This is just the initial shell for a **while** loop that repeats 10 times. The **while** loop's repeat expression is true if the **iterations** variable is below the value of **10**. The first time the expression is evaluated, the **iterations** variable is **0**. Inside the **while** loop, the **iterations** variable is incremented by **1** on the first line and will increase from **0** to **9** on each iteration of the loop.

4. Reload the **while-statement.html** web page in your web browser with the **console window** open.

   The results show the **iterations** variable increasing from **0** to **9** for **10** iterations:

```
iterations: 0
iterations: 1
iterations: 2
iterations: 3
iterations: 4
iterations: 5
iterations: 6
iterations: 7
iterations: 8
iterations: 9
```

5. Edit the **while-statement.js** document using the following bolded lines and then save it. This adds the line to show a dice roll for each iteration:

```
die = Math.floor(Math.random() * 6) + 1;
console.log("die:", die);
iterations ++;
```

6. Reload the **while-statement.html** web page in your web browser with the console window open.

7. You will see a list of 10 dice values. Your values will differ:

```
die: 2
die: 5
die: 2
die: 4
die: 2
die: 3
die: 4
die: 2
die: 6
die: 1
```

8. Edit the **while-statement.js** document using the following bolded lines and then save it.

    This adds an **if** block to test for an even number of the dice roll. If **true**, the **break** statement terminates the **while** loop and the line following it is processed. The two lines following the **while** loop display how many iterations occurred and the value of the dice roll for that iteration:

```
let die;
while (iterations <10){
  die = Math.floor(Math.random() * 6) + 1;
  if (die % 2 == 0){
    break;
  }
  iterations ++;
}
console.log("Number of iterations: ", iterations + 1);
console.log("Die value: ", die);
```

9. Run a few tests by reloading the **while-statement.html** web page in your web browser with the console window open:

```
Number of iterations:   1
Die value:   2
```

The **while-loop** use a Boolean expression to determine whether any iterations of the code it contains occurred. In this case, if the iterations variable was greater than 10, no iterations would have occurred.

for...in Statement

The **for...in** statement allows us to iterate over an object data type. The variable in the **for** expression holds one of the names of the name-value pairs of the object, which are the names of the properties and methods of the object. The syntax is as follows:

```
for (variable in object){
    //Statement
    //Statement
}

for (variable in object)
    //Single statement
```

You can declare the variable with **const**, **var**, or **let**.

Exercise 3.12: Writing a for...in Loop and Testing It

This exercise applies the for...in loop to the ready-made location object and to a programmer-created object. You can access object names and values by using them. Let's get started:

1. Open the **for-in-statement.html** document in your web browser.

2. Open the web developer console window using your web browser.

3. Open the **for-in-statement.js** document in your code editor, replace all of its content with the following code, and then save it:

```
for (let name in location) {
  console.log(name);
};
```

This iterates the web browser-created **location** object.

4. Reload the **for-in-statement.html** web page in your web browser with the console window open.

The following output shows the names of all the **location** object's properties and methods:

```
replace
href
ancestorOrigins
origin
protocol
host
hostname
port
pathname
search
hash
assign
reload
toString
```

5. Edit the **for-in-statement.js** document, add the following bolded text, and then save it:

```
for (let name in location) {
  console.log(name, ":", location[name]);
};
```

This will add the value of the property or method.

6. Reload the **for-in-statement.html** web page in your web browser with the console window open. The values may differ, assuming the web page was opened from a local file folder and not using http or https:

```
replace : ƒ () { [native code] }
href : file://PATH_TO/for-in-statement.html
ancestorOrigins :DOMStringList {length: 0}
origin : file://
protocol :
host :
hostname :
port :
```

pathname : /PATH_TO/for-in-statement.html

```
search :
hash :
assign : ƒ assign() { [native code] }
reload : ƒ reload() { [native code] }
toString : ƒ toString() { [native code] }
```

7. Edit the **for-in-statement.js** document, replace it with the following code, and then save it:

```
var stopWatch = {
  elapsedTime: 0,
  resultsHistory: [],
  isTiming: true,
  isPaused: true,
  start: function(){console.log("start");},
  pause: function(){console.log("pause");},
  resume: function(){console.log("resume");},
  stop: function(){console.log("stop");}
};
```

8. Below that, add the following code so that we can iterate through the object:

```
for (const name in stopWatch) {
  console.log(name, ":", stopWatch[name]);
};
```

9. Reload the **for-in-statement.html** web page in your web browser with the console window open.

    The following is an example of the output in the console window:

```
elapsedTime : 0
resultsHistory : []
isTiming : true
isPaused : true
start : ƒ (){console.log("start");}
pause : ƒ (){console.log("pause");}
resume : ƒ (){console.log("resume");}
stop : ƒ (){console.log("stop");}
```

Looping through the methods and properties of objects can be helpful when the code depends on a specific property or name that needs to be present for it to work.

for...of Statement

The **for...of** statement focuses on iterable objects. Not all objects are iterable. Although we will not cover how to create our own iterable objects, there are some ready-made iterable objects that you may find the **for...of** block useful for. The syntax is as follows:

```
for (variable of object){
    //Statement
    //Statement
}

for (variable of object)
    //Single statement
```

You can declare the variable with **const**, **var**, or **let**.

Exercise 3.13: Writing a for...of Loop and Testing It

This exercise uses the **for...of** statement, which is designed for iterable objects. You will learn how some objects may not be iterable objects and generate errors. For iterable objects, arrays and strings are used. Let's get started:

1. Open the **for-of-statement.html** document in your web browser.

2. Open the web developer console window using your web browser.

3. Open the **for-of-statement.js** document in your code editor, replace all of its content with the following code, and then save it:

```javascript
var stopWatch = {
  elapsedTime: 0,
  resultsHistory: [],
  isTiming: true,
  isPaused: true,
  start: function(){console.log("start");},
  pause: function(){console.log("pause");},
  resume: function(){console.log("resume");},
  stop: function(){console.log("stop");}
};
```

4. Below that, add the following code so that we can iterate through the object:

```javascript
for (let name of stopWatch) {
  console.log(name, ":", stopWatch[name]);
};
```

5. Reload the **for-of-statement.html** web page in your web browser with the console window open.

An error will occur. We need to code the object so that it's iterable for it to work; however, we are not learning how to do that at this point:

```
Uncaught TypeError: stopWatch is not iterable
```

6. Edit the **for-of-statement.js** document in your code editor, replace all of its content with the following code, and then save it.

A string turns out to be iterable:

```javascript
let anyString = 'abcxyz123';

for (const value of anyString) {
  console.log(value);
}
```

7. Reload the **for-of-statement.html** web page in your web browser with the console window open:

```
a
b
c
x
y
z
1
2
3
```

8. Edit the **for-of-statement.js** document in your code editor, make the changes shown in bold in the following code, and then save it.

   A string turns out to be iterable:

```
let anyString = 'abcxyz123';


/*
for (let value of anyString) {
  console.log(value);
}
*/


for (var i = 0; i<anyString.length; i++) {
  console.log(anyString.charAt(i));
}
```

9. Reload the **for-of-statement.html** web page in your web browser with the console window open. You will get the same results. The advantage of the **for of** loop is that it is more streamlined:

```
a
b
c
x
y
z
1
2
3
```

10. Edit the **for-of-statement.js** document in your code editor, replace all of its content with the following code, and then save it.

An array is iterable:

```
let bowlingScores = [150, 160, 144, 190, 210, 185];

for (const value of bowlingScores) {
  console.log(value);
}
```

11. Reload the **for-of-statement.html** web page in your web browser with the **console** window open:

```
150
160
144
190
210
185
```

12. Edit the **for-of-statement.js** document in your code editor, make the changes shown in bold in the following code, and then save it.

An array is iterable:

```
let bowlingScores = [150, 160, 144, 190, 210, 185];

/*
for (const value of bowlingScores) {
  console.log(value);
}
*/

for (var i = 0; i<bowlingScores.length; i++) {
  console.log(bowlingScores[i]);
}
```

13. Reload the **for-of-statement.html** web page in your web browser with the console window open. You will get the same results:

```
150
160
144
190
210
185
```

Looping through the methods and properties of objects can be helpful when the code depends on a specific property or name that needs to be present for it to work.

continue Statement

The **continue** statement stops execution inside a loop or a labeled loop for the current iteration and starts the execution of the next loop iteration. The **loop** statements then determine whether another iteration should occur. The syntax is as follows:

```
continue

continue label
```

The second syntax is for use within a labeled statement block. We will learn more about labeled statements later in this chapter.

Labeled Statement

The **Labeled** statement is used to create loop flows and conditional flows. It names either **block** statements or **loop** statements. The syntax is as follows:

```
label : {
    //Statement
    //Statement
}

label : loop statement
```

When a **loop** statement is named, the statements are processed until a **break** statement or **continue** statement is encountered inside the block that references the label.

When a **break** statement is encountered, the program flow continues on the line after the labeled statement block referenced by the **break** statement. If a **continue** statement is encountered, the program flow continues on the first line of the block referenced by the **continue** statement. A **continue** statement requires the labeled statement to be a loop. Both **break** statements and **continue** statements must appear within the labeled statement block that they reference. They cannot appear outside the labeled statement block that they reference. They can appear in nested labeled blocks and reference outer labeled blocks. Labeled statements are less commonly used because they are prone to creating confusing or difficult to follow program flow.

> **Note**
>
> It is good practice to avoid or find ways to eliminate all labeled statements from code. Conditional statements and dividing code into functions or object methods are alternatives to labeled statements.

Let's have a look at an example of using a labeled loop statement. The loop labels the **for** statement, which runs 10 iterations. Each iteration generates a random number from **1** to **12**. If the number is even, the **continue** statement starts the beginning of the **for** statement:

```
console.log("Odd number count started!");
let oddsCount = 0;
odd_number:
 for (let i = 1; i<= 10; i++){
   console.log("Iteration:", i);
   var number = Math.floor(Math.random() * 12) + 1;
   if (number % 2 == 0){
    continue odd_number;
   }
   oddsCount ++;
   console.log("Number:", number);
 }
 console.log(oddsCount + " odd numbers found!");
```

The output of the preceding code snippet is as follows:

```
Odd number count started!
Iteration: 1
Iteration: 2
Iteration: 3
Iteration: 4
Number: 7
Iteration: 5
Iteration: 6
Number: 5
Iteration: 7
Iteration: 8
Iteration: 9
Number: 3
3 odd numbers found!
```

The label can be eliminated with a better use of the **if** statement to achieve the same result:

```
console.log("Odd number count started!");
let oddsCount = 0;
for (let i = 1; i<= 10; i++){
  console.log("Iteration:", i);
  var number = Math.floor(Math.random() * 12) + 1;
  if (number % 2 != 0){
    oddsCount ++;
    console.log("Number:", number);
  }
}
console.log(oddsCount + " odd numbers found!");
```

The output is the same, but with different values:

```
Odd number count started!
Iteration: 1
Iteration: 2
Number: 9
Iteration: 3
Number: 5
Iteration: 4
Iteration: 5
Number: 5
Iteration: 6
```

```
Iteration: 7
Number: 9
Iteration: 8
Iteration: 9
Number: 1
Iteration: 10
Number: 7
6 odd numbers found!
```

Writing and Invoking Functions

Functions are the basic building blocks when it comes to writing JavaScript programs. A function is one or more statements that can optionally receive data input and provide data output. The statements in a function are not used until the function is invoked. Invoking a function is also known as calling the function.

Defining Functions

JavaScript offers a few ways to define a function. We are going to look at function declarations, function expressions, and arrow function expressions as ways to define a function.

Function Declaration

You can define a function as a statement. This is called a function definition or declaration. The syntax is as follows:

```
function name(optional parameter list) {
    //Statements
    //Optional return statement
}
```

It starts a line of code with the function keyword. It is followed by a name. The name is how the function will appear in other code. The list of comma-separated parameters are names for the input values to a function. Parameters are essentially variables within the function. They are enclosed in parentheses. The block statement then contains the code. Once a function is declared, it can be invoked either on a line of code by itself or within an expression. In the case of its use in an expression, the function typically returns data.

When a JavaScript function is declared as a statement, it can be invoked by statements that appear before it. This is called hoisting.

Let's have a look at an example of defining and invoking a function declaration. This example has no parameters and returns the value of a single dice roll:

```
function getDiceRollValue(){
   return Math.floor(Math.random() * 6) + 1;
}
```

Since it returns a value, we can use it as an expression. Here is an example where it is used in an addition expression to get the roll value of two dice:

```
var rollValue = getDiceRollValue() + getDiceRollValue();
```

We could improve the function so that it returns the value of a set number of dice by creating a parameter. Here, the parameter is the number of dice being rolled:

```
function getDiceRoll(numberOfDice){
  var rollValue = 0;
  for (let i = 1; i<= numberOfDice; i++){
   rollValue += Math.floor(Math.random() * 6) + 1;
  }
  return rollValue;
}
```

The revised expression to invoke for simulating a two-dice roll just requires us to pass the parameter values. In this example, the parameter is expressed as a number literal:

```
var rollValue = getDiceRollValue(2);
```

In this example, the parameter is expressed as a variable:

```
var numberOfDice = 2;
var rollValue = getDiceRollValue(numberOfDice);
```

Parameters can be optional, otherwise the wrong data can be passed. So, functions often have code that validates the parameter or provides a default value. In this example, the argument of the JavaScript built-in function known as **parseInt** is used to convert the argument into an integer. Its results are tested using the **isNaN** built-in function, which returns **true** or **false** if the number is not a number or the number is less than **1**. If any of that is true, the argument value is set to **1**. If not, the supplied number is passed through:

```
function getDiceRoll(numberOfDice){
  numberOfDice = (isNaN(parseInt(numberOfDice)) || numberOfDice< 1) ?1
  :numberOfDice;
  var rollValue = 0;
  for (let i = 1; i<= numberOfDice; i++){
   rollValue += Math.floor(Math.random() * 6) + 1;
```

```
  }
  return rollValue;
}
```

Now, the function always returns a roll of one dice, regardless of an incorrect parameter or no parameter. In both of these examples, the value of the roll of one dice is returned:

```
var rollValue = getDiceRoll();
var rollValue = getDiceRoll("BOGUS");
```

Exercise 3.14: Writing a Function as a Statement and Invoking It

This exercise will define a function as a statement and then use it. The function we will create will accept one parameter and return an array. If the parameter can be validated as a number, then each item in the array has one digit from the number starting with the **0** index item holding the digit for the ones place value, the 1 index item holding the digit for the **tens** place value, and so on.

We will use the **log** method of the **console** object in this exercise. Remember that a method is a function that belongs to an object, so it can have parameters. The **log** method takes an unlimited number of parameters. Let's get started:

1. Open the **function-declare.html** document in your web browser.

2. Open the web developer console window using your web browser.

3. Open the **function-declare.js** document in your code editor, replace all of its content with the following code, and then save it.

    This declares the function. Its name is **getDigitsOfNumber**. It has one parameter named **num**. It returns the **digits** array:

    ```
    function getDigitsOfNumber(num) {
      var digits = [];
      console.log("num:", num);
      return digits;
    }
    ```

4. Reload the **function-declare.html** web page in your web browser with the console window open.

    There is no output because the function was not invoked.

5. Edit the **function-declare.js** document, add the following bolded text to the end of the file, and then save it.

In this example, the function is being expressed and is not being invoked. Invoking a function requires to append parentheses around the function's name:

```
  return digits;
}
console.log("getDigitsOfNumber:", getDigitsOfNumber);
```

6. Reload the **function-declare.html** web page in your web browser with the console window open.

The function is treated as data and is displayed:

```
getDigitsOfNumber: ƒ getDigitsOfNumber(num){
  var digits = [];
  console.log("num:", num);
  return digits;
}
```

7. Edit the **function-declare.js** document, update it using the following bolded text at the end of the file, and then save it.

This invokes the function in an assignment statement to create the **test456** variable:

```
  return digits;
}
var test456 = getDigitsOfNumber(456);
console.log("test456:", test456);
```

This will add the value of the property or method.

8. Reload the **function-declare.html** web page in your web browser with the console window open. The first line of output shows the **num** parameter being displayed when the function was invoked. The second output line is the **test456** variable being set to the empty array that was returned by the function:

```
num: 456
test456: =>[]
```

9. Edit the **function-declare.js** document, add the following bolded text to the beginning of the file, and then save it. This shows invoking the function before it is declared. This demonstrates hoisting:

```
var test123 = getDigitsOfNumber(123);
console.log("test123:", test123);
function getDigitsOfNumber_1(num){
```

10. Reload the **function-declare.html** web page in your web browser with the console window open. These are the results for the invocations of the function before and after it was declared:

```
num: 123
test123: =>[]
num: 456
test456: =>[]
```

11. Edit the **function-declare.js** document, update it using the following bolded text, and then save it.

The second line in the function converts any negative numbers into positive numbers and truncates any decimals. The **if** statement tests to assure that the **num** parameter contains a number. The **while** loop repeats until the **num** parameter becomes zero. Inside the loop, the ones place value is added to the **digits** array by dividing by 10 and using the remainder. Then, the ones place value is stripped from the **num** parameter:

```
function getDigitsOfNumber(num){
  var digits = [];
  num = Math.floor(Math.abs(num));
  if(!isNaN(num)){
    while(num != 0) {
      digits.push(num % 10);
      num = Math.floor(num / 10);
    }
  }
  return digits;
}
```

12. Reload the **function-declare.html** web page in your web browser with the console window open.

Each array shows the test value digits split into arrays. The zero-array index has the ones place value, the one array index has the tens place value, and the two-index position has the hundreds place value:

```
test123: =>(3) [3, 2, 1]
test456: =>(3) [6, 5, 4]
```

13. Edit the **function-declare.js** document, add the following bolded text to the end of the file, and then save it. You can run various tests on your functions based on the possible inputs and expected outputs. These are a few for you to try.

An intermediate variable is not used for these new lines. A function can be used wherever an expression can be used. In these additions, it is used as an expression for a **log** method parameter:

```
var test456 = getDigitsOfNumber(456);
console.log("test456:", test456);
console.log('5:', getDigitsOfNumber(5));
console.log('4563:', getDigitsOfNumber(4563));
console.log('123.654:', getDigitsOfNumber(123.654));
console.log('-123.654:', getDigitsOfNumber(-123.654));
console.log('"1000"', getDigitsOfNumber("1000"));
console.log('"1,000"', getDigitsOfNumber("1,000"));
console.log('"B37"', getDigitsOfNumber("B37"));
console.log('"37B"', getDigitsOfNumber("37B"));
```

14. Reload the **function-declare.html** web page in your web browser with the console window open.

Here are the outputs. The expected results should be an array with all the digits or an empty array. Evaluate each output and verify that this was the result. If the output was an empty array, determine why:

```
test123: =>(3) [3, 2, 1]
test456: =>(3) [6, 5, 4]
5: =>[5]
4563: =>(4) [3, 6, 5, 4]
123.654: =>(3) [3, 2, 1]
-123.654: =>(3) [3, 2, 1]
"1000" =>(4) [0, 0, 0, 1]
"1,000" =>[]
"B37" =>[]
"37B" =>[]
```

In this exercise, we defined a function as a statement that accepts one parameter and return an array. We used the **log** method of the **console** object in this exercise.

Function Expression

In this variation, you can define a function as part of an expression. There is no name for the function. However, because a function is a data type, it can be assigned to a variable. The variable can then be used to invoke the function. The syntax is as follows:

```
function(optional parameter list) {
    //Statements
    //Optional return statement
}
```

The syntax is the same, except no function name is needed. A JavaScript function declared as an expression cannot be invoked by statements that appear before it.

Here is an example of defining and invoking a function expression.

This example shows the function as part of an assignment expression. The right-hand side of the assignment is the function without a name. The left-hand side is the variable:

```
var getDiceValue = function(){
  return Math.floor(Math.random() * 6) + 1;
}
```

In this case, the variable can be used to invoke the function:

```
var rollValue = getDiceValue() + getDiceValue();
```

Exercise 3.15: Writing a Function as an Expression and Invoking It

This exercise defines a function as an expression and then uses it.

The function returns a single random character from a string. The string is the function's only parameter. If the parameter is not a string or is an empty string, then an empty string is returned. Let's get started:

1. Open the **function-expression.html** document in your web browser.

2. Open the web developer console window using your web browser.

3. Open the **function-expression.js** document in your code editor, replace all of its contents with the following code, and then save it.

   The function, as a literal value, is assigned to the **getRandomStringCharacter** variable.

Then, the variable is displayed in the console. Remember, a function is not invoked unless you include parentheses:

```
var getRandomStringCharacter = function(source){
  var returnCharacter = '';
  console.log("source:", source);
  return returnCharacter;
}
console.log('getRandomStringCharacter', getRandomStringCharacter);
```

4. Reload the **function-expression.html** web page in your web browser with the console window open. The actual function is displayed but not invoked, as expected:

```
getRandomStringCharacter ƒ (source){
  var returnCharacter = '';
  console.log("source:", source);
  return returnCharacter;
}
```

5. Edit the **function-expression.js** document, update the lines with the following bolded text, and then save it.

Now, we will invoke the function:

```
  return returnCharacter;
}
getRandomStringCharacter();
getRandomStringCharacter("AEIOU");
```

6. Reload the **function-expression.html** web page in your web browser with the console window open.

The **console.log** statement in the function displays the **source** parameter value for each invocation. No parameter was passed in the first invocation. The **source** parameter data type is undefined:

```
source: undefined
source: AEIOU
```

7. Edit the **function-expression.js** document, add the following bolded text above the function, and then save it.

Now, we will invoke the function before it is defined:

```
getRandomStringCharacter();
var getRandomStringCharacter = function(source){
  var returnCharacter = '';
```

8. Reload the **function-expression.html** web page in your web browser with the console window open.

You should see an error in the console. Functions that are defined as expressions cannot be invoked before they are defined:

```
Uncaught TypeError: getRandomStringCharacter is not a function
    at function-expression.js:1
```

9. Edit the **function-expression.js** document, update the bolded text, and then save it.

We can remove the line that invokes the function before it is defined and finish coding the function. The **if** block tests whether the source parameter is not undefined and contains characters. In the **if** block, the **Math.floor(Math. random() * source.length** expression finds a random character position as a value from 0 to the length of the **source** parameter minus 1. The **charAt** string method extracts the character at that position it will be returned at:

```
var getRandomStringCharacter = function(source){
  if (source !=undefined &&source.length> 0){
    returnCharacter = source.charAt(Math.floor(Math.random() * source.
length));
  }
  return returnCharacter;
}
```

These lines are a set of tests of various source values. The first passes no parameter. The second, third, and fourth pass a string. The fifth is passing a number and the last is passing a Boolean:

```
console.log('():', getRandomStringCharacter());
console.log('("AEIOU"):', getRandomStringCharacter('AEIOU'));
console.log('("JavaScript"):',
getRandomStringCharacter('JavaScript'));
console.log('("124678"):', getRandomStringCharacter('124678'));
console.log('(124678):', getRandomStringCharacter(124678));
console.log('(true):', getRandomStringCharacter(true));
```

10. Reload the **function-expression.html** web page in your web browser with the **console** window open.

The function's output expects a random character in the source parameter. If it is not empty, it will return a string and will return an empty string for all other values. Reload the web page a few times to get different test results:

```
():
("AEIOU"): U
("124678"): 6
("JavaScript"): a
(124678):
(true):
```

Arrow Function Expression

Arrow functions were introduced in ES6. They are defined similarly in an expression, such as when defining function expressions. They offer syntactically compact alternatives over defining a function expression. There is nothing different in how they are invoked. The **=>** symbol is the telltale sign of an arrow function being defined. Also, the **function** keyword is not used. The concise variation, without a function body, can return an expression with or without a **return** statement. This differs from a function expression, which requires the **return** statement to return a value. The syntax is as follows:

```
(optional parameter list) => {
    //Statements
    //Optional return statement
}
(optional parameter list) => //Expression or return statement
```

Parameter parentheses are optional when a single parameter is named:

```
parameter => {
    //Statements
    //Optional return statement
}
parameter => //Expression or return statement
```

Parentheses are required if there is no parameter:

```
() => {
   //Statements
   //Optional return statement
}
() =>//Expression or return statement
```

JavaScript arrow functions cannot be invoked by statements that appear before it.

Defining and Invoking an Arrow Function Expression

This example shows a single statement arrow function with no parameters. The right-hand side of the assignment is the function without a name. The left-hand side is the variable:

```
var getDiceValue = ()=> Math.floor(Math.random() * 6) + 1;
```

In this case, the variable can be used to invoke the function:

```
var rollValue = getDiceValue() + getDiceValue();
```

This example shows a multiple statement arrow function with one parameter. The right-hand side of the assignment is the function without a name. The left-hand side is the variable:

```
var getDiceRoll = (numberOfDice) => {
  numberOfDice = (isNaN(parseInt(numberOfDice)) || numberOfDice< 1) ?1
:numberOfDice;
  var rollValue = 0;
  for (let i = 1; i<= numberOfDice; i++){
    rollValue += Math.floor(Math.random() * 6) + 1;
  }
  return rollValue;
}
```

The following is the output of invoking and passing a parameter:

```
var rollValue = getDiceRoll(2);
```

Exercise 3.16: Writing an Arrow Function and Invoking It

This exercise will show you how to convert a function expression into an arrow function. The JavaScript file we'll be using already contains the function. Let's get started:

1. Open the **function-arrow.html** document in your web browser.

2. Open the web developer **console window** using your web browser.

3. Reload the **function-arrow.html** web page in your web browser with the **console window** open.

    The first, second from last, and last results are an empty string. The second, third, and fourth results show a random character from the string:

    ```
    ():
    ("AEIOU"): U
    ("124678"): 6
    ("JavaScript"): a
    (124678):
    (true):
    ```

4. Open the **function-arrow.js** document in your code editor, make changes to the bolded lines, and then save it:

    ```
    var getRandomStringCharacter = (source) => {
     var returnCharacter = '';
     if (source !=undefined &&source.length> 0){
       returnCharacter = source.charAt(Math.floor(Math.random() * source.
    length);
     }
     return returnCharacter;
    }
    ```

5. Reload the **function-arrow.html** web page in your web browser with the **console window** open.

    The results are the same. The first, second from last, and last results are an empty string. The second, third, and fourth results show a random character from the string:

    ```
    ():
    ("AEIOU"): I
    ("124678"): 2
    ("JavaScript"): J
    (124678):
    (true):
    ```

Reacting to User Input Events and Updating the DOM

JavaScript is used to interact with the DOM. This entails responding to DOM-generated events such as a user clicking a button. It also entails updating content and HTML elements, such as displaying a notification message.

Elements in the DOM are objects. The **document** object that's provided by JavaScript contains the element objects. It also contains methods for accessing the elements and updating them.

The DOM HTML Element Object

The HTML elements are represented as objects. Since they are objects, there are methods and properties we can use for them. These properties and methods are inherited from a hierarchy of DOM objects that are provided by the web browser, starting with an object called **Node**. For example, the **ol** element shares methods and properties from the following hierarchy of DOM objects:

```
Node⇒Element⇒HTMLElement⇒HTMLOListElement
```

It is not necessary to understand all the objects involved, but it is good to be aware of them. It's better to learn about some of the properties and methods that are derived from all of those objects. The following are a few of the properties and methods that are inherited from a hierarchy of DOM elements above it:

- **innerHTML**: With the source element, this is the HTML and content contained in an element.

- **innerText**: With the source HTMLElement, this is the rendered text of an element.

- **addEventListener(...)**: With the source element event target, this is used to register a function to respond to events such as a user clicking on the element.

- **appendChild(...)**: With the source node, this adds a node to a parent node; for example, to add an **li** element to the end of an **ol** element, or to add a **p** element to the end of a **div** element.

Getting Access to Elements in the DOM

The following are **document** objects that contain methods that we can use to get one or more **HTMLElement** objects from the DOM:

- **getElementById(element-id)**: The element ID is the ID attribute of the element. Returned as an HTMLElement object.

- **getElementsByTagName(element-name)**: The element name is the static name of HTML elements such as **body, div, p, footer, ol, and ul**. This returns a **NodeList** object. A **NodeList** object is similar to an array of objects.

- **getElementsByClassName(css-class-name)**: The css class name is the class attribute of the elements. This returns a **NodeList** object. A **NodeList** object is similar to an array of objects.

- **querySelector(selectors)**: The selectors are like the selectors that are used in CSS. This returns an HTMLElement object for the first element that's matched.

- **querySelectorAll(selectors)**: The selectors are like the selectors that are used in CSS. This returns a **NodeList** object. A **NodeList** object is similar to an array of objects for each element that's matched.

- **createElement(tag name)**: This creates an **HTMLElement** object for the HTML tag name that's supplied.

- **createTextNode(data)**: This creates a **Text** object that can be placed inside an HTML element, for example, inside an **h1** or a **p** element. The data argument is a string.

The following is an example of the **document** object's **getElementById** method being used to access a DOM element. This creates an object from an element DOM that has the **id** attribute of **user-id**:

```
let userIdEle = getElementById("user-id");
```

This is an example of the **document** object's **getElementByTagName** method being used to access DOM elements. This creates a collection of objects representing all the **div** elements in the document. Further steps are needed to access each element, such as a loop:

```
let divEles = getElementByTagName("div");
```

This creates a collection of objects representing all the elements that use the **notice** class in the document. Further steps are needed to access each element, such as a loop:

```
let noticeEles = getElementByClassName("notice");
```

This is an example of the **document** object's **getElementByClassName** method being used to access DOM elements. This creates a collection of objects representing all the elements that use the **notice** class in the document. Further steps are needed to access each element, such as a loop:

```
let noticeEles = getElementByClassName("notice");
```

Creating Elements and Content in the DOM

You may want JavaScript to add HTML elements and content to a web page. This is done by updating the DOM. The **document** object has two methods that are useful for this:

- **createElement(tag name)**: Creates an **HTMLElement** object for the HTML tag name that's supplied.

- **createTextNode(data)**: Creates a text object that can be placed inside an HTML element, for example, inside an **h1** or a **p** element. The data argument is a string.

The following is an example of the **document** object's **createElement** method being used to create an **li** element:

```
let liEle = document.createElement("li");
```

The following is an example of the **document** object's **createTextNode** method being used to create a **Milk Moon** element:

```
let elementTextNode = document.createTextNode("Milk Moon");
```

Putting this all together, we can append elements and text nodes to the DOM. Consider the following HTML list of names for the November full moons:

```
<ul>
 <li>Flower Moon</li>
 <li>Planting Moon</li>
/ul>
```

Suppose we want to append another **li** element to the Milk Moon. To do that, we use the **document** object's **createElement** method to create an **li** element:

```
let liEle = document.createElement("li");
```

The **createElement** method returns an **HTMLElement** object. It provides the **appendChild** method, which we can use in this instance. For the **appendChild** method argument, the **document** object's **createTextNode** method can supply the required text node:

```
liEle.appendChild(document.createTextNode("Milk Moon"));
```

The resulting DOM is as follows:

```
<ul>
 <li>Flower Moon</li>
 <li>Planting Moon</li>
 <li>Milk Moon</li>
</ul>
```

Let's take this a bit further and assume that we have a list of full moon names in an array:

```
let mayMoons = [
  "Flower Moon",
  "Planting Moon",
  "Milk Moon"
];
```

Now, we want to use the array to populate a **ul** element that has the **id** attribute of **full-moons**:

```
<ul id ="full-moons">
 <li>Grass Moon</li>
 <li>Egg Moon</li>
 <li>Pink Moon</li>
</ul>
```

First, you may want to remove the existing **li** elements from the **ul** element. You can do that by using the **document.getElementById** method and the **innerHTML** property of the element:

```
let moonsEle = document.getElementById("full-moons");
moonsEle.innerHTML = "";
```

Next, we can loop through the array, appending `li` elements to the moon names:

```
for (let i= 0; i<= mayMoons.length - 1; i++){
  let liEle = document.createElement("li");
  liEle.appendChild(document.createTextNode(mayMoons.length[i]));
  listEle.appendChild(liEle);
}
```

The resulting DOM is as follows:

```
<ul id ="full-moons">
  li>Flower Moon</li>
  <li>Planting Moon</li>
  <li>Milk Moon</li>
</ul>
```

DOM Events

Events are messages that you can provide to code so that it can handle it; for example, the user clicking a button on an HTML page. The document model objects use the **addEventListener** method to add your code so that it is processed when the event occurs. The syntax is as follows:

```
target.addEventListener(event-type, listener)
```

The target is an object that has the **addEventListener** method. Objects representing elements in the DOM have this method.

The event type parameter is a predefined name for the event. For example, **click** is the name for a mouse click event. The listener is an object that has the ability to "listen" to events. Functions are objects that can "listen" to events. Functions that are used as event listeners have one parameter, which is an **Event** object.

For example, the **addEventListener** method for a click event that uses a function literal can be written as follows:

```
helpButtonEle.addEventListener("click", function(e){
  console.log("Something was clicked");
}
```

Exercise 3.17: Working with DOM Manipulation and Events

This exercise will accept an input value from a web page that aims to guess a number from 1 to 10. A button is used to check the input value against a random number that's generated from 1 to 10. Depending on whether there's a match, the **display** property of the other elements on the web page is toggled to hide or show the element. Also, the number that's generated is displayed on the page. Let's get started:

1. Open the **number-guess.html** document in your web browser.

2. Open the web developer console window using your web browser.

3. First, we can start with the web browser **document** object.

4. Type the items on the lines beginning with the **>** symbol. The console window will show a response on the lines beginning with the **<·** symbol.

5. Open the **number-guess.html** document in your code editor.

   Let's review some of the elements that will be accessed in JavaScript. First is the **input** element, which is used for entering the guess value. Note that its **id** attribute value is **number-guessed**. We are going to use the **id** attributes to get access to all the elements we use in JavaScript:

   ```
   <input id="number-guessed" type="text" maxlength="2">
   ```

   The next is the **button** element. The **id** attribute is **test-button**:

   ```
   <button id="test-button">Test Your Guess</button>
   ```

   The next is the **p** element. The **id** attribute is **results-msg**. This is the container for all the result messages. It has a **class** value of **hidden**. The **number-guess.css** file has the **display** property set to **none** for the **hidden** class:

   ```
   .hidden{
     display:none;
   }
   ```

   When the web page loads, this **p** element is not shown. The JavaScript will either hide or unhide this element:

   ```
   <p id="results-msg"  class="hidden" ...</p>
   ```

Inside the **p** element, there are two **span** elements that contain the message for a guess that either matches or does not. They also use the **hidden** class. This is because, if their parent element is unhidden, these remain hidden until the code determines which to unhide. Each **span** element has an **id** attribute. The JavaScript will either hide or unhide each of these **span** elements:

```
<span id="match-msg" class="hidden">Congratulations!</span><span
id="no-match-msg" class="hidden">Sorry!</span>
```

One more element inside the **p** element is a **span** element to show the number to guess. The JavaScript will update this:

```
<span id="number-to-guess"></span>
```

6. Open the **number-guess.js** document in your code editor, replace all of its content with the following code, and then save it.

   The first line creates an object for the element with **idtest-button** using the **document** object's **getElementByID** method.

   The second line adds the function named **testMatch** as the listener for the click event on the button.

   The following is the **testMatch** function and a message to the console so that we can test it:

```
let testButtonEle = document.getElementById('test-button');
testButtonEle.addEventListener('click', testMatch);


function testMatch(e){
  console.log("Clicked!");
}
```

7. Reload the **number-guess.html** web page in your web browser with the console window open and click the **Test Your Guess** button.

   You should see the following message in the console window:

```
Clicked!
```

8. Edit the **number-guess.js** document, update it using the bolded text, and then save it.

At the top of the file, all the elements we need to access in the HTML have been assigned to a variable:

```
let resultsMsgEle = document.getElementById('results-msg');
let matchedMsgEle = document.getElementById('match-msg');
let noMatchMsgEle = document.getElementById('no-match-msg');
let numberToGuessEle = document.getElementById('number-to-guess');
let guessInputEle = document.getElementById('number-guessed');
let testButtonEle = document.getElementById('test-button');
```

Next, add the DOM interface to get the **value** property from the input element's **guessInputEle** object. In case the user did not enter an integer, the **parseInt** JavaScript built-in function will flag that as not a number. Then, the **if** statement expression is true only if the number is between 1 and 10 inclusive:

```
function testMatch(e){
 let numberGuessed = parseInt(guessInputEle.value);
 if(!isNaN(numberGuessed) &&numberGuessed> 0 &&numberGuessed<= 10){
 }
}
```

In the **if** statement block, the first step is to get a random integer from **1** to **10**. Then, we use an **if...else** statement block if the input number matches the generated number.

For now, we can test this with outputs to the console window:

```
if(!isNaN(numberGuessed) &&numberGuessed> 0 &&numberGuessed<= 10){
 let numberToGuess = Math.floor(Math.random() * 10 + 1);
 if (numberGuessed == numberToGuess){
  console.log("MATCHED!");
 }else{
  console.log("NOT MATCHED!");
 }
 console.log("Number guessed:", numberGuessed);
 console.log("Number to match:", numberToGuess);
}
```

9. Reload the **number-guess.html** web page in your web browser with the console window open, enter an integer from **1** to **10**, and click the **Test Your Guess** button a few times.

Here are two test results:

```
NOT MATCHED!
Number guessed: 1
Number to match: 9
MATCHED!
Number guessed: 1
Number to match: 1
```

Try invalid values such as letters. There should be no output to the console.

10. Edit the **number-guess.js** document, update it using the bolded text, and then save it.

Now, we can add in the steps for updating the DOM elements with the results. To start, all the result elements are hidden when the button is clicked:

```javascript
function testMatch(e){
  matchedMsgEle.style.display = 'none';
  noMatchMsgEle.style.display = 'none';
  resultsMsgEle.style.display = 'none';
  let numberGuessed = parseInt(guessInputEle.value);
```

First, the hidden container for the message elements is displayed. Then, depending on whether there is a match or not, the element showing that result is displayed. Finally, the number to guess is updated in the element that was created for it:

```javascript
  if(!isNaN(numberGuessed) &&numberGuessed> 0 &&numberGuessed<= 10){
    resultsMsgEle.style.display = 'block';
    let numberToGuess = Math.floor(Math.random() * 10 + 1);
    if (numberGuessed == numberToGuess){
      matchedMsgEle.style.display = 'inline';
    }else{
      noMatchMsgEle.style.display = 'inline';
    }
    numberToGuessEle.innerText = numberToGuess;
  }
```

11. Reload the **number-guess.html** web page in your web browser with the console window open and repeatedly click the **Test Your Guess** button with a value entered.

The result of a matching output is as follows:

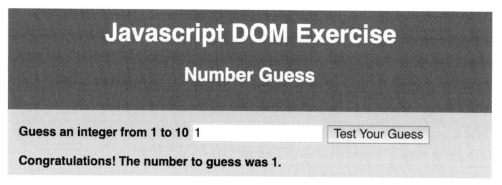

Figure 3.13: Matched value

The result of a non-matching output is as follows:

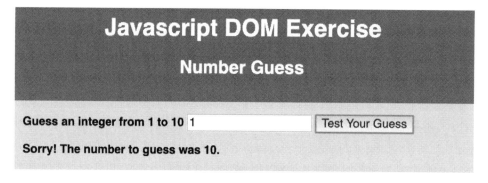

Figure 3.14: Non matched value

The result of an invalid entry output is as follows:

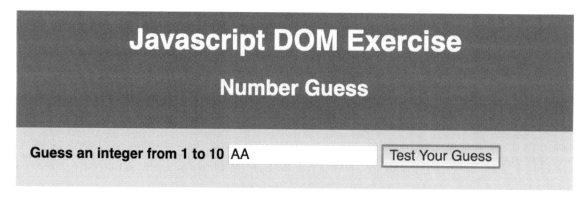

Figure 3.15: Invalid entry

Debugging

JavaScript programs may not work as intended. When that happens, it is usually called a bug.

Silent Fail

The people viewing your web page will not see any error message unless they know about the web developer console. This is called a silent fail approach. Silent fails keep web pages free of messages that would be cryptic to visitors. However, visitors may be puzzled when they try to interact with the web page and nothing happens and there are no messages.

There are two general categories of bugs: syntax and logic:

- Syntax: A syntax bug is a malformed JavaScript code.

- Logic: A logic error occurs when code that is syntactically correct does not perform as intended.

Syntax Bugs

Your console window will show you syntax errors so that they are easy to find and correct. Here is an example that shows an error at line 25 of the JavaScript file named `convert-celsius-fahrenheit.js`:

Figure 3.16: Syntax errors in the console window

The error code has a description and a link to the line number in the file. When you click that link, the source code file is opened in a window and the line that's involved is brought into view, as shown here:

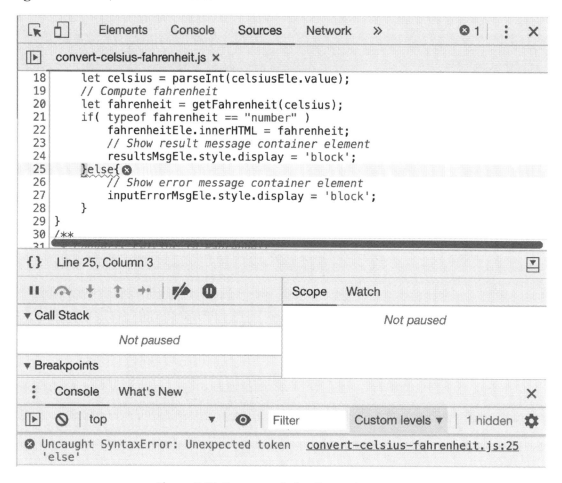

Figure 3.17: Source code for the syntax error

In this case, the error reports an **Unexpected token else**. Now, you need to look at the code to find out where the syntax is malformed. In this case, it is a missing **{** following the **if** statement on line 21.

Now, you can fix the syntax error in the source file and then reload the page:

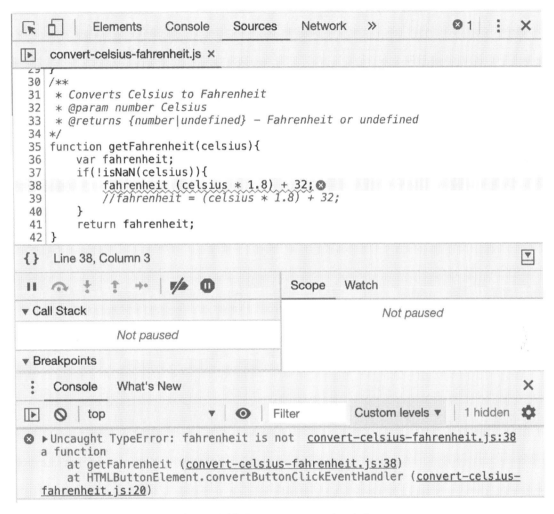

Figure 3.18: Syntax error at load time

The syntax error appeared at load time. This means that when the JavaScript file was loaded by the web browser, the syntax error was revealed.

However, a syntax error can appear at runtime. This happens while the code is executing, which does not need to happen when it's loaded, such as with a button click, as shown in the following screenshot:

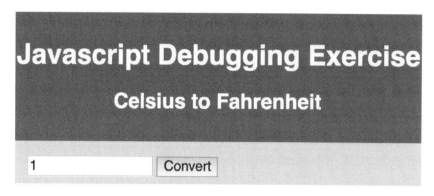

Figure 3.19: Code executed on the web page

Here is an example of where the code is executed after the user clicks the Convert button on the web page, the user sees no error. Nothing appears to happen when the button is clicked. If the web browser console window is open, we will see the offending syntax error.

The error message also includes a call stack. A call stack is a list of functions and methods that were called to reach the line that was reported in the error message. This call stack shows the **getFahrenheit** function containing the failed line. Then, it shows that the function was called inside the **convertButtonClickEventHandler** method that was assigned to an **HTMLButtonElement** object. Notice that each item in the call stack will branch you to a line in the file.

We start at the link that is part of the error message, which opens the source view window and takes you to line 38. The incorrect line is followed by a comment showing the correct line. You can see that it is a simple omission of the assignment operator. The code line now has to be fixed in the source file and then reloaded. Then, the **Convert** button is clicked again to see whether the syntax error has been fixed.

Logic Bugs

A logic error occurs when code that is syntactically correct does not perform as intended. Logic errors often occur due to data and expressions not using or computing the correct values.

When a JavaScript program encounters a logic bug, it stops executing the remaining code statements. There is often no error message to pursue.

This makes logic errors more challenging to resolve and you want to use debugging tools to aid in their resolution.

Debugging

Fixing bugs is called debugging. Debugging requires tools, skills, and techniques. It usually involves correcting the source code.

Using the `console.log` method and showing the values in the console window is one tool we can use. This allows you to view values at certain points in the program to see whether they are the expected values. One of the drawbacks of this approach is that this requires you to put the `console.log` method in your source code, which ultimately needs to be removed as a best practice. Another issue is that arguments to the `console.log` methods are potentially bugs themselves.

The other alternative is to use a debugger. The top desktop web browsers have a JavaScript debugger.

Debuggers

To help resolve logical errors, you usually need a debugger. A debugger is a tool that lets you pause a program, follow each step, and examine the data values at those steps. Most desktop web browsers have a debugger built into its web developer view. Here is an example of the debugger for the Chrome web browser's developer tools:

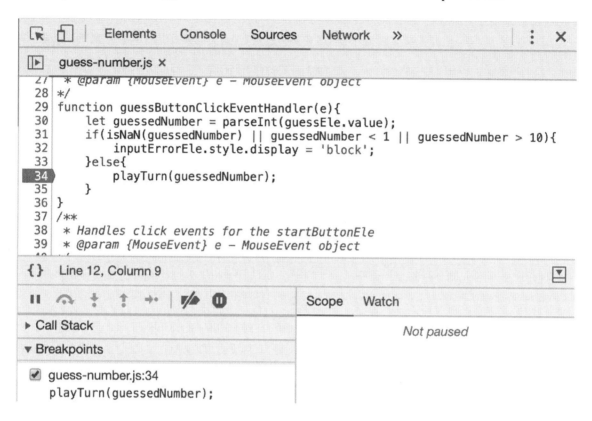

Figure 3.20: Setting breaking points for the Chrome web browser

One of its most important features is setting breakpoints. A breakpoint pauses the code's execution. In this example, there is a breakpoint at line 34. It is shown not only in a **Breakpoints** panel but also in the source window, with a symbol on the line number. The symbol on the line number is actually a toggle to set or unset breakpoints. The **Breakpoints** panel is handy when you have multiple breakpoints spread out in the code and you need to enable or disable them without having to find the code line in the source window.

Once the code execution hits the breakpoint, then you can inspect the expressions by hovering a mouse pointer over the code. There is also a window that keeps all the data values organized, ready for inspection. For example, the **guessedNumber** variable is shown as **5** in two places in the following screenshot:

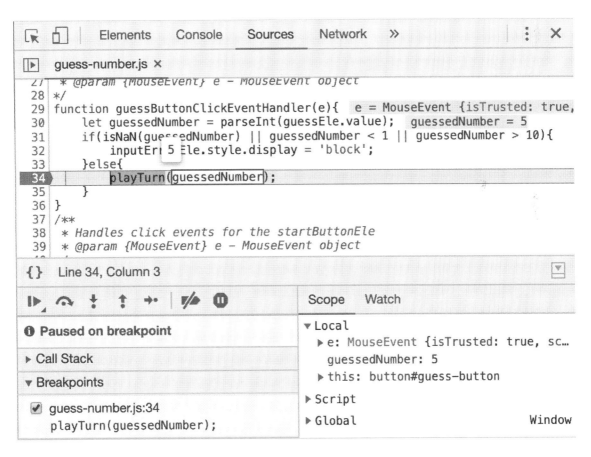

Figure 3.21: Data value organized in the debugger tool

Once the execution has been paused, you can control the execution of the code using the debugger menu:

Figure 3.22: Debugger Menu

The first four choices are a good place to start:

- **Resume**: The first choice restarts the JavaScript code's execution until it ends or reaches another breakpoint.

- **Step Over**: The second choice will not step into a function, but into all the code in a function it calls is executed. This is useful because there may not only be many functions you have written but also third-party functions that have been written that do not require a step-by-step investigation.

- **Step Into**: The third choice does step into a function where you can proceed. You can think of this as executing one line at a time.

- **Step Out**: The fourth choice is a way to step out of a function to the line that called it.

Activity 3.01: The To-Do List Shuffle Program

This activity will help you build a **todo** list web page. We will use JavaScript to load the list and shuffle the list after it has been loaded. A button labeled Shuffle has been added to the HTML file and the **ol** element has been assigned the ID, **todo-list**.

The high-level steps for the activity are as follows:

1. Use the **activity.js** file to write your code. This contains coding hint comments you may use if you desire. It also includes a function named **getNewShuffledArray**.

2. You need to load the **li** element **todo** items from JavaScript and then allow the user to randomize the list. You may approach the activity in two parts.

   In **Part 1**, you need to use an array for the **todo** list items and create a function that updates the HTML DOM list items using an **ol** element and an array as parameters. The function will remove the previous **li** elements and iterate through the array to add new **li** elements with the values in the array parameter. Test before proceeding. You can find the HTML file at https://packt.live/2XcP1GU

3. In **Part 2**, add a function to respond to the Shuffle button's click event. The function will use the original array of `todo` items and your previous function to update the `ol` element's list items. It also will use the `getNewShuffledArray` function to randomly shuffle an array and return the shuffled array.

The output of this activity is as follows:

Figure 3.23: The To-Do list Shuffle program

> **Note**
>
> The solution to this activity can be found on page 715.

Summary

JavaScript programming is a problem-solving endeavor. It relies heavily on data and data expressions. At the start of this chapter, we mentioned that data could be people's names, temperature, image dimensions, the amount of disk storage, and total likes on a discussion group post. Data can be values for a user interface, such as screen coordinates, sizes, scroll values, colors, and fonts.

A JavaScript program is a series of steps that use data. A program starts with an event. An event could be when a web browser finishes loading the web page, a mouse event, such as a click or rolling over a spot on the screen, such as a button or image, or when some data is received from a web server that was requested by JavaScript.

Once the program begins, it executes the code statements sequentially and is directed by flow control statements such as `if`, `switch`, `for`, and `while`.

The code is organized into units called functions. Functions contain code that may need to be repeated in more than one part of a program, but with different data and different results. Functions can take data as input values and return a result; for example, Fahrenheit as input and Celsius as output.

JavaScript programs for web pages generally deal with the DOM. The DOM is just a large object that's created by the web browser. It is made up of all the data and functions

Before you try to solve every coding problem, you may find that other programmers have already solved many common problems and make their code available for you to use in the form of libraries and frameworks. For example, you could use JavaScript and the DOM to write code to animate user interface elements by sliding or fading them in and out of view. However, if someone has already solved that coding problem, you may want to use their code. In the next chapter, we will look at some popular libraries and frameworks that solve a wide range of problems for a web page.

JavaScript Libraries and Frameworks

Overview

By the end of this chapter, you will be able to use JavaScript frameworks and libraries to perform different tasks; demonstrate event handling with jQuery; use popular JavaScript Frameworks; name the do's and don'ts of using a framework; and build a library

In this chapter, you will learn how and when to combine your source code with external software.

Introduction

In the previous chapters, you learned how to utilize conditional logic, loops, and the most common data structures. These form the groundwork and essentials for writing programs and building complex JavaScript applications. Still, building actual software is an inherently challenging task; focusing on only business logic is even more so. Therefore, as developers, we often rely on external software that lets us dedicate ourselves to the source code that's the most relevant to our product or business. This software does this by simplifying specific tasks and abstracting away complexity for us. Those pieces of external software are what we refer to as **frameworks** or **libraries**.

The following are some of the tasks that modern JavaScript frameworks can support us with:

- Performance rendering of complex or dynamic single-page applications (SPAs)

- Managing ongoing dataflow between the controllers and views of client-side applications

- Creating sophisticated animations

- Creating with fast and straightforward server APIs

Before we dive deeper into the whys and the wherefores of using external code, we need to clarify what the difference is between the terms "framework" and "library." This will be the topic of the following section.

Framework versus Library

Library describes an external collection of functions that perform a given task. These functions are made accessible to us as users of the library via APIs. One useful library is `lodash`, which can, for example, remove all duplicated values from an array:

```
const duplicatedArray = [1,2,1,2,3];
const uniqueArray = lodash.uniq(duplicatedArray)
// => [1,2,3]
```

Frameworks, on the other hand, are a particular form of library. They are reusable code frames that build the foundation of a JavaScript application. In contrast to libraries, which extend your code with functionality, a framework can stand alone and is enhanced with your source code to create an app as you like.

A popular framework is **Vue.js**, which we can use as follows:

library-vue.js

```
1  // example.html
2  <div id="example">
3  <input :value="text" @input="update"/>
4  <div v-html="myOwnText"></div>
5  </div>
6  //———————————————————————————————————
7  // example.js
8  new Vue({
9  el: '#example',
10 data: {
11 text: 'My first framework'
12 },
13   computed: {
14 myOwnText: function () {
15 return this.text
16 }
```

The full code is available at: https://packt.live/32MD4IN

As you can see, in general, there is more complexity to a framework than there is to a library. Nonetheless, both are equally important to software development.

Despite the technical differences between libraries and frameworks, we are going to use those terms interchangeably. Another synonym you'll encounter in the JavaScript world to describe external source code is "package." One of those packages you may encounter in JS resources is **Vanilla.js**. We'll have a look at it in the next section.

Vanilla.js

This specific framework follows the informal convention of including the JavaScript file extension with the name **nameOfFramework.js**. However, vanilla.js is not a framework; it's not even a library. People referring to **vanilla.js** are talking about plain JavaScript without any external code or tooling. The name is a running gag within the JavaScript community because some developers and non-developers think we need to use a framework for everything we build. We will discuss why this isn't the case later.

Popular JavaScript Frameworks

We have just looked at lodash.js, a library that helps developers handle data structures; (to be used, for example, making arrays unique) and Vue.js, a framework for building modular and dynamic user interfaces. These are just two examples of quite popular and widely used JS frameworks/libraries. In addition to those, there is a vast and ever-growing number of external packages you can choose from. Each one of them is useful for solving one specialized set of problems.

A few modern and often used alternatives that support creating browser applications are, for instance, React.js, Vue.js, and Angular.js. Other libraries that help you store and manage data in your app are MobX, VueX, and Redux.

Again, others can transform source code so that it supports older browser engines, for example, **Babel**, or handle and manipulate time for you, such as moment.js.

Then, there are frameworks such as Express.js or Hapi that let you create simple, easy-to-maintain, and performant REST APIs for Node.js.

Some packages make building **command-line interfaces (CLIs)** or desktop applications easy.

Most build and productivity tools for the JavaScript ecosystem are provided to the community as a library, too. Webpack, Parcel, and Gulp are a few of these tools.

Not all of the available libraries are equally popular or useful. Their popularity depends on a few key facts:

- Whether they fix a problem that bothers many developers
- How well their API is defined and structured
- The quality of their documentation
- The level of performance optimization

Keep these in mind when crafting a package that you want to become well known.

Everlasting jQuery

One evergreen library that has been around for over a decade is jQuery. It touches almost every web app in one way or another and belongs in the toolkit of everybody who builds browser applications:

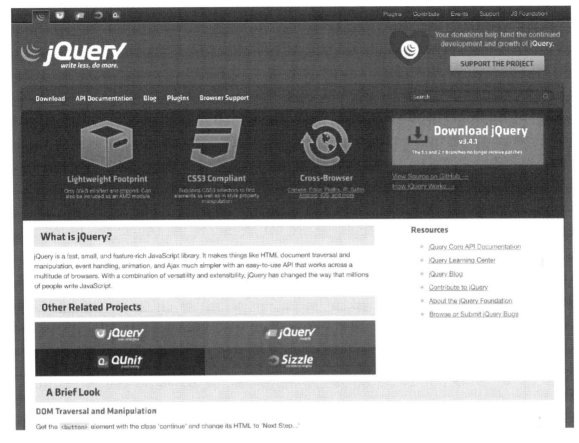

Figure 4.1: jQuery documentation

jQuery was not the first but was definitely among the earliest JavaScript libraries ever to be used by developers all over the world to make their jobs easier. Since it was first released, a lot of maintainers and engineers have contributed to making jQuery what it is today – namely, a robust and essential part of the modern internet that offers lots of different functionalities.

jQuery provides, but is not limited to providing, the following features:

- DOM manipulations

- Event handling

- Animated effects and transitions

We will see how to do these things when we look at jQuery in more detail later in this chapter.

Where to Find and How to Use External Code

There are a few different approaches when it comes to including libraries in your program. Depending on those approaches, we get packages from different places.

One is to copy the library's source code and to handle it as we wish. This approach is the most secure in the sense that we have all the control of the software and can customize it to fit our needs. However, by doing so, we give up compatibility and automated updates and patches. Most open-source projects host their code on GitHub or any other version control platform. Therefore, it's rather easy to access and fork the package's code. As soon as we download the source code, we can do whatever we want to get it working with our software. Possible solutions could be hosting it on our **cloud distribution network (CDN)** and accessing it from there or bundling it with our source code.

Another approach is downloading the package from a CDN from the client at runtime. The most popular CDN to exclusively host JavaScript libraries is cdnjs.com. It hosts thousands of libraries you can include in your markup without you having to worry about where to store it or how to upgrade it:

Figure 4.2: Downloading a package from cdnjs.com

The following is an example of how you'd include Vue.js with your markup:

```
// myApplicationMarkup.html
<html>
<script src="https://cdn.com/vue.js"></script>
<script type="text/javascript">
console.log("Vue was loaded: ", !!Vue)
```

```
// => Vue was loaded: true
</script>
</html>
```

> **Note**
>
> If you include packages by loading them from the browser during runtime, you have to be aware of the order of the script tags. They're loaded from top to bottom. Therefore, if you switched the two script tags in the preceding example, console.log would print that there is no **Vue.js** loaded, even though, eventually, it will be.

The previous approach gained lots of popularity and is now by far the most common due to the development of the JavaScript ecosystem in recent years. It involves the **Node.js Package Manager (npm)**. npm is a tool that, as its name suggests, takes care of JavaScript packages within the Node.js ecosystem. npm itself consists of three parts:

- The website npmjs.com, for hosting all the documentation and package searches

- The CLI that gets installed with **Node.js**

- The registry, which is where all of the modules are stored and made installable:

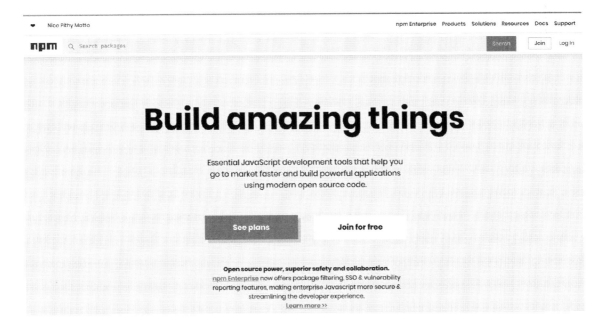

Figure 4.3: NPM website

Using npm requires a `Node.js` version to be installed on your machine and any tool to bundle all your JavaScript together to make it executable in the browser.

Then, all you have to do is install any module you can find on npm:

```
// in your terminal
$ npm install <package>
```

This command then stores the package in a particular folder, called **node_modules**. This folder contains all the source code of the libraries you installed, and from there, the bundler will join it into your application during build time.

All of the aforementioned methods to include libraries and frameworks with your source code are valid and have their preferred use cases. However, it's likely that you are going to use the latter the most as new projects are set up within the `Node.js` ecosystem, which is where modules and npm come from, naturally. Nonetheless, knowing how to use external resources without npm can come in handy when you want something much more comfortable and quicker than an entire project setup. Therefore, let's perform an exercise in which we will load a third-party library into our code.

Exercise 4.01: Using a Third-Party Library in Your Code

As we've already discovered, using external software, namely libraries and frameworks, is an extremely useful skill as it can save a lot of resources and help you build highly functional apps. In this exercise, we are going to find and utilize a library ourselves. We'll use the `lodash` library to create an array of unique values. Let's get started:

1. Create a new HTML file:

```
<html>
<head></head>
</html>
```

2. Find the CDN URL for the latest `lodash` version. To do so, navigate to `cdnjs.com` and search for lodash, and then copy the URL highlighted in the figure:

Figure 4.4: Search result of lodash at cdnjs.com

3. To look at the **lodash** documentation, navigate to <u>lodash.com</u>. There, you can use the search bar to find the "**uniq**" function:

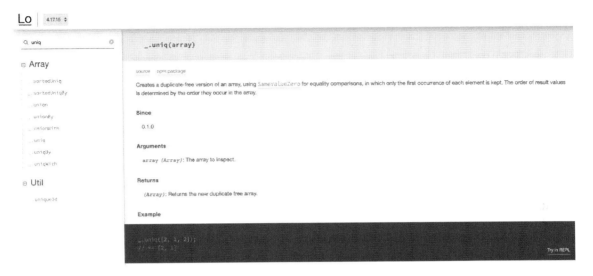

Figure 4.5: lodash.com documentation for uniq function

4. Load the CDN URL in a script tag's **src** attribute. To do so, paste the URL you previously copied in *step* 2:

```
<html>
  <head>
    <script src="https://cdnjs.cloudflare.com/ajax/libs/lodash.
js/4.17.15/lodash.min.
    js"></script>
  </head>
</html>
```

5. Create another **script** tag and write JS code using *lodash* to make an array, **[1,5,5,2,6,7,2,1]**, that contains **unique** values:

```
<html>
  <head>
    <script src="https://cdnjs.cloudflare.com/ajax/libs/lodash.
js/4.17.15/lodash.min.
    js"></script><script type=„text/javascript">
      // create an array with duplicated values
      const exampleArray = [1,5,5,2,6,7,2,1];
      // use lodash.uniq to make the array contain unique values
      const uniqueArray = _.uniq(exampleArray);
      // print the unique array to the console
      console.log(uniqueArray);
```

```
      // => [1,5,2,6,7]
    </script>
  </head>
</html>
```

6. Open your HTML, including the JavaScript, in a browser and verify that you created an array with unique values inside the browser's development tools console:

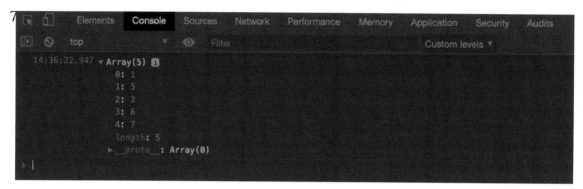

Figure 4.6: Unique array values in the browser's development tools console

In this exercise, we used the *lodash* library to create an array that contains sole unique values.

jQuery versus Vanilla.js

Earlier, in the *Everlasting jQuery* section of this chapter, we had a look at jQuery and how it has an exceptional standing in the JavaScript community. To demonstrate why libraries and frameworks, but mainly jQuery, became popular, we will compare it to `Vanilla.js` (plain JS).

Manipulating the DOM

If we wanted to fade out and then remove one element in plain JavaScript, we would write verbose and less comprehensive code:

```
// Vanilla.js
const styles = document.querySelector('#example').style;
styles.opacity = 1;(function fade() {
styles.opacity -= .1;

styles.opacity< 0
? styles.display = "none"
: setTimeout(fade, 40)
})();
```

On the other hand, with jQuery, we could have all this in just one line of understandable code:

```
// jQuery
$('#example').fadeOut();
```

Making XHR Requests

A fundamental functionality of modern web pages and applications is requesting additional resources or data from remote servers. Every browser provides interfaces to execute these so-called XHR requests. Those interfaces can be used from JavaScript. As we can see in the following code examples, jQuery, compared to vanilla.js, lets us write clean and self-explanatory code:

```
// Vanilla.js
const request = new XMLHttpRequest();
request.open("POST", "/example/api", true);
request.onreadystatechange = function() {
if (request.readyState != 4 || request.status != 200) return;
console.log("Successful XHR!");
};
request.send("example=payload");
```

In comparison to the preceding snippet, the code for making calls to a server is much clear and readable in jQuery. It is more readable in the sense that it is very clear and understandable regarding what exactly the function needs as parameters and what it is going to do. Let's have a look at a **POST** Ajax request to the **/example/api** URL with a specified payload data and also a function that gets triggered when the request is successful:

```
// jQuery
$.ajax({
type: "POST",
url: "/example/api",
data: "example=payload",
success: function() {
console.log("Successful XHR!");
}
});
```

> **Note**
>
> jQuery assigns itself to the $ variable. Hence, in the code examples,$.
> **functionName** could be replaced with **jquery.functionName**.

We could go on and show you more use cases where jQuery gets us faster to our goal than raw JS would. Instead, in the following exercises, we will use the library and gain some first-hand experience with it. Specifically, we will be writing code to handle a button-click event, once with jQuery and once with plain JavaScript.

> **Note**
>
> The dev tools in all modern major browsers have adapted to **$**, but only as a wrapper for **document.querySelector**.

Exercise 4.02: Handling Click Events with jQuery

In this exercise, we will identify how jQuery can help us react to events that get propagated when the target (in our case, a button) gets clicked. Let's get started:

1. Create a new HTML file including a button tag with the ID **exampleButton**. This button will be our target:

```
<html>
  <body>
    <button id="exampleButton">Click me.</button>
  </body>
</html>
```

2. Find the latest jQuery CDN URL on cdnjs.com.

3. Read the jQuery documentation for **.on ()** (https://api.jquery.com/on/) erytion:

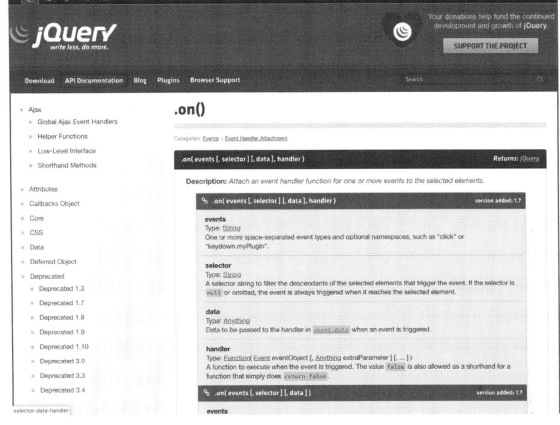

Figure 4.7: jquery.com Documentation for .on()

4. Load in the CDN URL:

```
<html>
  <head>
    <script src="https://cdnjs.cloudflare.com/ajax/libs/jquery/3.4.1/
jquery.min.
    js"></script>
  </head>
  <body>
    <button id="exampleButton">Click me.</button>
  </body>
</html>
```

5. Create a script tag containing code that logs a **Hello World** message to the console when you click the button:

```html
<html>
  <head>
    <script src="https://cdnjs.cloudflare.com/ajax/libs/jquery/3.4.1/
jquery.min.
    js"></script>
  </head>
  <body>
    <button id="exampleButton">Click me.</button>
    <script type="text/javascript">
      $('#exampleButton').on('click', function() {
        console.log('Hello World')
      })
    </script>
  </body>
</html>
```

6. Make sure you place the **script** tag after the button tag.

7. Open the HTML in your browser and open the dev tool console.

8. Press the **Click me.** button and verify that it prints **Hello World** to the console:

Figure 4.8: Hello world output using jQuery click events

In this exercise, you handled an event that got fired by the browser on a button click using jQuery. The handler you implemented prints **Hello World** to the browser's console as soon as the **click me** button is pressed.

You also saw how easy it is to use a library such as jQuery to do work that, otherwise, you would need to do manually.

Handling a click event, however, is not particularly hard to do in vanilla.js either, as you'll see in the next exercise.

Exercise 4.03: Handling the Same Event with Vanilla.js

In contrast to the previous exercise, this one demonstrates how to create a handler that gets triggered on a click event using plain JavaScript. Let's get started:

1. Create a new HTML file that includes a button tag with the ID exampleButton:

```html
<html>
  <body>
    <button id="exampleButton">Click me.</button>
  </body>
</html>
```

2. Create a script tag containing vanilla.js code that logs a **Hello World** message to the dev tools console when you click the button. **addEventListener** is a vanilla API provided to us by the browser. It takes **eventType** and **handlerFunction** as parameters:

```html
<html>
  <body>
    <button id="exampleButton">Click me.</button>
    <script type="text/javascript">
      const button = document.querySelector('#exampleButton')
      button.addEventListener('click', function() {
        console.log('Hello World')
      })
    </script>
  </body>
</html>
```

Again, make sure you place the **script** tag after the button tag.

3. Open the HTML in your browser and open the dev tools console. Press the "Click me." button and verify that it prints "Hello World" to the console:

Figure 4.9: Hello World output using Vanilla.js

In the previous two exercises, we added an event listener to a button. We did so once with the help of jQuery and the other time with no external code and instead used the native APIs that the browser provided us with.

UI Animation Using jQuery

In addition to the use cases for jQuery that we have seen in the code examples in the Manipulating the DOM and Making XHR Requests sections and in *Exercise 4.02: Handling Click Events with jQuery*, there is another important functionality that **jQuery** provides us with: animating the user interface (UI).

Animations contribute to a more engaging website and can mean that your users enjoy the experience of using your application more. Often reactions to user input are animated to highlight the fact that the interaction has been acknowledged or that something has changed. For example, appearing elements could be animated or placeholders inside of input fields. Proceed with the following exercise to implement the former UI animation example yourself.

Exercise 4.04: Animating a "Peek-a-boo" on Button Click

In this exercise, you will build on the knowledge you have gained regarding how to handle events using jQuery. The relevant part, however, will be animating an element on the page.

Whenever the **"Peek..."** button is clicked, the **...a-boo** headline will show up. Let's get started:

1. Create a new HTML file that includes a button tag with the ID **Peek...**, a headline with the ID **...a-boo**, and a **display: none** style attribute:

```
<html>
  <head></head>
  <body>
    <button id="peek">Peek...</button>
    <h1 id="aboo" style="display: none;">...a-boo</h1>
  </body>
</html>
```

2. Load the latest **jQuery** CDN URL, from **cdnjs.com** (see *Exercise 2, Handling Click Events with jQuery, step 2*), inside a script tag:

```
<html>
<html>
  <head>
    <script src="https://cdnjs.cloudflare.com/ajax/libs/jquery/3.4.1/jquer
y.min.js"></script>
  </head>
  <body>
    <button id="peek">Peek...</button>
```

```
      <h1 id="aboo" style="display: none;">...a-boo</h1>
   </body>
</html><head>
      <script src="https://cdnjs.cloudflare.com/ajax/libs/jquery/3.4.1/
jquer
      y.min.js"></script>
   </head>
   <body>
      <button id="peek">Peek...</button>
      <h1 id="aboo" style="display: none;">...a-boo</h1>
   </body>
</html>
```

3. Create a script tag containing the code to select the peek button and add an
   onClick event listener:

```
<html>
   <head>
      <script src="https://cdnjs.cloudflare.com/ajax/libs/jquery/3.4.1/
jquery.min.
      js"></script>
   </head>
   <body>
      <button id="peek">Peek...</button>
      <h1 id="aboo" style="display: none;">...a-boo</h1>
      <script type="text/javascript">
        const peekButton = $(,#peek');
        peekButton.on('click', function() {});
      </script>
   </body>
</html>
```

4. Inside the new script tag, write additional code to select the **aboo** headline and use
   the **jQuery.fadeToggle** function to animate the headline so that it's fading in and
   fading out:

```
<html>
   <head>
      <script src="https://cdnjs.cloudflare.com/ajax/libs/jquery/3.4.1/
jquery.min.
      js"></script>
   </head>
   <body>
      <button id="peek">Peek...</button>
      <h1 id="aboo" style="display: none;">...a-boo</h1>
```

```
<script type="text/javascript">
  const peekButton = $('#peek');
  const abooHeadline = $('#aboo');
  peekButton.on('click', function() {
    abooHeadline.fadeToggle();
  });
</script>
</body>
</html>
```

5. Open the HTML page in your browser and click the **peek** button.

6. You should see the **aboo** headline fading in and fading out whenever you click the **peek** button:

Figure 4.10: Animated output using the Click button

In this exercise, you used **jQuery** to execute yet another type of task in the browser. Animations in UIs can be as simple as our fading example, but they can also be very complex when building games or creating 3D animations.

By now, you have an idea of what jQuery, and also other libraries or frameworks, can help you do. In the next section, we will explore why and when it may be wiser to renounce external source code.

Frameworks versus Core JavaScript

So far, we've spoken a lot about why, how, and in what situations to use libraries. But we are yet to discuss when and why it would be a better idea not to rely on them.

First of all, all of the things that frameworks and libraries do can be done by ourselves. In a business context, or for the sake of development speed, however, we usually decide to buy them when facing the "make-or-buy" decision. But sometimes, we should keep in mind that adding external sources to our program or even founding it on top of these sources expands the amount of source code we have. Increasing the overall size of the necessary resources is particularly unpleasant for us JavaScript developers who build client-facing applications since we should be optimizing for delivering performance (how fast the app loads on the client). In general, more JavaScript code leads to the following:

- Longer download times

- Longer parsing times

- More delayed execution

- Potentially blocked rendering or usability of the app

Though we have complex optimization algorithms such as tree shaking or dead code elimination, which help us cope with huge bundle sizes in these cases, often, the better choice is to do the task at hand on our own.

Another aspect to consider is the security of our application. Some libraries or frameworks may open up attack vectors that we cannot control because we do not have full ownership or understanding of the involved code. However, the most popular libraries are concerned with the security of their packages and are also very fast at releasing patches for known vulnerabilities.

To provide an actual use case that spells out the negative impact a library or framework may have on our application, in the following two exercises, we will create a list and render it to the screen. The first one will make use of an external library, whereas the second one will be written in raw JavaScript.

Exercise 4.05: Rendering a List of To-Dos Using React

In this exercise, we're going to display a few list tags as bullet points of an imaginary **todo** list. To do so, we'll be using a massively popular library called **react.js** and its complementary **react-dom.js**. Let's get started:

1. Create a new empty HTML file with a head and a div tag with the **root** ID inside the HTML body:

```
<html>
  <head></head>
  <body>
    <div id="root"></div>
  </body>
</html>
```

2. Go to **cdnjs.com** and to get the latest **react.js** and **react-dom.js** CDN URLs and load the URLs into a script tag inside the HTML head:

```
<script src="https://cdnjs.cloudflare.com/ajax/libs/react/16.9.0/umd/
react.
production.min.js" charset="utf-8"></script>

<script src="https://cdnjs.cloudflare.com/ajax/libs/react-dom/16.8.6/
umd/react-dom.production.min.js" charset="utf-8"></script>
```

3. Use **react.js** and **react-dom** to create three list items and render them to the **root div**-element:

```
<script type="text/javascript">
  const todoListItems = [
    'buy flowers',
    'tidy up',
    'go to the gym'
  ];

  const todoListElements = todoListItems.map(item =>
    React.createElement('li', null, item)
  );
  ReactDOM.render(todoListElements,
    document.getElementById('root'));
</script>
```

4. Open the HTML page inside your browser and make sure that your **todo** list items are displayed correctly.

5. Open the network tab of your browser's dev tools and have a glance at how many kilobytes of JavaScript was loaded:

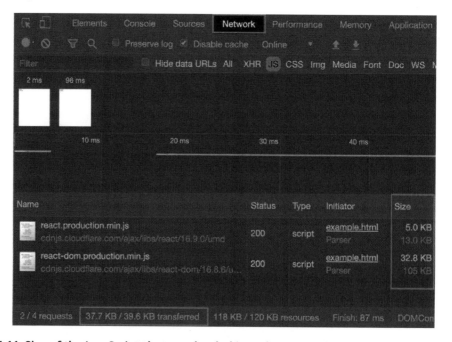

Figure 4.11: Size of the JavaScript that was loaded into the Network tab

In this exercise, you learned where to find and how to use React.js. Although in this exercise you simply created a small, static list of To-Dos, **React.js** lets you create complex, dynamic UIs without you having to worry about native browser APIs that you would normally need to create such UIs. However, as we mentioned previously, using a framework also comes at a cost, measured in kilobytes.

Next, you will learn how to do the same task without React. Afterward, you will be able to understand the kilobytes versus complexity trade-off when building applications.

Exercise 4.06: Rendering a List of To-Dos without a Library

In the previous exercise, we used the trendy library known as React.js to load more than **37 KB** (in ZIP format) and a couple of hundred bytes for the HTML, including the script tags, to create and render a list of three items. In this exercise, we are going to do the same thing, except we will utilize all the functionality that's already provided by the browser. Let's get started:

1. Create a new empty HTML file with a div tag with an ID of **root** inside the HTML body:

```
<html>
  <body>
    <div id="root"></div>
  </body>
</html>
```

2. Create a script tag and write some JS to create three list items and render them to the **root** div element:

index.html

```
4 <script type="text/javascript">
5  const todoListItems = [
6    'buy flowers',
7    'tidy up',
8    'go to the gym'
9  ];
10  const rootElement = document.getElementById('root');
11  const listFragment = document.createDocumentFragment();
12  todoListItems.forEach(item => {
13    const currentItemElement = document.createElement('li');
14    currentItemElement.innerText = item;
15    listFragment.appendChild(currentItemElement)
16  });
```

The full code is available at: https://packt.live/2QYfUxb

3. Open the HTML page inside your browser and make sure your **todoListItems** are presented correctly.

4. Open the network tab of your browser's dev tools and have a glance at how many kilobytes of JavaScript was loaded:

- buy flowers
- tidy up
- go to the gym

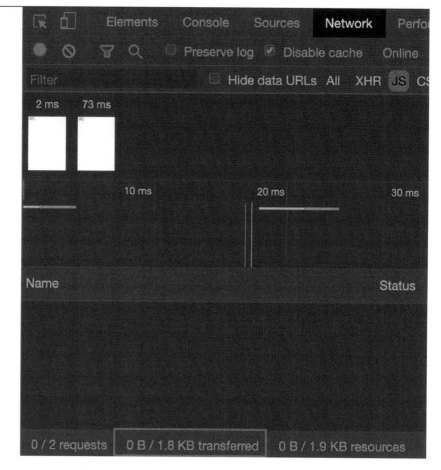

Figure 4.12: Loading the JavaScript's download size without using a library

There's exactly no, that is, 0 KB, additional JavaScript. That gives us 37 KB of downloading, parsing, and execution advantage over the method using `react.js`, all while achieving the same thing.

Of course, this is a simplified example. In general, real-world applications are more complex than our exercise. Nonetheless, you may often find yourself in an analogous situation where performance is a thing to consider and the task can plausibly be done using `vanilla.js`.

We have spoken in detail about what libraries and frameworks are and what they can help us to do. In order to really grasp what libraries may look like internally and how easy it actually is to build one, we'll be creating one ourselves in the following exercise.

Exercise 4.07: Creating a Library Yourself

Our library won't be capable of much at first, but you may want to put some effort into it and extend it as you wish.

HeadlineCreator.js is our library's name. It's a good name because it already hints at what it does; that is, it creates headlines. Technically speaking, our library will do the following:

- Be accessible on the global window object of the current browser tab, just as we've seen with jQuery before: window.headlineCreator.

- Provide a single method called createHeadline.

- Allow us (through the createHeadline method) to create a headline with the given text and append it to a given parent element.

- Take care of error handling for us, for instance, if we forgot to define some text to be displayed or passed an invalid selector for the parent element

- To verify that our library is working and having an example of its usage, we will create, additional to creating the library itself, an HTML page including script tags using our HeadlineCreator.js library.

  Let's get started:

1. Create an empty HTML file with a head tag, a body tag, and a div tag with an ID of **root** inside it:

```
<html>
  <head></head>
  <body>
    <div id="root"></div>
  </body>
</html>
```

2. Load a local JS file with the name **headlineCreator.js** inside a **script** tag:

```
<html>
  <head>
    <script src="./headlineCreator.js"></script>
  </head>
  <body>
    <div id="root"></div>
  </body>
</html>
```

3. Create the **headlineCreator.js** file inside of the same directory you created the empty HTML file in.

4. Inside the JavaScript file, create an IIFE and assign it to the **headlineCreator** variable:

```
// headlineCreator.js
const headlineCreator = (function(){}) ();
```

> **Note**
>
> IIFE stands for "immediately invoked function expression." This sounds more complicated than it is. IIFEs are functions that are executed at the very same moment they are defined. One use case for them in frameworks or libraries is to prevent name collisions with variables that are used in the source code. This includes the library. For example, using a create function within your library can cause weird side effects since this is a very common and ambiguous name. Hence, the library could be a different function than it was supposed to be.

5. Within the IIFE, create another function and name it **createHeadline**. This function takes two parameters, **text** and **parentElementSelector**:

```
// headlineCreator.js
const headlineCreator = (() => {
  function createHeadline(text, parentElementSelector = '#root') {}
}) ();
```

6. Inside the IIFE **headlineCreator**, add a **return** statement. This **return** statement will return an object with a single key named **createHeadline** that has the value of the same name (just like the function name we created in the previous step):

```
{}return {
createHeadline: createHeadline
  };;
```

7. Extend the new function with a DOM query to look for an element with the **parentElementSelector** that is passed as an argument to the **createHeadline** function.

8. Assign the result of the DOM query to a variable called **parentElement**:

```
{{const parentElement = document.
querySelector(parentElementSelector);{e;;
```

9. Next, create an **h1** tag element and set the **innerText** attribute of this element to the **text** parameter that is passed to the function:

```
{{; const headlineToInsert = document.createElement('h1');
headlineToInsert.innerText = text;}{e;;
```

10. Lastly, append the created headline to the node that we stored in **parentElement**:

```
{{;;;parentElement.appendChild(headlineToInsert);}{e;;
```

11. Refresh your HTML page and inside the dev tools console, call the **window. headlineCreator.createHeadline** function with any parameter you'd like. Then, view the result:

Figure 4.13: The window.headlineCreator.createHeadline function in the console and its output

12. If you'd like to, you can add some error handling and return the newly created headline element since that's considered good practice in such a case:

headlineCreator.js

```
1  // headlineCreator.js
2  window.headlineCreator = (function() {
3    function createHeadline(text, parentElementSelector = '#root') {
4      const parentElement = 5 document.querySelector(parentElementSelector);
5      if (!text) {
6        throw new Error('You forgot to pass the "text" parameter');
7      }
8      if (!parentElement) {
9        throw new Error(
10          `There was no node found for the Selector: "${parentElementSelector}"`
11        );
12      }
```

The full code is available at: https://packt.live/2OIR6q0

13. To test the error handling, simply call the **headlineCreator** function without the text parameter:

Figure 4.14: Error message in the console

14. Last but not least, add a script tag to the HTML file and call the **headlineCreator** library from there so that every time the HTML is loaded, a headline is created:

```html
<html>
  <head>
    <script src="./headlineCreator.js" charset="utf-8"></script>
  </head>
  <body>
    <div id="root"></div>
    <script type="text/javascript">
      headlineCreator.createHeadline('This is the HeadlineCreator');
    </script>
  </body>
</html>
```

This results in the following output:

This is the HeadlineCreator

Figure 4.15: The HeadlineCreator.js library created

Going through this exercise has taught you that the inner workings of a library don't have to be complex and hard to understand. The **headlineCreator** library lets the user create and append a headline to a given parent element. Even though this is a simplified and almost trivial use case, it demonstrates the basic process of building and using a library – that is, having a programmatic problem, finding a solution to it, abstracting the complexity, and providing it to others through a library.

Activity 4.01: Adding an Animation to the To-Do List Application

In this activity, you have been asked to animate the **todo** list application that you have been building in the activities from the preceding chapters. Do so using one of the following three libraries:

- jQuery
- Velocity.js
- Anime.js

The resulting **todo** list should animate the to-dos whenever you click the Shuffle button. It's up to you what exact animation you use, but nonetheless, I advise you to start with something simple, such as fading the to-dos.

The high-level steps for the activity are as follows:

Choose one of the frameworks. To gain a better understanding of how to use them, search for them online and have a look at their documentation (https://jquery.com, http://velocityjs.org, https://animejs.com):

1. Go to cdnjs.com and get the jQuery CDN URL.

2. Load the library into the head tag of your existing Todo-List-HTML using a script tag. This will enable you to use jQuery within your code.

3. Inside **activity.js**, you need to change the **todoEle** variable. Change it to a jQuery element.

4. Inside the **replaceListElements** function, you can now use functions on the **todoEle** element that jQuery provides to you.

5. Hide and clear what's inside the element using the jQuery functions.

6. Inside the for loop, create the **liEle** list item element, set the text contest, and append it to the **listEle** list element.

7. Finally, slowly fade in the new sorted **todo** list, that is, **listEle**.

8. Now, open the HTML in your browser and click the **Shuffle** button. The to-do list should fade out, shuffle, and fade in again. You will see the expected output.

9. Now, we'll use the **Velocity.js** method. Go to cdnjs.com and get the **velocity.js** CDN URL.

10. Load the library into the head tag of your existing Todo-List-HTML using a script tag. This will allow you to use **velocity.js** within your code.

11. Inside the **replaceListElements** function, you can now use **Velocity.js** to hide (by setting opacity to 0) the list element, **listEle**, and then empty the elements inside of it.

12. To fade the list element back in, animate **listEle** using **Velocity.js** and set the opacity to 1. Set the code after the **for** loop.

13. Now, open the HTML in your browser and click the **Shuffle** button. The to-do list should fade out, shuffle, and fade in again.

14. Finally, using the **Animae** method, go to cdnjs.com and get the **Anime.js** CDN URL.

15. Load the library into the head tag of your existing Todo-List-HTML using a **script** tag. This will allow you to use **Anime.js** within your code.

16. Inside the **replaceListElements** function, you can now use **Anime.js** to move (by using **translateX = -1000**) the list element, **listEle**, out of view and then empty the elements inside of it.

17. To show the newly shuffled to-do list, use Anime.js to animate the **listEle** list element back into view (**translateX = 0**). Do so inside a timeout to ensure that the shuffling has been done already.

Now, open the HTML in your browser and click the **Shuffle** button. The to-do list should fade out, shuffle, and fade in again. It should appear as follows:

Figure 4.16: Animated to-do list on click

> **Note**
>
> The solution to this activity can be found on page 719.

Summary

In this chapter, we took a dive into the vast world of JavaScript libraries. We started with an explanation of the terms library and framework. From there, we had a look at a few popular frameworks and what they can help us with. The exercises in this chapter demonstrated where we can find external packages and how we can make use of them. Some of the things we did with these libraries included creating fading effects, removing duplicated entries from a list, and rendering DOM elements to the document. We discussed the disadvantages of using external source code as well. However, the biggest achievement of this chapter was creating our own library that helped us create headlines. We finished this chapter by making use of various libraries to enhance our to-do list with some nice UI effects.

The next chapter will show us how to work with data in JavaScript. We will gain an understanding of how data is represented, how it can be passed around, and how specific types can be cast into different types.

5

Beyond the Fundamentals

Overview

By the end of this chapter, you will be able to identify the difference between JavaScript's mutable and immutable types; manipulate each of the built-in data types confidently; convert data from one type to another; format data types for presentation; and differentiate between an expression and a statement.

Introduction

In the previous chapter, you were given a tour of JavaScript, its runtimes, and its history. Using a high-level topography, that chapter will have given you an idea as to what JavaScript is, what it can do, and its ubiquity within the internet software development industry.

Understanding code can be difficult for beginners. JavaScript is no exception. Its flexibility, extensive language syntax, and varying coding patterns can prove daunting to the uninitiated.

This chapter will take you a step closer to writing your own software applications in JavaScript. By explaining the fundamentals, you will be empowered to not only understand what scripts do, but how to reason about problems using JavaScript syntax.

In this chapter, you will take a close look at JavaScript's type system. All programming languages have a type system. Types literally dictate the type of data stored in a variable or function parameter. Types are typically separated into two categories: **primitive** and **complex** types.

In JavaScript, all primitive data types are immutable. This means that the value cannot be changed in memory. New values can be assigned to a variable, but the underlying data stored in memory cannot be modified directly. This differs from the case in languages such as C++, where values can be directly altered in memory using pointers and helper functions. In JavaScript, when passing a primitive value from one variable to another, the data is copied in memory to the new variable. Therefore, updating one variable does not affect the other.

Complex data types work differently. They are also known as reference types. Reference types include the **Object** type and all of its derivatives, such as **Array**, **Date**, and **Function**. All reference types are passed by reference, hence the name. Therefore, if an object is modified through one reference, all the other references that share the same object will see it as updated too, since all of the references point to the same data in memory.

A complex type is simply a type that has more functionality than a primitive. For instance, a `Date` value provides additional means of representation, while objects can contain many nested values, such as primitives and other complex types.

> **Note**
>
> Function types will not be explained in detail in this chapter and will instead be covered in a later chapter when prototypes are introduced.

All primitives, and preexisting reference types are known as built-in data types. Each of these types has a corresponding object that provides functions for manipulating that type. These functions may be applied externally to data by passing the value as a parameter to a function, or they may be applied by calling the function as if it were a method of that type. The latter is also applicable to several primitives, despite them not existing as literal objects within the JavaScript type system. However, this is made possible through the syntactical context of the data. More will be explained about this feature throughout this chapter.

Creating Variables

Variable creation is the means to assign a value to a symbol. In this circumstance, a symbol is a textual representation of the data, much like a container, which can be used to move data through your program. It also improves the legibility of your code. There are multiple ways to create variables, including assignment to the global scope or through the use of either the **var**, **let**, or **const** keywords.

A Note on Referencing

Even at this early stage, it must be highlighted that JavaScript's referencing functionality can get rather confusing. The presence of **closures**, **prototypes**, **global** and **local memory stacks**, **variable assignment variations**, and **function invocation options** can leave even seasoned programmers scratching their heads. Each of the aforementioned features supports JavaScript as a formidable and flexible programming language that's able to challenge most other platforms for almost any purpose. While it does deepen JavaScript's learning curve, mastering these concepts can be extremely rewarding.

This chapter highlights the very basics of data referencing and attempts to not confuse matters any more than necessary. Only referencing with regard to data at the global level will be discussed.

Global Assignment

Assigning a variable without the use of **var**, **let**, or **const** will place the variable into the global scope. This value will then be accessible anywhere in your application unless a variable of the same name exists within that scope. Redeclaring the same variable name without the use of a preceding keyword will overwrite the global reference, even if it's assigned within a different scope.

Declaring globally in a browser environment is equivalent to declaring the value on the global window object as a field.

Declaring with var

Preceding variable assignment with the **var** keyword places the variable into function scope. This means the variable only exists at the same function as the assignment, but not outside that function. Declaring with **var** in the global scope is equivalent to declaring without the **var** keyword.

Redeclaring a variable with **var**, but in a nested scope, will not overwrite the variable of the same name in the outer scope.

Using the **var** keyword, variables can be scoped (declared) even after they are used within the same scope. This is due to variable hoisting. Hoisting was explained in *Chapter 4*, JavaScript Libraries and Frameworks.

Declaring with let

The **let** keyword has a narrower scope. While **var** is considered to be functionally scoped, the **let** keyword is block scoped. This means that variables that are created with **var** exist throughout a function's scope level, while let-declared variables are created and used at the block level, such as in **if** conditional blocks or **for** loops.

For example, using **let**, a variable can be temporarily overwritten within a **for loop** while not changing a variable of the same name in the outer function. However, if **var** is used instead, the outer variable will be changed:

```
var a=0;
for(var a in [0, 1]);
console.log( a ); // ==> a is now 1 (as modified by the loop)
```

In the preceding example, the variable declared in the **for loop** matches the symbol declared outside of it. As such, the same variable reference is modified. However, in the following example, the result is different, as the let-declared variable only exists within the context of the for loop, meaning the outside variable of the same name is left untouched:

```
var a=0;
for(let a in [0, 1]);
console.log( a ); // ==> a is still 0 (not modified by the loop)
```

Contrary to **var**, let-declared variables are not hoisted. If a scope declares a variable with **let**, accessing that variable before that let declaration statement (within the same scope or in any inner scope) will raise an error (this is regardless of whether a variable with the same name has been created in an outer scope):

```
glob=1; {glob=2; let glob=3;}   // ==> can't access lexical declaration
`glob' before
initialization
glob=1; {glob=2; var glob=3;} // ==> accepted syntax
```

Declaring with const

The **const** keyword works with the same scoping and hoisting rules as the **let** keyword. The difference with **const** is that it is assumed the variable will not change throughout its lifetime. Using **const** allows the JavaScript engine to make certain optimizations at compile time since it expects the data to remain constant at runtime.

It is possible to create a new variable assignment with the same name in a nested function scope, but it will not be possible to modify a variable of the same name using global scoping rules.

> **Note**
>
> Declaring a variable with var or let, but without assigning a value, will result in the variable containing **undefined**. The undefined value will be covered a little later in this chapter.

Exercise 5.01: Variables and Scope

In this exercise, we will use the browser's JavaScript **Read-Eval-Print Loop** (**REPL**) to experiment with variable assignment and scope. Let's get started:

1. Launch your browser and open the developer tools console. In Chrome, you can do this by pressing the F12 key.

2. Ensure the **Console** tab is selected:

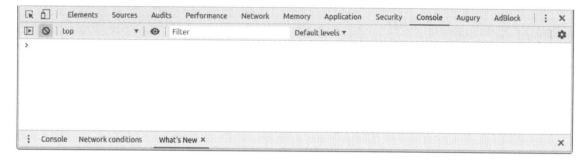

Figure 5.1: The Console tab

3. At the **prompt**, enter the following commands, pressing *Enter* at the end of each line:

```
const i = 10;
console.log(i);
// ->     10
```

The **console.log** command writes the value of **i** to the console.

4. Next, create a function that also initializes a variable of the same name, as follows:

```
const f = function() {
    var i = 20;
    console.log(i);
};
```

5. Invoke the function to print the variable that exists within the function scope. If you then print the global variable, you will see it has not been modified:

```
f();
// ->     20
console.log(i);
// ->     10
```

6. Next, try the **let** keyword:

```
if (true) {
    let i = 15;
    console.log(i);
}
// ->    15
  console.log(i);
// ->    10
```

As you can see, the **let** assignment only exists for the lifetime of the block that follows the if statement.

7. Close the browser tab. Open a new tab and open the console again (otherwise, you won't be able to re-assign **i** as a variable). Now, try the same with **var**. You will see that the variable declaration raises an error because it conflicts with the **i** variable outside of the conditional block:

```
i = 10;
if (true) {
    var i = 15;
    console.log(i);
}
// ->    15
console.log(i);
// ->    15
```

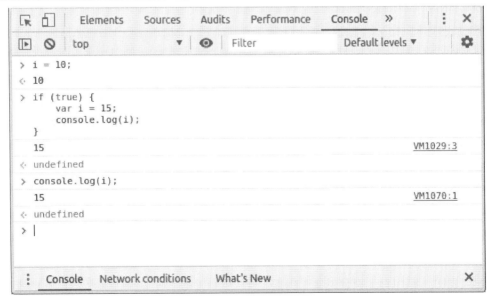

Figure 5.2: Exercise 5.01 output

Understanding the scope surrounding a variable is important for the correct execution of your application, as well as for minimizing bugs. Try to keep a mental note of the positioning and use of each variable as you work. Utilizing functional paradigms, as discussed in *Chapter 13, JavaScript Programming Paradigms*, will also help alleviate any discrepancies in variable scoping.

Identifying a Variable's Type

So far, you have created variables and output their value to the browser's console. In order to get the most out of the content of this chapter, however, it would be helpful to be able to identify the content of a variable. JavaScript is known as a weakly typed language because a variable can hold a **string** one moment, but then an **integer** the next. By being able to identify the type of value stored in a variable, you prevent errors occurring where you attempt to process a value you expected to be of a different type.

The **typeof** keyword exists to do just that. By preceding a variable with the **typeof** keyword, the returned value is the type of the variable represented as a **string**.

The **typeof** keyword evaluates with the following type mapping:

Type	Type of response
Undefined	`undefined`
Null	`object`
Boolean	`boolean`
Number	`number`
String	`string`
Function	`function`
Object (Including Date, Array, XM, and so on)	`object`

Figure 5.3: Types and responses

The **null** type evaluates as "**object**". This anomaly originates from the earliest incarnations of JavaScript where data types were tagged internally with an integer value. Object types were tagged with 0, while the **null** value existed as a **null pointer** (or **0x00** as a value). As the two expressions were identical, determining the type of **null** resulted in the same type as Object. This same anomaly still exists in JavaScript today. Therefore, when determining whether a type is an Object, we must also compare it with **null**:

```
var value = [1, 2, 3]; // an array - which is also an object
if (typeof value === "object" && value != null) {
    console.log("value is an object");
}
```

Exercise 5.02: Evaluating Types from Variables

In this exercise, we will create a function that outputs the type of whatever variable is passed to it. Let's get started:

1. At the command prompt, enter the following line to declare the function signature:

```
var printType = function(val) {
```

This function accepts a single variable, which will be the variable to analyze.

2. Due to the Null value caveat, you must check for this, first. Here, compare **val** to **Null** and output the appropriate message. If the value is indeed **Null**, then the function must be returned so that no further comparisons can be made:

```
if (val === null) {
    console.log("Value is null");
    return;
}
```

Here, you are comparing **val** to **Null** and outputting the appropriate message. If the value is indeed **Null**, then the function must be returned so that no further comparisons can be made.

3. If the value is **not Null**, then you can safely return the type of the value itself:

```
    console.log("Value is", typeof val);
}
```

console.log(...) will output however many values are passed into it and concatenate them onto the same line. Here, you output the generic message but then concatenate it with the type of the variable. Since no value is required to be passed from this function, and as there is no more logic to perform, no return statement is required to close out the function.

4. To test this function, execute it in the console with different values:

```
printType(12);
printType("I am a string");
printType({});
printType(null);
```

The preceding code will result in the following output:

```
Value is number
Value is string
Value is object
Value is null
```

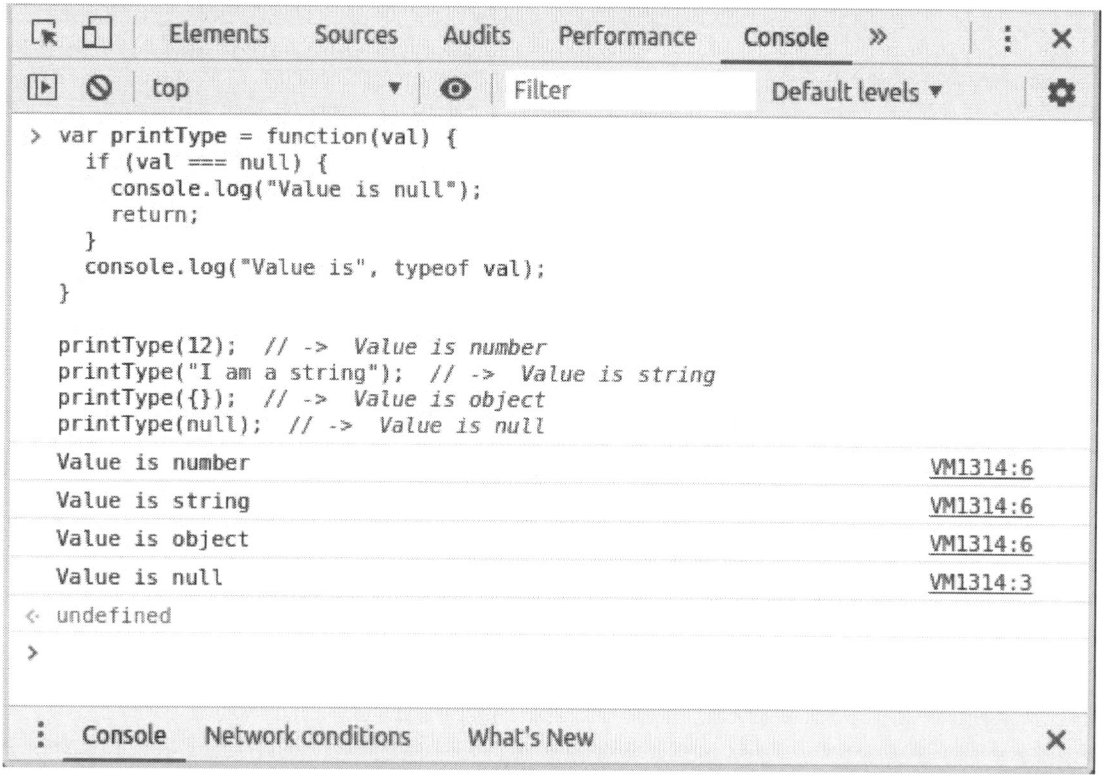

Figure 5.4: Exercise 5.02 output

The function you have just created is rather light in terms of introspection. It essentially enables you to determine the general type of a passed in value, but it isn't powerful enough to differentiate object types, including JavaScript's built-in objects. Whether you pass in a **Date** or an **Array**, you will get the same output.

You will discover how to be more thorough in determining data types later in this module.

Fixed Types

Fixed types are types that have no variation of value. Unlike numbers, which may have any combination of digits, an optional minus sign (for negative numbers), a decimal point, or a scientific notation, a fixed type is always one simple value or value group.

In JavaScript, the available fixed types include `null`, `undefined`, and `Boolean`s (`true` and `false`). These values are `static` and cannot change. If a variable contains one of these values, it is then strictly equal to the value itself. Fixed types are more of a representation of a situation than actual data. For instance, `true` is a fixed representation of truthfulness and `false` is a fixed representation of falsehood. The values are not quantifiable in the real world but are representative of logic that software directly deals with.

The null Value

`null`, in mathematical terms, denotes a value that is not present. In JavaScript, `null` is a static value that's used to mean no value. In other languages, this would be equivalent to nil or void.

`null` is a useful value for dereferencing variables or for returning a value from a function when no value can be returned. For instance, a function may return an object from an array if the item is present but may return `null` if it is not.

The undefined Value

`undefined` is similar to `null` in many ways and, due to this, the two values are often misused. `undefined` is the value contained in any variable that is declared first, but not assigned a value. It is also the value that's been returned from a function that does not explicitly return a value using the `return` keyword and it is the value that's returned from a statement (an action with no resulting value).

When working with `undefined`, you should always anticipate it, but never assign it to a variable or return it explicitly from a function. In such circumstances, you should use `null`.

Boolean Values

`Boolean` is a term named after George Boole, a nineteenth-century English mathematician and philosopher. It is used to denote the values `true` and `false`. These values may be assigned to variables and are strictly equivalent to their value, like null.

Booleans are unique among the types supported by JavaScript because they are indirectly comparable to other types and expressions. The logical operators described in *Chapter 3, Programming Fundamentals*, of this book, for instance, all result in a `Boolean` value.

Boolean Operators

Boolean operators are operators that, when combined into an expression, return a **Boolean** value. Most Boolean operators are "**binary**" operators that accept two values, each of which sit either side of the operator. Like other operators, each value can be an expression and can be of any value type. As **Boolean** operators themselves form expressions, they can be used as input to other **Boolean** operators.

Boolean operators fit into two categories; namely, comparison operators and logical operators.

Comparison Operators

Comparison operators are used for comparing one value, or the result of an expression, with another. The operator in this circumstance may be considered a rule. If the rule succeeds, then the response of the combined expression returns **true**. Otherwise, it returns **false**.

Comparison operators include the following symbols:

Symbol	Name	Description
==	"Is equal to" or "equality"	Returns **true** if both sides have an equal value.
i=	"Is not equal to" or "negated equality"	Returns **true** if both sides do not have an equal value.
>	"Is greater than"	Returns **true** if the left-hand expression is of greater value than the right-hand expression.
>=	"Is greater or equal to"	Returns **true** if the left-hand expression is of greater or equal value than the right-hand expression.
<	"Is less than"	Returns **true** if the left-hand expression is of less value than the right-hand expression.
<=	"Is less or equal to"	Returns **true** if the left-hand expression is of less or equal value than the right-hand expression.

Figure 5.5: Comparison operators and their descriptions

Comparison operators are often used as the condition parameters of if conditionals and while loop statements. If or while the condition expression returns true, the body block of the expression will execute.

The following example expressions will all return the value true:

```
21 == 9+12;
false != true;
6 > 1;
5 >= 5;
"1" == 1;
```

If you look at the last example in the list, you may be a little surprised. The **==** operator is a "value comparison operator". In the example shown, the numeric value 1 and the string value "1" are considered the same value. As such, the equality operator, which is a "value comparison" operator, will compare them as equal.

In order to determine whether values are of the same type, as well as the same value, "strict comparison operators" should be used:

Symbol	Name	Description
===	"Strictly equal to" or "strict equality"	Returns **true** only if both the value and the type are equal.
!==	"Strictly not equal to" or "strict negated equality"	Returns **true** if either the value or the type is not equal.

Figure 5.6: Equality operators and their descriptions

Logical Operators

Logical operators are often used to concatenate **Boolean** expressions together. For instance, when comparing the qualities of a **string** value, you may wish to execute code if the **string** is longer than one value but shorter than another. In order to do this, you need to join two comparison expressions using the **&&** operator. In another condition, you may wish to execute the code if only one of the expressions is **true**, in which case, you would use the **||** operator.

The following table lists each of the logical operators and what they do:

Symbol	Name	Description
&&	AND	Returns **true** if the expressions either side of the operator is true.
||	OR	Returns **true** if one or both operators return true.
!	NOT	Negates a **Boolean** value or expression.

Figure 5.7: Logical operators and their description

Exercise 5.03: Odds and Evens

In this exercise, we will process a series of numbers and output messages describing whether a number is either odd or even.

We'll fulfill this exercise using a function so that you can experiment with different starting values. Let's get started:

1. At the command prompt, create the **odd_or_even** function with a couple of parameters:

```
function odd_or_even(counter, last) {
```

The **last** parameter will be the ceiling value of the numerical series, while the **counter** parameter is both the starting value and the current index variable for each loop.

2. Next, create your loop using the **while** keyword. while will process a block of code as long as the conditional expression is truthy. As the conditional in this exercise, you will simply compare **counter** with the **last** parameter:

```
while (counter <= last) {
```

If the **counter** variable is ever larger than the **last** parameter, then the **while** loop will exit, which will also exit the function.

3. With the **while** conditional in place, you can now begin describing the counter value with each iteration. To do this, you simply examine the value of **counter** and respond with an appropriate message, depending on its content:

```
    if (counter % 2 == 0) { // is true if the remainder of 'counter /
2' is
equal to zero
        console.log(counter, "is an even number");
    } else {
        console.log(counter, "is an odd number");
    }
```

4. Now, increment the **counter** variable by **1** before you close the **while** loop block. If you fail to increment, the condition of the **while** loop would always be **true**, and the loop will never exit. Also, each iteration of the loop would process identically, which is not the result you require:

```
counter = counter + 1;
```

5. Close out both the **while** block and the function. There is no need to return anything from this function as we are not interested in any final values:

```
    }
}
```

6. Now, execute the function, passing a **counter** value and **last** value as required. The output should accurately describe all the numbers from **counter** to **last**, inclusively.

Here's the output:

```
odd_or_even(1, 5);
//    1 "is an odd number"
//    2 "is an even number"
//    3 "is an odd number"
//    4 "is an even number"
//    5 "is an odd number"
```

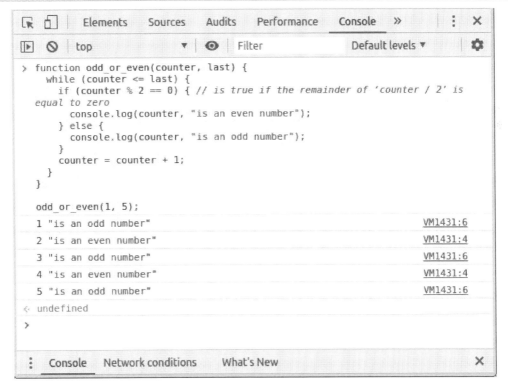

Figure 5.8: Exercise 5.03 output

Have a go at changing the passed parameters when calling the function. However, be sure to keep **counter** to a value less than or equal to the **last** parameter or the **while** loop will not execute.

Testing the Truth of Values

When writing programs with JavaScript, you will often need to compare values, typically when working with conditionals. Often, values will be compared with other values, but it is just as likely that you will need to check the truthiness of a value.

Testing for truthiness can mean many things:

- Is there a value present?
- Are there any items in an array?
- Does the string have a length greater than 0?
- Does the passed expression return **true**?

JavaScript provides a means to pass in a solitary value to conditional statements to test for truthiness. However, this can sometimes be an area of confusion. For instance, examine the following example:

```
if (0) console.log("reached");   // doesn't succeed
console.log( 0 == false ); // prints true
console.log( 0 === false ); // prints false
```

The **if** statement body executes if the conditional is truthy. In the first example in the preceding code, the numeric value zero is seen as falsey. As the second and third examples show, **false** is equal to numeric zero, but only non-strictly. However, in the third example, the numeric value zero is not strictly equivalent to **false**. The reason for this is that there is a difference between a **false** value and a falsey value. A **false** value is always false, but a falsey value may be one of several values, including the following:

- false
- **undefined**
- **null**
- -0, +0, or NaN
- An **empty** string

If the value is not in the preceding list, then it is considered truthy.

The NOT Operator

The **!** or **NOT** operator is rather unique. It is considered a "unary" operator because it only accepts one value to the right of it. By using the **NOT** operator, you essentially negate the value that precedes it. Here's an example:

```
var falseValue = !true;
```

In the preceding example, the **falseValue** variable will contain a value of **false**.

A very useful feature of the **NOT** operator is the "**double NOT**." This is when two **NOT** operators are combined to double negate an expression; a true expression is negated to **false**, then back to **true**, while a **false** expression is negated to **true**, then back to **false**.

When working with truthy or falsey expressions, using the **double NOT** operator alters the resulting value of these expressions to actual Boolean values. Here's an example:

```
if (!!1 === true) {
   console.log("this code will execute");
}
```

Boolean Operator Precedence

All operators have an order of execution known as "**precedence**." This precedence is also apparent in mathematics and is a means to ensure that expressions are executed in a predictable manner.

Consider the following code:

```
if (true || false && false)
```

The preceding example could be read in two different ways. This is the first way:

```
if ((true || false) && false)
```

This is the second way:

```
if (true || (false && false))
```

If you follow the code from left to right, as in the first example of interpretation, it will return **false**, because the **&&** operator is executed last. There, the code will be reduced to the following:

```
    true || false && false
= true && false
= false
```

The second interpretation, however, will produce a different result:

```
   true || false && false
= true || false
= true
```

To prevent such ambiguity, operator order precedence exists. Precedence is applicable to all the operators in the JavaScript language, but we'll list just those that are applicable to **Boolean** expressions here:

Operators	Associativity
(,)	Not applicable
! (NOT)	Right to left
<, <=, >, >=	Left to right
==, !=, ===, !==	Left to right
&&	Left to right
||	Left to right

Figure 5.9: Boolean operators and their associativity

In the preceding table, the top row has the highest precedence and so is evaluated first, while the bottom row has the lowest precedence and is evaluated last.

Boolean Operator Associativity

In the previous table, each operator is given an associativity description. Associativity relates to the execution direction of an expression. Most operators have "left-to-right" associativity, which means the left-hand side expression is executed before the right-hand side expression. The **NOT** operator, however, executes its right-hand expression first.

Associativity can be very important, especially when side effects occur within an expression. In the following example, the expressions present on either side of a || operator log the parameter and return it:

```
function logAndReturn( value ) {
   console.log( "logAndReturn: " +value );
   return value;
}
if ( logAndReturn (true) || logAndReturn (false)) {
   console.log("|| operator returned truthy.");
}
```

When executed, if the **log_and_return** function returns a truthy value, then only the first execution will occur and so only that call logs a message with **log_and_return:** concatenated with the value passed in. Since the || operator is left-to-right associative, the entire expression is considered truthy if the left-hand side returns **true**. As such, the right-hand side is never executed. For this particular operator, the right-hand side only ever executes if the left-hand side is false. This behavior is also called a short circuit.

Since the side effect of **logAndReturn** is only logging the value, this provides a useful tool for debugging. However, consider a function that receives an object as a parameter, modifies it, and then returns a value:

```
// Following two variables are set to "anonymous" (simple) objects,
// each with two fields, 'name' and 'happy', set to initial values (both
sad)
var john= {name: "John", happy: false};
var lucy= {name: "Lucy", happy: false};

function make_happy( person ) {
   console.log("Making " +person.name+ " happy.");
   person.happy= true;
   return true;
}
if (make_happy(john) || make_happy(lucy)) {
   console.log("John is happy: " +john.happy+ ", Lucy is happy: " +lucy.
happy);
}
```

Both objects follow the same structure and the **make_happy** function could possibly work with either object. However, when the conditional is called, only **john** will be updated since the || condition in the conditional expression is satisfied on its left-hand side.

The right-hand side is never executed. Therefore, if the code is dependent on both objects being modified at a later date, it will fail.

This same caveat is true for the **&&** operator. Since an **&&** operator expression is considered **true** if both sides are truthy, then both sides will only execute if the left-hand side execution returns **true**.

The associative execution rule for the **||** operator is particularly useful when working with variables. In some circumstances, it is preferable to assign a default value to a variable if, and only if, it does not already contain a value. In this instance, using the **||** operator can make light work of this task:

```
distanceLimit = distanceLimit || 5;
```

If the variable already contains a value, then it will keep that value. However, if its value is **null**, **undefined**, or some other falsey value, then it will be assigned the value 5.

Similarly, using the **&&** operator is great if you wish to execute a function if a preceding variable is truthy:

```
items.length && processItems(items);
```

Exercise 5.04: Free Home Delivery Eligibility Validation

In this exercise, we will create a function that will determine whether the customers of a grocery store are eligible for free home delivery. The store only delivers to customers who are located within 5 miles of the store. To make this exercise more interesting, the store recently decided to provide free delivery for customers located within 10 miles of the store, but only if those customers have an active membership for their loyalty program. Moreover, if customers are within 1 mile of the store, they aren't eligible for free home delivery, regardless of their membership status. Let's get started:

1. Define your function signature. The function should accept the distance of the customer's house from the store and their membership status:

```
function isEligible(distance, membershipstatus) {
```

Based on the store's criteria, the function will return **true** if the customer is eligible for free delivery and **false** if they are not. Functions that describe something in a **Boolean** fashion are often labeled **is**, such as **isValid**, **isEnabled**, or **isGoingToReturnABoolean**.

2. There are two ways to build the body of this function; either break the problem up into small chunks and test the parameters bit by bit or create a single conditional that detects all the appropriate outcomes. We'll work with the latter in order to appropriately demonstrate the content of this chapter thus far. The following if statement is a negative check – it checks whether a customer is not eligible for free home delivery:

```
if (distance < 1 || membershipstatus === "active" && distance > 10 ||
membershipstatus === "inactive" && distance > 5 ) {
```

This is the crux of the exercise. The **Boolean** operators are executed in the following order, but only those that are necessary to determine the overall result. First and always is the relative check for houses within **1** mile of the store. If the house is within **1** mile of the store, the overall result is **true**, and the rest of the expression is not evaluated at all. Only if the distance is **1** mile or more is the overall result not determined yet and the following goes ahead. Only if the membership status is active does the check for a distance greater than **10** miles come. Otherwise, if the membership status is inactive, there comes the check for a **distance** of greater than **5** miles. Then, those results are with the less-than-1-mile check. Due to operator precedence, no grouping using parentheses was required.

3. If the conditional evaluates as truthy, then we want to report that the person is not eligible for free delivery:

```
return false;
```

4. Since the function will simply halt here, if the conditional block is executed, simply return **true** for anything that slips past:

```
    }
    return true;
}
```

5. With the function complete, try different parameter variations to test it:

```
console.log( isEligible(.5, "active") );
// =>    false
console.log( isEligible(7, "inactive") );
// =>    false
console.log( isEligible(7, "active") );
// =>    true
```

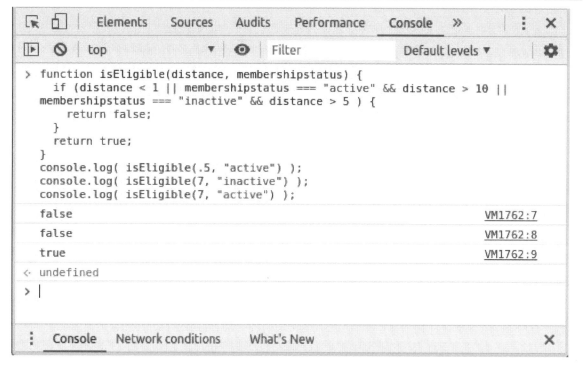

Figure 5.10: Exercise 5.04 output

Why You Shouldn't Compare Boolean and Non-Boolean Expressions

While many non-Boolean values and objects are considered truthy, they may not be equal to **Boolean true**:

```
console.log( 1 == true ); // => true, but:
console.log( 2 == true ); // => false, because true first converts to 1
console.log( 2 == false ); // => also false, because false converts to 0
```

A good rule of thumb is to convert the non-Boolean expression into a **Boolean** type with **!!** – the double negation:

```
console.log( !!2 == true ); // => true
console.log( !!2 == false ); // => false
```

Why You Shouldn't Chain Comparison Expressions

Repeated applications of the same operator to more than two expressions are called chaining. Usually, this is practical and clear:

```
console.log( 1 + 2 + 3 ); // => 6
console.log( true && true && false ); // => false
```

It may also be tempting to use this process with comparison operators, but that would give a surprising, and incorrect, result. In such circumstances, the intermediary result of the first **Boolean** comparison would provide a **Boolean** outcome. Therefore, when it is compared with the next number in the chain, it will be converted by the JavaScript engine into a **1** (if it is **true**) or a **0** (if it is **false**):

```
console.log( 1 < 3 < 2 ); // 1<3 => true, but then: true<2 => 1<2 => true!
```

Similar confusion arises when using comparison operators:

```
console.log( 2==2==2 ); // 2==2 => true, but then: true==2 => 1==2 =>
false!
// Similarly with 0:
console.log( 0==0==0 ); // 0==0 => true, but then: true==0 => 1==0 =>
false!
// However, not the same with 1:
console.log( 1==1==1 ); // 1==1 => true, then: true==1 => 1==1 => true
```

Therefore, avoid chaining any comparison operators unless you're explicitly working with **Boolean** values.

The Ternary Operator

So far, we have looked at unary and binary operators, but another operator is also supported in JavaScript. Known simply as the ternary operator, it performs a similar role to **if...else**, but in a much more compact fashion. The **ternary** operator consists of a question mark (**?**) and a colon (**:**), which are used to denote a conditional expression **?**, a true expression with if **false** expression. For example:

```
var action = (score < 40) ? "Fail" : "Pass";
```

This, of course, is the same as the following:

```
var action;
if (score < 40) {
   action = "Fail";
} else {
   action = "Pass";
}
```

The primary difference here is that the **ternary** operator is an expression in itself. This differs from **if**, which is a statement (it does not return a value).

The conditional segment of the **ternary** operator does not need to be enclosed in parentheses but is often seen as such so that it closely resembles an **if** expression. The rules for each of the three expressions are simply that they must be expressions; you cannot use **if**, **while**, or another such statement, otherwise an error will be thrown.

As ternary operators are expressions, they can be nested. Each question mark segment of the operator expects a colon segment to follow, much like nesting groups of brackets. Therefore, it is possible, and acceptable, to do the following:

```
var status = (score < 40) ? "Fail" : (score > 90) ? "Outstanding Score" :
"Pass";
```

This is equivalent to the following:

```
var status;
if (score < 40) {
   status = "Fail";
} else if (score > 90) {
   status = "Outstanding Score";
} else {
   status = "Pass";
}
```

Ternary operators are very useful for keeping your code succinct. Sometimes, utilizing a complete **if...else** statement detracts from the purpose of the code and makes it harder to understand. Feel free to use the **ternary** operator where you see fit.

Working with Numbers

All numbers in JavaScript are 64-bit floating-point values. Unlike other languages, there is no internal differentiation between floating-point values and integers. JavaScript provides several objects containing functions that are orientated specifically around floating-point values and integers. However, these objects are semantic. Therefore, applying integer-specific functions to a number will still result in a floating-point value.

Numbers are the simplest form of data represented by the JavaScript engine. Number values are immutable, which means their value cannot be modified in memory. If you assign a new number to a variable, you are simply overwriting the old value with the new. The existing value is not modified.

Since **`numbers`** are passed to variables by value, it is not possible for two variables to point to the same **`number`** address space. Therefore, working with **`number`** values is considered pure, providing you do not reassign values to variables.

Arithmetic Limitations

Floating-point values can pose something of a problem in JavaScript. Due to their **`binary`** encoding, which is how the **`number`** is represented in bits within the JavaScript engine, simply adding two floats together may not produce the result you are expecting. Consider the following:

```
0.1 + 0.2;  // outputs 0.30000000000000004
```

Here, the response should be **`0.3`**, but it is not. The underlying runtime simply does not handle values in a way that allows them to be accurate, even with a single **`decimal`** place.

If accuracy is necessary for your application, there are a number of tricks that provide the correct output. With regards to the preceding example, simply converting the values into decimals before the addition will yield better accuracy. You can then convert the resulting value back into a floating-point number afterward, like so:

```
((0.1 * 10) + (0.2 * 10)) / 10;  // outputs 0.3
```

The same is also true for multiplication and division:

```
0.0032 * 13;  // outputs 0.041600000000000005
```

However, if you convert into an **integer** first, then the result is more accurate:

```
0.0032 * 1000 * 13 / 1000; // outputs 0.0416
```

This limitation is not restricted to JavaScript. In fact, any language that works with 64-bit IEEE 754 floating-point numbers will have the same limitations. There are numerous libraries available on the internet that help with these issues, if you would prefer not to tackle them yourself.

> **Note**
>
> The largest integer values that JavaScript can represent as numbers are
> **9,007,199,254,740,991** and **-9,007,199,254,740,991**.

The Number Object

As we mentioned previously, numbers in JavaScript are primitives. As such, they have no properties or methods. Contrary to this, however, the JavaScript engine maintains an awareness of where numerical literals and variables are used within your application and provides syntactic support for methods via the **number** object. It is even possible to extend this object using prototypes, which will be explained in full in Part Four. Any extension imposed on the **Number** object will be usable against numeric values in your application:

```
5.123.toPrecision(3);
  // returns "5.12"
```

Note that while it may seem as though numerical values are objects, this is not actually the case. In memory, numbers are very simple values. The **Number** object, and its implementation by the JavaScript runtime, merely provides many of the benefits afforded with objects against these values.

Number Functions

The **Number** object contains an assortment of functions that work with numeric values. Like all objects, the **Number** object provides a constructor that, if invoked with the **new** keyword, creates a **Number** object instance. Numbers that are created with the **Number** constructor are actual objects, which is contrary to the previous statement, that is, that numbers are not objects, and is the cause of a lot of confusion. To make things even more interesting, the resulting object instance can be treated just like any other number.

In addition to the constructor is the **Number** function. This is used in the same manner as the **Number** constructor but without the **new** keyword. Invoking this function returns a **number**, not an **object**:

```
var num1 = 99;
var num2 = Number(99);
var num3 = new Number(99);
console.log(num1 == num2); // outputs 'true'
console.log(num1 == num3); // outputs 'true'
console.log(num2 == num3); // outputs 'true'

console.log(num1, num2, num3); // outputs '99 99 Number {99}'
```

In all the instances detailed in the preceding code, the resulting values can be worked with in the same manner and with the same rules, except when dealing with truthy conditionals. Typically, conditionals see the value **0** (zero) as a falsey value, but the value returned from **new Number(0)** is truthy, even though it is also zero.

```
console.log( false==new Number(0) ); // => true, meaning that Number(0)
equals to false, but:

if( new Number(0) ) { // => truthy
   console.log("truthy");
}
else {
   console.log("falsey");
}
```

Likewise, when comparing by type, the value that's returned from **new Number(0)** is an object, not a number, so strict comparisons against numeric literals will fail.

Both the **Number** function and constructor will accept any value type. If the value type cannot be converted into a number, then **NaN** (not a number) is returned:

```
console.log( Number(true) ); // 1
console.log( Number(false) ); // 0
console.log( Number("5") ); // 5
console.log( Number([]) ); // 0
console.log( Number([1, 2, 3]) ); // NaN
```

When working with JavaScript, it is advised not to use the **Number** constructor at all so that your code is more readable.

Aside from the **Number** function and constructor, the global **Number** object also provides a variety of functions to help us identify or parse numeric values:

Function	Description
`Number.isNaN(<value>)`	Returns **true** if the passed value is NaN. Only use this to compare a value with NaN. This is because NaN is special in that it's not equal to any number, not even itself: NaN==NaN evaluates to **false**.
`Number.isFinite(<value>)`	Returns **true** if the passed value is a representation of a finite value (not infinite).
`Number.isInteger(<value>)`	Returns **true** if the passed value is an integer. This will also occur if a **float** is passed with a zero mantissa but will return **false** if the mantissa is greater than zero.
`Number_isSafelnteger(<va iLl e>)`	Returns true if the passed integer is between 9,007,199,254,740,991 and -9,007,199,254,740,991 inclusive.
`Number.parseFloat(<value>)`	Converts a passed value into a **float**, if possible, or NaN if it is unable to.
`Number.parseint(<value>)`	Converts a passed value into an **integer**, if possible, or NaN if it is unable to.

Figure 5.11: Number functions and their descriptions

Each of these functions is **static** and so must be preceded with the global **Number** object (which acts as a class in many languages), except when using **parseFloat** or **parseInt**. These functions are also global and therefore can be invoked without the preceding **Number**, like so:

```
console.log( Number.parseFloat("1.235e+2") ); // outputs 123.5
console.log( parseFloat("1.235e+2") ); // outputs 123.5 again
```

Number Methods

Since the JavaScript parser semantically identifies numeric values, it is possible to invoke instance methods of the Number object against them, just like we can with actual objects. The majority of these methods are used to format **numeric** values as **string** representations, which is very useful for presentation in web pages:

Method	Description
`toExponential()`	Formats the number as a **string** with **exponential** notation.
`toFixed(<places>)`	Formats the number as a **string** with **fixed-point** notation.
`toLocaleString(<fractionDigits>)`	Formats the number as a **string** with language sensitivity.
`toString0`	Returns a direct **string** representation of the **number**.

Figure 5.12: Number methods and their descriptions

Using a combination of the **Number** functions and methods, it is possible to convert to and from numeric values as necessary, though some precision may be lost:

```
console.log( 123.456.toLocaleString() ); // outputs "123.456"
console.log( 123.456.toFixed(1) ); // outputs "123.5"
console.log( 123.456.toExponential(3) ); // outputs "1.235e+2"
```

However, calling those functions on integer literals (rather than floats) fails:

```
console.log( 123.toString() ); // => Uncaught SyntaxError: Invalid or
unexpected token
```

When JavaScript sees the first dot right after one or more digits, it assumes you want to write a float literal. There are some workarounds to this:

```
console.log( 123.0.toString() ); // Append .0. It will still be
represented as an integer (as far as it fits in the integer range)
console.log( (123).toExponential(2) ); // Wrap within parentheses (..)
```

Number Properties

The global **Number** object provides a variety of constant properties, which is useful when comparing your numeric values. The most important of these is **NaN**. Being able to identify numeric discrepancies outside of the JavaScript runtime's ability to calculate provides you with a means to reduce bugs in your code. For instance, observe the following example:

```
var num = 999 / 0;
```

When executed, the result of **num** is the constant value known as Infinity. Since it is not possible to add, deduct, multiply, or divide other values from infinity, any further math against that value will also be Infinity. Therefore, being able to deduce this restriction within your code will provide an early warning that something may be amiss in your logic.

Other properties of Number include the following:

Property	Description
EPSILON	The smallest value possible between two numbers that are representable by JavaScript.
MAX SAFE INTEGER	This is the largest possible **integer** that can be used in calculations.
MAX VALUE	The largest number possible that can be represented as a double-precision floating-point number.
MIN SAFE INTEGER	This is the smallest possible **integer** that can be used in calculations.
MIN_VALUE	The smallest number possible that can be represented as a **double** floating-point number.

Figure 5.13: Number properties and their descriptions

Both **MAX_SAFE_INTEGER** and **MIN_SAFE_INTEGER** are interesting values. Consider the following code:

```
Number.MAX_SAFE_INTEGER + 1 === Number.MAX_SAFE_INTEGER + 2;
```

Surprisingly, the result of the preceding expression is **true**. This is simply because the numbers exceed safety boundaries and are therefore no longer accurately represented. The precision that's used in both sides of the preceding expression results in the same value and thus are considered equal.

Exercise 5.05: Currency Formatter

In this exercise, we will create a function that can take a numeric value parameter as a **number** or **string** and format it into a price value with two-decimal precision. In order to prepend a **currency** symbol, the function will accept it as a parameter. Let's get started:

1. Define your function signature. This function will accept two parameters. The first of these will be the decimal value and the second will be the currency symbol:

```
function formatPrice(value, currency) {
```

2. When executing, the first task that the function performs should be to validate the quality of the passed parameter values. The **value** parameter must be able to be converted into a numeric value, while the **currency** parameter should be a character **string**. If the **currency** is falsey, such as when no parameter has been passed, then we can default its value to the dollar symbol:

```
value = Number(value);
currency = currency || "$";
```

3. When responding to errors, there are many ways we can notify the caller that something went wrong. In this instance, we'll simply return **null**. This way, the caller will know that anything other than a **string** response means that something wasn't quite right:

```
if (Number.isNaN(value) || typeof currency != "string") {
    return null;
}
```

4. Now that we know the parameters are usable, combine them into the correct format and return the value:

```
    return currency + value.toFixed(2);
}
```

5. If you go ahead and execute this function, you will see the appropriate responses:

```
console.log( formatPrice(1.99, 32) ); // => null
console.log( formatPrice(5, "£") ); // => £5.00
console.log( formatPrice(9.9) ); // => $9.90
console.log( formatPrice("Ted") ); // => null
```

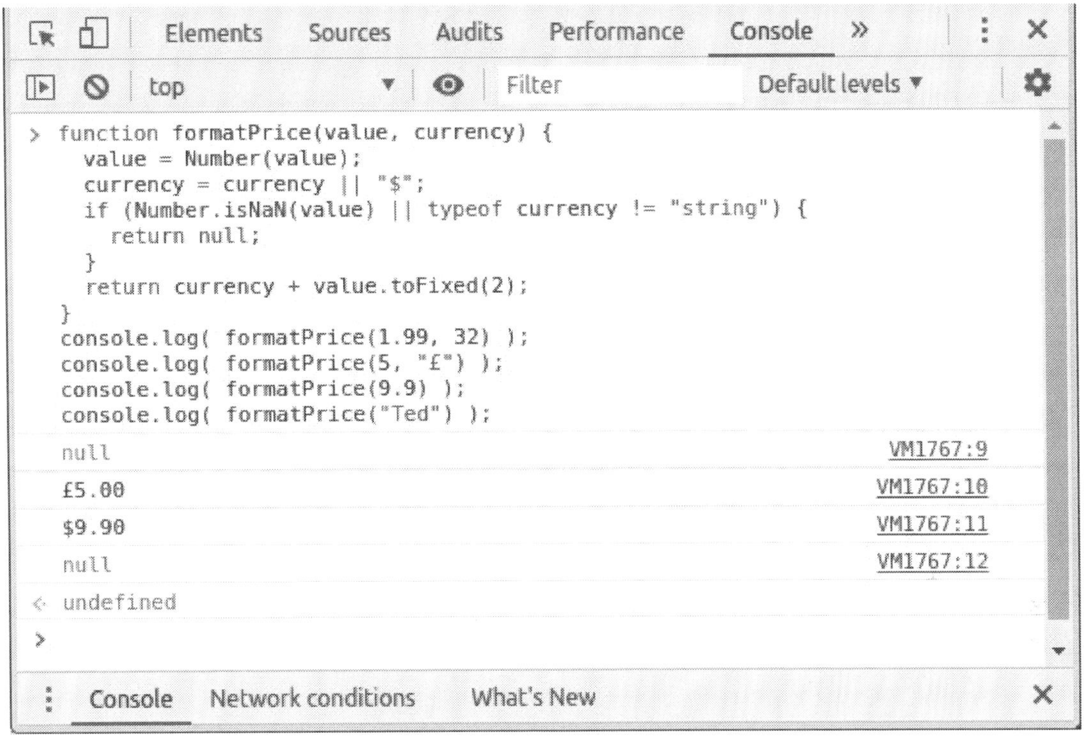

Figure 5.14: Exercise 5.05 output

We can see the output once all four functions are run in the preceding figure. In this exercise, we created a function that took a numeric value parameter as a **number** or **string** and formatted it into a price value with two-decimal precision.

Working with Strings

Like **numbers**, **strings** are simple immutable data types that are managed within the JavaScript runtime as a list of binary values, which are representable as characters. Since they are immutable, they cannot be altered. If you modify a **string**, using one of the various methods provided, you are actually creating a new string with the changes applied.

The literal representation of strings is a list of characters surrounded by quotes. These quotes can be double quotes, single quotes (apostrophes), or backticks:

```
console.log( "I am a string" );
console.log( 'I am also a string' );
console.log( `I am a special string` );
```

Strings can be thought of as a long list of single characters, much like arrays, which will be discussed later. As such, it is possible to query individual, or groups of, characters:

```
["H", "e", "l", "l", "o", ",", " ", "W", "o", "r", "l", "d", "!"]
```

The preceding code is not a literal representation, but simply an analogy of how strings may be perceived. Since strings are lists, it is possible to retrieve characters from them using the character index. This is performed by enclosing the index with square bracket symbols. The index of a character string starts at **0** (zero):

```
"Hello, World!"[7];
// =>    "W"
```

Since strings are immutable, you cannot assign a replacement character to an index, like so:

```
var msg = "Hello, World!";
console.log( msg[7] = "Z" ); // => "Z"
msg; // =>   "Hello, World!"
```

It is not possible to modify a **string**. Instead, you can only create a new one based on the original. You can either reconstruct it using operators or use one of the many **string** functions provided by the **String** object, which will be described shortly.

Special Characters

Since strings are contained in quotes, placing the same quotes within the string can be problematic. Simply typing the quote in the string is the same as terminating that string. This will then mean that any proceeding characters may be seen as malformed JavaScript code or, possibly worse, executable JavaScript code.

One way to avoid terminating the **string** is to use a different quote to the type used to contain the **string**. For instance, if the string is contained in double quotes, then single quotes can be used freely. Likewise, containing the **string** in single quotes will allow double quotes to be used freely:

```
console.log( "I can contain 'single' quotes" );
console.log( 'I can contain "double" quotes' );
```

This will work for simple text but is not as foolproof for strings that need to contain both quote types.

The JavaScript language provides a means to **escape** characters included within strings so that they are treated differently. This is performed by preceding the character to escape with a backslash (\) character. In the case of quotes, escaping ensures that the quote character is not seen as the string termination character:

```
"It's useful to be able to \"escape\" quotes"
```

The **escape character** can be used with several other characters for varying effects. It is even used to escape the escape character, for times when a backslash must exist within a **string**:

```
"This \\ will create a single backslash"
```

Other supported escape characters include the following:

Escaped Character	Description
\b	The backspace character, which is used to overwrite the previous character with the following character.
\f	The form feed character, which is used when printing to move content onto a new page (depending on the browser).
\n	The newline character, which moves proceeding text onto a new line.
\r	The carriage return character, which works similarly to the newline character.
\t	The tab character, which is used to insert a tabular space into the string.
\v	The vertical tab character, which is used to position the form at the next line tab stop.

Figure 5.15: Escape Characters

Concatenation

Concatenating is a means of combining elements, end to end, to form a new element. With regards to strings, this is simply combining strings together to form a larger string.

String concatenation is performed using the plus (**+**) symbol. This is known as method overloading:

```
"This string " + "and " + "this string " + "are concatenated";
// =>  "This string and this string are concatenated"
```

When concatenating strings, it is important to pay attention to the presence of space characters. No additional characters are added at the point of concatenation. Therefore, if you require spaces between combined strings, you must add these yourself.

Since strings are immutable, concatenating strings creates a new string, which you can assign to a variable or pass as a parameter to a function. The original strings remain unaffected.

Template Literals

Template literals are a more recent addition to the JavaScript language. Surrounding strings with backtick quotes (`) alter the translation of the literal by the JavaScript engine and afford some additional new features.

The first interesting feature, and the one that's the most commonly used, is the ability to interpolate expressions within a **string**. This is performed by embedding blocks within the string preceded with the dollar (**$**) character. Combining strings in this fashion provides the benefit of making string literals easier to read, but can also greatly simplify more complex string concatenation requirements:

```
var str = `2 + 2 = ${2 + 2}`;
console.log( str ); // =>  "2 + 2 = 4"
var name = "Jonny";
welcomeStr = `Hello, ${name}!`;
console.log( welcomeStr );  // => "Hello, Jonny!"
```

Another useful feature of template literals is the ability to use physical line breaks. By applying line breaks to the JavaScript code, those same breaks appear within the resolved string:

```
var str = `This is line one
and this is line two`;
console.log( str );
// => "This is line one
// =>  and this is line two"
```

Finally, a template expression can contain inner template literals within it too, thereby providing a nested template literal implementation. You'll see them in the next example. This caters to more complex expressions within the **string** itself, such as conditionals or loops.

The result of template literals is a feature within JavaScript that lends itself very nicely to processing pages, and other string data content, in a manner that is more manageable. Where JavaScript developers once looked toward third-party libraries to perform such feats, such libraries are no longer required.

Exercise 5.06: Email Templates

In this exercise, you will create a function that accepts the components of an email sending service and combines them into an email body template. To make things more interesting, only adults are eligible to post comments on the website. Accordingly, the message text will change. Let's get started:

1. Start off by creating a function signature. The parameters of the function determine the values that can be entered into the email body. As stated in the description, we will require an **age** parameter:

```
function sendEmail(name, age, comments) {
```

2. With this in place, check the passed parameters now. If any are invalid, the function will simply return **null**:

```
var age = Number(age);
if (Number.isNaN(age)
|| typeof name != "string"
|| typeof comments != "string") {
  return null;
}
```

Here, we're checking whether the number can be used as a valid numerical value and whether the **name** and **comments** are **strings**. We could also choose to check the length of the strings to ensure they have content, but that is not necessary for this exercise.

3. Now that we have valid parameters, we'll need to create our **body** text with the alluded-to nested template expression:

```
var body = `A user has posted a comment from the website:
name: ${name}
age: ${age}
status: ${(age < 18) ? `${name} is not a valid user` : `${name} is a
  valid user`}
comments: ${comments}`;
```

As you can see, a **ternary** operator expression is used to populate the content of the interpolation in the **status** line. It would also be possible to invoke a function here, but it would not have been acceptable to use an actual **if** condition. The reason for this is that an **if** condition is composed of one or more blocks, which is not accepted in template interpolation syntax.

4. Finally, we can close the function by returning the variable. If you now execute the function and pass in some arbitrary parameters, you should see the complete interpolated string:

```
   return body;
}


sendEmail("Jane", 27, "Your website is fantastic!");
// =>  "A user has posted a comment from the website:
// =>  name: Jane
// =>  age: 27
// =>  status: Jane is a valid user
// =>  comments Your website is fantastic!"
```

The expected output will be as follows:

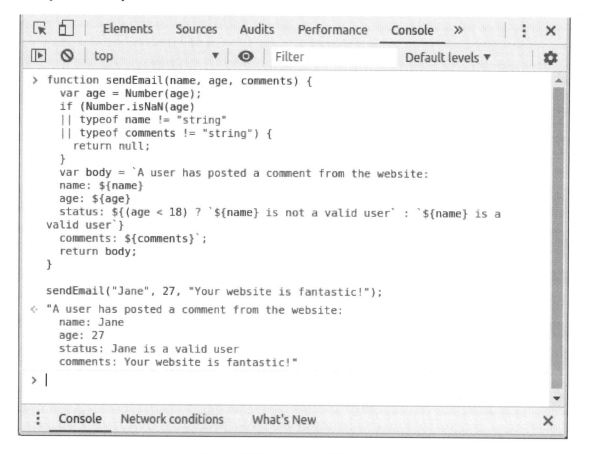

Figure 5.16: Exercise 5.06 output

How and where you choose to concatenate or interpolate strings is up to you. When tackling a problem, consider whether the code is more readable using one form of quotation over another, especially if more than one developer will be working with the code.

The String Object

Like number values, character strings also come with a useful object called the String object. Similarly, the String object provides numerous functions, methods, and properties oriented around strings.

Also similar to the **Number** object is the **String** function, which converts any passed value into a **string**. The **String** function works by calling the value's **toString** function, which we'll discuss a little later.

The length Property

The **String** object, and thus strings themselves, have only one property: the **length** property. As the name suggests, the **length** property returns the **length** of the **string** as an **integer**. As the indexing of a **string** starts at zero, the length is always one more than the last character index:

```
"Hello, World!".length;
// =>  13
```

The **length** property is particularly useful for iterating over the **string**, or when working with many of the **string** methods when its **length** is not already known.

String Methods

The **String** object does not have any **static** functions, but it does support strings with numerous available methods – far more than those available in the **Number** object. This chapter will not attempt to cover them all but will look at the more useful methods.

Working with and manipulating strings is a common requirement in JavaScript; not just for displaying text, but for working with data in general. It is often necessary to clip, sort, modify, add, and remove segments of strings using varying criteria. As such, JavaScript provides just about every method you could think of to make these tasks simple.

The following table lists the most commonly used methods that are provided by the String object:

Method	Description
charAt(<index>)	Returns a character at a given index. This produces the same result as accessing using the square bracket syntax. Index starts from 0 – this applies to other methods, too.
charCodeAt(<index>)	The same as charAt(); but returns the Unicode value as an integer.
concat(<string1>, <string2>[, ...])	Combines two or more strings passed as parameters and returns a new string. Similar to using the + operator.
endsWith(<string>)	Returns true if the current string ends with the same characters as the parameter string. Otherwise, false is returned.
startsWith(<string>)	Returns true if the current string starts with the same characters as the parameter string. Otherwise, false is returned.
indexOf(<string>)	Returns the index of the first occurrence of the given parameter string. If no occurrence exists, –1 is returned.
lastIndexOf(<string>)	Similar to indexOf(): but returns the index of the last occurrence of the given parameter string. If no occurrence exists, –1 is returned.
split(<string>)	Splits the string into an array of substrings. Each substring ends/starts at the index of the occurrence of the passed string parameter.
substr(<start>, <count>)	Returns a substring from the string, starting at the start index and encompassing the count characters that follow.
substring(<start>, <end>)	Returns a substring from the string, starting at the start index and ending at the end index (excluding the character at the end index).
trim()	Removes any whitespace characters at the start or end of the string.
toLowerCase()	Returns a version of the string with all characters converted into lowercase.
toUpperCase()	Returns a version of the string with all characters converted into uppercase.

Figure 5.17: String Methods

Exercise 5.07: Sentence Reversal

In this exercise, you will create a function that accepts a string of any size, trims any whitespace characters, reverses its content, and then capitalizes the first character of the string or of those following a period character. The result should look like a normal sentence from a reversed dimension. The purpose of the exercise is to understand data transformation. Transforming data is ubiquitous in software development. The JavaScript runtime transforms data when it reads your code and converts it into a running application. Being able to transform data in a simple manner will prove to be a valuable skill. Let's get started:

1. Start off with the function signature. We only want to accept a single parameter, which we'll call **str**; this is an abbreviation of "string":

```
function reverse(str) {
```

2. Next, perform the simplest task first, that is, removing any trailing whitespace characters from the beginning and end of the string. While doing this, you should also ensure that you are actually working with a string value:

```
str = String(str).trim();
```

3. With the parameter prepared, you should now start a loop. The loop will build a new string by walking the parameter string in reverse. Therefore, you will also need to declare four additional variables, namely, a temporary variable to hold the resulting value, a variable to keep track of the current string index, a variable to store the current character, and a variable to keep track of whether the next non-whitespace character is at the start of a sentence:

```
var result = "", index = str.length - 1, chr, isStart = true;
while (index >= 0) {
```

In the preceding code, we ensure that the counter starts at one less than the **length** of the string (the last index of the string) and that the loop iterates as long as the counter is greater than or equal to **0** (zero).

4. With the loop in progress, store the character at the index into the **chr** variable:

```
chr = str[index];
```

5. With the character stored, check whether the previous iteration is found at the end of a sentence. If it was, then you will need to uppercase the next non-whitespace character. Otherwise, you will need to **lowercase** it:

```
if (isStart && chr != " ") {
  chr = chr.toUpperCase();
  isStart = false;
} else {
  chr = chr.toLowerCase();
}
```

If the character is the start of a sentence, then the **isStart** flag needs to be set back to **false** so that the next iteration doesn't repeat the uppercasing.

6. Since the uppercasing occurred for the previous iteration, check whether you should flag a new sentence in this iteration:

```
if (chr == ".") {
  isStart = true;
  if (index == str.length - 1) {
    index--;
    continue;
```

You detect the start of a new sentence by checking for the period character. If it is the start of a new sentence, then you set the **isStart** flag, but you also need to determine whether this is the very end of the original string. The reason for this is that you do not want to copy the last period of the original string to the start of the new string, or the result will start with a period, which will not make sense. If it is, you simply skip the character altogether by decrementing the **index** and continuing the loop.

7. If the period was not at the end of the original string, make some adjustments. You will not want the new sentences to end with a space and then a period – you will require the reversal of that. Since the space will have already been applied to the result, you need to backtrack by one character and re-add the required output. As the result string has now been modified, you will need to continue to the next iteration once more:

```
} else {
  result = result.substr(0, result.length-1) + ". ";
  index--;
  continue;
  }
}
```

8. If the loop does not continue, then the current iteration results in a regular character, which should simply be appended to the result. Decrement the index for the next iteration and close out the loop. End the function by returning the result to the caller:

```
    result = result + chr;
    index--;
  }
  return result + ".";
}
```

9. Now, go ahead and execute the function. Try passing multiple sentences to it inside a single string to see the full result:

```
reverse("This is the first sentence. This is the second.");
// =>  "Dnoces eht si siht. Ecnetnes tsrif eht si siht."
```

```
> function reverse(str) {
    str = String(str).trim();
    var result = "", index = str.length - 1, chr, isStart = true;
    while (index >= 0) {
      chr = str[index];
      if (isStart && chr != " ") {
        chr = chr.toUpperCase();
        isStart = false;
      } else {
        chr = chr.toLowerCase();
      }
      if (chr == ".") {
        isStart = true;
        if (index == str.length - 1) {
          index--;
          continue;
        } else {
          result = result.substr(0, result.length-1) + ". ";
          index--;
          continue;
        }
      }
      result = result + chr;
      index--;
    }
    return result + ".";
  }
  reverse("This is the first sentence. This is the second.");
< "Dnoces eht si siht. Ecnetnes tsrif eht si siht."
>
```

Figure 5.18: Exercise 5.07 output

There you have it. You have just created a string manipulation function using methods from the **String** global object. Certainly, the function will not win any awards and may not work well if provided with strings containing consecutive whitespace characters, but it does work.

The toString Method

Every primitive type in JavaScript can be converted into a string using the **String** function. When working with more complex types, however, this is not always the case. For instance, with a typical object, converting it into a **string** will produce a set result, regardless of the object's content:

```
var obj = {name: "Bob"};
String(obj);
// =>   "[object Object]"
```

The reason for this is that the JavaScript engine doesn't understand how you wish the data to be parsed. It could simply be that you require the output to form a table of keys and values, or you may simply want a list of the values themselves and to discard the keys. The possibilities are endless.

As such, JavaScript provides the concept of the **toString** value method.

toString is a method that exists on all data types but is required to be overridden on some of the complex types, providing that you have your own parsing logic. When calling the **String** function and passing it a value, you are in fact invoking the **toString** method on that value:

```
console.log( String(99) );
// =>   "99"
console.log(  (99).toString() ); // See above about invoking methods on
integer literals
// =>   "99"
console.log( [1, 2, 3].toString() );
// =>   "[1, 2, 3]"
```

Overriding the **toString** method is simply a case of supplying an alternative function of the same name to the data value. For instance, to override the **toString** method in a custom object, you could simply do the following:

```
var obj = {ted: "bob", toString: function() { return "I am Bob!" }};
obj.toString();
// =>   "I am Bob!"
String(obj);
   "I am Bob!"
```

Working with complex objects and object functions will be described fully later in this chapter.

Numbers with Strings

Numbers and **strings** are both primitive data types and both overload the + (addition) operator. However, there is much more of a relationship between the two that can prove useful or catch you out if you are not careful.

Interestingly, numbers and strings in JavaScript can often be interchangeable, thanks to an intelligent context-based system. Depending on the circumstances, JavaScript will attempt to deduce the resulting type of an expression based on the available parameters.

You have already seen that strings can be concatenated using the + operator, but numbers can also be concatenated into strings:

```
"I am " + 21 + " years old";
// =>   "I am 21 years old"
```

When the JavaScript parser identifies a numeric value and a string value passed as expressions to the + operator, it will convert the number into a string so that the result is a simple string concatenation. This is otherwise known as context-based casting.

When the string expression is also a representation of a numerical value and is used with other numerical associated operators, such as / or *, the reverse action will occur. At such times, JavaScript's context-based casting will instead convert the string number into an actual number. Here's an example:

```
"42.7" * 2;
// =>   85.4
```

JavaScript will always convert the non-string value into a string when we use the + operator in order to produce an expected result. It would be too confusing if the + operator worked differently based on the content of the string expression.

Numbers can also be mathematically calculated when both expressions are a string, but again, this will only occur if you're not utilizing the + operator:

```
console.log( "10" * "10" );
// =>   100
console.log( "10" + "10" );
// =>   "1010"
```

If it is expected that you will need to add together two numbers represented as strings, such as values read from text input fields, always convert them into numbers first:

```
Number ("10") + Number ("10");
// =>  20
```

Working with Functions

As you've already seen, JavaScript functions are blocks of code with signatures naming the variables that were passed to them when invoked. As with any block, functions have their own stacks that encapsulate and protect data declared within them.

In JavaScript, functions are considered first-class types. This means that, much like any other type, they can be assigned to variables, passed as parameters to other functions, and returned from functions. They are also able to call themselves, which is known as recursive and is the quality that helps make JavaScript a functional language.

There are many forms of function in JavaScript:

- Anonymous functions
- Named functions
- Arrow functions
- Generator functions

The differences between them are mostly slight syntactical changes that affect how they are used. We will briefly cover each of the function types in this chapter.

Anonymous Functions

Since functions in JavaScript are first class, they exist as a transferable resource, much like primitives and objects. Until now, functions have been declared and assigned, which means they have a callable name. However, a function is also an expression with two states: its **declared format** and its **invocation**.

A function can exist without providing a name in the signature, whereby it has the following format:

```
function (...parameters) {
    ...body
}
```

In JavaScript, it is possible to code a function without providing a name at declaration time. Creating functions in this way allows them to be created in place, such as in a call to another function:

```
otherFunction( function(a, b) { /* do something */ } );
```

Functions can also be assigned to variables and, of course, be received as parameters in a function call. Once an anonymous function has been assigned to a variable, it becomes a named **function**, since the variable constitutes its name:

```
var echo = function(subject) { console.log(subject); };
echo("Hello, World!");
// =>  "Hello, World!"
```

In fact, up until now, you have been writing functions with a global scope. Declaring a named function simply means that a variable of the same name will be declared in the current scope and will point to that function. For instance, the following two syntaxes are equivalent:

```
var myFunc = function(i) { return i + 1; };
function myFunc(i) { return i + 1; };
```

Declaring a function without assigning a name can be considered a function literal. Since the function exists at the point of definition, it can also be executed in place. How could that be useful? It can encapsulate entire programs and avoid dirtying the global namespace:

```
( function(a, b) { console.log(a + b); }
) (2, 4);
// =>  6
```

Namespace dirtying is a term to describe functions and variables declared globally. While doing so is not disallowed, it can be problematic. If two libraries within the same web page create global variables of the same name, there can be unexpected results. Creating applications that honor a clean global environment will be discussed in a later chapter.

Callbacks

An important use case for anonymous functions has often been asynchronous execution callbacks. When calling code that does not immediately return a value, but also does not stop the execution of code that immediately proceeds it, that code is considered **asynchronous**.

Applications that contain asynchronous code need a means to alert the rest of the application once the asynchronous code has finished running and a value must be returned. In JavaScript, callbacks have long been used for this purpose:

```
function doSomethingAsync(data, callback) {
   async_task(data).then(     // do async request
     function(result) {     // then on return
       callback(result);     // execute callback, passing result data!
     }
   );
   //.. continue with other code ..
}
```

The issue with callbacks is that should numerous asynchronous calls need to occur sequentially, the resulting code file has a tendency to indent catastrophically. This issue is sometimes fondly known as the pyramid of doom or callback hell:

```
asyncOne(data, function(res1) {
   asyncTwo(res1, function(res2) {
     asyncThree(res2, function(res3) {
       //... ad infinitum ..
     });
   });
});
```

As you can see, each new request indents a further two characters. It is not uncommon for an application to possess callback chains of several tens of requests, thereby reaching the far side of the screen while coding. Developers can choose not to indent, as indentation is not a requirement, but not doing so results in harder-to-read code. To resolve this, generator functions were introduced. You will learn more about generator functions later in this chapter.

Exercise 5.08: Functional Parameters

In this exercise, you will create a function that accepts two parameters: a primitive data type and a function. This function will then combine those parameters and return a function as a result. The returned function will work identically to the function that was passed as a parameter, with the exception that it will always receive the original primitive parameter as its argument. Let's get started:

1. Start off by creating the function signature. You know that it will accept two parameters and, since it will act as a kind of currying process (a term used in functional programming), that's the name that will be used here:

```
function curry(prim, fun) {
```

There is nothing special here. The **curry** function is just like any named function.

In this circumstance, it's not important what value the first parameter contains. Even if it contained **null**, that would still be valid in this instance, so you can accept whatever comes through.

2. Now, check if the second parameter is a function. Otherwise, when it is invoked, an error may occur if it is some other value type:

```
if (typeof fun != "function") return;
```

3. Now for the fun part. The intention is to always populate the parameter list of the passed-in function with the first parameter of this function, however many times it is called. To do this, use a local function definition:

```
var ret = function() {
  return fun(prim);
};
```

As you can see, the result here is a function that, whenever it is called, will simply call the **fun** function. The **prim** parameter will always remain the same here, so the invocation will always produce the same result.

4. Now, return the new function:

```
    return ret;
}
```

5. Let's give this a spin. Try calling the function while trying different values as parameters:

```
var fun = function(val) { return val + 50 };
var curry1 = curry(99, fun);
console.log( curry1() );
// =>  149
console.log( curry1() );
// =>  149
// calling curry1 will produce the same output however many times
// it is called, because it is a fixed, pure function.
var curry2 = curry("Bob", fun);
console.log( curry2() );
// =>  "Bob50"
```

The expected output will be as follows:

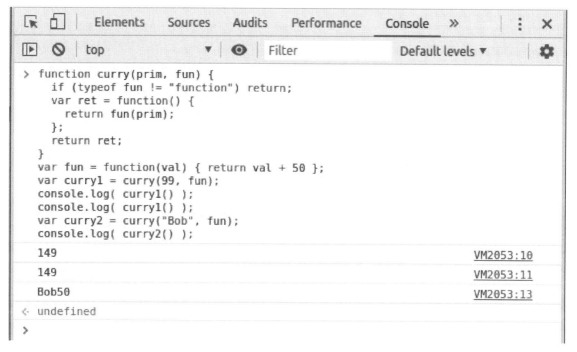

Figure 5.19: Exercise 5.08 output

Arrow Functions

Arrow functions, sometimes called **fat arrow** functions, are a simplified syntax for function declaration:

```
var myFun = (param) => param + 1;
```

As shown in the preceding example, arrow functions don't need to provide a block of code and can instead be replaced with an expression. If an expression is used, then no **return** keyword is required since expressions already return a value. However, the **return** keyword is required if a block is used, since blocks are not expressions:

```
var myFun = (param) => {
   return param + 1;
};
```

As well as functioning without a block, arrow functions can also be declared without the parentheses surrounding the parameter list:

```
var myFun = param => param + 1;
```

However, the preceding code only works if the parameters are a list of one. This is because a list of two or more parameters forms a rather ambiguous statement. For instance, consider the following:

```
var myFun = a, b, c => a + b + c;
```

When reading the preceding declaration, the compiler will not know which of the following declaration strings you are trying to achieve:

```
var myFun = a, b = undefined, (c) => { return a + b + c };
var myFun = a, (b, c) => { return a + b + c };
var myFun = (a, b, c) => { return a + b + c };
```

> **Note**
>
> The first two examples will give an error since they attempt to define an arrow function in a **var** statement, but without being assigned to a variable.

Arrow Function Caveats

While arrow functions appear much cleaner and more flexible than regular function declarations, there are disadvantages to their use. The first disadvantage is that arrow functions cannot be used as an object constructor and it's ill-advised to use them as object methods. The reason for this has to do with the second limitation; arrow functions have no access to their own this, arguments, or super objects (discussed later in this chapter).

The purpose of arrow functions is simply to enable a cleaner syntax when working with anonymous functions. Arrow functions were the first syntactical weapon against callback hell, which we described previously. As such, arrow functions should be used wisely.

Generator Functions

Generators are a recent and rather complex addition to the JavaScript language. They are incredibly useful functions once you begin to understand them, though that may take some effort. Generators do not facilitate any means that cannot be carried out in some other fashion within the JavaScript language. As such, this section will merely touch upon the subject of generator functions in order to alert you to their usefulness.

Generators provide additional power to sequence iteration. Here's an example:

```
for (let i = 0; i < 3; i++) {
   callback(i);
};
```

The preceding code is an iterator. The loop iterates three times, from 0 to 2. Each time the iteration occurs, the **callback** function is called, and the iteration result is passed to it.

Now, the problem with loops is that they are a closed stack. For any custom code to execute within the loop, the loop needs to have knowledge of what to do with the iterated data. This is a restriction that generators aim to overcome.

Generator functions are declared much like named and anonymous functions, but with a slight difference; an asterisk must be placed after the **function** keyword:

```
var myFun = function*(params) { /*body*/ };
```

> **Note**
>
> The arrow function format cannot be used for generator functions.

When creating the function body, the same rules for named and anonymous functions apply. However, there are some differences. Take a look at the following example, based on the preceding loop:

```
var myFun = function*() {
   for (let i = 0; i < 3; i++) {
     yield i;
   }
};
```

In particular, note the **yield** keyword. **yield** is a keyword that's been borrowed from multithreaded languages such as C++. Its usage in those languages is similar to its usage here. Essentially, by calling **yield**, you are asking the runtime engine to pass control back to the caller. In JavaScript, "passing back of control" includes sending a value to the caller. In the preceding example, a value will be sent each time the function yields, which will be three times in total.

To use the function, you must create an instance of the generator by invoking the function:

```
var myGen = myFun();
```

Once you have a generator instance, you can acquire a value:

```
var firstValue = myGen.next().value;
console.log( firstValue );   // firstValue will equal 0;
```

You can call the **next** function many times, until the stream is exhausted. Once exhausted, the returned value will be undefined:

```
console.log(myGen.next().value);
// =>   1
console.log(myGen.next().value);
// =>   2
console.log(myGen.next().value);
// =>   undefined
```

The return value of the **next()** function is an object with two fields:

```
{value: <value>, done: <boolean>}
```

The **object** is hidden from the previous examples and we simply return the value in order to keep things simple. The done value will return true as long as there are more yields to return from the generator. Once the generator is exhausted, it will return the following for all successive calls to **next()**:

```
{value: undefined, done: true}
```

One point to keep in mind is that the **yield** keyword may be called as many times as necessary in the **generator** function. In the previous example, the **yield** keyword was used in a loop, but it may just as easily be called elsewhere, too:

```
var myFun = function*() {
  var count = 0
  for (let i = 0; i < 3; i++) {
    yield i;
    count += i;
  }
  yield count;
};
```

Generator functions may also use the **return** keyword. If **return** is used, then the returned value will be retrieved with a call to **next()**, just like yielded values. However, calling return will end the generator, meaning that no more values will be returned from calls to **next()**, even if further **yield** keywords exist in the function.

The this Keyword

All functions, apart from arrow functions, have access to additional objects related to the functions' stack. As we mentioned previously, functions provide a stack that ring-fences the memory that's used by variables that are declared within it, while allowing access to variables declared in the functions or blocks surrounding the function being called. This is otherwise known as encapsulation and protects the outer stacks from being inadvertently corrupted by function body-related processes, while also protecting the data within the function from outside processes.

The **this** keyword exists as a means to be able to directly target the context present within the execution of the function. While the variables that are declared within a function are direct members of the functions stack, the context of the function body may specifically be that of another block or object and may even be changed at invocation time to be a specific context other than the one the function is defined within:

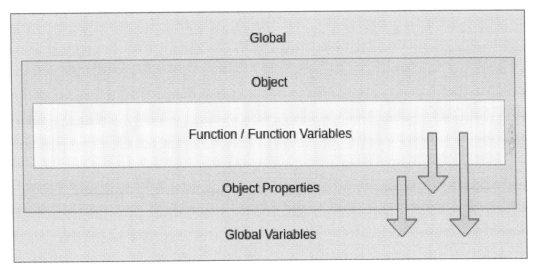

Figure 5.20: Global, object, and function diagram

The arguments Keyword

Another keyword that's available to functions is the **arguments** keyword. When defining a function signature, the parameters listed within the brackets of the signature are known as "named parameters" while the values that are passed to the function during invocation are considered the "functions arguments". Named parameters map to arguments, where possible, during the execution of the function.

When calling a function, you may pass in as many or as few arguments as you like, but they do not need to total the number of parameters listed in the function signature. If you specify fewer parameters than are named in the function signature, those parameters that are not provided for will simply have a value of undefined:

```
function myFun(param1, param2) {
  console.log(param1, param2);
};
myFun(99);
// =>  99, undefined
```

If, on the other hand, you specify more parameters than are listed for that function, those parameters are still made available to the function, despite not having enough named parameters; they are simply not named. In such circumstances, you can access the additional parameters using the arguments keyword.

> **Note**
>
> The **arguments** keyword is very much like an array. You can access it like an array, and you can use it in functions that expect an array. It even has built-in array-like functions. However, the **arguments** keyword is not an array.

To access additional function parameters, you can target them specifically by index against the **arguments** keyword. For instance, if four arguments were passed to the function, you could access the **fourth** argument with the following code:

```
var someValue = arguments[3];
```

As you'll see later with arrays, you can find out just how many arguments were passed to the function invocation by calling the **length** property:

```
var numParams = arguments.length;
```

The **arguments** object can be extremely useful when working with functions of a more dynamic nature.

Call and Apply

As we mentioned previously, JavaScript is an exceptionally flexible language. Since functions are first-class citizens in JavaScript, facilities are provided by the language to manipulate functions.

Two of the most commonly used tools for this endeavor are **call** and **apply**.

Both **call** and apply function in very much the same way: by enabling the invocation of functions while changing the function stack's context.

The differences between **call** and **apply** are simply that **call** is solely used to manipulate the invoked functions context and **apply** is used for the same thing and also to supply an arbitrary number of arguments:

```
var fun = function () { return arguments.length; };
fun.call(this, 1, 2, 3);
// => 3
fun.apply(this, [1, 2, 3]);
// => 3
```

As you can see, to use **call**, you need to know the number of arguments at development time. The arguments that are used in **apply** can be of any **length** and do not have to be known.

Exercise 5.09: Dynamic Currying

This exercise will be a continuation of the previous exercise. Since you now know much more about how functions work in JavaScript, we will take the **curry** concept to a much higher level by supporting arbitrary numbers of arguments. Let's get started:

1. Start off with your **function** signature. However, since you would like to support an arbitrary number of arguments, the function parameter will need to come first. Also, as the remaining parameters are **arbitrary**, there is no need to define them:

```
var curry = function(fun) {
```

Check that the first parameter is a **function** before continuing with the rest of the logic:

```
if (typeof fun != "function") return;
```

2. As you may have guessed, you will use the arguments object to acquire the parameters. However, you will need to manipulate the arguments list since you will not want to pass the function parameter to itself. As we mentioned previously, the **arguments** object is not an array, so you'll need to convert it into one first by manipulating it with an **array** function:

```
var args = Array.prototype.slice.call(arguments);
args.shift();
```

In order to convert **arguments** into an **array**, you need to call a native function of **array** instances that copies the array. The **slice** function creates a shallow copy of an array. In this case, it doesn't know that the **arguments** object is not an array, but still works fine, which is perfect for this use case. The **args.shift()** code removes the first item in the array using the newly created array's shift function. Since arrays are mutable, like objects, the **args** array value is permanently modified.

3. Now that you have your parameters list, create your function wrapper, like you did previously. This time, however, the **fun** parameter will be invoked using **apply**:

```
var ret = function() {
   var nested_args = Array.prototype.slice.call(arguments);
   return fun.apply(this, args.concat(nested_args));
}
```

Since parameters will be supplied to the **curry** function and the returned function, the arguments of each must be joined into a single array. This is what **concat** does. The resulting array is then used as the arguments of the **fun** function.

4. Finally, return the new function and close the **curry** function:

```
    return ret;
}
```

5. Now, let's give this a spin:

```
var fun = function() { return arguments.length; };
var cur1 = curry(fun, 1, 2, 3);
console.log( cur1(4, 5, 6) );
// =>  6
var cur2 = curry(fun, 1, 2, 3, 4, 5, 6);
console.log( cur2(9, 8, 7, 6, 5) );
// =>  11
```

The expected output will be as follows:

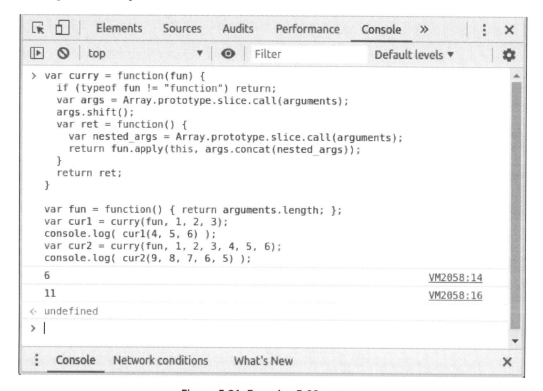

Figure 5.21: Exercise 5.09 output

What you have just achieved is no small feat. **Currying** is a powerful tool in functional programming, and you have achieved this task with very few lines of code.

Activity 5.01: Simple Number Comparison

A lot has been covered so far, so it's time for an activity. In this activity, you have been tasked with writing a function that will receive the grades for a student's coursework for an entire year as percentages. The function must average the result of each grade in order to determine whether the student has passed the course for the entire year. The calculation will assume the following:

- An average below 35% is an F grade.

- An average of 35 – 44% is a D grade.

- An average of 45% – 59% is a C grade.

- An average of 60% – 74% is a B grade.

- An average of 75% and over is an A grade.

Grades for each coursework assignment may be passed as a **Number** or a **String**. No other data type is expected, so error handling is not necessary.

The high-level steps for the activity are as follows:

1. Create a function. Argument labels aren't necessary as we won't know how many arguments there will be.

2. Extract the arguments for the function.

3. Get the number of arguments that were passed and store it as a variable.

4. Add all the arguments together and calculate the average. Store this in a variable.

> **Note**
>
> The final condition will always be true if the others have failed, so the condition itself can be skipped. Each condition will not be evaluated if the previous condition has been returned from the function.

5. Determine the **grade** from the student based on the **average** and return it.

> **Note**
>
> The solution to this activity can be found on page 724.

This activity should highlight the flexibility and simplicity of common problem-solving using JavaScript functions and data types. There are, in fact, many ways to solve this problem, but attempting this in a logical, easy-to-read manner is always preferable.

Working with Objects

In JavaScript, objects are the primary configurable data structures from which all other complex data types extend, including **Array** and **Date**. Objects work like a **hash map**; they contain **key/value** properties that can contain any data type, including functions and other objects.

An object is defined using curly braces, much like a block:

```
var myObject = {};
```

The values that are added to an object are "members" of that object. Those members are accessible using dot notation:

```
var myObject = {foo: "bar"};
console.log(myObject.foo);
// =>   "bar"
```

The key of a property may be specified with or without quotes. However, the result is exactly the same:

```
var myObject = {param1: 1, "param2": 2};
```

JavaScript is known as a prototype language, which means its object-oriented capabilities are provided by prototyping values to objects prior to instantiation. As such, JavaScript objects support the **prototype** keyword. Prototypes are too advanced for this chapter and will be discussed at length in further chapters.

Objects as Hashtables

Objects are very much like key/value **hashtables**: you assign a value to an object with a given **name** or **key**. These values are arbitrary, and they can be primitives, functions, objects, arrays, and so on. Once an object has been defined, you can further assign properties to them using dot notation:

```
var myObject = {};
myObject.age = 21;
console.log(myObject.age);
// =>   21
```

As well as assigning values via dot notation, they can also be assigned by named index, much like an **array**:

```
myObject["age"] = 32;
console.log(myObject.age);
// =>   32
```

The result is exactly the same, but there are some differences between these approaches.

When using dot notation, the parameters of an object must use standard variable naming rules. These include the following:

- Only use letters, digits, underscores, and dollar symbols.

- Must start with a letter, dollar, or underscore symbol.

- Names are case-sensitive (a and A are different variables).

- Must not match a reserved word, such as "**while**" or "**if**".

Objects keys, however, are not limited by this convention. By using square brackets and passing the name as a **string**, the scope for naming keys becomes much broader. In fact, you can seemingly use any **ASCII** character of your choice, including whitespace characters, with up to **2²⁷** characters in length. That's **134,217,728** characters!

```
var obj = {};
obj["    "] = 99;
console.log(obj["    "]);
// =>    99
```

Aside from strings, digits may also be used as keys. This results in objects appearing much like arrays. In fact, for the most part, arrays themselves are simply objects, albeit with some superpowers of their own.

> **Note**
>
> Just as strings can be used with square brackets, values can be written and read from objects dynamically simply by using variables (or expressions) between square brackets instead.

Object Keys and Memory

When working with objects as data stores, it can be tempting to add and retrieve all kinds of data. Objects are extremely versatile containers and their use is the foundation of many applications. However, as with any language platform, data consumes memory. Every time a new key is added to an object, more memory is used on the host computer.

JavaScript uses a rather intelligent **garbage collector**; whose job is to clean up discarded data. The issue is, however, that data may not be considered discarded if a reference to it exists in an object. If it isn't handled properly, then memory will continue to be consumed as you add more data, eventually resulting in your browser crashing. This is known as a memory leak!

One way to remove a reference to data from an object is to simply replace it with something else. For instance, it is common in JavaScript applications to see **null** assigned to object parameters when they are no longer needed. The problem with this approach, though, is that while the original value has been detached from the object, the new **null** value has now taken its place. null is a value, after all. This may not be overly problematic as all **null** values point to the same data space, but the contained value is not the only part of the property occupying memory; the **key** is also an overhead:

```
var obj = {key: 99};
obj.key = null;
console.log(obj);
// =>   {key: null}
```

In order to fully delete the reference from the object, which includes **key** and **value**, the **delete** keyword should be utilized:

```
var obj = {key: "data"};
delete obj.key;
console.log(obj);
// =>    {}
```

Object and Pass-By Reference

As we mentioned at the beginning of this chapter, primitive values are immutable and exist by value. When passing them to functions or modifying them, a new copy is made of the data, which occupies a different location in memory.

Objects differ from primitive values in this regard.

Objects are **mutable** data. This means that instead of a copy of the object data being passed to functions or variable assignments within your applications, a reference to the original object data is always passed. When modifying an object, it is the actual original object being altered. No new object is created:

```
var myObj = {key: 99};
function update(obj) {
   obj.key = 22;
   console.log(obj === myObj);   // check they are the same object
}
update(myObj);
// =>    true
console.log(myObj.key);
// =>    22
```

The reason objects work so differently is that copying object data is slow and CPU-intensive. Since objects can be nested, attempting to copy an object that has a tree of descendants linked to it can be agonizingly laborious for the host machine and is therefore completely impractical.

Since objects are presented differently, care must be taken with their use. Modifying object data by passing the object to functions can be the cause of hard-to-find bugs.

Object Iteration

Since objects work like **hash arrays**, it makes sense that functions exist to work with objects as **iterables**. The JavaScript language provides a number of functions for use when iterating over objects, but it also provides operators to this end, as seen with the in operator.

The in operator converts an object into an **iterable** by iterating over its keys:

```
var myObj= {key: "value"};
for (const key in myObj) {
   console.log(myObj[key]);
}
```

The same feat can also be accomplished with the **Object.keys(myObj)** function. The difference here is that it returns the object's keys as an array, so it also has other usefulness when working with objects:

```
var keys = Object.keys(myObj);
for (let i=0; i<keys.length; i++) {
   var key = keys[i];
   console.log(myObj[key]);
}
```

It can also be used like so:

```
var keys = Object.keys(myObj);
for (const key of keys) {
  console.log(myObj[key]);
}
```

As well as a means to get the object keys as an array, there is a function to retrieve the object's values as an array, too:

```
var values = Object.values(myObj);
for (const value of values) {
  console.log(value);
}
```

Finally, should you require both keys and values as associated pairs, JavaScript provides the entries function to do just that. The **key/value** pairs are provided as arrays, with the first item being the key and the second item being the value:

```
var keyValues = Object.entries(myObj);
for (const kv of keyValues) {
  console.log(kv[0], kv[1]);
}
```

Object Accessors

As you may have seen, writing to and reading from objects is allowed freely, but it may not be what you want. Let's suggest, for example, that you wish to create a **gameState** object that will keep track of the player's score and the remaining **enemies** in play. By allowing data to be read and written randomly, you provide an avenue for bugs to creep into your application.

Let's look at an example:

```
var gameState = {
  score: 0,
  enemies: 99,
  lives: 3
}
```

Now, one solution to restricting access to these properties would be to incorporate functions. Here's an example:

```
var gameState = {
  _score: 0,
  _enemies: 99,
  _lives: 3,
```

```
  addToScore: function(value) {
    this._score += value;
  },
  killEnemies: function(num) {
    this._enemies -= num;
  },
  killPlayer: function() {
    this._lives -= 1;
  }
}
```

Here, the member variables have been renamed to start with an underscore. This is a common practice as it is deemed that any values starting with an underscore are values that should not be accessed directly. In *Chapter 4, JavaScript Libraries and Frameworks*, you will find out how to protect object variables absolutely, such that direct access becomes impossible.

Now, while the preceding implementation is perfectly reasonable, the properties of the objects are no longer assignable but invoked. If you needed to read back the values of those properties, you would need yet another set of functions, and those would also need to be invoked. In short, it's not very clean.

JavaScript provides a solution to this conundrum through the use of accessors, also known as getters and setters. Accessors are a way to add functions that can be used like variables, whereby a getter allows for the retrieval of data and a setter enables the setting of data.

The syntax for accessors is as follows:

```
<accessor_type> <accessor_name>() {
   .. body..
}
```

Let's rework the previous example to utilize getters and setters:

```
var gameState = {
  _score: 0,
  _enemies: 99,
  _lives: 3,
  get score() {
    return this._score;
  },
  set score(value) {
    this._score += value;
  },
```

Here, we can see that the **get.score()** allows getting the score and **set.score(value)** allows to set a value to the data.

```
      get enemies() {
        return this._enemies;
      },
      get killEnemies() {
        this._enemies--;
      },
      set killEnemies(num) {
        this._enemies -= num;
      },
      get lives() {
        return this._lives;
      },
      get killPlayer() {
        if (this.enemies <= 0) {
          this._lives = 3;
        } else {
          this._lives--;
        }
      }
    }
```

Here, a bit of creative license has been utilized. The **score** can be read and written to, just like any other value, except when writing, instead of replacing the value, the value is added to the original value, like so:

```
console.log(gameState.score);
// =>    0
gameState.score = 100;
gameState.score = 99;
console.log(gameState.score);
// =>    199
```

The **enemies** value can be read as normal, but by calling **killEnemies**, passing a value will deduct it from the current value, but passing no total will deduct **1** from the value:

```
console.log(gameState.enemies);
// =>    99
gameState.killEnemies = 3;
console.log(gameState.enemies);
// =>    96
gameState.killEnemies;
console.log(gameState.enemies);
// =>    95
```

Finally, reading the player's lives property will return the current number of lives, but reading **killPlayer** will either deduct a life or it will reset it back to **3** lives should there be no enemies left. This may be useful, for instance, if you wanted to reset the player's lives after they've completed the game:

```
console.log(gameState.lives);
// =>    3
gameState.killPlayer;
console.log(gameState.lives);
// =>    2
gameState.killEnemies = 99;
gameState.killPlayer;
console.log(gameState.lives);
// =>    3
```

Note that if you assign the value of a setter to another variable, that other variable will contain whatever was passed to the setter, not the value that was determined within the setter logic. If no value is passed, then the accessor is not a getter, and so **undefined** is returned.

Exercise 5.10: Converting Objects to toString

In this exercise, you will create a function within an object that provides a "pretty print" facility when using the object in circumstances that require a **string** value. The function will utilize the **toString** capability, which we detailed earlier in this chapter:

1. To begin, create an object with a bunch of different values. Add some nested objects to make things more interesting:

```
var obj = {meaningOfLife: 42, foo: "bar", child: {me: "you", other:
{him: "her"}}, toString: Object.prototype.toString};
```

2. Now, if you output this with `console.log`, then it should show up just fine as the console is designed to parse complex objects for debugging purposes. However, if you concatenate the object data into a string, you'll get unwanted results:

```
var str = obj + "";
console.log(str);
// =>    [object Object]
```

3. To rectify this, create a function that parses objects into a string representation:

```
var objToString = function(obj, indent) {
  obj = obj || this;
  indent = indent || "";
  var res = "";
```

The first thing you do here is accept both the passing of an object and utilize the current object context. This way, the function can be called against the object it exists in it, but also as a passed parameter. You'll need to do this so that you can recursively **stringify** any child objects that exist within the parent. The **indent** parameter is used to keep track of the child object indentation. For each level of child, you meet, you will want to indent it further still. This helps you visualize your object structure when printed. Finally, you also need the **res** variable to store the resulting string representation as it's being built.

4. Iterate through all of the object's keys and build the string representation:

```
for (var k in obj) {
```

5. Now, this is where things get a little tricky. If a value for the **k** key is also an object, you will want to pretty print that, too. Therefore, just pass it to the same function:

```
if (typeof obj[k] == "object") {
  res += indent + k + " = {\n";
  res += objToString(obj[k], indent + "- ");
  res += indent + "}";
```

To nest the child, the key for that child is prefixed with the value of the current indent parameter. An open curly brace is used to denote an object in the returned string. The indent is then increased in length and passed to the recursive call to the **objToString** function for the nested iteration. The child print is then closed with a closing curly brace, which is also indented.

6. If the value of the key is not an object, then it might be a function. You will want to skip those as you can't cleanly print them. Everything else can be appended like a string, but will also need to be indented in case it's the value of a field in a child object:

```
    } else if (typeof obj[k] != "function") {
        res += indent + k + " = " + obj[k];
    } else {
        continue;
    }
```

7. Next, apply a delimiter so that each of the keys is separated. A newline character should suffice:

```
    res += "\n";
```

8. Finally, close the loop and return the value:

```
    }
    return res;
}
```

9. To make this work, append the **objToString** function to the starting object as a **toString** function:

```
obj.toString = objToString;
```

10. Finally, to test this out, simply concatenate the object to a string, forcing the object to be cast to a string value:

```
obj + "";
```

The output should be as follows:

```
"meaningOfLife = 4
foo = bar
child = {
    - me = you
    - other = {
    - - him = her
    - }
}"
```

The expected output will be as follows:

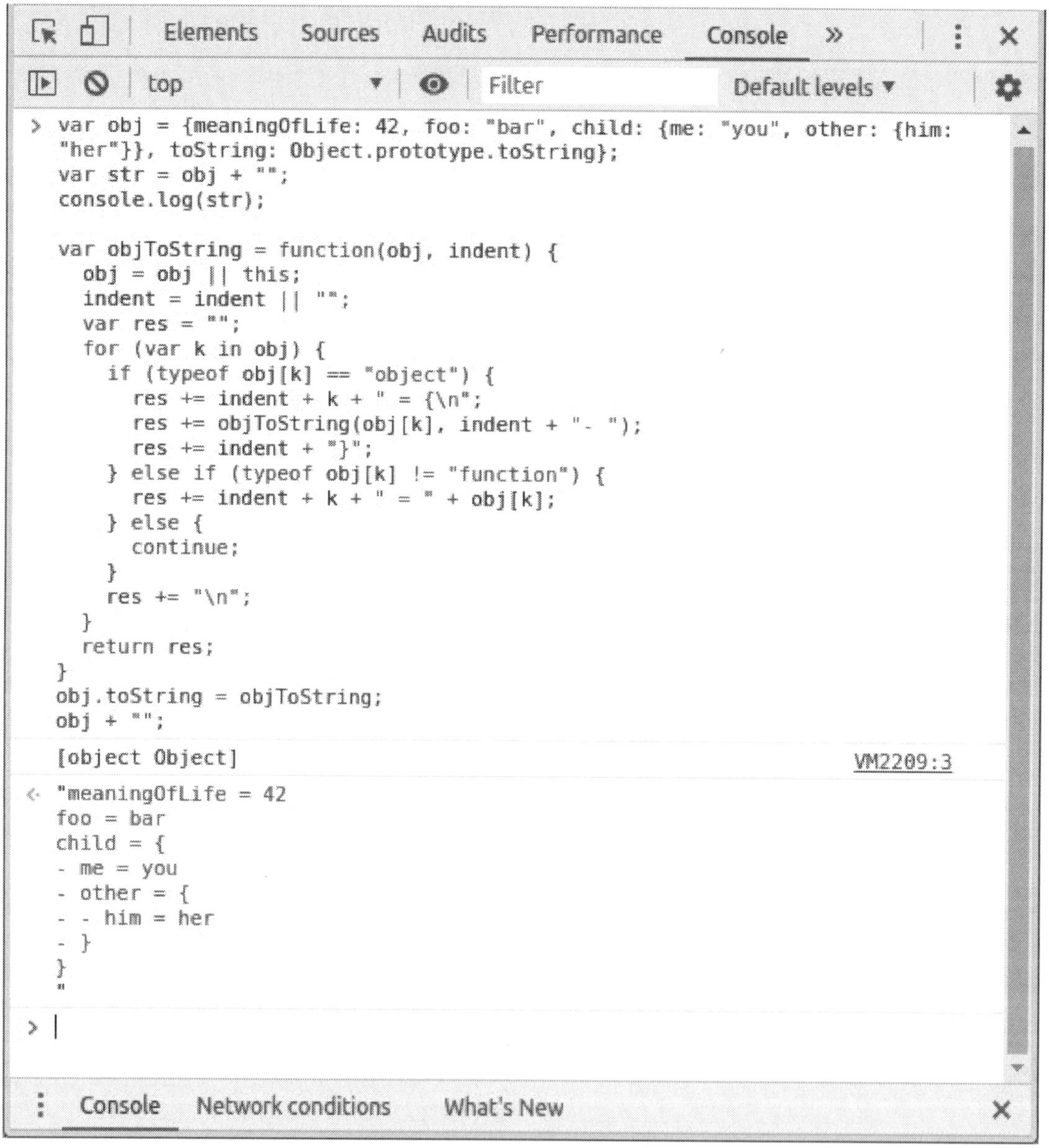

Figure 5.22: Exercise 5.10 output

You have created a useable object **stringifier** function that works with complex objects of any depth.

Working with Arrays

Arrays are another complex object type built on top of objects. Unlike objects, arrays are designed to work with lists of data. Arrays may be created in several ways. The first is known as an Array literal and, similarly to object literals, is simply a means of passing a defined Array value to a variable:

```
var myArray = [1, 2, 3];
var myEmptyArray = [];
```

The values of an array have no keys, and are instead accessed using integer indexes with the square bracket form:

```
myValue = myArray[3];
```

As with other types, the array type also has a constructor function that's used to create array instances. The array constructor can be passed values to prepopulate the **Array**. Therefore, the following examples are equivalent:

```
var arr1 = [1, 2, 3];
var arr2 = new Array(1, 2, 3);
```

However, when using the constructor form, passing a single integer value will create an array with a set number of values set to undefined:

```
var arr = new Array(3);
console.log( arr );
// =>    (3) [empty x3]
```

Note that the **Array** constructor can lead to unintended results, should the developer intend to create an **Array** with one value as a single integer type. As such, it is considered a good practice to initialize all arrays using the literal form.

Arrays and Mutability

Like objects, arrays are mutable objects. If you update an array that is passed into a function, the original **Array** is also modified.

The **Array** object has a number of built-in functions that are useful in maintaining immutability when using arrays. They do not make the array immutable but provide a means to work with arrays while ensuring that they are copied rather than modified.

The Array's immutability functions will be discussed at length in *Chapter 4, JavaScript Libraries and Frameworks*, when functional programming methodologies are discussed.

Array Iteration

Arrays can be iterated in much the same way as objects. If you're using the **for...in** syntax, the element of the **Array** is the index, which is the same result when working with objects that have numerical keys:

```
for (var i in myArray) {
    console.log(myArray[i]);
}
```

This format works well if you need to iterate an array from start to finish, but this isn't very flexible. To aid the traversal of an Array, JavaScript provides a number of additional features.

Since an array is a linear list, it has a **length**. The array object provides the length property, which returns the number of elements in the array:

```
for (let i = 0; i < myArray.length; i++) {
    console.log(myArray [i]);
}
```

The starting index of an array is always **0**, while the **length** of an array is always one more than the last index of the **Array**.

As well as retrieving a value from an array by index, it is also possible to search an array for a value and return its index using the **indexOf** function. **indexOf** takes a single parameter, that is, the value to find within the array:

```
var arr = [1, "b", true];
arr.indexOf("b");
// =>    1
```

indexOf will return the index of the value if it is found but will return **-1** if it does not. A match can be at **index 0** or above, up to but exclusive of **arr.length**. To use a result of **indexOf(...)** in a conditional statement, compare it and check whether it's higher than **-1**:

```
var searchedValue= "b";
  if ( arr.indexOf(searchedValue)>-1 ) {
    console.log( "match found" );
}
```

Note that **indexOf** looks for the matching value of an element. Therefore, complex types will only be found within the Array if they exist within the Array by reference. Here's an example:

```
var obj = {name: "bob"};
var arr = ["a", 99, obj];
console.log( arr.indexOf(obj) );
// =>   2
console.log( arr.indexOf({name: "bob"}) );
// =>   -1
```

Since complex types of identical structure are not considered the same by value, it is not possible to find occurrences of complex objects within an Array in this manner.

If multiple occurrences of a value exist within an Array, **indexOf** will return the first discovered item index. All other instances of that value will be ignored.

A companion of the **indexOf** function is the **lastIndexOf** function. This function works identically to **indexOf**, with the exception that the index search starts at the end of the Array.

Built-In Array Functions

The array type provides many more functions that are useful in traversing, copying, concatenating, and presenting array structures. The following table lists some important and useful functions that are available as members of the array type:

Method	Description
push(<value>)	Appends a value to the end of the Array.
pop()	Removes the last value from the end of the Array and returns it.
unshift(<value>)	Appends a value to the beginning of the Array.
shift()	Removes the first value from the beginning of the Array and returns it.
splice(<index>, <num>, ...<elems>)	Enables adding and removing values within an Array. The first parameter is the index where elements should be added/removed. The second parameter is an integer requesting the number of items to be removed. The rest of the parameters will be values to be added as new entries within the Array at that index.
concat(<array>)	Appends the passed Array to the current Array, creating a new Array. Unlike many Array functions, the result of this function is a new Array.

Figure 5.23: Built-in array functions and their descriptions

Working with Dates

The Date object is an important type in JavaScript but is a complicated type in any language. Like the **Array** type, the **Date** type is built on top of a JavaScript object.

Dates have no literal format. As such, they must be created using the **Date** constructor. There are four ways to do this:

- An empty constructor creates a date with the current date and time.
- The constructor may be passed an integer representing the number of milliseconds to have passed since the beginning of **January 1st, 1970**.
- Supplying multiple integer parameters will specify date segments, for example:

  (year, month, day, hour, minute, second, millisecond)

  (year, month, day, hour, minute, second)

  (year, month, day, hour, minute)

  (year, month, day, hour)

  (year, month, day)

  (year, month)

  Be aware that the month is specified by the numbers **0 - 11**.

- Supplying a string representation of a date:

  ISO 8601 date format ("**2019-04-25**" or "**2019-04-25T12:00:00Z**", where months, days, and time are padded to two-digit lengths)

  US short date format ("**04/25/2019**" with padded day and month)

  US long date format ("**Apr 25 2019**" and so on)

> **Note**
>
> You cannot create a **Date** instance by simply passing the year value as an integer since the JavaScript engine will not know whether you meant year or milliseconds. However, you can create a Date instance from simply passing a year string.

Once a **Date** object has been constructed, it can be queried. The **Date** object provides numerous functions for extracting the elements of the **date**. The following table lists the functions that are available:

Method	Description
getDay()	Get the weekday as a number from 0 to 6
getTime()	Get the current timestamp in milliseconds since January 1st, 1970
getMilliseconds()	Get the current millisecond of the current second (0-999)
getSeconds()	Get the current second of the current minute (0-59)
getMinutes()	Get the current minute of the current hour (0-59)
getHours()	Get the current hour of the current day (0-23)
getDate()	Get the current day of the month (1-31)
getMonth()	Get the current month of the year (0-11)
getFullYear()	Get the current year as a four-digit value

Figure 5.24: The Date object methods and their descriptions

> **Note**
>
> Each of the functions provided by Date returns a value starting from 0, with the exception of the **getDate** method. This often leads to confusion and bugs, so be sure to keep this in mind.

Each of the functions detailed in the preceding table also has a set equivalent, with the exception of **getDay**. Therefore, to update the hour of the **Date** instance, you simply call **setHour** and pass it an integer:

```
var d = new Date();
d.setHours(12);
```

Parsing Date Strings

As we mentioned previously, the **Date** constructor can accept a date string and convert it into an instance of the **Date** object. Dates are represented internally within the Date type as integers. Thus, the **getDate** method returns the true interpretation of the date value.

If you have a valid date string, as detailed previously, you can convert it into a date by calling the **parse** method:

```
var greatDate = Date.parse("November 3, 1976");
```

However, the return value of the **Date.parse** method does not return a **Date** instance. Instead, it returns the number of milliseconds since **January 1st, 1970** until that date. In order to create a **Date** instance, you must, therefore, pass that resulting value to the **Date** constructor:

```
var millis = Date.parse("November 3, 1976");
var greatDate = new Date(millis);
```

Formatting Dates into Strings

The **Date** object provides its own **toString** function. If you attempt to use a **Date** instance as a **string**, you will receive a formatted string instead:

```
var d = new Date();
console.log(d);
//  => current time in local timezone, for example:
// Thu Apr 25 2019 12:00:00 GMT+0100 (British Summer Time)
```

However, this is often not the format you require. If you wish to provide your own date string format, you can override the **toString** function of the object, much like in the *Working with Object* section of this chapter. Here's an example:

```
var toString = function(date) {
  date = date || this;
  var months = [
    "Jan", "Feb", "Mar",
    "Apr", "May", "Jun",
    "Jul", "Aug", "Sep",
    "Oct", "Nov", "Dec"
  ];
  var day = date.getDate();
  var mnth = date.getMonth();
  var year = date.getFullYear();
  return day + ' ' + months[mnth] + ' ' + year;
}
var d = new Date();
d.toString = toString;
console.log(d);
```

The output of this code will be as follows:

```
current date in format 25 Apr 2019
```

Date Math

JavaScript provides no functions for comparing, adding, or subtracting dates. However, working out date differences or combining dates is not hard in JavaScript.

Typically, there are two tasks that need to be considered when comparing dates:

- What the difference is between two dates

- Adding or subtracting time to/from a date

The first task is relatively simple. Since the date can be converted into a simple integer representing the number of milliseconds since **January 1st, 1970**, the dates you wish to difference can simply be represented as milliseconds and that value can be compared. Here's an example:

```
var date1 = new Date("Dec 25 2001").getTime();
var date2 = new Date("Dec 25 2019").getTime();
var diff = date2 - date1;
diff
// =>    567993600000
```

Now, with the number of milliseconds in each, you can convert that into a time unit. For example, if you wanted to find out the number of days that difference represents, you would simply do the following:

```
var day = 1000 * 60 * 60 * 24;
var numDays = diff / day;
numDays
// =>    6574
```

To get the unit, you simply start with milliseconds and work up. Therefore, a day is **1,000 milliseconds * 60 seconds * 60 minutes * 24 hours**.

Adding or subtracting time from dates is also very simple. The set* methods provided by the **Date** object provide a means for us to roll over values that exceed the next largest unit. For instance, if the current date is **April 25, 2019**, adding **10** days will change the date to **May 5, 2019**. This feature is applicable to all of the **set** functions. Thus, to add time, simply get the unit of time you wish to add to and add to it:

```
var d = new Date("Apr 25 2019");
d.setMonth(d.getMonth() + 60);
d
// =>   Thu Apr 25 2024 00:00:00 GMT+0100 (British Summer Time)
// The above result will use your local timezone.
```

Activity 5.02: Creating a To-Do Model

Let's utilize all the information we have learned about in this chapter and see what we have retained. For this activity, imagine that you are working with a team of developers and your project is to create a stateful model that stores entries for a To-Do application. The model will be a primary function, though other functions can be created and used by it. The function will need to store one or more entries and will receive "actions" that tell the state to change.

These actions will include the following:

- Create a new To-Do
- Remove a To-Do
- Modify a To-Do

Actions will be passed to the state with a given action keyword of either **CREATE**, **REMOVE**, or **MODIFY**.

Each To-Do item in the state will have the following fields:

Name	Data Type	Description
id	String	The id is a unique string value. It should never be duplicated. However, many entries can be added to it. It is used to identify the entry.
title	String	The user-defined name of the To-Do.
description	String	A user-defined message that explains the To-Do entry in more detail.
createdAt	Date	The date the To-Do entry is created. The user will not supply this. It will be created dynamically.
updatedAt	Date	The date the To-Do entry is updated. The user will not supply this. It will be updated dynamically.
completed	Boolean	Typically, this defaults to false. The user should be allowed to toggle this value.

Figure 5.25: Activity fields

The data will be passed to the state function with the action type. If the action is a **CREATE** action, then all of the preceding fields will be passed, with the exception of the **id** field. If it is a **REMOVE** action, then only the **id** is passed. It will be passed as a string value. Finally, if the **MODIFY** action is passed, then all of the data is passed, with the exception of the **created_at** value. This is because the **created_at** value shouldn't change.

An important part of this task is to ensure that the state data is treated as immutable since the project manager is a fan of functional programming and wants to ensure that as few bugs as possible are added to the application. No objects, including **Arrays** and **Dates**, should be changed in this activity. Instead, new objects, **Arrays**, and **Dates** must be created, replacing the old values. This must also be true of the Array containing the **TODO** entries.

> **Note**
>
> The Array **concat** function returns a new Array, but any objects within it will still be references to the original values.

Finally, when each action is received, the state function will need to pretty-print the data to the console. For **CREATE** actions, this will be the incoming data and for **REMOVE** actions, this will be the removed data. For **MODIFY** actions, both the removed and created data should be printed.

If all goes to plan, you will be able to add, remove, and modify entries in your state function without worrying about corrupted data. You can prove this by modifying the values you send to the state function. If the entries in the state function are also modified, your model is not immutable.

This activity highlights a common means to handle application data effectively and in a way that will not introduce bugs to your application. By managing data in a pure manner, you will ensure that your development practices produce reliable results in a short period of time.

The high-level steps for the activity are as follows:

1. Create the function signature to accept the following:

- The current state, which is the current list of To-Do items

- The action, which is simply a string value

- The data to apply to the state change

    The function signature will look as follows:

```
function modelStateChange(state, action, data)
```

    Here, **state** is the current Array of **ToDo** items in the model, **action** is either **CREATE**, **MODIFY**, or **REMOVE**, and **data** is either new **ToDo** data or simply the parameter to match a **ToDo** item to remove.

2. Create a conditional for each action type. Then, in the body of the condition, manipulate the state as needed. Remember to return the new state within the condition body. You may want to create a secondary function that does the lookup of a **ToDo** within the state as you'll need this functionality in the **MODIFY** and **REMOVE** actions.

    Remember, this function should always return a new state value. That way, it is possible to cleanly test the function predictably and ensure that it works as intended.

    An example of how this function may be called is as follows:

```
todoState = modelStateChange(_todoState, "MODIFY", {id: curTodo.id,
completed: true});
```

> **Note**
>
> The solution to this activity can be found on page 726.

Summary

A lot has been covered in this chapter. You should now have a deeper understanding of the types provided by JavaScript, but also the subtle ways in which each type is related. Understanding how data is represented in a language provides a solid foundation for building applications more quickly and with fewer bugs.

As well as understanding the data types, you also saw how to manipulate them, both with methods and with helper functions provided by the JavaScript engine. You also saw how to convert data into different types, in order to enable data interoperability.

Finally, you saw how you can debug your data using the console and using string-based data formatting capabilities provided by the language.

In the next chapter, you will start down the path of user interactivity and see how events can be triggered to force your code to do something. You will also be introduced to the relationship between the JavaScript language and the HTML DOM in the browser environment.

Understanding Core Concepts

Overview

By the end of this chapter, you will be able to apply timeouts and intervals to include asynchronous functionality in applications; identify the different browser event types; capture and handle user interaction; intercept and prevent events; impersonate events to improve application user experience; summarize the different browser supported input controls; and work with forms, form submission, and form event handling.

Introduction

In the previous chapter, you were introduced to the many data types supported by the JavaScript language and runtime, including functions, JavaScript's most impressive first-class data type. Understanding the differences between data types is an important first step for building practical, efficient, and bug-free applications. Software applications have many forms and may have many uses. In its simplest form, an application may read parameters on execution, process the data, and return a response. It may not even interact with any other applications or outside services. Terminal commands are a good example of this. For instance, executing **dir** in a Windows command window or **ls** in a **Linux Terminal** would simply read the contents of a directory on the hard disk and display the details of those files and directories within the Terminal window. The Linux operating system is built on the premise of such very small and simple applications working together to create a much larger ecosystem. The converse of this may be modern multiplayer video games, which typically react to user interaction and receive streamed data from remote locations. The former of these concepts can be considered much like a function: input enters from the top and is output somewhere within the body, typically, the end of the function.

JavaScript applications can facilitate both ends of this spectrum, and indeed, anything in between. Modern browsers are now fully capable of providing the foundations for immense and processor-intensive 3D multiplayer games, responding to data from numerous sources, but JavaScript is also frequently used for the simplest of tasks, such as formatting a **string** or rounding a **number**.

At the core of all of these applications are **events**. Events, conceptually speaking, are triggers that execute code. This might, for example, be the ready state when a page has finished loading or a mouse event when the user clicks an element within the page. Typically, without events, functions won't know when to execute and, therefore, nothing can happen.

Throughout this chapter, we will examine the options JavaScript provides for listening to and handling different types of events within the browser environment.

Event Types

An event is simply a notification or a "**triggered**" alert within the JavaScript runtime. These notifications can represent practically anything but are a means to invoke one or more of your own functions when such an event occurs.

When a web page loads, the browser will typically display content as soon as it is available. This means some content will be presented to the user before the entire page has finished downloading. The browser does this to prevent long-loading assets from withholding other content from being available to the user.

Now, imagine you want to invoke a function immediately within a web page to rotate an image. JavaScript code embedded into a web page is able to run immediately once it has been parsed by the JavaScript engine, which could possibly be before the image in question is available. To overcome this conundrum, JavaScript provides an `onload` event, which is dispatched as soon as all the page's content has finished downloading. By refraining from invoking your function until this event has been dispatched, you can ensure that your image can be rotated.

Of course, there are many other such events. Arguably, there are four specific types of events within the JavaScript ecosystem:

- **Timer events** provide forced asynchronous functionality within your applications. They allow you to invoke a function after a period of time, either once or repeatedly.

- **Asynchronous events**, such as `callbacks`, are dispatched when something has finished executing but has occurred in parallel to any other function execution in your application. This means the process has not stopped your application from doing other tasks.

- **Interaction events**, such as `DOM` or keyboard events, are events that are dispatched due to the user interacting with your application.

- **Custom events** are events that you create yourself. These can be almost anything but are usually created as a response to one of the JavaScript event types listed previously.

The type of event you will require is very specific to a given use case. In this chapter, we will examine both timer-based events and interaction events.

Timer Events

In some languages, such as C, the base application may be run using a continuous loop. In C, specifically, an application runs during the lifetime of its `main` function; when this function returns, the application exits. Typically, applications that need to run for some time and respond to events would utilize a simple loop. In fact, it's not uncommon to see applications start with something like this:

```c
int main(int ac, char** av) {
    while (true) {
        // .. do stuff ..
    }
    return 1;
}
```

Here, the application simply enters an indefinite loop. If the application needs to quit, it would call a command similar to JavaScript's **break** keyword. Otherwise, the application would quite happily run and invoke functions as needed.

Applications written in C are able to do this for several reasons. The first is that C is a multi-threaded platform. This means that several processes, known as threads, can be created within a C application and may run concurrently, providing the underlying hardware it supports. In the worst-case scenario, these threads are cycled, allowing each one to utilize a period of execution time within the CPU. Another reason this is possible is that C applications run very close to the hardware and, unlike JavaScript, are unencumbered by a lower-level engine that dictates execution flow.

Since a program can exist with a loop at its core, it stands to reason that functions will, or can, be called with each iteration. However, if a function was called indefinitely with every iteration, such a process may be overly resource-intensive or simply run too fast. An alternative is to make the function conditional by requiring it to execute only when enough time has passed since its last execution. This is the essential basis of a timer event.

Unlike C, JavaScript is a **single-threaded** platform, meaning it can only execute a single thread throughout your entire application. A thread is an execution space in the CPU. If you have one thread, then only a single series of function executions can occur at once. In JavaScript, this does not mean the underlying engine doesn't use, or have access to, more than one thread; only that your application has programmatic access to one single thread.

Since JavaScript runs within an engine, known as a virtual machine, it is driven by a number of rules that determine how your code is run. The JavaScript virtual machine follows an architecture known as an event loop. This means that the loop in the preceding C example is already occurring within the JavaScript engine that your application runs within. However, within that loop, the JavaScript engine manages code execution for each of the function calls your application makes, among other things, regardless of whether those calls invoke your own functions or those native to JavaScript.

Exercise 6.01: Custom Timer

As we mentioned previously, many developers coming from lower-level languages will consider a loop as a means to create timed function invocations. If a loop can occur indefinitely, then we only need to check the current system time and invoke functions when sufficient time has passed. For instance, when animating, in order to control the **speed** of the animation, you may want to ensure your frame update functions are executed with a sufficient period of time between each invocation. Without this control, your animation frames will update with every possible cycle of the JavaScript runtime, which may be very fast on some machines, while not so fast on weaker machines. In this exercise, you will implement one such loop. Let's get started:

1. To begin, you'll need three variables. The first will store the current time in milliseconds for each iteration, the second variable will contain the time in milliseconds of the last time the custom timer function executed, and the third variable will be the required minimal interval between timer function calls in milliseconds:

```
var curTime, lastTime,
  interval = 500;
```

2. Next, we open the **main** function and the indefinite loop. Similar to the preceding example, we'll simply use a **while** loop and pass it a decrementing value:

```
function main() {  // primary function
  let running = true;  // loop running flag
  while (running) {  // enter loop
```

3. Now, the first thing that needs to happen with each iteration is that we need to get the current time in milliseconds and compare it to the last stored time:

```
curTime = new Date().getTime();
lastTime = lastTime || curTime;
if (curTime - lastTime > interval) {
```

The **lastTime** variable, if it is **null**, will be passed the value of **curTime**. This way, it will execute correctly from its first iteration since **null** cannot be deducted from an **integer**.

4. If the values are sufficiently different (greater than the **interval** amount), you can invoke your timed functions. You will then need to update the **lastTime** variable to equal the current time so that the function doesn't execute again in succession and instead waits for the next duration to occur:

```
console.log(curTime);
lastTime = curTime;
running = false;
```

5. Finally, you close out the conditional, loop, and function:

```
        }
    }
}
```

6. That's it. If you execute the function by calling **main()**, you will see the current time in milliseconds output to the console every **500** milliseconds:

```
main(); // ==> 1558632112316
```

What you have just created is similar to an application loop. Many programming languages support the notion of an application loop. In fact, languages such as C++ require such a loop in order to prevent an application from exiting. In such circumstances, the loop is a simple "**keep-alive**" mechanism whereby checks for potential events occur manually within the loop. In JavaScript, such loops are unnecessary. This is because the JavaScript engine already enlists the help of such a loop under the hood, known as the event loop.

Event Timers

The previous exercise exhibits perfectly legitimate code and would facilitate a working function invocation timer. However, creating timers in this fashion has a number of drawbacks. The first issue here is that since JavaScript is single-threaded, the entire application will be contained within the loop. There is no way to continue processing data outside of the loop without breaking out of it.

The second issue in the previous exercise is that since the JavaScript engine is already running its own event loop, the example code is actually performing two infinite loops, one nested within the other:

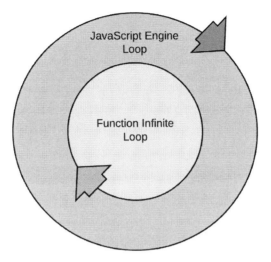

Figure 6.1: Nested infinite event loop

Since delayed and repeated function invocation is a common programming requirement, the JavaScript language provides two functions that make timers simple without us having to construct our own loops. These are **setInterval** and **setTimeout**.

The setInterval Function

setInterval is a native implementation of our previous infinite loop. The premise is that, given a function and an interval value in milliseconds, JavaScript will repeatedly execute the function whenever the interval time has passed:

```
intervalReference = setInterval(timerFun, milliseconds);
```

> **Note**
>
> The time-based execution in JavaScript is "as near to" the interval value as possible. JavaScript is unable to guarantee absolute accuracy when executing triggers due to various limitations with the underlying hardware, operating system, and resource availability.

We can reproduce our previous example with the following code:

```
var timerFunction = function() {
  var time = new Date().getTime();
  console.log(time);
}
setInterval(timerFunction, 500);
// ==> 1558632112316
```

The function expression in this example will be executed **500** milliseconds after we call **setInterval** and every **500** milliseconds thereafter. It is executed asynchronously, so the code that follows the **setInterval** call is executed without delay:

```
function main() {
  setInterval(() => console.log("executed"), 500);
  console.log("after execution");
  console.log("another message");
}();
// ==>    after execution
// ==>    another message
// ==>    executed
// ==>    executed
```

The **setInterval** function itself, when invoked, returns a reference to the resulting interval handler, that is, the execution stack that invokes the passed **callback** function. This reference may be used to terminate the interval loop at any time using the **clearInterval** function:

```
var ref = setInterval(someFunc, 100);
clearInterval(ref);
```

The setTimeout Function

The **setTimeout** function works identically to the **setInterval** function, the difference being that its passed **callback** function is only ever called once. The **setTimeout** function is useful when animating elements within an HTML page, or when you wish to delay a process for a period of time, such as clearing a visible error message or dialog:

```
setTimeout(someFunc, 500);
```

Like **setInterval**, the **setTimeout** function also returns a reference to its execution handler so that the timer can be cleared with **clearTimeout**. Since the **setTimeout** callback is only executed once, calling **clearTimeout** after the **callback** has executed has no effect. It is, however, possible to cancel **setTimeout** before it executes, which is a perfectly reasonable requirement:

```
var ref = setTimeout(() => console.log("fire!"), 200);
setInterval(function() {
  console.log("waiting...");
  clearTimeout(ref);
}, 100);
// ==> waiting...
// ==> waiting...
// ==> waiting...
```

The **setTimeout** function can be mimicked by the **setInterval** function by simply clearing its reference after its first timer iteration, like so:

```
var ref = setInterval(function() {
  console.log("Boo!");
  clearInterval(ref);
}, 500);
// ==> Boo!
```

Timer Parameters

In modern browsers (excluding **IE9** and below), the **setInterval** and **setTimeout** functions may receive additional parameters. If any are supplied proceeding the interval parameter, those additional parameters will be passed as parameters to the **callback** function when it is invoked. This provides a useful means to customize timer functions:

```
var handler = function(p1, p2) {
  console.log(p1, p2);
};
setTimeout(handler, 100, "Hello,", "World!");
// ==> Hello, World!
```

If you anticipate older browsers running your scripts, the same effect may be attained by wrapping the passed **callback** within an anonymous function call:

```
setTimeout(function() {
  handler("Hello,", "World!");
}, 100);
// ==> Hello, World!
```

Exercise 6.02: Real-Time Clock

It is now time to put your knowledge of timers to use. In this exercise, you will be creating a real-time in-page clock display that will count up in seconds and show the full time using a 24-hour digital clock format. This exercise will make use of an HTML file, albeit a simple one. Let's get started:

1. Create a new file called **clock.html**. Here, you'll add some very simple HTML. Firstly, add the opening document tag and the **script** tag:

```
<html>
  <script>
```

The **script** tag will contain the JavaScript to be executed within the page.

2. Next, you'll need some placeholder variables for the **seconds**, **minutes**, **hours**, and the current **Date** object instance:

```
var secs, mins, hrs, date,
```

3. The **handler** function you'll use for the timer will also be assigned to a variable called **setTime**. In it, you will simply populate the preceding variables with the current time components:

```
setTime = function() {
  date = new Date();
  hrs = date.getHours();
  mins = date.getMinutes();
  secs = date.getSeconds();
```

4. To output the time to the page, you'll simply need to update the **body** content. There are better solutions to this that will be explained later in this module:

```
document.body.innerHTML = `${hrs}:${mins}:${secs}`;
```

5. Finally, close the function and assign it to an interval. Set the interval to run every **500** milliseconds to ensure better accuracy:

```
    }
    setInterval(setTime, 500);
```

6. With the **script** complete, you should close out the **script** tag block:

```
    </script>
```

7. The page should end with a **body** tag block, which will contain the clock and the closing **html** tag:

```
    <body>
    </body>
  </html>
```

8. Now, save the page and load it (or drag it) into your browser. You should see the time displayed in the top left-hand corner of the page, and it should update every second. You have successfully built your first timer-based JavaScript application.

Displaying a real-time clock on a web page is a practical application, particularly within corporate websites and intranets that may exhibit times for several time zones around the world. However, utilizing a timer to update page content is not limited to clocks. This same process could be utilized to update stock market prices, real-time chat forums, or just about any kind of real-time presentation.

The JavaScript Events Model

As we noted previously, the JavaScript engine utilizes an event loop. In fact, events are at the center point of the JavaScript engine and its language. At its simplest definition, an event is a notification that something has occurred. This may be interaction by the user with a web page or the completion of some process that occurs within the browser.

To make use of events, a **callback** function must be assigned to the event type, much like with the timer-based function. However, typically, events are a little more complex and feature-rich than simple timers.

An event notification is known in programming as a dispatched event. When JavaScript events are dispatched, they are passed an event object. This is true of all JavaScript events. The event object contains useful details about the dispatched event, including the name of the event, a reference to the object that holds the context of the event, and a reference to the object that triggered the event.

The following table lists the properties of the event object:

Property	Type	Description
bubbles	Boolean	Returns true if the event will bubble, otherwise false.
cancelable	Boolean	Returns true is the event is cancelable, otherwise false.
currentTarget	DOM element	Returns the element that handled the event.
target	DOM element	Returns the element that dispatched the event.
defaultPrevented	Boolean	Returns true if the preventDefault() function was called for this event.
eventPhase	Integer	Returns: 0: The event has no phase. 1: The event is being handled by a handler. 2: No event handler was found on the target, so the event is dispatched to the target element. 3: The event is bubbling up the parent element hierarchy.
isTrusted	Boolean	Returns true if the event is trusted, otherwise false. An event is trusted if it was triggered by the user, but not trusted if the event was triggered dynamically by the script.
Type	String	The name of the event.
timeStamp	Integer	The time, in milliseconds, when the event was dispatched.

Figure 6.2: Event Object properties

Event Bubbling

In order to understand event bubbling, it helps if we understand browser-based HTML. HTML is an abbreviation for HyperText Markup Language, which itself is a derivative of eXtensible Markup Language (XML). HTML is not really a language at all, but a declarative information markup that structures data, which, in the case of websites, is page content.

HTML is a hierarchical construct that can be best envisaged as a data tree. Imagine the following page content:

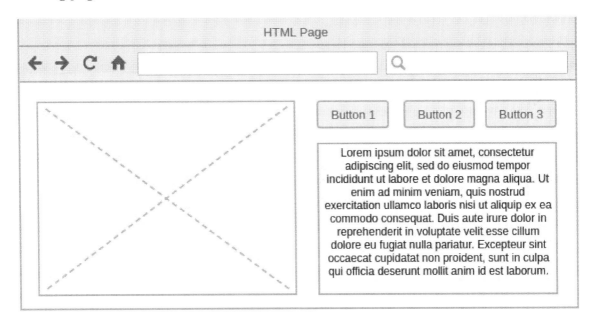

Figure 6.3: HTML mockup

The structure of the page consists of two columns. On the left is an image and on the right is a container with two rows; the first row contains three buttons and the second row contains a block of text. Like a tree, this layout may look something like this:

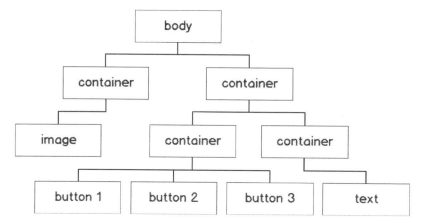

Figure 6.4: HTML data tree

The preceding tree outlines the visible content of the page, but the **body** node is not the actual top of the literal HTML tree. Instead, the page content tree starts with a node called the **document**. This then has a child called **html**, and that node contains the **body** node.

Each node within the HTML tree will raise events if interacted with, even if that node is not immediately visible. When clicking the page with your mouse, for instance, the visible node beneath the mouse arrow that is closest to the bottom of the tree will raise a **click** event. If one or more event handlers have been assigned to that node, then those handlers will be invoked and will be passed an **event** object.

Event bubbling occurs when event handlers are not assigned to the node for that event type or if the event is handled but the event is allowed to continue propagating. At this point, the handlers of the parent node for that specific event are called, and the same process occurs. If the event continues to not be explicitly halted, it will **bubble** through each parent node until it reaches the **document** node.

If multiple handlers exist on a given node for a specific event, any one of those handlers may halt the event, preventing it from bubbling. It is not required for all handlers to halt the event.

Traversing the Node Tree

In order to handle an event, you first need to add an event type handler to a node. However, to do that, you need some way to acquire a reference to the node on which you wish to listen. JavaScript provides numerous functions for selecting and acquiring nodes based on many different factors, including direct named access, acquisition through node tree traversal, and acquisition by attribute value.

Of all the nodes within your HTML pages, the easiest to acquire are the **body** and **document** nodes. Both of these nodes have simple attribute accessors on the global **document** object:

```
var document = document.documentElement;
var bodyNode = document.body;
console.log(bodyNode);
// ==> <body></body>
```

Once you have a reference to the top of the tree, acquiring a node elsewhere within the tree is simply a matter of traversing it. JavaScript provides several properties for acquiring a node's parent, siblings, or children, each of which uses the **familiar relationship** metaphor:

Method	Returns	Description
parentNode	Node	Returns the node immediately above the current node.
childNodes	Array	Returns an array of all child nodes immediately beneath the current node.
firstChild	Node	Returns the first child in the array of child nodes immediately beneath the current node.
lastChild	Node	Returns the last child in the array of child nodes immediately beneath the current node.
nextSibling	Node	Returns the next child to the right/below the current node.
previousSibling	Node	Returns the previous child to the left/above the current node.

Figure 6.5: Node properties and their description

Each of these properties can be read from the given node. If a corresponding node cannot be found, then the property will return **null** (or an empty array in the case of **childNodes**):

```
var image = document.body.firstChild.firstChild;
image
// ==> <img src="./logo/packt.png" >
var btn = image.parentNode.nextSibling.firstChild.childNodes[1];
btn
// ==> <button>button 2</button>
```

Direct Node Acquisition

Aside from node tree traversal, JavaScript also provides a means to specify the node reference you require by supplying a node property filter, which is a string value describing the node you require using a specific format.

All HTML nodes follow a certain pattern:

- They are opened and closed, sometimes in a single tag.
- They have a node name or type.
- They may have an optional **id** property, which should be unique to the page.
- They may have one or more optional **class** names.
- They may have other optional known properties, such as **name**, **styles**, **type**, **value**, or **src**.
- They may have optional custom properties, named by the page creator.

The node's signature is known as its **tag**, which is defined within angle brackets, with a left-facing angle bracket at the start of the node and a right-facing bracket at the end of the node. Immediately after the left-facing bracket is the node's name. Properties are appended to the node as **attribute="value"**:

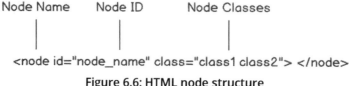

Figure 6.6: HTML node structure

The closing tag of a node contains the node's name and is also wrapped with a left-facing and right-facing angle bracket. However, to differentiate it from a new opening tag, its left-facing angle bracket is preceded by a forward-slash (**/**) character.

If a node has no children, it is acceptable to immediately close the node without supplying a distinct closing tag. This is accomplished by providing the forward-slash character immediately before the right-facing angle bracket:

```
<img src="/images/flower.png" />
```

The properties of a node are its description. Later, these values allow you to style the node's look-and-feel, but they specifically facilitate the node's data and identity. As such, it is perfectly legitimate to add attributes to nodes in order to make them easily acquirable. The **id** attribute is one such value that exists solely to differentiate tags and it is important that all the tags that are used within a page have a unique **id** attribute, if they have one at all. If an **id** attribute is present, the associated node can be acquired using the **getElementById** method of the **document** object:

```
var node = document.getElementById("myTagId");
```

Since node IDs are deemed to be unique, the **getElementById** method returns a single node, or **null** if a matching node is not found. If, for some reason, a page contains multiple nodes with the same ID attribute value, then calling **getElementById** with that value will return the first element found within the page.

Other similar functions exist in order to query using other tag descriptors, such as the **name** or **class**. The majority of these return an array since it is expected that many tags may share matching descriptors. The following table lists some of the common functions for acquiring tag references:

Method	Context	Description
getElementById(<string>)	Document	Returns a single node if found. Otherwise, **null** is returned.
getElementsByTagName(<string>)	Document, node	Returns an array of elements that have a **name** attribute matching the passed parameter.
getElementsByClassName(<string>)	Document, node	Returns an array of elements that have a class matching the passed parameter.
querySelectorAll(<string>)	Document, node	Returns an array of elements that match a query (discussed later in this module).

Figure 6.7: Common functions for tag references

Assigning and Removing an Event Handler

Once you have a node reference, you are then able to assign listeners (or handlers) for specific event types. Listeners can be assigned to a node using the **addEventListener** function, which accepts two parameters, the type of the event as a string value and the handler of the event as a function:

```
document.body.addEventListener("click", () => alert("I was clicked"));
```

When an event is dispatched, the event handler is passed a single value, known as an event object. Event objects may have slightly different parameters depending on the event type being handled. The object is actually an instance of a specific event object type. For instance, mouse-based events, such as **click** or **mousedown**, generate **MouseEvent** objects. These differ from many other events in that they contain **x** and **y** values detailing the mouse coordinates within the web document at the time the event was dispatched:

```
document.body.addEventListener("click", function(evt) { console.log(evt);
});
// ==> MouseEvent {isTrusted: true, screenX: 230, screenY: 499, clientX:
163,
clientY: 400, …}
```

When attaching an event handler, it will not overwrite existing handlers attached to that node, even if the handler is assigned to the same event type. In fact, a node may have any number of event listeners attached at any one time. This way, multiple facets of your application can independently access the same event notifications for the same object, as needed. What is not possible, however, is for the same **function reference** to be assigned more than once to the same event type, like so:

```
var display = () => console.log("Clicked");
document.body.addEventHandler("click", () => console.log("I was clicked");
document.body.addEventHandler("click", () => console.log("I was clicked");
document.body.addEventHandler("click", display);
document.body.addEventHandler("click", display);   // this one will not be
output
// ==> I was clicked
// ==> I was clicked
// ==> Clicked
```

In the preceding example, since the **display** function is a single reference, the second listener assignment was simply ignored. JavaScript will not repeat the function invocation more than once. However, the previous assignments were both invoked because, although the functionality was the same, the functions themselves possessed different references.

If you wish to remove an event handler, you can do so with the **removeEventListener** method, which takes identical parameters to its counterpart:

```
document.body.removeEventListener("click", display);
```

The **removeEventListener** method finds the handler association by reference. This means that any event listener assignments you make using anonymous functions cannot be removed using the **removeEventListener** method.

> **Note**
>
> If you dispose of a node that has event handlers attached to it, it will not be cleaned up by the JavaScript engine's **garbage Collector**. Removing nodes without cleaning up their event handlers is a common cause of memory leaks in JavaScript, which leads to poor application performance. If you know a node may be removed from the **DOM**, do not add event listeners to it, or its children, using anonymous functions.

Exercise 6.03: Tabbed Content

In this exercise, you'll use what you have learned so far to create a tabbed display. The display will utilize three buttons at the top of the page, with a container **div** tag at the bottom. When a button is pressed, content associated with the button handler will be displayed within the container **div** tag. Let's get started:

1. First, create a new document called **tabs.html** and add the starting HTML:

```
<html>
  <head>
    <title>Tabbed Display</title>
  </head>
  <body>
```

2. The three buttons will sit side by side in a single container **div**. Each one will have a unique ID so that we can easily reference them:

```
<div>
    <button id="btn1">Tab One</button>
    <button id="btn2">Tab Two</button>
    <button id="btn3">Tab Three</button>
</div>
```

3. Next, add the container **div**. We'll add a descriptive body to inform the user of the page. However, once a button has been pressed, that content will disappear for good and will be replaced by dynamic content:

```
<div id="container">Click a button!</div>
```

4. With the structure of the page in place, you can now close out the body and begin the **script** block:

```
</body>
<script>
  var btn1 = document.getElementById("btn1"),
    btn2 = document.getElementById("btn2"),
    btn3 = document.getElementById("btn3"),
    container = document.getElementById("container");
```

Here, we've created a variable for each element in the page we need to interact with. This makes the code neater and cleaner.

5. Next, you'll need some content to add when the buttons are pressed, one for each button:

```
var content1 = "Button 1 was pressed",
  content2 = "Button 2 was pressed",
  content3 = "Button 3 was pressed";
```

6. Now, we need to wire up the content. To do this, simply add an event listener to each button, updating the container **div** content in each one:

```
btn1.addEventListener("click", () => container.innerHTML =
content1);
btn2.addEventListener("click", () => container.innerHTML =
content2);
btn3.addEventListener("click", () => container.innerHTML =
content3);
```

7. Now, simply close out the open tags and save the page:

```
</script>
</html>
```

8. That's it. If you now run the page in your browser and click each button, you should see that the content has been updated.

The interactive page is as follows:

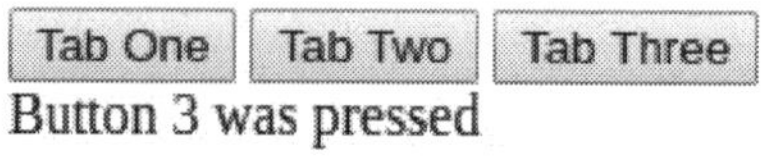

Figure 6.8: Tabbed control exercise

This has been your first exploration of interactive content. Manipulating page content based on user interactivity is a common requirement for JavaScript and is something it excels at. Through careful planning and good coding practices, it is possible to create JavaScript applications that can mimic almost any kind of native software application.

Bubbling versus Capturing

So far, you've seen that event bubbling is where an event bubbles up from the node that dispatched it to the top of the tree, but JavaScript also provides an alternative to bubbling called capturing.

Event capturing is where events are handled in the reverse order to bubbling, capturing notifications from the node that dispatched it to the bottom of the tree. This means that, when a node is interacted with, its attached event handlers may not be the first to intercept the event. Instead, a parent (or ancestor) may receive the event first, instead. If one of those ancestral handlers halts the event, then the handlers on the node that gave rise to the event may never actually be invoked at all:

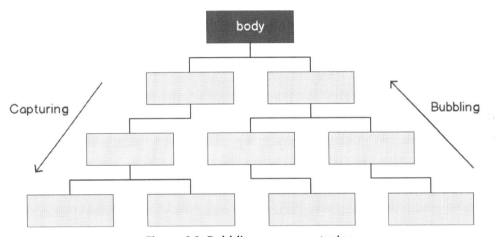

Figure 6.9: Bubbling versus capturing

To attach an event handler to a capture event, you simply need to pass a third parameter to the **addEventListener** method. This third parameter is known as the **useCapture** parameter and is a Boolean. If set to **true**, the attached event will be assigned in **capture** mode. Thus, not supplying the **useCapture** parameter to the **addEventListener** method is the same as supplying **false** for that parameter:

```
var clickHandler = () => console.log("clicked");
document.body.addEventListener("click", clickHandler);
// ==> clicked
```

Event handlers that are attached to capture events sit in a different space to bubbling event listeners. When assigning capturing events, they will not conflict with bubbling events. Therefore, assigning a function reference as an event handler as both bubbling and capturing, using the same event type on the same node, will mean that function will be called twice when that event is dispatched:

```
var clickHandler = () => console.log("clicked");
document.body.addEventListener("click", clickHandler);
document.body.addEventListener("click", clickHandler, true);
// ==> clicked
// ==> clicked
```

To remove an event that's been added with **useCapture** set to **true**, you simply pass the same **useCapture** value to the **removeEventListener** method:

```
document.body.removeEventListener("click", clickHandler, true);
```

The JavaScript Event Life Cycle

Regardless of which node has dispatched the event, all event notifications start at the **document** node. They then travel in capture mode through the tree branches toward the node that dispatched it (the **target** node). Once all the appropriate capture handlers along that path have been invoked, the event then travels back to the **document** node, invoking all the appropriate bubbling handlers.

When traveling down the tree, the event is said to be in its capture phase and is said to be in its bubbling phase when returning to the **document** node. It is in its target phase when the target nodes handlers are invoked, regardless of whether it is its capturing handler or bubbling handler.

At any point in an event's round-trip travels, it may be halted by a handler, preventing all further event handlers from being invoked.

Halting Event Propagation

Sometimes, when handling events, you may need to stop an event in its tracks. Knowing an event may be acted upon elsewhere in your page, it may make sense to halt an event if the conditions within your app are not in a state to allow the event to continue.

For instance, if an event is dispatched when a user enters a new password within a **textfield** control, the event may be useless if the password does not meet certain requirements, such as consisting of too few characters or including characters that are not allowed.

JavaScript provides two similar functions to halt events: **stopPropagation** and **stopImmediatePropagation**. Both functions are methods of the event object that are passed to event handlers as their sole parameters.

The **stopPropagation** method will prevent event handlers on further nodes along its journey from being invoked, regardless of whether the event is in its capturing phase or bubbling phase. However, it will still allow all remaining as-yet-uninvoked event handlers for the current event type to execute if they are on the same node as the event handler that called **stopPropagation**. The **stopImmediatePropagation** method will stop all further handlers, including those as-yet-uninvoked on the current node:

```
var handler = function(ev) {
  if (ev.target.value.length < 6) {
    ev.stopImmediatePropagation();
  }
};
```

Either method may be invoked anywhere within a handler and may be called in multiple handlers, though only the first instance will execute.

Halting Event Actions

Some events within the JavaScript engine result in an action. An action is a browser-specific response to an event, outside of your own custom event handlers. Examples of this include the submission of a **form** or a page redirection when clicking a link.

Actions occur after the event bubbling phase, once the event has finished its journey through the node tree. If an event is stopped due to the invocation of either **stopPropagation** or **stopImmediatePropagation**, the action will still occur.

To prevent an action, the event object's **preventDefault** method must be called:

```
var handler = function(ev) {
  ev.preventDefault();
}
```

Calling **preventDefault** does not halt the event passing through the capture or bubbling phases. Therefore, if you want to stop an event in its tracks and prevent its action, you must call both types of method:

```
var handler = function(ev) {
  ev.stopPropagation();
  ev.preventDefault();
}
```

Note that not all events can be prevented from initiating an action. Each dispatched event contains a property called cancelable. If this property is **true**, then it can be canceled by calling its **preventDefault** method. If, however, the property is **false**, then calling **preventDefault** will do nothing to change its behavior:

```
var handler = function(ev) {
  if (ev.cancelable) {
    ev.preventDefault();
  }
};
```

The **onload** event is one such event that can't be canceled, and with good reason, since it is imperative that the event completes its life cycle to ensure the proper functionality of the browser. Conversely, a form **onsubmit** event is cancelable since its success must be at the discretion of the page's business logic.

Exercise 6.04: Conditional Event Prevention

In this exercise, you will create a group of links. Each link, when clicked, will raise a **click** event. Above these links, the containing **div** will listen for the event each one raises and will determine if it should stop the event propagation, stop its action, or stop both. Let's get started:

1. Let's start by creating a document called **ev-prev.html** and adding some HTML code:

```
<html>
  <body>
    <div id="container">
      <a href="https://google.com">Google</a>
      <a href="https://bing.com">Bing</a>
      <a href="https://yahoo.com">Yahoo</a>
    </div>
    <div id="message"></div>
  </body>
```

   Here, we have a container with three links and a secondary container for output messages.

2. Next, open a **script** tag for the JavaScript and create variables to reference the **link** container, the links themselves, and the **message** container:

```
<script>
  var container = document.getElementById("container"),
      links = container.children,
      msg = document.getElementById("message");
```

3. When each link is clicked, we want a message to display, showing which link was clicked. Therefore, we will attach an **event listener** to the **link** container so that when the events bubble up, the handler will be there to catch the event object and identify which link dispatched the event:

```
container.addEventListener("click", function(ev) {
  msg.innerHTML = `${ev.target.text} clicked`;
  console.log(`${ev.target.text} clicked`);
});
```

4. Then, we will add a behavior for each link. The first will prevent actions, the second will stop **propagation**, and the third will do both:

```
links[0].addEventListener("click", function(ev) {
  ev.preventDefault();
});
links[1].addEventListener("click", function(ev) {
  ev.stopPropagation();
});
links[2].addEventListener("click", function(ev) {
  ev.preventDefault();
  ev.stopPropagation();
});
```

5. Finally, close out the **script** tag and **html** tag:

```
</script>
</html>
```

6. By running this page in a browser, you should see that the first link will print **Google** clicked in the message container, the second will redirect the user to the **Bing** website, and the third will do nothing at all. When clicking the second link, the message is never displayed because the event propagation is stopped in the handler.

You have now successfully marshaled events and caught them as they bubbled up through the node tree:

Google Bing Yahoo

Figure 6.10: Event prevention

Event Triggers

You have seen that events are dispatched dynamically when interacting with a web page, but events can also be triggered manually, through your own code.

As we mentioned previously, events in JavaScript are typed objects. When a dynamic event is raised, the JavaScript engine creates such an object and dispatches it. The object contains a type value that stores the event type as a string, such as **click**.

It is possible to instantiate your own event objects and dispatch them, rather than simply relying on events being created dynamically. There are many reasons why you might like to do this, such as to simulate user interaction or to easily invoke code already assigned as an event handler without duplicating code. To do so, you simply create an instance of an **Event** using the **new** keyword and pass it the type of event you wish to raise:

```
var ev = new Event("click");
```

Once created, you then simply dispatch it using the node's **dispatchEvent** method:

```
someNode.dispatchEvent(ev);
```

The node that the **dispatchEvent** method is called from becomes the event object's target property. Once dispatched, the event enters the capture phase down through the DOM to this node, then the bubbling phase back up from it as normal, triggering event listeners as it goes.

Custom Events

The **Event** object is the simplest type of event provided by the JavaScript framework. In fact, all the other events provided by JavaScript extend the simple **Event** type. However, the **Event** object by itself is not very flexible and does not provide a means of easily attaching additional data for an event. To alleviate this, the JavaScript language supplies the **CustomEvent** type, that is, an event specifically designed for custom developer events.

When instantiated, the **CustomEvent** object accepts an additional named parameter called **detail**. By providing an object with a **detail** property as the second constructor parameter, the value of that property is then available to all event handlers that intercept it, like so:

```
var event = new CustomEvent("click", {detail: 123});
```

Now, any event handlers that may intercept this event can retrieve the detail value by simply referencing it:

```
var handler = function(ev) {
  var value = ev.detail;   // value is now 123
};
```

CustomEvent exists for more than just manually triggering native event types; it is also possible to create your own event types. The name that's passed to an event object when it is created may be any string you choose. By listening for that event, you are able to handle it just like events built into the JavaScript engine:

```
var event = new CustomEvent("myEvent", {detail: 42});
someContainer.addEventListener("myEvent", someEventHandler);
someNode.dispatchEvent(event);
```

Native Event Triggers

There are many native event types in the JavaScript language, some with actions and some without. So far, you have seen the **click** event being used, but there are far more than that. The mouse events group alone includes **15** different event types, and there are over **40** different groups of events, including the following:

- Network
- Element focus
- Web sockets
- CSS animations and transitions
- Forms
- Printing
- Keyboard interactivity
- Element drag and drop
- Window and document events

There are even events that occur through touch screen display interaction, virtual reality headsets, device battery changes, smartcard events, and many, many more.

Event Hander Attributes

When building out your HTML page, the HTML specification also caters to infix event handling notation. This is where event handlers are assigned within the HTML nodes themselves. Infix event notation is known in HTML as event attributes. There are numerous available event attribute types, though not as many as there are event types provided by JavaScript.

Event attributes typically have names that are identical to their native JavaScript event type counterparts but are prepended with the word **on**. For instance, the **click** event would be assigned to a node as the **onclick** attribute:

```
<div id="someNode" onclick="someFunction();"></div>
```

The value of the event attribute is an executable JavaScript statement, such as a function invocation.

DOM nodes can only support one event attribute of each type; it is not possible, for instance, to provide two **onclick** attributes in a single node. However, event attributes can execute multiple statements within a single attribute by ensuring the correct use of the semi-colon character to distinguish the separate statements:

```
<div id="someNode" onclick="someFun1(); someFun2();"></div>
```

Functions called as event attribute handlers are not passed an event object. However, unlike typical event handlers, they can be called with additional parameters. For instance, to pass a reference to the node containing the event attribute, the event attribute function statement can be passed the **this** context:

```
<div id="someNode" onclick="someFunction(this);"></div>
```

In this instance, **this** resolves as the first parameter, which is a reference to the **div** node.

Many developers consider event attributes to be a last resort since their inclusion mixes the view (HTML) with the logic (JavaScript). The recommended option is to always assign event handlers dynamically using **addEventListener**.

Events and Memory

In the previous chapter, the **delete** keyword was introduced and a chapter regarding memory management was touched upon. When working with event handlers, managing memory becomes very important. If an event handler is attached to a node but that node is then removed from the page **DOM**, it may not be cleaned up by the JavaScript engine's **garbage collector** (cleaned from memory) until the handler is removed from the node. This is particularly true if the event handler is not an anonymous function.

When using events against nodes that may be deleted from the **DOM**, ensure you perform a proper cleanup of your nodes and handlers. This may mean removing the event handlers and properly deleting a variable's contents prior to removal.

Working with Forms

Forms are an integral part of the HTML specification and exist separately to the JavaScript engine, though they are also fully interactive with JavaScript. HTML forms are declarative structures are defined using the **form** tag. This tag outlines a context that can be submitted, and its data is sent to a remote server location.

To understand how the **form** tag works, it helps to understand HTTP requests, their type differentiation, and how data is sent within the request.

HTTP

HTTP is a specification, the long form of which is **HyperText Transfer Protocol**. It was originally released as **HTTP 1.0** in 1990 and detailed in the **RFC 1945** specification (where 1945 is the specification number, not a year). This transport format was designed for the transfer of HyperText documents across the internet, such as **HyperText Markup Language** (HTML) documents.

Within the HTTP specification, numerous metadata is identified that can be sent with an **HTTP request**. This metadata is known as **headers**, as it sits within the starting bytes of a request packet and is used to identify how the request is read.

The HTTP protocol provides an option to identify the purpose of the request packet, known as the **Method**. There are numerous **Method** options available, some of which are parsed and read differently by the HTTP servers that receive them, though their use may also be simply contextual. Two of the most common HTTP **Methods** are **GET** and **POST**.

GET is a method that simply means "**get me information at this address**", where the address is the URL the request was sent from. When making a **GET** request, parameters may be appended to the address in the form of query variables or as part of the path itself, which the server could then make use of in some way. However, in early versions of the **HTTP protocol**, **Uniform Resource Locator** (**URL**) addresses were only supplied with up to **255** characters, including the protocol and domain address, which proved tricky for larger amounts of data, including file uploads. To alleviate this problem, the specification also provides a **Method** called **POST**.

POST is an extension of **GET** and allows us to include a request **body**. In an HTTP request, a **body** is the packet content that is included after the headers; thus, it is the literal packet body:

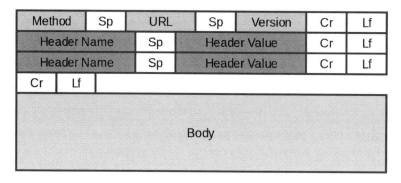

Figure 6.11: HTTP packet

Since nothing follows the **body** in the request packet, the **body** is able to be much larger than the **GET** limitation of **255** characters.

When sending a **body** with a request, the sender is able to provide a **Content-Type** header, which describes the format (or MIME type) of the **body**. For instance, if the body is a **JavaScript Object Notation (JSON)** string, then the request's **Content-Type** may be **application/json**, while a body with a JPEG image could be **application/jpeg**.

The Form Tag

The **form** tag has existed in HTML since its public inception and is detailed in the **HTML RFC 1866** specification. The **form** tag typically encloses elements of a literal form, presented visibly to users of an HTML page. As with any HTML node, a **form** tag may be styled visually or left invisible as required:

```
<form method="POST" action="/data/form-handler.php" enctype="text/plain">
    ...
</form>
```

The attributes of the form tag include the following:

Attribute	Values	Description
method	GET, POST, PUT, and so on	The HTTP protocol method of the data request.
action	URL string	The URL of the endpoint or handler to receive the request.
enctype	MIME string	The MIME type of the request. This may be something like **application/x-www-form-urlencoded** **text/plain** **multipart/form-data/**
target	Display parameter string	Signifies where the response of the form submission will be displayed. Some possible values are as follows: _blank _self _parent _top
autocomplete	on or off	If on, the browser may attempt to help prepopulate the form controls based on data provided by the user when filling in similar internet forms. Defaults to off.
novalidate	true or false	If true, prevents automatic browser validation of some controls. Defaults to false.

Figure 6.12: Form Tag attributes and their description

In comparison to the HTTP packet specification, the **method** attribute is equivalent to the method of the HTTP packet itself, the **action** is the same as the URL parameter, and the **enctype** is the same as the **Content-Type** header value.

The **form** tag provides a logical request block around groups of input controls. Each **form** tag within a web page needs to be submitted for a request to be formulated and sent. Submission can occur dynamically with JavaScript or via user interaction through the use of a **submit** button control:

```
<form method="POST" action="/data/form-handler.php" target="_top">
  <input type="submit" value="submit" />
</form>
```

When you prefer direct user interaction, forms may be submitted using either a **submit** or an **image** input control, where the latter provides a means to display a styled graphic as the submission button:

```
<form method="POST" action="/data/form-handler.php" target="_top">
  <input type="image" src="images/send-btn.png" />
</form>
```

Submitting a Form with JavaScript

Sometimes, it is not appropriate to send a **form** request via user interaction. Instead, forms may send data after an animation has completed or perhaps redirect a user once their browser capabilities have been discovered. At such times, it helps to be able to trigger a form's submission dynamically using JavaScript.

As with all DOM-based interaction, submitting a form first requires the acquisition of the form node. Once acquired, a form can be submitted by simply calling its **submit** function:

```
var form = document.getElementsByTagName("form")[0];
form.submit();
```

Note that more than one form tag may exist within a page. Form tags may include identification and style-based attributes, the same as any other tag, such as **name**, **id**, **class**, and **style**.

Form Submission Events

The **form** tag supports a number of useful events oriented around controls and form handling. The most useful of these events is the **submit** event.

The **submit** event is dispatched when the form is submitted, but prior to the request actually being sent to the designated endpoint. This event is typically used for validating the user-supplied values of the form to ensure that no obvious mistakes were made or to ensure that the required fields have been completed.

> **Note**
>
> Since the **submit** event is dispatched before the request is sent, be sure not to redirect the user to another page using this event or to do anything that will prevent the form submission from completing. If you wish to halt the form's submission, see the Preventing Form Submission section.

Like many events, the **submit** event handler may be assigned to a form node using explicit HTML attribute syntax:

```
<form method="GET" action="/endpoint" onsubmit="myFormHandler()">
```

The **submit** event functions just like any other event, meaning that it captures from and bubbles to the **document** node.

Preventing Form Submission

Stopping a **form** from submitting is a common requirement in HTML and JavaScript. Often, if the validation of the **form** fails, it is preferable to cancel the submission and display appropriate messages to the user. To cancel a **form** submission, we could call the **preventDefault** method of the event, which stops the eventual action of the event, just like it does with other event types. An alternative method is to return the **false** value from the function.

Returning **false** from an event handler has the same effect as calling the event's **preventDefault** function, but it doesn't halt the capturing/bubbling.

If your function is handling a jQuery event, returning **false** is the same as performing both the **preventDefault** and **stopPropagation** method calls:

```
function formHandler(ev) {
  if (document.getElementById("password").value().length < 3) {
    alert("Password is too short");
    return false;
  }
};
```

Resetting a Form

Resetting a form means returning the form to its initial state. This feature is provided as a way to restore a form to a clean state, or if the form was loaded with default or original values, then it returns those values to each of the controls.

Website users may sometimes require a reset capability if they're working with complex values. Being able to reset a form saves the user from having to memorize the initial values present in the form, or at least to quickly return to the original state prior to repopulating the form.

Like submitting, resetting a form may be carried out via user interaction through the use of a reset input control:

```
<form method="GET" action="/endpoint">
  <input type="reset" value="Reset Form" />
</form>
```

Once the control has been clicked, the **form** will revert to its initial state.

Another means to reset a form is by using the **reset** method of the **form** node:

```
document.getElementByTagName("form")[0].reset();
```

> **Note**
>
> A **form reset** cannot be reversed automatically. If such a feature is required, all the values of the form will need to be saved first and then individually reapplied to the controls.

Form Reset Event

When resetting a form, the browser will raise the **reset** event. The handler for the reset event may be applied explicitly within the HTML node's declaration:

```
<form method="GET" action="/endpoint" onreset="myResetHandler()">
```

Similarly, form reset events may be handled by simply assigning the event handler with JavaScript:

```
document.getElementByTagName("form")[0].addEventListener("reset",
myResetHandler);
```

Exercise 6.05: Simple Form Handling

In this exercise, you will create a simple form with **submit** and **reset** buttons. When submitting, the form action will be canceled, but the submitted values will still be handled and displayed on the screen. This is the first step to creating a form validation system. Let's get started:

1. Let's begin with the standard opening HTML boilerplate:

```
<html>
  <body>
```

2. Next, create the opening form tag. This will be given an ID, for ease of acquisition, and will provide a random action URL since it won't be used in this exercise:

```
<form id="myForm" method="GET" action="http://google.com">
```

3. To make this more interesting, let's introduce a simple **text** field control. It won't be used, per se, but it will help demonstrate the reset functionality:

```
<input type="text" value="original text" />
```

Input controls will be discussed in the next section of this chapter.

4. Now, you will need the two buttons: one for **submit** and one for **reset**:

```
<input type="submit" value="Submit" />
<input type="reset" value="Reset" />
```

5. Finally, let's close out the **form** tag and open the **script** tag, ready for our JavaScript:

```
</form>
<script>
```

6. The **reset** button handler will be simple. Once clicked, display a message in the console. However, you won't be attaching the handler to the button's **click** event as doing that will not provide the power to stop the **reset**, should you wish to. Instead, the event will be assigned to the form's **reset** event:

```
function resetHandler(ev) {
    console.log("form has been reset");
};
document.getElementById("myForm").addEventListener("reset",
resetHandler);
```

7. Likewise, with the **submit** handler, the form's **submit** event will be listened to. In this instance, however, you will call **ev.preventDefault()** from the handler to prevent the form from actually submitting:

```
function submitHandler(ev) {
    console.log("form has been submitted");
    ev.preventDefault();
};
document.getElementById("myForm").addEventListener("submit",
submitHandler);
```

8. Finally, close out the **script** tag and the page:

```
    </script>
  </body>
</html>
```

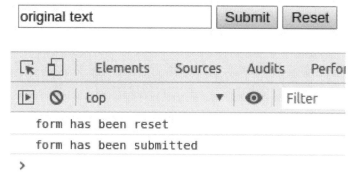

Figure 6.13: Form buttons

That's it. Now, if you run the page in the browser, you will see that clicking **submit** will display one message in the console, while the **reset** button will show another. Also, clicking **reset** will always revert the text in the text field to the words original text.

Form Controls

Form tags are pretty useless without data to send. This data is typically provided using the various form controls or widgets that are available in the HTML specification. Where possible, and where the control has no child nodes, a form control typically utilizes the **input** node tag type. Other controls include **select**, **textarea**, **button**, and **datalist**. We will look at each of these control types throughout the rest of this chapter.

Input Controls

The majority of the controls that are available to HTML forms are provided using the **input** tag. The **input** tag requires a **type** parameter, which displays a relative control within the HTML page:

```
<input type="text" />
```

The following are the types that are available in modern browsers when using the **input** control.

The Button Control

The **button** control appears very much like the **submit** and **reset** form buttons. However, unlike **submit** and **reset**, the **button** control has no default action:

```
<input type="button" onclick="buttonHandler();" value="Clickable Button"
/>
```

The **button** control also has an alternative tag format, which we can use by using the **button** tag:

```
<button onclick="buttonHandler();">Clickable Button</button>
```

Note that the **input** format requires a label to be passed in the **value** attribute, while the **button** tag format requires the button text to be passed as content using a closing **button** tag, like so:

Clickable Button

Figure 6.14: Button input control

The button control supports the **click** event, or the **onclick** attribute, as we explained earlier in this chapter.

The Checkbox Control

The **checkbox** control represents a "true or false," "on or off," or "yes or no" control:

```
<input type="checkbox" checked />
```

The **checked** parameter in the preceding example is a valueless attribute. When supplied, the **checkbox** is presented checked by default and will be set to check whether the encompassing **form** is reset.

An alternative implementation of this is to supply a value for **checked**:

```
<input type="checkbox" checked="checked" />
```

Any values supplied with valueless attributes are disregarded, and thus any value may be provided:

Figure 6.15: Checkbox input control

The **checkbox** control supports the **change** and **input** events. The **input** event will be dispatched whenever the **value** parameter of a control is changed, while the **change** event is raised only when the **value** of that control is committed, such as when losing focus or when the *Enter* key is pressed. Typically, there is very little difference between the two events when they're used with the **checkbox** control, though it is deemed preferable to always use the **change** event.

When a **checkbox** is present in a form, its value is only submitted if it is **checked**. When unchecked, no value is passed to the handling script at all.

To check the checked status of a checkbox using JavaScript, simply query its **checked** parameter:

```
<input type="checkbox" id="check" value="1" checked />
<script>
   var chk = document.getElementById("check");
   console.log(chk.checked);   // ==> true
</script>
```

The value of **checked** will be **true** if the control is checked, or **false** if it isn't.

To set the **checked** state of the control, simply pass a **Boolean** value to the **checked** parameter.

The Radio Control

The **radio** control is similar to the **checkbox** control, with the exception that it handles multiple-choice options. Unlike a **checkbox** control, a **radio** control cannot be deselected by clicking on it. Instead, a different option must be selected, thereby providing at least one result when submitting the **form**:

```
<input type="radio" name="color" value="red" checked />
<input type="radio" name="color" value="blue" />
<input type="radio" name="color" value="green" />
```

The **name** attribute of the **radio** control provides the grouping functionality. If a different **name** is provided from previous **radio** controls, then that new control belongs to a different group. Only by clicking the **radio** controls within the same group can the previously selected **radio** control be deselected:

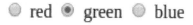

Figure 6.16: Radio input control

Like the **checkbox** controls, the **radio** control is selected using the **checked** attribute. If a **radio** control group is present within a page, but none of the controls have been set to **checked**, none of those **radio** controls will be selected. At such times, submitting the parent form will mean that the **radio** group is absent from the sent data.

To dynamically check a specific **radio** button (and thus uncheck the currently selected one), there needs to be a means to reference the specific **radio** control you wish to check. There are several ways to do this, such as providing a unique **id** for each **radio** control in a group, but by far the most efficient is to simply reference its index in the group. For instance, to select the second **radio** button in a group, we may do this:

```
<input type="radio" name="color" value="red" checked /> red
<input type="radio" name="color" value="blue" /> green
<input type="radio" name="color" value="green" /> blue
<script>
  var chk = document.getElementsByName("color")[1];  // select index 1
  chk.checked = true;
</script>
```

getElementsByName returns an array of all the elements matching the passed criteria. Therefore, providing an index enables direct access to a given element index.

radio control supports the **input** and **change** events, much like the **checkbox** control.

The Text Control

The **text** control is the most basic of all **input** control types and is used to create free-text fields. These fields allow for single-line text strings to be entered using the keyboard, though text may also be pasted into it using the browser context menu. Text fields are created by setting the **type** attribute of the **input** control to **text**:

```
<input type="text" name="color" value="red" />
```

The permissible content of a **text** control may be restricted by supplying a **pattern** attribute value in the form of a regular expression. As an example, a text field can be restricted to accept only numerical values with the following code:

```
<input type="text" name="num" pattern="[0-9]" title="Enter a number" />
```

When using the preceding text field, submitting a value other than a number will result in the form submission terminating and a tooltip displaying alongside the **text** field with the text **Enter a number**. The form data will not be submitted under this circumstance:

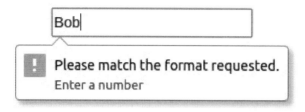

Figure 6.17: Text input control with the pattern attribute

Another feature of the **text** field is the **placeholder** attribute. Placeholders allow for temporary text to exist within the field itself:

```
<input type="text" name="num" placeholder="Enter a number" />
```

This text does not constitute a value of the control, so the submission of the container form will not yield the **placeholder** value. Likewise, querying the text control's **value** attribute will not return the **placeholder** value if it is visible:

Enter a number

Figure 6.18: Text input control with placeholder attribute

The Password Control

The **password** control works very similarly to the **text** field control, but with a couple of differences:

```
<input type="password" name="pass" />
```

The primary difference with the **password** control is that any value present in the control is presented to the user as a series of dots, known as a hash, rather than as the value text itself. The purpose of the hash is for the value to be unreadable by the user and, thus, provide a level of security from unwanted attention. The user is, therefore, expected to already know the value contained within the field. When submitting the form, the value is correctly passed with the form data as clear text:

Figure 6.19: Password input control

Another difference with the **password** control over the **text** control is that it is not possible to highlight its content and copy it. Any attempt to copy the content of a **password** control is ignored. This prevents malicious users from copying and pasting the value of a **password** control into a text editor, or other such software, thus making the value text clearly readable. However, despite this, it is still possible to reference the control with JavaScript and output its value that way, like so:

```
<input type="password" id="secureValue" value="secret" />
<script>
var pass = document.getElementById("secureValue");
console.log(pass.value);   // ==> "secret"
</script>
```

email, tel, and url Controls

The **email**, **tel**, and **url** controls are modern variations of the text field control. They can be created by simply passing email, tel, or url as the type attribute of the input control:

```
<input type="email" />
<input type="tel" />
<input type="url" />
```

By themselves, each of these controls provides no additional functionality over the standard **text** control. All of the attributes, events, and visual look-and-feel of these controls are identical to the **text** control and to one another. However, the benefit of these types becomes apparent when they're used with devices that present an on-screen keyboard, such as mobile phones and tablets. By using one of these **input** types, rather than a **text** control, the visible keyboard that's presented to input text into them is typically oriented toward the control's content type:

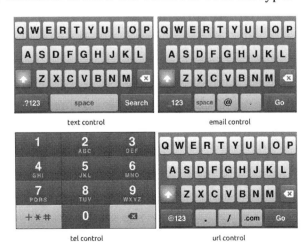

Figure 6.20: Mobile keyboards for the text, email, tel, and url controls

Note that additional work is needed to ensure that the content of the field is appropriate for the field format. This can be accomplished using the **pattern** attribute and form validation logic.

The Hidden Control

The **hidden** control is a very useful field for storing data to be passed to the handler of a form, such as a remote server endpoint, without the user of the web page being aware of its existence. As its name implies, the **hidden** field is hidden from the user and has no visible presence:

```
<input type="hidden" />
```

Many of the attributes provided by the input tag are irrelevant when using the **hidden** control since it is not a control that a user will interact with. However, its **value**, **id**, and **name** attributes will prove useful and can be used and manipulated in the same way as the **text** control.

The Number Control

A **number** field appears similar to a **text** field but will naturally constrain all text input to numerical values, the addition and subtraction symbols, and the period symbol:

```
<input type="number" />
```

In some browsers, the number control will also present small up and down arrow buttons, which can be used to increment or decrement the contained value:

Figure 6.21: Number control

The content of a **number** control can be further constrained by using its **min**, **max**, and **step** attributes. The **min** and **max** attributes are self-explanatory and constrain possible numeric entry values to these attributes. For instance, providing a **min** value of 0 will ensure a negative number cannot be entered, while a **max** value of 100 will ensure the value never exceeds 100:

```
<input type="number" min="0" max="100" />
```

Using **min** and **max** does not mean a value outside of these constraints cannot be physically entered as input into the control from the keyboard, but merely that the constraints cannot be breached when clicking on the provided arrow buttons or that any provided value outside of these parameters will be accepted when submitting the form:

Figure 6.22: Number control constraints

The step attribute provides a means to increase the rate at which the arrow buttons increase or decrease the value. For instance, if large numbers are allowed within the control, incrementing by 1 with each click may be impractical. Therefore, setting a larger step size would allow the value change to happen with fewer clicks:

```
<input type="number" min="-100000" max="100000" max="100" />
```

When using step, the change in value when clicking the arrow buttons will change at a rate of the step value from whatever value is currently present within the control. Therefore, setting a step of 5 will not constrain the contained value to multiples of 5.

The Image Control

The **image** control works as a hybrid of an **img** tag and a **submit** input control. The idea here is that you can use a graphical image as a submit button. You specify the image source using the **src** attribute, much like we do with the **img** tag:

```
<input type="image" src="/path/to/img.png" />
```

An additional benefit to using an **image** input control is that once it's clicked, the x and y coordinates of the mouse in relation to the image are also sent with the form data as an **x** and **y** value. This can prove very useful if, for instance, you wish to register a location on a map as part of form submission, or if you wish to determine the area of the image that the user clicked on:

```
<form method="GET" action="/handler.php">
  <input type="image" src="/path/to/img.png" />
</form>
// will submit to a URL like "/handler.php?x=14&y=27
```

The availability of the **image** control means forms can be stylized beyond the confines provided by HTML button controls and can be very popular with web designers.

The File Control

The **file** control is a requirement when uploading files to a remote server. In fact, it is not actually possible to upload a file dynamically without using the **file** control in some way. This is due to security as it is unethical to be able to dynamically upload files from a user's machine without their knowledge:

```
<input type="file" name="file" />
```

The **file** control is typically presented to the user as a **text** field and **label** pair. It is possible to style the control so that one of these items, or both, is not visible to the user. The text that's supplied within the button and label is fixed by the browser and requires some extreme styling to be changed.

Choose file   No file chosen

Figure 6.23: File control

When using the **file** control to upload files to a server, it is important to set the **enctype** parameter of the surrounding form to **"multipart/form-data"**. This value informs the form submission on how to encode the data when sending it to the server. Failure to do this will prevent the file from uploading since files typically require multiple packets to successfully transfer all of the file's data bytes.

The file control supports an accept attribute value, which enables the filtering of accepted file format types. This attribute can support more than one value, but they must be supplied as MIME types (a predefined string representation of a file's type):

```
<input type="file" name="file" accept="image/png, image/jpeg" />
```

In the preceding example, only files with a .png, .jpg, or .jpeg extension will be visible when selecting files through the control.

The Textarea Control

While the **text** control is great for accepting single lines of text, the **textarea** control is required for capturing multiline text values:

```
<textarea name="description">
    Some default text.
</textarea>
```

As the name implies, the **textarea** control supports an area of text and is, therefore, a larger control than many of the **input** controls. Like the **button** tag, the **textarea** control consists of both an opening and a closing tag. Any text that's supplied between the tags makes up its text content.

Although the textarea doesn't utilize a value attribute, its content may still be read and set using the **value** attribute in JavaScript, like so:

```
var desc = document.getElementsByName("description")[0];
console.log(desc.value) // ==> outputs "Some default text"
desc.value = "Some other text"; // ==> updates the value of the textarea
to "Some other text"
```

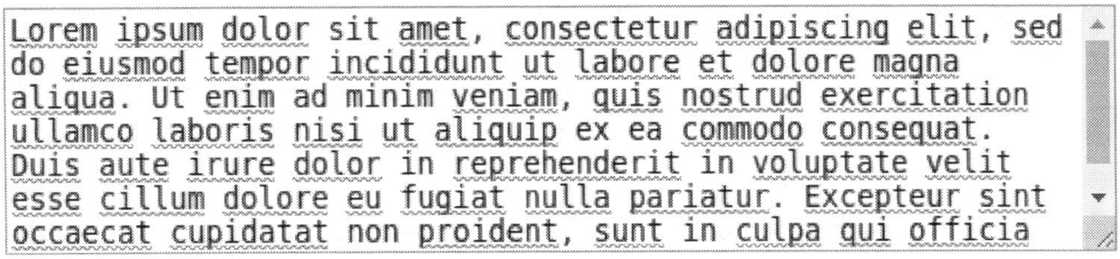

Lorem ipsum dolor sit amet, consectetur adipiscing elit, sed do eiusmod tempor incididunt ut labore et dolore magna aliqua. Ut enim ad minim veniam, quis nostrud exercitation ullamco laboris nisi ut aliquip ex ea commodo consequat. Duis aute irure dolor in reprehenderit in voluptate velit esse cillum dolore eu fugiat nulla pariatur. Excepteur sint occaecat cupidatat non proident, sunt in culpa qui officia

Figure 6.24: Textarea control

The Select Control

The **select** control provides the functionality of a drop-down list control. Like **textarea**, the **select** control utilizes an opening and closing tag, both of which form the body of the control. However, the items within the control are provided as an additional tag, called **option**:

```
<select name="colors">
   <option value="">--Please choose an option--</option>
   <option value="red">Red</option>
   <option value="blue">Blue</option>
   <option value="green">Green</option>
</select>
```

The **option** elements of a **select** control typically contain two values: the **value** attribute and the **text** body. These are known simply as the **value** and **text**. The text contained between the opening and closing **option** tags is the string that's visible to the user within the control, while the **value** attribute is the string to be sent when the form is submitted if that particular **option** element is selected. When adding **option** elements, the **value** attribute may be omitted, but this will mean the **text** value will be sent with the form data instead.

Similar to checkboxes and radio buttons, an option value may be preselected by passing the selected attribute to one of the option values:

```
<select name="colors">
  <option value="">--Please choose an option--</option>
  <option value="red" selected>Red</option>
  <option value="blue">Blue</option>
  <option value="green">Green</option>
</select>
```

The select control can be displayed in two formats. The standard format is as a dropdown (or combo) list control:

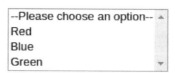

Figure 6.25: Select control

The secondary format is displayed if the control needs to support multiple simultaneously selected options. As such, the control is displayed as a permanently open list control, with scrollable options. The **select** control can support multiple selected options by supplying the **multiple** attribute:

```
<select name="colors" multiple>
  <option value="">--Please choose an option--</option>
  <option value="red">Red</option>
  <option value="blue">Blue</option>
  <option value="green">Green</option>
</select>
```

When displayed, the user must press and hold the Ctrl key on the keyboard while selecting items. If the Ctrl key is not pressed, then selecting an item will deselect any previously selected items:

```
--Please choose an option--
Red
Blue
Green
```

Figure 6.26: Select control with multiple attributes

When working with a dropdown **select** control, it is possible to get the value of the selected **option** by simply querying the **select** control's **value** property:

```
var select = document.getElementsByName("colors")[0];
console.log(select.value); // ==> outputs selected color
```

It is also possible to output the index of the selected item by querying the **selectedIndex** property. Index values start at 0 (zero) for the first element:

```
var select = document.getElementsByName("colors")[0];
console.log(select.selectedIndex); // ==> outputs numerical index of
selected option
```

However, when querying a multi-select list, things aren't so easy. If multiple items are selected, querying the **value** property would simply return the first selected item in the list, thus ignoring all the other selected items. Instead, developers need to make use of the **options** property of the **select** control and the **option** item's **selected** property to discern which items are selected.

The **select** control's **options** property returns all the **option** elements contained within it, regardless of their selected state. The **option** item's **selected** property is simply the condition of its selected status; it's true if it is selected and false if it is not. Thus, by combining these two values, the selected **option** elements can be discerned with a simple loop, like so:

```
var selectedItems = [];
var select = document.getElementsByName("colors")[0];
for (let opt of select.options) {
  if (opt.selected) {
    selectedItems.push(opt.value);
  }
}
console.log(selectedItems); // ==> outputs array of selected values
```

Activity 6.01: Making Changes to the Model

A lot has been covered in this chapter, but you should now have the knowledge that's required to make something visual. In this activity, your role will be to create a simple form that requests the title and description for a new **To-Do** entry which, when submitted, feeds the data to the action handler we created in the previous chapter.

Once your form is in place and its data is being handled, the model functions must be updated to receive this data. Create an event handler that's able to receive **CREATE** action events and pass them appropriately to the model.

Since there is no visual cue that data has been successfully stored within the model, any updates to the model should result in a notification event being dispatched. This way, other areas of your application can respond accordingly as data changes. Your project manager has requested that a custom event be dispatched from the model, called **CHANGED**. This will notify any interested party that data has either been added, updated, or removed from the model.

To verify that the **CHANGED** event works, create a message banner at the top of the page that briefly displays the message "**The To-Do model has been updated**". This message should be present for three seconds, before being removed.

Your project manager has asked that this information is dispatched as a custom event, to be caught by the action handler. This event should match the action types already recognized by the model. Therefore, be sure to send the object as a **CREATE** event.

Save the following HTML in a file called **index.html**:

```html
<html>
  <head>
    <title>Create TODO</title>
    <script src="model.js"></script>
    <script src="create_todo.js"></script>
  </head>
  <body onload="loadHandler();">
    <div id="notifications"></div>
    <form id="todo_form" />
      <label>Title:
        <input type="text" id="title" />
      </label>
      <label>Description:
        <textarea id="description"></textarea>
      </label>
      <input type="submit" value="Create TODO" />
    </form>
  </body>
</html>
```

This HTML should include the model from the previous chapter, but also a new JavaScript file that will contain the logic for this activity.

The following is the expected output for this activity:

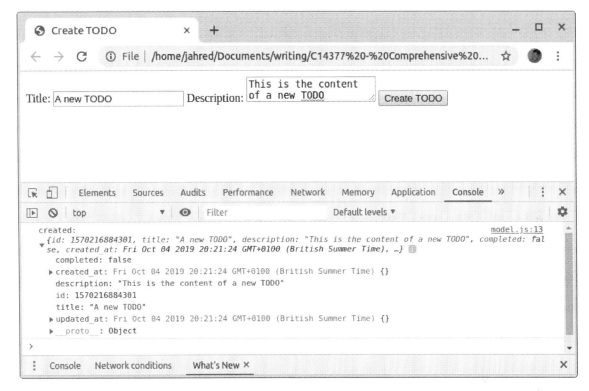

Figure 6.27: TODO submission form

Follow these steps to complete this activity:

1. Add a custom event handler to the model. This handler should receive the **CREATE** state change and update the model with the new **TODO** details from the event body.

2. Add a **loadHandler** function to the **create_todo.js** file. This handler should listen for the submit button's **click** event, but also the custom **CHANGED** event from the model.

3. Add a handler function in **create_todo.js** to handle the **CHANGED** event itself. This handler should temporarily display a **The TODO model has been updated** message within the **notifications** tag.

4. Add the **TODO** to the `create_todo.js` file. This will be executed when the **submit** button click event is raised. This handler should parse the values of the form controls and dispatch them in a new **CREATE** custom event if they are valid. If any of the data is not valid, then sufficient error messages should be temporarily displayed in the **notifications** tag.

5. Add a **CHANGED** event dispatch when the model is updated. The event body should contain a type added and a value containing the details of the new **TODO**.

If you run the HTML page, you will expect to see messages to be written to the screen when you submit the form. Remember that the model will receive and send events. It will not be contacted directly. The handler functions will ensure that the events are attached correctly and that the data has been correctly parsed so that it can be sent to the model.

> **Note**
>
> The solution to this activity can be found on page 728.

Summary

This has been the first chapter to have utilized an HTML page using JavaScript in this book, as well as the first to explain the abstract nature of the event messaging system. Understanding these concepts is very valuable when building a useful web application in JavaScript.

Throughout this chapter, you have explored the various nuances of event message bubbling and capturing, along with how they can be used to control the flow of information within an application. You have also seen how to halt these events in their tracks and how to create your own custom events.

By adopting the tools and skills you've learned about in this chapter, you will have a foundational arsenal at your disposal so that you can tackle applications of any size or complexity. These skills will be honed throughout the rest of this book while broadening your perspective as to what is possible with this powerful language.

In the next chapter, you will dive deeper into the JavaScript event loop and gain a greater understanding of the underlying technology.

Popping the Hood

Overview

By the end of this chapter, you will be able to differentiate between single-threaded and multi-threaded execution; describe JavaScript's execution process; show how the call stack and memory heap interact with the other elements of the runtime; write code that works in tandem with JavaScript's garbage collection process; and debug memory-related issues in the browser.

In this chapter, we'll look at how JavaScript is executed in the browser and how it manages important system resources such as memory.

Introduction

In the previous two chapters, you learned about some of the core concepts of JavaScript, were introduced to the ideas of the `event` loop, and looked at how JavaScript handles the process of **memory management**. In this chapter, we'll look at those aspects of the language in more detail and learn how we can write code that works in concert with some underlying features of JavaScript.

It is common for developers to get quite far in their careers without having a solid understanding of some of the core concepts underlying (and surrounding) JavaScript. Indeed, it's quite possible to be a successful developer who writes solid, commercially viable applications, without ever fully grasping the topics that are covered in this chapter.

So, why should we learn about the inner workings of JavaScript? Can't we just write our code and let JavaScript handle the nitty-gritty? Well, the problem with that approach is that, sometimes, things don't quite go according to plan, and we need to be able to understand what's happening under the hood in order to rewrite the part of our code that is making the application buggy or less performant. Imagine you're a rally driver. You can drive your car along the track with just a rudimentary level of knowledge of how to drive a car. This skill level may get you to the finish line, but it definitely won't have you winning any races.

To set yourself apart from other drivers, you need to increase your skill and experience levels. Sure, simply practicing the skill will help you improve over time, and allow you to intuit a lot of what's happening behind the scenes – this is true for driving a car and programming computers with JavaScript – but having a deeper understanding of the actual processes involved will allow you to plan and make decisions with confidence so that you know specifically what parts of the system you want to control.

To give you a more concrete programming example, imagine you're testing a co-worker's code and you can't understand why a page seems to take so long to load, why it becomes unresponsive during a certain operation, or why the application takes up excessive system resources. These kinds of performance issues don't necessarily break an application, and they may not even be noticeable to every user. But they do affect the software's usability and the user experience, which has knock-on effects on things such as SEO page ranking and a site's popularity with its end users. Understanding what's going on under the hood can help you write better code and debug code faster, making your life as a developer easier, and making for smoother user experience and more successful applications.

Arming yourself with the knowledge covered in this chapter means that the code you write will make the best use of the JavaScript programming language and its runtime environments.

JavaScript Execution and the Event Loop

JavaScript is a single-threaded language, meaning it lines up all of its operations in a single thread and executes them one at a time. Many other languages are multi-threaded, that is, they are able to execute more than one thread of operations at a time. There are pros and cons to each method of execution, mostly revolving around efficiency versus complexity, but we won't look at these in-depth here. As we'll see in a moment, JavaScript's call stack processes operations one at a time, on a last in, first out (LIFO) basis.

LIFO describes a process of adding and removing elements from a data structure – in this case, from a stack. As the name suggests, the last thing that's added is the first thing taken away – much like stacking books on a desk.

The JavaScript Runtime

A runtime environment is an application that allows the software to be run on a system. It's the bridge between the software being run and the system on which it is being run and provides access to system resources such as memory and filesystem, and to runtime and environment variables. In the case of JavaScript, the runtime is often – but not always – the browser.

There are different implementations of the JavaScript runtime, and the exact way they handle executions differs between each. Each one makes use of optimization, which can make real-life processes differ from those described here.

However, from a theoretical standpoint, a JavaScript runtime can be usefully broken down into several key components and processes:

- The JavaScript engine
- Environment/Browser APIs
- The Message Queue/Callback Queue
- The **event** loop

The JavaScript runtime environment and execution broken down into these key components can be displayed as follows:

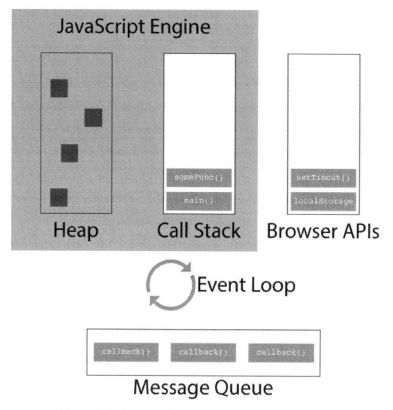

Figure 7.1: An overview of the JavaScript runtime

Let's look at each of these in turn to get a better understanding of their functionality.

JavaScript Engine

A JavaScript engine is a piece of software that runs JavaScript code, turning the high-level JavaScript source code into low-level machine code via the process of **compilation**. A common JavaScript engine is Google's V8 engine, which is found in the Chrome browser as well as in **Node.js** (used in server-side JavaScript execution) among other places. V8, like most modern browsers, uses a **Just-In-Time compilation** process to execute JavaScript code, meaning that the code is compiled at runtime and not ahead of time, like with older compilation processes.

The two elements of a JavaScript engine that we're concerned with here are the **memory heap** and the **call stack**, both of which will be explained shortly. Note that the preceding diagram shows the event loop as being separate from the JavaScript engine as it's generally expected that the JavaScript runtime will implement and manage the event loop. However, many JavaScript engines implement their own event loop process, which can be used as a fallback for the runtime environment.

> **Note**
>
> By default, Node runs on the V8 JavaScript engine. However, alternate implementations of Node using different engines are being worked on. **Node-ChakraCore**, which uses Microsoft's ChakraCore JavaScript engine, is one such project and is under active development. Another is **SpiderNode**, although the development of this project has stalled at the time of writing.

Environment APIs

Often called Web APIs or Browser APIs in the context of a browser, these are the interfaces that are made available to JavaScript by the environment in which it is being run. For example, the browser gives access to the **Document Object Model (DOM)**, `LocalStorage`, and methods such as `setTimeout()` and `setInterval()`, which we've covered in previous chapters. JavaScript running outside of a browser will have different needs, and therefore the runtime will expose different interfaces for it to use. Node.js is a popular server-side JavaScript runtime environment, which we will cover later on in this book. It usually wouldn't make much sense for Node.js to have a Document Object Model (DOM), so instead, Node provides APIs that are more relevant to server-side code such as the `FileSystem` API for performing **CRUD** (create, read, update and delete) operations on the `filesystem`.

As we'll see shortly, environment APIs are a crucial component of JavaScript's ability to run **asynchronous operations**.

Message Queue

The message queue (also known as the **callback queue** or task queue) is simply a list of messages with corresponding functions that are due to be executed. Callback functions are added to the message queue at the appropriate time, for example, when a `setTimeout` function's delay time has expired, or when an event occurs and there is a corresponding event listener, such as when a user clicks on a button and the button has a click event listener attached to it. These operations occur in a **first in, first out**(FIFO) sequence, much like the queue you find at a supermarket checkout. The message queue doesn't actually execute the functions itself – it's simply a place to keep them on hold until the call stack has finished doing what it's doing. The time at which the operation is executed is decided by the event loop.

Event Loop

The event loop is the process by which messages are added from the message queue to the call stack. The event loop watches the call stack and the message queue, and if the call stack is empty, then the oldest message from the message queue (the first in) will be pushed onto the stack for execution. Only when all the function calls on the stack have returned will subsequent messages (function calls) be pushed onto the stack.

Call Stack

The call stack keeps track of JavaScript's function invocations. When a function is called, a **stack frame**, consisting of the function's name (or 'anonymous," for anonymous functions), and a reference to the function caller's address, is pushed onto the top of the stack. If this function calls another function, then a new frame for the second function is pushed to the top of the stack, on top of the previous frame. When the function returns – either explicitly or implicitly – the function's corresponding stack frame is popped off the call stack, and code execution carries on from where it was before the function call. Unlike the message queue, the call stack processes frames in a LIFO sequence: stack frames are added to and taken from, the top of the stack, much like stacking books on a desk. When the call stack is empty, the event loop will decide whether to push messages from the message queue or to allow new stack frames to be added to the call stack for subsequent function calls.

Memory Heap

The memory heap is an unsorted area of memory that the JavaScript engine uses to dynamically read and write objects at runtime. We will look at memory management in JavaScript in detail later in this chapter.

Event Loop in Action

This section explains the code we will use to demonstrate the event loop in action and also provide a brief precursor regarding how asynchronous code is executed.

In your browser's JavaScript console or your code editor of choice, the three simple function declarations are as follows:

```
function firstCall() {
   console.log('I'm logged first!!");
   secondCall();
}

function secondCall() {
   console.log('I'm second...");
   thirdCall();
}

function thirdCall() {
   console.log('I'm last.");
}
firstCall();
```

In this simple code snippet, we are declaring three functions and then calling the first of the three. The **firstCall** function logs the **'I'm logged first"** string in the console, and then calls the next function, **secondCall()**. This function logs the **'I'm second..."** string, and subsequently calls the third of our functions, **thirdCall()**. **thirdCall()** simply logs the **'I'm last."** string

What do you expect to see in the console when we run this code? Hopefully, it's quite obvious that we will see the following logged:

```
>I'm logged first!!
>I'm second...
>I'm last.
>undefined
```

In this case, each function invocation is added to the call stack, executed in turn, and then popped off the top of the stack. Therefore, we get the strings from the three functions logged in their correct order. You can see the stack frames for each of the function invocations in the following screenshot:

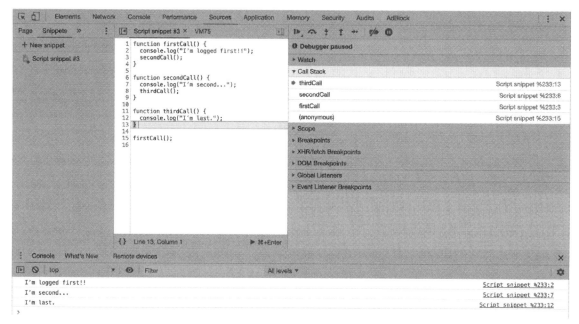

Figure 7.2: Demonstrating the sequence of execution in the call stack

Now, let's make a small change to our code by adding a **setTimout()** function in the second function block. So, let's take a look at what the three strings will be logged in this time if you write and run the code:

```
function firstCall() {
   console.log('I'm logged first!!");
   secondCall();
}
function secondCall() {
   setTimeout(function() {
     console.log('I'm second...");
   }, 0);
   thirdCall();
}

function thirdCall() {
   console.log('I'm last.");
}
firstCall();
```

Logic dictates that the order of our console logs will remain the same – after all, the `setTimeout` delay is `0` milliseconds, so it will execute on the console log straight away, right?

However, we find that the order has changed:

```
>I'm logged first!!
>I'm last.
>undefined
>I'm second...
```

So, what do you think is going on here? We will go through the source code line by line and see how the JavaScript runtime is handling each function.

First of all, the `firstCall()` function is invoked and a new stack frame is pushed to the top of the call stack of this function invocation. The function contains a call to the `log()` method of the console object, with an argument of the string type with the value `'I'm logged first!!'`. This is highlighted in the following figure:

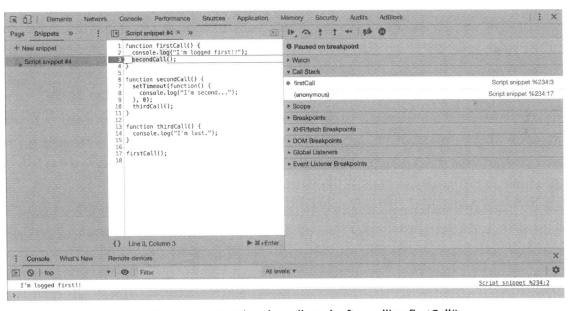

Figure 7.3: Demonstrating the call stack after calling firstCall()

The **'I'm logged first!!"** string is logged to the console, the **secondCall()** function is invoked, and a new stack frame is pushed onto the top of the stack for **secondCall()**. Here is where things are different from the original code snippet. This function contains a call to the **setTimeout()** function, which is a part of the browser's API, so this function is taken outside of the main JavaScript execution thread for now. The **setTimeout()** function is called with a delay of 0 milliseconds, after which a message is passed to the message queue with a reference to the **console.log()** call contained within the **secondCall()** function. Now, this message sits in the message queue, waiting patiently to be dealt with by the **event** loop:

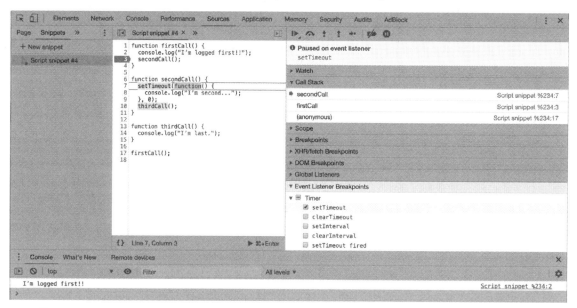

Figure 7.4: Demonstrating the setTimeout() method being assigned to the message queue

Now, let's look at how the **secondCall()** function calls **thirdCall()**. Another new stack frame is pushed onto the call stack for this function invocation. It calls **console.log()** with the **'I'm last."** string, which is printed to the console:

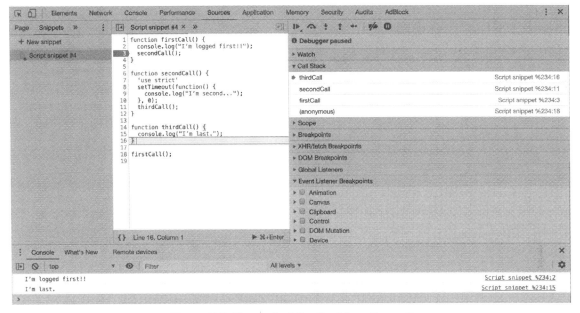

Figure 7.5: The end of the final function call

At this point, **thirdCall()** has no other operations to execute, so it implicitly returns the value **undefined** back to **secondCall()**, and the stack frame for **thirdCall()** is popped off the call stack. Then **secondCall()** returns **undefined** to **firstCall()**, and the stack frame for **secondCall()** is popped off the stack. Next, the stack frame for **firstCall()** is popped off the stack, and **undefined** is returned back to the main process:

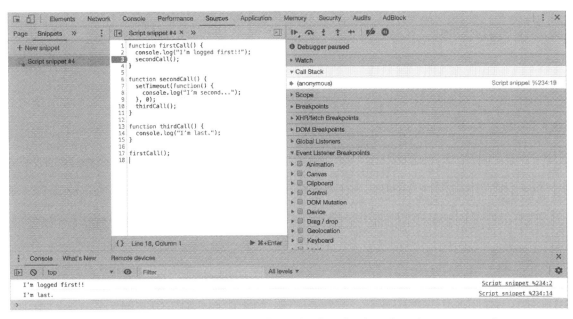

Figure 7.6: Showing the empty call stack after the functions have returned

Now, we can see that the only remaining frame on the call stack is the anonymous main process and that no other functions are being called by the main process. The event loop sees that the call stack is available and that there is a message waiting in the message queue, so it pushes a new stack frame for the callback function referenced in the pending message. This callback function is our remaining `console.log()` call, with the `'I'm second...'`: string:

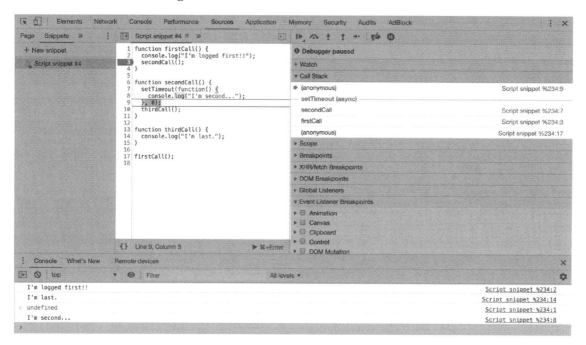

Figure 7.7: Showing the console.log stack frame

The final `console.log` call is executed, with the string being printed to the console, and the stack frame is then popped off the call stack, again leaving only the anonymous main process left on the stack.

This demonstrates how, despite JavaScript being single-threaded, it's possible to continue executing code while a previously invoked function is waiting to be completed. There are many other functions and APIs built into the browser besides `setTimeout`, and we will look at more of these in the next chapter.

Exercise 7.01: Working with the Event Loop

Let's take a look at how we can apply this knowledge to a more realistic (albeit simple) application. The goal of this exercise is to illustrate how the **event** loop can produce some unexpected behavior in our applications and also to see how we can work with the **event** loop to give useful functionality to our apps. Let's get started:

1. We'll have an HTML file with two **\<div\>** elements in the body with IDs of **status** and **result**. The purpose of the application is going to be to run a function and display the result in the **result** div. We know that our function will take a not-insignificant amount of time to run, so we will also incorporate a status feature so as to keep the user aware of what's happening in the application. For this example, our main function will be an arbitrary calculation that takes a few seconds to complete. In real life, this could be any kind of complex calculation, or a function for fetching data from an external source, such as a database or an API. Load the **index.html** file:

```html
<!-- index.html -->
<!DOCTYPE html>
<html>
  <head>
    <script src='event-loop.js'></script>
  </head>
  <body>
    <span id='status'></span>
    <span id='result'></span>
  </body>
</html>
```

2. In a separate JavaScript file, called **event-loop.js**, we'll write a collection of functions to make up our application. First, we're adding an event listener to the window object so that the rest of the code won't run until the DOM's content has loaded (**DOMContentLoaded** is triggered when the browser completes the DOM tree structure, not including any style sheets or images):

```js
// event-loop.js
document.addEventListener('DOMContentLoaded', () => {
```

3. After this, we are assigning our two **\<span\>** elements with the IDs of **status** and **result** to two aptly named variables:

```
let statusSpan = document.getElementById('status');
let resultSpan = document.getElementById('result');
```

4. Next, we are defining two functions, **showStatus()** and **doCalculation()**. The **showStatus()** function takes in an argument of **statusText**, which will be set to the **innerText** property of **statusSpan**, thereby displaying whatever text we pass to **showStatus()** on the page:

```
let showStatus = (statusText) => {
   statusSpan.innerText = statusText;
};
```

5. The other function, **doCalculation()**, runs our calculation and then sets the result to the **innerText** property of the **resultSpan** variable:

```
let doCalculation = () => {
   let result = 0;
   for(var i = 0; i< 10000000000; i++) {
     result = result + i;
   };
   resultSpan.innerText = `The result is ${result}`;
};
});
```

6. So, to join these together, we could call the functions at the end of the **DOMContentLoaded** callback function like this:

```
showStatus('Calculation running, please wait... Maybe for quite a
while...');
doCalculation();
showStatus('Calculation finished, here is the result:');
```

7. Try running this code and see whether it works as we expect. Not very good, is it? When we first open the page, it loads for a while and then displays the **Calculation finished** status and the result. But we never see the **Calculation running** status:

Calculation finished, here is the result: The result is 49999999990067860000

Figure 7.8: The output from the first version of the application

Why is it, then, that don't we get to see the first status? When we update the DOM by doing something such as setting the **innerText** property of a DOM node, the DOM tree itself is updated, and then the browser repaints the render tree to the browser window. These are two separate steps, and the repaint step happens after the current call stack has finished. So, with our new knowledge of the event loop, we should be able to see what's happening. When we call **showStatus()** for the first time, the DOM is updated, but the browser doesn't redraw the page yet. Then, **doCalculation()** is called, and the execution thread is blocked until the calculation has finished. The **showStatus()** function is called a second time with the **Calculation finished** string, and at this point, the browser repaints the render tree with the **Calculation finished** string that we passed to the second call of **showStatus()**.

To get our application to work more in line with our specifications, have a go at this yourself before checking out the solution:

```
showStatus('Calculation running, please wait... Maybe for quite a
while...');
setTimeout(() => {
   doCalculation();
   showStatus('Calculation finished, here is the result:');
},0);
```

By adding the call to **doCalculation()** and the second call to **showStatus()** to a **setTimout()** function, the call stack is emptied after the first **showStatus()** function executes, at which point the browser repaints the page, displaying the **Calculation running** string as expected. This is a much better implementation since it keeps the user informed of what the application is doing:

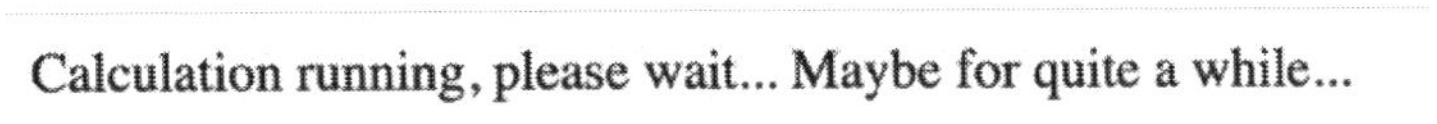

Calculation running, please wait... Maybe for quite a while...

Figure 7.9: Showing the status while the calculation is running

Stack Overflow

The call stack is an example of a data type called – you guessed it – a stack. You can think of a stack simply as a container of objects (stack frames, representing functions and arguments, in the case of a call stack). There's a limit to the number of frames a call stack can hold. We'll now look at what happens when the call stack gets full, a common problem that developers face, and what's known as a stack overflow. (In the V8 JavaScript engine, it has a different name, but the theory is the same.)

This can happen, for example, when developers are trying to write a recursive function but fail to code in a base case and/or a termination condition, at which point the recursion should stop. It can be tricky – especially for new developers – to account for every edge case that may bypass these points.

Let's take a look at a simple example of a stack overflow first, after which we'll explore a more true-to-life example.

Given the following code, let's take a look at what will happen in the JavaScript engine when we call the **callMe()** function:

```
function callMe() {
    nowCallMe();
}


function nowCallMe() {
    callMe();
}
```

It should be fairly obvious what will happen with this code, but still, let's look through a few steps of the process on the call stack.

When we call **callMe()**, a new stack frame is added to the call stack for that invocation:

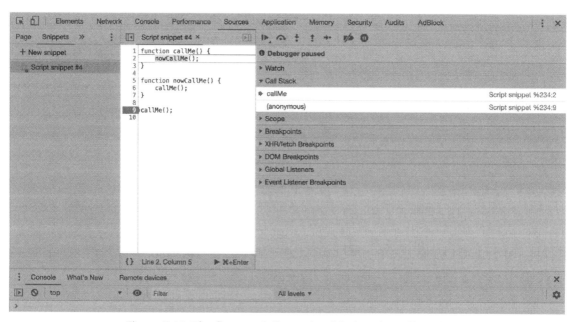

Figure 7.10: The first stack frame is added to the call stack

Inside **callMe()**, the other function, **nowCallMe()**, is called, adding a stack frame for that function invocation to the stack. **nowCallMe()** in turn calls **callMe()**, adding a new stack frame to the call stack, and on and on it goes, with both functions calling each other in turn, and a new stack frame is added to the stack every time. In this scenario, the JavaScript execution thread has nowhere else to go – there is no condition in the code that will cause the thread to move on from this loop:

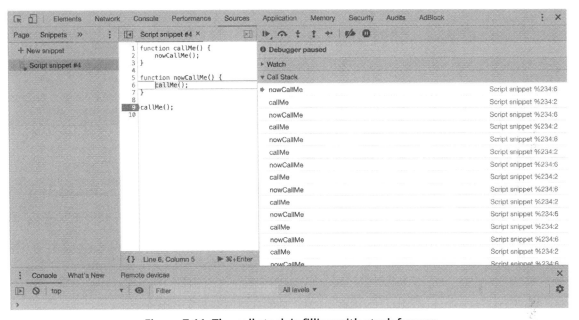

Figure 7.11: The call stack is filling with stack frames

This loop will continue to add stack frames to the call stack until the stack's limit is reached. In the V8 implementation of the JavaScript engine, the limit for the number of frames in the stack is often somewhere around 16,000, although it can be higher or lower, depending on the content of each frame, the variables being used, and other factors. (At the end of this chapter, we'll write a function to calculate the stack limit for different JavaScript engines and environments.) If this limit is exceeded, the engine throws a stack overflow error, referred to by V8 as **Maximum call stack size exceeded**:

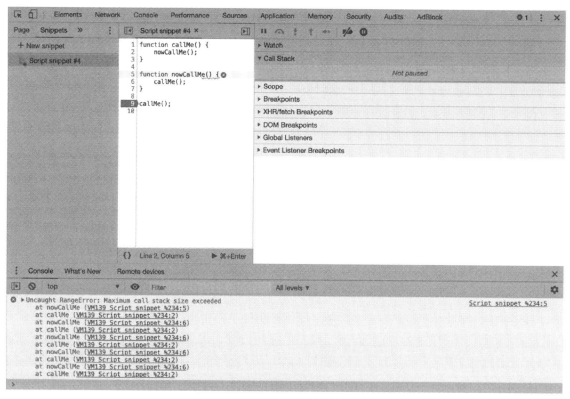

Figure 7.12: Stack overflow error

> **Note**
>
> It's possible to change the call stack size limit in the V8 JavaScript engine. To do so, simply launch the environment – be it Node, Chrome, or another implementation – with the **stack-size=[value]** flag. Bear in mind, though, that this should only be used for debugging or for experimentation – you certainly don't want to write code with the expectation that it will be run with anything other than the default call stack size.

Now, let's take a look at a more real-life example, and later see how we can fix it:

```
function countdownByTwo (num) {
  if (num === 0) return console.log(num);
  console.log(num);
  countdownByTwo (num - 2);
}
```

This function is an example of **recursion**, which we'll look at in more detail later on in this book. It may not be immediately obvious what this function is doing, so let's break it down into steps.

The function takes in a number and calls itself recursively, subtracting 2 from the **num** argument for each call. Let's say we call it with the argument of **10**, like so:

```
countdownByTwo (10);
```

The function first checks to see whether **num** is equal to **0**, and if it is, it will return a console log with the value of **0**, and this function's execution will finish (this line is our termination condition). Right now, **num** is equal to **10**, so this **if** statement is **false**, and the execution proceeds to the next line.

The next line logs the value of **num** to the console and then proceeds to the next line.

Now, the function calls itself again, with the value of **num minus 2** – so **8**, in our case. This continues.

By calling the preceding function with the argument of **10**, we'll see the numbers **10**, **8**, **6**, **4**, **2**, and **0** are logged to the console, as expected.

But what happens if we call the function with an odd number? Try calling the same function with **11** as the input. You'll see that our termination condition of **num=== 0** never occurs since **num** goes from **1** to **-1**.

Exercise 7.02: Stack Overflow

The goal of this exercise is to rewrite the stack overflow function so that it accounts for as many other inputs as it can. Think about all the possible arguments this function could be called with, and how the function will handle each one. Let's get started:

1. Let's go through a few possible inputs to make sure we're accounting for all eventualities, thereby minimizing the risk of an error occurring. Here are some of the edge cases we need to be careful of:

*   The **num** input is odd.

*   The input is 0.

*   This input is less than 0.

*   The input is null or is not of a **number** type.

2. For now, let's assume that we want the function to return whenever the input is not a number or is a negative number, and if it's 0, then we want the function to log 0 to the console and return. Write the function as follows:

```
function countdownByTwo(num) {
   if (typeof num !== 'number' || num< 0) return;
   console.log(num);
   countdownByTwo(num - 2);
}
```

Here, we've added a termination condition using the **typeof** operator to determine whether the input, **num**, is a number as expected. We will return **undefined** if it's not of a **number** type or if it's a number less than **0**. If **num** is a number, and it's greater than or equal to **0**, then the function will log the value of **num** and call itself again with **num −2**, and so the cycle repeats.

3. By making these changes to the function, we are accounting for the initial input of an odd number, which would have bypassed our termination condition in the original function. We're also accounting for inputs where **num** is not of type **number**; say, a string or an object. But there are also some less obvious edge cases we need to be aware of. Let's see what happens when we call a function like this:

```
countdownByTwo('bananas' * 2)
```

It turns out that multiplying **bananas** by **2** doesn't make any sense: JavaScript cannot coerce the result to a numerical value, and therefore it results in a value of **NaN**.

And what does this mean for our function? To answer that question, we need to establish what data type the **NaN** property is. You'd be forgiven for assuming that running **typeof NaN** would return something – anything – other than **number**, but you'd be wrong. As we saw in the previous chapter, **NaN** is a property of the **Number** object and is indeed of the **number** type. This results in yet another stack overflow, with the function logging **NaN** repeatedly until the maximum call stack size is reached.

4. A similar problem would also occur when calling the function with Infinity, so it's clear that we need to add another check in our **isFinite()** function that returns true if its input is a finite and legal number to handle these edge cases:

```
function countdownByTwo(num) {
    if (typeof num !== 'number' || num< 0 || !isFinite(num)) return;
    console.log(num);
    countdownByTwo(num - 2);
}
```

5. This function is used so that we can remove the **typeof** operator check. Now, we have a fairly robust set of termination cases for this function. There may still be other checks we would want to implement, such as limiting the size of the number that the function will count down from. For example, if we wanted to make sure the input is less than **10,000**, we could amend our **if** statement to the following:

```
if (num< 0 || num> 10000 || !isFinite(num)) return;
```

This results in the following output:

Figure 7.13: Outputs from various inputs to countdownByTwo()

In this exercise, we've seen a basic example of how we may inadvertently write code that works poorly with the JavaScript engine, and that we should handle as many different edge cases that our code may be presented with as possible.

So far in this chapter, we've looked at the JavaScript runtime, what it is conceptually, and the processes and components it comprises. We've looked at the JavaScript engine in detail – particularly the V8 implementation – and how its call stack and memory heap interact with the other elements of the runtime.

We've also looked at a common call stack error that developers face, and at the ways, we can ensure our code doesn't reach the maximum call stack size.

Memory Management

We'll now move our attention to another core aspect of a computer's hardware – its memory. Memory management is an important, but often overlooked, aspect of developing software in JavaScript. Memory management simply refers to the allocation, use, and deallocation of system memory for the various data structures that make up our programs.

There are two main approaches that are used by different programming languages to handle memory management: **explicit allocation and deallocation** and **automatic allocation and deallocation**. When writing software in an explicit memory management language, such as C-like languages, it's the software developer's job to tell the compiler when to allocate memory and how much to allocate to the software at any given stage. The developer also has to decide when that memory is no longer needed and explicitly tell the compiler to deallocate it. This increases the workload for the developer and can lead to frustrating bugs being introduced.

Automatic memory management, on the other hand, removes the need for developers to explicitly allocate and deallocate memory, which, for the most part, makes the developer's job easier. The compiler requests memory from the operating system in two main stages: static allocation at compilation time and dynamic allocation at runtime. Modern JavaScript engines use **Just-in-Time compilation**, which makes use of more than one compiler – a baseline compiler – and one or more optimization compilers, which recompile and cache parts of the code so that it's more efficient. This forms a continuous loop of compilation, optimization, and decompilation/recompilation. The result of this is that JavaScript code is compiled and recompiled continuously at runtime, somewhat blurring the static and dynamic memory allocation stages.

The memory allocation step is basically straightforward: the JavaScript engine identifies the amount of memory it needs and requests it from the operating system. Memory is then read from and written to as required by the program. The final stage of memory management, that is, deallocation, is the stage we need to focus on here.

The Garbage Collector

JavaScript engines have an additional application called a garbage collector, which deals with the automatic deallocation of memory at runtime. The garbage collector uses a process called mark-and-sweep to identify objects that are no longer needed and remove them from memory. It does this by starting at a root object – for example, the global window object – and traversing each object that is referenced by the root. It then checks all child and grandchild objects referenced by those objects, and thus maps out all the objects that are reachable from the root. Anything that is cut off from this map, thus being unreachable by the root object, is marked for deletion and subsequently removed from memory:

```
let cat = {
    name: 'Professor Meow"
}
```

Let's look at the following diagram:

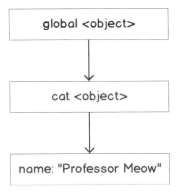

Figure 7.14: References between objects

In this simple case, the root object has a reference to the **cat** object, and the **cat** object has a reference to its **name** property, which is a string with the **Professor Meow** value. The garbage collector will see these references and will mark the **cat** object and its **name** property as reachable, and they will not be collected.

If we now reassign **cat** to **null**, we will have removed the reference chain between the root object and the **name** property of **cat**:

```
cat = null;
```

Let's look at the following diagram:

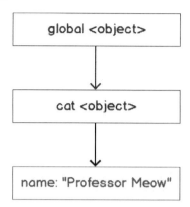

Figure 7.15: The reference is lost, and the memory is freed

The `cat` object remains property of the global object, with a value of `null`, but any properties of `cat` that are not also referenced by another object linked to the root are removed from memory by the garbage collector.

We can expand on this example to show how referencing an object from more than one other object can preserve its place in memory:

```
let mammal = {
   hasTeeth: true,
   furry: true
}

let cat = {
   name: 'Professor Meow",
   class: mammal
}

let dog = {
   name: 'Captain Woof",
   class: mammal
}
```

Let's look at the following diagram:

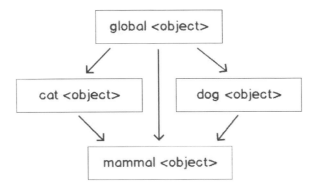

Figure 7.16: Multiple references to the same object

The **cat**, **dog**, and **mammal** objects are all properties of the global object (the **root**, in garbage collector speak), and the **cat** and **dog** objects reference the **mammal** object through their **class** property.

If we now reassign the **mammal** object to **null**, and once again the **cat** object to **null**, the reference from the **global** object to the **mammal** object via the **cat** object will be broken, as will its direct reference. However, since we have another reference to the **mammal** object via the **dog** object, the **mammal** object is still 'reachable" from the **global** object and is not collected by the garbage collector.

You can see that, by inadvertently maintaining object references, you can make a program take up more memory than it needs. This is especially troubling for large datasets.

Memory Leaks

Garbage collection is a handy process for us developers since it reduces the workload that comes with manually managing memory. But it's a double-edged sword; garbage collection happens automatically – we have no way of triggering the garbage collection process, nor do we know when the JavaScript engine will decide to do a garbage collection run – so it's easy for us to forget all about the potential pitfalls of memory management. But garbage collection is not a perfect process, or at least it doesn't always behave as we may expect it to. It will often fail to free up memory which, in actuality, is no longer needed. This is not a bug or mistake in the garbage collection process, it's just a symptom of a problem: the question of whether an object will be needed again later on during execution can only be answered with certainty by the developer.

When a piece of memory is allocated but maintains a link to the root object, even after it's no longer needed in the program, it will never be freed and will remain allocated, thereby taking up system memory until the software's execution ends. This is a memory leak, and it's not hard to imagine that they can become big issues with large objects, or frequent reoccurrences. It's not always obvious when our application is suffering from a memory leak, especially if we're developing our applications on a powerful machine, so it's important to avoid the common mistakes and to keep an eye on our application's memory usage.

Let's look at a few common memory leak scenarios and look at how we can avoid them.

Event Listeners

One of the most common ways in which memory leaks occur comes from event listeners. Consider the following code:

```
document.getElementById('scrollable').addEventListener('scroll',
function() {
  console.log('I've been scrolled!")
})
```

It's quite common to see event listeners being added with an anonymous callback function, and it will work as expected (as long as there is an element with an ID of **scrollable**). However, by using an anonymous function, we are unable to remove the event listener at a later date should we need to, meaning that once this event listener is added, it will remain in place for the entirety of the program's execution, and, depending on the function, could be adding objects to memory every time it's called. To tackle this, let's declare a named function and then pass that function to the event listener:

```
let scrollHandler = function () {
  console.log('I've been scrolled!")
}

document.getElementById('scrollable').addEventListener('click',
scrollHandler)
```

Now that we have the handler function instead of an anonymous function, we can make use of the **removeEventListener** method if we want to remove the event listener later on in our program:

```
document.getElementById('scrollable').removeEventListener('scroll',
scrollHandler)
```

Detached DOM Nodes

Any reference to a DOM node that's made by JavaScript will prevent that node's memory allocation from being freed, even if the node is subsequently removed from the DOM.

For example, let's say we have an array of image sources that we want to add to the DOM. It would make sense to store the parent DOM node in a variable and add the images via this variable reference:

```javascript
let imageParent = document.getElementById('image-wrapper');
imageSources.forEach(imgSrc => {
  let tempImg = document.createElement('img');
  tempImg.src = imgSrc;
  imageParent.appendChild(tempImg);
});
```

So, now, we have all of the images attached to the DOM, but we have also created an additional reference to the image parent element; there is one reference in the DOM tree, and one via the JavaScript variable, that is, **imageParent**. Let's say that, later on in the program, we need to remove the image parent element:

```javascript
document.body.removeChild(imageParent);
```

This would remove the DOM node with the ID of **image-wrapper** from the DOM tree, but the variable, along with all its appended child **img** elements, is still referenced by the **imageParent** variable, and will still occupy memory, never to be collected by the garbage collector.

The simple solution in this situation is to reassign the **imageParent** variable an **undefined** value after removing **imageParent** from the DOM.

Global Variables

Since the mark-and-sweep algorithm looks for all the references connected to the roots of the memory object graph, any variables of the global object (the **window** object, in browser-based JavaScript, or the **global** object, in Node.js), will always be referenced and will therefore never be collected by the garbage collector.

It's good practice to avoid declaring variables on the global object wherever possible, in other words, don't pollute the global namespace. There are a few good reasons for avoiding this, one of which is to avoid the resulting memory leaks.

It's fairly obvious when variables are explicitly declared on the global object, but there are a couple of situations that can lead to unexpected global variables:

```
function makeGlobalCat() {
   cat = 'I'm a cat"
}
makeGlobalCat();
```

This function creates an undeclared variable called `cat` that will implicitly be a property of the **global** object, even though it was created inside the function:

```
function makeGlobalDog() {
   this.dog = 'I'm a dog"
}
makeGlobalDog();
```

Likewise, using the **this** keyword will create a global variable. You can declare a variable with **var**, **let**, or **const** inside a function, and it will have a function-level scope of that function, instead of having global scope, like it would with an undeclared variable. It's also a good idea to use the **use strict** statement at the top of your JavaScript files, which will result in an error being thrown if you try to create an undeclared variable.

Identifying Memory Leaks

Despite our best efforts, memory leaks can creep into our code. They're often not obvious because the amount of memory they consume can be small, and they may grow relatively slowly, meaning they may not impact an application's performance unless they're kept running over many hours or days. And even when you find that you have a memory leak, it can be tricky to find the root cause.

Exercise 7.03: Identifying Memory Leaks

Let's take a simple example and see how Chrome's developer tools can help us identify that we have a memory leak. Let's get started.

1. Open a new tab in Chrome, open **Menu** > **More Tools** > **Developer tools**, and go to the **Sources** tab:

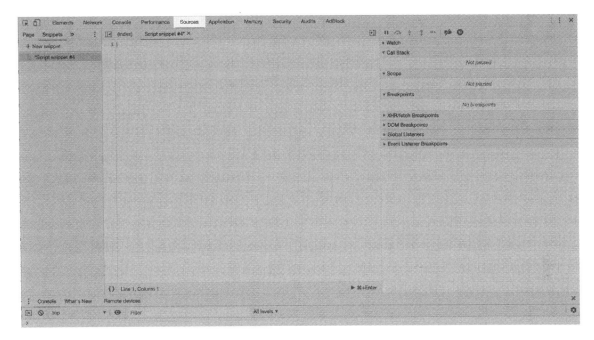

Figure 7.17: An empty code snippet

2. Click '+ New snippet' at the top left of this window and add the following code to set up our memory leak: First of all, we are creating a new DOM element of the div type and assigning it to a variable called imageWrapper:

```
// Create a div element
let imageWrapper = document.createElement('div');
```

> **Note**
>
> Every modern browser has its own set of developer tools. However, for dealing with memory leaks, Chrome's developer tools are the most useful.

3. Next, we declare three functions that simulate some user interaction with our page. The first function, **loadImages()**, creates 50 new image elements and adds a data property to them of a string containing **1,024 b** characters. This is analogous to loading images and adding them to **imageWrapper**:

```
function loadImages() {
   for (let i = 0; I < 50; +i) {
      let img = document.createElement('img');
      img.data = new Array(1024).join('b');
      imageWrapper.appendChild(img);
   } // Add 50 child images to the 'imageWrapper'
}
```

4. The next function, **add()**, simply adds the **imageWrapper** element to the end of the document body, and our third function **remove()** will be used to remove that image wrapper.

```
function add() {
   document.body.appendChild(imageWrapper);
} // Add the 'imageWrapper' div to the end of body

function remove() {
   document.body.removeChild(imageWrapper);
} // Remove the 'imageWrapper' div from the body
```

5. Now, let's write one last function to tie these three together:

```
function process() {
   for (let i=0;i<1000;i++) {
      loadImages();
      add();
      remove();
   }
}
```

6. This last function simulates adding and removing the image wrapper multiple times, thus loading 50 new images to it each time. A real-world example may be that we have a gallery of images and the user is clicking the '**next**" button to load the next set of images (in our scenario, they'd be clicking it 1,000 times!). Clearly, this would be a rather poor implementation of such a feature, but our aim here is to demonstrate how memory leaks can occur in a simple way. Your final code snippet should look something like this:

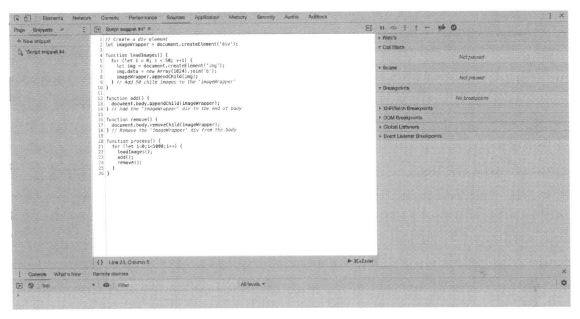

Figure 7.18: Code snippet with all the process() code

7. Now, click the **run snippet** button to execute the code.

8. Next, we will go to the performance tab of the dev tools and have a look at what's happening in the memory heap as we add and remove our images. From the performance tab, click the record button to start recording a performance profile. While it's recording, in the console, call the **process()** function, say, three times, and then hit the **stop** button. You should now see a screen that looks something like this:

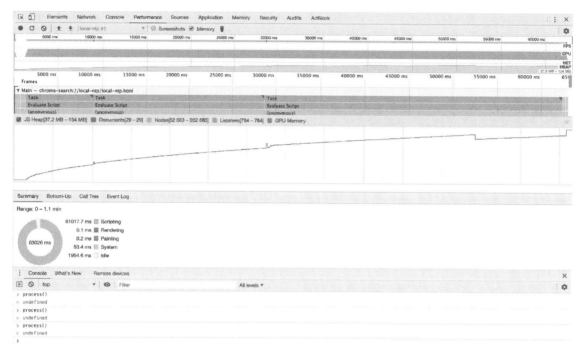

Figure 7.19: Memory heap of the performance tab of the developer tools

This is the performance profile we have just recorded. It can tell us lots of information about the system resources that are being used by our application over the duration of the recording. The blue line here shows us how much of JavaScript's memory heap is being used over time. In an application without memory leaks, we would expect the memory usage to repeatedly go up with memory allocation and back down again to a base level with memory deallocation, giving us a **sawtooth graph**. In our case, though, it's only going in one direction – up. This is a sure sign that we have a memory leak in our code. The garbage collector is unable to determine that the **images** we've loaded are no longer needed after each call of **process()**, and so they stay in the memory heap. If you notice a real-life application becoming less performant over time, or using higher than expected system resources, then this is a good place to come to check for a memory leak.

Exercise 7.04: Fixing the Memory Leak

Now that we've established that we have a memory leak – as shown by the JavaScript memory heap graph in the preceding screenshot – our next task is to fix our code so that it no longer contains the leak. Given what you know of the garbage collector and the reason for our leak, try to implement a fix for the previous code so that the garbage collector can see when our objects are no longer needed. After each function call, record a performance profile to see whether the garbage collector is able to free up the memory. What you're looking for is that the blue heap-memory allocation line goes up with memory allocation, but then comes back down again at regular intervals, showing that the memory is being deallocated. This is a sign of a garbage collector being able to deallocate the memory after each execution of the **process()** function. Let's get started:

1. Write a function and add it to the existing three functions that are called in the **process**:

```
function resetImageWrapper() {
    imageWrapper = document.createElement('div');
}
```

Here, we've added one more function that is called **resetImageWrapper()**, which resets the **imageWrapper** object to an empty **div** element and added the function to our **process()** function's **for…loop**. Now, each time a set of images is removed from the DOM, its reference in JavaScript is also removed, and it can be marked by the garbage collector for deletion.

2. The next step is to call this new function each time we process our images, so we will add it to our main **process()** function:

```
function process() {
    for (let i = 0; i< 1000; i++) {
        loadImages();
        add();
        remove();
        resetImageWrapper();
    }
}
```

3. Once again, we'll run the performance profiler. Go to the dev tools, then to the **Performance** tab, and click the record button to begin a performance profile recording. Then, call the **process()** function a few times and take a look at the memory heap usage:

Figure 7.20: Memory heap usage

> **Note**
>
> As you probably noticed, the problem with our code was that we were storing references to each image element, and, therefore, the contents of its data attribute, inside the **imageWrapper** variable. The simple solution to this problem is to reassign the **imageWrapper** variable each time we remove it from the DOM.

This is a much healthier memory heap profile. After each of the three **process()** function calls, the garbage collector could see that the images were no longer referenced by either the DOM or by JavaScript, and the space they were allocated in memory was freed up and given back to the memory pool.

In this section, we've covered the two main techniques for dealing with memory management in different programming languages – manual and automatic – and looked at the browser's garbage collector processes. We then looked at the major con of automatic memory management and modern browsers' garbage collection algorithms, namely memory leaks, in more detail. Finally, we had an overview of one of the techniques we can use to identify when our application has such a leak.

Activity 7.01: Finding out the Number of Stack Frames

Earlier in this chapter, we learned about JavaScript's call stack and saw that it's possible to generate an error if too many stack frames are added to the stack. Each implementation of a JavaScript engine can have a different limit regarding the size of the stack. In this activity, we'll write a function that will tell us when the maximum number of stack frames has been reached in the stack before the stack overflow error is triggered.

The high-level steps for the activity are as follows:

1. Add a function that calls itself repeatedly, causing the stack overflow.

2. Keep count of the number of times the function calls itself. (This is like counting the number of stack frames getting pushed to the call stack.)

3. Display the final number after the stack overflow error has occurred. Remember that no new functions can be called after a stack overflow error!

   The output of this activity will be as follows:

Figure 7.21: Showing the number of stack frames pushed before a stack overflow was triggered

> **Note**
>
> The solution to this activity can be found on page 731.

Summary

In this chapter, we have seen how the blocks of code many people think of as just 'JavaScript" can actually be broken down into separate components: the JavaScript engine, consisting of the call stack, memory heap, and the garbage collector (as well as other important components not covered by this chapter); and the JavaScript runtime environment, such as a browser, or Node.js, which contains the JavaScript engine, and gives the engine access to additional functions and interfaces, such as `setTimeout()` or a filesystem interface.

We also looked at how JavaScript manages memory allocation and deallocation, and how even though it is managed automatically, it's important for developers to bear the processes involved in mind in order to write code that enables the garbage collector to work correctly.

In the next chapter, we will look at different aspects of the environment API in more detail so that we can learn about some of the less commonly used features we can find in the browser and in Node.js.

8

Browser APIs

Overview

By the end of this chapter, you will be able to explain what a web/browser API is; draw in HTML using JavaScript; create and control audio in the browser; store data in the browser; decide on the type of storage to use in different circumstances; measure and track a website's performance; and create and manage a sustained, two-way connection between the browser and server.

In this chapter, you will learn about interesting browser APIs and look at JavaScript's extended capabilities.

Introduction

In the previous chapter, we looked at the different examples of JavaScript runtime environments and had an overview of their components. We'll now look at one of those components in greater depth, that is, the **Browser Object Model (BOM)**, and the APIs it exposes to JavaScript.

The BOM is a set of properties and methods that are made available to JavaScript by the browser. Now, you've come across many parts of the BOM already, with methods such as **setTimeout()**, and the document property, with its many methods, such as **addEventListener()**. It's a subtle but important point that the methods and properties we'll cover in this chapter are not part of the JavaScript programming language; that is to say, they're not part of the ECMAScript specification – the specification to which JavaScript engines are built – but they are methods and properties of the browser, and they form the interface between JavaScript and the browser (and by extension, between JavaScript and the rest of the system it's being run on).

In the same way that every browser has its own implementation of the JavaScript engine, each browser implements the BOM in a slightly different way. So, it's important to check cross-browser compatibility for the features you want to use as a developer and implement **fallbacks** or **polyfills** for browsers that don't support certain features. It's often the case that the current version of a particular browser supports a certain functionality, but older versions do not.

As we've already mentioned, you've seen many of the more commonly used methods of the BOM. Here, we will look at some of the most commonly used and useful browser APIs in more detail, as well as some less frequently used yet powerful aspects of the BOM that will greatly increase the number and functionality of tools at your disposal, and which can allow you to build some super cool and possibly even useful features into your sites and apps.

Canvas

Images and diagrams are a fundamental part of creating engaging websites and applications. We already know how to include images and videos in our pages, but we can also draw our own images, diagrams, and even complex visuals such as charts or game elements by using JavaScript and the **Canvas API**. The Canvas API allows us to draw graphics programmatically inside an HTML **<canvas>** element using JavaScript. With it, we can draw paths and rectangles, and control things such as stroke and fill color, line dashes, and arc radiuses (or radii, if that's your flavor).

The process of drawing inside an HTML canvas using JavaScript can be broken down into a few distinct steps:

- Get a reference to the HTML's canvas element.

- Get a new canvas rendering context that the graphic is drawn onto.

- Set various drawing styles and options as required (for example, line width and fill color).

- Define the paths that will make up the graphics.

- "Stroke" or fill the defined paths and shapes – this is the step where the actual drawing takes place.

In the following exercise, we will start by using the **fillRect()** method. This method is one of the methods we can use for drawing on the canvas and, as its name suggests, draws a rectangle and fills it with color. To describe the rectangle, we require four pieces of information: the **x** and **y** coordinates of the top-left corner, the rectangle's width, and its height. Therefore, the parameters we will pass to **fillRect()** are an **x** coordinate, a **y** coordinate, the width, and the height.

Exercise 8.01: Drawing Shapes Using Canvas Elements

Let's get started with an exercise in which we'll learn how to work with a Canvas element, some of the components that make up the API, and how we can use it to draw simple shapes. The Canvas API has many methods and interfaces. In this exercise, we'll look at a few of the most commonly used ones. Let's get started:

1. Create an HTML file called **index.html** with a **<canvas>** element and a reference to a JavaScript file in the HTML body in the **DevTools** console. We'll call the JavaScript file **canvas.js**:

```
<!-- index.html -->
<!DOCTYPE html>
<html>
  <head>
  </head>
  <body>
    <canvas id='canvas' style="border: 1px solid"></canvas>
    <script src='canvas.js'></script>
  </body>
</html>
```

We've given the canvas element an ID of **'canvas'** so that we can select it easily in JavaScript, and an inline style of **"border: 1px solid"** so that we can see the area that the canvas takes up on the HTML page.

2. Next, we'll create our **canvas.js** file in the same directory as **index.html** and declare a variable that will hold a reference to our HTML canvas element:

```
// canvas.js
let canvas = document.getElementById('canvas');
```

3. Now, we'll create a rendering context by calling the **getContext()** method with the **'2d'** parameter since we will be drawing 2D graphics. This method takes in a string to denote the context type and returns a drawing context that's used to draw and modify the graphics we want to display. There are several types of context, but for this introduction to Canvas, we will be looking only at **'2d'** contexts:

```
let context = canvas.getContext('2d');
```

Now that we have the context, we can start drawing. The canvas object works on a grid system, with its origin in the top left, so that the **0,0** coordinates are at the top left of the canvas. It's from this origin that we can draw our graphics.

4. Finally, we'll use the **fillRect()** method to draw a **100** by **100** pixel rectangle on the canvas:

```
context.fillRect(10,10, 100, 100);
```

Now, open the HTML file in your browser. You should see something like this:

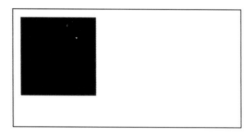

Figure 8.1: Simple canvas with a square inside

5. You've probably already noticed that the canvas element is fairly small. By default, a canvas is **300** by **150** pixels, so let's add a couple of lines to our JavaScript so that the canvas' dimensions match the size of our window when we load the HTML page. We'll use the window object's **innerWidth** and **innerHeight** properties – which tell us the viewport's width and height – to set the canvas' width and height:

```
// canvas.js
let canvas = document.getElementById('canvas');
canvas.width = window.innerWidth;
canvas.height = window.innerHeight;
let context = canvas.getContext('2d');
context.fillRect(10,10, 100, 100);
```

6. Now that we have a much larger canvas (assuming your browser window is bigger than **300** x **150** pixels), we can start to play around with this and other drawing methods. Let's add a few more rectangles but mix things up a bit:

canvas.js

```
let canvas = document.getElementById('canvas');
canvas.width = window.innerWidth;
canvas.height = window.innerHeight;
let context = canvas.getContext('2d');
context.fillStyle = 'yellow';
context.fillRect(10,10,200,200);
context.fillStyle = 'black';
context.strokeRect(230, 10, 200, 200);
context.setLineDash([10]);
context.strokeRect(450, 10, 200, 200);
context.setLineDash([0]);
context.strokeStyle = 'red';
context.strokeRect(10, 230, 200, 200);
context.fillRect(450, 230, 200, 200);
context.clearRect(500, 280, 100, 100);
```

7. We should now have five new rectangles that look something like this (there's actually six if you include **clearRect()** inside the filled black rectangle at the end):

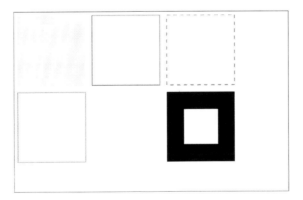

Figure 8.2: Six more rectangles

In this exercise, we learned how to draw all formats of rectangles using the `canvas` element.

The additional lines of code in the exercise are pretty self-explanatory, but there are still a few things to point out:

- The `fillStyle` and `strokeStyle` properties can take any valid CSS color value (hexadecimal, RBG, RGBA, HSL, HSLA, or named color).

- The `setLineDash` property takes an array of numbers that determine the distances of drawn lines and spaces. The list is repeated, so if you pass [5], the lines and spaces will repeat at 5 pixels in length each. If you pass [5, 15], then all the lines will be 5 pixels, and all the spaces will be 15 pixels.

- Once set, `fillStyle`, `strokeStyle`, and `setLineDashvalues` persist for anything drawn in the same context, so you need to make sure that you reset the value if you need to, as we have with the `setLineDash` property (otherwise the red rectangle will be dashed) and `fillStyle`.

- The `clearRect` method can be used to remove a drawn area from another part of the canvas.

Manipulate Shapes Using Path

Now that we've mastered drawing rectangles, we'll start drawing more interesting shapes with paths using some of the other methods available on the context object. A path is a list of points that are joined by lines. We can manipulate the properties of these paths, such as their curvature, color, and thickness. This time, we'll go through the methods first, and then see them in action:

- `beginPath()`: Starts a new path list
- `moveTo(x,y)`: Sets the point at which the next path will be drawn from
- `lineTo(x,y)`: Creates a line from the current point to the coordinates passed to the method
- `closePath()`: Creates a line from the most recent point to the first point, thereby closing off the shape
- `stroke()`: Draws the shape that's been described
- `fill()`: Fills in the described shape with a solid color

These methods can be used to draw a big triangle that takes up most of the canvas' width and height. You can replace the previous code in canvas.js with the following, or create a new JavaScript file and change the **<script>** tag's source attribute in the HTML file to reflect the new JavaScript file:

canvas-1.js

```
let canvas = document.getElementById('canvas');
const width = window.innerWidth;
const height = window.innerHeight;
canvas.width = width
canvas.height = height
let context = canvas.getContext('2d');
context.beginPath();
context.moveTo(50, 50);
context.lineTo(width - 50, 50);
context.lineTo(width / 2, height - 50);
context.closePath();
context.stroke();
```

First of all, we assigned the window's innerWidth and innerHeight values to a variable because we'll be using them more than once. After getting a reference to the canvas object, we begin a new path and move our starting point to **50** pixels on both axes. Next, we plot a line from our current point to a point **50** pixels less than the innerWidth, and **50** pixels from the top. Then, we plot a line to a point half the innerWidth, and **50** pixels from the bottom. The final two methods are used to close the path and draw the entire shape with the **stroke()** method.

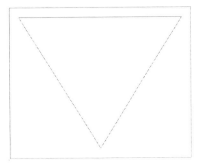

Figure 8.3: A triangle

The steps to create a fractal pattern are fairly straightforward, but here are some pointers to keep in mind:

- The starting point should be the middle of the **canvas** element.

- The line is drawn in one of four directions.

- The line drawing part of the function should repeat as long as the point is within the bounds of the canvas.

- In the preceding example, the lines increase in length after every two plots of a line. You can, however, get a similar result by increasing the line length on every line.

Activity 8.01: Creating a Simple Fractal

We're now going to put what we've learned about HTML Canvas into practice. This time, we'll be using JavaScript to repeat the drawing steps to create a very **simple fractal**. Have a go at creating a pattern like this:

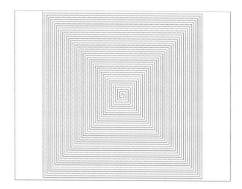

Figure 8.4: A basic pattern

Follow these steps to create a fractal:

1. Initialize a variable with coordinates for a starting point in the middle of the canvas.

2. Create a loop. For every iteration of the loop, alternate between increasing and decreasing the coordinates and drawing the line:

- Increase or decrease the coordinate values to move the point outward in a spiral

- Draw a line from the previous point to the new one

3. End the loop when the point reaches any edge of the canvas.

Spend some time trying to do this on your own before checking the solution.

> **Note**
>
> The solution to this activity can be found on page 732.

For now, we'll move on to another web API: the Web Audio API.

Web Audio API

This API provides a set of methods and objects that we can use to add audio to HTML from a variety of sources, even allowing developers to create new sounds from scratch. The API is feature-rich and supports effects such as panning, low-pass filters, and many others that can be combined to create different kinds of audio applications.

Like the Canvas API, the **Audio API** starts with an audio context, and then multiple audio nodes are created within the context to form an audio processing graph:

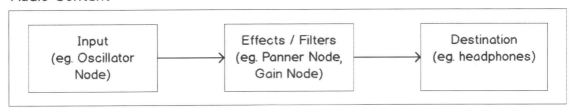

Figure 8.5. The audio context and its audio processing graph

An **audio node** can be a source, a destination, or an audio processor, such as a filter or a gain node, and they can be combined to create the desired audio output, which can then be passed to the user's speakers or headphones.

Exercise 8.02: Creating an Oscillator Waveform

In this exercise, we will see how we can create **a simple oscillator waveform** in JavaScript and output it to the system's audio output device. Let's get started:

1. Let's start by creating an audio context and adding a volume and oscillator node. Type or copy and paste the following code into the console window of Google Chrome's Developer Tools (accessible using the F12 key):

```
// create the audio context
let context = new AudioContext();
// create a gain node
let gain = context.createGain();
// connect the gain node to the context destination
gain.connect(context.destination);
// create an oscillator node
let osci = context.createOscillator();
```

2. Now, we'll set the oscillator type to **'sawtooth'** and set the frequency of oscillation to **100**. Instead of **'sawtooth'**, you can set the oscillator type to **'sine'**, **'square'**, or **'triangle'**. Feel free to experiment with the frequencies as well:

```
// set the oscillation type
osci.type = 'sawtooth';
// set the oscillation frequency
osci.frequency.value = 100;
```

> **Note**
>
> The frequency of a waveform refers to how often the waveform completes one cycle or period, with **1 Hertz** (1 Hz) being 1 cycle per second. We perceive higher frequency sound waves as being higher pitched.

3. Finally, we'll connect the oscillator to the gain node and call the oscillator's **start()** method:

```
// connect the oscillator node to the gain node
osci.connect(gain);
// start the oscillation node playing
osci.start();
```

If you run this code with the volume up, you should hear a continuous oscillating sound (the sound is similar to the static noise you hear on the radio when the channel you want cannot be found). Some browsers will not play a sound with the Audio API until the user has interacted in some way with the screen. This is to stop developers from making annoying pages that play unwanted sounds. If you encounter an error, just click somewhere on the screen before running the code.

We can add multiple source nodes, either of the same type (an oscillator, in our example) or of different types, and they can each be controlled separately, or share other audio nodes such as gain or pan nodes. Of course, we can also make our audio contexts respond to some external input, such as user inputs or time events.

Activity 8.02: Playing Sound and Controlling Frequency Using Two Oscillators

Let's make better use of the audio API by adding some interactivity. In this activity, we will have two oscillators playing a sound, and the user will be able to control their frequencies by moving their cursor around on an HTML page. One oscillator's frequency will be controlled by the cursor's **x** position, with the frequency increasing as the cursor moves toward the right of the page, and the other oscillator's frequency is controlled by the **y** position, with the frequency increasing as the cursor moves toward the bottom of the page.

Before checking the solution, see if you can achieve this goal; it'll be good practice for the activity at the end of this chapter.

Some points to get you started:

- The two oscillators should be in the same context and be connected to the same volume node.

- There are four preset oscillator types available to the oscillator node interface: `'sine'` (default), `'square'`, `'sawtooth'`, and `'triangle'`. Both our oscillators can have different types, so play around with them.

The high-level steps for the activity are as follows:

1. Initialize an audio context and a volume node.

2. Create a gain node and connect it to the context's destination.

3. Initialize two oscillators (one for each coordinate of the cursor).

4. Set the oscillator types, connect them to the gain node, and call their **start()** methods.

5. Create an **event listener** that listens for the **mousemove** event on the **document**.

6. Set the oscillators' frequencies based on the cursor's position.

> **Note**
>
> The solution to this activity can be found on page 733.

Before we move on to the next web API, here's some information on how we can extract data from a currently playing sound and use it to visualize that sound in our app.

Audio Visualization

Audio visualization is a graphical representation of a sound. It's common to see this in an audio program, and it can produce very interesting patterns and shapes. Web audio has many kinds of audio nodes. One that opens up a lot of possibilities for audio visualization is the analyzer node, which gives you access to the waveform and frequency data of its audio input. Unless you're a sound technician, the inner workings of the node are quite arcane, so we'll just get straight into how we access the data. There is one additional property and one method we'll use to get some data that is useful for visualization:

*   **frequencyBinCount**: This essentially tells us how many data points we have available to us for our data visualizations.

*   **getFloatTimeDomainData()**: This method takes in a **Float32Array** as a parameter and copies the current waveform data to it. (A Float32Array is a special kind of array that takes in 32-bit floating-point numbers. The array represents the waveform when broken up into however many items there are in the array. Each item represents the amplitude of that part of the waveform, from –1 to 1).

If we have, for example, an oscillator node, we can create an analyzer node, connect it to the oscillator, and use the preceding two properties to get the waveform data for the sound that's playing at that precise moment:

```
let oscillator = audioContect.createOscillator(); // create the oscillator
let analyser = audioContect.createAnalyser(); // create the analyser node
oscillator.connect(analyser); // connect the oscillator and the analyser
oscillator.start(); // start the oscillator playing
let waveform = new Float32Array(analyser.frequencyBinCount);
```

```
// create a Float32Array which will hold the waveform data in the next
step

analyser.getFloatTimeDomainData(waveform); // get the waveform data for
the sounds at this precise moment.
```

The **getFloatTimeDomainData** function would be called every frame when creating an audio visualization. The information in this subsection will be useful for the activity at the end of this chapter, so refer back to it then.

Web Storage API

Storing data in the browser can be a great way of improving the user's experience. It can save the user having to wait while the same data is fetched from the server, and it can be used to instantly bring a previously visited page back to the state it was left in, meaning, for example, that the user doesn't have to refill in the same parts of a form. The **Web Storage API** is used to store data in the browser in the form of key/value pairs. It can be used to store data that a user has entered into a form to allow them to easily come back to it and complete it later, or it could be preferences a user has chosen in the web app, data that you want to pass from one page to another within the same origin, or any other piece of data that you think would be useful to store. The Web Storage API is synchronous, so setting and retrieving data will block other JavaScript code until the web storage methods have completed. Web storage is intended for storing relatively small amounts of data, in which case being synchronous won't have a noticeable effect on performance.

You've probably heard of cookies as being an example of data storage within a browser. Web storage is somewhat similar to cookies, although their respective use cases are different: cookies are meant for sending data to the server, whereas web storage is designed for storage on the client-side only. Also, web storage allows for much more data to be stored – typically, web storage has a limit of **10 MB** (although, like with so much in the world of web development, this depends entirely on the browser in question), while cookies are limited to **4 KB**. Another key difference is that cookies must either have an expiration date set, or they will expire at the end of the session, while on the other hand, one kind of web storage is only removed via JavaScript, or by clearing the browser's cache.

The Web Storage API is very simple, but before we get into that, let's look at the two variants of web storage and cover some other key points about the interface.

There are two kinds of web storage available through the API: **sessionStorage** and **localStorage**. The main difference between these two is that **sessionStorage** will only persist for as long as the current session is active; that is to say until the browser window is closed. **localStorage**, on the other hand, has no expiration date and will live on the client machine until cleared, either via JavaScript or by clearing the browser's cache. Both **sessionStorage** and **localStorage** work on the same origin principle, meaning that data that's stored by a particular domain is only available to that domain.

The methods that are available to both **sessionStorage** and **localStorage** are the same, and the API is very simple to use. There are five methods at our disposal, but only three or four are commonly used:

- The **setItem()** method is how we store a key/value pair in web storage. It takes two parameters, both of the string type. The first is the item's key, while the second is its value:

```
// Sets key 'dog' with value 'woof'
sessionStorage.setItem('dog', 'woof');
```

- The **getItem()** method allows us to get any item set in the store. It takes a single parameter, that is, the key of the item we want to retrieve. If an item of the supplied key doesn't exist in the store, then it will return null:

```
sessionStorge.getItem('dog');
// gets the value of key 'dog'
```

- The **removeItem()** method takes one parameter, that is, the key of the item you wish to remove:

```
sessionStorage.removeItem('dog');
// removes the key 'dog' and its value
```

- The **clear()** method clears the whole storage for the current page's origin and takes no parameters:

```
sessionStorage.clear();
// clears all sessionStorage for the current origin
```

- The **key()** method takes an index as its parameter and returns the key of the items at that index, or **null** if no item exists for the index:

```
sessionStorage.key(0);
// returns the key of item at index 0 (if any)
```

There are also the **sessionStorage.length** and **localStorage.length** properties, which return the number of items stored in the browser storage object.

Web storage objects behave much like JavaScript objects in that we can access their properties through dot notation as well as by using the **setItem** and **getItem** methods:

```
sessionStorage.planet = 'Mars';
// sets an item with the key 'planet'
sessionStorage.planet;
// returns the string 'Mars'
```

An important point to note is that the value of an item must be a primitive data type, but that doesn't mean we can't store more complicated objects using web storage. If we want to store an object in web storage, we can stringify it using the JSON object **obj** when we set it, and then parse it when we want to retrieve it again:

```
let obj = {
  name: 'Japan',
  continent: 'Asia'
};
sessionStorage.setItem('country', JSON.stringify(obj));
```

We can then combine **sessionStorage.getItem()** with **JSON.parse()** to retrieve the object:

```
JSON.parse(sessionStorage.getItem('country'));
// Outputs the country object 'obj' defined above.
```

Exercise 8.03: Storing and Populating Name Using the localStorage API

Let's make a simple web page that takes some user information and stores it using the **localStorageAPI** so that it will be displayed when the user visits the page next. Browser support for web storage is very strong these days. Still, it's important to account for the possibility that web storage is not supported, so make sure to warn the user in case web storage is unsupported in their browser. In this exercise, let's ask the user for their first name and last name. Let's get started:

1. First of all, let's create an HTML file with standard boilerplate HTML, and add a couple of input boxes for the user's first and last name, along with a warning message in case the browser doesn't support web storage. We'll set the **<p>** tags' display style to none by default:

```
<!-- index.html -->
<!DOCTYPE html>
<html>
  <head>
```

```
    </head>
    <body>
      <input type="text" id='first-name' placeholder='First name'>
      <input type="text" id='last-name' placeholder='Last name'>
      <p style='display: none;' id='warning'>Your browser doesn't
support local storage</p>
      <script src='storage.js'></script>
    </body>
</html>
```

If you open this HTML file in the browser, it will look like this:

| Fist name | Last name |

Figure 8.6. The HTML page with two input boxes

2. Next, we'll create a JavaScript file, starting off with a check to see whether the **localStorage** method is available on the window object. If it's not available, we simply return and set the warning message to display block, thus alerting the user that there will be reduced functionality on the page:

```
// storage.js
if (!window.localStorage) {
    // if localStorage is not supported then display the warning and
return out to stop the rest of the code from being run.
    document.getElementById('warning').style.display = 'block';
} else {
```

3. If the browser does support localStorage, we'll proceed to assigning any values for the **firstName** and **lastName** keys that are currently held in **localStorage** to variables of the same name:

```
    let firstName = localStorage.getItem('firstName');
    let lastName = localStorage.getItem('lastName');
```

4. Then, we'll grab the two input elements, and if **firstName** or **lastName** have a value, then that value is set as the respective text input's value, thereby populating any string saved in **localStorage** back into the relevant text input:

```
    let inputFName = document.getElementById('first-name');
    let inputLName = document.getElementById('last-name');
    if (firstName) {
      inputFName.value = firstName;
    }
```

```
    if (lastName) {
        inputLName.value = lastName;
    }
```

5. The final thing we need to do is add an event listener to the two text inputs and store their current values in **localStorage** each time the input event is fired:

```
    inputFName.addEventListener('input', event => {
        localStorage.setItem('firstName', event.target.value);
    });
    inputLName.addEventListener('input', event => {
        localStorage.setItem('lastName', event.target.value);
    });
}
```

The error output will be displayed as follows:

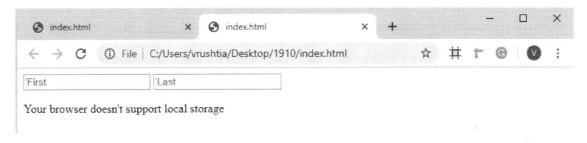

Figure 8.7: Output error

The output is displayed as follows, with the two names stored:

Figure 8.8: The HTML page with two input variables stored and populated

This completes our simple application. Assuming `localStorage` is supported, any string that's entered into either of the text inputs will be saved and repopulated, even after the page is refreshed or the browser or tab is closed.

> **Note**
>
> Here, our method of feature detection is not robust, and it will not detect, for example, when the feature has been disabled in the browser. A better approach for production code is to attempt to set and get an item in `localStorage`. If the get value is as expected, then we know that local storage is working.

While the web storage API is extremely useful for storing relatively small amounts of data, it's not well suited for storing larger files or data structures. Firstly, we can only store string values in web storage, and more importantly, since the API is synchronous, an application would take a performance hit if it were storing and retrieving large amounts of data.

In cases where we want the client to store large datasets, files, or blobs, we can make use of anther browser API: the `IndexedDB` API.

IndexedDB

IndexedDB is another form of client-side data storage that differs from web storage in some important ways:

- Unlike web storage, it is well suited to storing large amounts of data, and for storing many different data types.

- The API has much greater functionality than the web storage API, allowing us to do things such as perform queries against indexed data.

- It's an asynchronous API, so working with data stored in indexedDB won't block the execution of other code.

These last two points hint at the biggest drawback with using indexedDB over web storage: its API and workflow are more complex than the simple get and set methods we use for web storage. IndexedDB is often criticized for having an overly complex API, but it's necessary to ensure data integrity (more on that soon), and anyway, if we take the time to understand some core concepts, then we'll see that it's actually not that complex after all.

Like web storage, indexedDB follows the same origin rule, meaning that only pages at the same domain, protocol, and port can access a particular instance of indexedDB. Before we start working with indexedDB, let's examine some of its components and core concepts.

An indexedDB database comprises one or more **object stores**. An object store, as its name suggests, is a container for the objects we are storing in the database. Like web storage, objects in indexedDB are stored as key/value pairs, but unlike web storage, the value doesn't need to be of the string type. The value could be any JavaScript data type, or even blobs or files.

These objects are typically all of the same type, but they do not need to have the exact same structure as each other, as you may expect with traditional databases. For example, let's say we're storing data on employees. Two objects in the object store may have the salary property, but one's value could be 30,000 and the other could be thirty thousand.

Object stores can be linked to indexes (which are actually just a different kind of object store). These indexes are used to efficiently query the data we store in the database. The indexes are maintained automatically. We'll look at how we can use them in more detail shortly:

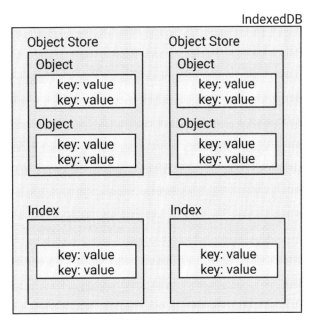

Figure 8.9: Layout of indexedDB

With indexedDB, all of our **Create, Read, Update, and Delete (CRUD)** operations are performed inside of a **transaction**, which we'll look at in detail soon. Working inside of a transaction can seem like a convoluted way of doing things, but it's an effective way of preventing write operations happening on the same record at the same time. Consider two pages open on the same page, both of which are trying to update the same record. When a transaction is open on one page, the other is unable to perform operations on the same record.

The process of working with indexedDB can be broken down into four steps:

1. Open the database.

2. Create an object store if the required store doesn't exist yet.

3. Process the transaction: create, read, update, or delete a record or records.

4. Close the transaction.

Exercise 8.04: Creating an Object Store and Adding Data

Let's create a database that will hold records of animals. We'll go through the preceding steps in more detail to create a database, create an object store, start a transaction, and add some data to the database. Add the code that follows into the console of the Google Chrome developer tools:

1. We'll initialize a variable called request with the **indexedDB.open()** method and pass the database name **animals** and the database version number **1** as parameters. It returns a request object, which in turn will receive one of three events: **success**, **error**, or **upgradeneeded**:

```
let request = window.indexedDB.open('animals', 1);
```

When we call open for the first time, the **upgradeneeded** event is triggered, and we can attach an **onupgradeneeded** event handler function, in which we will define our object store.

2. Then, we'll define a function to handle the **onupgradeneeded** event, assign the database at **event.target.results** in a **db** variable, and create a **'mammals'** object store:

```
request.onupgradeneeded = event => { // handle the upgradeneeded event
  let db = event.target.result;
  db.createObjectStore('mammals', {
    keyPath: 'species'
  });
};
```

Notice that we pass a second parameter, **1**, to the open method. This is the database's version number, which we can change to allow changes to object stores, or to add new object stores. We'll see how this works later.

The database itself is accessible at the request object's result property. We can access it either through the event object at event.target, or through the request object (the event target is the request object).

We then use the **createObjectStore()** method of the database to create a new store. We pass this method a name, which can be any string, but which should typically describe what kind of data is being stored. We also pass in an object, with a key of keypath and a value of the key we want to use to address the objects we store, and for accessing the objects stored.

3. Now that we've created our database, we can go ahead and insert some objects. This time, when we call the open method of the indexedDB object -- assuming there are no errors -- the success event will be triggered, and we access the database and proceed with the transaction. Let's run through what we are doing with the **onsuccess** handler. Assign the database to a **db** variable again and handle the errors that may occur (for now, we'll just log them to the console):

```
request.onsuccess = event => {
  let db = event.target.result;
  db.onerror = error => {
    console.log(error);
  }
}
```

4. Create a transaction with the **storeName** property of **'mammals'** and the type of **'readwrite'**. This limits the transaction to only be able to perform read/write operations to the **'mammals'** object store:

```
let transaction= db.transaction('mammals', 'readwrite');
```

5. Next, we assign the object store to the store variable and add two records to the store:

```
let store = transaction.objectStore('mammals');
store.put({
  species: "Canis lupus",
  commonName: "Wolf",
  traits: ["Furry", "Likes to howl at moon"]
});
store.put({
  species: "Nycticebuscoucang",
```

```
    commonName: "Slow Loris",
    traits: ["Furry", "Every day is Sunday"]
  });
```

6. Then, we define the action that should happen when the transaction receives the **'complete'** event, which is to close the database, thereby completing our transaction:

```
transaction.oncomplete = () => {
  db.close();
};
};
```

7. After running this code, and assuming there were no errors, you can open Chrome's developer tools, navigate to the **Application** tab, and expand the IndexedDB storage item on the left-hand side. In here, you'll see your newly created **animals** database, containing its mammals object store, and the two entries we added previously:

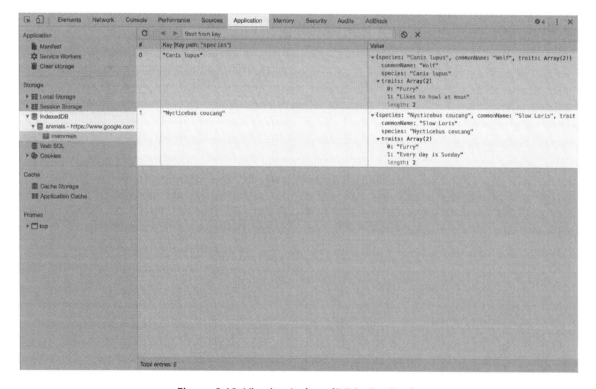

Figure 8.10: Viewing IndexedDB in DevTools

8. Now that you've saved some data in the database, let's learn how to retrieve it again. The process of retrieving data follows a similar pattern to storing it in the first place. When we created the object store, we set the **keyPath** to species as we know this will be a unique property. We can use this property to access a particular entry in the object store:

`indexedDB-v2.js`

```
1  let request = window.indexedDB.open('animals', 1);
2
3  request.onsuccess = event => {
4    let db = event.target.result;
5    db.onerror = error => {
6      // handle an error
7      console.log(error);
8    }
9    let trx = db.transaction('mammals', 'readonly');
10   let store = trx.objectStore('mammals');
11   let animalReq = store.get('Nycticebuscoucang');
12   animalReq.onsuccess = (event) => {
13     console.log(event.target.result);
14   };
```

The full code is available at: https://packt.live/2q8v5bX

9. Like we did previously, we must initiate a request to open the database and attach an **onsuccess** handler to that request. When the success event is emitted, we can access the database through either request.result or through the event object, that is, event.target.result. We can now create a transaction by calling the database's **transaction()** method and specify the object store and transaction type we want with mammals and readwrite.

10. Next, we access the store by calling the **objectStore()** method of the transaction. We can now call the **get()** method and pass in the keyPath value of the entry we want to access. This **get()** method returns another request object, which also receives events for successes and errors. We attach one final success handler to the **onsuccess** property, which will access the **event.target.result** property. This contains the entry we are looking for.

When we first created the database, and every time we subsequently made a request to open it, we passed a database version number as the second parameter to the **indexedDB.open()** method. As long as we keep the version number the same, the database will open with consistent object stores, but we will not be allowed to make any changes to the structure of the stores, nor will we be able to add new object stores to the database. If we want to modify an object store or add a new one, we need to upgrade our database. We do this by simply creating an open request and passing a new version number to the second parameter.

This will trigger the request's onupgradeneeded event and allow us to create a version change transaction, which is the only type of transaction in which we can modify or add an object store. Version numbers must be integers, and any new version must be of a higher value than the database's current version number.

Let's say we want to add another object store, this time for animals in the **cephalopod class**. The process of handling the **upgradeneeded** event is the same as when we first created the database. When a new object store is added, the success event will be triggered on the request object. This means we can add entries to our new object store immediately after creating it:

`indexedDB-v3.js`

```
2  let request = window.indexedDB.open('animals', 2);
3
4  // handle the upgradeneeded event
5  request.onupgradeneeded = event => {
6    let db = event.target.result;
7    // Our new cephalopods store
8    db.createObjectStore('cephalopods', {
9      keyPath: 'species'
10    });
11  };
12
13  request.onsuccess = event => {
14    let db = event.target.result;
15    db.onerror = error => {
16      console.log(error)
```

`The full code is available at: https://packt.live/2pdYCAr`

Looking again at the Application tab of Chrome's developer tools, we will see our newly created cephalopod store and its two new entries:

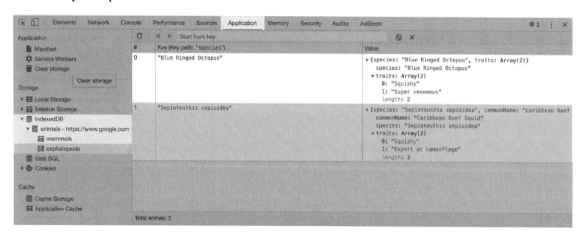

Figure 8.11: New object store and entries in indexedDB

In this exercise, we created a database that holds records of animals. You can further try to add different object stores and add data to it.

Querying IndexedDB

As well as accessing data by its key (species, in our examples so far), we can run simple queries against an object store to return multiple entries that match our query term. The data in indexedDB needs to be indexed by any key that we want to use for queries; unlike other databases, there is no in-built search functionality with indexedDB. If we decided we wanted to use a different key than the keyPath we set when we created our objectStore, we would need to create a new index.

Exercise 8.05: Querying the Database

In this exercise, we will see how we can use a different key to the **keyPath** that we used when we created our **objectStore**. To do so, we will use the **createIndex** method, which takes in two parameters and an **options** object as the third parameter. The first is the name we want to associate the new index with, while the second is the data key we want to link to the index. Doing this requires updating the database version once again when we create the database open request. Let's work through the exercise to see how we can achieve this. Like we did previously, follow along in a code snippet in Google Chrome's developer tools:

1. Make a new request to open the animals database and assign a function to the **onupgradeneeded** event:

```
let request = window.indexedDB.open('animals', 3); // version 3 of the
DB
request.onupgradeneeded = event => {
```

2. Access the mammals store through **event.target.transaction.objectStore** and call the **createIndex()** method on it:

```
let store = event.target.transaction.objectStore('mammals');
  store.createIndex('traits', 'traits', {multiEntry: true, unique:
false});
};
```

As we mentioned previously, the **createIndex** method takes in two parameters. In our example, we use traits for both of these parameters. The third parameter is an **options** object. Here, you can set the unique property to true so that the database does not allow duplicates of this key to be stored, or to **false** to allow multiple records with the same value for this key. You can also set a **multiEntry** parameter. If it's set to **true**, then the database will add an entry for every item in an array; if it's set to **false**, then the entire array will be indexed as one entry. Setting this to true will allow us to query entries by a single trait, as we'll see now.

3. Next, we instantiate a database open request object for version 3 of our database and create another **onsuccess** event handler function:

```
let request = window.indexedDB.open('animals', 3);
request.onsuccess = event => {
```

4. We then get hold of the resulting database, create a transaction, access the store, and call the store's **index()** method with the name of the index we wish to query against:

```
let db = event.target.result;
let trx = db.transaction('mammals', 'readonly');
let store = trx.objectStore('mammals');
let index = store.index('traits')
```

5. Then, we call **index.getAll()** with the value of **Furry** and assign the returned value to the **animalReq** variable. As usual, this object receives a success event, through which we can access an array of all the records matching our query:

```
let animalReq = index.getAll('Furry');
animalReq.onsuccess = (event) => {
   console.log(event.target.result);
};
```

6. Lastly, we create an error event handler to deal with any errors that may arise:

```
animalReq.onerror = (error) => {
   console.log(error); // handle any error
   };
};
```

7. If we run this code, we should get all the database entries that match our query:

Figure 8.12: The result from accessing all the Furry mammals in the database

In this exercise, we learned to use a different key to the **keyPath** and the **createIndex** method, which took two parameters and an **options** object as the third parameter.

IndexedDB Cursor

As we mentioned previously, indexedDB does not have native record search functionality for unindexed record keys. If we want this functionality in our database, we're on our own. IndexedDB does, however, provide us with a cursor, which is an object representing a location in an object store, and which we can use to iterate through objects in the database. Like other parts of the indexedDB API, the cursor object is event-based, so we must wait for a success event to be fired before proceeding with our operations:

```
let request = window.indexedDB.open('animals', 3);
request.onsuccess = event => {
   let db = event.target.result;
   let trx = db.transaction('mammals', 'readonly');
   let store = trx.objectStore('mammals');
   let cursorReq = store.openCursor();
   cursorReq.onsuccess = e => {
     let cursor = e.target.result;
     if (cursor) {
       console.log(cursor.value); // do something with this entry.
       cursor.continue();
     } else {
       console.log('end of entries');
     };
   };
};
```

Once again, we'll walk through the processes of gaining access to the database, opening a transaction, and accessing the store we're interested in. We can now use the **openCursor()** method of the object store to create our cursor. This method can take two optional parameters: a range of keys within which the cursor can iterate, and a direction that tells the cursor which direction to move in through the records when its **continue()** method or **advance()** method is called. The possible values for the direction parameter are **next**, **nextunique**, **prev**, and **prevunique**, with the default of next.

In our case, we haven't provided any parameters to the **openCursor()** method, so it will iterate through all the keys and will move forward over each individual record.

We then define an **anonymous callback function** that will be fired on the cursor request's success event. This method is where we would process the record according to our needs. We can do things such as conditionally adding a record to an array based on certain property values, which would turn the whole process into a custom search method or delete particular records by calling the `cursor.delete()` method. In our example, we are simply logging the record to the console and then calling the `continue()` method. Calling `continue()` moves the cursor on to the next record, which then triggers the `cursorReq` object's success event, starting this part of the process again. If the cursor has reached the end of the records, the cursor object will be `null`, and we can terminate the process.

There's been a lot to cover in indexedDB – this is unsurprising, really, given that it's a comprehensive client-side database that comes with a lot more functionality, and therefore complexity, than the Web Storage API we looked at previously.

Before we move on to an exercise to solidify our understanding of indexedDB, here is a quick recap of what we've covered:

- IndexedDB is suitable for storing large amounts of data.

- It can store many more data types than web storage (any JavaScript data type, files, or blobs).

- It's event-based – pretty much all operations are requested from the database and receive various events.

- It's asynchronous.

- It comprises the database, one or more object stores, data objects, and indexes (a kind of object store).

- All operations happen inside of a transaction, which ensures that all the operations complete successfully or that the object store is reverted back to its pre-transaction state.

- We can query records against specified indexes.

- We can use a cursor to iterate through records in an object store and use this to create our own search features, as required for our application.

Exercise 8.06: Fetching, Storing, and Querying Data

In this exercise, we'll be fetching some data from a remote API, storing it in an indexedDB database, and then writing our own function to query the database for a particular subset of data. We'll do this by adding 200 **todo** items to the database and retrieving the tasks that are not complete.

The API we'll be calling can be found at https://jsonplaceholder.typicode.com. If we make a get request to its **todos** route, we will get a list of **todo** items in response.

We will then create an indexedDB database and an object store and store all this data in the store. In this example, we will use the fetch API, which is another Browser API that's used for making HTTP requests in JavaScript. Let's get started:

1. In a new snippet in Google Chrome's developer tools, we'll get the data from the API:

```
const http = new XMLHttpRequest();
http.open('GET', 'https://jsonplaceholder.typicode.com/todos');
http.send();

http.onload = event => {
    let todos = JSON.parse(event.target.responseText);
```

Here, we're using the **XMLHttpRequest()** constructor to make a new HTTP get request to our API endpoint.

2. Then, we're setting a function to the load event listener of the HTTP request object. This event handler is where we receive our **todos** data from the API and is where we will write the rest of our code. If we were to console log the **todos** variable, we would see an array of objects in the following format:

```
{
    userId: 1,
    id: 1,
    completed: false,
    title: "delectusautautem"
}
```

3. Once we have our data in the **todos** variable, we'll create a new database called tasks and a new object store called **todos** and set the object store's **keyPath** to the id property of our **todo** items (again, everything is happening inside the http object's onload handler):

```
let dbRequest = window.indexedDB.open('tasks', 1);
dbRequest.onupgradeneeded = event => {
    // handle the upgradeneeded event
    let db = event.target.result;
    db.createObjectStore('todos', {
        keyPath: 'id'
    });
};
```

4. We can now go ahead and add our **todo** items to the database. Like we did previously, we'll add some lines of code to our http.onload event handler. This time, we'll add an **onsuccess** function to our **dbRequest** object, in which we'll get the database from the success event object and start a **readwrite** transaction targeting the **todos** store. We'll access the store from the transaction use a **forEach** loop to loop through the items in the **todos** array, and push each one into the database:

```
dbRequest.onsuccess = event => {
    let db = event.target.result;
    let trx = db.transaction('todos', 'readwrite');
    let store = trx.objectStore('todos');
    todos.forEach(item => {
        store.put(item);
    });
    trx.oncomplete = () => {
        console.log('close');
        db.close();
    };
};
```

5. Select the **Application** tab of the developer tools and expand the IndexedDB list on the left-hand side. Here, you should find our tasks database containing the **todos** object store, which should now have our 200 **todo** items:

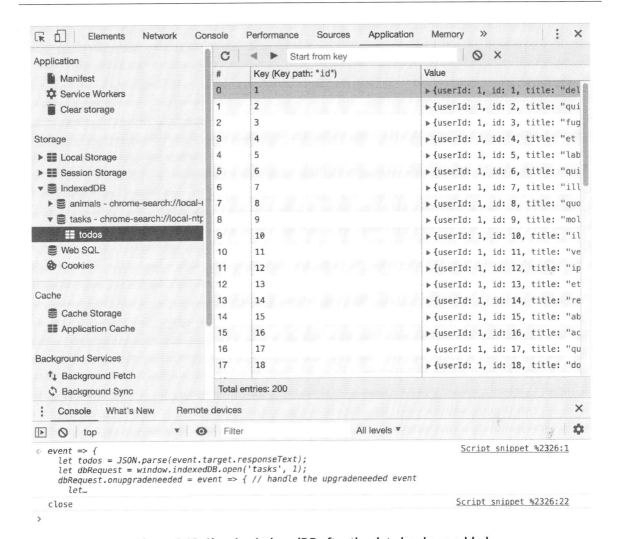

Figure 8.13: Showing indexedDB after the data has been added

6. With our data safely in the database, we'll write a query function to get all of our **todo** items that have completed set to false. First, we'll instantiate an empty array to hold our uncompleted **todos**. Then, we'll use the indexedDB cursor interface to iterate through the records. For each record, we'll check to see whether the completed property is **false**. If it is, we'll push the record into the array. Since we already have our data in the database, it's best to comment out the last block of code, otherwise, we'll make the HTTP request again and save duplicates of all the **todos**:

exercise-8_06_1.js

```
1 let dbRequest = window.indexedDB.open('tasks', 1);
2 let outstandingTodos = [];
3 dbRequest.onsuccess = event => {
4   let db = event.target.result;
5   let trx = db.transaction('todos', 'readonly');
6   let store = trx.objectStore('todos');
7   let cursorReq = store.openCursor();
8   cursorReq.onsuccess = e => {
9     let cursor = e.target.result;
10    if (cursor) {
11       console.log(cursor.value)
12       if (!cursor.value.completed) outstandingTodos.push(cursor.value);
```

The full code is available at: https://packt.live/2qRT6Ek

This results in the following output:

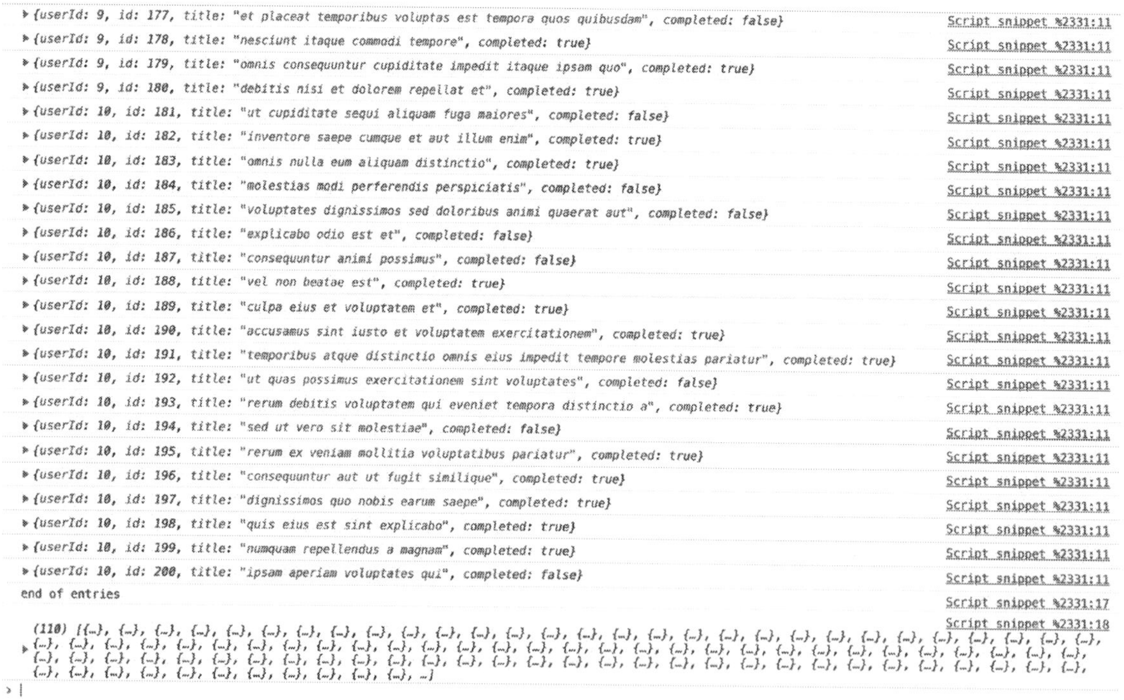

Figure 8.14: The console output from our query function

We can see that the completed property is **false** from the preceding figure and uncompleted are **true**. In this exercise, we learned to fetch some data from a remote API, storing it in an **indexedDB** database, and then writing our own function to query the database for a particular subset of data.

This section has covered one of the more complicated web APIs. Here's a quick recap of the IndexedDB API's core principles:

- IndexedDB databases comprise the database, which contains one or more object stores, which contain the actual data objects

- (Almost) everything happens with events, so you use event handlers a lot.

- Transactions are where the business happens. Transactions apply to only one object store and can be read-only, read-write, or version-change.

- You can fetch items by their key name if they have been indexed by that key, or you can use a cursor to iterate through a set of records.

Now, we'll look at a browser API we can use to give us information on how performant a site or application is. This API is surprisingly called the Performance API.

Performance API

When we're building sites and web apps, it's important to be able to measure the performance of our applications to help ensure good user experiences. We do this during development, testing stages, and in production. As our application grows and we add new features, it's equally important to make sure that the changes we're making aren't negatively affecting performance. There are a number of ways to measure this and some useful tools to help us. One such set of tools is the browser's **Performance API** and other closely related APIs.

The Performance API allows us to time events with extreme accuracy: the time measurements we have access to are expressed in milliseconds but are accurate to about 5 microseconds. With these APIs, we can accurately measure the time it takes to complete specific actions, such as the following:

- The time it took to render the first pixel on our page

- The time between a user clicking an element and the next action (for example, the start of an animation, or sending a request to the server)

- The time it takes for various page resources to load

- The time it takes for information to be sent from the browser to the server, and then to get a reply

The API also gives us access to particular data that the browser collects during events leading up to our site being loaded, such as the following:

- The type of navigation that leads to the page being loaded (from history, navigation event, or page reload)

- How long it took for the DNS to respond with the IP address of the webserver

- How long it took to establish a TCP connection

You can also create custom measurements to see how long particular processes take in the application. Together, all of this information can be used to create detailed accounts of a site's performance, help identify areas of the application which need optimization, and track the performance improvements (or hits) as you make changes to your site.

Let's say you want to know how long your page takes to load. That's a reasonable question to ask, but you have to be a bit more specific about what you mean before answering this question accurately and usefully. First, you need to ask yourself what information you actually want: from a developer's point of view, this question could be interpreted as "how long does it take for my webserver to send all the requested resources to the browser, and for the browser to then process and render them?", but from the user's perspective, the question would be more akin to, "how long does it take from the moment I click a link to the moment the page has fully loaded?". Both of these questions are important, but the user's question requires more information to answer than the developer's. So, we can start to see that we need to break down all the events taking place to be able to answer these, and other, questions. This is where the Performance API comes in: it gives us many metrics we can use, including from processes that happen before our page is requested.

First, let's break down some of the key steps that take place when a user clicks on a link to a site at a new domain. In practice, there are more steps involved than those shown here, but it's not really necessary to unpick the whole process for this example:

Figure 8.15: Overview of processes after a user clicks a link

Let's go through the following steps:

1. When a user clicks on a link – say a Google search result – the browser sends a request to the **domain name server** (**DNS**) and receives the IP address of the webserver for that domain.

2. The browser then opens a TCP connection with the server at the IP address.

3. When this connection process has finished, the browser requests the page data.

4. The server responds with that data and the browser process and displays the page to the user. This is a very high-level, stripped-down, simplified account of what happens when a browser wants to load a page, and it assumes nothing went wrong. The takeaway here is that there's a lot going on and that there are many potential areas for navigation and page loads to be slowed down. Using the Performance API gives us the timings for many key events.

Open your browser to any page. In the console, you can view the performance data for that page. We can get a navigation timing object from the browser, which will give us much of the information we're looking for. First, we'll assign the navigation entry of the Performance API to a variable:

```
let navTiming = performance.getEntriesByType("navigation")[0]; // this
returns an array, but we're only interested in one object.
```

The **getEntriesByType** method returns all the performance timing entries that the browser has stored of the specified type. Here, we've said we want all the navigation type entries (there's only one entry, so we'll get an array with one object).

After assigning a reference to the **0th** object in the returned array, we can view the object by entering the variable's name (that is, **navTiming**) in the console:

Figure 8.16: Expanded navigation timing object

Expanding the navigation entry object, we can see many properties that we can use to calculate how long the various actions took during navigation and loading the current page. Let's run through a couple of examples so that you get the idea:

```
let dnsLookupTime = navTiming.domainLookupEnd - navTiming.
domainLookupStart;
```

This will give us the total time take for the domain name service to respond with the IP address of the requested domain. The browser will typically cache the IP address of a particular domain, so it may well result in zero if you've previously visited the page you're testing. Let's take a look at the following code:

```
let tcpConnectTime = navTiming.connectEnd - navTiming.connectStart
```

The **connectStart** and **connectEnd** properties are the times at which the client established a TCP connection with the server and the time at which the connection process was complete. Taking one from the other gives us the total connection time. Let's take a look at the following code:

```
navTiming.domComplete;
```

The **domComplete** property is the time at which the browser finished loading the document and all its resources, such as CSS and images, and the **document. readyState** property is set to complete. This would be the answer to our user's question: "how long does it take from the moment I click a link to the moment page has fully loaded?".

As you can see, there are many other metrics you can use in this navigation timing entry for timing the navigation and loading a page. But what about once our page has loaded and the user is interacting with it? We obviously want to be able to measure the performance of our site during its usage, and the Performance API gives us some useful methods for doing just that.

We can use the Performance API to measure the performance of any part of our site or application by making use of the **mark()** and **measure()** methods of the interface. For example, let's say part of your application involves some CPU-intensive processing that you want to optimize. You can use performance marks to measure the time it takes to a high degree of precision and measure the success of different optimization approaches:

```
function complicatedFunction() {
  let n = 0;
  for (let i = 0; i< 1e9;) {
    n = n + i++;
  }
  return n;
};
```

Here, we've defined a function that performs some arbitrary calculation **1,000,000,000 times (1 x 109 times)** and returns the result, n. If we want to know how long it takes to complete the **for** loop, we can use the **performance.mark()** method at the beginning and end of the loop, then use the **performance.measure()** method to measure the two marks and return the resulting measure:

```
functioncomplicatedFunction() {
  let n = 0;
  performance.mark('compStart');
  for (let i = 0; i< 1e9;) {
    n = n + i++;
```

```
  };
  performance.mark('compEnd');
  console.log(n);
  performance.measure('compMeasure', 'compStart', 'compEnd');
  console.log(performance.getEntriesByName('compMeasure')[0].duration);
};
```

Calling the mark method creates a performance timeline entry with the name provided (we called our **compStart** and **compEnd**). We can then use **performance.measure()** to create a **performance.measure** entry, which will give us the precise times between the start and end marks. Running **complicatedFunction()** will give us the following output:

```
⟨ undefined
> complicatedFunction()                                                    Script snippet %2331:1
  499999999067109000                                                       Script snippet %2331:8
  1283.1200000364333                                                       Script snippet %2331:10
⟨ undefined
>
```

Figure 8.17: Output from running the function

Exercise 8.07: Assessing Performance

Let's say we want to add a new feature to our app that involves a similar CPU-intensive process to our preceding example, so we want to make sure we write the function in the most efficient way possible. We can use the Performance API's **mark()** and **measure()** methods to find the precise time taken to run a particular section of code, and we can then compare two different implementations of the same logic. In this exercise, we will use the **mark()** method to mark the start and endpoints of the blocks of code we want to compare, and we will use the **measure()** method to measure the exact time between the marks. Our output will be the time difference.

Let's take the preceding example and compare the performance of different looping functions in JavaScript. Let's get started:

1. This first function will measure the performance of a **for** loop. Start by declaring a function and initializing a variable that will hold a value that was used in the loop:

    ```
    function complicatedForLoop() {
       let n = 0;
    ```

2. Now, we'll use the **performance.mark()** method to mark the start of the looping function, and we'll give the mark a name of **forLoopStart**:

    ```
    performance.mark('forLoopStart');
    ```

3. Next, we'll run the for loop, which does the same calculations as it did in the preceding example:

```
for (let i = 0; i< 1e9;) {
   n = n + i++;
}
performance.mark('forLoopEnd');
console.log(n);
performance.measure('forLoopMeasure', 'forLoopStart', 'forLoopEnd');
console.log(`for loop: ${performance.
getEntriesByName('forLoopMeasure')[0].duration}`);
};
```

4. This second function will measure the performance of a while loop:

```
function complicatedWhileLoop() {
   let n = 0;
   let i = 0;
   performance.mark('whileLoopStart');
   while(i<1e9) {
      n = n + i++;
   }
   performance.mark('whileLoopEnd');
   console.log(n);
   performance.measure('whileLoopMeasure', 'whileLoopStart',
'whileLoopEnd');
   console.log(`while loop: ${performance.
getEntriesByName('whileLoopMeasure')[0].duration}`)
}
```

5. Now, let's run both of these functions and see how the performance compares:

```
complicatedForLoop();
complicatedWhileLoop();
```

Here, we have declared two functions, both of which produce the same result, but using different JavaScript looping functions: a **for** loop and a **while** loop. We are marking the moment before each loop starts, and again marking the moment the loops end. We then measure the marks and log the measured duration to the console. What results did you get?

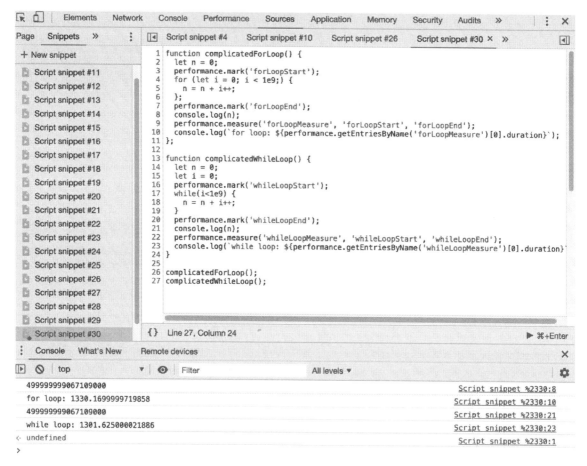

Figure 8.18: Results from the performance tests on a for loop and a while loop

Your results may be quite different, depending on the system and the JavaScript engine you're running the code on, but you should still see a marked difference between the two loop statements. This section has dipped into a fairly advanced topic and one that may not be quite as exciting as, say, drawing triangles. However, application performance is important to keep in mind as failing to do so can lead to slow apps that people will find frustrating and may ultimately abandon.

Web Socket API

Typically, when a browser connects to a server during normal browsing, it does so over HTTP or HTTPS. For the purposes of this topic, all we really need to know about HTTP is that each time a browser wants to send or receive a piece of information from the server, it has to open a new connection to that server, make its request, and then close the connection. This is fine for most situations, but it's a one-way street; the server cannot open a connection with the browser. This means that if the server receives some new data, it has no way of alerting the browser, and instead has to rely on the browser querying the server at some point and asking for the data. A lot of the time, this is ok because we developers know when we can expect new data to be available, or we know when in our application we want to request any new data.

Relying on a developers' savviness falls short, of course, in situations where we don't have full control over when or how often new data is made available to the server. The classic example of such a situation is with real-time chat apps, for example, Facebook's instant messaging or WeChat. We're probably all familiar with the basic functionality of these apps: two or more people can send messages to each other, and they will appear on the receiver's device instantly (minus the network latency and processing time).

But how is this functionality achieved? If we think about this in terms of HTTP, there's no elegant solution: Client A wants to send a message to Client B via the server. Sending the message from Client A to the server is no problem – the client can open an HTTP connection, send the message over, and the server will receive the message. But when it comes to the server relaying that message to Client B, the server is unable to open the connection on its end. In this situation, the solution would be for all connected clients to ask the server whether there are any new messages at regular intervals, say every 30 seconds. This is not a great solution; it means there will be lots of unnecessary opening and closing of connections, each one carrying a relatively large amount of data, in the form of HTTP headers. Also, if a client sends a message at second 1, then the receiving client won't know about that message for at least 29 seconds – and what if it's something important?

WebSockets are an alternative way for browsers and clients to communicate with each other and allow for bidirectional communication; that is to say that the server can send a message to the client at any time. The connection process is fairly simple at a high level: the client connects to a server over HTTP with a WebSocket handshake request containing an Upgrade header (which basically tells the server that the client wants to upgrade the protocol to WebSocket), the server sends a handshake response, and the HTTP connection is upgraded to a WebSocket connection. And then the party starts.

This WebSocket connection stays active indefinitely, and the server keeps a list of connected clients that it can talk to at any moment. If a connection breaks, then the client can try to open the connection again. As long as the connection is active, then either side can send messages to the other at any moment, and the other side can reply to those messages if necessary. It's an open, bidirectional channel of communication, and it's up to us developers to decide what we're going to use it for.

WebSocket messages can contain data of several types, including **Strings**, **ArrayBuffers**, and **Blobs**. To send and receive JavaScript objects, we can easily convert them into strings by using the JSON object before sending them and then parse them on the receiving side.

Setting up a WebSocket server is fairly involved and would be too much detail to include in this chapter. However, we can easily set up a WebSocket client and connect to one of a number of WebSocket testing servers online.

There are several WebSocket testing servers that we can use. In this example, we will use the server at **wss://echo.websocket.org**. If it's not working, feel free to find another online. One thing to note is that the client and server must start on the same HTTP protocol, so if the page that you've opened the console on is on HTTPS, then the WebSocket server must be on the WSS protocol (and not WS).

Open your browser to any page of your choosing, open the developer tools, and open the console.

WebSocket connections are event-driven, so when we create a connection, we must assign functions to the events we want to handle.

To start off, let's create a new WebSocket connection using the browser's WebSocket constructor function. It takes the server address as a parameter:

```
let socket = new WebSocket('wss://echo.websocket.org');
```

If you run this code, and then access the socket object in the console, you will see the new connection object we have created:

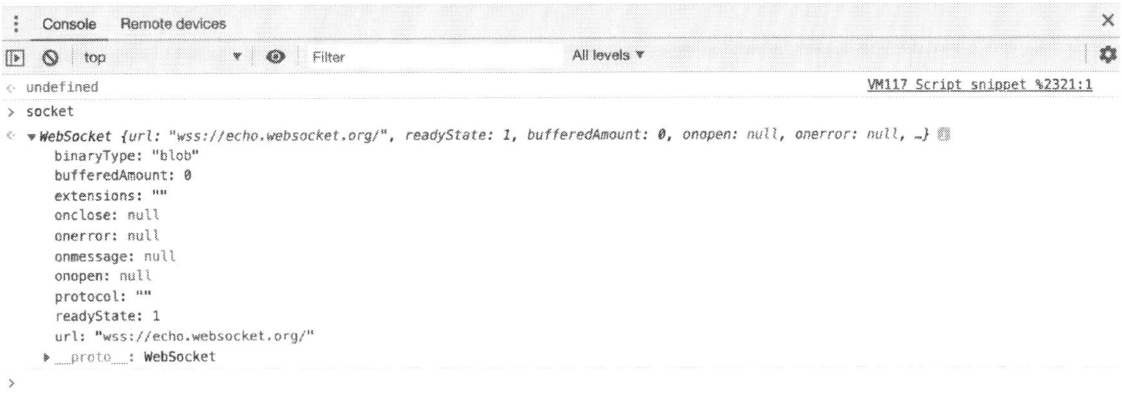

Figure 8.19: The WebSocket connection object

Here, we can see the URL of the server we're connected to, and also that there are event listeners for **open and close events**, **error events**, and **message events**. For now, we will just declare a handler for the **onmessage** property:

```
socket.onmessage = event => console.log(event);
```

Now, we are ready to send a message to the WebSocket server:

```
socket.send("Hello websocket server");
```

The server I have chosen – and surely any other WebSocket testing server – will simply output whatever message you send to it back as a response. Since we have an event handler attached to the message event, which will log the event to the console, we should get this event object logged to our console soon after we send the message:

Figure 8.20: The response from the WebSocket server

We now have a functioning WebSocket connection. If the server were programmed to do so, it would be able to send us messages at any time, as long as the connection stays open. Because WebSockets are useful for many different kinds of applications, there is no specific functionality built into them, even though there are some very common use cases. It's up to us to develop systems to handle different kinds of messages, for example, sending a message with a "join chat group" action versus a regular "send message to the user" action.

Exercise 8.08: Creating Chat Rooms Using Websockets

Let's create a small application to make some extended use of this WebSocket server. We'll be creating an application with two chat rooms: one is a group chat and one is a direct message chat room with a single user. We're a bit limited by the WebSocket server's functionality since all it does it send the message it receives back to the client. Since we're only one client, and the server will only respond with the message we send, it'll be a bit of a lonely chat.

For this application, we'll need an HTML page with two lists of chat messages: one for the group chat and one for the direct messaging chat. We'll also need an input box for both chat threads so that we can type our messages in, as well as a few other elements along the way. We'll give most of the elements relevant IDs so that we can easily get hold of them in JavaScript later on. Let's get started:

1. Let's start off by creating an HTML page, adding our opening HTML tag, adding a head tag with a script referencing a JavaScript file in the **DevTools** console, and adding our opening body tag:

```
<!-- index.html -->
<!DOCTYPE html>
<html>
  <head>
    <script src='scripts.js'></script>
  </head>
  <body>
```

2. Now, inside the body, we'll add an **<h1>** element as our page's title:

```
<h1>The Echo Chamber</h1>
```

3. Let's add an **<h4>** element, which will let us know if the socket is open or closed (the default is closed):

```
<h4 id='socket-status'>Socket is closed</h4>
```

4. Let's add an **<h6>** element for our group chat message list header:

```
<h6>Group Chat</h6>
```

5. Let's add a **`<ul>`** element to which we will append new group messages:

```
<ul id='group-list'></ul>
```

6. Let's add an **`<input>`** element in which we will write messages to the group chat:

```
<input type="text" id='group-input'>
```

7. Let's add another **`<h6>`** element for the private chat room:

```
<h6>Private Chat</h6>
```

8. Let's add a **`<ul>`** element for the private chat messages list:

```
<ul id='dm-list'></ul>
```

9. The following is the input we need for writing private messages:

```
<input type="text" id='dm-input'>
```

10. Finally, we need to add our closing **`<body>`** and **`<html>`** tags:

```
  </body>
</html>
```

This results in the following output:

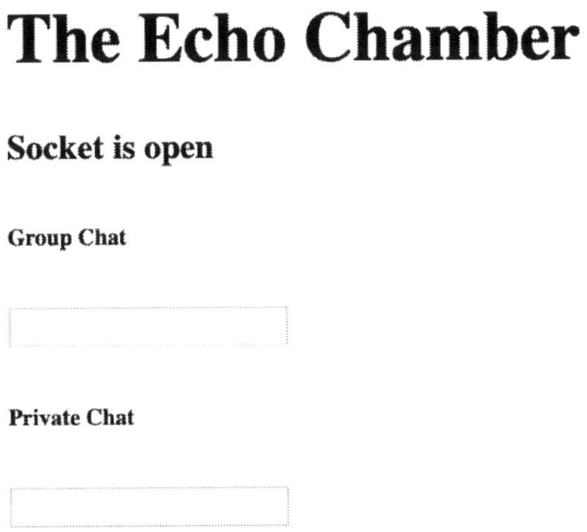

The Echo Chamber

Socket is open

Group Chat

Private Chat

Figure 8.21: Our new chat app's HTML

Now for the JavaScript: let's go through the functionality we need in a bit more detail. We'll need to get hold of some of our HTML elements so that we can work with them in our JavaScript. We need to open a new web socket connection to our server, that is, **`wss://echo.websocket.org`**. We'll want to notify the user when the socket is open or closed, so we'll add socket event handlers for **`onopen`** and **`onclose`** and set our **`<h4>`** element's text accordingly.

We'll listen for when a user has pressed the *Enter* key on either of the input boxes and then send a message to the socket server. The server will echo our messages back to us, so we'll want to listen for incoming messages, decode them, and attach them to the end of the correct message list.

That's a high-level breakdown of what our JavaScript will do, so let's walk through the code.

11. We'll start the JavaScript file with an event listener listening for the **DOMContentLoaded** event, and we'll put our code inside the event listener's callback function:

```
// scripts.js


// wait for page load
document.addEventListener('DOMContentLoaded', () => {
```

12. Next, we'll create a new socket connection to our chosen server:

```
let socket = new WebSocket("wss://echo.websocket.org"); // create new
  socket connection
```

13. Let's grab the references to the various HTML elements we'll need:

```
let dmInput = document.getElementById('dm-id'); // get the DM text
    input
let groupInput = document.getElementById('group-input'); // get the
    group text input
let dmList = document.getElementById('dm-list'); // get the dm
    messages list
let groupList = document.getElementById('group-list'); // get the
    group messages list
```

14. Now, we'll set the socket's onopen event handler function, which will set the socket-status element's inner text to Socket is open:

```
socket.onopen = event => {
  document.getElementById('socket-status').innerText = "Socket is
    open";
  // set the status on open
};
```

15. We'll also set a function for the socket's **onclose** event, which will revert the status to Socket is closed:

```
socket.onclose = event => {
  document.getElementById('socket-status').innerText = "Socket is
    closed";
  // set the status on close
};
```

16. Next, we'll set the socket's **onmessage** function. This event is triggered when a message is received from the websocket server:

```
// prepare to receive socket messages
socket.onmessage = event => {
```

17. We'll parse the incoming data from a string back to a JavaScript object using the JSON object's **parse()** method and assign the result to a variable:

```
// parse the data
let messageData = JSON.parse(event.data);
```

18. We'll create a new **<li>** element and assign it to a variable called **newMessage**:

```
// create a new HTML <li> element
let newMessage = document.createElement('li');
```

19. Next, we'll set the inner text value of **newMessage <li>** to the value of the message data's message property:

```
// set the <li> element's innerText to the message text
newMessage.innerText = messageData.message;
```

20. Now, we'll check whether the message is meant for the group chat, and if it is, we'll append it to the **groupList**:

```
// if it's a group message
if (messageData.action === 'group') {
  // append to the group list
  groupList.append(newMessage);
```

21. If it's not meant for the group chat, then we'll append it to the DM list instead, and then close off this event handler function:

```
} else {
  // append to the dm list
  dmList.append(newMessage);
};
};
```

22. Next, will iterate through both of the HTML's input elements:

```
// For each input element
Array.from(document.getElementsByTagName('input')).forEach(input =>
{
```

23. We'll add a **keydown** event listener to the input elements and assign a handler function to the event:

```
// add a keydown event listener
input.addEventListener('keydown', event => {
```

24. If the **keydown** event was triggered by the key with **ascii code 13** (the carriage return key), then we'll begin the process of sending the message to the socket server. The first thing we need to do is create an object with a message key called message and the value of the input box's text. We can get this from the event object's target.value properties. We'll name the message object **messageData**:

```
// if it's keyCode 13 (the enter key)
if (event.keyCode === 13) {
  // declare the message data object
  let messageData = {
    message: event.target.value,
  };
```

25. Now, we'll check whether the target input is the one with the ID of **group-input**, in which case we'll set an action property on the **messageData** variable with a value of group:

```
// check the message type by looking at the input element's ID
if (event.target.id === 'group-input') {
  messageData.action = 'group';
```

26. Otherwise, we'll assign the same property, but with a value of dm:

```
} else {
  messageData.action = 'dm';
};
```

27. Then, we'll turn the **messageData** object into a string with the **JSON.stringify()** method and send it to the websocket server with the **send()** method of the socket connection object we created at the start:

```
// stringify the message and send it through the socket
connection
  socket.send(JSON.stringify(messageData));
```

28. Finally, we'll clear the target input box and close off the functions:

```
        // clear the input element
        event.target.value = '';
      };
    });
  });
});
```

Open the HTML file in your browser and if you type a message into either of the input boxes, you should see it echoed back in the chat list:

The Echo Chamber

Socket is open

Group Chat

- Hello eveyone!

Private Chat

- Hi there friend.

Figure 8.22: The Echo Chamber chat app with message

This is a quick insight into how we can add our own functionality to the WebSocket API. Websockets can be useful any time we need real-time data to be shown in the browser, such as stock market price updates, or when it makes sense to have a sustained open connection with the server, such as in a chat app.

Activity 8.03: Audio Visualization

We're going to tie together a couple of the interfaces we looked at right at the start of this chapter, that is, the Canvas API and the Web Audio API. The aim of this activity is to create a page that is displaying a graphic, and for that graphic to animate based on the Audio **API's getFloatTimeDomainData** method that we looked in the *Audio* API section. The Audio API's sound should be controlled by the user, and the graphic should represent the audio in some way (the animation could change based on the sound's volume, or its frequency, for example).

This is quite a broad specification for the activity, but you can build the exercises for the two APIs to come up with something, or you can make use of information in the *Audio Visualization* subsection of the *Web Audio API* section earlier in this chapter. See what you can come up with before checking out the solution.

The high-level steps for the activity are as follows:

1. Create a simple HTML file with a link to a JavaScript file.

2. Add an event listener on the document that's listening for a click event.

3. Set up an HTML canvas element and a canvas rendering context.

4. Set up an Audio context with one or more oscillators, or other audio sources if you like.

5. Connect an audio analyzer to the audio context.

6. Start the audio source.

7. Inside a continuous loop, draw in the Canvas context using the output from the audio API's **getFloatTimeDomainData()** method to modify one or more of the parameters of the graphic on each iteration of the loop.

The expected output should be as follows:

Figure 8.23: One frame of the audio visualization output image

> **Note**
>
> The solution to this activity can be found on page 734.

Summary

In this chapter, we've looked at a few of the most useful and interesting browser APIs that open up a wide range of functionality that we can make use of in our JavaScript applications. We've seen that while these APIs are commonly accessed through JavaScript, they are not a part of the ECMAScript specification to which JavaScript engines are programmed and are not part of JavaScript's core functionality. Even though we covered quite a lot of information in this chapter, there are many more APIs available to us. When working with browser APIs, it's important to check how much browser support there is for that particular feature, as some APIs are experimental or non-standard, while others are deprecated or obsolete. Often, some browsers will fully support a feature, others will support certain aspects of the same interface, and then others will not support it at all. It is a bit of a minefield, but make use of caniuse.com, which you looked at earlier in this book, to steer yourself and your projects in the right direction.

For a list of available Web APIs, check out the Mozilla Developer Network's page: https://developer.mozilla.org/en-US/docs/Web/API.

So far, you have been mostly learning about traditional, browser-based JavaScript. However, there are many other environments outside of the browser where JavaScript can run. In the next chapter, we'll look at some of these other environments, notably **Node.js**, which is typically used for server-side JavaScript execution.

9

Working with Node.js

Overview

By the end of this chapter, you will be able to describe the basics of and use **Node.js** to build basic web applications; differentiate between synchronous and asynchronous processing; use **Node Package Manager (npm)** to add, remove, and update the packages with your command-line interface; use built-in and third-party node modules; run MySQL and MongoDB databases; and build real-time web applications using **WebSocket**, and more.

Introduction

So far, you have covered the fundamentals and core basics of JavaScript. This includes understanding the core syntax of building interactive web-based programs using JavaScript code. A strong understanding of the foundation of this programming language will enable us to take a look at Node.js, which is beyond the browser. It forms the basis for the popularity of JavaScript.

In this chapter, you will be introduced to Node.js. Before Node.js, JavaScript was used primarily for client-side scripting as part of the browser. In 2009, Ryan Dahl developed Node.js, a cross-platform, open-source JavaScript runtime environment that executes JavaScript outside the browser. It allows developers to use command-line tools and carry out server-side scripting. Basically, it unites the entire process of web application development through a single programming language as opposed to the developer having to learn different languages and build different projects for the server-side and the client-side.

Node.js is not just considered a programming language but an environment in which you can execute JavaScript. It is a popular programming language with a huge repository on GitHub that is sustained by contributions from thousands of developers all around the world. In this chapter, you will start with the installation of Node.js on all platforms, and then you will go through how it works in the background and how it processes requests asynchronously. Furthermore, you will study the different types of modules and how to use them. You will also do a lot of important exercises to get some practical exposure to Node.js. There are a lot of things to learn, so let's begin.

The Node.js Environment

Node.js has an event-driven architecture that is capable of processing requests asynchronously. Node.js has a single-threaded architecture. Traditional servers had multi-threaded architectures and they spawned a new thread as soon as a new request landed, but Node.js handles everything on a single thread. You may wonder how a single-threaded Node.js handles millions of requests. Well, the answer is the event loop. JavaScript works on a single thread and handles async operations thanks to its event-loop architecture. Any request that is taking a long time is sent to the background and the next request is addressed and processed. Before proceeding, let's understand the difference between synchronous and asynchronous processing.

Sync versus Async

If the execution of a program takes place in a linear sequence, it is synchronous processing. For example, in the following code block, an entire line will be read and executed before the process moves to the next line:

```
var fs = require('fs');
var contents = fs.readFileSync('fake.js', 'utf8');
console.log(contents);
```

This process works best with only one request. In the case of multiple requests, you have to wait for the previous request to finish. This can be as exciting as watching grass grow. To overcome this, you can handle the request asynchronously. This way, you will push any process that is taking too long from the execution stack to the background so that other code can be executed. Once the background work is done, the program will be pushed back again to the execution stack and processed further:

```
var fs = require('fs');

fs.readFile('DATA', 'utf8', function(err, contents) {
    console.log(contents);
});

console.log('after calling readFile');
```

Background of Request Processing

Node.js uses a library named **llibuv**. It handles asynchronous I/O very well. Instead of spawning multiple threads for each request, it manages a thread pool very efficiently with the help of the OS kernel. As soon as a new request lands on a Node.js server, it delegates most of the work to other system workers. As soon as the background workers finish their job, they emit events to Node.js callbacks registered on that event. This process is visualized in the following figure:

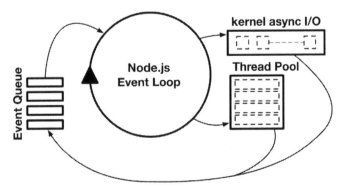

Figure 9.1: Node.js event loop architecture

Node.js is much faster than multithreaded systems, even with a single thread. Therefore, Node.js uses event loop architecture with thread pool management, which makes it powerful and faster than its competitors.

What Are Callbacks?

Callbacks are a very important concept when it comes to asynchronous programming. A callback is a function that can be executed as soon as its primary function finishes. Callbacks are heavily used in Node.js.

A typical example of where a callback would be useful is reading text from a file. While a file is read, you do not want the server to wait for it to finish first. Reading a file can be handled by a background worker and as soon as it finishes, it will execute an event, which will be processed by the event loop. This event will then execute the callback.

The Node.js Shell

Node.js comes with a virtual terminal shell. It provides a quick way to use Node.js. You can execute expressions in the shell. You can also execute loops and define functions in the shell. To enter the shell, open your terminal and type node.

> **Note**
>
> **REPL** is also a built-in module. You can also import it to your module.

Exercise 9.01: Your First Program

Now that you know about the Node.js environment and its workings, you are ready to write your first script and execute it with Node.js. Let's write our first very simple Node.js script in which we will just perform the sum of two numbers and will show the output on the screen:

1. Create a file named **first.js**. Open the terminal in the same directory and add the following lines:

```
// 1. define the function
let add = (a, b) => {
    return a + b;
}

// 2. Call the defined function
console.log("Sum of 12 and 34 is", add(12, 34));
```

2. Run the function to get the output:

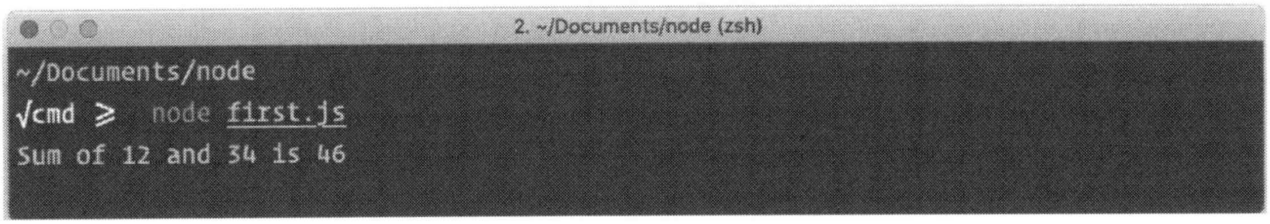

Figure 9.2: Output of your first program

Here, you have written a simple function to add the two numbers, which you will pass when you call the function. Then, you will execute this script with Node.js and the output will be printed in the console.

How to Import/Require a Module in a Node.js Application

Importing/requiring other modules in your program is very easy in Node.js. You can use **require** to import other modules into your Node.js application. Let's say we need one of the built-in modules of Node.js in our script. We would use the following syntax:

```
const path = require('path');
```

This will look for the package within Node.js modules along with any globally or locally installed packages in the project. If it is found, it will import it; otherwise, it will throw an exception. When writing modularized code, you can create your own custom packages and import them using **require** with a relative path, like so:

```
const myModule = require('./modules/myModule');
```

Node Package Manager (npm)

One of the good things about working with Node.js is that you can write highly modularized code. There are millions of packages available on the internet that can be used in your projects. But as the number of packages used in your projects grows, so too does the difficulty of handling them. Node.js comes with its own package manager, which is called npm.

npm has thousands of packages, and all are easily available through its web portal and through your command-line interface. It is used to manage the packages your application needs. You can add, remove, and update packages with your command-line interface.

> **Note**
>
> **npm** is preconfigured at the time of node installation on all major platforms. In the case of Linux, if you are facing issues while accessing **npm** after successfully installing Node.js, then you have to add the path of **npm** to the **$PATH** variables. Check the Linux installation part in the *Preface* of the book for more details. In the case of Windows and Mac, it's most likely that you will not face any issues.

Flags

Some of the useful command-line flags are:

- **-g** = Install the package globally, that is, in the system.

- **-S** = Save the package as a project dependency. Similar to **--save**.

- **-D** = Save the package as a **dev** dependency. Similar to **--save-dev**.

- **-v** = Check the currently installed version.

Commands

Some of the very useful commands of **npm** are given here:

- **Install**:

  In order to install a package, you can use the install or **i** parameters of **npm**. For instance, say you wanted to add **express.js** to your program – you would do that as follows:

  ```
  $ npm install express //i is the shortcut to install. (npm i express)
  ```

- **Update**:

  To update a package, you can use the update parameter of **npm**. For instance, you would use this if you wanted to update **express.js** in your program:

  ```
  $ npm update express
  ```

- **Remove**:

  To remove a package, you can use the remove or **rm** parameters of **npm**. For instance, say you wanted to remove the previously installed package (**express.js**) from your program – you could do so this way:

  ```
  $ npm remove express // rm is the shortcut to remove.  (npm rm express)
  ```

- **Publish**:

  You can publish your own packages to the **npm** registry. Use the **publish** parameter to push the package to the **npm** registry:

  ```
  $ npm publish
  ```

- **Search**:

  You can even search the registry using the **search** parameter:

  ```
  $ npm search express
  ```

package.json

package.json is a file that always stays in the root of the project. It is a manifest file that almost all **Node.js** projects have. This is the file that **npm** uses to manage dependencies. Before starting development in **Node.js**, everybody should understand what **package.json** is and what it does. It basically serves two main purposes:

- Managing the dependencies of your project
- Providing scripts that help to generate builds, run tests, and other stuff related to your project

You can define start scripts in this file, which will help you to inject environment variables into your project. You can even use this file to configure the production and development environments.

To create this file in the project root, execute the following in your terminal:

```
$ npminit
```

You will be prompted to answer a question. You can simply press *Enter* to skip it and a file named **package.json** will be created in your current directory:

```
● ◌ ◌                        2. ~/Documents/node (zsh)
~/Documents/node
√cmd ≥  npm init -y
Wrote to /Users/gauravmehla/Documents/node/package.json:

{
  "name": "node",
  "version": "1.0.0",
  "main": "first.js",
  "scripts": {
    "test": "echo \"Error: no test specified\" && exit 1",
    "start": "node server.js"
  },
  "keywords": [],
  "author": "",
  "license": "ISC",
  "description": ""
}
```

Figure 9.3: Sample output of package.json

Publishing a Package

The **npm** registry is completely open to new packages. You can build and upload your own package to the **npm** registry, and to do that, you just need a directory with a **package.json** file in it. You can just write your module and update the **package.json** parameters. Then, you use the following command to push it to the registry:

```
$ npm publish
```

You can now search for your package at https://www.npmjs.com and anyone can install your package as a dependency in their project.

In this section, you were introduced to Node.js and its workings, and you wrote and executed your first Node.js program. You learned how to handle Node.js packages efficiently. You understood the purpose and importance of **package.json**. This was just the introduction. Now that we've introduced you to Node.js, let's dive deeper into managing Node.js packages and using them in your projects.

Node Modules

To start with, we can say that Node.js modules can vividly comprehend the dependencies of an application. Suppose that you have created an easy-to-use payment application, say, for a restaurant. You have developed a payment app. Now, you get the idea to implement a QR scanner inside your app to make bill payments even easier. Well, you have two choices. Either create the entire feature yourself by spending time developing, or you can install the same functionality in your application using **npm**'s vast inventory of modules.

All you need to do is follow these steps:

1. You need to search for the module name, say, **QR scanner**, to use in your Node or Angular application on Google.

2. The very first link you need is https://www.npmjs.com/. In this inventory, you can see many efficient Node.js modules. You can find a vast variety of modules there to use for anything from beautifying your terminal to rectifying your code. When you have got the module you need, you will have to install and merge it with your application.

3. Now that you have the module, you just need to implement it in your application. Finally, the last step is to install the module in your application by entering the following command in your terminal:

```
$ npm install <module_name> --save
```

4. This will add your module as a dependency in your **package.json** file. You just need to import or require it as per the tech syntax. Just copy and paste the functions as per the installed module's guidelines. Now is the time to run your application:

```
$ npm start
```

You now have some wonderful new features in your application, added in a matter of minutes.

To summarize this, a Node.js module is a properly bundled magical box consisting of one or more JavaScript files destined to fulfill a specific operation in your application, in the most efficient and sustainable way, that are maintained by its developers consistently.

You can even make your own Node.js modules and publish them. That makes you an open source contributor. Before moving onto that, let's jump into an interesting discussion about built-in node modules.

Node.js Modules

There are numerous modules included with Node.js that do not require installation. One such basic module is the URL module.

URL

URL is a module provided by Node.js that is used to split complicated URL strings into a more readable format. It can be used as follows:

```
const url = require('url');
```

There are some utilities provided by this module that you can use to resolve and parse a URL. If you look at any URL closely, you will find that it contains some particular components written in a complex format:

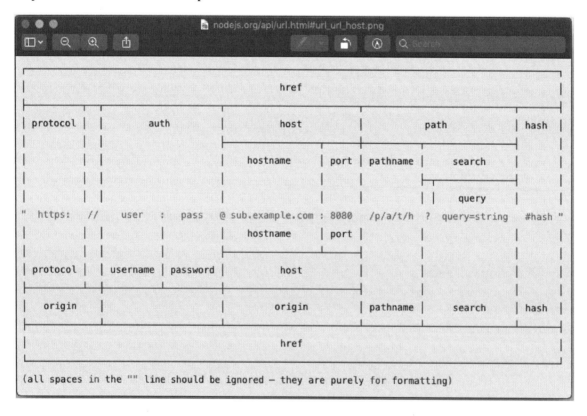

Figure 9.4: Breakdown of URL into different terms

You can use the URL module to solve any difficulty that you're having. The module treats the URL as an object and each component inside the URL is treated as a property of the object, meaning you can access each and every part of the URL without difficulty.

Some of the useful properties of URL are shown in this table:

URL Properties	Uses
Parse	Converts any URL string into a processable URL object.
Protocol	Identifies and changes the protocol of the URL. For example, changes **https** to **ftp** or **http**.
Host	Helps to get and update the host of the URL.
Pathname	Changes the path string of the URL.
Search	Helps to search the entire URL.
Format	Converts a URL object into a URL string.

Figure 9.5: URL Properties

Exercise 9.02: Updating URL Information Using the URL Module

To try and understand the different properties of a URL, let's do an exercise where we will try to update the information of a URL, such as the pathname and host. This will help us understand how to manipulate the properties of the URL object to alter URLs when we need to:

1. Create an empty file and save it with the **.js** extension. For this exercise, let's create **url.js**.

2. The first thing to do is to import the URL module:

```
const url = require('url');
```

3. Now, let's use the **parse** function of the URL module and try to process a URL:

```
const url = url.parse('https://www.google.com/maps#horizontal');
```

4. After calling the **parse** function, in return, you will get a processable object. This object will contain all the metadata of that URL. We can then use this object to manipulate the URL. Let's change the host, pathname, and hash of the URL:

```
url.host ='maps.google.com'; // https://maps.google.com/
maps#horizontal
url.pathname = '/q'; // https://maps.google.com/q
url.hash = 'vertical'; // https://maps.google.com/q#vertical
```

5. Now let's use the **format** function of the processable URL object to format it into a string and print it using the **console.log** function:

```
console.log(URL.format(url));
```

6. Finally, just execute the script using Node.js. It will print the new URL, which you have updated using the properties of the URL object:

```
2. ~/Documents/node/modules (zsh)
modules: vim url.js (zsh)
1 const URL = require('url');
2 const url = URL.parse('https://www.google.com/maps#horizontal');
3
4 url.host = 'maps.google.com';
5 url.pathname = '/q'
6 url.hash = 'vertical';
7
8 console.log(URL.format(url));

~/Documents/node/modules
~/Documents/node/modules
√cmd ≥   node url.js
https://maps.google.com/q#vertical
```

Figure 9.6: Output of the URL program

In this exercise, we learned how to manipulate the properties of a URL. We modified the different components of a URL by using different functions provided by the URL module.

Filesystem

There is a Node.js section that you can use to work with the filesystem. You can perform various operations on files and directories using this module, such as create, update, read, and delete operations. The **try...catch** statement is a block of statements that are used to handle the exceptions that occur using synchronous operations. These exceptions may also be allowed to bubble up.

> **Note**
>
> Before proceeding further, know that you will perform all of these operations on an **intro.txt** file, which contains the introduction of Node.js. So, make sure that you have the **intro.txt** file with some content in the root of the project where you will write these scripts. You can run and test scripts by simply typing **node NameofYourFile.js** in your terminal window, making sure that you have the appropriate rights.

The various ways in which you can use this module are as follows:

- **read** is used to read files in the filesystem using the **fs.open()** method:

```
var fs = require('fs');
fs.readFile('sample.txt', 'utf-8', (err, data) => {
        if (err) { console.log(err) }
        console.log('Data read from file: ', data);
});
```

This will print all the data of the file to the console.

- **append** adds specific content to files using **fs.appendFile()**:

```
var fs = require('fs');
var data = "\nLearn Node.js with the help of a well built Node.js
tutorial.";
fs.appendFile('sample.txt', data, 'utf8',
// using the callback function
function (err) {
if (err) throw err;
// if there is no error
    console.log("New data was appended to file successfully.")
});
```

It will append the line that you passed as the second parameter to the **appendFile** function to the file of the file.

- Renaming the files in the filesystem is done using the **fs.rename()** method:

```
var fs = require('fs');
fs.rename('sample.txt', 'introduction.txt', (err) => {
        if (err) { console.log(err) }
        console.log('Done');
})
```

This code will rename the **intro.txt** file to **introduction.txt** file.

- Files can be deleted using the **fs.unlink()** method:

```
var fs = require('fs');
fs.unlink('introduction.txt', (err) => {
        if (err) { console.log(err) }
        console.log('Done');
})
```

You use **unlink** to remove any file from the filesystem. Just pass the relative path or filename that you want to remove, and it will unlink that file/path from the filesystem.

Operating System

This section provides a number of operating system-related utility methods. It can be imported using:

```
const os = require('os');
```

Some of the important functions of this module are:

- **os.arch()**

    This method will return the operating system's CPU architecture for which the Node.js binary was compiled, that is, **arm**, **arm64**, **x32**, **x64**, and so on. This module is very helpful if you are designing any architecture-dependent module.

- **os.cpus()**

    This method will return an array of objects that contains all the information about each CPU core.

- **os.hostname()**

    This method will return the hostname of the operating system.

- **os.platform()**

    This method will return the operating system platform for which Node.js is compiled. This will be set during the compile time of Node.js. Some of the famous platforms are Darwin, freebsd, linux, openbsd, and win32.

- **os.networkInterfaces()**

    This method will give us all the information regarding network interfaces that have been assigned a network address. It will return an object, and each key will identify a network interface.

Exercise 9.03: Fetching Details about the Operating System

Let's explore this module with a simple exercise. In this exercise, you will use Node.js' **os** module to get details about the operating system:

1. You have to import the os module using **require** in your Node.js script:

```
const os = require('os');
```

2. Then, you can access this **os** object to call its properties and get the information necessary:

```
console.log(os.arch()); //x32, x64
console.log(os.platform()); //win32, Win64, Darwin, Linux
```

3. You can then change the flow of your code execution based on the architecture on which the script is running.

The output will be visible as follows:

```
●●●                          2. Activity: node (node)
~/Documents/node/The-JavaScript-Workshop/lession-9/Activity master ↓
√cmd ≥  node
> os.arch()
'x64'
> os.hostname()
'Gauravs-MacBook-Air.local'
> os.platform()
'darwin'
> os.cpus()
[ { model: 'Intel(R) Core(TM) i5-5350U CPU @ 1.80GHz',
    speed: 1800,
    times:
     { user: 44339640, nice: 0, sys: 15061540, idle: 52457440, irq: 0 } },
  { model: 'Intel(R) Core(TM) i5-5350U CPU @ 1.80GHz',
    speed: 1800,
    times:
     { user: 20734370, nice: 0, sys: 6343180, idle: 84778430, irq: 0 } },
  { model: 'Intel(R) Core(TM) i5-5350U CPU @ 1.80GHz',
    speed: 1800,
    times:
     { user: 44940190, nice: 0, sys: 13801100, idle: 53114700, irq: 0 } },
  { model: 'Intel(R) Core(TM) i5-5350U CPU @ 1.80GHz',
    speed: 1800,
    times:
     { user: 17917910, nice: 0, sys: 5885830, idle: 88052230, irq: 0 } } ]
>
```

Figure 9.7: Some useful methods of the built-in os module in REPL mode of node

In this exercise, we learned some useful methods to change the flow of code execution based on the architecture of the script and fetch details about the operating system.

Path Module

The **path** module provides utilities for working with file and directory paths. It can be imported as follows:

```
const path = require('path');
```

Some of the important functions of this module are:

`path.dirname(pathString)`

This method will return the directory name of a path. It is similar to Unix's **`dirname`** command.

`path.extname(pathString)`

This method will return the extension of the path. It will move from the last occurrence of the . (period) character of the entered path to the end of the path.

`path.format(pathObject)`

This method will return a path string from an object with specific keys. This is the opposite of **`path.parse()`**.

`path.join([...pathStrings, pathString... ])`

This method joins all the given path segments together using a platform-specific separator as a delimiter, then normalizes the resulting path. It's very useful when you are switching directories programmatically.

Exercise 9.04: How to Extract and Join Directories

Let's explore the **`path`** module in detail by working on an exercise. In this exercise, you will extract the directory from absolute and relative paths, join directories, and extract file extensions from a path:

1. Create an empty file and save it with a **`.js`** extension. For this exercise, let's name it **`path.js`**.

2. Now, let's take some sample directories and filenames for you to use to observe how the **`path`** module manipulates paths. Note that these paths are related to Windows:

```
let dir = 'C:/Packt';
let otherDir = '/assets/images/';
let file = path.js';
```

3. First, let's get the directory from a path. Let's say that you have one path of a file (**`/Users/YourUserName/Documents/node/modules/myFile.js`**) and you want to extract the directory where this file exists:

```
// On Windows: "C:/Packt"
path.dirname(dir+file);
```

4. Now, let's extract the file extension from the path string. For that, you have to use the `'extname'` function of the **path** module:

```
path.extname(file); // ".js"
```

5. Finally, let's try to join multiple directories and files to create a path. You can use the **join** method of the **path** module for this:

```
path.join(dir, otherDir + file)
```

6. Now that you have the finished code snippet, run **node path.js** in your terminal:

```
const path = require('path');
let dir = "C:/Packt";
let otherDir = "/assets/images/";
let file = "path.js";
console.log(path.dirname(dir + file));
console.log(path.extname(file));
console.log(path.join(dir, otherDir + file));
```

The screenshot of this preceding code will be displayed as follows:

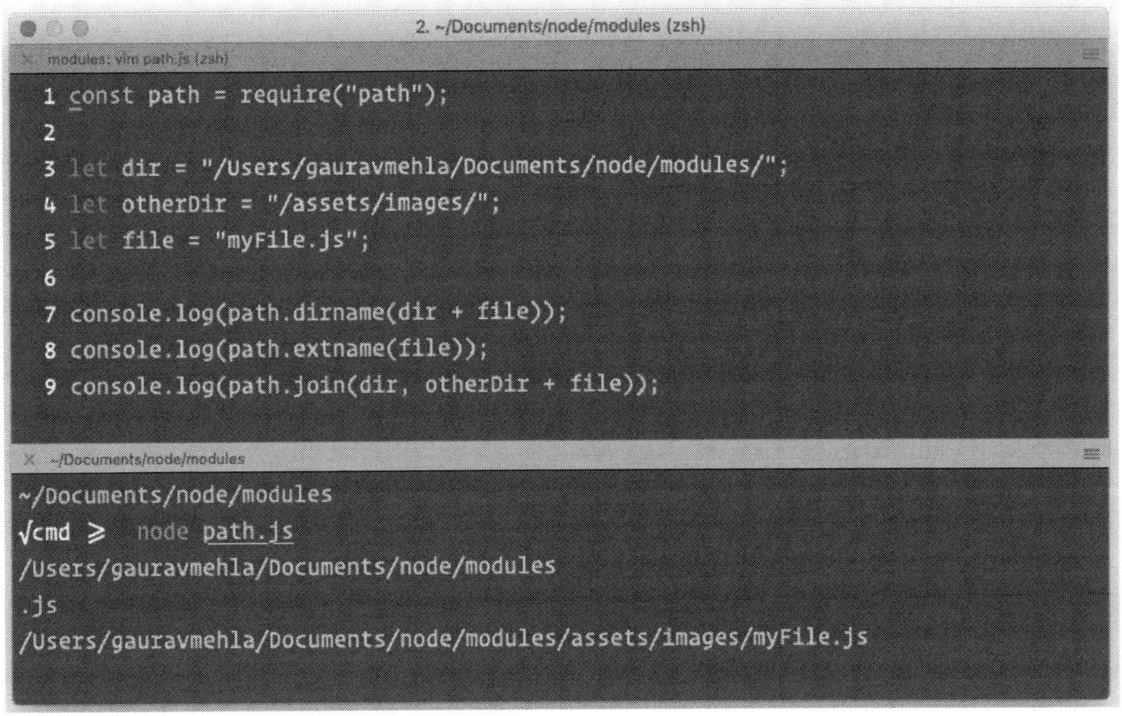

Figure 9.8: Output of the path program

We can see the path to the directory in the preceding figure. We also learned to extract file extensions from a path.

HTTP

http is the most important module of Node.js. It helps you to spin up a server that will listen to one specific port. It will let you transfer information over **Hypertext Transfer Protocol (HTTP)**.

The **createServer** function takes one function as a parameter, which will be called when you make any request to the server. That function has two parameters: **req** and **res**. The first, the request parameter, is a stream that holds all the details of the request. For instance, if you are using a **POST** request to submit a form, then this object will hold all the values in it. The response parameter is also a stream, and you can use it to update the response header, status, and more:

```
res.writeHead(200, {'Content-Type': 'application/json'});
```

Here, you are updating one key in the header and writing the status code as **200**, which is "OK." The difference between a parameter and a query is highlighted in the following figure:

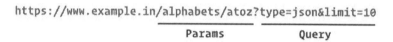

Figure 9.9: Difference between a parameter and a query

You can also get the parameter and the query from the same **req** object, which will help you to process the request.

Exercise 9.05: Using a Node.js Server

Let's start our first Node.js server. This will be a very basic server that will just greet all requests with a "Hello World!" response. We will learn how to start up a server on a particular port and how to write responses to requests. Let's jump straight into coding:

1. Create a file named **http_server.js** and copy the following content into the file, then save it:

```
var http = require('http');
var port = 3000;

// Start the server instance
let server = http.createServer( function (req, res) {
        res.write( 'Hello World!' ); // Response content
        res.end(); // End response
});

server.listen( port ); // the server object listens on port 3000
```

It should display as follows:

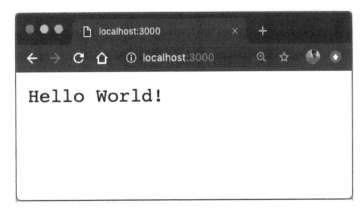

```
1  var http = require('http');
2  var port = 3000;
3
4  // Spin-up a server instance
5  let server = http.createServer(function (req, res) {
6    res.write('Hello World!'); // Response body
7    res.end(); // End the response
8  });
9
10 server.listen(port); //the server object listens on port 3000
```

```
~/Documents/node/modules
√cmd ≥   node path.js
/Users/gauravmehla/Documents/node/modules
.js
/Users/gauravmehla/Documents/node/modules/assets/images/myFile.js
```

Figure 9.10: Node.js server

2. Run the **http_server.js** file using the following command in your terminal:

```
$ npm i express
```

3. Then open the browser and go to **http://localhost:3000**:

```
localhost:3000        ×   +
← → C ⌂  ⓘ localhost:3000      Q ☆

Hello World!
```

Figure 9.11: Output from the Node.js server in Chrome

We can see the **Hello World** response in the browser by starting the server. We learned how to use a Node.js server and how to write responses to requests.

Third-Party Modules

Node has a huge library of packages where a lot of developers have written and published useful modules for you to use. You can simply download these modules using **npm** and use them in your projects. There are thousands of packages available in the **npm** repository. Let's look at some of the useful third-party packages available for Node.js.

Express.js

Express is one of the most popular frameworks of node.js. It is one of the reasons why Node.js is so popular. It is a minimal, open-source, and flexible web application framework that provides a robust set of features for web and mobile applications.

You can install it using:

```
$ npm i express
```

Starting up a web server is extremely simple in **Express**:

```
const express = require('express')
const app = express()
app.get('/', (req, res) => res.send('Hello World!'))
app.listen(3000, () => console.log('Example app listening on port
3000)));}!'))
```

The server is up and running in just four lines of code.

Routing in Express

Express has taken care of routing very well. You can write modularized routes in Express. The following code can be used to set up **basic routing**:

```
const express = require('express')
const app = express()
// GET
app.get('/', function (req, res) {
  res.send('Hello World!')
})

// POST
app.post('/', function (req, res) {
  res.send('Got a POST request')
})

// PUT
app.put('/user', function (req, res) {
  res.send('Got a PUT request at /user')
```

```
})

// DELETE
app.delete('/user', function (req, res) {
  res.send('Got a DELETE request at /user')
})
```

The bodyParser Module

JSON is a very common data sharing format that is used by over 90% of the web applications on the internet. Managing JSON is very easy in JavaScript, but when it comes to sharing JSON online, it becomes a little more difficult. For this purpose, we use the **bodyParser** module. Data is shared as buffer on the internet. This module works as a middleware between the request received and your application. It converts the buffer to plain JSON and binds it to the request:

```
var express = require('express')
var bodyParser = require('body-parser')

var app = express()

// parse application/x-www-form-urlencoded
app.use(bodyParser.urlencoded({ extended: false }))

// parse application/json
app.use(bodyParser.json())

app.use(function (req, res) {
  res.setHeader('Content-Type', 'text/plain')
  res.write('you posted:\n')
  res.end(JSON.stringify(req.body, null, 2))
})
```

Morgan Logger

morgan is a logging module. Every time a request hits on the server, your application logs the request to reveal the real status of your server. A server can handle multiple types of requests. So, the application must log all the requests to check the health of the server. There are a lot of benefits to using loggers on a server. Some of them are listed here:

- You can track how many requests the server is processing in a day, week, month, and so on.

- You can see how much time each request is taking to process.

- You can see the types of requests that are getting hit, such as **GET**, **POST**, and **PUT**.

- You can see what endpoints are being used frequently.

- The module will maintain all the error logs.

morgan is very easy to use and is a configured middleware **npm** module for node applications. You can install it by entering the following command in your terminal:

```
$ npm install morgan --save
```

Then use it in your application as follows:

```
var morgan = require('morgan')
```

Finally, you just need to add this one line to create a middleware between **morgan** and your Node.js application:

```
app.use(morgan(':method :status :url - :response-time ms'));
```

This will print the following log:

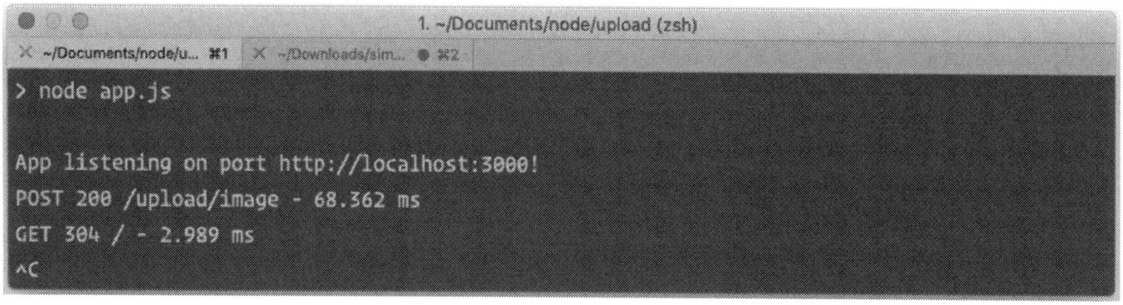

Figure 9.12: Output from the Node.js server in the terminal

In this section, we learned how to use built-in and third-party node packages in your project. You learned how to use routing and how to log requests on the server. It does not end here, though; you can write your own custom modules as well. The only thing you need to do is export one of the entry functions. An example is shown in the following figure:

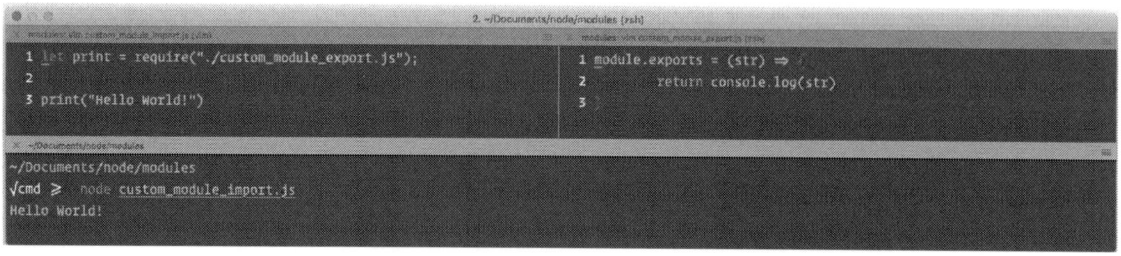

Figure 9.13: Example of export and require using Node.js

Think of a module export as a variable. A module export is a variable in which you will put some value and you can get the same data wherever your application requires this file. You can export functions, JSON, strings, or any type of data from any JavaScript file to any other JavaScript file in your application.

Working with Databases

When it comes to the server-side, databases are very important. All the data that your applications need to store for future reference have to be stored somewhere. In this topic, you will learn how to use two of the most popular databases: MySQL and MongoDB.

Setting up Databases

In this section, we will work with two of the major database types present today. Before proceeding further, let's go through different ways in which we can connect with databases. There are two ways to connect with databases:

- Locally: When a database server is running on your machine.

- Remotely: When a database server is running on some other machine and you are accessing it through the internet.

You can have your database server running somewhere in the cloud and you can access it using a URL along with credentials. But for this section, let's set up both databases locally on the machine and let's connect to them using Node.js.

The installation of both databases is pretty straightforward. You can download the latest bundles from their official websites and install them as you install other applications. For installation guidelines, you can follow their official documentation, which is very easy to understand. They have also covered installation on all different types of platforms, such as Windows and Linux.

MySQL : https://packt.live/32ypsRH MongoDB: https://packt.live/2PY7SDV

Connecting with Databases

After installing, you have to start both the database servers and configure a user. This is the user whose credentials you will use to get access to the database. For learning purposes, give this user administrator privileges so that you will have all the permissions to perform various types of actions.

In order to connect with databases, we require some information about the server machine:

Host: The host will be the domain name or the IP address of the server where the database is running.

Port: This will be the port number on which the database server is listening. By default, MySQL database runs on port 3306 and MongoDB runs on port 27017.

User: Here, we have to specify the username of any active user of the database. We always create an administrator user just after finishing the installation. It is not recommended to use an administrator account with applications in production, but for learning purposes, we can use it. In a production environment, we must create a database user that has limited and necessary access only.

Password: The password of the user will go here.

Database: Here, we have to mention the name of the database with which we want to initialize the connection.

We have to specify this configuration to the database driver that we will use when making connection with database. For example, when making a connection with MySQL, we have to specify this configuration:

```
var connection = MySQL.createConnection({
        host: 'localhost', // 127.0.0.1
        user: 'me',
        password: 'secret',
        database: 'my_db'
});
```

> **Note**
>
> If the port is not mentioned, it will pick the default value of the port number.

We will learn more about how to make a connection and how to use this connection to fetch and save data for both MySQL and MongoDB in the next sections.

MySQL

MySQL is a relational SQL database management system. It is one of the oldest, most successful, and most popular open-source databases in the world. It is widely used for developing various web-based software applications.

The MySQL library is one of the most widely used **npm** libraries. Millions of developers use this library worldwide. The best way to learn about configuring the database is with practice. Let's go through a very useful exercise that will help you to learn about database setup in any Node.js project.

Exercise 9.06: Install, Connect, and Process Responses with a MySQL Server

Let's do an exercise in which we will install a MySQL driver and connect it to a MySQL server. We will also take a look at how to fire MySQL queries to the database and how to process the responses:

1. In order to use this module with node, you can install it into your project as a dependency:

```
$ npm install mysql
```

2. After installing it, you can require it in the project using:

```
var MySQL = require('mysql');
```

3. After importing it into the project, you have to make a connection with the database. For that, you can use the **createConnection** method.

4. If everything went fine, the connection will be ready. You can fire the MySQL query using:

```
var connection = MySQL.createConnection({
        host: 'localhost',
        user: 'me',
        password: 'secret',
        database: 'my_db'
});
connection.connect(function (err) {
        if (err) {
                console.error('error connecting: ' + err.stack);
                return;
        }

        console.log('connected as id ' + connection.threadId);
}
);
Code runs connection and logs thread ID to console. From here on, the
reader should be able to run queries like, connection.query('SELECT *
FROM table, function(err, result, fields)
```

```
{
  if (err) throw err;
  console.log(result);
});
```

Note

Before closing the connection, note that port 3307 is the author's local port. The standard MySQL port is 3306.

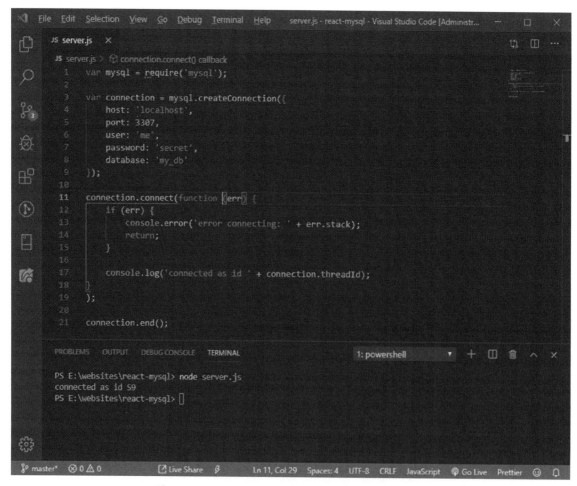

Figure 9.14: Passing credentials in MySQL Server

5. Make sure that you pass the credentials of the user you created earlier while going through the previous section (*Setting Up Databases*):

```
connection.query('SELECT 1 + 1 AS solution', function (error, results,
fields) {
        if (error) throw error;
        console.log('The solution is: ', results[0].solution);
    });
```

6. When done querying the database, you can close the connection using:

```
connection.end();
```

7. To check the connection, use the following query to the database:

```
if(connection.state === 'disconnected'){
    return respond(null, { status: 'fail', message: 'server down'});
    } else ("continue with app code")
```

In this exercise, we connected to a MySQL server and fired MySQL queries to the database to process the responses.

MongoDB

MongoDB is a leading open-source NoSQL database. It is a document-oriented database program written in C++. It uses a JSON-like structure to store data, which is why it is most popular for use with node apps. It is also a part of the MEAN stack, which is one of the most popular tech stacks in the world today. The MEAN stack is a combination of the four major technologies of MongoDB, Express.js, AngularJS, and Node.js. In MongoDB, tables are referred to as collections, and data rows are referred to as documents. Documents are formatted in JSON format and are, by default, schema independent.

> **Note**
>
> Make sure to run the local MongoDB server first, and then get the URI to the connection. A URI contains the protocol, authentication, port, and database name a single string. You will learn about the format of the URI soon.

Exercise 9.07: Installing and Configuring a Connection in MongoDB

Let's write some code in Node.js to help us connect our application with MongoDB. After this exercise, you will be able to install MongoDB and configure a connection with MongoDB using Node.js:

1. In order to install the driver, use the following command in your terminal:

```
$ npm install mongodb --save
```

2. Then, in your application, make it a requirement:

```
const MongoClient = require('mongodb').MongoClient;
```

3. Then you have to prepare a connection URL. It must be in the following form:

```
mongodb://[username:password@]host1[:port1][,...hostN[:portN]]][/
[database][?options]]
```

4. You can use this URI to connect with MongoDB:

```
const url = 'mongodb://localhost:27017';

MongoClient.connect(url, function(err, client) {
  assert.equal(null, err);
  console.log("Connected successfully to server");

  const db = client.db(dbName);

  client.close();
});
```

The output will be displayed as follows:

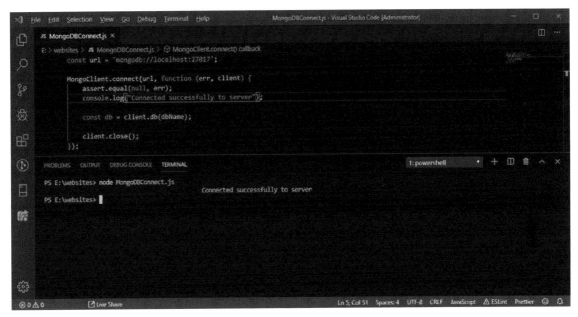

Figure 9.15: Successful connection with MongoDB

Make sure you pass the credentials of the user you created earlier while going through the *Setting Up Databases* section.

In this exercise, you learned about one of the main database that we have in the industry today. So far, you have learned about what MySQL and MongoDB are and how to use them with node apps.

Making Real-Time Web Apps

Our world is very dynamic, and we are living in an era where live communication is crucial. Whether talking to another person in real life or following cricket scores, real-time communication, and data are very important. The best thing about Node.js is its support for streams and WebSocket. Node.js is the perfect tool for creating a real-time web application.

WebSocket

WebSocket provides a continuous full-duplex communication channel. This means that both the server and the client communicate and exchange data at the same time over a single TCP connection. With WebSocket, clients do not have to refresh a page to see changes. The server will push the date back to the client. WebSocket helps facilitate the dynamic flow of connections, resulting in communication at both ends being achieved at considerable speeds. It means that you can now receive and send data on one connection only.

A server can configure the client in real-time because of the lack of lag in communication, and the client can continuously share its data with the server, which will allow it to analyze and optimize the project:

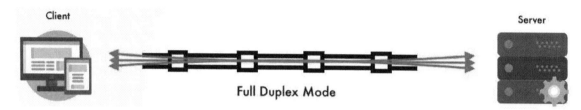

Figure 9.16: Duplex tunnel between client and server with WebSocket connection

The WebSocket connection is made through a process known as the WebSocket handshake. This process starts with the client initiating a regular HTTP request to the server. Any additional information will be included in the header of this request, which informs the server that the client wishes to establish a WebSocket connection. If the server has WebSocket configured, it will accept the request. When the handshake is complete, the initial HTTP connection is replaced by a WebSocket connection. This connection uses the same underlying TCP/IP connection that HTTP uses. Now, either the frontend or backend can start sending data.

Socket.IO

Socket.IO is a library that enables real-time, bidirectional, and event-based communication between the browser and the server. It is built to make the use of WebSocket easier. It only requires two things:

- A Node.js server
- A JavaScript library for the browser

It supports auto-connect, which means if one client disconnects for any reason, it will continuously try to reconnect with the server.

Let's look at how to install it in your project. Use the following command in your terminal:

```
$ npm install socket.io --save
```

Next, configure it with your app server:

```
const express = require('express')
const app = express();
server.listen(3000);
const io = require('socket.io')(server)
```

socket.io is now configured with the app server. You can bind events and listeners using the **io** variable. Now, whenever a new client connects with the server, it executes a connection event where you can get all the information regarding the sockets:

```
io.on('connection', client => {
      client.on('event', data => { /* … */ });
      client.on('disconnect', () => { /* … */ });
    });
```

That's it. It is really that simple to configure socket.io with your app server.

Exercise 9.08: Building a Chat Application

Let's make a real-time chat application using node and socket.io. In this exercise, we will create an app that will allow us to start multiple sessions for different users and develop a real-time chat experience between users. This will be a very basic and simple chat application where you will be able to create a group where:

- You can chat in real-time.
- More than one person can join the group.
- Each member will be assigned fake names by default.
- You can change your name.
- You can see who is typing at any time.

Before proceeding further, let's go through the file structure of our project:

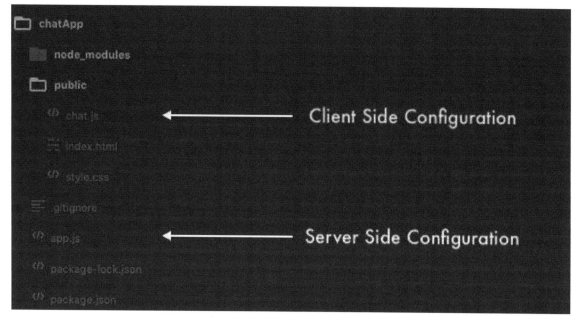

Figure 9.17: File structure of this exercise

There are two main files:

- **App.js**: This file contains all the server-side configuration. In this file, we will configure **socket.io**, write all events and listeners, and perform the routing of the requests.

- **Chat.js**: This file contains all the code required for the client-side.

1. Start the server and configure it to use **socket.io** in **app.js** by adding the following code:

```
const express = require('express')
const app = express()
// Listen on port 3000
server = app.listen(3000)
// Configuring Socket
const io = require('socket.io')(server)
```

2. Now, WebSocket is configured with the server. Let's create some events and listeners that will help us communicate with the client (frontend) and listen on every connection:

```
io.on('connection', (socket) => {

        //listen on change_username
```

```
        socket.on('change_username', (data) => {
            socket.username = data.username
        })

        //listen on typing
        socket.on('typing', (data) => {
            socket.broadcast.emit('typing',{username : socket.username
    })
    })
    })
```

The application is listening for two events, **typing** and **change_username**. They will be executed whenever a socket emits these events.

3. Now, you are done with your server-side code. Let's work on the frontend (client). First, import the socket.io library to the client-side. After a successful configuration of the server, you can open **http://localhost:3000/socket.io/socket. io.js** in your browser, which will download a script file. This is the file that you have to import on the client-side.

4. Add the following **script** tag inside **index.html**:

```
<script src='/socket.io/socket.io.js'></script>
```

5. The complete file will look like this:

index.html

```
2  <html>
3  <head>
4      <meta http-equiv="Content-Type" const="text/html;charset=UTF-8" />
5      <link rel="stylesheet" href="https://stackpath.bootstrapcdn.com/
           bootstrap/4.3.1/css/boot strap.min.css"
6           integrity="sha384-ggOyR0iXCbMQv3Xipma34MD+dH/1fQ784/j6cY/
               iJTQUOhcWr7x9JvoRxT2MZw1T" crossorigin="anonymous">
7      <link rel="stylesheet" type="text/css" href="style.css">
8      <script src="/socket.io/socket.io.js"></script>
9      <title>Packt - Chat App Exercise</title>
10 </head>
11
12 <body>
13     <header>
14         <h1>Avengers Chatroom</h1>
15     </header>
```

The full code is available at: https://packt.live/2NIGAjn

6. Let's configure the client-side by connecting the client-side to the server. Create a file named **chat.js** and make sure that both **index.html** and **chat.js** are in the same directory or folder. If you want to move the files to different locations, then you have to reflect this in the **import** link in your **index.html** as well.

7. You have to declare the link to the server where the request will be forwarded to in **chat.js**:

```
var socket = io.connect('http://localhost:3000');
```

8. We are using **localhost** because the server is running on our local machine. It listens for events that are executed by the server. In this case, we need to listen for **keyboard typing**. Enter the following code snippet below the declared connection in the **chat.js** file:

```
socket.on('typing', (data) => {
feedback.html("<p><i><b>" + data.username + "</b> is typing a
message..." + "</i></p>")
})


//Listen on typing
socket.on('stop_typing', (data) => {
feedback.html("")
})
```

9. Execute the server file with the following command in your terminal to start the server and listen to all requests:

```
$ npm start
```

10. Now, open two instances of Chrome and visit **http://localhost:3000**. These two instances of Chrome will create two sessions, which will mimic two different users. Just start typing and sending messages to have a good conversation in real-time:

> **Note**
>
> The code will be available in the GitHub repository for this book at https://packt.live/36KWlh0.

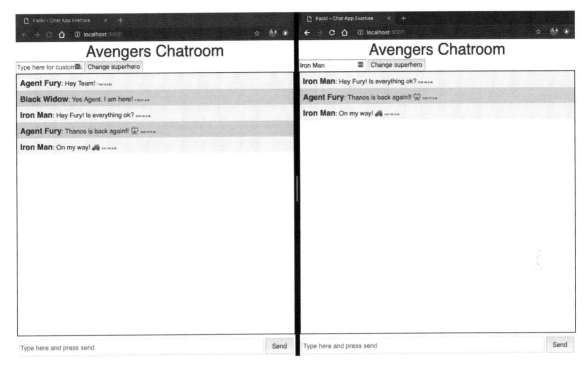

Figure 9.18: Two Chrome sessions conducting a real-time chat

As you can see in this figure, there are two sessions of Chrome running. These two sessions represent two users. Both can chat in real-time. They can even see whether the other person is typing or not.

In this section, you were introduced to building real-time web applications in node using socket.io and you built a cool chat app.

Activity 9.01: Create a Web Application to Upload, Store, and Save Image Details

A major part of web development is uploading media and referring to it in the future. In this activity, you'll create a web application that will allow you to upload images to a server and store them in a directory. To make it even more challenging, you'll need to save the image details in a database for further use and analytics.

> **Note**
>
> This activity requires a MySQL database server to be running on the system. Please make sure that a MySQL server is installed and running on your machine before executing this script.

When the request reaches the server, it will first rename the file and then upload the image to the directory, before sending the path of the images as a response back to the client:

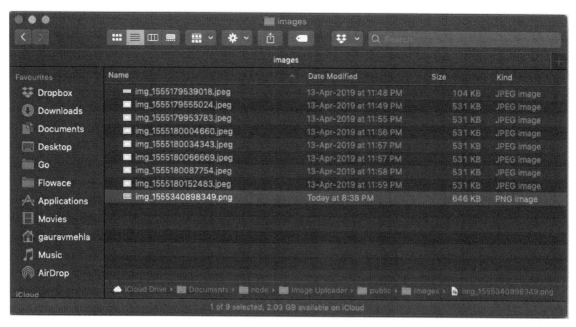

Figure 9.19: Output of the node server

You should get the following log from the server-side:

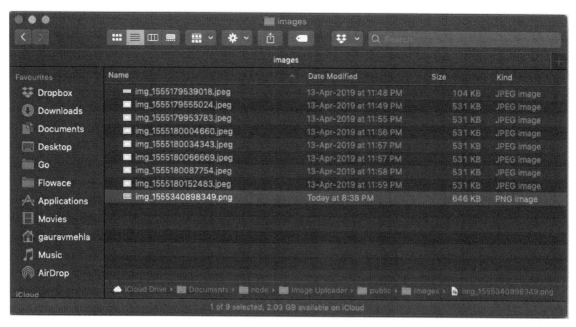

Figure 9.20: File is uploaded in the image's directory on the server

Once the file is uploaded to the directory successfully, you should see the following MySQL output:

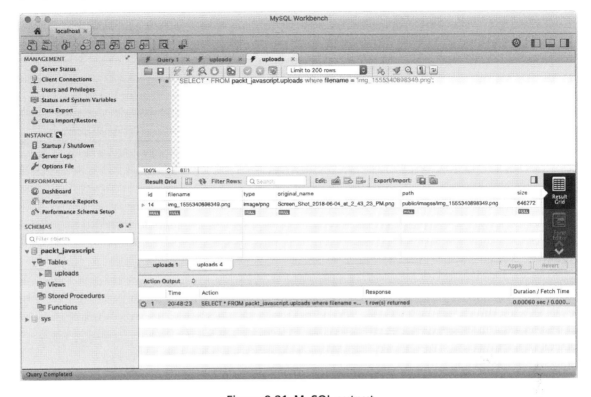

Figure 9.21: MySQL output

> **Note**
>
> Details about the image file are also successfully stored in the database.

Here are the steps that will help you complete the activity:

1. Define the directory structure.

2. Import all of the dependencies.

3. Configure the Node.js **morgan** module to log each of the request details in the console.

4. Configure your application to use the MySQL database.

5. Establish the database connection to configure **Multer**.

6. Add routing to the application.

7. Start the server.

8. Send a request to upload the image to the server.

> **Note**
>
> The solution to this activity can be found on page 738.

Summary

So far, you have covered nearly all the basics of web development with Node.js.

You started with an introduction to Node.js, wrote your first program, and ran it. You learned about Node's package manager and the Node.js environments. You were guided through some of the useful built-in and third-party Node.js modules and discovered how you can import these modules in your application and use common modules such as **body parse** and **auth**. You created connections with databases using Node.js and learned how to make queries in the databases.

Finally, you learned how to make a real-time web application and learned how to build a chat application. There are a lot of concepts still to cover because node is huge, however, you have the required knowledge to explore node further with ease. In the next chapter, you will learn how to use requests to communicate with other services. You will look into different types of requests and how to process and display data. You will also take a look at **RESTful APIs**.

Let's move on to the next chapter.

10
Accessing External Resources

Overview

By the end of this chapter, you will be able to describe AJAX, REST, JSON, and HTTP to APIs; perform service calls using a library such as jQuery and native XMLHttpRequest and be familiar with the pros and cons of each approach; use an external API to retrieve data using JavaScript; use some jQuery functionality for the UI and events; and identify cross-domain-capable APIs and use cross-domain requests.

In this chapter, we will cover various approaches to using AJAX to obtain data, primarily from RESTful services.

Introduction

In the previous chapter, you learned about Node.js, which runs on the server-side. This chapter will cover the other side of services – you will learn how to call them from the client-side. There's a good chance that services being accessed are, in fact, implemented in Node.js, but it is common for them to run on other platforms as well, such as Java, C#, and Python.

Web pages are static and of limited use without fresh data. Web services are a set of technologies that provide standards for your web page to communicate with other servers and sites to exchange data.

To enable services implemented in different languages to communicate with each other, they need to have common rules regarding how the requests and responses being exchanged should look and be structured. For this reason, there are a number of different standards and approaches to web services out there that define the format of data being exchanged. The most popular combination used for websites today is **REST** with **JSON**, which stands for **Representational State Transfer** with **JavaScript Object Notation**. This chapter will describe in detail all you need to know in order to call REST services to provide data for your web pages.

Before web services came about, web servers needed to gather all required data on the server-side before rendering the final HTML they would serve. To get a fresh update, the entire page had to be redrawn. The user experience of the pages was constantly affected, especially if the data involved complex calculations or queries, as the user would need to wait until redrawing was complete and didn't have the ability to use any other functionality on the page in the meantime.

For example, think of a page that displays stock quotes or email messages. In the old days, you would have to reload or refresh the whole page in the browser to see whether there were any updates to the stock quotes or whether you had any new mail. Web services and dynamic HTML changed this, as it is now common for pages to only update portions at a time without needing to reload and redraw the entire page.

Note that many web services use a different technology, known as **SOAP**, which stands for **Simple Object Access Protocol** with an **XML (eXtensible Markup Language)** format. There are some emerging standards as well that are gaining traction, such as Google's protocol buffers. While each of these technologies has its advantages and disadvantages and use cases where they are appropriate, we will only focus on REST and JSON in this book as they are the most widespread methods in use today.

JSON

As you have been using JavaScript up until now in this book, you should feel right at home with the syntax of JSON, as it is derived from JavaScript and closely resembles object structures you have already learned in previous chapters. JSON, usually pronounced like the name Jason, is lightweight, easy for humans to read and write, and easy for machines to parse and work with.

There are two main data structures used in JSON:

- A collection of key-value pairs enclosed in curly-braces **{ }**

- A list of values enclosed in square brackets **[ ]**

Here's a sample JSON object that shows different structures and value types:

sample_json.json

```
1  {
2      "twitter_username": "@LeoDiCaprio",
3      "first_name": "Leonardo",
4      "last_name": "DiCaprio",
5      "famous_movies": [{
6          "title": "Titanic",
7          "director": "James Cameron",
8          "costars": [
9              "Kate Winslet",
10               "Billy Zane"
11         ],
12          "year": 1997
13     }, {
14          "title": "The Great Gatsby",
15          "director": "Baz Luhrmann",
```

The full code is available at: https://packt.live/2CDXhWC

Each key-value pair has the key wrapped in double quotation marks, as in **"key"**, and a colon is placed between the key and the value. For example, the following would be incorrect, as the key does not have double quotation marks:

```
first_name: "Leonardo"
```

Keys must be unique within each object, can be any valid string, and allow space characters (though it is not always the best idea to use spaces in keys, as programming is sometimes easier if other characters, such as underscores, are used instead). Each key-value pair is separated by a comma.

The values can be one of the following types:

- **String**: Such as **"twitter_username": "@LeoDiCaprio"** in the preceding example. String values are enclosed in double-quotes.

- **Number**: Such as **"year": 1997** in the preceding example. Sign (+ or -) and decimal fractions are also permitted. Numbers are not enclosed in double-quotes.

- **Boolean (true or false)**: Such as `"active": true` in the preceding example (Boolean values are not enclosed in double-quotes).

- **Nested array**: This is a value that is itself an array of strings. Each of the strings is enclosed in double-quotes and separated by a comma. (An array is used here to allow any number of costars to be specified). Have a look at the example block:

```
"costars": [
    "Kate Winslet",
    "Billy Zane"
],
```

- **Nested object**: Such as the elements in the preceding `famous_movies` list. Each element in the array is a nested object that contains fields related to a movie, including `title, director, costars`, and `year`. The nested objects in the array are separated by a comma.

- **Null**: Such as `"eye_color": null` in the preceding code snippet. `Null` can be used to indicate an unknown or inapplicable value. `Null` is indicated with no quotes.

> **Note**
>
> There is some debate on how to best represent such scenarios, with many opinions being that if a value is unknown, the field should not appear at all rather than assigning a value of `null`. We can leave this debate aside for the purposes of this book.

Whitespace (spaces, tabs, and carriage returns) is generally ignored in JSON (except in strings) and can be used liberally to increase readability.

There are some important limitations with JSON syntax as well:

- Values must be one of the types previously specified, and cannot have more complex expressions, calculations, or function calls.

- Comments are not permitted.

REST

An **Application Programming Interface** (**API**) defines the formats and rules of how programs talk to each other. REST is a software architectural style that has become the de facto standard for most web services used by websites today. In this book, rather than getting bogged down with the academic theory behind REST, we'll focus on the practical aspects of how to invoke and use RESTful services from the client-side.

What Is HTTP?

In order to understand REST, it is important to touch a bit on the underlying technology of the World Wide Web and how resources are identified and communicated. Very briefly, **HyperText Transfer Protocol (HTTP)** defines what actions web browsers and servers should take in response to various commands.

Resources such as HTML pages, images, documents, or video files are identified by using a **Uniform Resource Locator (URL)**. URLs have the following parts:

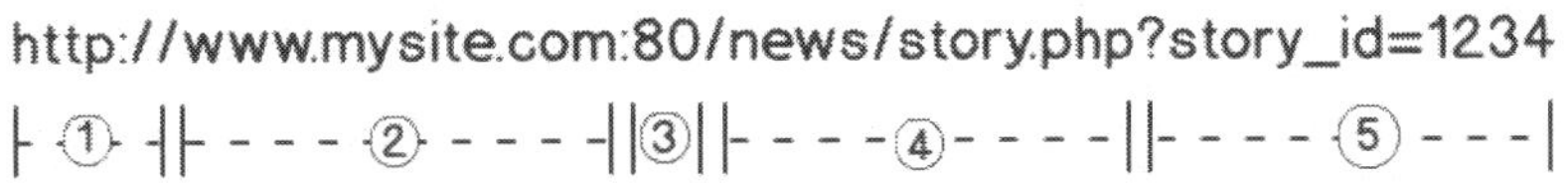

http://www.mysite.com:80/news/story.php?story_id=1234

├ ① ┤├ - - - ② - - - -┤│③│├ - - -④- - - -│├ - - - ⑤ - - -│

Figure 10.1: Parts of a URL

1. **Protocol identifier**: Typically, `http` (insecure) or `https` (for secure communication).

2. **Host Name**: Specifies the location of the IP address or domain name.

3. **Port (optional)**: If no port is specified, port **80** is assumed by default for `http` (**443** for `https`).

4. **Path**: To a file or location on the webserver.

5. **Query**: Parameters in a query string that follow a question mark (**?**). The parameter name is separated from the value by an equals sign (**=**). Multiple parameters can also be present, usually separated by an ampersand (**&**).

Most REST APIs favor URLs that combine identifiers with other elements of the URL rather than using parameters in the query string, for example, a URL such as `http://myserver.com/user/1234`.

The preceding URL code is often preferred over `http://myserver.com/user?user_id=1234`.

But this latter style is still perfectly valid and definitely considered RESTful!

On a basic level, REST utilizes HTTP verbs to perform actions with data or resources: `GET` is used to retrieve a resource, `PUT` is used to update a resource, `POST` is used to create a new resource, and `DELETE` is used to remove data.

HTTP requests frequently require different values to be passed through headers as well. The HTTP header format contains name-value pairs separated by a colon. For example, to indicate that you desire the data in your HTTP response to be in JSON format, it is often necessary to provide the following header:

```
Accept: application/json
```

TheSportsDB

There are many websites and services that provide data of various types through APIs. TheSportsDB (https://www.thesportsdb.com) is one such site that provides sports-related data through its simple JSON REST API.

TheSportsDB is a community database of sports data and artwork that covers hundreds of professional and non-professional sports, such as soccer, basketball, baseball, tennis, cricket, and motorsport. It provides live scores, logos, rosters, stats, schedules, and much more:

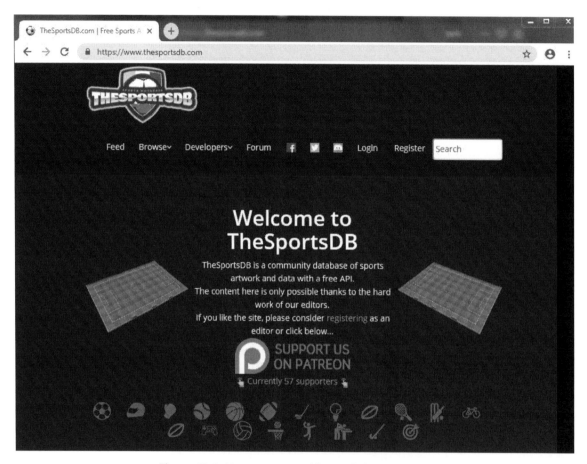

Figure 10.2: Home page and logo of TheSportsDB

Many APIs require users to obtain an API key in order to use their services. The good news is access to TheSportsDB API is free with a test API key, **1**, for educational purposes or smaller applications. (Commercial applications and larger users are encouraged to sign up if the API will be used frequently. Donations are also accepted, though are not required, through Patreon.)

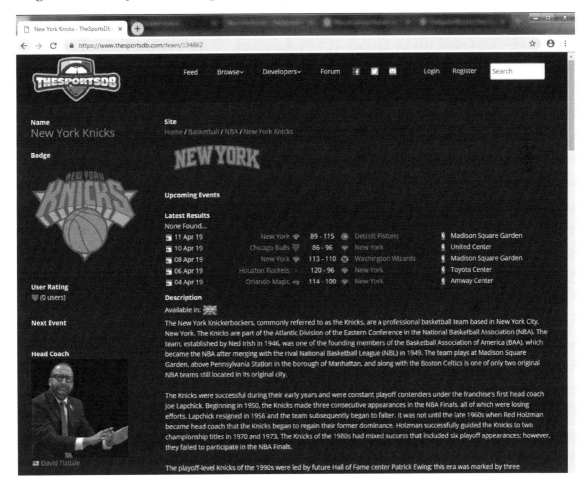

Figure 10.3: Sample page showing how the data from various API calls are combined to present team info

Note

The full API is documented at https://packt.live/2NuwMtd.

468 | Accessing External Resources

Exercise 10.01: Using a REST API to Make Calls

To get a good feel for this REST API and how it works before learning how to invoke it programmatically, we are going to make some calls right in our web browser.

Calls to TheSportsDB API have `https://www.thesportsdb.com/api/v1/json/{APIKEY}/resource_path` as the base form. Since we are using the free test API key, substitute `{APIKEY}` with the value of `1`.

The following is a summary of the API calls we will be using in the exercises. A string of **XXXX**'s indicate where an appropriate identifier or value should be substituted:

- **List all leagues**: `https://www.thesportsdb.com/api/v1/json/1/all_leagues.php`

- **List all teams' details in a league by ID**: `https://www.thesportsdb.com/api/v1/json/1/lookup_all_teams.php?id=XXXX`, where **XXXX** is a value of `idLeague` from the list of leagues

- **Last 5 events by team ID**: `https://www.thesportsdb.com/api/v1/json/1/eventslast.php?id=XXXX`, where **XXXX** is a value of `idTeam` from the list of teams

- **Team details by ID**: `https://www.thesportsdb.com/api/v1/json/1/lookupteam.php?id=XXXX`, where, again, **XXXX** is a value of `idTeam` from the list of teams

The following are other useful methods the API provides (but will not be specifically covered here):

- **Search for the team by name**: `https://www.thesportsdb.com/api/v1/json/1/searchteams.php?t=XXXX`, where **XXXX** is a search string

- **List all players in a team by team ID**: `https://www.thesportsdb.com/api/v1/json/1/lookup_all_players.php?id=XXXX`, where **XXXX** is a value of `idTeam` from the list of teams

- **Player details by player ID**: `https://www.thesportsdb.com/api/v1/json/1/lookupplayer.php?id=XXXX`, where **XXXX** is a value of `idPlayer` from the list of players

- **Player honors by player ID**: `https://www.thesportsdb.com/api/v1/json/1/lookuphonors.php?id= XXXX`, where **XXXX** is a value of `idPlayer` from the list of players

- **Next 5 events by team ID**: `https://www.thesportsdb.com/api/v1/json/1/eventsnext.php?id= XXXX`, where **XXXX** is a value of `idTeam` from the list of teams

- **Event details by ID**: `https://www.thesportsdb.com/api/v1/json/1/lookupevent.php?id=XXXX`, where **XXXX** is an `idEvent` from the list of events

- **Next 15 events by league ID**: `https://www.thesportsdb.com/api/v1/json/1/eventsnextleague.php?id=XXXX`, where **XXXX** is a value of `idLeague` from the list of leagues

- **Events on a specific day**: `https://www.thesportsdb.com/api/v1/json/1/eventsday.php?d=2019-10-10`

In order to obtain useful data regarding our favorite sports team, it is necessary to first look up the ID for that team. The easiest way to do this is by obtaining a list of all available leagues, finding the ID we are interested in, then doing another call with this ID.

TheSportsDB provides the following service call to obtain our list of all available leagues. The following instructions are for Google Chrome, but any major browser supports similar functionality:

1. Launch a new instance of the browser.

2. Press the F12 key to launch the debugger (or select **More Tools | Developer Tools** from the menu).

3. Select the **Network** tab and make sure the circle icon is red (to indicate that network traffic is being logged). Your screen should now look similar to this:

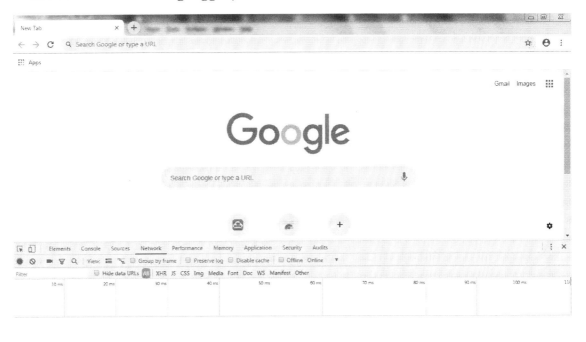

Figure 10.4: Network tab in the debugger of Chrome Developer Tools

4. Type **https://www.thesportsdb.com/api/v1/json/1/all_leagues.php** as the URL into the address bar and press *Enter*. Your screen should now look similar to this:

Figure 10.5: Raw JSON response with league data

Notice the JSON response in the main window lists all the league data, but it is unformatted and not very user-friendly. Luckily, the debugger provides a nicer way of viewing the data in a collapsible tree. In the **Network** tab, select the line with **all_leagues.php** and select the **Preview** tab.

You should see the first line of JSON data in your **Preview** window. Place your mouse over this line and right-click the mouse button to open the context menu. From the context menu, select **Expand recursively**. You will now see a lot more data, like the screenshot that follows. Note that you may need to select **Expand recursively** two or three times to get the data to fully expand.

5. Let's find the data for the league we are interested in. Press *Ctrl* + F and type **NBA** to find the entry for the National Basketball Association. Your screen should now look similar to this:

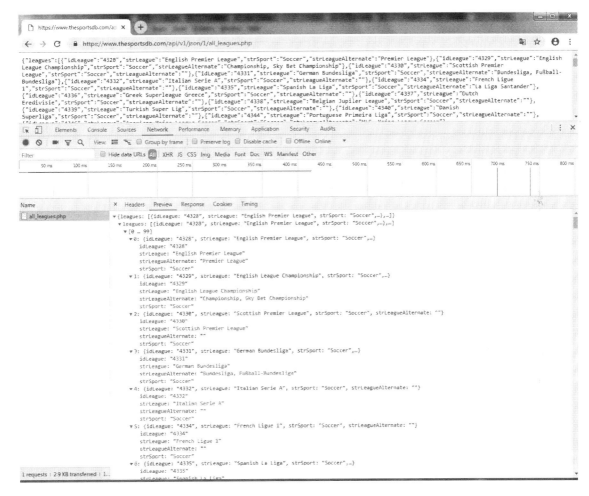

Figure 10.6: Expanded and formatted JSON

6. Focusing on the entry for our leaguc, the full JSON for the entry looks like this (formatted for clarity):

```
{
    idLeague: "4387"
    strLeague: "NBA"
    strLeagueAlternate: "National Basketball Association"
    strSport: "Basketball"
}
```

This entry only has a few key-value pairs, but with the **idLeague** key, we now know that the league ID of **4387** represents the NBA in this API. This ID can now be used for another service call to obtain further details regarding the NBA.

7. Following a similar process to the one previously described, enter the following as the URL:

    `https://www.thesportsdb.com/api/v1/json/1/lookup_all_teams.php?id=4387`

    Notice the **id** parameter placed at the end of the URL, for which we plugged in the ID of **4387** that we found in the previous steps.

8. Once you have expanded the result set, search for the word **Knicks**. This time, you will need to search through several of the matches until you find the correct one, as the word **Knicks** appears in several irrelevant entries as part of long descriptions. Also, there will be many more key-value pairs available in the resulting entry compared to last time, but we will only focus on some of them.

The relevant JSON looks something like this, with many of the fields removed:

```
{
  "idTeam": "134862",
  "strTeam": "New York Knicks",
  "strTeamShort": "NYK",
  "intFormedYear": "1946",
  "strSport": "Basketball",
  "strLeague": "NBA",
  "idLeague": "4387",
  "strStadium": "Madison Square Garden",
  "strStadiumLocation": "New York City, New York",
  "intStadiumCapacity": "19812",
  "strWebsite": "www.nba.com/knicks/?tmd=1",
  "strFacebook": "www.facebook.com/NYKnicks",
  "strTwitter": "twitter.com/nyknicks",
  "strInstagram": "instagram.com/nyknicks",
  "strCountry": "USA",
```

Here, we see the team ID and name in the **idTeam** and **strTeam** keys, followed by other fields related to team history, stadium info, and website and social media URLs.

```
  "strTeamBadge": "https://www.thesportsdb.com/images/media/team/badge/wyhpuf1511810435.png",
  "strTeamJersey": "https://www.thesportsdb.com/images/media/team/jersey/jfktrl1507048454.png",
```

```
  "strTeamLogo": "https://www.thesportsdb.com/images/media/team/logo/
yqtrrt1421884766.png",
  "strTeamBanner": "https://www.thesportsdb.com/images/media/team/banner/
wvrwup1421885325.jpg",
}
```

Finally, there are links to various available images for the team badge, jersey, logo, and banner, which we can use to display on our site if we wish. We will be making use of these values in the upcoming exercises.

HTTP Headers

While we have the network monitor open, it would be a good time to take note of some other useful information. Click on the **Headers** tab, and you will see all the HTTP request headers, response headers, and some other details that were involved in the interaction, similar to this:

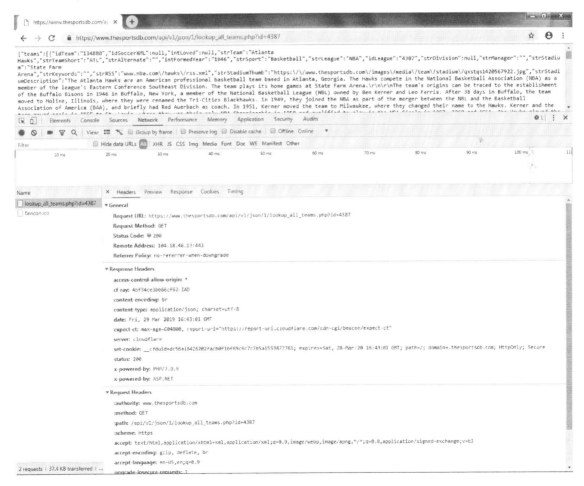

Figure 10.7: HTTP Headers

The following are of particular note:

- **Request Method: GET**: URLs entered into the address line of a browser are **GET** by default.

- **Status Code: 200**: This indicates the interaction was successful. There are several status codes, and the following are some of the most common ones. The later status codes, with a number of **400** or greater, indicate various error conditions that occurred:

Status Code	Meaning
200	Ok
201	Created
202	Accepted
204	No content
301	Moved permanently
304	Not modified
400	Bad request
401	Unauthorized
403	Forbidden
404	Not found
409	Conflict
500	Internal server error
503	Service unavailable

Figure 10.8: Status code and their meanings

- **content-type: application/json; charset=utf-8**: This indicates to the caller that the response is in JSON format in UTF-8 encoding.

- **Remote Address: 104.18.46.13:443**: This indicates the IP address and port of the remote server that processed the request.

- **access-control-allow-origin: ***: This is a header that enables cross-site requests. More on this in a later section.

- `accept: text/html,application/xhtml+xml,application/xml;`…: This header advises the server what formats the caller would accept for the response. This requires a bit of explanation in our case. TheSportsDB is designed to be a JSON-only API, so even though JSON is not indicated in the list of accepted formats the browser sent, the response is still in JSON. (This is not the case for other APIs that may support multiple formats such as HTML, XML, or JSON. So, this header would be used for the caller to indicate which format they desire.)

There are other available HTTP headers that were not part of this request but deserve to be mentioned. To briefly summarize some of the most common headers:

- `Authorization`: Many resources are protected and require credentials to access them, such as with a user/password combination or a token. This header is used to send the credentials in various formats.

- `Cache-Control`: Static resources or data that is not expected to change in the near future can be cached by the browser or client, so the resource is not fetched unnecessarily if requested again. This response header indicates whether caching is allowed. Some of the most common values are `no-cache` and `max-age=<seconds>`, which indicate whether the object can be cached and for how long, respectively.

- `Last-Modified`: This response header indicates when the object was last modified.

- `Keep-Alive`: Controls how long a persistent connection should stay open. A persistent connection is a special type that is used when multiple requests are made with the same connection, making it unnecessary to close and re-establish connections.

- `Cookie/Set-Cookie`: A cookie is a small piece of data sent by a website to save state or track user authentication, devices, and activity. The next time the browser or client makes a request to the server, the previously sent cookie value is included.

In this section, we introduced the basics of HTTP, JSON, and REST web services. We learned about the parts of a URL, HTTP status codes, HTTP headers, and how to use the browser debugger to invoke REST services and glean the data we need.

In the next topic, we will introduce AJAX and how to invoke services with JavaScript code using the jQuery library.

AJAX

AJAX stands for Asynchronous JavaScript and XML and is an umbrella term for a set of technologies to communicate with servers and other sites in various formats, including JSON and XML.

Most JavaScript is synchronous, which means there is only a single thread of execution, and only one operation can be executed at a time. If browsers were truly synchronous, websites would be a drag to use, as only one resource would be able to load at a time. Imagine if the images on websites only drew one at a time after loading! Sometimes, requests can take a long time, such as to do a calculation or a complex database query. You wouldn't want your site to become non-responsive while a request is processing!

Luckily, service calls were designed to allow multiple calls to occur asynchronously. Also, in between requests being made and a response is received, the main thread of execution can continue to execute and potentially issue more service calls. This is the "A" in AJAX.

JavaScript has developed several techniques and approaches to accomplish synchronicity, and the most straightforward and widespread is by using callbacks. This chapter will use callbacks, but other techniques, such as promises, will be explored in *Chapter 15, Asynchronous Tasks*

JavaScript has a means of natively performing service calls via an object called **XMLHttpRequest**. Normally, there is a preference to use native functionality that is built-in to JavaScript, but in my opinion, **XMLHttpRequest** is too low-level and difficult to use most of the time. This is a use case where utilizing a library makes more sense and really simplifies your code. (However, we will also cover **XMLHttpRequest** later in this chapter.)

There are several libraries available that make REST calls, and we'll start with exploring jQuery's **ajax()** and **getJSON()** calls.

jQuery

jQuery is one of the most popular JavaScript libraries out there. It is lightweight and greatly simplifies programming JavaScript for many functions related to websites. These include:

- HTML/DOM manipulation

- CSS styling helpers

- HTML event handling

- AJAX service call helpers and much more

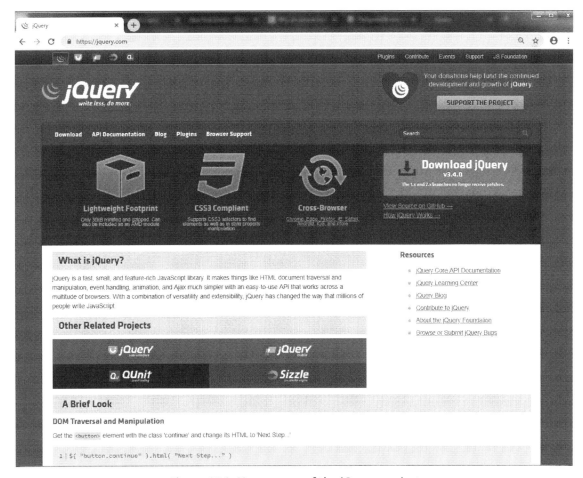

Figure 10.9: Home page of the jQuery project

For HTML/DOM and CSS manipulation, jQuery syntax typically follows a pattern of *selecting* HTML elements and calling methods to perform *actions* on the elements.

The basic syntax is `$(selector).action()`, where:

- The **$** sign defines/accesses jQuery.

- **(selector)** locates HTML elements.

- **action()** denotes the jQuery action to be performed on the elements.

Selectors start with the dollar sign and parentheses: `$()`. They follow a very similar syntax to selecting elements in CSS code. The most basic case for using a selector is an element by HTML ID, for which you prefix the ID with a pound sign (**#**). For example, if you start with the following HTML:

```
<div id="test_div">
    <button class="testbutton">Click Me</button>
</div>
```

The `$("#test_div"").hide()` code would cause the **<div>** with an ID of **test_div** to be hidden from view. Multiple actions can also be performed in a chained fashion on the same elements. For example, `$("#test_div"").html(""Hello World"").show()` would assign the text **Hello World** as the body of the **<div>** and cause it to reappear.

The following are common methods provided by jQuery for UI purposes:

Methods	Description
.focus()	Asynchronously sets focus on an element.
.hide()	With the use of custom effects, it hides the matched elements.
.show()	With the use of custom effects, it displays the matched elements.
.toggle()	With the use of custom effects, it displays or hides the matched elements.
.addClass()	It animates all style changes and adds the specified CSS class(es) to each of the sets of matched elements.
.removeClass()	It animates all style changes and removes the specified class(es) from each of the sets of matched elements.
.effect()	Applies an animation effect to an element. Supports many different types of animations, such as fade in/fade out, slide up/ slide down, at different speeds and easing.

Figure 10.10: Common jQuery Methods for UI purpose

jQuery can also be used to define functions to handle events on HTML elements; for example:

```
$(".testbutton").click(function() {
    alert("Button Clicked!");
}
```

The preceding code would cause an alert with the message **Button Clicked** to appear if the button was clicked. Also note that a class selector was used in this case, not one to select by ID as was used previously. Class selectors start with a period (.) and result in selecting all elements in the document that have that class in its list of classes (in this case, only one element).

It is also possible to select multiple elements by type, attributes, values, and much more.

The following are common methods provided by jQuery for event handlers:

Methods	Description
.click()	Attaches an event handler to the click event of JavaScript. It can also trigger the click event on an element.
.dblclick()	Attaches an event handler to the dblclick event of JavaScript. It can also trigger the dblcick event on an element.
.focus()	Attaches an event handler to the focus event of JavaScript. It can also trigger the focus event on an element.
.hover()	Attaches one or two handlers to the matched elements that will be executed when the mouse pointer enters and leaves the elements.
.keydown()	Attaches an event handler to the keydown event of JavaScript. It can also trigger the keydown event on an element.
.keyup()	Attaches an event handler to the keyup event of JavaScript. It can also trigger the keyup event on an element.
.ready()	Specify a function to execute when the DOM is fully loaded.

Figure 10.11: Common jQuery methods for event handlers

Finally, jQuery offers a complete suite of helpers to perform AJAX service calls. These will be introduced in the next exercise.

The previous paragraphs were only a brief introduction to jQuery, but there are many good tutorials and resources available to learn about it in more depth.

Exercise 10.02: Using AJAX and the jQuery ajax() Method to Invoke a Service

Now that we understand the mechanics of HTTP and REST, we are ready to write some code.

jQuery has very nice methods available that greatly simplify AJAX interactions. In this exercise, we will first use the **$.ajax()** method to make a TheSportsDB service call to find out how our favorite team scored in its last game. We will use the team ID obtained in the previous section as a parameter.

1. First, we enter the HTML code. Open a text editor or IDE and create a new file (**exercise2.html**).

2. Add the **<html>** tag and the **<head>** element, which simply includes the JavaScript files for the jQuery library and our JavaScript source file, which will be shown shortly using the file **exercise2.html**:

```
<html>
  <head>
    <meta charset="utf-8"/>
    <script src="https://ajax.googleapis.com/ajax/libs/jquery/3.3.1/
      jquery.min.js"></scr ipt>
    <script src="exercise2.js"></script>
  </head>
```

3. Next, add the **<body>** tag. The **<table>** contains the HTML tags to display the last game data:

```
<body>

    <table id="game_table" style="display: none">
```

We use a table to aid the layout. The table is initially specified with a style of **display: none** since the data is incomplete when the page is loaded, and we don't want it to be shown yet. We will make it visible only once the service call returns and provides us with the data.

4. Fill in the table rows and columns until the end of the HTML:

exercise2.html

```
11    <tr>
12        <td>Last Game Score:</td>
13        <td></td>
14        <td id="game_date"></td>
15    </tr>
16    <tr>
17        <td id="away_team"></td>
18        <td>vs</td>
19        <td id="home_team"></td>
20    </tr>
21    <tr>
22        <td id="away_score"></td>
23        <td></td>
24        <td id="home_score"></td>
25    </tr>
```

The full code is available at: https://packt.live/37aWtH4

Most of the table columns are given IDs such as **away_team** and **away_score** so they can be referenced later to fill in the data once available. This also allows us to treat each value separately and define different styling for each if we desire.

5. Finally, we get to the actual JavaScript code. Save the first file as **exercise2.html** and create a new file in the text editor or IDE.

6. Enter the first line of the file **exercise2.js**:

```
$(document).ready(function () {
```

All jQuery functions begin with the dollar sign, **$**, as a shortcut, followed by a dot and the function name. The **$(document).ready()** function is called once the page is fully loaded. It's important to use this function here, since this JavaScript file was included in the document via a **<script>** tag in the **<head>** section of the HTML before the **<body>** tag. This code could potentially be loaded and executed before the full body of the HTML is parsed and processed. If we did not enclose our logic in a **$(document).ready()** function, there is potential for errors if an HTML element is referenced that hasn't been loaded yet.

7. Start the **$.ajax()** call as follows:

```
$.ajax({
    method: 'GET',
```

The **$.ajax()** call includes a listing of various settings. The **method** setting indicates that the type of call we desire is **GET**. (In truth, it is not really necessary to specify the **method** setting as **GET** is the default value if it is not present. But sometimes it is more beneficial to be more explicit.)

8. We next enter the **dataType** setting:

```
dataType: 'json',
```

This specifies that we expect the call response to be in JSON format, and to return the JSON parsed to a JavaScript object. This also causes a request header similar to **Accept: application/json** to be sent.

9. Type the **url** setting next, which indicates the URL for our call:

```
url: 'https://www.thesportsdb.com/api/v1/json/1/eventslast.
php',
```

10. Next is the **data** setting:

```
data: {id: 134862},
```

The **data** setting indicates the parameters that should be sent in the request. Since this is a **GET**, under the hood, jQuery will add the parameter key-value pairs to the URL query string, resulting in **?id=134862** in this case. We could have added this value to the URL ourselves if we wanted but specifying parameters in the **data** setting allows the parameters to be separate from the URL itself. Another reason is so that the library will handle any URL encoding needed for more complex values.

11. Next, begin the **success** function, which is a callback function called by jQuery once the service call returns with a response. By this point, jQuery will have processed the response and parsed the JSON into a JavaScript object:

```
success: function (data) {
```

12. This **eventslast.php** service call returns the last five events for the team, ordered by latest date first, in the **data.results[]** array. However, for our purposes, we only require the latest game. There is a quirk in the API we need to account for: if the game is currently in progress, the event will be present in the array, but the score may not have a value yet. For our page, we'd prefer to only show games that actually have a score. Enter the following code:

```
// find the most recent game that had a score reported
const lastGame = data.results.find(g => g.intAwayScore !=
null &&
                                        g.intHomeScore !=
null);
```

We use the **data.results.find()** function to iterate through the array and locate the first element with a score. Specifically, we look for the first event for which the **intAwayScore** and **intHomeScore** values are non-null. We will next set various table cell data with the following code:

```
$("#game_date").html(lastGame.dateEvent);
$("#away_team").html(lastGame.strAwayTeam);
$("#home_team").html(lastGame.strHomeTeam);
$("#away_score").html(lastGame.intAwayScore);
$("#home_score").html(lastGame.intHomeScore);
```

These lines set the table cell corresponding to the ID to the specified value. HTML elements can be selected by ID in jQuery by placing a pound (**#**) character before the ID. So, for example, **$("#game_date")** would result in **<td>** with the **game_date** ID being selected, and method calls that come afterward will apply to that element. Finally, the **html()** call would result in the value being assigned to that table cell.

13. Once all the data is assigned in the table, we are finally ready to show the table to the user. Enter the following final code:

```
$("#game_table").show();
        }
    });
});
```

jQuery has a **show()** function, which results in the **display: none** style being made visible. So, **$("#game_table").show()** would select the table represented by the **game_table** ID and cause it to show.

14. Save the file as **exercise2.js**.

15. Load the **exercise2.html** file into a browser. The output should look something like the following screenshot:

Figure 10.12: Result of exercise 10.02

Note there is no styling yet (but that will be added in the next exercise). We can see the results of the favourite team scored using the **$.ajax()** method.

In this section, we introduced AJAX and the jQuery `ajax()` method to invoke a service. We also introduced the basic jQuery functions to add dynamic content to HTML elements and show/hide them as needed.

In the next topic, we will go further and use the results of one service as an input to another service call. We will also invoke multiple services asynchronously.

Exercise 10.03: More AJAX and Some CSS Styling

The previous exercise was a good starting point, but now we'd like to build on it to do the following:

- Use the results obtained from the first service call to show additional items related to the game and teams, such as team logos.

- Make the site more visually appealing by adding CSS styling.

We'll enhance the code in these steps:

1. Open a text editor or IDE and create a new file.

2. First, add the **<html>** tag and the **<head>** element. It is almost the same code as in *Exercise 10.02: Using AJAX and the jQuery ajax() Method to Invoke a Service*, but with the addition of a stylesheet using the file **exercise3.html**:

```
<html>
<head>
  <meta charset="utf-8"/>
  <script src="https://ajax.googleapis.com/ajax/libs/jquery/3.3.1/
      jquery.min.js"> </script>
  <script src="exercise3.js"></script>
  <link rel="stylesheet" href="exercise3.css" />
</head>
```

3. Next, add **<body>**. In **<table>**, the first **<tr>** row is the same as *Exercise 10.02: Using AJAX and the jQuery ajax() Method to Invoke a Service*:

```
<body>
  <table id="game_table" style="display: none">
  <tr>
      <td>Last Game Score:</td>
      <td></td>
      <td id="game_date"></td>
  </tr>
```

4. Add the next table row. This is new code and has two **<img>** elements that contain the team's banner images. Also, notice that these images have also been marked with **class="team_banner"**, as we will define CSS styles for them later:

```
<tr>
    <td><img id="away_img" class="team_banner" /></td>
    <td>vs</td>
    <td><img id="home_img" class="team_banner" /></td>
</tr>
```

5. The last row and the remainder of the HTML is the same as the last exercise as well, as are the slots where the home and away scores will be displayed:

```
<tr>
    <td id="away_score"></td>
    <td></td>
    <td id="home_score"></td>
</tr>
</table>

</body>

</html>
```

6. Save the file and create a new one for the JavaScript code. Copy the initial code from the previous exercise:

```
$(document).ready(function () {
    $.ajax({
        method: 'GET',
        dataType: 'json',
        url: 'https://www.thesportsdb.com/api/v1/json/1/eventslast.
php',
        data: {id: 134862},
        success: function (data) {

            // find the most recent game that had a score reported
            const lastGame = data.results.find(g => g.intAwayScore !=
null &&
                                                   g.intHomeScore !=
null);

            $("#game_date").html(lastGame.dateEvent);
```

7. A cool feature would be to apply special styling to the winning score, or to both scores in the event of a tie. We do this by assigning a dynamic style to the appropriate score element with the following code. Firstly, add the Boolean expressions to determine whether the home team had the winning score or there was a tie:

```
const homeScore = parseInt(lastGame.intHomeScore);
const awayScore = parseInt(lastGame.intAwayScore);
const homeWinner = homeScore > awayScore;
const tie = homeScore == awayScore;
```

If the home score is greater than the away score, then **homewinner** will equal **true**. Notice you need to call **parseInt()** to convert the data values to integers before performing the comparison, as the service returns the scores as string types.

Note

If you had trouble following why, let's break it down a bit more. Say the relevant key-value pairs in the JSON returned from the service call looked like the following within the larger JSON object:

```
"intHomeScore": "113",

"intAwayScore": "85"
```

Notice that the values **"113"** and **"85"** have double quotes around them. This indicates that the values are string types, not numbers. Comparing these as string values will lead to incorrect results since string comparisons are character by character and the initial **"8"** character of **"85"** is greater than the **"1"** character of **"113"**. (If you still don't believe it, try entering **print("85" > "113")** in a JavaScript console. Your result will be **true**!)

For this reason, we must first convert the strings to integers by calling **parseInt()**. Let's expand on the preceding code for clarity:

```
// convert string "113" to int 113

const homeScore = parseInt(lastGame.intHomeScore);

// convert string "85" to int 85

const awayScore = parseInt(lastGame.intAwayScore);

// will evaluate to the Boolean value true, since 113 > 85

const homeWinner = homeScore > awayScore;
```

Now that we know whether the home team won the game or not, we add the **homeWinner** value to determine which element should have the **winning_score** CSS class added for special styling:

```
$("#home_score").html(homeScore)
    .addClass( (homeWinner || tie) ? "winning_score" :
"")
$("#away_score").html(awayScore)
    .addClass( (!homeWinner || tie) ? "winning_score" :
"");
```

Notice the expression with the conditional ternary operator. This shortcut has the same effect as the following code:

```
if (homeWinner == true || tie == true) {
    $("#home_score").addClass("winning_score");
}
```

> **Note**
>
> This can actually be improved a bit further if we wish. jQuery has a function called **toggleClass()** for this specific use case where a class should be added conditionally. This code can be rewritten as follows:
>
> ```
> $("#home_score").html(homeScore)
>     .toggleClass("winning_score", homeWinner || tie);
> ```
>
> The **toggleClass()** method takes two parameters. The first parameter is the name of the class that will be conditionally added (or removed). The second parameter is the Boolean value or expression itself.

8. Next, we add the code to get the team's banner images:

```
getTeamImage(lastGame.idHomeTeam, "#home_img");
getTeamImage(lastGame.idAwayTeam, "#away_img");
```

The **lastGame.idHomeTeam** and **lastGame.idAwayTeam** fields contain the IDs of the home and away teams of the most recent game. Using these IDs, we are going to call the **getTeamImage()** function, which will load the banner image for each of the teams, passing in the HTML IDs of the images as well. (This function will be defined soon.)

9. Type in the remainder of the function, which is the same as in the last exercise, to actually show the table:

```
            $("#game_table").show();
        }
    });

});
```

10. Finally, we come to the **getTeamImage()** function:

```
function getTeamImage(teamId, imageId) {

    $.getJSON('https://www.thesportsdb.com/api/v1/json/1/lookupteam.
php',
        {id: teamId},
         function(data) {
             const teamData = data.teams[0];
             $(imageId).attr("src", teamData.strTeamBanner);
         }
    );
}
```

Once the exercise is complete, the final result should look something like the following screenshot:

Figure 10.13: Final result of exercise

There are a number of items to notice here:

* We used **$.getJSON()** instead of **$.ajax()** this time. The **$.getJSON()** function is a shortcut that can be used for requests that are **JSON GET**. Using this shortcut, **dataType="json"** is assumed by default. There is no need to specify the URL, data parameters, and **success** function as separate settings, as the signature of the function is the following, with the brackets indicating that the last two parameters are optional: **$.getJSON(url [, data] [, success])**.

- **imageId** is passed in to represent the ID of the HTML image element that will be set. We will use jQuery to select this image element and call **attr("src", value)**, which is jQuery's utility method to set the **src** field of the **<img>** HTML element (similar to **<img src="...."/>**). We will set this **src** with the value returned by the service call in the **teamData.strTeamBanner** element. Setting the **src** field will trigger the browser to load the corresponding image dynamically.

- **$.getJSON()** is an asynchronous call, which means that after the request is made, the browser will not wait for the response and execution will continue even while the service call is in progress (and execute the **success** callback when the response is received). The implication of this is that the calls to **getTeamImage()** will effectively issue two simultaneous service calls and not lock the browser while the requests are in flight.

CSS

We will now briefly cover the CSS and styling that was added to the page in the preceding exercise to make it visually appealing. As this is not really a book on CSS, we will only give a brief overview. (There are many excellent books and resources available that cover CSS in depth.)

The stylesheet is included in the head element with the following tag:

```
<link rel="stylesheet" href="exercise3.css" />
```

The contents of the CSS file follow here:

exercise3.css

```
1  #game_table {
2      border: 1px solid;
3      display: none;
4  }
5
6  #game_table td {
7      text-align: right;
8  }
9
10 #away_score, #home_score {
11     font-size: 24px;
12 }
13
14  team_banner {
15      width: 275px;
```

The full code is available at: https://packt.live/33K3gVY

- The **#game_table** selector indicates that all styles in this block will apply to the HTML element with an ID of **game_table**.

- Places a border around the table to make it appear more contained.

- We move the **display:none** style (to prevent display until the data is loaded) into the stylesheet itself, to keep the HTML code less cluttered of styling code.

- The **#game_table td** selector indicates that the styles in the block will apply to all **<td>** elements that appear within the table with an ID of **game_table**. Here, we are saying that all text in table rows should be aligned to the right.

- A comma in the selector allows you to select multiple elements. Here, we are indicating that scores should have a larger, 24-pixel font.

- Selectors that begin with a dot (such as **.team_banner** here) are a different type of selector. This is a **class** selector, which would apply to all HTML elements that have **class="team_banner"** specified.

- The banner images from the server are quite large, but we only want a scaled-down image of 275 x 50 pixels.

- A distinctive style that indicates the winning score in green and bold.

In the last section, we explored different types of responses from services (JSON and images) and how to use jQuery to display them using the helpers for dynamic DOM manipulation. We also saw how to use CSS to add colors, fonts, and other styles to make our screen more visually appealing.

Other Libraries and XMLHttpRequest

This section explores other approaches to AJAX with JavaScript. The approach to making REST calls using jQuery and callbacks is just one of many different options available and was presented first as it's the most straightforward and easy-to-understand option for novice users. This is not to say the approach is not powerful though. And it is really all that is needed in many cases. Remember that jQuery offers other functionality you may want to use in your application as well.

Axios and the Fetch API

At this point in the book, we'd like to mention two other popular choices that may be appropriate to be used in your projects, Axios and the Fetch API. These use advanced concepts such as promises, so they will not be covered here but will be covered in *Chapter 15, Asynchronous Tasks* of the advanced module. (Note that even jQuery itself offers variations on the AJAX methods that return promises instead of using callbacks, but this usage is not in the scope of this chapter either.)

But for now, we'll compare jQuery with the native **XMLHttpRequest** JavaScript object in the next section.

For Comparison: XMLHttpRequest and jQuery

XMLHttpRequest is a low-level class built into JavaScript to handle service calls. Despite having XML in its name, **XMLHttpRequest** can actually be used for other protocols as well, including JSON and HTML.

The following is equivalent code to *Exercise 10.02: Using AJAX and the jQuery ajax() Method to Invoke a Service* so you can compare how code using **XMLHttpRequest** looks in comparison to that of jQuery (**xml_http_request_example.js**):

> **Note**
>
> HTML part is the same as above in *exercise 10.02* in file **exercise2.html**, but omit the jQuery lib in **<head>** and change the **js** script **src** file to **xml_http_request_example.js** rather than **exercise2.js**

xml_http_request_example.js

```
1 const url = "https://www.thesportsdb.com/api/v1/json/1/eventslast.php?id=134862"";
2 var xhttp = new XMLHttpRequest();
3 xhttp.open('GET', url);
4 xhttp.setRequestHeader('Accept', 'application/json');
5 xhttp.onreadystatechange = function() {
6     if (this.readyState == 4 && this.status == 200) {
7         const data = JSON.parse(this.response);
8
9         // find the most recent game that had a score reported
10        const lastGame = data.results.find(g => g.intAwayScore != null &&
11                                 g.intHomeScore != null);
12
13        document.getElementById("game_date").innerHTML = lastGame.dateEvent;
14        document.getElementById("away_team").innerHTML = lastGame.strAwayTeam;
15        document.getElementById("home_team").innerHTML = lastGame.strHomeTeam;
```

The full code is available at: https://packt.live/2q9dErM

Let's examine the preceding example in detail:

```
const url = "https://www.thesportsdb.com/api/v1/json/1/eventslast.
php?id=134862";
```

When using **XMLHttpRequest**, we need to append query parameters ourselves to the end of the URL. Here, it is straightforward to do so, since the value is just a simple number, but more complex values will require HTTP encoding by calling **encodeURI()**:

```
var xhttp = new XMLHttpRequest();
xhttp.open('GET', url);
```

We instantiate the **XMLHttpRequest** object and call the open method, specifying the method (**GET**, **POST**, and so on) and the URL:

```
xhttp.setRequestHeader('Accept', 'application/json');
```

This low-level API doesn't take care of setting headers like jQuery did:

```
xhttp.onreadystatechange = function() {...}
```

This is the callback function that will be called when there is a ready state change. There are a number of states the request can have, so we need to check the current state, as in the following line:

```
if (this.readyState == 4 && this.status == 200) {...}
```

Unlike the jQuery implementation, there is no **success()** function that gets called. We have to check the **readyState** and **status** code explicitly.

A **readyState** of **4** indicates the request finished and the response is ready. Possible states are:

- **0**: Request not initialized
- **1**: Server connection established
- **2**: Request received
- **3**: Processing request
- **4**: Request finished, and response is ready

A **status** of **200** indicates **OK**. See the HTTP *Headers* section for a list of the most common HTTP status codes:

```
const data = JSON.parse(this.response);
```

Unlike with jQuery, we need to parse the JSON text ourselves by calling **JSON.parse()** from the response field:

```
document.getElementById("game_date").innerHTML = lastGame.dateEvent;
```

The **document.getElementById()** function is the native way to select DOM elements in JavaScript by ID (equivalent to jQuery's **$("#game_date")** function). You would set the text for the element by setting the **innerHTML** field directly (rather than calling an **html()** function as in jQuery):

```
document.getElementById("game_table").style.display = 'block';
```

Setting **style.display** is the native way to make a hidden element visible again, equivalent to jQuery's **show()** method (though obviously not as simple):

```
xhttp.send();
```

The request does not actually get sent until the **send()** method is actually invoked, so it is important we do not forget to call it. (Unlike jQuery, where the request is automatically sent.)

Using jQuery and XMLHttpRequest for POST Requests

Using **$.ajax()** for **POST** requests with regular parameters is much the same as for **GET**, apart from specifying **method="POST"**. However, a **POST** request has an additional capability – sending the request data in **JSON** format rather than the default **'application/x-www-form-urlencoded'** content type. If you wish to do so, the **contentType** setting should be set to **'application/json'** and the data object should be wrapped in **JSON.stringify()**. Here's an example:

```
$.ajax({
    url: 'http://example.do',
    dataType: 'json',
    type: 'post',
    contentType: 'application/json',
    data: JSON.stringify( {"firstname": "George", "lastname": "Cloony"} ),
    success: function(data){
...
```

Like **$.getJSON()**, jQuery also provides a shortcut for **POST** requests, called **$.post()**. It has one additional parameter, though, to indicate the data type of the response. Here's an example:

```
$.post("http://example.do", {
        "firstname": "George",
        "lastname": "Cloony"
    }, function (data) {
        // process the response
    }, 'json'
);
```

For **XMLHttpRequest**:

- If you are just sending standard parameters, use **setRequestHeader("Content-Type", "application/x-www-form-urlencoded")** and send the encoded parameters when calling **send()**. (You may need to also call **encodeURI()** if your data is complex.)

- If you are sending your input as JSON, use **setRequestHeader("Content-type", "application/json")** and send the data wrapped in **JSON.stringify()** when calling **send()**.

- For either method, one caveat is that the return code from the service will frequently be **201 (Created)** rather than **200 (OK)**, so you want to make sure your code looks out for the correct return code.

Here's an example:

```
xhttp.setRequestHeader("Content-type", "application/json");
var data = JSON.stringify({
    "firstname": "George",
    "lastname": "Clooney"
});
xhttp.send(data);
```

Cross-Domain Requests

When selecting or implementing a REST API, there is an important rule to be aware of that can impact whether the API can be used for your site. Browsers have a security feature known as the **Same Origin Policy**. This policy only allows scripts running on a site to access data from URLs on the same site with no specific restrictions but prevents scripts from accessing data that is hosted on a different domain. The reason for this policy is to prevent different types of attacks unscrupulous people can make by exploiting browser security weaknesses to steal your data or invoke malicious service calls.

For instance, if your page is hosted at https://www.mygreatsite.com/foo.html, you would be able to access data or call the service with a URL such as https://www.mygreatsite.com/my_data.json. However, if the domain differs, even just in a different subdomain such as https://www.foobar.mygreatsite.com/my_data.json, the browser would respond with an error such as the following:

```
XMLHttpRequest cannot load https://www.foobar.mygreatsite.com/my_data.
json. Origin null is not allowed by Access-Control-Allow-Origin.
```

Luckily, there are a few ways around this restriction that APIs can implement. The details of the implementation of these workarounds are on the server side and are not in the scope of this chapter. But it is sufficient to know that APIs can be designed in a way that makes them data available across sites. So, when selecting APIs to use for your project, you'll need to investigate whether it is cross-domain capable. (The API we used in the earlier exercise, TheSportsDB, is such a site.)

CORS Header

If you are really curious, the main technique that allows cross-site requests is by the service sending something called a **CORS** header, which stands for **Cross-Origin Resource Sharing**. If the API wants to make its service available from any domain, the server can send the following response header when serving the response:

```
Access-Control-Allow-Origin: *
```

The * value indicates "any origin," but the server could also be more restrictive in what sites have access to as per its desire. This is only a very brief description of a larger subject. There are some other techniques to achieve cross-domain requests, such as using JSONP, **postMessage()** between frames, or local server-side proxies, but we will not detail them here.

Activity 10.01: Implement REST Service Calls Using Various Techniques

So far, we have only coded for HTTP **GET** requests. Let's get some practice using **POST**. The API we have been using in the previous exercises, TheSportsDB, only contains GET requests, making it unsuitable for testing other HTTP methods. Luckily, there are several dummy REST APIs out there made specifically for testing and prototyping that can be used for our purposes. We will use one such free API called **REQ | RES** (at https://reqres.in/):

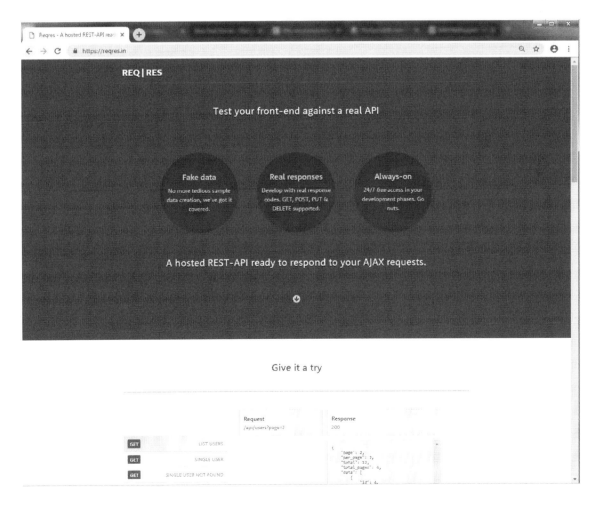

Figure 10.14: Home page of REQ|RES

The API supplies a POST method at https://reqres.in/api/users for which you supply a JSON object with any fields you wish. You include the object as the data of your service call, and the service responds with the same object but with additional `id` and `createdAt` fields.

For instance, if you have the following data:

The request will be similar to:	The response will be similar to:
{ "first_name": "Beyonce", "last_name": "Knowles", "occupation": "artist" }	{ "first_name": "Beyonce", "last_name": "Knowles", "occupation": "artist", "id": "3", "createdAt": "2019-04-11T01:36:14.969Z" }

Figure 10.15: Request and Response example

Your task is to implement the code for this service call using the `$.ajax()` method followed by the `$.post()` method, and finally execute it using the `XMLHttpRequest` method. Then, print out the `id` and `createdAt` fields returned to the console.

Keep in mind that the **REQ | RES** API is really just a dummy service for testing and does not actually persist any data, so don't expect to be able to retrieve the data you sent later.

The high-level steps for the activity are as follows:

1. Use `$.ajax()` with `method: 'post'` and `dataType: 'json'`.

2. Enclose your data fields in an object, `{}`.

3. Create a **success** function to output the expected values.

4. Now, use `$.post()`.

5. Enclose your data fields in an object, `{}`.

6. Create a **success** function to output the expected values.

7. As the last parameter to `$.post()`, use the `'json'` value to indicate the expected JSON return type.

8. Finally, create a new **XMLHttpRequest** object.

9. Call **open('POST')**.

10. Set the **Content-type** and **Accept** request headers to the appropriate values.

11. Create a function for **onreadystatechange** that checks for a status code of **201 (Created)** and parses the JSON data with **JSON.parse()**.

12. Call **JSON.stringify()** on the input data to convert it to JSON format.

13. Send the JSON data when calling **send()**.

The code should result in something like the following in the JavaScript console in Google Chrome:

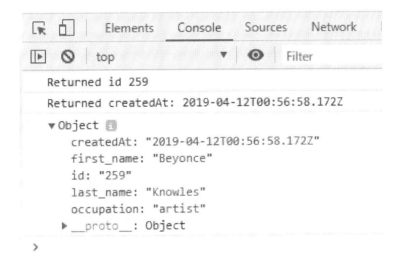

Figure 10.16: JavaScript Console output

Note

The solution to this activity can be found on page 742.

Summary

In the last section, we explored the native **XMLHttpRequest** object and how it differs from other libraries for making service calls. In summary, as you can see, compared to jQuery, the native approach is a lot more verbose, difficult to work with, and low-level for most use cases. Unless you have a specific need where more control is required, I do not recommend its use.

In the next chapter, we will describe regular expressions, which are commonly used to match patterns in a concise, flexible, and efficient manner. We will also explore best practices for writing clean and understandable code, which is critical if you want your code to be easily maintainable and live for a long time.

11

Creating Clean and Maintainable Code

Overview

By the end of this chapter, you will be able to identify and implement basic regular expressions (regex); use best practices to produce clean and maintainable code; utilize code quality tools such as `ESLint`, `JSLint`, and `JSHint` and implement strategies for refactoring code.

Introduction

In this chapter, you will learn about the techniques that can be used for pattern matching and clean coding, which have many uses, perhaps even to facilitate your testing as well.

Regular expressions (**regex** for short) are a concise and powerful method to search for and match patterns. They may appear alien and intimidating at first, but once you learn the basics, they will quickly appear less difficult, and so you are likely to recognize their usefulness. Regexes are common in many languages and in tools where text and data are involved. So, it is a worthwhile investment to take the time to learn them. A pattern that's expressed as a regex is usually much shorter than the equivalent code that's required to parse and match the same pattern using conventional techniques.

Making use of regexes also leads to clean and maintainable coding practices. For programming projects to be successful, it is critical that the code is easily understood by others and that it is orderly, focused, and flexible. This chapter introduces techniques and best practices for coding, starting with choosing the clearest and most understandable names for your variables and methods.

What Is a Regex?

A **regex** is a sequence of characters that form a pattern that's used to search. Each character in the pattern either has special meaning (a metacharacter) or is meant to match the character itself (a literal). This is perhaps best understood by the following example.

As a demonstration of the difference between pattern matching with conventional coding versus regex techniques, consider the following code for matching phone number format patterns in a conventional way. We'll then rewrite the matching logic using a regex for comparison. To keep things simple, we will only look for phone numbers that match the following pattern, which is common for phone numbers, particularly in the United States:

```
[2-9]XX-XXX-XXXX
```

Here, **X** can be any digit from **0-9**, and the first digit cannot be a zero or one (only **2-9** are permitted). For example, **234-567-8901** is a valid phone number in this format.

You can use the following code to do the matching using conventional methods:

conventional.html

```
1 <html>
2 <head>
3   <meta charset="utf-8"/>
4 </head>
5 <body>
6 Enter a phone number in format XXX-XXX-XXXX:
7 <input type="text" id="phone">
8 <div id="msg"></div>
9 <script>
10 var phone = document.getElementById("phone");
11 phone.addEventListener("input", validatePhoneNumber);
12 function isDigit(character) {
13     return character >= '0' && character <= '9';
14 }
```

The full code is available at: https://packt.live/2CFKQtK

The following screenshot show the output of the preceding code when a number is entered in an invalid format:

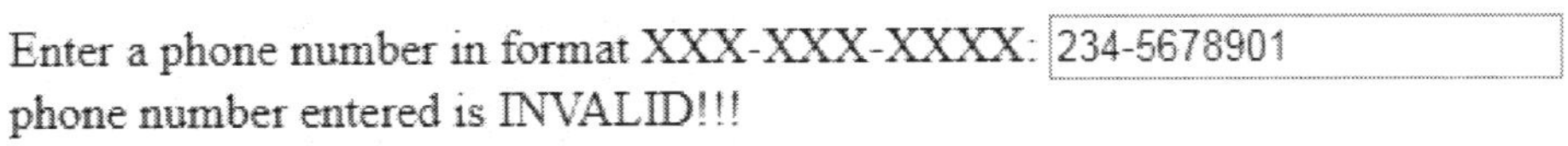

Enter a phone number in format XXX-XXX-XXXX: 234-5678901
phone number entered is INVALID!!!

Figure 11.1: Sample output when a number is input in an incorrect format

Here's the output when a number is entered in a valid format:

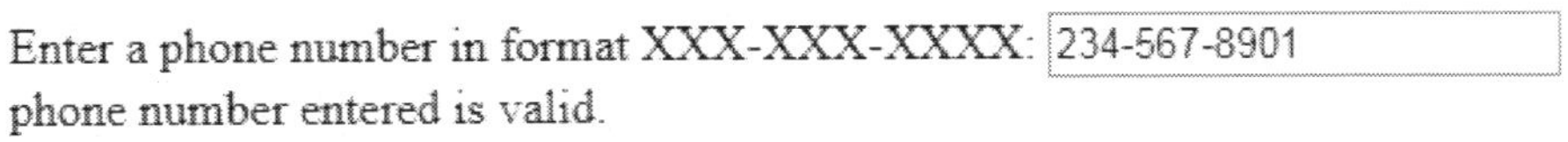

Enter a phone number in format XXX-XXX-XXXX: 234-567-8901
phone number entered is valid.

Figure 11.2: Sample output when a number is input correctly

Let's focus on the important parts of the JavaScript code:

```
var phone = document.getElementById("phone");
phone.addEventListener("input", validatePhoneNumber);
```

These lines set up the phone number validation, which is to be done as the user enters a value. It finds the DOM element of the input text and adds an event listener for the **input** event. This event occurs when the value of **<input>** is changed, such as with a keypress or even if a value is pasted in using cut/paste. When triggered, the **validatePhoneNumber()** function is called.

Note the code that checks whether a character is a digit:

```
function isDigit(character) {
    return character >= '0' && character <= '9';
}
```

This function has a parameter that must be just one character. What may not be intuitive is that JavaScript allows greater than or less than operators on character types. This allows us to check that the character is any digit in the range between the 0 and 9 characters.

The following is the code for the **validatePhoneNumber()** method:

```
var phoneNum = phone.value.trim();
// check if phone number matches format  [2-9]XX-XXX-XXXX
var valid =
    phoneNum.length == 12 &&
    phoneNum.charAt(0) != '0' &&
    isDigit(phoneNum.charAt(0)) &&
    isDigit(phoneNum.charAt(1)) &&
    isDigit(phoneNum.charAt(2)) &&
    phoneNum.charAt(3) == '-' &&
```

This code does the following:

- Checks the expected length of the phone number to make sure there are no extraneous characters, such as additional digits, alphabetic characters, or symbols. Note that since we're calling the **trim()** function when we initially read the phone number value, this check is forgiving of leading and trailing whitespace.

- Checks that the first character is not a 0.

- Checks that the first three characters are digits (indices 0-2).

> **Note**
>
> Rather than calling the **isDigit()** function multiple times, we could have added parameters to the function so that multiple characters would be checked in one invocation. However, for the purposes of this exercise, we chose to keep the code simpler and easier to understand.

- Checks for the – character afterward.

The rest of the validation repeats and is similar for the rest of the characters.

Finally, the validation message is formed and set in the **<div>**:

```
    var validMsg = "phone number entered is " +
        (valid ? "valid." : "INVALID!!!");
    document.getElementById("msg").innerHTML = validMsg;
```

We will now compare this logic to an equivalent implementation using regexes. We'll describe regexes more methodically and in more depth in the next section, but for now, we'll look at how to code with regex techniques, even though it may not make much sense to you yet. We will code an alternative to the phone number validation function we presented, which uses regexes. So, don't worry if you don't quite understand all the concepts yet, as they will be explained in detail later.

Consider the preceding code, which is for pattern matching with conventional methods. Let's modify it so that it uses a regex.

To do this, find the **validatePhoneNumber()** function and the declaration of the **valid** variable. Then, delete the entire expression all the way to the semicolon (**;**) character until the comment above it. Replace the area you deleted with the following:

```
// check if phone number matches format [2-9]XX-XXX-XXXX
var valid = phoneNum.match(//);
```

At this point, you only have a shell of a regex in the area between the two forward slash marks.

After the first forward slash, add a ^ character (called a caret). Your code should now look like this:

```
var valid = phoneNum.match(/^/);
```

The ^ symbol is an **anchor** that indicates matching should begin at the start of the string.

Now, add the characters **[2-9]** so that the code now looks like this:

```
var valid = phoneNum.match(/^[2-9]/);
```

The **[2-9]** characters specify a **character range** to indicate that it must match a character between **2** and **9**.

By now, you will be able to see how you are progressively adding more characters with each step. In a similar fashion, add the remaining characters one by one, as shown in the left column of the following table:

Character	Explanation
\d	This is a **character class** that specifies to match a digit character. This is equivalent to the character range [0-9]. (In the previous character, you did not use **\d** since zeros are not permitted in the first character of a phone number.)
{2}	This is a **fixed quantifier** that indicates that the previous character (**token**) needs to repeat twice for it to be considered a match.
-	This is a **literal character** that simply indicates a dash character that is required to be in the pattern.
	To recap, up until this point, you are expecting three digits and a dash character, for example, the first four characters of **987**-654-3210. The remainder of the regex is mostly a repeat of the pattern up to this point.
\d{3}	A sequence of three digits.
-	A dash character.
\d{4}	A sequence of four digits.
$	This symbol is an **anchor** that indicates matching should terminate at the end of the string and that the string is not permitted to have any other characters after this point. (This is the counterpart to the ^ anchor)..

Figure 11.3: Table of characters

The complete code should now look like this:

```
// check if phone number matches format [2-9]XX-XXX-XXXX
var valid = phoneNum.match(/^[2-9]\d{2}-\d{3}-\d{4}$/);
```

Here, you have seen the power of regular expressions and that all of them can be expressed in just one line of code. The different concepts of a regular expressions are shown in the following figure:

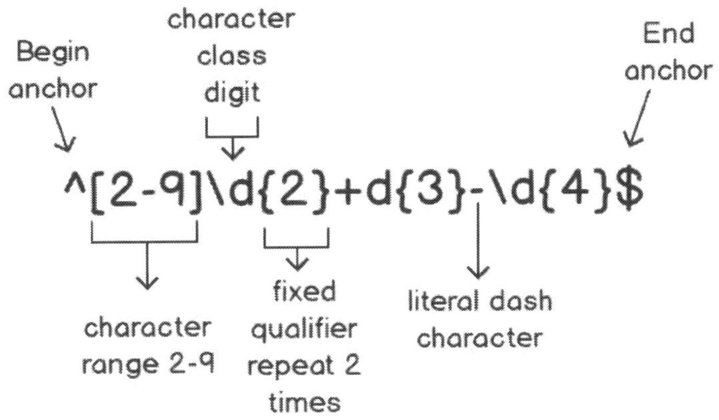

Figure 11.4: Showing different concepts in the regular expression

Regexes in Detail

In the upcoming sections, the following sample phrase is used for illustration:

"The ships were loaded with all these belongings of the mother"

This phrase will be used to demonstrate various regex concepts, including literal characters, word boundaries, character classes, and others.

Literal Characters

The simplest regex is one of more **literal characters**, such as **the**. This indicates a pattern that is a match if the **t** character is immediately followed by **h** and finally an **e** character. This expression would have four matches in the sample phrase: the initial **the**, the second to last word, **the**, **the** in the word **these**, and the sequence of **the** as part of the word **mother**.

Special Characters, Anchors, and Escaping

If a regex only had literals, its usefulness would be limited. In most cases, you do not want to only match literals; therefore, regexes have a number of characters that have special meanings. These are also known as metacharacters. Two of these special characters are the **^** and **$ anchors** that you saw earlier, which indicate the beginning and end of a string, respectively.

So, if you change the regex to **^the**, only the initial **the** of the phrase would now be a match since this is the only instance of **the** in the phrase that is at the beginning of the string. Anchors are often important in situations where you need to avoid matching too much that is not intended to be matched.

The following are the most common characters that have special meaning in regexes:

Character	Character Name
^	The caret
$	The dollar sign
\	The backslash
(and)	Parenthesis
[and]	Brackets
{ and }	Braces
.	The period, or dot
		The pipe symbol
?	The question mark
*	The asterisk, or star
+	The plus sign

Figure 11.5: Special characters

Note

If you need to use any of these characters in your regexes as a literal character, in most cases, the character will need to be escaped. You do that by placing a backslash \ before the character.

Here are two examples:

- If you need to match a dollar sign as part of your pattern, you would use \$.

- Some less obvious escapes are the backslash character itself (you would just use two consecutive backslashes, for example, \\), and a dot, where \. is the correct escaping sequence.

Word Boundary

Another type of anchor is a **word boundary**, which is denoted by \b (a backslash followed by a b). A word boundary is defined as either of the following:

- The beginning of a string, followed by a word character

- The character between whitespace and a word character, or after a word character leading to either whitespace or the end of the string

Note that the word characters are defined as follows.

- If the preceding regex was changed to **\bthe**, there would only be three matches in the sample phrase: the four previous matches, minus **the** in **mother**. (The initial **\b** of the pattern are special characters, and the remainder are literal characters.)

- If the regex was changed to **\bthe\b**, only the two standalone **the** words would be matches, and not the ones in **these** or **mother**. This is one way to specify to search for whole words, but with no other leading or trailing characters in a given word.

Shorthand Character Classes and Word Characters

There are a number of **character classes** that are available in a sort of shorthand notation due to how commonly they are used. One is the **\d** sequence, which denotes any digit **[0-9]**.

Another is the **word character, \w**, which is defined as **[A-Za-z0-9_]**. (Character classes and ranges will be defined in more detail next. For now, this is read as a character in the range of uppercase characters **A-Z**, range of characters **a-z**, range of digits **0-9**, or the underscore **_** character.) Here are some examples:

- If the **the\w** regex were used on the preceding sample phrase, only the sequence of **the** in the words **these** and **mother** would be a match, since the other two **the** words do not have a word character following it.

- If the **\wthe\w** regex were used, only the sequence of **the** in the word **mother** would match, as it is the only place in the string where the sequence **the** is both preceded and followed by a word character. This is one way to specify how to search for characters that are only contained within a word.

- Combining the word boundary and word character shortcuts, if the regex **\bthe\w** were used, only the sequence of **the** in the word **these** would match as it is the only place in the string where the sequence **the** starts on a word boundary and is followed by a word character.

Another common shorthand character class is **\s**, which is shorthand for whitespace, including space characters, tabs, and newlines.

Inverse Classes

Every shorthand character class has an inverse class as well, denoted by making the letter uppercase:

- **\B**: The opposite of a word boundary, such as in the middle of a word

- **\D**: Represents any non-digit character

- `\W`: Any character that is not included in `[A-Za-z0-9_]`
- `\S`: Any non-whitespace character

For example, as the inverse of the first example in the previous section, if the `the\W` regex were used on the preceding sample phrase, only the two **the** characters would match, including the trailing space character. The words **these** and **mother** would be a match, since in both cases there is a word character following **the**.

Dot Character

The dot, `.`, matches any character except newlines. For instance, the `.h.` regex looks for any **h** and matches it with the character before and after it, as long as it is not a newline. The highlighted characters that follow are the result of applying the regex to the earlier sample phrase:

"The ships were loaded with all these belongings of the mother"

Take special note of the third match of the last two letters of the word **with**, along with the space character that follows it. It is easy to forget that a dot matches any character, including a space. This can be a common error if you do intend to allow spaces in your pattern.

Sets

One or more characters or character classes enclosed in square brackets, `[...]`, indicates we should match any of the given characters. This is called a **set**. Here are two examples:

- The `[AEIOUaeiou]` regex can be used to match vowel characters.
- When combining a set followed by two literal characters, the `[oi]ng` regex would match the **ong** and the **ing** in the word **belongings** (from the sample phrase).

Ranges

One **range** you saw earlier was `[2-9]`, which indicated a character between **2** and **9**. Similar to sets, ranges are specified within square brackets, `[...]`, and use a dash character to separate the characters that indicate the range.

Another range you saw earlier was `[A-Za-z0-9_]`, which specified the word characters. This also shows how multiple ranges and even a character that's not part of a range can be indicated in one expression, as this allows characters from **A-Z**, **a-z**, and **0-9**, as well as the underscore character.

Excluding Sets and Ranges

The opposite of regular sets and ranges, an excluding range indicates to "match a character except for the following". Excluding sets or ranges is indicated by placing a caret character, ^, immediately after the first square bracket in the expression.

For instance, `[^AEIOUaeiou]` would match any character that is NOT a vowel.

The dash can also be included in the exclusion to indicate a range of characters to be excluded. For example, `[^0-9]` would indicate to match any character that is not a digit (similar to `\d`).

Quantifiers

A **quantifier** specifies how many of a given character, character class, or token are required for a match.

Perhaps the most straightforward is a **fixed quantifier**, which requires an exact number of occurrences for it to be a match, as you saw at the beginning of this section. This type is specified by placing a number inside a pair of curly braces, such as `{4}`. For example, the `a{4}` regex would require the letter `a` to be repeated four times, and `\d{3}` would require three digits in sequence.

Its close cousin, the range quantifier, can be specified using a format similar to `{min,max}`. This one would match if anything between the specified minimum and maximum number of occurrences was present. For example, the `a{2,5}` regex would match any of `aa`, `aaa`, `aaaa`, or `aaaaa`.

A special type of range allows for an unbounded upper limit if the numeral after the comma is omitted. For example, `a{3,}` would match any number of consecutive `a` characters of at least three occurrences.

Shorthand Quantifiers

There are three quantifiers that are used so often that they have special shortcut characters designated to denote them. They are as follows:

Symbol	Meaning	Equivalent to
+	One or more	{1,}
*	Zero or more	{0,}
?	Zero or exactly one	{0,1}

Figure 11.6: Quantifiers

Combining these shorthand qualifiers with the concepts we previously covered (literals, character classes, sets, ranges, and so on), the following are example regexes and what they would match:

Regex	Matches
a+	a, aa, aaa, aaaa, ...
a*	<empty string>, a, aa, aaa, aaaa, ...
a?	<empty string>, a (only).
[ab]+	a, b, aa, bb, ab, ba, aaa, bbb, aba, bab, aab, bba, ...
[ab]*	<empty string>, a, b, aa, bb, ab, ba, aaa, bbb, aba, bab, aab, bba, ...
[ab]?	<empty string>, a, b (only).
[1-3]+	1, 2, 3, 11, 12, 13, 111, 222, 333, 123, 122, 321, 1233, 12333, 1233333, ...
[1-3]*	<empty string>, 1, 2, 3, 11, 12, 13, 111, 222, 333, 123, 122, 321, 1233, 12333, 1233333, ...
[1-3]?	<empty string>, 1, 2, 3 (only).
[ab3-5]?	<empty string>, a, b, 3, 4, 5 (only). Notice that both a set and a range are specified in the same expression. This is to be read as an a, b, or character in the range between 3 and 5.
.+	Any sequence of characters (besides a newline).
.*	<empty string> or any sequence of characters (besides a newline).
.?	<empty string> or exactly one character (besides a newline).

Figure 11.7: Regex and their Matches

Alternation

Let's say you want your pattern to allow either of two (or more) words. You can do this by separating the words with a pipe | character, which is equivalent to an **OR** indicating **expression1 OR expression2**.

In most cases, it is also a good idea to enclose the alternative expressions in parenthesis, for example, **(expression1|expression2)**, to separate them from the rest of the pattern. For example, to scan for either a word, **the**, followed by one or more whitespace characters, which would be either **mother** or **father**, the regex would be as follows:

```
the\s+(mother|father)
```

Many More Regex Concepts

This chapter covers only a brief overview of basic regex concepts and provides a good background so that you can get started with them. You are encouraged to explore more advanced features using the many available resources. These include the following concepts:

- Greedy versus lazy quantifiers: https://packt.live/33vxqvQ
- Capturing groups: https://packt.live/34Iq0G0
- Backreferences: https://packt.live/2NqrDCe
- Lookahead and lookbehind: https://packt.live/2NrkMbR
- Sticky flag: https://packt.live/32q86Gw
- The internals of how regex engines actually work: https://packt.live/2oXQUKE

Pattern Specification and Flags

So far, we have covered the elements that comprise regex patterns, but now, we will cover how these patterns are conveyed in JavaScript code. The most common method is to enclose the pattern in a pair of slash characters, for example, **/pattern/**. Flags can also be added after the second slash, though this is optional.

Flags can change the behavior of how matching and searching occurs. The most common flags are as follows:

- **g**: If specified, all matches are returned (if not specified, only the first match is returned by default).
- **i**: Makes the matching case-insensitive; there's no differentiation between uppercase and lowercase letters.

Others include **m** (multiline search), **s** (dot . matches newline), **u** (Unicode support), and **y** (sticky mode).

Finding Matches with String.match()

The JavaScript **String** class has a number of built-in methods that accept regex parameters. This section outlines some of them.

The most common method you would use is **String.match()**. This method behaves differently, and its return value varies depending on whether the **g** flag is included:

- If there is no **g** flag: Searching stops after the first match is found. The result is an array with the match returned as the array element, the additional property **index**, indicating the position where the match was found, and some additional properties. (Note that it has other functionalities if the regex contains groupings, but groups are not covered in this chapter)

- If there is a **g** flag: Searches for all possible matches and returns those found in an array. There are no other properties in the return value.

Exercise 11.01: The Effect of the g Flag

The following code illustrates the difference regarding whether the **g** flag is present or not. It matches words that begin with the letter **t**. (The **i** flag is also demonstrated to make the match case insensitive.) Let's get started:

1. In the Google Chrome browser, go into **Developer Tools** (Menu (the three dots in the upper right of the screen), **More Tools | Developer Tools**, or just hit the **F12** key).

2. Type the following into the console to set up our test string:

```
const str = "Here's the food for Tommy today";
let match;
```

3. **Case #1**: This is where the **g** flag is not present. Type the following:

```
let match = str.match(/\bt\w+/i);
```

In the steps that follow, the lines of the code snippets that begin with **>** indicate what you should type in. The lines that begin with **<-** is the output you are expected to see.

4. Let's see what was matched. To do that, type the following:

```
> match[0]
<- "the"
```

5. Check at what character index the match was made:

```
> match.index
<- 7
```

6. Since there is no **g**, we are not expecting any further matches. To verify this, use the following code:

```
> match[1]
<- undefined
```

The matches from the first expression will be displayed as follows:

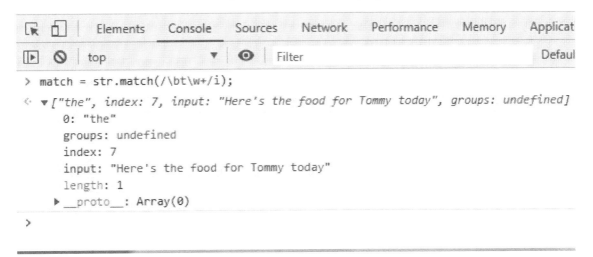

Figure 11.8: Full output of the first match expression

7. **Case #2**: This is where the **g** flag is present. Type the following to reassign the match variable to include **g** (and **i**):

```
match = str.match(/\bt\w+/gi);
```

8. Type the remaining lines in succession, checking the expected output of each:

```
> match[0]
<- "the"
> match[1]
<- "Tommy"
> match[2]
<- "today"
> match[3]
<- undefined
```

The matches of the expression with a **g** will be displayed as follows:

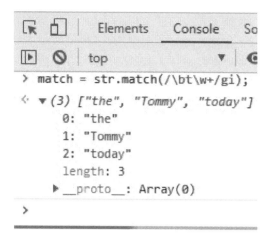

Figure 11.9: Full output of the match expression with the g flag

In this exercise, you saw how to use the **g** flag of the **String.match()** method to can obtain multiple matches. Next, you will learn about other methods that involve regexes.

Other String Methods for Regexes

The following table briefly describes some of the other methods in the String object related to regexes:

`String.search(regex)`	Returns the position of the first match, or −1 if no match is found.
`String.split(regex)`	Splits a string using the regex as a separating delimiter. Returns an array of substrings.
`String.replace(regex, str)`	Searches for characters that match the regex and replaces them with the given string. Only the first occurrence is replaced, unless the **g** flag is indicated with the regex.

Figure 11.10: String methods

There is another useful method to take note of when using regexes in JavaScript. The **test()** method returns a simple **true** or **false** that indicates whether a match has been found. You can use it in code such as the following to test whether a string begins with the characters **hello**:

```
if (/^hello/.test(str)) {


}
```

> **Note**
>
> There are other more advanced methods of the String object that are not covered here. JavaScript also has a dedicated built-in RegExp object that supports advanced use cases (the **test()** method actually belongs to RegExp).

Exercise 11.02: Modifying Regex to Match a Pattern

Recall the regex pattern we presented at the beginning of this chapter, which we used to match phone numbers in the format **XXX-XXX-XXXX**:

```
^[2-9]\d{2}-\d{3}-\d{4}$
```

Using what you've learned so far, in this exercise, you will modify the regex to match phone numbers of a slightly different format:

```
(XXX) XXX-XXXX
```

There are many sites that help you craft and test regexes. We will use https://regex101.com/ to work on our regex. Let's get started:

1. First, compare the two formats to see how similar they are. Notice that the new format, **(XXX) XXX-XXXX**, is identical to the original format, **XXX-XXX-XXXX** , for the last seven digits and is only different at the beginning of the pattern. We only need to replace the first four characters of the original pattern (the three digits and a dash, **XXX-**) with the new characters (an open parenthesis, three digits, a close parenthesis, and a space).

2. We need to come up with a regex that corresponds to **(XXX)**, including a trailing space character that is not displayed:

```
\([2-9]\d{2}\)
```

    Let's break this code down:

    -   **\(**: The first character you need to match is a parenthesis. Remember that parentheses are special characters (metacharacters) in a regex, so they need to be escaped with a backslash to indicate that you really intend for the parenthesis character to be matched.

    -   **[2-9]**: A character range to match a character between 2 and 9.

- **\d**: This is a character class that specifies to match a digit character.

- **{2}**: A fixed quantifier that indicates that the previous digit character (\d) needs to repeat twice for it to be considered a match.

- **\)**: The closing parenthesis, also escaped.

3. By combining this with the rest of the original regex, you get the final regex:

```
^\([2-9]\d{2}\) \d{3}-\d{4}$
```

To test this solution, there are many sites that help you craft and test regexes. You can go to https://regex101.com/ and enter the regex in the input box. Also, enter **(234) 567-8910** in the TEST STRING area, as shown here:

Figure 11.11: Screenshot of https://regex101.com/

As you can see, the MATCH INFORMATION section indicates that our test string is a full match.

There is quite a bit happening on this screen, and a lot of information that helps you understand and work with regexes. If you look at the REGULAR EXPRESSION input box, you will see that the various elements of the regex have been color-coded to help break it down to its constituent parts. The EXPLANATION area goes even further and provides detailed explanations of each character or token. Since the full text was not visible in the preceding screenshot, here are the explanations that were provided:

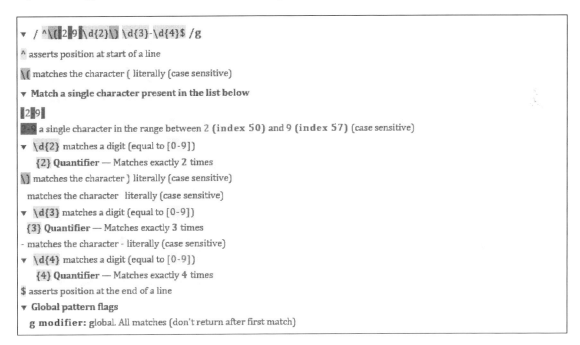

Figure 11.12: The EXPLANATION area

Adding More Strings to the Regex

Besides having a test string that passes matching, it is a good idea to also put in other test strings that are similar but are not expected to pass. The following screenshot shows some other such patterns in the TEST STRING area, but notice that only the first one of those patterns shows a match (as expected):

Figure 11.13: More test strings that are not expected to match

The pattern to match phone numbers in the previous exercise works okay, but it looks for a very specific pattern. The following activity will challenge you into making the regex more flexible so that it accepts multiple phone number formats.

What if you were asked to come up with one regex that can be used to match either of the **xxx-xxx-xxxx** or **(xxx) xxx-xxxx** patterns?

The challenge is to come up with just one regex that can match either phone number format. Before presenting a good solution, let's consider an incorrect and naive one that, at first glance, seems like the most obvious approach to take, but is actually flawed and fraught with pitfalls.

Observe that the second format is mostly similar to the original one, with the exception that the first set of three digits begins and end with parenthesis characters (**(** and **)**) and is followed by a space rather than a dash character. You may begin to think of representing these differences by adding parenthesis to the regular expression and simply making them optional (using the ? quantifier) and placing the dash and space in a set (using **[]** syntax). Such a regex would look like this (the additions are emphasized):

```
^\(?[2-9]\d{2}\)?[- ]\d{3}-\d{4}$
```

The problem is that this regex is incomplete and would also allow matches of some incorrect and undesirable formats, such as the following:

- **(234 567-8901** (no ending parenthesis)
- **234) 567-8901** (no starting parenthesis)
- **234 567-8901** (using a space character inappropriately)
- **(234)-567-8901** (using a dash inappropriately)

This can be seen if you enter these test strings into the tool as well:

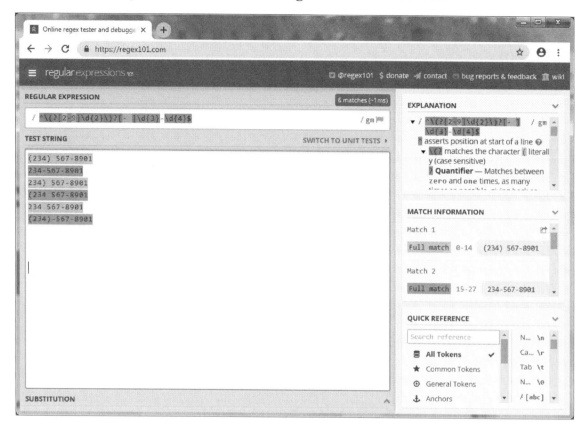

Figure 11.14: All the test strings match due to a flawed regex

Only the first two test strings should have matched, but they all did (indicated by them all being highlighted in blue).

Activity 11.01: Expanding Phone Number Matching Patterns to Accept Multiple Formats

In the previous exercise, we modified a regex to match phone numbers that have the following format: **(XXX) XXX-XXXX**. In this activity, we will create one regex that can be used to match either of the **XXX-XXX-XXXX** or **(XXX) XXX-XXXX** patterns. Once you have completed this activity, you should have a regex that accepts either of the **(XXX) XXX-XXXX** or **XXX-XXX-XXXX** number formats.

The high-level steps for the activity are as follows:

1. Indicate that the regex snippets corresponding to each format are alternate expressions of an alternation.

2. Combine them with the rest of the original regex in the previous exercise to get the complete regex.

3. Now, test the regex with the following numbers: (234) 567-8901; 234-567-8907; 234) 567-8901; (234 567-8901; 234 567-8901; and (234)-567-8901.

The expected output of this activity should be as follows:

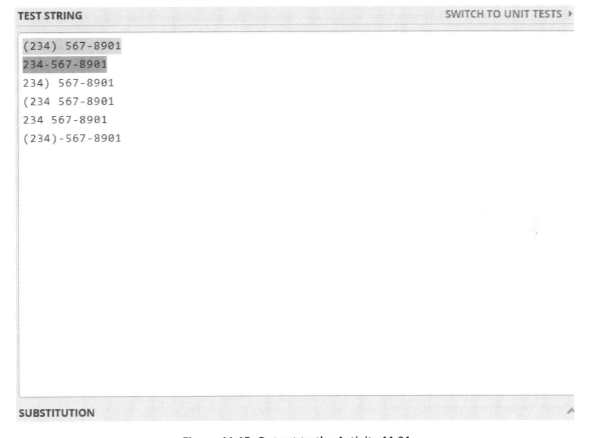

Figure 11.15: Output to the Activity 11.01

> **Note**
>
> The solution to the activity can be found on page 745.

Activity 11.02: Expanding Phone Number Matching Patterns to Accept a Particular Format

In this activity, we will expand the pattern from the previous activity to allow a format that's used in many non-US countries that optionally prepends a plus sign, 1-3 digits, and a space (for example, **+XXX**), such as one of the following:

```
+97 (234) 567-8910
+97 234-567-8910
```

Once you've completed this activity, you should have a regex that successfully tests for the **+xxx** format.

Steps:

1. Construct the regex for the **+XXX** pattern (where between 1-3 digits are acceptable).

2. Combine this with the original regex to get the complete regex.

3. Modify the regex to allow the use of space or dot characters as digit separators rather than only dashes.

4. Test the patterns with the following numbers:

Figure 11.16: Many of the patterns that match the regular expression

> **Note**
>
> The solution to this activity can be found on page 747.

Useful Regexes

The following table presents a number of regexes for different purposes. You should be able to understand them using the concepts we've covered, but in most cases, no further explanation will be given besides for the regex itself:

Regex	Purpose
`^([01]?\d|2[0-3]):[0-5]\d$`	Time in 24-hour format. Leading zero required in the minutes portion if less than 10.
`^(0?[1-9]|1[0-2]):[0-5]\d [AaPp][Mm]$`	Time in 12-hour format (with an optional leading zero). If the number starts with a 1, the second number can only be a 0, 1, or 2, since 12 is the max hour. Must have AM or PM at the end, separated by a space (lowercase is OK too).
`^.+@.+$`	Simple pattern for email addresses (but is very forgiving. More restrictive and precise patterns exist as well to make sure a domain is specified, but the pattern that's presented should suffice for many use cases).
`^[a-z\d_]{3,16}$`	A username between 3 and 16 characters long consisting of just lowercase letters, numbers, or underscore characters.
`^\d{5}(-\d{4})?$`	US Postal five-digit zip code (with an optional four-digit extension). Other countries will require other regexes for their specific formats.
`^\d+\.\d+$`	Decimal numbers (as a minimum, it needs one whole number and one decimal place, for example, 0.0).
`^\d+(\.\d+)?$`	Whole number with an optional decimal place.
`^-?\d+(\.\d+)?$`	Whole number or decimal, may optionally be negative.
`([12]\d{3}-(0[1-9]|1[0-2])-(0[1-9]|[12]\d|3[01]))`	Date format of YYYY-MM-dd.
`^\$(\d{1,3}(\,\d{3})*|(\d+))(\.\d{2})?$`	Matches US currency with a leading $ sign. The dollar value may be separated by commas for thousands and so on, but this is not required. Cents portion is optional. Adjustments can be made for other currencies as well, such as replacing \$ with £ for British Pounds Sterling. (Does not restrict leading zeros.)
`^(\d{1,3}(\.\d{3})*|(\d+))(\,\d{2})?$`	European-style currency. Different from the US or UK, the symbols are inverted. A dot "." is used to optionally group the thousands and a comma "," is used for the coin portion, for example, 10.456.000,50. This regex has no specific currency symbol, but one can be added as needed.

Figure 11.17: Regex and their purpose

In this topic, you learned about the basics of regular expressions and their usefulness. Just a word of caution, though: while regexes are very powerful, they can also be very tricky to implement, and it can take some practice to get them right.

Now, for a bit of an admission. While our exercise presented regexes for validating phone numbers, they were for the sake of learning and education about regexes. In a real-world application, you would probably want to consider using a dedicated library for such validation. Several such libraries are available, and the advantages of using such libraries are that they are well thought out, tested, and support a wide variety of options and phone number formats from different countries around the world. One such library is Google's libphonenumber.

In the next topic, you'll get into clean coding.

Best Practices for Clean Coding

Code often has a way of living longer than anyone would think it would. Just look at all the mainframe systems that are still in use today. At times, even experienced developers are baffled by it and have a difficult time understanding code they themselves wrote when looking at the code just a few weeks or months later. It behooves software developers to adopt a mindset of good practices and habits when coding.

Code is almost never written just once to never be used again. Often, you or someone else will need to work on the code at a later date. If you write clean code, you are helping your future self and co-workers work more efficiently when that time comes. You are also making it easier to maintain the system and fix bugs.

Many of the ideas and practices in this section are based on the books and blogs of Robert C. Martin, also known as "Uncle Bob," who is a recognized expert in the field of clean coding and has produced popular books, blogs, and training videos. We will only present a brief overview and highlights, but entire books have been written on the subject. You are encouraged to delve deeper into this subject.

Look at the following code:

```
function circ(r) {
    return r * 2 * Math.PI;
}
```

The purpose of this code is to calculate the circumference of a circle, but I'll bet this was not very obvious to you based on how it is written. Perhaps adding some explanatory comments would help, but compare the preceding code to this:

```
function circumference(radius) {
    return radius * 2 * Math.PI;
}
```

You would agree that this code was much more understandable and leaves little doubt about what it does, what the parameter is, and what is returned. Renaming the function from `circ` to `circumference` and the parameter from `r` to `radius` is all it took to achieve understanding. This was all done without the need to add any explanatory comments.

We've improved our code so far by using better naming, but here's another improvement worth making. The usual formula for circumference is `c = πd`, where `d` is the diameter. If you split our calculation into two steps, the code would be clearer. Compare the preceding code to the following:

```
function circumference(radius) {
    let diameter = radius * 2;
    return diameter * Math.PI;
}
```

This simple change makes it clearer why the calculation needed to multiply the radius by 2, namely, to calculate the diameter before multiplying it by pi to get the circumference.

This may not seem like a big improvement, and arguably the extra line of code does not add much value or clarity. You would probably be correct in this simple instance. But consider how coding in such a way could potentially simplify scenarios where more complex calculations or logic is required.

Good Naming Practices

Use the following guidelines when naming variables, functions, or other objects:

- **Use intention revealing names**: Your names should be clear enough that no comments should be needed to explain them, for example, `timeElapsedInDays`, `daysSinceCreation`, and `ageInDays`. In general, code should be as self-documenting as possible and comments should be kept to a minimum. Comments have a way of becoming outdated as code is refactored and logic is changed over time, and programmers tend to forget to update them.

- **Avoid disinformation**: Don't call your variable `bookList` if it is in fact an array of books. Just calling it `books` is preferred.

- **Make meaningful distinctions**: If you have two different classes with similar names, such as `BookInfo` and `BookData`, you have made the names different without making them mean anything different. Use more specific names that differentiate what the purpose of each class is.

- **Use pronounceable names**: Let's take a bad example:

```
const yyyymmdstr = moment().format("YYYY/MM/DD");
```

Now, let's compare it with a good one:

```
const currentDate = moment().format("YYYY/MM/DD");
```

- **Use constants and searchable names**: You will read code more than you will ever write it. A variable named **SECONDS_IN_DAY** is more meaningful than **86400** and explains what that number represents better. It also makes it easier to locate later when searching over the body of text.

- **Class names**: Classes should have noun or noun phrase names such as **Customer**, **Account**, and **AddressParser**. Avoid words such as **Manager**, **Processor**, **Data**, or **Info**, which are either verbs or too generic.

- **Method names**: Methods should have verb or verb phrase names such as **addFunds**, **deleteUser**, or **save**. Accessors and mutators should be prefixed with **get** or **set**.

- **Pick one word per concept**: It is confusing to have **fetch**, **retrieve**, and **get**, which do the same thing. It's best to pick one word and use it consistently across your code.

- **Don't be cute**: If names are too humorous or specific to one culture, they may not make sense to other people who don't share the same culture or sense of humor. This is like using **eatMyShorts()** to mean **abort()**.

- **Don't add unneeded context**: If your class or object is already named descriptively, there is no need to repeat the name in the variables within. Take a look at the following examples.

This is bad:

```
const employee = {
    employeeFirstName: "Daniel",
    employeenLastName: "Rosenbaum",
    employeeActive: true
};

function fireEmployee(employee) {
    employee.employeeActive = false;
}
```

Whereas this is good:

```
const employee = {
    firstName: "John",
    lastName: "Smith",
    active: true
```

```
};

function fireEmployee(employee) {
    employee.active = false;
}
```

Following are the best practices for functions:

- **Functions should only do one thing and be small**: When functions are concise and limited in what they do, they are easier to understand, test, and work with. They would also read cleaner and be refactored easily. Coupled with a good function name, they are self-documenting as well.

Here's a bad function:

```
function phoneSubscribers(subscribers) {
    subscribers.forEach(subscriber => {
        const subscriberRecord = database.lookup(subscriber);
        if (subscriberRecord.isActive()) {
            phoneSubscriber(subscriber);
        }
    });
}
```

Here's a good function:

```
function phoneActiveSubscribers(subscribers) {
    clients.filter(isActiveSubscriber).forEach(phone);
}

function isActiveSubscriber(subscriber) {
    const subscriberRecord = database.lookup(subscriber);
    return subscriberRecord.isActive();
}
```

- **Limit the number of function arguments**: Ideally, there should be no more than two or three arguments. This makes testing easier. If there are more arguments, consider that your function is probably trying to tackle too much and should be split into multiple functions.

- **Function names should say what they do**: Here's an example of a bad function name:

```
function addToDate(date, month) {
    // ...
}
```

```
const date = new Date();

// It's hard to tell from the function name what is added
addToDate(date, 1);
```

This is a good function name:

```
function addMonthToDate(month, date) {
  // ...
}

const date = new Date();
addMonthToDate(1, date);
```

- **Don't use boolean flags as function parameters**: If at some point, a function's behavior will be completely altered due to the value of a flag, it is an indication that it would be better to split it into two separate functions. As a guideline, if the name of the function can no longer reasonably be called **doSomething()** and instead turns into **doSomethingOrSomethingDifferentIfAFlagIsSet()**, it's time to split the function.

Take a look at the following code:

```
function createFile(name, temp) {
  if (temp) {
    fs.create(`./temp/${name}`);
  } else {
    fs.create(name);
  }
}
```

Rather than using the preceding code, use the following instead:

```
function createFile(name) {
  fs.create(name);
}

function createTempFile(name) {
  createFile(`./temp/${name}`);
}
```

- **Write your functions to avoid side effects**: Very briefly, a side effect is if, during the execution of a function, something is modified, or an action is done that does not involve the values the function will return. This may be something such as changing the value of a global variable, writing to a file, or making a service call.

Of course, there will be times where such actions are needed, such as to make a service call to obtain data or write results to a file. However, the best practice here is to isolate such logic into dedicated functions but to take care and keep the majority of your functions as pure and side-effect-free as possible.

As an example, the following function modifies a global variable and therefore has side effects. (This could be code in a game where the player's character is located somewhere on a grid.) The **playerX** and **playerY** variables represent the character's current coordinates:

```
let playerX = 45, playerY = 100;
const moveRight = (numSlots) => {
  playerX += numSlots;
}
moveRight(5);
```

It is better to take x as a parameter and reassign the result to a global variable outside the function so that the function remains pure and maintains predictable return values (and makes it easier to test):

```
let playerX = 45, playerY=100;
const moveRight = (playerX, numSlots) => playerX + numSlots;
playerX = moveRight(playerX, 5);
```

> **Note**
>
> Side effects and pure functions are covered in more detail in *Chapter 14, Understanding Functional Programming*, on functional programming. Another important example is to clone objects, arrays, or lists when making modifications, rather than directly doing the modification itself on the input.

- **Create functions to capture conditional clauses**: Your code could become cluttered, unfocused, and hard to follow if you have complex conditions. Creating dedicated functions for your conditions and naming them descriptively makes the code self-documenting and easier to follow.

An example of a bad function:

```
if (serviceCall.state === "loading" && isEmpty(result)) {
    // ...
}
```

An example of a good function:

```
function shouldShowSpinner(serviceCall, result) {
    return serviceCall.state === "loading" && isEmpty(result);
}

if (shouldShowSpinner(serviceCall, result)) {
    // ...
}
```

JavaScript Linters

A linter is a tool that analyzes source code to help you debug your code, find potential issues and bugs and check coding styles (which is often subjective). Using a linter in your projects could help you and your team improve the quality of your code and provide consistent styling, which could help smooth out differences of code that different team members write.

Linters can typically be used in three different ways:

- Typing or pasting your code into the online version of a tool via a browser page. This is the simplest way, but it is not convenient for anything but small spot checks.

- Using a plugin for your IDE or text editor, either to show your errors and warnings as you type or separately.

- Running scans and generating reports as part of your automated build process every time your source code is built, or periodically. (If desired, you can even cause builds to fail if the scan results in errors of sufficient severity.)

There are several linters available for JavaScript, including the following:

- **ESLint**: This is very configurable and customizable. This perhaps makes it the most complex and hardest linter to just pick up and start using.

- **JSLint**: This is somewhat configurable but highly opinionated on a popular but particular coding style, as described in the tool's documentation.

- **JSHint**: This is somewhere between the other two in terms of customizability.

Exercise 11.03: JSLint

This exercise will describe **JSLint** in more detail since it is the easiest to set up and start using, uses a good coding style, and is a good fit for many projects. Let's get started:

1. Open a web browser such as Google Chrome and go to www.jslint.com.

2. In the Options section on the lower part of the screen, select **Assume → a browser** (this sets the scan to define certain objects that are usually available in a browser, such as a **document** object):

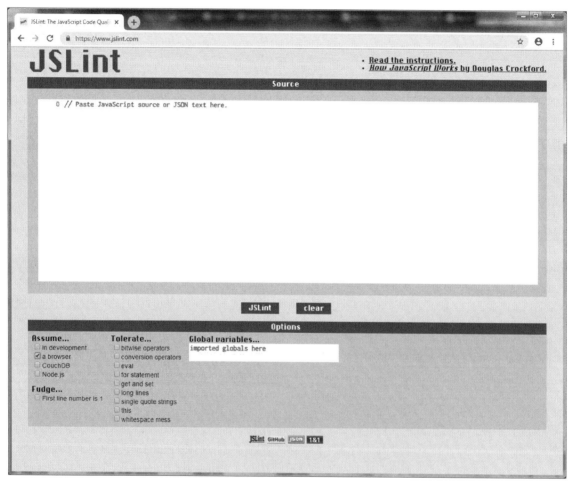

Figure 11.18: Online version of JSLint

3. Paste in the code from **conventional.html** file into the *Source* window.

4. Press the *JSLint* button, which will result in an output that's similar to what's shown in the following screenshot:

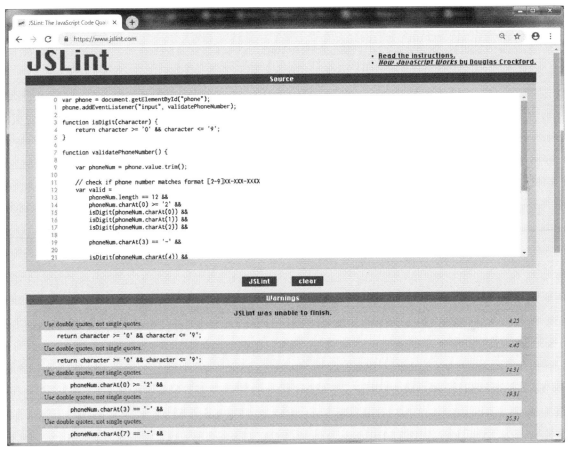

Figure 11.19: Result of the scan

5. The scan results have multiple warnings of the following: `Use double quotes, not single quotes`. This is perhaps an example of a subjective preference as it is common in many languages for single characters to use single quotes, not double-quotes. Luckily, this is a configurable option if you select **Tolerate → single quote strings** in the Options section, as shown in the following screenshot. After clicking the *JSLint* button once again, this will result in all the warnings being removed:

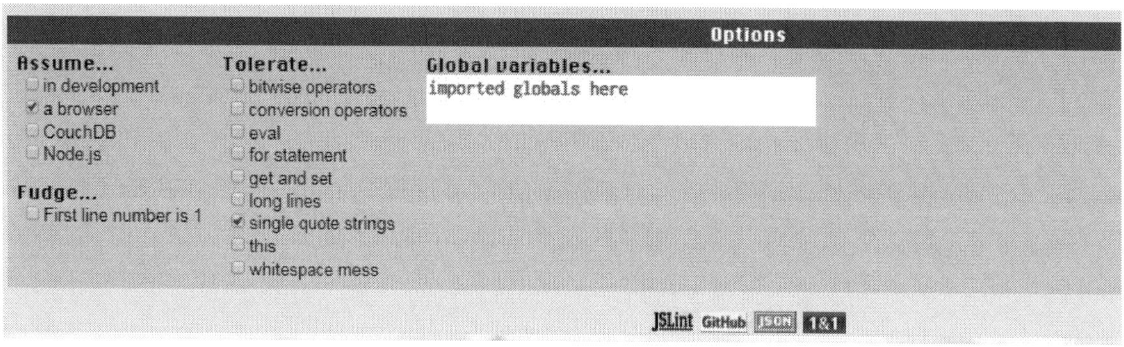

Figure 11.20: Tolerate → single quote strings option

6. An alternative way of specifying the option to allow single quote strings (and a number of other options) is by means of a special comment syntax that begins with **/*jslint**. Uncheck the **Tolerate → single quote strings** option and add the following to the top of the code:

```
/*jslint
      single
*/
```

The warnings will continue to be empty upon clicking the JSLint button.

This exercise explains how your JavaScript code compiles using the **Jslint** tool. It also helps to decrease the debugging time by providing a fixing issues report.

Activity 11.03: Refactoring to Clean Code

Making a habit of using clean coding best practices is an essential skill. We are now ready to put our newly acquired clean coding skills to test.

Look at the JavaScript code in the **<script>** section of the following file and figure out how you can refactor it to be cleaner and easier to maintain and test.

`activity_original_code.html`

```
1  <html>
2  <head>
3  <meta charset="utf-8"/>
4  </head>
5  <body>
5  <span id="error" style="color: red"></span>
6  <table>
7    <tr>
8      <td># of hours:</td>
9      <td><input id="numHours" /></td>
10   </tr>
11   <tr>
12     <td>Pay rate per hour:</td>
13     <td><input id="payRate" /></td>
14     <td>(in ####.## format)</td>
15   </tr>
```

In short, this is a simple web page that calculates worker pay based on the number of hours, pay rate per hour, and worker type. There are three types of workers that have different rules regarding how their pay is determined: **Standard**, who gets overtime pay at **1.5x** after **40** hours, **No Overtime**, who do not get any overtime, and **Double Overtime** workers, who are paid **2x** after **50** hours.

There are also format checks for the two number fields (implemented with regexes) and a facility to show validation error messages. The following screenshot shows the output with valid inputs (there is only minimal color and styling in this implementation):

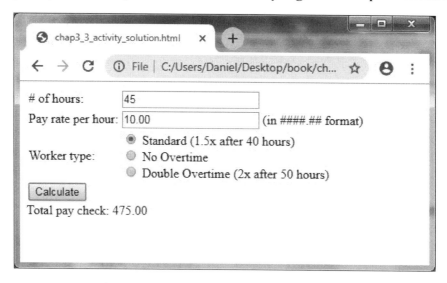

Figure 11.21: Sample output with valid inputs

The following screenshot shows the output with a validation error:

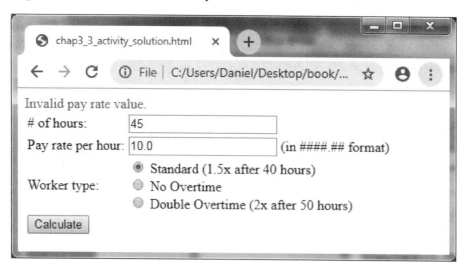

Figure 11.22: Sample output with a validation error

Note

The solution to this activity can be found on page 748.

The high-level steps for the activity are as follows:

1. To refactor the code, create a function called **processForm()**.

2. Create a function called **resetErrorsAndResults()**.

3. Create a class to hold form field values and perform validations.

4. Next, create a function called **getFormFields()**. This function is limited to getting the values from the form and creating an instance of the **FormFields** class.

5. Create the **displayError()** and **displayResult()** functions to display errors and results.

6. Finally, create the **calculateStandardWorkerPay()**, **calculateNoOvertimeWorkerPay()**, and **calculateDoubleOvertimeWorkerPay()** functions, which take the same two parameters and have the same return value definition so that they can be called abstractly in **doCalculation()**.

Summary

In this chapter, you learned about the best practices for clean and maintainable coding. As you saw in this chapter's activity, the refactored code that used clean coding techniques resulted in code that was much longer than before. However, you can see that the code as-is is much cleaner and is easier to understand and test compared to the original.

It is arguably overkill to refactor to the degree that we presented for our simple application, and many developers feel this way. But the value of this programming style really shows itself more in a complex real-world application, and it is good practice to do work in this way. Developers and tech leads need to decide what standards and clean coding practices make sense for their particular project.

In the next chapter, you will explore the current trends and cutting-edge features that JavaScript has to offer.

12

Using Next-Generation JavaScript

Overview

By the end of this chapter, you will be able to identify and select from the tools available for advanced JavaScript development; use the latest JavaScript syntax in older browsers; select from useful frameworks for client-side and server-side application development; use **npm** and **Yarn** within a project; apply config-free asset management using **Parcel**; and implement configurable asset management using webpack.

Introduction

In the previous chapter, you looked at creating clean, maintainable code by utilizing coding best practices, ensuring pure function implementation, and keeping your code simple. Now, while your code may be concise and correct, there are numerous factors that can cause problems when it's time to deploy your application.

Writing JavaScript applications is not natively a simple "**write and deploy**" practice. There are many caveats that need to be overcome; for instance, managing incorporated third-party modules, ensuring the proper directory structure of your project, and ensuring your code runs without error in all the necessary environments.

It is important to remember that JavaScript is a constantly evolving platform. Since its creation, JavaScript has always had differences between the available runtimes and, most notably, between browser types and versions. In the early years of its existence, JavaScript was quite unruly, with obvious differences between browsers. During those times, developers needed to repeatedly test their applications in each browser frequently to ensure it ran successfully and without bugs. Even now, each available modern browser has a different list of supported features and, awkwardly, very small variations in how similar features are implemented, which can trip up an unsuspecting developer. Attempting to write code that works in all modern browsers can be time-consuming and may require some patience.

Thankfully, there are ways to overcome these differences through tooling and libraries. These include the following:

- **Polyfill** libraries, which add missing features to runtimes, ensuring a better match between environments

- Libraries that support coding methodologies, ensuring a practical cross-runtime development experience

- **Transpilers**, which convert a singular language implementation into code supported in multiple different runtime environments

By including these tools in your project workspaces, you can not only save hours of frustration and needless headaches when deploying your code but also ensure a pleasant development experience from its inception. The idea is to support your creativity rather than to fight with the tools.

This chapter will highlight those libraries and tools that make light work of coding with JavaScript, as well as to inform you of where to look so that you can customize your development experience.

Browser Differences

When a user views a website or web application, it is important that it works as expected and, preferably, works similarly within all browsers. However, ensuring this occurs is a difficult task for many developers. Not only do browsers provide slightly varying implementations of JavaScript, but also of HTML5 features, **Cascading Style Sheet (CSS)** support, and more. Overcoming such differences have been an important task in every JavaScript developers working life, with experience playing a key part in ensuring applications work similarly in all environments.

To see what works on different browser types and versions, you can use the *Can I Use* website, which lists every browser's features and their compatibility: https://caniuse.com/.

In recent years, Microsoft has worked to eradicate these differences. For instance, on iOS devices, Microsoft's Edge browser uses **WebKit**, which is the same technology that's used by Google's Chrome and Apple's Safari browsers. As such, the future of web application development is looking much brighter, with fewer caveats between browsers. The problem will be, though, that not all users are up to date with the latest versions of their internet browser, meaning backward compatibility is still a necessity.

polyfills

A solution to browser incompatibilities is to use polyfills. These are libraries that are created by third parties to bridge the gaps between browsers, ensuring the functionality they provide is matched. There are many polyfill libraries, each asserting a given list of features across a range of browsers and browser versions. The most popular of these polyfills is **Polyfill.io** (https://polyfill.io/v3).

Polyfill.io was created by the *Financial Times* to cover a broad range of discrepancies among browsers. It is an open-source library that can be configured to include just the features you require, or you can simply import everything. By including it in your project, you can smooth over the cracks in browser differences.

Including Polyfill.io in your application is as simple as adding it with a **script** tag:

```
<script crossorigin="anonymous" src="https://polyfill.io/v3/polyfill.min.
js"></script>
```

However, to make full use of Polyfill.io, it is best to appropriately configure it to your needs using the **Create a Polyfill Bundle** page on the Polyfill.io website.

Transpilers

Transpilers are tools that convert one language into another. They are similar to compilers, except compilers typically convert a language into machine code or into intermediate byte code. There are many transpilers that convert a different language into JavaScript, but one of the most popular in web development is the **Babel transpiler**, which converts JavaScript into JavaScript. This may sound strange but imagine being able to utilize all of the latest features of JavaScript, then transpile it to work on all major browsers from the last 5 years, without having to utilize a polyfill library. This is essentially what Babel does.

The Babel transpiler, as well as several other transpilers, will be discussed later in this chapter.

Development Methodology Libraries

An alternative to covering the cracks in browser differences is to utilize libraries that offer a uniform development methodology that is supported in older browsers. There are many libraries that provide an arsenal of functionality, thereby making it easier to code in a predefined, opinionated manner. Some of these include the following:

- The **Underscore**, **Lodash**, **RxJS**, and **Ramda** functional programming libraries
- The **React**, **Polymer**, and **Riot** component-based UI libraries
- The **Backbone** and **Knockout MVC** frameworks
- The **jQuery** and **MooTools DOM** manipulation libraries

Each of the preceding libraries may be used in tandem with each other and with a transpiler, so choosing your libraries can be an important step to getting the results you require. We will be looking at some useful libraries later in this chapter.

Package Managers

Package managers are tools that provide managed support for your included libraries. These package managers may provide functionality that can be used in your production code, provide functionality externally to your application that helps test your code, or even provide tools you can use to make development easier but that is discarded from the eventual production code.

When implementing a package manager, a manifest is kept that keeps track of each of the libraries that have been imported into your project, as well as their version numbers. This way, if you were to remove all of the libraries from your project, you could easily reinstall the libraries that were used instantly. This is very useful when storing your application source code in a source repository such as GitHub, as you only need to store your own code. Any libraries you have used in the past can be easily installed by other developers in your team using the package manifest, ensuring your source repository is streamlined.

For many years, the most popular package manager that's been used by JavaScript developers has been Node Package Manager (npm). However, additional managers are available, with some gaining popularity, including Yarn.

The Node Package Manager

The node package manager (npm) is automatically installed when you install Node.js. Therefore, if you followed along in *Chapter 9, Working with Node.js*, then you should already have it. To test for it, simply run the following in your Terminal:

```
npm -v
```

This will output version information if you do indeed have it installed on your system:

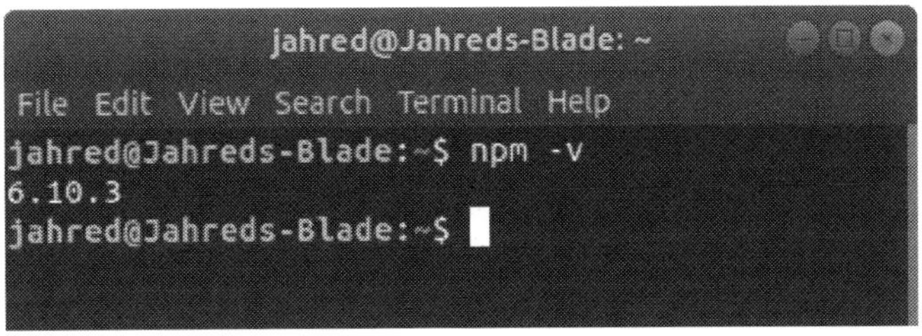

Figure 12.1: npm version

When using npm with a project, it creates a manifest file called **package.json**, which maintains a list of production and development libraries to be used with your project. Any installed packages are stored in a directory called **node_modules**, which npm also creates, and which lives in the root of your project. It is advisable to ensure that the **node_modules** directory is never stored in your project's source code repository, for streamlining purposes.

To begin using npm, you simply navigate to your project directory using your Terminal and execute the following command:

```
npm init
```

This will prompt you to answer a number of questions. It's okay if you don't know what to put for these, and you can simply press the Enter key to skip them and use the provided default values if you wish:

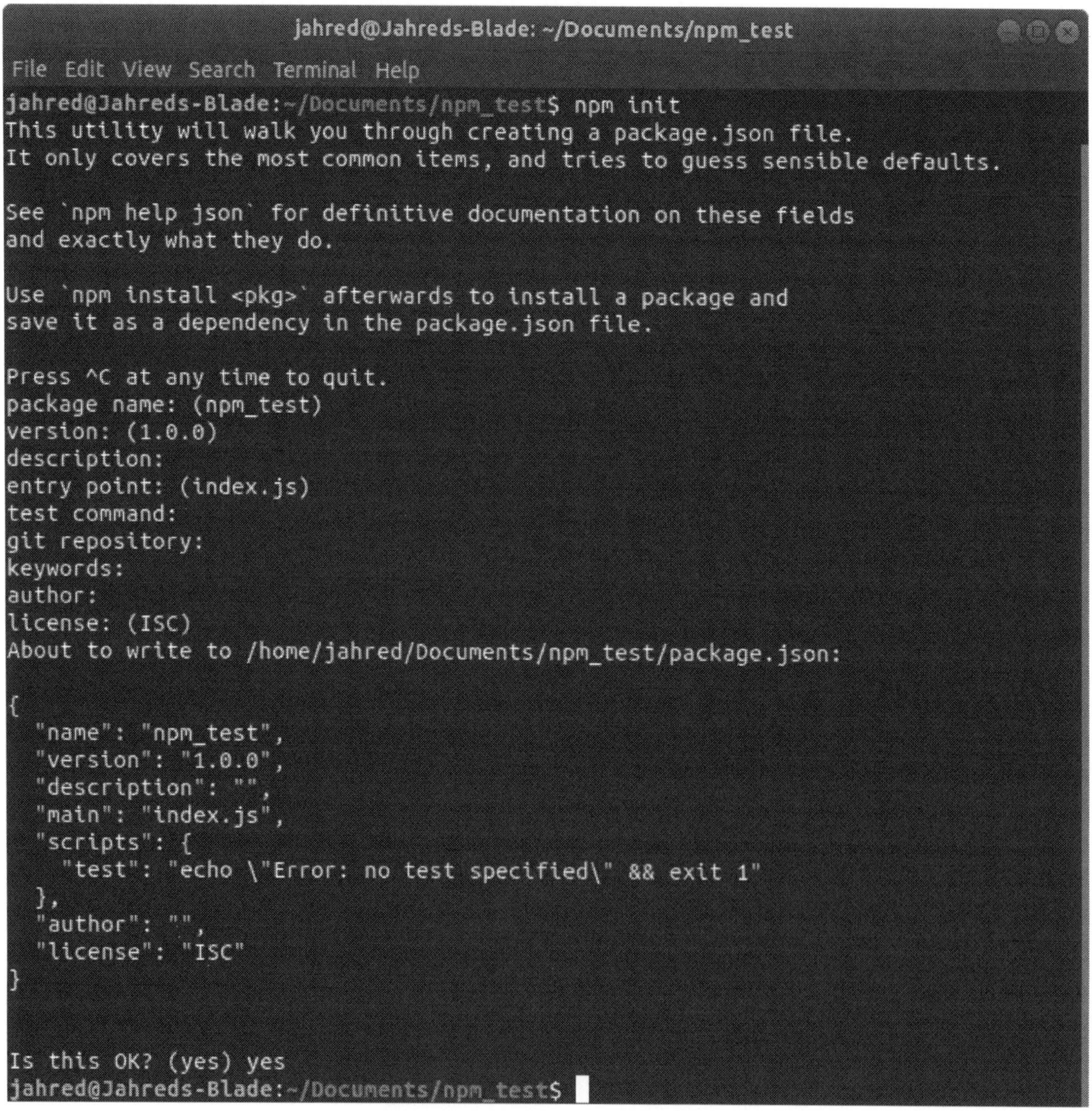

```
jahred@Jahreds-Blade: ~/Documents/npm_test
File Edit View Search Terminal Help
jahred@Jahreds-Blade:~/Documents/npm_test$ npm init
This utility will walk you through creating a package.json file.
It only covers the most common items, and tries to guess sensible defaults.

See `npm help json` for definitive documentation on these fields
and exactly what they do.

Use `npm install <pkg>` afterwards to install a package and
save it as a dependency in the package.json file.

Press ^C at any time to quit.
package name: (npm_test)
version: (1.0.0)
description:
entry point: (index.js)
test command:
git repository:
keywords:
author:
license: (ISC)
About to write to /home/jahred/Documents/npm_test/package.json:

{
  "name": "npm_test",
  "version": "1.0.0",
  "description": "",
  "main": "index.js",
  "scripts": {
    "test": "echo \"Error: no test specified\" && exit 1"
  },
  "author": "",
  "license": "ISC"
}


Is this OK? (yes) yes
jahred@Jahreds-Blade:~/Documents/npm_test$
```

Figure 12.2: npm initialization

Once completed, it will create a barebones **package.json** file containing the JSON code detailed in the preceding screenshot. Now, at this time, this JSON will not contain any modules, but that's fine. What it does and can contain is metadata about your project, such as its version, the initial index or starting script, and other such important information.

One of the predefined metadata properties is the **scripts** object. This is an important entry and one you will soon become familiar with. Each entry within this object is an executable command shortcut that you can invoke using the npm Terminal command. The one that's provided initially doesn't really do anything except output an error, but you can run it anyway if you wish so that you can see it in action. Do this by executing the following in the Terminal:

```
npm run test
```

With the current JSON, this will simply output the following error:

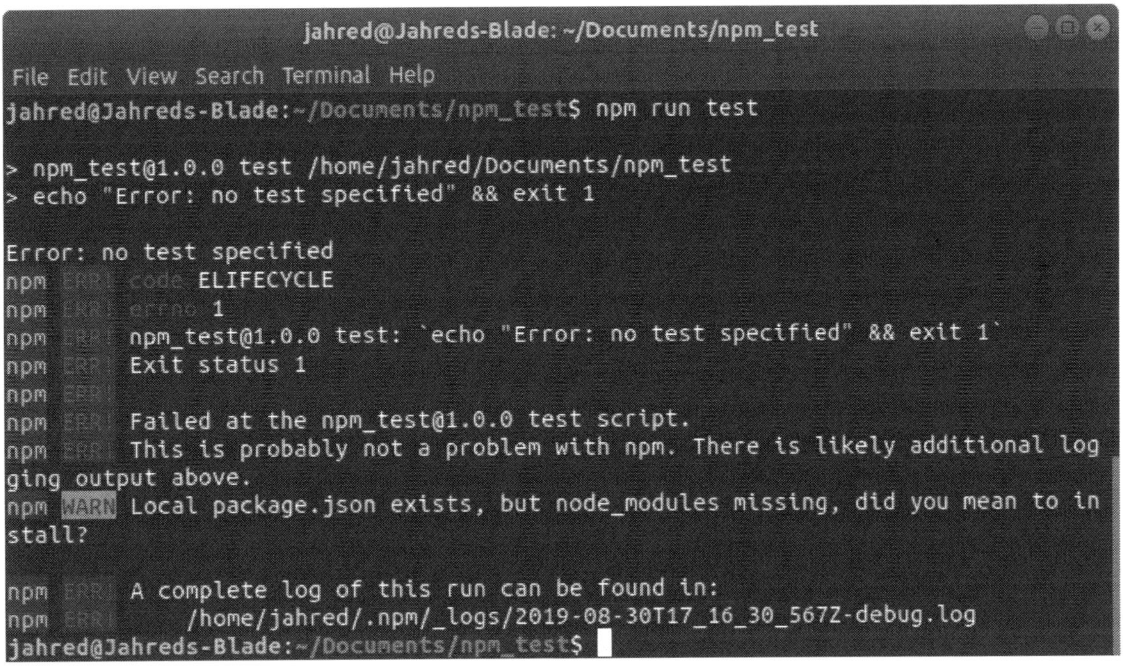

Figure 12.3: Initial package.json output

The **scripts** section of the **package.json** file is extremely useful for implementing your own shortcut commands so that you can run common tasks. You will be utilizing this a lot later in this chapter.

Installing Modules

The key task of a package manager is to install modules. As we stated previously, there are two primary ways to install a module into your project. The first is to install it as a production-level module. This means it may be incorporated into your deployment scripts during a build phase:

```
npm install --save-prod <module>
```

Similarly, to install it as a development module, you would simply execute the following code:

```
npm install --save-dev <module>
```

Each installed module will be added to a list within the **package.json** file; either **dependencies** for production modules or **devDependencies** for development modules.

At any time, once your module list exists within the **package.json** file, you can install all the modules by simply invoking the following in the Terminal:

```
npm install
```

If no **node_modules** folder exists in your project, this command will create it and proceed to download all the modules contained in both the **dependencies** and **devDependencies** lists.

The Yarn Package Manager

Yarn is a more recent addition to the available JavaScript package managers but is increasing in popularity. It was conceived by Facebook, in collaboration with Google, Tilde Inc., and Exponent Inc., and works as a different frontend to the npm repository. It was created primarily to provide a safer alternative to npm since the npm command-line tool can allow modules to run code upon installation, which can be a security risk.

Whether you should use Yarn is simply a preference. The issues that are exposed by the Yarn project are likely to be patched by npm over time and may already be irrelevant. Since Yarn doesn't replace much in the npm ecosystem, there isn't a big requirement to use it over the **npm CLI**.

The Babel Transpiler

Babel is a set of tools and libraries that transpiles JavaScript into JavaScript. Its benefit is that you can use cutting-edge JavaScript features today and still ensure that they run on a wide range of browsers and browser versions, all while ensuring minimally produced code.

> **Note**
>
> When working on exceptionally small projects, it is still possible to create much shorter scripts than what's run on most browsers. Using Babel is mostly beneficial for medium-to-large projects, which many modern JavaScript applications tend to be. Therefore, if all you are doing is reading some values from a field or two and validating them using a handful of lines of JavaScript, then you may be better off skipping modules and transpilers altogether.

A simple Babel installation provides three development-time tools and a polyfill library to be compiled into your application. These are as follows:

- The Babel engine core
- The Babel command-line interface
- The Babel environment preset engine
- The Babel/polyfill library

Each of the Babel tools can be installed using the npm CLI and use package names that are prefixed with `@babel/`. This is known as the package scope or namespace and ensures that other packages in the npm repository do not conflict should they have the same name.

@babel/core

The `@babel/core` tool provides the engine of the Babel transpiler. It contains functions that invoke the transformation of JavaScript code from one form to another, though the logic for various transformations may not be in the `@babel/core` package itself. All Babel installations must include the `@babel/core` package in order to function.

@babel/cli

@babel/cli provides command-line functionality for Babel projects. This can be used to invoke the transpilation of your source code, as well as to incorporate additional plugins and configuration. However, you will not typically use this CLI directly. Instead, you will create a new **scripts** entry and provide the configuration in a separate file.

@babel/preset-env

The **@babel/preset-env** tool provides intelligent directives for transpiling your code for specific environments, such as browser types and versions. Typically, the wider the range of environments you wish to support, the larger your resulting deployable transpiled code will be. The configuration for this tool will exist in a configuration file so that you only need to specify it once.

@babel/polyfill

@babel/polyfill is a library that is at least partly compiled into your deployable code. Through using **@babel/preset-env**, Babel selects elements from **@babel/ polyfill** to include in the transpiled code.

.babelrc Configuration File

The **.babelrc** file (note the period character at the start of the filename) is a JSON configuration file that sits in the root of your project directory. This file can store information about the presets, plugins, and various other bits of information that are useful for Babel's installation.

The most common configuration you will apply to this file will be the environments you wish to support:

```
{
"presets": [
    [
"@babel/preset-env", {
"targets": "> 0.25%, not dead"
        }
    ]
  ]
}
```

The preceding example requests that Babel transpiles code to support browsers that are used globally by more than 0.25% of the population. Otherwise, those browsers are not considered dead, which means browsers that are still actively supported.

A full explanation of the environment queries that are supported by the **.babelrc** configuration file can be found at https://packt.live/2NVxWwP.

Exercise 12.01: A Basic Babel Project

In this exercise, you will create a usable install of the Babel transpiler using npm. This will be a simple setup that will result in a working environment that's able to transpile a source modularized JavaScript application into a deployable repository of files. Let's get started:

1. Begin by creating a new directory called **babel_app** in your operating system's **Documents** folder using the Terminal. Then, navigate into that directory:

```
cd ~/Documents/
mkdir babel_app
cd babel_app/
```

2. Then, initialize the folder as an npm project. You can use all of the default settings for this:

```
npm init
```

You should see something similar to the following output:

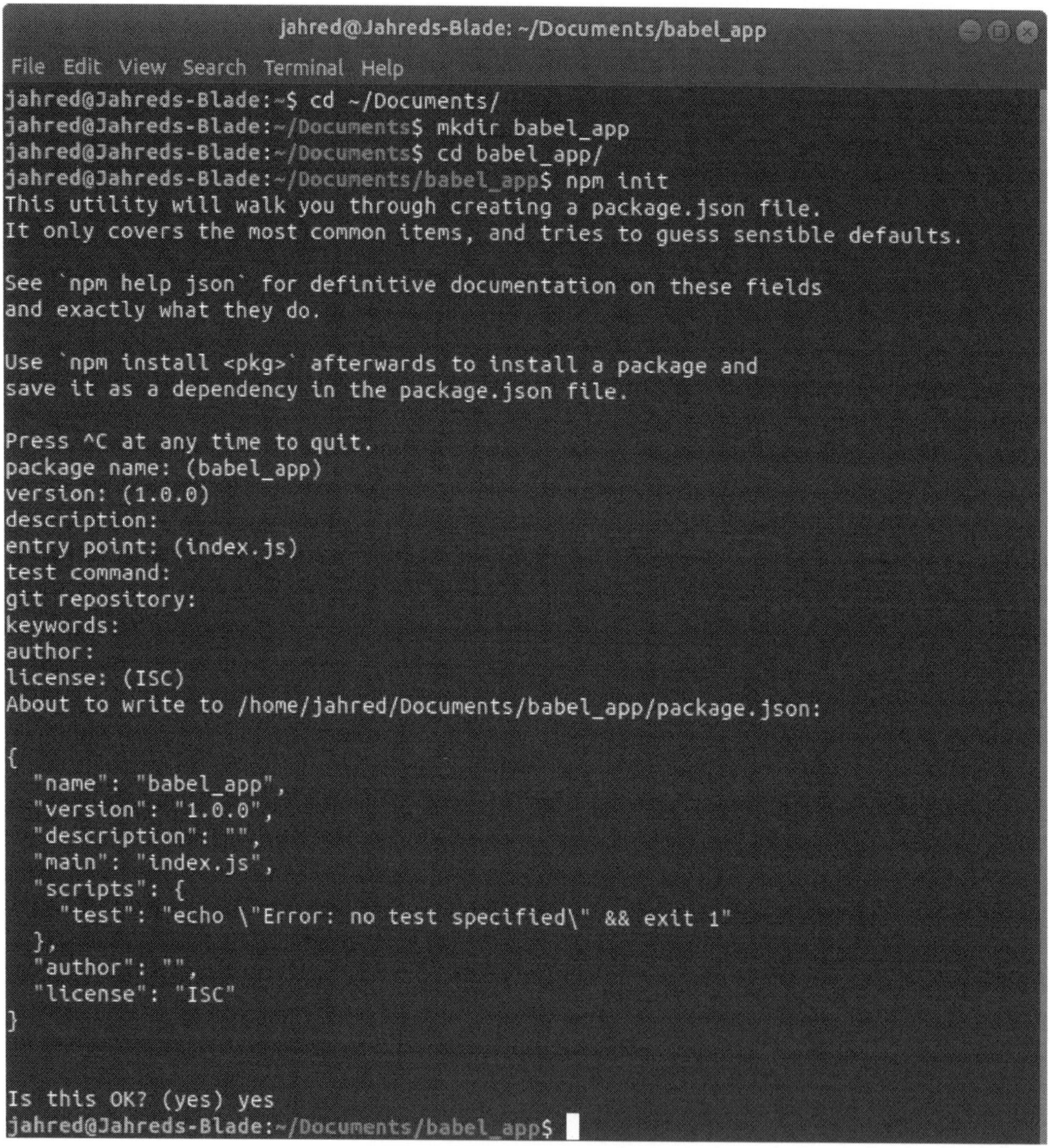

```
                    jahred@Jahreds-Blade: ~/Documents/babel_app
File  Edit  View  Search  Terminal  Help
jahred@Jahreds-Blade:~$ cd ~/Documents/
jahred@Jahreds-Blade:~/Documents$ mkdir babel_app
jahred@Jahreds-Blade:~/Documents$ cd babel_app/
jahred@Jahreds-Blade:~/Documents/babel_app$ npm init
This utility will walk you through creating a package.json file.
It only covers the most common items, and tries to guess sensible defaults.

See `npm help json` for definitive documentation on these fields
and exactly what they do.

Use `npm install <pkg>` afterwards to install a package and
save it as a dependency in the package.json file.

Press ^C at any time to quit.
package name: (babel_app)
version: (1.0.0)
description:
entry point: (index.js)
test command:
git repository:
keywords:
author:
license: (ISC)
About to write to /home/jahred/Documents/babel_app/package.json:

{
  "name": "babel_app",
  "version": "1.0.0",
  "description": "",
  "main": "index.js",
  "scripts": {
    "test": "echo \"Error: no test specified\" && exit 1"
  },
  "author": "",
  "license": "ISC"
}


Is this OK? (yes) yes
jahred@Jahreds-Blade:~/Documents/babel_app$ 
```

Figure 12.4: npm initialization

3. Now that npm is set up, you can install the Babel development libraries. These will need to be saved in the **devDependencies** list:

```
npm install --save-dev @babel/core @babel/cli @babel/preset-env
```

You will see some information pertaining to downloading the modules to the **node_ modules** directory:

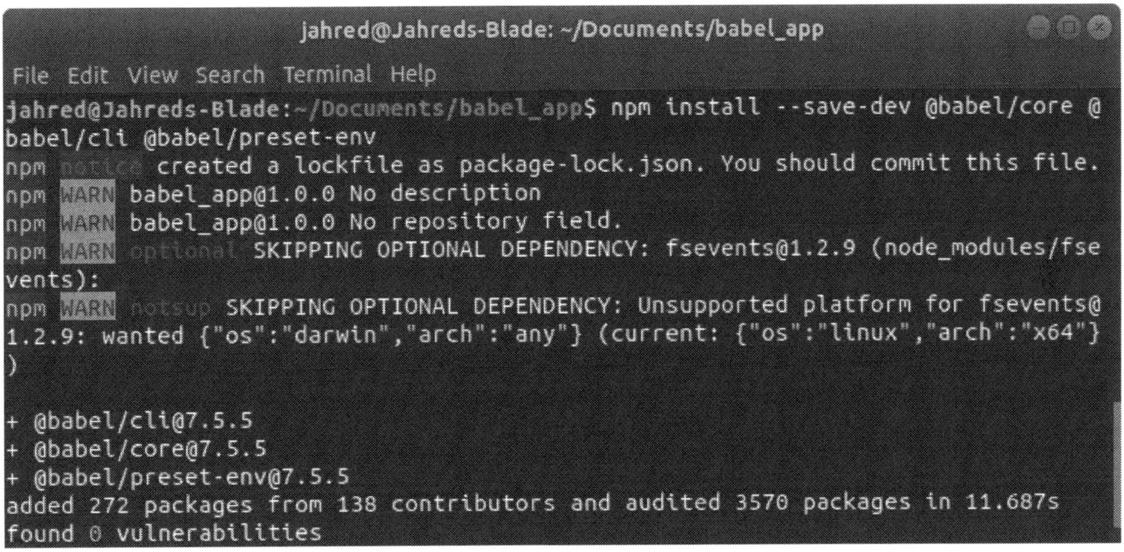

```
jahred@Jahreds-Blade: ~/Documents/babel_app

File  Edit  View  Search  Terminal  Help
jahred@Jahreds-Blade:~/Documents/babel_app$ npm install --save-dev @babel/core @
babel/cli @babel/preset-env
npm notice    created a lockfile as package-lock.json. You should commit this file.
npm WARN  babel_app@1.0.0 No description
npm WARN  babel_app@1.0.0 No repository field.
npm WARN  optional SKIPPING OPTIONAL DEPENDENCY: fsevents@1.2.9 (node_modules/fse
vents):
npm WARN  notsup SKIPPING OPTIONAL DEPENDENCY: Unsupported platform for fsevents@
1.2.9: wanted {"os":"darwin","arch":"any"} (current: {"os":"linux","arch":"x64"}
)

+ @babel/cli@7.5.5
+ @babel/core@7.5.5
+ @babel/preset-env@7.5.5
added 272 packages from 138 contributors and audited 3570 packages in 11.687s
found 0 vulnerabilities
```

Figure 12.5: Development modules installed

These files will not be compiled into your resulting transpiled application since they are used to perform the transpiling itself.

4. Now, you will need to install the Babel polyfill library. This library will be transpiled into your resulting application, as required by the transpiler:

```
npm install --save @babel/polyfill
```

Again, this module will be saved in the **node_modules** directory:

```
jahred@Jahreds-Blade: ~/Documents/babel_app

File Edit View Search Terminal Help
jahred@Jahreds-Blade:~/Documents/babel_app$ npm install --save @babel/polyfill

> core-js@2.6.9 postinstall /home/jahred/Documents/babel_app/node_modules/core-j
s
> node scripts/postinstall || echo "ignore"

Thank you for using core-js ( https://github.com/zloirock/core-js ) for polyfill
ing JavaScript standard library!

The project needs your help! Please consider supporting of core-js on Open Colle
ctive or Patreon:
> https://opencollective.com/core-js
> https://www.patreon.com/zloirock

Also, the author of core-js ( https://github.com/zloirock ) is looking for a goo
d job -)

npm WARN babel_app@1.0.0 No description
npm WARN babel_app@1.0.0 No repository field.
npm WARN optional SKIPPING OPTIONAL DEPENDENCY: fsevents@1.2.9 (node_modules/fse
vents):
npm WARN notsup SKIPPING OPTIONAL DEPENDENCY: Unsupported platform for fsevents@
1.2.9: wanted {"os":"darwin","arch":"any"} (current: {"os":"linux","arch":"x64"}
)

+ @babel/polyfill@7.4.4
added 3 packages from 2 contributors and audited 3573 packages in 2.026s
found 0 vulnerabilities
```

Figure 12.6: Polyfill module installation

5. With the modules installed, you will now need to configure Babel. This requires a
    new file called **.babelrc**, which will contain the appropriate JSON. There are many
    possible configurable features of Babel, but for this exercise, you will simply need
    to specify the environment presets. Create a new file called **.babelrc** in the root
    of the project directory and populate it with the following content:

```json
{
    "presets": [

        "@babel/preset-env", {
            "targets": "> 0.25%, not dead"
        }

    ]
}
```

6. With everything in place, you will now need to create your project work files and directories. You can layout your project however you like, but for this example, you'll utilize two directories: an **src** directory for source files and a **dist** directory for transpiled files. Go ahead and create these in the root of the project directory:

```
mkdir src dist
```

7. Next, you'll need a project file to transpile. In the **src** directory, add a file called **index.js** and add the following JavaScript:

```
[1, 2, 3].map((value) => console.log("Mapping value ", value));
```

This JavaScript uses a little of the ES2015 specification, in the form of the fat arrow function. This means, when transpiled, you should see a difference between what is in the source file and what is in the transpiled file.

8. Now, in order to get everything working, you'll need to modify the **package.json** file to include a script that executes the Babel transpiler. Go ahead and open that file up, and then add the following line to the **scripts** array:

```
"build": "npx babel src --out-dir dist"
```

This line means that when you run it, it will call the Babel CLI tool using the npm package runner and will pass it the **src** directory for input and the **dist** directory for output. Don't forget to add a comma at the end of the previous line or your JSON will be invalid. Your **package.json** file should now look as follows:

package.json

```
1  {
2  "name": "babel_app",
3  "version": "1.0.0",
4  "description": "",
5  "main": "index.js",
6  "scripts": {
7  "test": "echo \"Error: no test specified\"&& exit 1",
8  "build": "npx babel src --out-dir dist"
9    },
10 "author": "",
11 "license": "ISC",
12 "devDependencies": {
13 "@babel/cli": "^7.5.5",
14 "@babel/core": "^7.5.5",
15 "@babel/preset-env": "^7.5.5"
```

The full code is available at: https://packt.live/32DKdv6

Notice the version numbers next to each of the module entries. If your version numbers are different, don't panic. The steps that were used to install these modules ensured that the latest versions were downloaded. Any differences in your own file compared to the preceding code simply mean those modules have been updated since this chapter was written. However, everything should still work fine.

9. Finally, it's time to run the transpiler. To do this, simply call the script through the npm CLI tool:

```
npm run build
```

Once executed, take a look at the **dist** directory. It should now also contain an **index.js** file. However, the contents of this file will differ slightly to the code you entered in the **index.js** file in the **src** directory:

```
"use strict";
[1, 2, 3].map(function (value) {
  return console.log("Mapping value ", value);
});
```

Notice that the Babel transpiler stripped out the fat arrow function syntax and replaced it with a standard function definition. This is so that the transpiled code will work in the environments you specified in the **.babelrc** configuration file. Babel allows you to utilize any of the cutting-edge features you want to use while being comforted by the knowledge that your resulting transpiled application should work exactly where you need it to.

The basic setup we've described here provides a powerful starting point for even the largest of applications. Many professional JavaScript development companies use Babel to ensure code correctness, portability, and a flexible working environment that can be managed by teams of developers without having each developer stepping on the toes of another.

While what you have accomplished is a great starting point for a robust, team-driven application, there is more that can be accomplished to improve this even further. We will look at some of these additional steps throughout the rest of this chapter.

Babel Applications with Parcel

npm works very well as a package manager, but its project management capabilities are limited. In the previous exercise, you set up a script in the npm **package.json** file that executed the Babel transpiler. The transpiler can translate JavaScript files one at a time and place the resulting translated files in the **dist** directory, but that's about the extent of it. Often, your projects will have other requirements, such as the following:

* Ensuring your files are combined into fewer resulting JavaScript files

* Defining hot modules (breaking the compiled output into smaller chunks with dynamic loading)

* Processing CSS files

* Compressing images

* Ensuring files aren't cached between builds

It is possible to write your own scripts to manage your projects and execute them from npm from a parent script, but this is a lot of repetitive work that has already been solved by others. **Parcel** is a solution to this.

What is Parcel?

Parcel is considered a web application bundler. It is, essentially, a packaging module that performs the tasks that were listed in the previous section. What makes Parcel unique is that it is a zero-configuration bundler. You simply call it from your project directory, and it figures out how your application should be readied for distribution. The only requirement, then, is to call the Parcel CLI command to launch it.

Parcel is typically installed in your project as a global module. This means it is not stored in the **node_modules** directory in your project folder, but in a **node_modules** directory that exists on your operating system's environment path. To do this, instead of supplying a **--save** or **--save-dev** flag, you supply a **-g** flag, for global:

```
npm install -g parcel
```

Since Parcel is globally installed, the installation will not modify the **package.json** file as it will not need to be added to the **dependencies** or **devDependencies** lists.

Using Parcel

To make use of Parcel, you will need to add new scripts to the **package.json scripts** object. There are several ways Parcel can be called. The first is simply to pass the main JavaScript file as the only parameter to the **parcel** CLI tool:

```
parcel src/index.js
```

This will request that Parcel processes the JavaScript file and for it to output a development build of it. Parcel traverses this file and determines whether any other files also need processing. During the processing phase, Parcel will also analyze any configuration files present within the project directory. The **.babelrc** configuration file is one such file Parcel understands. Therefore, by its very presence, Parcel will ensure that any JavaScript files are transpiled by Babel. The same will be true if common configuration files are present for other tools, but also with files of a given type within the source tree, such as HTML and CSS files:

Figure 12.7: Parcel development build

When processing as a development build, Parcel includes additional code within the transpiled JavaScript. Additionally, a call to Parcel to process your files in development mode will not return. As you can see in the preceding screenshot, running Parcel in development mode launches a special development server, which you can navigate to by going to http://localhost:1234 in your web browser. This simply presents your transpiled application as though it were running on a remote webserver.

The running service also utilizes a filesystem listener so that, when you update a file within your project, that file is then automatically reprocessed, and the resulting changes are made available immediately. If you then view your application within the browser at the time a file is changed, the browser will automatically be refreshed to include those changes. This feature greatly speeds up development time.

Another way to invoke the parcel CLI tool is to provide the **build** flag:

```
parcel build src/index.js
```

The **build** flag tells Parcel to process the source files so that they're ready for a production release. This version will not have the additional browser update code and there will be no development server running:

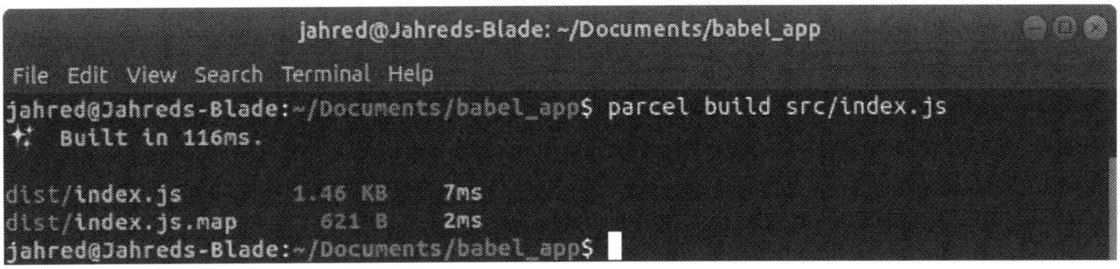

Figure 12.8: Parcel production build

When deploying your finished application to a production server, the development features are not necessary and simply add bloat to your code, so being able to compile your application without them is a necessary step.

Modular Applications in Parcel

Utilizing Parcel provides a lot of features for free. In *Chapter 9, Working with Node.js*, you saw how modules are acquired in a Node.js application. Transpiling with Babel and Parcel also provides module acquisition when using the **import** keyword.

When building your applications, it is preferable to break the application source into smaller files so that managing your code is simpler. The **import** keyword follows the ES2015 specification, whereby each module in your source directory **exports** one or more functions, which can then be imported into other modules as required using the **import** keyword. If a module **exports** only one function, then it can be exported simply as a **default** function:

```
// myModule.js
const myFun = () => console.log("Hello, World!");

export default myFun;
```

In another module, this function can then be imported with a named reference, like so:

```
// index.js
import fun from "./myModule";

fun();  // ==> Hello, World!
```

Notice how the `.js` extension was not required when naming the importing module, much like how Node.js imports modules. The transpiler automatically understands how to reference the external file using this format. When processing the `index.js` file, Parcel automatically traverses all imported files, transpiling those as well. Each module is followed, including their linked modules and so on. The resulting code is stored in a single JavaScript file in the `dist` directory.

If a module contains multiple functions, then it can export them using an object format. This foregoes the `default` keyword as, now, functions must be cherry-picked using their specific names:

```
// multiModule.js
const fun1 = () => console.log("I am function one");
const fun2 = () => console.log("I am function two");

export {fun1, fun2};
```

Now, in the calling module, each required function must be named explicitly:

```
// index.js
import {fun1, fun2} from "./multiModule";

fun1();
fun2();
```

Using this method, only those functions you intend to use need to be imported. The transpiler will ensure that any dead functions (functions that are never called) are not transpiled needlessly into the resulting `dist` code.

Exercise 12.02: A Basic Parcel Project

In this exercise, you will update the application you created in *Exercise 12.01: A Basic Babel Project* to incorporate a Parcel build system. You will also include an additional module so that you can experience how simple modular application development can be. Let's get started:

1. First, you will need to install the Parcel tools. If you have not already done so, install them globally:

    ```
    npm install -g parcel
    ```

    If you are on a Mac or Linux device and you receive an error stating that you have insufficient privileges, you will need to prepend the previous line with the `sudo` command:

    ```
    sudo npm install -g parcel
    ```

2. Next, create a new file in the **src** directory and call it **index.html**. Then, add the following markup:

```html
<html>
<head>
<title>Babel App</title>
<script src="./index.js"></script>
</head>
<body>
</body>
</html>
```

Parcel works by processing a file tree. By passing an HTML file as the master file, not only will JavaScript files be processed, but so will the HTML, CSS, and other such assets linked in your application.

3. Now, update the **package.json** file to include the new **build** command scripts:

```json
"dev": "parcel src/index.html",
"build": "parcel build src/index.html"
```

The **"build"** entry should replace the one we used previously, which called the Babel CLI directly. Your **package.json** file should now look as follows:

package.json

```json
1   {
2   "name": "babel_app",
3   "version": "1.0.0",
4   "description": "",
5   "main": "index.js",
6   "scripts": {
7   "test": "echo \"Error: no test specified\"&& exit 1",
8   "dev": "parcel src/index.html",
9   "build": "parcel build src/index.html"
10   },
11   "author": "",
12   "license": "ISC",
13   "devDependencies": {
14   "@babel/cli": "^7.5.5",
15   "@babel/core": "^7.5.5",
```

The full code is available at: https://packt.live/32LScpY

4. Next, add a new module in **src** called **module.js**. This file will demonstrate the module loading in Parcel. In this file, add the following code:

```javascript
export default () => {
   [1, 2, 3].map((value) => console.log("Mapping value ", value));
};
```

5. Now, import that module into the **index.js** file by replacing its content with the following:

```
import mapper from "./module";
mapper();
```

6. You can now run your application in development mode by simply calling the following:

```
npm run dev
```

You should then see the expected development server launch in the Terminal:

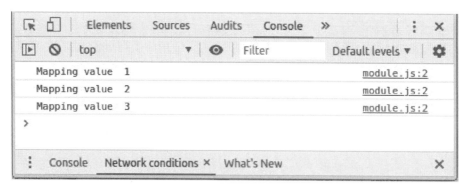

Figure 12.9: Running the development server

If you launch your browser with the console open, you will see the expected content:

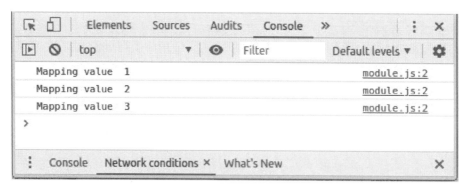

Figure 12.10: Console output

7. Finally, update **module.js** by adding additional value in the array. When you save the file, the browser should instantly refresh to show the latest changes:

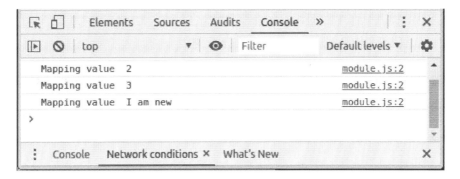

Figure 12.11: Updated console output

8. If you view the source of the HTML page, you will see that the HTML doesn't reference **index.js** as it does in the **src** directory. Instead, the JavaScript file will have a random name in order to prevent the browser from caching the file:

```
<html>
<head>
<title>Babel App</title>
<script src="/src.e31bb0bc.js"></script>
</head>
<body>
</body>
</html>
```

The setup we've created in this exercise is now a perfect starting point for many JavaScript projects. This simple build provides numerous development features that empower your coding and ensure optimal reliability in the production files.

Babel Applications with Webpack

Webpack is an application bundler for JavaScript applications that provides a much more configurable experience. In version 4, the webpack team introduced zero-configuration support in order to compete with Parcel specifically. While webpack is an excellent tool for bundling your JavaScript and other assets, it does take quite a lot of configuring and requires just as much patience.

To use a webpack, you simply install it, just like any JavaScript module. Webpack comes in two main parts: the webpack engine and the webpack CLI. Both can be installed simultaneously, like so:

```
npm install --save-dev webpack webpack-cli
```

If you install it using your Terminal, you should see the following output:

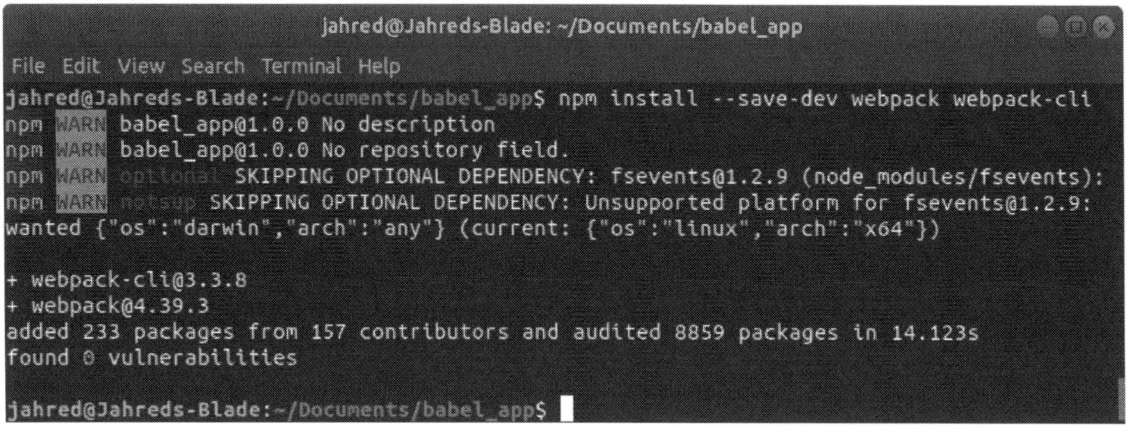

Figure 12.12: Webpack installation

With those downloaded, you can then add a script in the **package.json** file in order to execute them, like so:

```
"wp": "webpack"
```

Then, by running the script in the Terminal, it should compile your JavaScript:

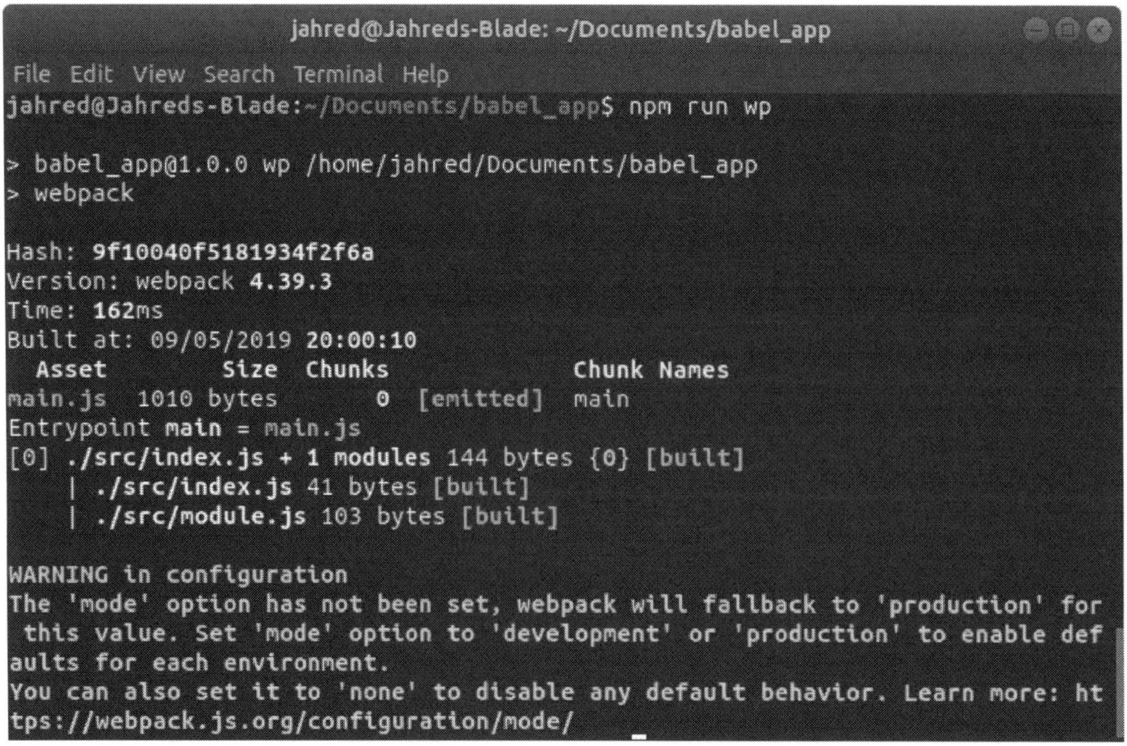

Figure 12.13: Executing Webpack zero configuration

As you can see, in the preceding screenshot, both the **index.js** and **module.js** files were compiled into a file called **main.js**. Webpack defaults its entry point path to **src/index.js** and its output path to **dist/main.js**.

Let's supply a source file and output file explicitly so as to try and mimic the Parcel build. Update your **wp** script to the following:

```
"wp": "webpack src/index.html -o dist/index.html"
```

This will set the input source as the **index.html** file and request the output to be placed in the **dist** directory, but with the same filename. If you run this, you should see something like the following:

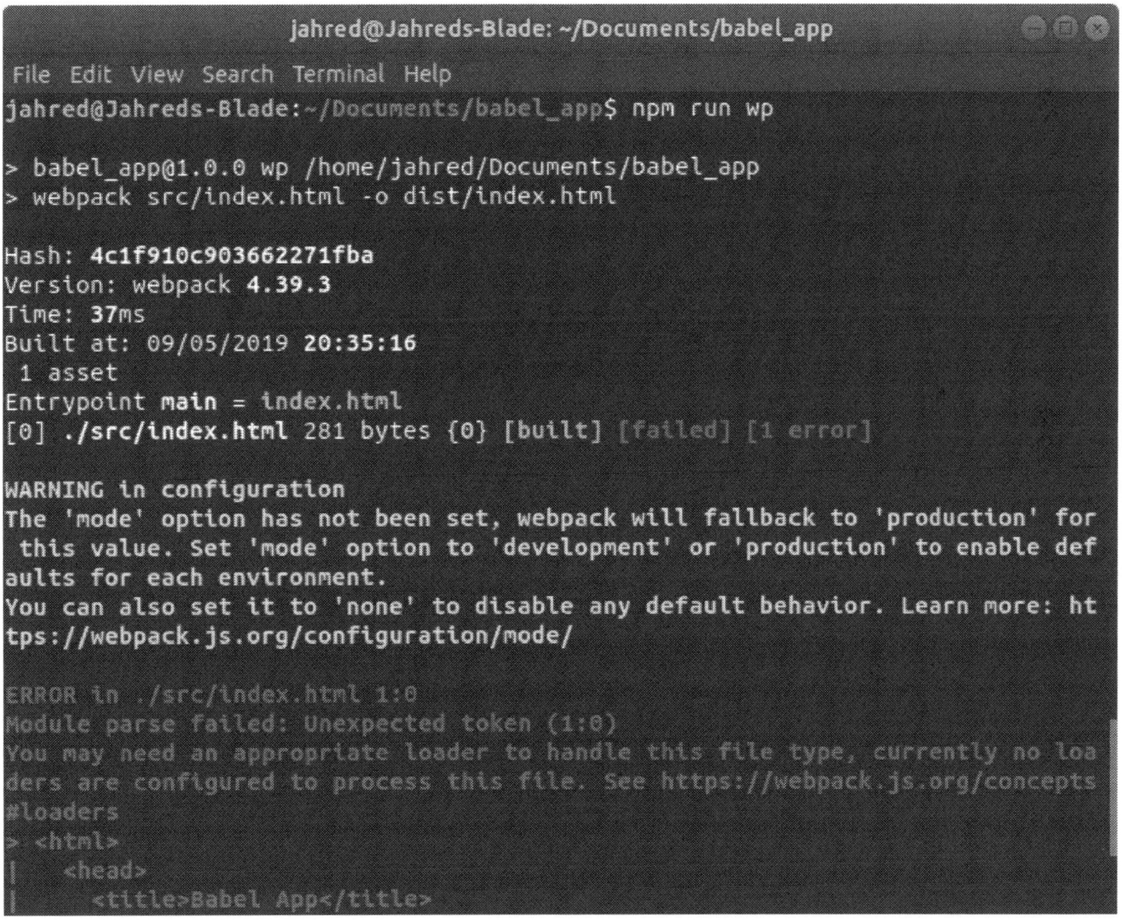

Figure 12.14: Webpack HTML parse error

As you can see, the webpack wasn't too happy about finding an HTML file.

Now, a caveat with a webpack is that it does not try to be intelligent. The compiled output of the previous execution would not have transpiled your code using Babel, so the fat arrow functions from the source files will have made it to the output folder. Also, webpack in zero-configuration mode will only compile your JavaScript, meaning any other assets included in your application require some configuration in order for them to be processed and sent to the **dist** directory, including any HTML files.

Webpack Architecture

Webpack provides a linear processing pipeline for your applications. Using a source input file, it will build a dependency tree, known as a dependency graph, and will process each file where configuration exists for that file type. The pipeline utilizes the following:

- Source input file or entry point
- Output file
- Loader modules
- Plugin modules

Webpack requires a specific configuration for each of the asset types in your application so that it knows how to process them.

Webpack Loaders and Plugins

Both **loaders** and **plugins** are modules of code that you include in a webpack pipeline. They can be considered the bolt-on functionality since webpack is a pipeline, they are like its "fixtures and fittings." Loaders and plugins both have an effect on how your application is processed by webpack, but they are also quite different from one another.

A loader is a module that works at the beginning of the webpack pipeline; sometimes even before it starts. These modules process assets individually. For instance, if you wanted to use Babel in a webpack configuration, you would need to include the babel-webpack loader, which transpiles each file individually as they are processed.

Plugins, on the other hand, tend to work at the end of the webpack pipeline. These modules affect the entire output bundle and allow you to have much greater control over your application output. Plugins are quite a bit more complex than loaders, and their configuration often reflects this.

Webpack Configuration

The configuration of a webpack pipeline is added to a file called **webpack.config.js**, which exists in the root of your project directory. As a JavaScript file, it is executed by the Node.js runtime and can, therefore, include Node.js-compatible JavaScript.

The webpack configuration is exported from the **webpack.config.js** file, much like any JavaScript module. The exported data can include information about the entry point path, destination path, loaders, and plugins, as is required.

As an example, a simple **webpack.config.js** file, which specifies the entry point and output paths, may look like this:

```
var path = require('path');
module.exports = {
  entry: path.join(__dirname, 'src', 'index.js'),
  output: {
    path: path.resolve(__dirname, 'dist'),
    filename: 'index.js'
  }
}
```

If you create a **webpack.config.js** file, be sure to reset your **package.json** script so that it is like so:

```
"wp": "webpack"
```

Failing to do so may cause confusing results.

Exercise 12.03: A Basic WebPack Project

In this exercise, you will set up your webpack installation so that it implements Babel transpiling and so that it includes and processes your **index.html** source file. As we stated previously, there are many configuration features you can apply to a webpack installation, but by completing this exercise, you will have a better understanding of how to implement any loaders you require. Let's get started:

1. Although your application includes the Babel transpiler in the **package.json** file, it is not enough for a webpack to be able to understand how and when to use it. To utilize Babel with webpack, you need to include and configure the **Babel loader module**. Run the following in your Terminal to download and install the Babel loader:

    ```
    npm install --save-dev babel-loader
    ```

2. Next, open up the **webpack.config.js** file, if you have it, and add a new **module** section to the **exports** object. If you don't have the **webpack.config.js** file yet, create it now and add the code from the previous section:

```
module: {
  rules: [
    {
      test: /\.js$/,
      exclude: /node_modules/,
      use: {
        loader: "babel-loader"
      }
    }
  ]
}
```

This new block provides the rule we can use to process files with Babel. Essentially, it's saying "test: for filenames that end with **.js**, exclude: any files in the **node_modules** folder, use: **babel-loader** on those files you find."

3. With Babel transpilation supported, you now need to include support for HTML files. HTML processing is both a pre- and post-JavaScript processing task and, therefore, is carried out using both a loader and a plugin. To install both of these, run the following code:

```
npm install --save-dev html-webpack-plugin html-loader
```

If all went well, you should see the following output:

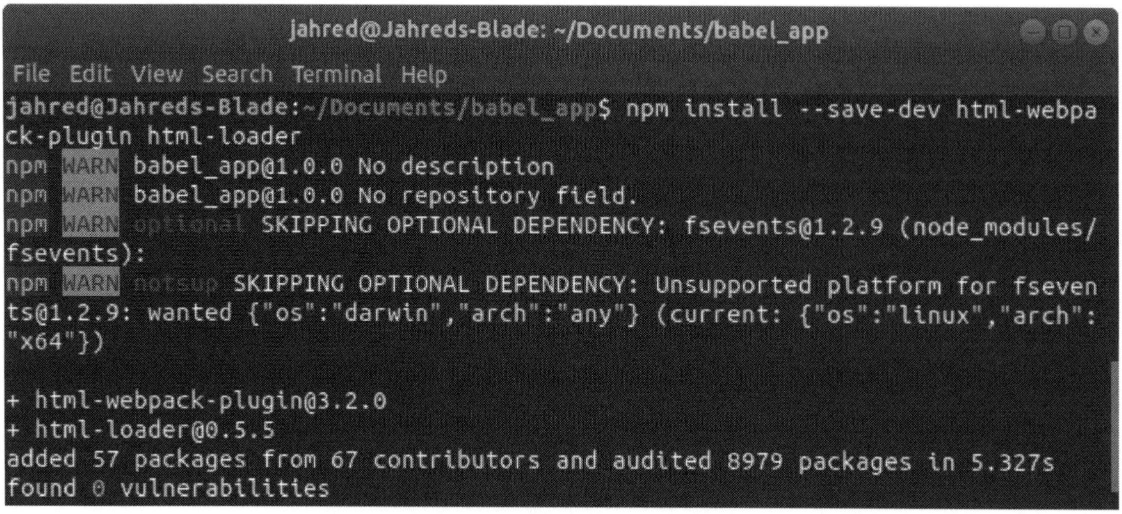

Figure 12.15: Webpack HTML loader and plugin installation

4. With these modules installed, they now need to be configured in the **webpack. config.js** file. Like the Babel loader, the HTML loader should be entered into the **modules** array of the **exports** object. Add it after the **babel-loader** configuration:

```
{
  test: /\.html$/,
  use: [
    {
      loader: "html-loader",
      options: { minimize: true }
    }
  ]
}
```

5. Implementing the HTML plugin requires a couple of steps. First, you will need to require it at the top of the page:

```
const HtmlWebPackPlugin = require("html-webpack-plugin");
```

6. With the module required, you can now configure it by adding it to the **plugins** section of the **exports** object:

```
plugins: [
  new HtmlWebPackPlugin({
    template: "./src/index.html",
    filename: "./index.html"
  })
]
```

Note that the directory of the output file is not required. The HTML plugin will place it in the **dist** folder, regardless.

Your **webpack.config.js** file should now look as follows:

`webpack.config.js`

```
10    module: {
11      rules: [
12        {
13          test: /\.js$/,
14          exclude: /node_modules/,
15          use: {
16            loader: "babel-loader"
17          }
18        },
19        {
20          test: /\.html$/,
21          use: [
22            {
23              loader: "html-loader",
24              options: { minimize: true }
25            }
```

The full code is available at: https://packt.live/2XckybQ

7. Finally, execute your webpack script. You should now find that the JavaScript output has been correctly transpiled by Babel and that the **index.html** file will also be present within the **dist** directory. Your Terminal window should look as follows:

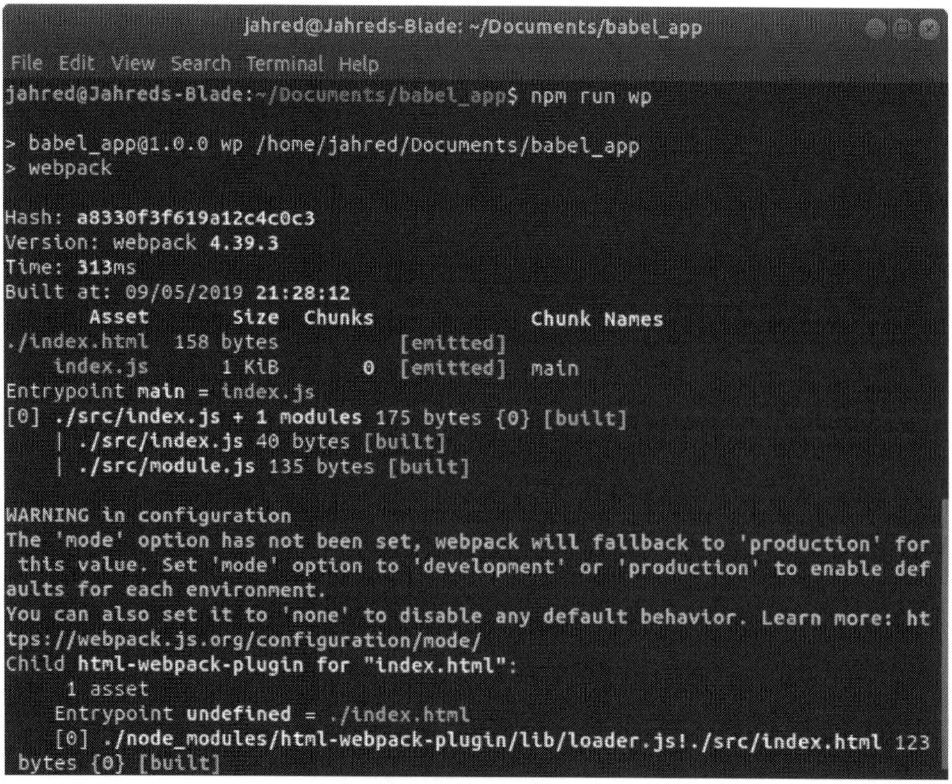

Figure 12.16: Successful webpack transpilation

Configuring webpack installations can be quite a lengthy process of trial and error. Even with this exercise, you may notice that the `index.html` file still does not implement a non-caching process whereby the JavaScript output is renamed randomly to avoid browser caching. While webpack is a must for medium-to-large projects that require that extra mile in configuration freedom, it is recommended that Parcel is used for those small projects that need a simple setup, without configuration headaches.

Other Popular Bundlers

There are many bundler tools available for your JavaScript project, each with their own benefits and caveats. Obviously, choosing a bundler may result from personal choice or it may be a requirement from the project manager, development team, or the organization that tendered the project. However, of those bundlers, two of the most popular tools that haven't been covered in this chapter yet are Gulp and Grunt.

Gulp and **Grunt** are a little different from the examples you've seen up until now as they don't use configuration files. Instead, they use JavaScript code that you write to accomplish tasks similar to what webpack and Parcel can accomplish.

Gulp and Grunt are known as task runners. This means that, instead of defining a coding environment for your project, they act as an application you write to manage the application you're writing; a kind of application wrapper, if you will. The toolsets for both these bundlers provide a framework to facilitate this, which runs on the Node.js runtime. You simply code what you would like to achieve and execute it.

The `gulp` bundler which runs on the Node.js runtime is as follows:

```
var gulp = require('gulp');
gulp.task('build', () => { /* Compile production application */ });
gulp.task('build.dev', () => { /* Compile development application */ });
gulp.task('test.unit', () => { /* Run all unit tests */});
gulp.task('test.e2e', () => { /* Run all end-to-end tests */});
gulp.task('test', ['test.unit', 'test.e2e']);
```

The `grunt` bundler which runs on the Node.js runtime is as follows:

```
module.exports = function(grunt) {
   grunt.initConfig(gruntConfig);
   grunt.loadNpmTasks('grunt-contrib-jshint');
   grunt.loadNpmTasks('grunt-contrib-uglify');
   grunt.loadNpmTasks('grunt-contrib-watch');
   grunt.registerTask('default', ['jshint', 'uglify']);
};
```

Other Language Transpiling

The JavaScript platform is an extremely popular one. After all, it is the de facto script runtime for the majority of browsers. However, the JavaScript language isn't necessarily loved by everyone. Some developers prefer a static typing system, while others prefer better interoperability with their favorite server-side language. Whatever the reason, this love/hate relationship, mixed with JavaScript's monopoly of the browser itself, has created a long list of alternative languages that each transpile to JavaScript. Some of the more popular of these languages include the following:

- TypeScript
- Dart
- CoffeeScript
- Elm
- ClojureScript
- Haxe
- Nim
- PureScript

Of course, the list is much longer than this, but the preceding list does highlight some of the more popular alternatives, each of which has its own set of benefits and drawbacks.

The TypeScript Language

TypeScript is an interesting and important alternative to the JavaScript language. A superset of the JavaScript language, TypeScript was developed by Microsoft and was released sometime in 2014. It is very similar to JavaScript but has a feature that is very important to some: strict typing with type inference.

Strict typing is where a variable has a fixed type. This may be a number, a string, or a Boolean. By being strictly typed, a variable is unable to contain a value of any other type. This prevents a number of bugs in your system.

Let's look at a JavaScript problem.

A developer builds a function that accepts two numbers and adds them together:

```
function add(a, b) {
if (a && b && a + b) {
    return a + b;
```

```
    } else {
        throw "invalid parameters passed to 'add' function";
    }
}
```

Now, the developer has thought to check the parameters, first, that both **a** and **b** are provided, and then that the two values can be added together. However, as you saw in *Chapter 5, Beyond the Fundamentals*, the addition operator is overloaded, so if a string is passed, it will be concatenated into a new string:

```
add(1, 2);   // ==> 3
add(true, false);   // ==> "invalid parameters passed to 'add' function"
add(1, "2");   // ==> "12"
```

While this is fine if the developer expected the outcome, it does raise potential hazards that could be missed by even seasoned developers. Such bugs are problematic because they do not resolve in an error at the source, but rather further in the application.

TypeScript's static typing could easily solve this issue by ensuring the values that are passed to the function are of a specific type:

```
function add(a: number, b: number): number {
    return a + b;
}
```

All types are checked at compile time. In the preceding example, checking the content of the type is not necessary as the compiler will ensure that the function is called with the correct number of arguments. If an argument were optional, then it could be marked as such with the **?** operator:

```
function fun(a: number, b?: boolean) {}
```

Such optional parameters must always appear at the tail end of the arguments list.

Of course, specifying the types of your variables is not required—the compiler will infer them. This means that based on the first value the variable contains, the compiler will then expect it to always contain a value of that type. Function arguments can still contain any type if you wish them to.

Exercise 12.04: A Basic TypeScript Project

TypeScript is a major player in the professional JavaScript world, so understanding how to set up a TypeScript project is an important skill. In this exercise, you will create a minimal webpack project by utilizing the TypeScript transpiler. Let's get started:

1. Create a new directory and initialize it with a webpack installation, as per *Exercise 12.03: A Basic Webpack Project*.

2. Next, install the TypeScript libraries from npm. These libraries will be saved as **devDependencies**, since TypeScript is not required by your project after transpiling:

```
npm install --save-dev typescript ts-loader
```

ts-loader is a webpack loader module since webpack doesn't know about or understand ***.ts** files out of the box.

3. The TypeScript transpiler utilizes configuration from a unique document in the root of your project called **tsconfig.json**. The possible values for this document are extensive, but for a simple project, simply enter the following:

```
{
"compilerOptions": {
"outDir": "./dist/",
"noImplicitAny": true,
"module": "es6",
"target": "es5",
"allowJs": true
  }
}
```

4. Open the **webpack.config.js** file and add the following rule to the **rules** list:

```
{
  test: /\.tsx?$/,
  use: 'ts-loader',
  exclude: /node_modules/,
},
```

5. Update the entry filename from **index.js** to **index.ts**. Your entire **webpack.config.js** file should now look as follows:

webpack.config.js

```
28  plugins: [
29    new HtmlWebPackPlugin({
30      template: "./src/index.html",
31      filename: "./index.html"
32    })
33  ],
34  resolve: {
35    extensions: [ '.tsx', '.ts', '.js' ],
36  },
37  output: {
38    filename: 'bundle.js',
39    path: path.resolve(__dirname, 'dist'),
40  },
41}
```

The full code is available at: https://packt.live/2KhPK3Y

6. Now, provide an **index.ts** file within the **src** directory and add the following content:

```
export function hello(name: string): string {
   return 'Hello ' + name;
}
```

7. You can now compile the application with the following code:

```
npm run wp
```

576 | Using Next-Generation JavaScript

You should now see a successful compilation output, as follows:

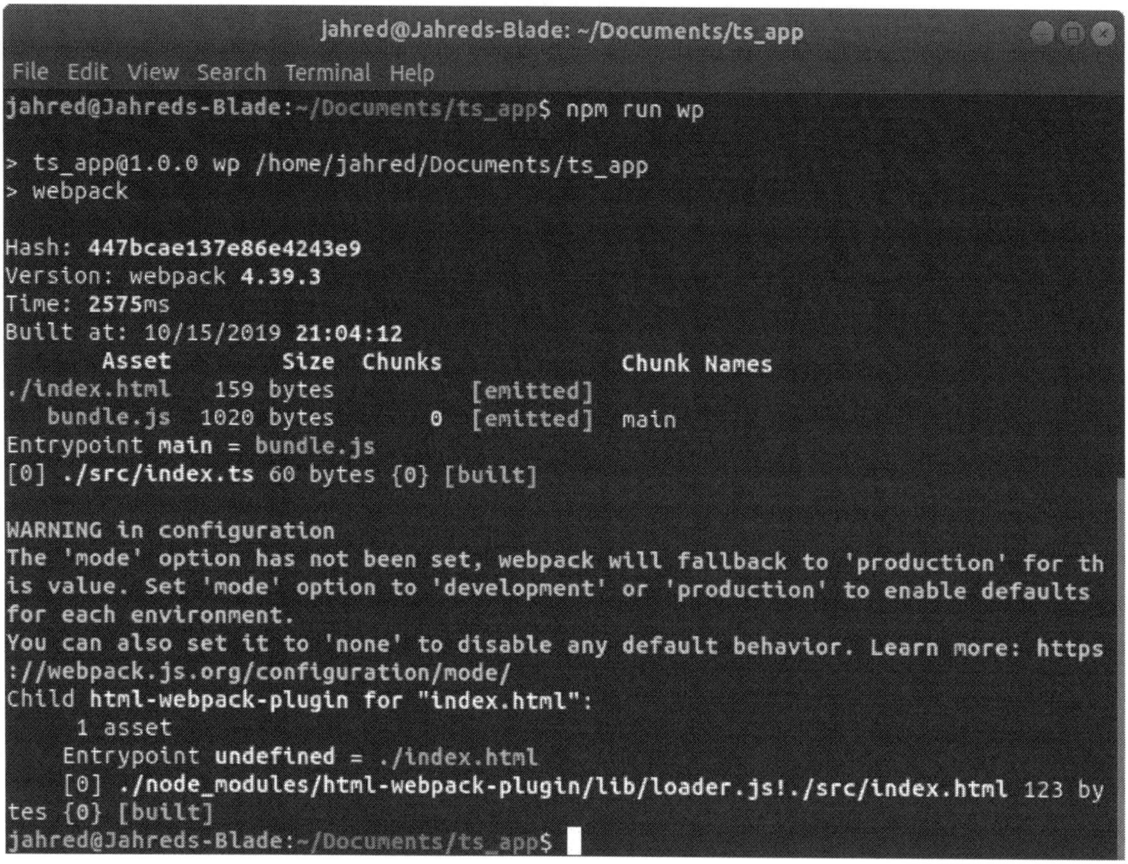

Figure 12.17: TypeScript with webpack

What you have just created is boilerplate for any kind of TypeScript application. Creating a webpack and TypeScript project may be something you do time and time again for many of your future projects.

Elm and ClojureScript

Both **Elm** and **ClojureScript** are interesting contenders for JavaScript replacement languages since they provide an entire ecosystem for browser application development. Elm and ClojureScript are declarative functional languages and promise a number of benefits out of the box, including smaller and faster code output and a greatly reduced possibility of runtime errors. Elm even does away with **null** and **undefined** values completely.

The intention of these languages is to empower the developer by outputting better code, but also improving the developer's coding ability. By thinking declaratively and functionally, problems can be solved more quickly and with better results.

Haxe

Haxe approaches JavaScript from a different angle. It was created as a unified language that could compile on many platforms, including the following:

- Flash ActionScript 3
- C++
- C# (.NET)
- Java
- JavaScript
- Neko (a small, native cross-platform virtual machine)
- HashLink (an even faster, more portable cross-platform virtual machine)
- PHP
- Python
- Lua

The platforms that are supported are continually increasing thanks to an enthusiastic community.

By compiling on many platforms, the source code of a Haxe application has the benefit of being potentially portable between those platforms. This means you could write a Haxe application for a JavaScript client, but also use much of the same code in a C# server application.

Code Support Libraries

Throughout its relatively long life, JavaScript has acquired a number of popular and useful libraries to aid engineers with their application development. Some of these libraries simply provide useful and reusable functions that reduce code complexity, while others offer extensive opinionated frameworks. Everything from user interfaces to database management is covered, with many overlapping libraries providing something a little different than competing libraries.

jQuery

jQuery is one of the oldest running utility libraries available. Functioning as a general-purpose tool, jQuery empowered developers with a simple means to manipulate the browser's Document Object Model (DOM), perform animations, send Asynchronous JavaScript and XML (AJAX) requests, manage events, and more.

Before jQuery was first released, finding and acquiring nodes within a web page was a laborious task, as was handling data and events from UI controls. The inception of jQuery alleviated a lot of the issues of earlier browsers, specifically with regard to cross-browser differences.

These days, much of the functionality provided by jQuery is now present in modern browsers, but the library itself is still a popular choice for many seeking a more uniform means to manage client-side application development.

jQuery provides a singular global reference object that can be accessed in two ways:

```
jquery(<context>)
$(<context>)
```

jQuery's ubiquity means that you're likely to see the solitary **$** symbol used throughout the internet and, indeed, very few libraries adopt this simple sigil, which is a valid variable symbol, for that reason.

The jQuery library has been covered somewhat in previous chapters, so no further information will be provided here.

Underscore, Lodash, and Ramda

Functional programming is becoming ever more important, with the benefits being realized in many different languages and platforms. While we can program in JavaScript functionally, it still does lack many features of more mature functional languages.

To overcome this shortcoming, the JavaScript community has provided numerous functional-oriented libraries, with the most popular being Underscore, Lodash, and Ramda.

Underscore and Lodash are named thus due to their use of the _ symbol. Just like jQuery's $ symbol, the _ symbol provides the single access point for either of these libraries. Both libraries provide a means to assign the primary object to a variable of a different name if there is a likelihood of a clash of library namespaces in an application, but since Underscore and Lodash provide much of the same functionality, it is not common to see both in use at the same time. The Ramda library uses the capital letter **R** as its library accessor:

```
let toString = (v) => `${v}`;

// Lodash
_.map([1, 2], toString);   // ==> ["1", "2"]

// Underscore
_.map([1, 2], toString);   // ==> ["1", "2"]

// Ramda
R.map(toString, [1, 2]);   // ==> ["1", "2"]
```

While each of these libraries provides a number of overlapping features, there are some functionalities that are unique to a library among the three. For instance, the Ramda library provides lensing functionality, which is a means to operate on subsets of a collection of data that match the given criteria.

Client Frameworks Overview

Recent years have seen an explosion in powerful JavaScript application frameworks. Many of these provide interesting ways to greatly simplify single-page application (SPA) development, as well as modular, dynamically loaded applications. While frameworks have long been an important requirement for reducing development complexity, supporting engineering teams, and facilitating common use cases with minimal fuss, modern frameworks often take things to a whole new level.

Thanks to mobile internet browsing, JavaScript applications often require increased functionality within the browser and less on the server. This greatly increases complexity and, while many such large applications require many engineers to work on such a JavaScript project, building these from scratch simply isn't conducive to a productive project. As such, frameworks are now becoming more and more important to reduce time to market, increase standards and best practices, and to raise creativity.

Models, Views, and Controllers

Most application frameworks implement an architecture that separates application logic into common units of functionality. The primary abstraction of these units typically consists of Models, Views, and Controllers (MVC), whereby the Model represents an application's data, the View represents how information is presented to the user, and the Controller is the functionality that facilitates processing between data and events:

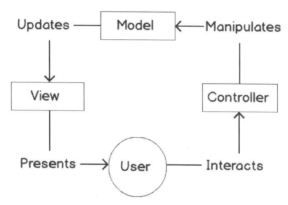

Figure 12.18: Model-View-Controller

The notion of an MVC was derived well before the inception of the JavaScript language and, indeed, frameworks often derive from an MVC to something a bit more appropriate to the browser, such as the Model-View-View-Model (MVVM) pattern. However, simply understanding that there is an abstraction, and knowing the roles of the actors therein, helps improve your adoption of any given framework.

Virtual DOMs

Another commonality of many newer frameworks is the inclusion of a virtual DOM. These are rendering engines that manage changes to nodes within the DOM. This means that, instead of manipulating the HTML within a web page directly, developers will instead utilize an API that sits between the application and the DOM. This way, when updates are needed, the virtual DOM will modify only those elements of the DOM that have changed by facilitating known low-latency, highly efficient methods.

A great benefit of virtual DOMs arises when implementing two-way data binding between a Model and a View. If a user inputs a value in a text field, the associated Model could be instantly and automatically updated. Likewise, when the model updates, this may also trigger another view to display this new value.

This is known as two-way data binding, which is the ability for a model and its views to equally update each other when one location changes. Such manipulations of the browser are greatly enhanced through the use of a virtual DOM, which may previously have resulted in user experience degradation.

Reactive Programming

Another feature that's commonly found in modern frameworks is reactive functionality. When two-way data binding occurs using a virtual DOM, it is typically a reactive code that facilitates it. Reactive programming is a methodology of facilitating responsiveness, resilience, and scalability through data messaging. The idea is that, instead of polling and pulling data, messages are pushed as changes to data occur or when new data is made available. These updates may occur within an application or between applications, such as between the browser and the server.

Reactive programming is such an important new paradigm that whole libraries and frameworks are named after it, such as RxJS (the Rx means Reactive) and ReactJS.

Popular Frameworks

Of the numerous frameworks available, there are three that are arguably the most popular among the JavaScript community. They are as follows:

- **AngularJS**
- **ReactJS**
- **Vue.js**

AngularJS

AngularJS was created by Google and released in October 2010 and was completely rewritten in 2014 as Angular2, changing many of its unique characteristics and adopting TypeScript as its preferred language; though it can be utilized with vanilla JavaScript with a bit of work. Since the rewrite, Angular2 is now incrementally updated with new releases regularly. Currently, Angular2 is on version 8 but is still called Angular2, which can get very confusing.

AngularJS (and its successor, Angular2) has a relatively high learning curve, flourishing many paradigms that are unique to the Angular community. However, it's an extremely opinionated library, helping to ensure that teams of developers utilize it in a common way, relieving any potential ambiguity of functionality. Additionally, AngularJS is a fully encompassing framework, providing almost all of the tools you may require when building complex browser-based applications.

ReactJS

ReactJS was conceived and developed by a single engineer at Facebook. In contrast to AngularJS, ReactJS does not try to do everything for you but purports to be merely the UI management layer, providing Virtual DOM functionality and other such goodies. The community that has formed around this framework has created additional libraries that can come together to form an ecosystem with similar capabilities to AngularJS. However, unlike AngularJS, ReactJS is not so opinionated, meaning applications can pick and choose what is implemented and, to some degree, how it is implemented. Developers also have greater freedom to decide from a range of libraries that compete to provide similar functionality.

Vue.js

Vue.js was developed by Evan You in 2013, a Google developer who had been using AngularJS while working for Google, but who decided he'd like to take only those elements of AngularJS that he liked and make his own lightweight framework. The result is a modular framework that provides almost all of the functionality of AngularJS, but in pieces that can be selected as needed, such as ReactJS, and with a total file size far smaller than either of the other two frameworks.

Vue.js has a very gentle learning curve and is steadily increasing in popularity as a framework that offers great application development structure, but without the rigid opinionated paradigms that work well in team environments. However, these often-hinder projects of a less vanilla nature.

Server-Side Libraries

Just like the browser, the server-side JavaScript ecosystem also has access to libraries and frameworks that aid an application's development. Since Node.js is JavaScript too, it is possible to utilize many libraries within both the browser and Node.js. For instance, Lodash, Underscore, and Ramda, having no browser-specific qualities, will function just as well in a Node.js application. This is one of the key reasons why the Node.js platform took off so quickly following its initial release; with so many libraries already usable on the platform that was created for browser applications, it was possible for developers to continue working in a style they were familiar with for server-side application development.

As well as all the possible browser-centric libraries, Node.js also has some key libraries of its own that provide functionality that is not possible in the browser, such as REST server functionality or database object relational mapping (ORM).

Express

Possibly the single most popular library for Node.js is called Express. This library makes it extremely easy to build webservers since it provides functions that are able to establish routes and serve content when requests are sent to those routes.

Express can be installed with the following command:

```
npm install --save express
```

Once installed, you can write a simple server application, such as the following:

```
const express = require('express')
const app = express()

const port = 4000;
app.get("/say_hello", (request, response) => response.send("Hello,
World!"))

app.listen(4000port, () => console.log(`Web server now listening on port:
${port}`))
```

Once built, the webserver can be launched just like any other Node.js application; for example:

```
node index.js
```

The Express object supports all possible HTTP call types, including **GET**, **PUT**, **POST**, and **DELETE**, thus empowering complete REST-capable servers, but is also capable of serving static HTML, JavaScript, CSS, and other such asset files, using a special **static** function.

The Express library is very complete, so reading the documentation and guides on its website is recommended so that you get a true feeling of its capabilities.

Request

While Express functions as a webserver, the Request library functions as a web client. Often, when creating web applications, it can become necessary to proxy content, data, or functionality from another remote webserver. The Request library enables communication with such servers for this purpose.

Request can be installed with the following command:

```
npm install --save request
```

Once installed, you can use Request as follows:

```
const request = require("request")

request("https://www.google.com", function (error, response, data) {
    // do something with data
});
```

Socket.IO

Working with HTTP can be slow. The client creates a request packet and sends it to the recipient server. This server then creates a response packet and sends it back to the caller. Each request/response transaction is atomic, meaning it occurs independently of any other request/response transactions, often requiring a unique connection setup and teardown.

Modern applications prefer to utilize web sockets more and more. These are "always connected" sockets that use a faster, more agile connection protocol for sending data and are wonderful for building applications such as online chat rooms, multiplayer games, and also for fast data storage and retrieval.

While web sockets utilize a protocol of their own, that protocol merely handles the security and reliability of the data transaction, and not with the specific requirements of an application's logic.

To address this, Socket.IO provides an additional layer to make working with web sockets much easier, thus providing functionality that's common to many applications that can utilize it how they see fit.

Socket.IO can be installed with the following command:

```
npm install --save socket.io
```

A simple Socket.IO server application looks as follows:

```
const app = require("express")()
const server = require("http").createServer(app)
const sio = require("socket.io")(server)

sio.on("connection", function(socket){
    console.log("Connection established");
});
```

Activity 12.01: Creating a Project to Recognize and Compile TypeScript Files

This chapter provided a lot of information regarding the investigation of the greater JavaScript world. Obviously, there is a lot you can learn beyond the basics of a language or platform but knowing where to look and how to integrate a new library or framework into your application provides the necessary foundation from which you can experiment and improve your coding skills.

In this activity, you have been tasked with setting up TypeScript for a new project. You are now aware of what TypeScript is. For the project at hand, both your project manager and your developer colleagues want to utilize TypeScript's static typing capabilities, among other things, in what will be a large project.

Your task for this activity is to create the initial project setup, ensuring that TypeScript files are recognized and compiled correctly to the output folder. It is not important to provide any code, merely to ensure everything compiles successfully. The project manager is happy for Parcel to be used in this project in order to keep things simple.

The high-level steps for the activity are as follows:

1. Create a new project that has **npm** initialized.

2. Install Parcel as a global library.

3. Install the TypeScript library in the application.

4. Create the necessary TypeScript configuration but keep it simple.

5. Create a temporary **.ts** file in the **src** directory.

6. Add the necessary script to the **package.json** file.

7. Run the transpiler and ensure that output is generated. You should see no errors. The TypeScript transpiler should show a **Built in <x>ms** response message if all went well.

The expected output for this activity is as follows:

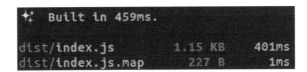

Figure 12.19: Parcel TypeScript Output

> **Note**
>
> The solution to the activity can be found on page 752.

Simply knowing how to utilize a package manager opens up vast amounts of power so that you can create functional applications quickly. When working in a professional environment, using the necessary tools in the correct fashion is paramount and will ensure that your application starts off on the right footing.

Summary

In this chapter, we had a look at the various tools that are available on the market for advanced development in JavaScript. We learned how to use the latest JavaScript syntax in older browsers and identified the different options that are available for the development of JavaScript applications in other languages. We also explored the various package managers, such as npm and Yarn, that are compatible with JavaScript, along with several different frameworks, such as AngularJS, ReactJS, and Vue.js. Finally, we looked at some server-side libraries such as Express, Request, and Socket.IO.

In the next chapter, we will look at some other areas of advanced JavaScript.

13

JavaScript Programming Paradigms

Overview

By the end of this chapter, you will be able to apply different JavaScript paradigms; use prototypes, inheritance, and anonymous functions; list different types of data scopes and closures; declare variables using hoisting; and explain JavaScript memory management.

In this chapter, we will dig deep into the core features of JavaScript that make it a very diverse and multi-paradigm programming language.

Introduction

So far, we know the importance of JavaScript at the browser level and its power at the server level. We have learned how to install Node.js on the system and how to write and execute code. Also, we have gained a huge amount of knowledge about the internal and external modules of Node.js. Moreover, web sockets and working with databases were also covered in the previous chapters. We learned all of this through interesting activities and exercises. Now it's time to strengthen this knowledge and learn about the root concepts of JavaScript.

In this chapter, we will go through the different types of JavaScript programming paradigms. During the learning phase of any programming language, people usually code in a procedural way; instead of planning, they put most of their focus on execution and understanding the concepts of that particular programming language. But when it comes to working on real-life problems, the procedural way is not a scalable option. Luckily, we have a lot of different types of code implementation techniques that we can use to model real-life entities with a programming language, such as the **object-oriented programming** paradigm, or **OOP**.

Let's take a real-world example in which we have to build a project for our college. There will be teachers, clerks, students, heads of departments, and so on. One way of implementing this project is to write the logic for each of these entities separately, which is not a scalable option, and it will not be a flexible solution either. Another way is to use the OOP approach, in which we will create one `Person` model that will hold a person's designations as keys in the object. This way, we are separating people from their designations. We can easily implement changes in either `Person` or entities, that is, heads, teachers, students, and so on. All the changes to `Person` will automatically be implemented on entities because they belong to the `Person` class. There are a lot of other approaches that we can use to solve the same types of problems. We will go through some of them in this chapter.

After that, you will learn what prototypes are and how to use them to achieve inheritance. There are a lot of other basics as well. Let's start.

JavaScript Paradigms

A programming paradigm is a way or method in which we write code to solve different types of problems. Since there are a lot of ways to code, there are a lot of programming paradigms that developers use to write code.

JavaScript is a multi-paradigm scripting language, which means that it is very dynamic in nature and supports various types of programming styles, such as object-oriented, imperative, and functional programming. In this book, we will discuss the three main programming paradigms that are popular among developers.

We can divide programming paradigms into two categories:

- Imperative, which includes **Procedural Programming** and **OOP**

- Declarative, which includes **Functional Programming**

In this chapter, we will discuss procedural and object-oriented programming. Functional programming is quite popular, and there are a lot of concepts to learn, so we have dedicated one chapter, named Functional Programming, to cover that topic.

The Procedural Paradigm

As the name suggests, this paradigm follows the procedural pattern. In this paradigm, we divide our whole program into routines and subroutines. The process flow is very linear and synchronous in this coding pattern. It follows a top-down approach to programming. It simply involves breaking down the desired result in some routines and smaller subroutines. These subroutines will be further divided into processes, which will then be executed to achieve the desired result.

Procedural programming uses a top-down approach to write an application, while OOP follows a zigzag approach to the data flow. Reusability is one of the most important factors when developing large applications. There is less reusability in procedural programming compared with OOP, and that is the reason why the object-oriented approach is more popular in scalable applications. When developing programs using procedural programming, we might plan out a program without thinking about recycling code.

The data flow is sequential in procedural programming, but that doesn't mean we do not have to plan the data flow. Planning is still involved in procedural programming. It takes a much more literal approach. Procedural programming applications are structured more like a story format. The procedural approach makes the development process much simpler, but it consumes more time.

The pros of adapting to the procedural paradigm are as follows:

- A lot of learning resources can be found online.

- It has an easier way to track process flow.

- The implementation of programs is very easy.

The cons of adapting to the procedural paradigm are as follows:

- It is difficult to relate to the real world.
- There is less data security.
- It is difficult to solve complex problems with this approach.

The procedural approach is one of the basic approaches that most people use when they start learning code. So, to strengthen our concepts, it's always better to practice what we have just learned. Let's do an exercise in which we will implement a very basic and simple function using straightforward procedural programming.

Exercise 13.01: Implementing Procedural Programming

In this exercise, we have a string and we have to capitalize every word in it. As per the procedural approach, we have to implement it in such a way that each statement executes in a top-down manner. This means that we will start with the first statement and by the last statement, we will have our result. In order to do that, we have to perform some operations. Let's look at them one by one:

1. First, let's create an empty file and call it **procedural.js**. You can change the name if you want.

2. Let's write a function called **toCapitalize()**, which will take one argument as an input. The input parameter will be of the string type only:

```
functiontoCapitalize(input){

}
```

3. Inside this function, let's first split the input string using spaces. This will divide the input string into words and will return an array of all those words:

```
let arrayOfString = input.split(' ');
```

After this statement, **arrayOfString** will hold an array of words, that is [**'Once'**, **'upon'**, **'a'**, **'time'**, **'in'**, **'new'**, **'york'**].

4. Let's loop over the array:

```
for(let i=0; i<arrayOfString.length; i++) {

}
```

5. Inside this **for** loop, extract the first letter of all the words and save the result in a variable:

```
letfirstChar = arrayOfString[i].charAt(0);
```

6. Let's make this letter uppercase using the **toUpperCase()** method:

```
firstChar.toUpperCase();
```

7. Now, remove the first letter of every word from the input string and replace it with the one we just made uppercase:

```
arrayOfString[i] = firstChar.toUpperCase() + arrayOfString[i].slice(1);
```

8. Finally, let's join all the words of the array, including the spaces, to make a sentence again and return it as the output of the function:

```
arrayOfString.join(' ');
```

9. Now we can pass any string to this function and it will return the string with all the words with the first letter in uppercase:

```
let string = "Once upon a time in new york.";
    console.log(toCapitalize(string));
```

10. Let's execute this script with Node.js and look at the output:

```
1 // Procedural
2 function toCapitalize(input) {
3         let arrayOfString = input.split(' ');
4
5         for(let i=0; i<arrayOfString.length; i++){
6                 let firstChar = arrayOfString[i].charAt(0)
7                 arrayOfString[i] = firstChar.toUpperCase() + arrayOfString[i].slice(1);
8         }
9
10        return arrayOfString.join(' ');
11 }
12
13 let string = "Once upon a time in new york."
14 console.log(toCapitalize(string))
```

```
~/Documents/node
√root ≥    node procedural.js
Once Upon A Time In New York.
```

Figure 13.1: Output of the procedural exercise

As you can see, we now have our desired output: the first letter of each word is uppercase. In the code, we have called a lot of methods, such as **split**, **toUpperCase**, **slice**, and **join**. All these functions were called in a top-down manner. We started with the first statement of this function, where we had our input string, and then we processed the input. After the execution of the last statement of this function, we have our desired result. This is a simple example of the implementation of procedural programming. Next, we will learn how to implement the object-oriented approach in programming.

The Object-Oriented Paradigm

The object-oriented paradigm is one of the most popular paradigms used by developers. A lot of programming languages are oriented to this paradigm. The reason for its popularity is its ability to model real-life things in code. In this paradigm, we can create objects that will represent entities in the real world.

We use classes to imitate real-world categories, and then we can create objects from those classes, which will act like entities. All classes in JavaScript have one constructor function that will execute every time we initiate new instances of that object. We use the **Class** keyword to create a class, and **constructor** is a default function inside each class:

```
class Animal{
constructor(category){

}

}
```

Whatever we are initializing in the **constructor** function will have a scope level of this whole class. We can use the **new** keyword to create instances of this object:

```
new Animal('Lion');
```

Here, the parameter passed when creating the new instance will get passed straight to the **constructor** function.

Exercise 13.02: Implementing OOP

The object-oriented paradigm is the best one to implement because we can relate the code to real life. We create classes of real-world entities, such as cars, furniture, and electronics, and create instances of those classes to represent real-world objects. For example, imagine you have a car from the manufacturer Audi. The car is an entity that we can represent as a class in OOP. We can create an instance of this **car** class, which will represent your car, and this instance will hold information about you, such as that the car's owner is you and the car's manufacturer is Audi. Each instance will act as the registration of that vehicle. That way, we can create relations between the code and the real world.

The best way to understand this is by taking an example from the real world and implementing it. Let's consider a simple program that displays information about the living beings on Earth. To do this, we have to make a class of living beings and we can create multiple instances of that class, such as **Humans**, **Animals**, and **Plants**.

To start this off, we have to first create a class of **Humans**. There are a lot of things that are common in humans, such as age, weight, height, and skin and hair color, but in this case, we are only interested in showing their age, name, and gender:

1. Let's create an empty file and call it **humans.js**.

2. Now, let's create a class called **Humans** and a **constructor** function, which will take **name**, **age**, and **gender** as parameters:

```
class Humans {
constructor(name, age, gender) {
        this.name = name;
this.age = age;
this.gender = gender;
    }
  }
```

3. Let's create one more method inside this class, which will print the values of **name**, **age**, and **gender** because only the methods of this class have access to class variables:

```
info() {
return console.log(this);
    }
```

4. From our **Humans** class, we can now create some instances that represent actual humans:

```
let Gaurav = new Humans('Gaurav', 24, 'Male');
let Nishi = new Humans('Nishi', 23, 'Female');
```

5. Now we will print both of these objects. They will contain all the information we passed to the constructor when we created them:

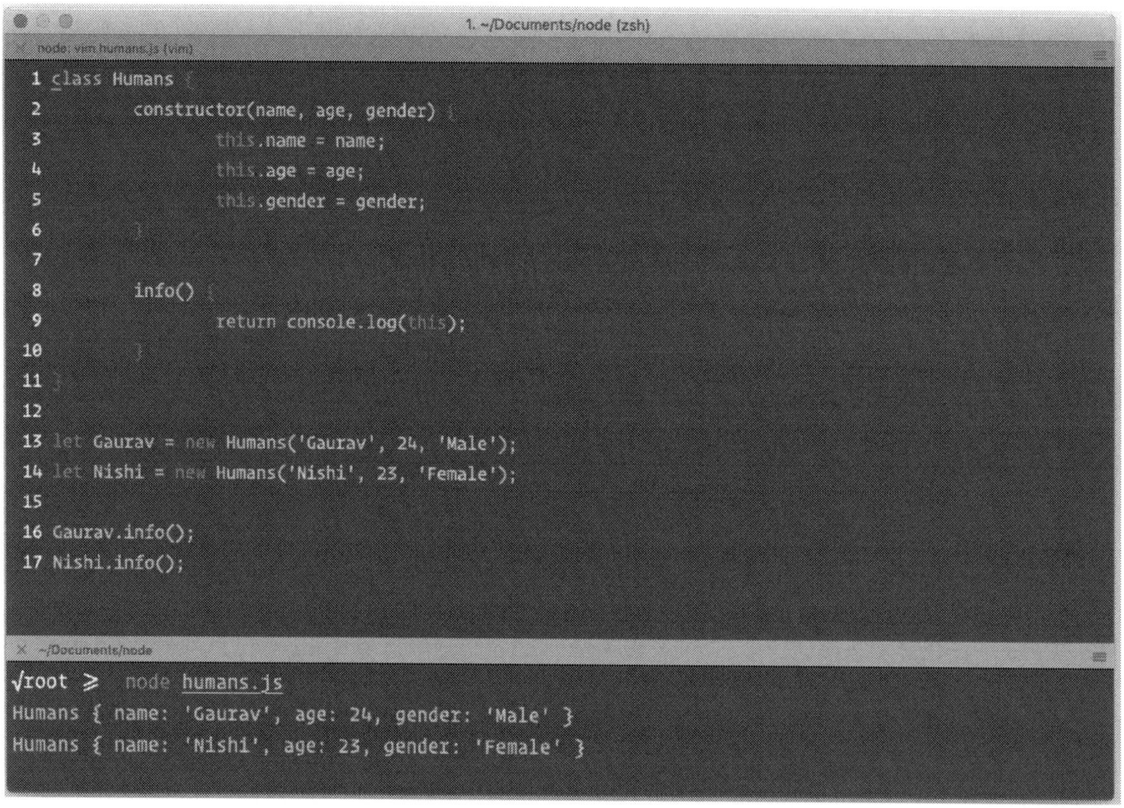

Figure 13.2: Output for the object-oriented exercise

As you can see, we now have two instances of the **Humans** class, each of which holds information about a human. We can treat these two instances as real humans. They have their own **name**, **age**, and **gender**. This will help you a lot when writing code because you know the object you are writing the logic for. Similarly, we can implement any real-world entity as a class and can create multiple objects of that class, which can represent real-world objects.

So far, we know there are a lot of benefits of using OOP, and some of them are very useful. Next, we'll look at two very important features that this paradigm provides – encapsulation and inheritance. Let's go through each of them and see how we can use these concepts with JavaScript.

Encapsulation

One benefit of using OOP is that it protects the data in classes. We can add data to classes that will only be available for the class' methods. Other classes will not be able to access that data. It works as a protective shield for the class.

As we saw in the previous example, the scope of the **name**, **age**, and **gender** variables was limited to the class. All the methods initialized in the class can have access to those variables. This is how we can protect data inside a class.

Inheritance

Inheritance is a way in which one class can have access to the properties of another class. In the last example, humans can have a lot of different types of professions. So, we can inherit the **Humans** class by professions as well. Let's examine this concept by doing an exercise. In the last exercise, we created a **Humans** class that holds the name, gender, and age information. We will extend this class further by creating a new class called **Teacher**. This class will hold all the properties of the **Humans** class along with some additional properties describing the subject they teach, grades, and more. This will give you an idea of how classes are extended and how parent class properties are inherited by other classes. Let's jump into the code now.

Exercise 13.03: Inheritance Implementation Using the extends Keyword

Let's create a class called **Teacher** that will inherit the properties of the **Humans** class. We will use the **extends** keyword to inherit from classes in this exercise:

1. Use the **extends** keyword to inherit from the class:

```
class Teacher extends Humans {
    }
```

2. Inside this class, we have to pass all the necessary parameters to the **constructor** function. Inside the **constructor** function, we will call the **super** function and pass the parameters required for the parent class:

```
constructor( name, age, gender, subject, grade ) {
        super(name, age, gender);
    this.subject = subject;
    this.grade = grade;
      }
```

3. Here, **name**, **age**, and **gender** are parameters of the **Humans** class. Using the **super** function, we passed these parameters to the **Humans** class and the rest of the variables, that is, **subject** and **grade**, are a part of the **Teacher** class.

4. Let's have an **info** method in the **Teacher** class that will print all the variables of that class:

```
info(){
        return console.log(this);
    }
```

5. After we have finished creating the **Teacher** class, let's create an instance of it:

```
let teacher = new Teacher('GauravMehla', 24, 'Male','Science', 'A');
```

6. Finally, let's run this script with Node.js:

Figure 13.3: Teacher instance after inheritance

As you can see in the output, there are some properties, such as **name**, **age**, and **gender**, that are not present in the **Teacher** class. These properties are inherited from the **Humans** class, which we implemented in *Exercise 13.02: Implementing OOP*.

Now that we know how to achieve inheritance using JavaScript, we can now create multiple objects of the **Teacher** class that will inherit all the properties of their parent class, **Humans**.

Let's look at some of the pros of adopting the object-oriented paradigm:

- **Reusability**: We can use already-created classes again and again without creating new classes.

- **Real-Life modeling**: We can model a real-world concept using OOP, such as a chair, person, or car. This makes understanding the implementation easy.

- **Parallel development**: Classes can be independent, which means we can develop more than one class at a time. This results in quicker project development.

- **Team independency**: As OOP supports parallel development, teams can work independently of each other.

- **Secured development**: OOP features, such as inheritance and encapsulation, hide data from other classes, thereby improving security. The internal data of a class can't be accessed by external functions.

The possible cons of using the object-oriented paradigm:

- **Unnecessary code:** It can create an enormous amount of unnecessary and bloated code if it's not implemented with proper planning.

- **Duplication**: As OOP can be implemented for each individual class, it can lead to code duplication.

- **Early planning**: Programmers should have a proper plan before designing a program.

- **Project size**: Projects developed with OOP are often larger than projects developed with other approaches, such as the procedural paradigm.

In this section, we have learned about different types of programming paradigms we can use with JavaScript. We dug deep into two of the most popular paradigms – procedural and object-oriented. We went through different pros and cons of both paradigms. We also learned about two of the most important features of OOP, which are encapsulation and inheritance.

Basic JavaScript Concepts

Programming paradigms are important, but to understand them in detail, we need a basic understanding of different JavaScript concepts. So, let's go through some of the core concepts of JavaScript, which will help you get a grasp of JavaScript and give you a better understanding of how we can use programming paradigms to build scalable solutions to problems.

Prototypes and Prototypical Inheritance

Objects are very important because they help us manipulate JavaScript to achieve the functionality we want. There are a lot of ways to create objects in JavaScript. One of the ways is by using a `constructor` function, and whenever we create a function, the JavaScript engine adds a `prototype` property to the function. This `prototype` property is an object that has a `constructor` property by default. This constructor points back to the parent functions. You can see this function by calling `functionName.prototype`.

Let's first create a function:

```
functionPersonName(first_name, last_name) {
this.first_name = first_name;
this.last_name = last_name;
this.fullName = function(){
 return [ this.first_name, this.last_name].join(" ");
    }
  }
```

Now, let's check its **prototype** property by entering **PersonName.prototype**.
The output will be as follows:

Figure 13.4: Prototype property of objects

As you can see, we have created a function named **Person** and JavaScript automatically
binds a **prototype** property to it. You can print the **prototype** and you can see that
there is a **constructor** property, which holds all the metadata of the parent function.

What Is Prototypical Inheritance?

As we know, everything in JavaScript is an object. Every string, integer, array, object, and function that you define is an object of its respective parent class. Each object in JavaScript holds a **proto** property (**__proto__** keys inside child objects are usually referred to as **proto** properties) that holds all the properties of its parent class. We can use these **proto** properties to implement inheritance. These **prototype** objects act as template objects from which all the child objects will inherit methods and properties. We can also override the properties of a parent class using this **prototype** property. This linking of prototypes is referred to as a prototype chain.

Exercise 13.04: Prototypical Inheritance Implementation

In this exercise, let's implement a very simple function that will take a first name and a last name as parameters and return the full name. After this exercise, you should be completely clear on how prototypical inheritance works and the differences between the two approaches to achieve this output:

1. We can implement **firstName** and **lastName** child functions inside the **PersonName** parent function that will have the scope to use the values of the parent function. We can bind the functions to their parent's prototype because the parent function can always access the scope of a child function. Let's implement and observe both approaches. Open the Google Chrome Developer Tools console using the **F12** key.

2. Use this constructor function to create some objects and paste the code in the console:

```
functionPersonName(firstName, lastName) {
this.firstName = firstName;
this.lastName = lastName;
this.fullName = function(){
  return [ this.firstName, this.lastName].join(" ");
    }
  }
let pName1 = new PersonName("Gaurav", "Mehla");
```

Whenever we use a **constructor** function to create objects, JavaScript adds a property to its object, which is **_proto_**. This **_proto_** property holds the link to the prototype of the main function, which can be seen in the following output:

Figure 13.5: Prototype property of instances created with the new keyword

As you can see here, the **pName1** object has a **__proto__** property that directly points to the prototype of its parent, **PersonName.prototype**. In the next step, we can use this **prototype** property to achieve inheritance using JavaScript.

3. Let's bind the **fullName** function with the **prototype** property of **Person** instead of defining it inside the function:

```
PersonName.prototype.fullName = function(){
    return [this.firstName, this.lastName].join(" ");
}
```

4. Now, create two objects of the **PersonName** method using the **new** keyword:

```
let pName1 = new PersonName("Gaurav", "Mehla");
let pName2 = new PersonName("Sarthak", "Sharma");
```

5. All the objects created here with the **new** keyword will now contain a **proto** property, which will point to its parent prototype, and all the functions and properties defined in the parent prototype will be accessible to all its child objects. In other words, if we create a function and bind it to the prototype of the parent function, that function will be accessible to all its objects using the prototype chain object. Now, call the **fullName** function, which is defined in the **prototype** property of the **Person** method, using its objects:

```
pName1.fullName();
pName2.fullName();
```

The output is as follows:

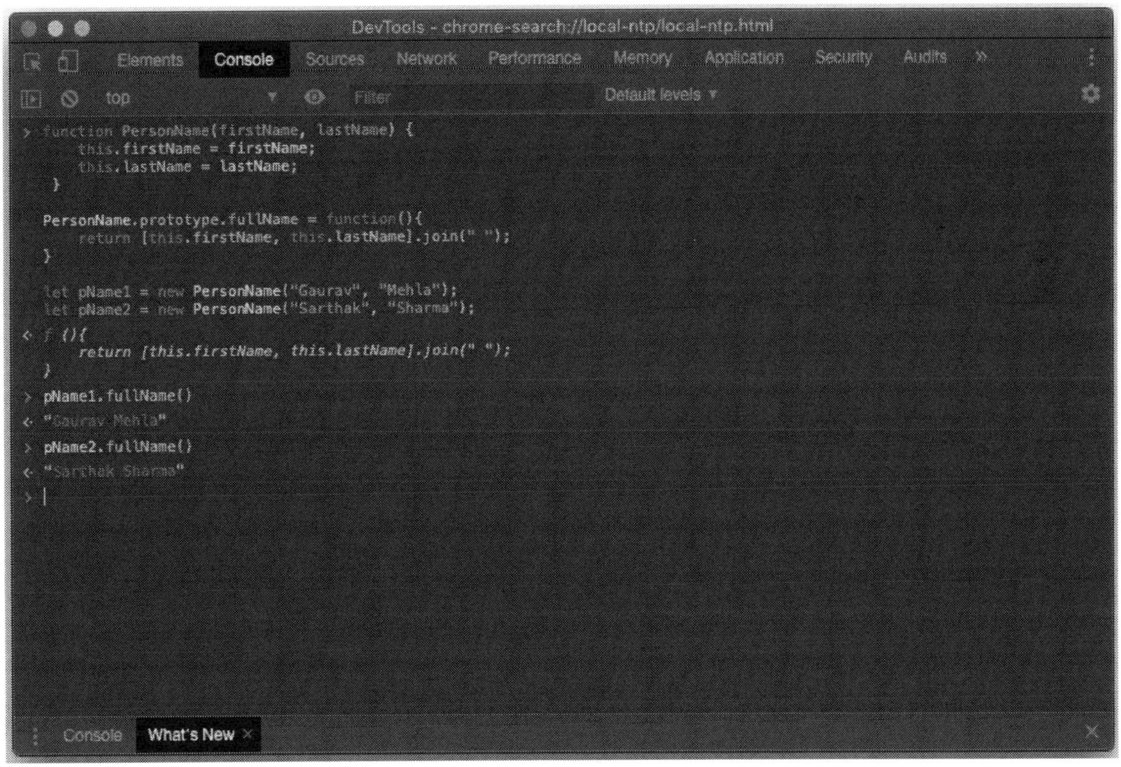

Figure 13.6: Example of a prototype chain

In this exercise, we declare a constructor function (**PersonName**), then we create a function (**fullName**) and bind it to its prototype. Then, we create two child objects using the function's constructor. You can see that both of these objects have access to the **fullName** function, which is in their parent's prototype. This way, we have achieved inheritance using a prototype chain, as visualized in *Figure 13.7*:

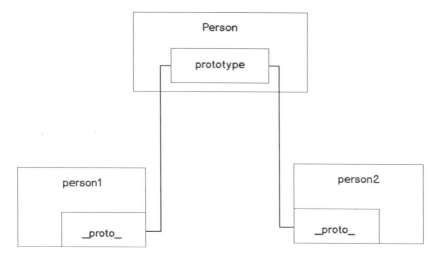

Figure 13.7: References of the __proto__ property

Now we can create as many instances of **PersonName** as we want, and all those instances will always have access to **PersonName.fullName**.

We can even modify the prototypes and the changes will be reflected in all of its child objects instantaneously.

Anonymous Functions

Objects in the JavaScript language are very tricky. Everything in JavaScript is an object. So, functions in JavaScript are considered functional objects and can be used in the same way as we use objects. Functions in JavaScript can be passed as arguments to other functions as well. Any function that also returns a function is called a function factory. Let's have a look at an example:

```
functioncalculateSum(a, b) {
    return () => {
        return a + b();
    }
}
let sum = calculateSum(10, () =>20);
```

In this example, we have called a function, **calculateSum**, and passed two parameters to it. One is a number and the other one is a function. This function will return a new function, which will display the passed function followed by the result, as can be seen in the following output:

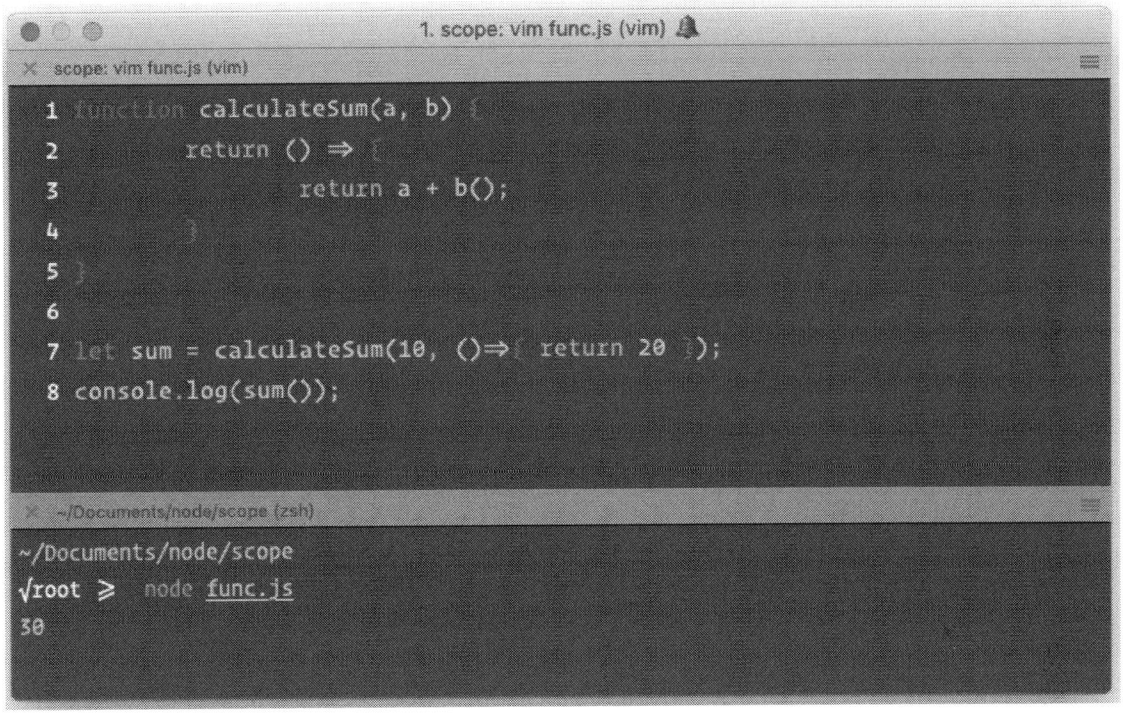

Figure 13.8: Examples of anonymous functions

In the example, you can see we have used a lot of functions without naming them. These functions are very important in JavaScript. A function declared with no particular name is called an anonymous function. We use anonymous functions a lot when programming in JavaScript. These types of functions are declared dynamically at runtime and can be passed as parameters to other functions. For example, **Function () {}** is a typical example of an anonymous function. You can assign the return value of this function to any variable. Creating functions with this approach allows us to create functions on the go. Anonymous functions are mainly used in callbacks.

The Differences between Named Functions and Anonymous Functions

The major difference between named and anonymous functions is that when you declare a named function, the compiler allocates a stored memory block to that function. So, if you have to call it, you can use the name to call it. But with anonymous functions, the memory block is assigned to them and the address is returned, which we can then store in a variable. This helps us initialize functions in places where we can't declare named functions. We can even change the name with which we can call this function by assigning the function to another variable. This can be visualized in the following diagram:

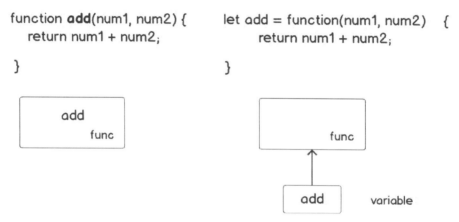

```
function add(num1, num2) {        let add = function(num1, num2)   {
    return num1 + num2;               return num1 + num2;

}                                 }
```

Figure 13.9: Named versus anonymous functions

Data Scope

Data scoping determines the accessibility of variables, functions, and objects in your code during runtime. This means the scope of a variable is controlled by the location of the variable declaration.

In JavaScript, there are two main types of scopes:

- Global scope
- Local scope, which includes **function level** and **block level**

Global Scope

Every JavaScript application has a global scope in which we can define anything that all the functions in our application can access. All the variables defined outside the functions, blocks, and modules have a global scope. Global variables are available for the lifetime of the application.

Another way of creating global variables is to use predefined global variables such as **process** (in Node.js) and **window** (in browsers). You can bind any value to these already defined global variables, and you can access them from anywhere inside the application. For example, let's add the **NODE_VERSION** value to the **env** property of **process**:

```
$ process.env.NODE_VERSION=10.8
```

The **process** variable has a global scope during the execution of the program. Now, we can access the value that we've set (**NODE_VERSION = 10.08**) anywhere in our program:

```
$ console.log(process.env.NODE_VERSION); // "10.08"
```

Local Scope

Variables defined within a function or a block are in a local scope. Only those functions that are defined inside that function or block can have access to those variables.

Function-Level Scope

In JavaScript, each function has its own scope. All the variables and functions defined inside that function will have access to only each other:

```
// Function A
function parent(arg1, arg2) {
let name = "gaurav";
let age = 24;

function print(){
console.log(name, age);
}
}

// Function B
function print(){
console.log(name, age); // Error : name, age variable not defined.
}
```

Here, both functions have different levels of scope. **Function B** can't access the variables defined in **Function A**. The scope of both functions is highlighted in the following figure:

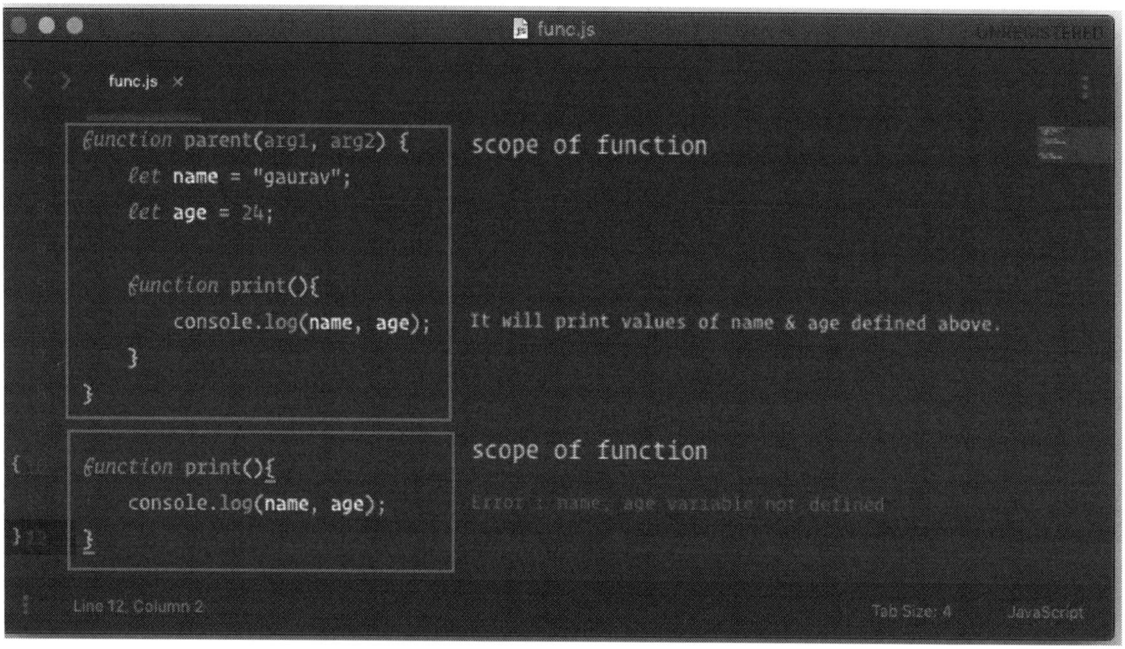

Figure 13.10: Example of function-level scope

Block-Level Scope

Block-level scope is similar to function-level scope, but in this type of scope we do not initialize any functions. We can separate the scope of variables by creating blocks in JavaScript:

```
// 1st block
{
let name = "gaurav";
let age = 24;
console.log(name, age);
}
```

```
// 2nd block
{
console.log(name, age);
}
```

> **Note**
>
> We use curly braces to create blocks in JavaScript. The second block can't access any variables created in the first block.

Hoisting

We now know that the scope of variables and functions depends on where they are declared, but there is an interesting concept in JavaScript, which is called **hoisting**. Hoisting is a feature in which the interpreter moves the declarations of functions and variables to the top of their scope. This means that variable declarations are processed before any code is executed. When any scope is processed, first, the whole scope is searched for variable and function declarations. Then, the memory space is allocated for each of the variables and functions. After this, the body of the function or block is executed line by line.

> **Note**
>
> Hoisting only moves the declaration of the variables and functions, not the assignment. The assignment stays in the same position.

Functions are hoisted first followed by the variables. So, it is a good practice to always first declare functions and then work on the implementation part:

```
// 1st block
{
var name;
console.log(name);
name="gaurav"
}
```

```
// 2nd block
{
console.log(name);
var name = "gaurav";
}
```

Here, both of the blocks will return **undefined**. The output of both blocks is the same. The position of the declaration doesn't matter inside a block. The first block will not throw any errors relating to variables not being defined.

The Difference between var and let

In the case of **var**, after creating variable definitions, each of the variables is initialized with an undefined value, but in the case of **let/const**, the initialization to undefined does not happen until the line of the declaration. In the following code, the variable is in the Temporal Dead Zone and accessing it results in a reference error:

```
// 1st block
{
let name;
console.log(name);
name="gaurav";
}

// 2nd block
{
console.log(name);
let name="gaurav"
}
```

Let's execute this and see the difference by observing the different outputs of **`var`** and **`let`**:

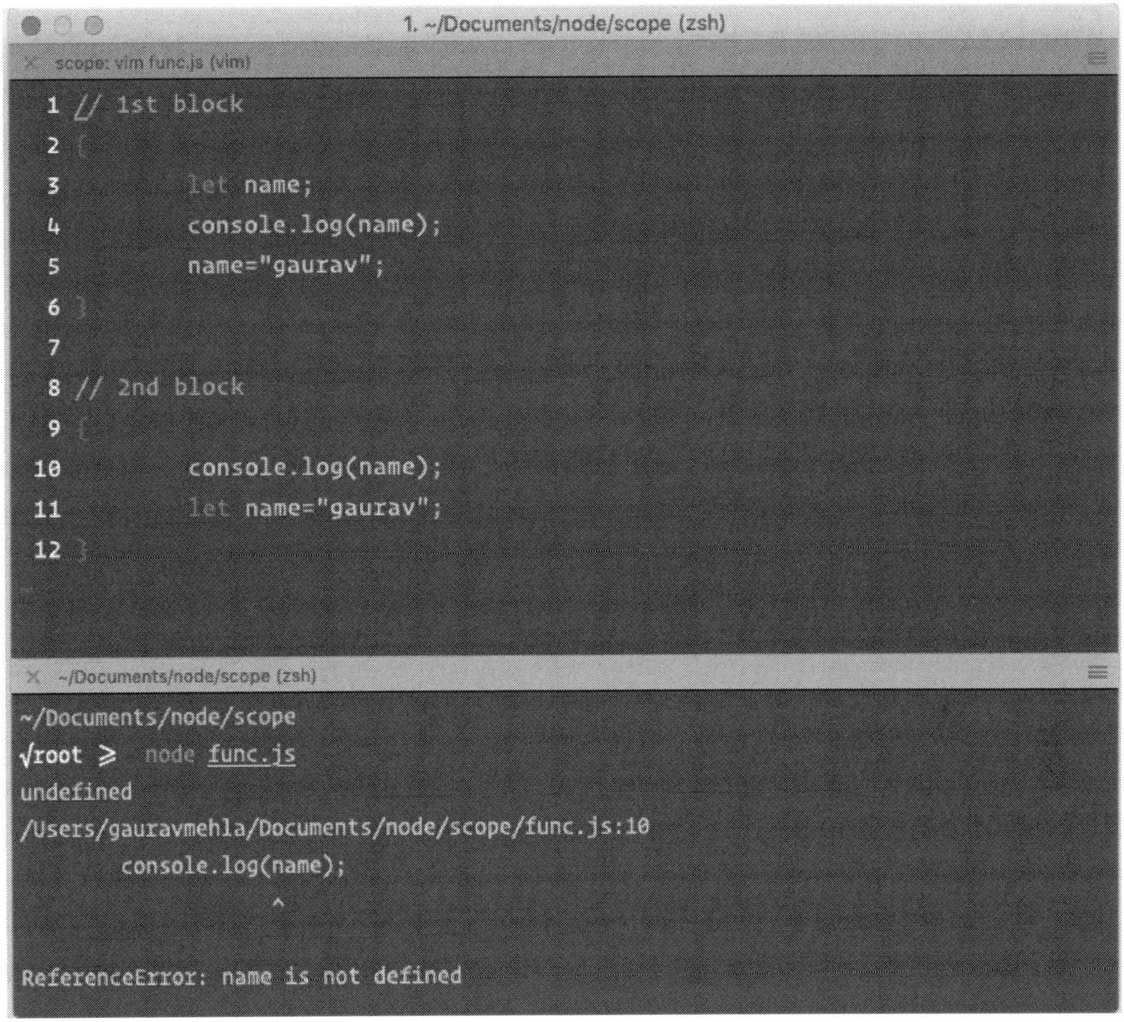
1. ~/Documents/node/scope (zsh)
scope: vim func.js (vim)
1 // 1st block
2 {
3 let name;
4 console.log(name);
5 name="gaurav";
6 }
7
8 // 2nd block
9 {
10 console.log(name);
11 let name="gaurav";
12 }
~/Documents/node/scope (zsh)
~/Documents/node/scope
√root ≥ node func.js
undefined
/Users/gauravmehla/Documents/node/scope/func.js:10
console.log(name);
^
ReferenceError: name is not defined

Figure 13.11: let keyword usage

In the preceding figure, you can see that if we use **`let`**, it throws a reference error. Let's look at the output using the **`var`** keyword:

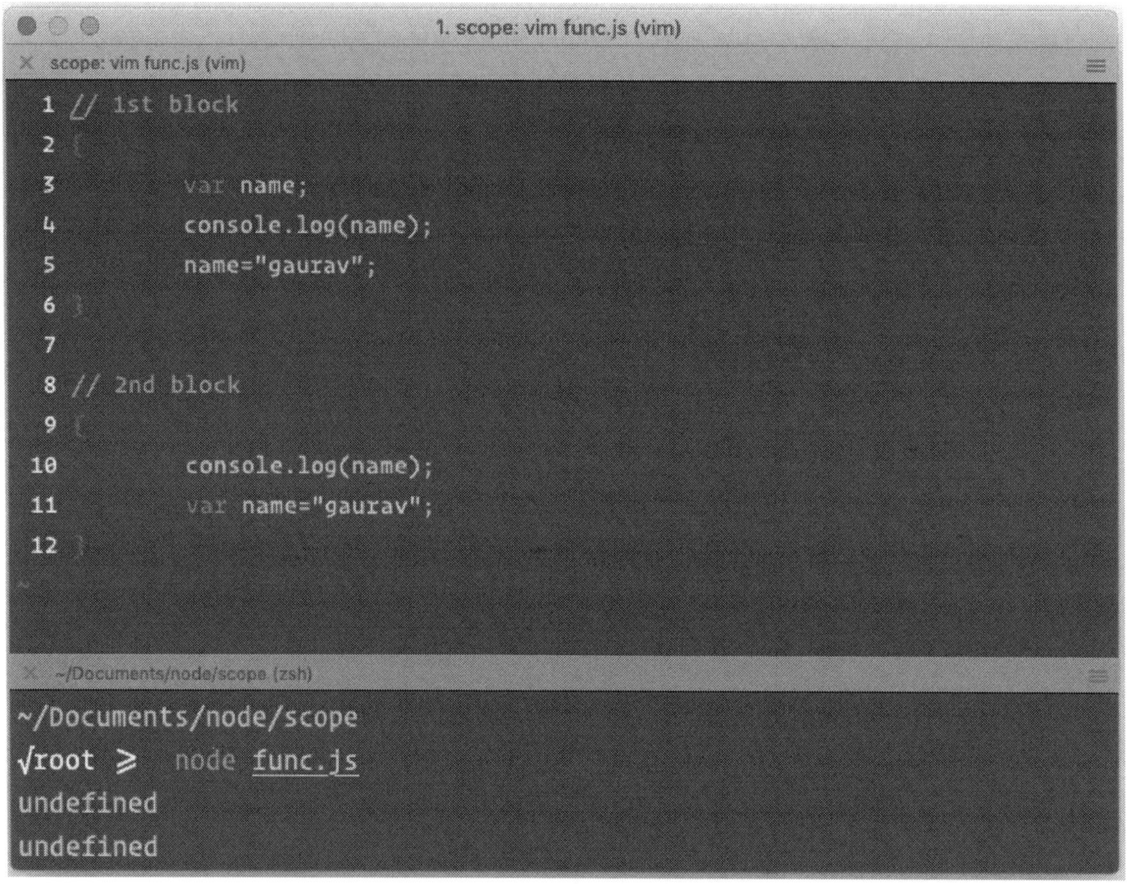
1. scope: vim func.js (vim)
scope: vim func.js (vim)
// 1st block
{
var name;
console.log(name);
name="gaurav";
}
// 2nd block
{
console.log(name);
var name="gaurav";
}
~/Documents/node/scope (zsh)
~/Documents/node/scope
√root ≥ node func.js
undefined
undefined

Figure 13.12: var keyword usage

We see that using the **`var`** keyword gives the same undefined output for both blocks.

Closures

A closure is a feature in JavaScript where a function defined inside another function has access to the parent function's variables. A closure has three scope chains:

- Own scope: Variables defined between its curly brackets
- Parent function: Properties defined in the parent function
- Global variables: Properties defined in the global scope

Let's have a look at an example:

```
function outer(arg) {
let count = 1;
function inner() {
console.log(arg, '=', count++);
    }
return inner;
}

varfunA = outer('A');   // outer() invoked the first time
varfunB = outer('B');   // outer() invoked the second time

funA(); // function funA called for first time
funA(); // function funA called for second time
funA(); // function funA called for third time
funB(); // function funB called for first time
```

We have one main function, which is **outer**. Then, we have declared a **count** variable with a value of **1**. We have one more function, **inner**, which is using and incrementing the value of **count**. Then, we return the **inner** function. The output of the preceding code is as follows:

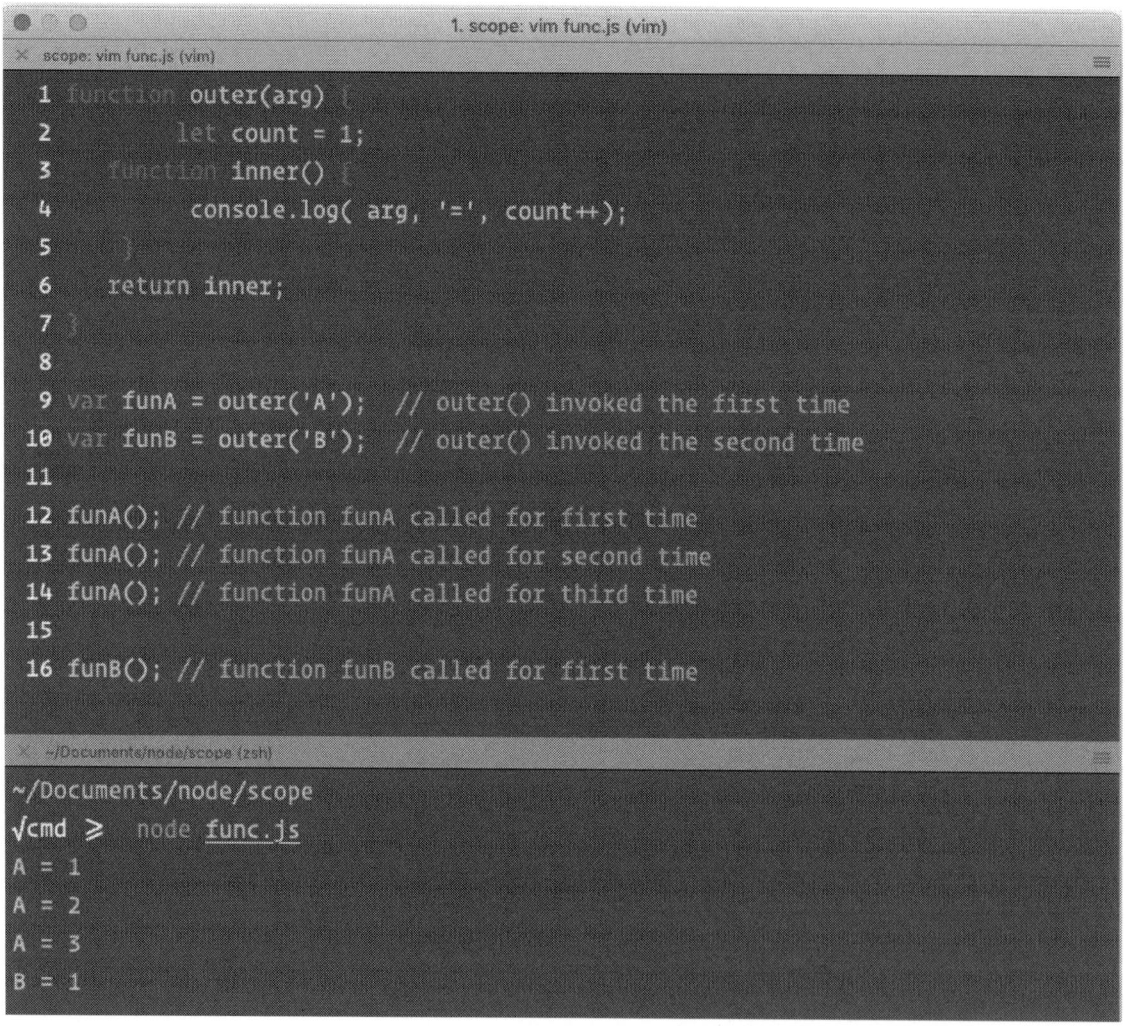

```
 1 function outer(arg) {
 2         let count = 1;
 3     function inner() {
 4             console.log( arg, '=', count++);
 5     }
 6     return inner;
 7 }
 8
 9 var funA = outer('A');  // outer() invoked the first time
10 var funB = outer('B');  // outer() invoked the second time
11
12 funA(); // function funA called for first time
13 funA(); // function funA called for second time
14 funA(); // function funA called for third time
15
16 funB(); // function funB called for first time
```

```
~/Documents/node/scope (zsh)
~/Documents/node/scope
√cmd ≥  node func.js
A = 1
A = 2
A = 3
B = 1
```

Figure 13.13: Example of closures

When we first call the **outer('A')** **function**, we are creating a scope for the **count** variable and the **inner** function. Then, we return the **inner** function and save its address in **funA()**. We did the same with **funB()**.

When we called **funA()** first, it had access to the **count** variable because it was in its parent function. So, it printed the value of **count** and updated it by adding **1**. When we called it again, it again accessed the parent scope and got the updated value of **count**. JavaScript is able to achieve this because of closures.

In this section, we have learned about a lot of the basic features of JavaScript. We started with prototypes and used them to implement inheritance. Then, we learned about anonymous and named functions and how to use them. We also learned about different types of data scopes in JavaScript. Finally, we learned about hoisting and closures, which are among the most complicated and important features provided by JavaScript.

JavaScript Memory Management

In other technical languages, such as C and C++, memory allocation and deallocation is an additional task. We have to use the **malloc()** and **free()** functions in C to allocate and deallocate memory for our variables. Thankfully, we do not have to take care of memory allocation in JavaScript anymore. JavaScript has a garbage collector built into it. JavaScript automatically allocates and frees up memory when objects are created and destroyed.

Memory Life Cycle

The memory life cycle of most programming languages is the same. It doesn't matter which language you are using, whether JavaScript, Python, or Java, the allocation and deallocation of memory is almost the same. They all follow three steps:

1. Allocate the memory.

2. Use the allocated memory.

3. Free the allocated memory.

The first and last parts are explicit in low-level languages, which means developers have to write code for the allocation and deallocation of memory, but it is mostly implicit in high-level languages such as JavaScript. During the compilation of your code, the compiler examines all primitive data types used in the code and calculates how much memory your program will take. It then allocates the required memory to the program in the call stack space. This process of the allocation of memory is called static memory allocation. During runtime, the memory allocation works in a LIFO (last-in, first-out) manner, which means as functions are called and terminated, their memory is added on top of the existing memory and is removed in a LIFO order.

Static versus Dynamic Allocation

There are two types of memory allocation, static and dynamic. Static allocation is performed at compile time only. When we compile our code, the compiler figures out all the static variables and assigns them memory at that time. Here's an example:

```
let num = 786;      // allocates memory for a number
let str = 'Hello World';   // allocates memory for a string
```

Dynamic allocation, as the name suggests, is done at runtime only because sometimes we do not know the exact size of the data, for example, when assigning the response of an API to a variable. In this case, we do not know exactly what the API will send us, so the memory will be allocated during runtime:

```
let res = response.json();   // allocates memory for json
```

In this example, we can't predict the size of the JSON object in advance, so this variable will be allocated dynamically. Some of the main differences between static and dynamic memory allocation are detailed in the next section.

The following are the features of static memory allocation:

- Allocates during compile time
- Uses stack storage
- Good to use when the required amount of memory is known
- Uses LIFO (Last In, First Out)
- Faster execution than a dynamic allocation
- More efficient
- Higher performance

The following are the features of dynamic memory allocation:

- Allocates during runtime
- Uses heap storage
- Good to use when the required amount of memory is unknown
- No order of assignment

- Slower execution than a static allocation

- Less efficient than a static allocation

- Slower performance because of memory allocation at runtime

Releasing Memory

The most difficult task is to discern situations when the allocated memory is no longer required. JavaScript's garbage collector comes in handy when it comes to finding and clearing out unused memory.

Reference-Counting Garbage Collection

One way of finding usable variables is by finding their references. If any variable has more than one reference, it means that it is possible to use this variable. But if we remove all the references to any variable, it becomes useless and it will be garbage collected by JavaScript in the next cycle.

Let's say we have a nested object, **obj**. It has a property called **a**, and another property, **b**. Now, **obj** is referencing **a** and **a** is referencing **b**. The only way to access **b** is through **a**:

```
let obj = {
a : {
 b : 2
  }
}
```

If we change the reference of **a** to **b**, then **b** will be garbage collected:

```
obj.a = null;
```

Now, as there is no reference to **b**, the garbage collector will delete it and free the memory.

In this section, we learned about how JavaScript automatically manages memory and does memory management for us. We learned about static and heap storage devices and had an overview of how the garbage collector in JavaScript works. We went through reference garbage collection as one of the many ways a garbage collector uses to find and clear unused memory in JavaScript programs.

Activity 13.01: Creating a Calculator App

In this chapter, we have learned about different types of paradigms that we can use when programming with JavaScript. Now it's time to sharpen our knowledge of these paradigms and make sure we know the difference between them when implementing paradigms in the real world.

Let's build a simple calculator application using both a procedural and object-oriented approach, which will give us a clear example of implementing the solution to a problem with different paradigms.

The high-level steps for the activity are as follows:

1. Create an empty file and call it **procedural.js**.

2. Initialize an array that will maintain the history of function calls.

3. Create simple **addition**, **subtraction**, **multiplication**, **division**, and **power** functions.

4. Create a **history** function that will maintain the history of function calls.

5. Call all the functions one by one with some random numbers as parameters.

6. Now print the history to check the output.

7. Now, build the app using OOP. Create a class and call it **calculator**.

8. Initialize a **historyList** array, which will maintain the history of all function calls.

9. Create simple **add**, **subtract**, **multiply**, **divide**, and **pow** methods.

10. Add one more method, which will show the history of the operations.

11. Create an instance of this class and call its method with simple numbers to perform mathematical operations.

12. Call the **history** method of the **calculator** class to check the history.

Using both a procedural and an object-oriented approach, the output of this code will be as follows:

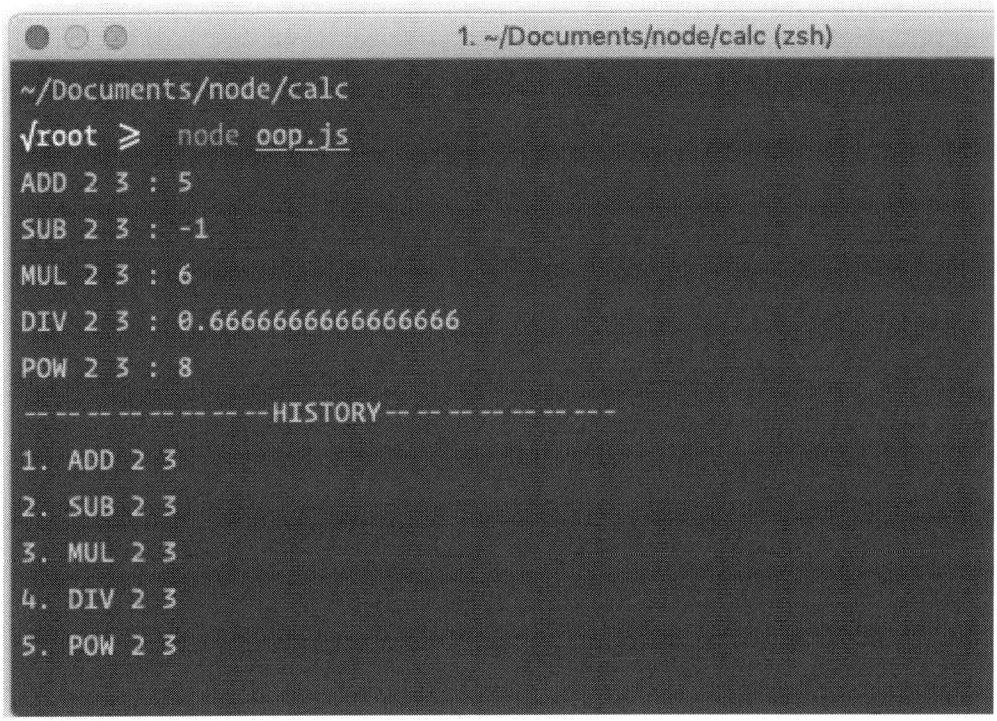

Figure 13.14: The same output using the procedural and the object-oriented approach

> **Note**
>
> The solution to this activity can be found on page 754.

You will see that, the outputs of both scripts are exactly the same, but the way we implemented them is completely different. This implementation tells us that there is more than one way to solve a problem. The best way depends on a lot of factors, such as team size, project plans, expectations of the project, and others. So, finally, we have achieved the same solution to the same problem.

Summary

So far in this book, we have covered client-side and server-side JavaScript execution. You learned about the importance of scope in JavaScript, along with the basics necessary for a solid foundation in JavaScript.

In this chapter, we learned about different programming paradigms. We discussed two of the popular approaches used by developers, namely procedural and object-oriented. Then, we explored the uses of prototypes, data scopes, hoisting, and closures.

Now, let's dig deep into the final and most important programming paradigm, which is used by a lot of developers: functional programming. In the next chapter, we will learn a lot about functional programming, including how and when to use it.

14

Understanding Functional Programming

Overview

By the end of this chapter, you will be able to use functional programming concepts such as pure functions, immutability, composition, and currying; use higher-order functions such as filter, map, and reduce; apply techniques such as cloning objects to reduce side effects in your code; and demonstrate strategies for reducing imperative logic and `for` loops in your code.

Introduction

In the previous chapter, we talked about how JavaScript is a multi-paradigm programming language. It's possible to write code with procedural, object-oriented, and functional design patterns. In this chapter, we'll look closely at the functional programming design pattern.

Functional programming is a programming paradigm that has become popular in the last few years, though most JavaScript developers were unfamiliar with it before then.

JavaScript is not a purely functional language like some others, such as Haskell, Scheme, and Clojure. However, JavaScript has support for functional structures and techniques if you choose to use them. It is worthwhile becoming familiar with its concepts and gaining a working knowledge of how to use them.

Functional programming has a set of features. Among others, here are some of the important ones:

- Pure functions
- Immutability and avoiding shared state, mutable data, and side effects
- Declarative rather than imperative
- Higher-order functions
- Function composition and piping
- Currying functions
- Reduces the use of traditional flow control structures such as `for`, `while`, and even `if`

These concepts will be covered over the course of this chapter. If implemented correctly, functional programming can result in code that is more predictable, less error-prone, and easier to test compared to other programming methods.

Pure Functions

Pure functions are one of the pillars of functional programming. A function is pure if it always returns the same result when it's given the same parameters. It also cannot depend on or modify variables or state outside of the function's scope.

A simple example of an impure function is as follows:

```
var positionX = 10;

function moveRight(numSlots) {
    positionX += numSlots;
```

```
}

moveRight(5);
```

You can plainly see how the function is manipulating a value outside of its scope in the **positionX** global variable. A pure function should only use the arguments that have been passed in for its logic, and should not directly modify them. Another issue is that the function doesn't actually return a value.

Consider the following code. Can you see why it would not be considered a pure function?

```
var positionX = 10;

function moveRight(numSlots) {
    return positionX + numSlots;
}

positionX = moveRight(5);
```

Though the function only reads the global variable value and does not manipulate the variable directly, it is still not pure. To see why think about what happens if you call the function multiple times with the value **5** for the **numSlots** parameter:

- The first time, the result is **15** (since **positionX** is **10** and **10 + 5 = 15**)

- The second time, the result would be **20**

- The third time, the result would be **25**

In other words, there is a different result for each invocation. For the function to be pure, the result would have had to resolve to the exact same value for the given parameter value, that is, **5**. Also, consider how difficult it would be to write tests for this function since the result is not predictable.

The correct way of making this function pure is as follows:

```
var positionX = 10;

function moveRight(x, numSlots) {
    return x + numSlots;
}

positionX = moveRight(positionX, 5);
```

In this version, all the data that the function uses in its logic is passed in as arguments, and it does not refer to any data outside of the function's scope. It will also always have the same result for a set of given parameters:

- If **x=10** and **numSlots=5**, the result will always be **15**.

- If **x=15** and **numSlots=5**, the result will always be **20**.

- If **x=20** and **numSlots=5**, the result will always be **25**.

The predictability of the result makes the code quality higher, makes it easier to reason about the function, and makes it easier to write tests. It also makes the code maintainable and less risky if the function ever needs to be refactored.

Side Effects

An important concept in functional programming that is closely related to pure functions is reducing side effects. A side effect is when a function performs some action, either directly or indirectly, that is not strictly for the purpose of the function or its return value.

Examples of side effects are actions such as showing an alert box, writing to a file, triggering a service call on the network, or making changes to the DOM. (Actually, when we manipulated the global variable in the impure function example in the previous section, we were also creating a type of side effect known as the shared state.)

> **Note**
>
> It is not possible or desirable to create programs that have no side effects whatsoever. After all, what good is the program if you can't see the output in some way? However, functional programmers aim to create pure functions most of the time and isolate the functions and parts of the code that require output or side effects. Keeping such code separate helps you understand your software better for debugging, to create better tests, and to ease future maintenance and extensions.

Immutability

Another concept in functional programming is to prefer immutable values and objects over mutable ones as much as possible. In short, immutable objects are those whose values cannot change once they are created, even if those objects are used. Going forward, we will perform a few exercises to demonstrate how certain objects such as strings and numbers are immutable, whereas arrays are not. We will begin with the immutability of strings in the following exercise.

Exercise 14.01: Immutable Values and Objects – Strings

In this exercise, we will demonstrate how strings are immutable. Let's get started:

1. In the Google Chrome browser, go to **Developer Tools** (go to the menu with the three dots at the upper-right of the screen | **More Tools** | **Developer Tools**, or just hit the F12 key).

2. JavaScript has several built-in immutable objects, such as strings. Create two constants, **string1** and **string2**, and assign the variable so that **string2** is a substring of **string1**:

```
const string1 = "Hello, World!";
const string2 = string1.substring(7, 12);
```

3. Display both strings. Type the following into the console:

```
console.log(`string1: ${string1}`);
console.log(`string2: ${string2}`);
```

4. This code results in the following output:

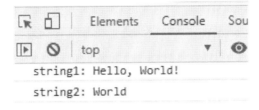

Figure 14.1: Output of strings

From this, you can see that the execution of **substring()** on **string1** did not change the value of **string1** in any way, demonstrating that the string is immutable. It actually results in a new string consisting of the characters of the partial string between the given indices. This result is then set as the value of the **string2** variable.

Exercise 14.02: Immutable Values and Objects – Numbers

Primitives such as numbers are also immutable. In this exercise, we will perform an operation on a number to demonstrate immutability in numbers.

1. Create two constants, **number1** and **number2**, and assign them numeric values such that **number2** is half of the value of **number1**:

```
const number1 = 500;
const number2 = number1 / 2;
```

2. Display both number objects. Type the following into the console:

```
console.log(`number1: ${number1}`);
console.log(`number2: ${number2}`);
```

3. This code results in the following output:

number1: 500

number2: 250

Figure 14.2: Output of numbers

We can see that performing a calculation with **number1** and setting the result to a new variable does not affect the original variable.

Exercise 14.03: Mutability – Arrays

So far, we have looked at immutable objects. From this point on, we will look at examples of objects that do not have this immutability. In this exercise, we'll create an array and assign its values to another array, and then we'll modify its value to demonstrate how arrays are mutable.

1. Create and define **array1** so that it has three value elements, namely, **'one'**, **'two'**, and **'three'**:

```
const array1 = ['one', 'two', 'three'];
```

2. Create another array, **array2**, with the value equal to **array1**:

```
const array2 = array1;
```

3. Now, append another element, **'four'**, to **array2**:

```
array2.push('four');
```

4. Display both outputs in the console, like so:

```
console.log(`array1: ${array1}`);
console.log(`array2: ${array2}`);
```

This code results in the following output:

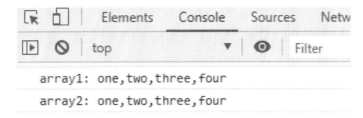

```
array1: one,two,three,four
array2: one,two,three,four
```

Figure 14.3: Output of arrays

Here, we assigned the **array2** variable to the same array as **array1**, and then appended another element to **array2** (the value **'four'**). It may surprise you that **array1** is affected and gets the element added to it as well, unlike the other examples so far. This is because when the assignment is made to **array2,** it does not create a new array. Rather, it assigns only a reference that points to the original array, that is, **array1**. Manipulating either array would affect both of the variables as they are in fact the same array.

Exercise 14.04: Mutability – Objects

In this exercise, we will assign values to properties in an object to demonstrate mutability in objects.

1. Create an object, **actor1**, with the properties **name** and **show**. Assign the value **Sheldon** and **BB Theory** to these properties:

```
const actor1 = {
    name: 'Sheldon',
    show: 'BB Theory'
};
```

2. Now, create another variable, **actor2**, and assign it to the same object as **actor1**. Then, also add a new property to **actor2** called **name**

```
const actor2 = actor1;
actor2.name = 'Leonard';
```

3. Type the following into the console:

```
console.log("actor1:", actor1);
console.log("actor2:", actor2);
```

4. This code results in the following output:

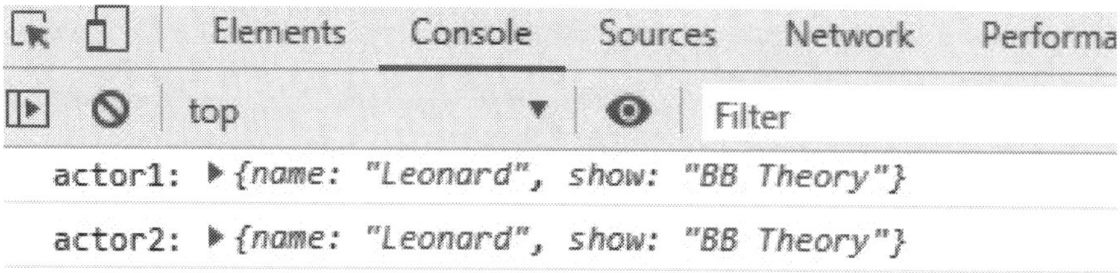

Figure 14.4: Output for objects

As you can see, both the objects in the **actor1** and **actor2** variables end up being exactly the same. The **name** property is not only in **actor2**, as you might expect. This is once again because **actor2** is only a reference to **actor1**, and is not its own object.

Another point is worth mentioning as well. In all these examples, the variables were defined as constants using the **const** keyword. However, as we have seen in the last two examples, we were able to make changes to the object and the compiler did not complain. This shows that the **const** keyword is *not* equivalent to saying the value is immutable!

All **const** means is that the compiler prevents you from being able to reassign the variable to a new object. It does not restrict you from changing the properties of the assigned object or adding array elements, though.

The next section will show you some strategies regarding how to handle mutable objects effectively.

Cloning Objects and Arrays

In the previous exercise, you saw how arrays and objects are mutable. What if you need to make modifications, though? How can you do this in a safe manner that avoids side effects?

First, there's a simple technique for arrays. If you are just adding an element to the array, you can use **Array.prototype.concat** rather than **Array.prototype. push**. The difference is that **concat** returns a new array copy with the element added, whereas **push** modifies the original array.

We can see this in the following code. Here, **array1** and **array2** are now, in fact, distinct objects:

```
const array1 = ['one', 'two', 'three'];
const array2 = array1.concat('four');
```

```
console.log(`array1: ${array1}`);    // output: array1: one,two,three
console.log(`array2: ${array2}`);    // output: array2: one,two,three,four
```

The output of the preceding code would be as follows:

```
array1: one,two,three
and
array2: one,two,three,four
```

For other array modifications or to manipulate objects, you would usually need to clone the array or object and operate on the clone. How do you make clones, you ask? Here's a neat trick: in newer JavaScript versions (since ECMAScript 2018), the spread syntax works for both arrays and objects. Using the spread syntax, you can do the following:

```
// Arrays
const array1 = ['one', 'two', 'three'];
const array2 = [...array1];
array2[0] = 'four';

console.log(`array1: ${array1}`);    // output: array1: one,two,three
console.log(`array2: ${array2}`);    // output: array2: four,two,three

// Objects
const actor1 = {
    name: 'Sheldon',
    show: 'BB Theory'
};

const actor2 = {...actor1};
actor2.name = 'Leonard';
//the output for variable actor1 will be displayed.
console.log("actor1:", actor1);
```

The output of **const actor1** will be as follows:

```
    // output: actor1: { name: "Sheldon", show: "BB Theory" }
//the output for variable actor2 will be displayed.
console.log("actor2:", actor2);
```

The output of **const actor2** will be as follows:

```
    // output: actor2: { name: "Leonard", show: "BB Theory" }
```

Notice that there are three consecutive dots in [...**array1**] and {...**actor1**}. These dots are known as spread operators. Using the spread syntax in this fashion effectively clones the array, or key-value pairs in the case of an object.

There is one caveat, though. This method only makes a shallow copy, which means only the top-level elements or properties are copied. Beyond the top level, only references are created. What this means is that, for example, multi-dimensional arrays or nested objects are not copied.

If a deep copy is required, one popular method is to convert the object into a JSON string and parse it right back, similar to the following code. This works for both objects and arrays:

```
let object2 = JSON.parse(JSON.stringify(object1));
```

The deep copy method also has the added benefit of working on older versions of JavaScript.

Sample Data for Examples and Exercises

Before we go further, we need to introduce a scenario with sample data. In the upcoming sections, the following data will be used in the examples and exercises:

```
const runners = [
    {name: "Courtney", gender: "F", age: 21, timeSeconds: 1505},
    {name: "Lelisa",   gender: "M", age: 24, timeSeconds: 1370},
    {name: "Anthony",  gender: "M", age: 32, timeSeconds: 1538},
    {name: "Halina",   gender: "F", age: 33, timeSeconds: 1576},
    {name: "Nilani ",  gender: "F", age: 27, timeSeconds: 1601},
    {name: "Laferne",  gender: "F", age: 35, timeSeconds: 1572},
    {name: "Jerome",   gender: "M", age: 22, timeSeconds: 1384},
    {name: "Yipeng",   gender: "M", age: 29, timeSeconds: 1347},
    {name: "Jyothi",   gender: "F", age: 39, timeSeconds: 1462},
    {name: "Chetan",   gender: "M", age: 36, timeSeconds: 1597},
    {name: "Giuseppe", gender: "M", age: 38, timeSeconds: 1570},
    {name: "Oksana",   gender: "F", age: 23, timeSeconds: 1617}
];
```

This is an array of objects that represents the results of runners in a 5 km race. The name, sex, age, and time are indicated for each runner in object fields. Time is recorded in seconds, allowing for easy minutes/seconds and pace calculations.

We will also define three helper functions to display the data. They will use some concepts that you may not be familiar with yet, particularly, arrow function notation and the **Array.prototype.map** method. But don't worry – these concepts will be covered in upcoming sections and they will become clear soon.

The purpose of our first helper function is to format seconds into **MM:SS**:

```
const minsSecs = timeSeconds =>
    Math.floor(timeSeconds / 60) + ":" +
    Math.round(timeSeconds % 60).toString().padStart(2, '0');
```

Let's understand the code in detail:

- The **minsSecs** variable defines an arrow function with a **timeSeconds** input parameter.

- For the minutes portion, the **Math.floor()** method removes the decimal part of the minutes when dividing seconds by 60, resulting in just a whole number integer.

- For the seconds portion, the **Math.round()** method returns the number rounded to the nearest integer. (Note that we only wish to round fractional seconds. For the minute portion, it would not be correct to round.)

- The **String.prototype.padStart** method pads the seconds value with a leading **0** if the value is less than 10. The seconds themselves are calculated using the remainder operator, **%**, which returns any remainder value in the division.

Our second helper function creates a string that prints the fields of the **runner** object in custom formats:

```
const printRunner = runner =>
    [`Name: ${runner.name}`,
     `gender: ${runner.gender}`,
     `age: ${runner.age}`,
     `time: ${minsSecs(runner.timeSeconds)}`
    ].join('\t');
```

Let's understand the code in detail:

- Once again, arrow function syntax is used. The function is named **printRunner** and has a **runner** input parameter.

- An array of formatted strings is created, one for each field in the **runner** object.

- Lastly, all the string elements are joined together with a tab character separator by calling **Array.prototype.join('\t')**, resulting in nice columns when printed.

The final helper function prints all the runners:

```
const printRunners = (runners, listType) =>
    `List of ${listType} (total ${runners.length}):\n` +
        runners.map(printRunner).join('\n');
```

Let's go through the different parts of the above code in detail:

- The function is called **printRunners** and takes two parameters: an array of **runners**, and **listType**, which is a description of what type of list is being printed. It returns a string.

- **Array.prototype.map** is used to form the runner details for printing.

- In short, the **Array.prototype.map** method iterates over every array element executes a callback function on them and results in a new array with the transformed values of each element. We'll explain how this works in detail later.

- But for now, the **Array.prototype.map** call here calls the **printRunner** function specified previously on each array element to get the formatted strings. Since the **printRunner** function only takes one parameter, in this case, it is not necessary to explicitly specify the parameter, since it is implied.

- The strings are then joined together with a newline character by calling **Array. prototype.join('\n')**.

To print all the runners to the console, invoke it like this:

```
console.log(printRunners(runners, "all runners"));
```

The output will look like this:

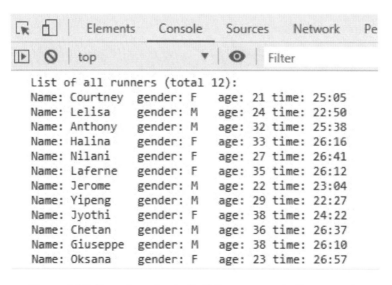

Figure 14.5: Sample output of all the runners in the console

Higher-Order Functions

Functions in JavaScript are first-class citizens. This means they can be passed as parameter values to other functions, or even assigned to a variable. This is one of the main characteristics that make JavaScript well-suited to the functional style of programming.

Higher-order functions are functions that operate on other functions. They can do this in one of three ways:

- If the function takes another function as an argument
- If the function returns another function as its result
- In both of these ways

In the previous chapters, we've already seen several higher-order functions, perhaps without you even realizing it. Remember the callback functions that get executed in response to DOM events, or the callbacks in *Chapter 10, Accessing External Resources*, which were called once the AJAX response was ready? These are all examples of higher-order functions since these functions are parameters that are passed into other functions.

The following sections will introduce three higher-order functions that are commonly used in functional programming: **Array.prototype.filter**, **Array.prototype.map**, and **Array.prototype.reduce**.

The Array.prototype.filter Method

The first function we will look at is the **Array.prototype.filter** method, which is simple. Given an existing array, **filter()** creates a new array with elements that fall under the specified criteria.

The syntax is as follows:

```
var newArray = array.filter(function(item) {
  return condition;
});
```

The callback function is called for each element of the array in turn. If the condition passes and the function returns **true**, the element is added to the new array. If the function returns **false**, the element is skipped and will not be added.

Note that the return value is a new array. The original array is not impacted at all by this operation. In other words, it is not the case that items are filtered out and removed from the original array if they don't pass the condition. Rather, a new array is created with the elements that pass the test.

The reason for creating a new array rather than modifying the existing one is due to the fundamental principles of functional programming you learned about earlier: immutability and avoiding side effects.

We will look at some examples of how **Array.prototype.filter** is used in the following section.

A Refresher

Before we look at these examples, though, it is prudent for us to take a step back and review basic JavaScript function syntax and arrow function notation. This will ensure that you have a good grounding for what's to come. We will do this review by showing you different ways that the filtering function can be specified for **Array.prototype. filter**.

Say we wanted to filter the array of runners (presented earlier in this chapter) for only female runners. The most straightforward filtering function looks like this:

```
function femaleFilter(runner) {
    if (runner.gender === "F") {
        return true;
    }
    return false;
}
```

This filtering function would be called from another function that actually invokes **filter()** with the following code:

```
const getFemaleRunners = runners => runners.filter(femaleFilter);
```

To make the function self-contained, it takes the **runners** array as a parameter. It is not good practice to require **runners** to be a global variable.

Note that we only pass in the name of the filtering function, **femaleFilter**, as the argument, and not with parentheses, like **femaleFilter()**. We do not want the function to be executed right away, which is what would happen if there were parentheses. Rather, when a function is passed by name without parentheses, you are passing the function object itself. The **filter** method is a higher-order function that takes a callback function as its input, which requires the actual function object.

The results of this filtering can be displayed with the following code:

```
console.log(
    printRunners(getFemaleRunners(runners), "female runners"));
```

```
// → List of female runners (total 6):
// → Name: Courtney  gender: F    age: 21   time: 25:05
// → Name: Halina    gender: F    age: 33   time: 26:16
// → Name: Nilani    gender: F    age: 27   time: 26:41
// → Name: Laferne   gender: F    age: 35   time: 26:12
// → Name: Jyothi    gender: F    age: 38   time: 24:22
// → Name: Oksana    gender: F    age: 23   time: 26:57
```

> **Note**
>
> This code should be used to display the results of the following examples as well.
> The same results are expected for each example.

We've done pretty well so far, but we could do better. As an alternative, the filtering function could be specified directly inline:

```
const getFemaleRunners = runners => runners.filter(
    function(runner) {
        if (runner.gender === "F") {
            return true;
        }
        return false;
    }
);
```

We can simplify this a bit more if we change the filtering test to a Boolean expression rather than explicitly returning **true** or **false** in an **if** statement:

```
const getFemaleRunners = runners => runners.filter(
    function(runner) {
        return runner.gender === "F";
    }
);
```

In newer versions of JavaScript, since ES6, this function can also be expressed more concisely using an arrow function expression:

```
const getFemaleRunners = runners => runners.filter(runner => {
    return runner.gender === "F";
});
```

Finally, note that this function has only one argument and a single **return** statement in its body. This allows us to make the code even more concise with the following one-liner, which omits the open/close brackets and the **return** keyword:

```
const getFemaleRunners = runners =>
    runners.filter(runner => runner.gender === "F");
```

If desired, the filtering function can also be split into its own function and stored in a variable, since functions are first-class objects in JavaScript:

```
const femaleFilter = runner => runner.gender === "F";
const getFemaleRunners = runners => runners.filter(femaleFilter);
```

Eliminating for Loops

The **Array.prototype.filter** function is a great demonstration of powerful functional programming techniques that are used to eliminate looping code, particularly the **for** loop. To get a feel of the potential pitfalls of the traditional **for** loop, consider the equivalent imperative code to filter female runners:

```
var femaleRunners = [];
for (var i = 0; i < runners.length; i++) {
    if (runners[i].gender == "F") {
        femaleRunners.push(runners[i]);
    }
}
```

Compare this to the one-liner we saw in the previous section, which does the same thing:

```
const femaleRunners = runners.filter(runner => runner.gender === "F");
```

The imperative looping code requires the use of the looping variable, **i**. This introduces mutation of the state into our code and is a potential source of bugs. Even though, in this case, it is a local state, it is best to avoid the state in all situations when possible. At some point in the future, there is a risk that a variable will change for an unknown reason, producing an issue that's difficult to debug.

With the functional equivalent, it is easier to see at a glance what the code does, is easier to test, and has more opportunity for potential reuse. It has no indentation, no loops, and the code is more concise and expressive.

This also demonstrates how functional code is most often declarative rather than imperative. It specifies "what to do" (declarative) rather than the steps and flow of "how to do it" (imperative). In this example, the functional code simply says, "filter the array elements passed in the **runners** parameter where gender is female". Compare this to imperative code that requires multiple variables, statements, loops, and so on, which describes "how" rather than "what."

In the upcoming sections, we will look at other array methods that eliminate loops as well, such as **Array.prototype.map** and **Array.prototype.reduce**.

The Array.prototype.map Method

The array **map()** method is used when you want to transform array elements. It applies a function to every element of the calling array and builds a new array consisting of the returned values. The new array will have the same length as the input array, but each element's contents will be transformed (mapped) into something else.

Say you wanted to calculate the average pace per mile of each runner of the 5 km race. Our dataset provides a **timeSeconds** field, which is the total amount of time in seconds the runner needs to complete the full distance. There are also 3.1 miles in 5 kilometers. Therefore, to get the pace per mile, you would divide the number of seconds by 3.1.

We can calculate the pace for all runners with the following code:

```
const getPaces = runners => runners.map(runner => runner.timeSeconds /
3.1);
const paces = getPaces(runners);
```

This code results in a new array with elements that have the **pace** value of the corresponding runner at the same index of the input array. In other words, the value of **paces[0]** corresponds to the runner in **runner[0]**, the value of **paces[1]** corresponds to the runner in **runner[1]**, and so on.

The pace results can be printed to the console as follows:

```
paces.forEach(pace => console.log(minsSecs(pace)));

// output:
// → 8:05
// → 7:22
// → 8:16
// → 8:27
// ...
```

Exercise 14.05: Another Way of Using Array.prototype.map

The results from the previous section in regards to mapping to an array of single-valued elements are useful as-is for some contexts, such as if you intend to subsequently calculate the sum or average of the values. This is okay when you just require the raw numbers and context isn't important. But what if you need more values or context for each element, such as the name of the runner that achieved the pace? This exercise shows another way we can use **Array.prototype.map** to achieve different results using the original dataset; for example, to get the calculated pace of each runner.

1. In the Google Chrome browser, go to **Developer Tools** (go to the menu with the three dots at the upper-right of the screen | **More Tools** | **Developer Tools**, or just hit the F12 key):

Figure 14.6: Developer Tools in the Google Chrome browser

2. In the console, paste in the sample runner data (beginning with **const runners = [...]**) from the *Sample Data for Examples* section of this chapter:

```
const runners = [
    {name: "Courtney", gender: "F", age: 21, timeSeconds: 1505},
    {name: "Lelisa",   gender: "M", age: 24, timeSeconds: 1370},
    {name: "Anthony",  gender: "M", age: 32, timeSeconds: 1538},
    {name: "Halina",   gender: "F", age: 33, timeSeconds: 1576},
    {name: "Nilani ",  gender: "F", age: 27, timeSeconds: 1601},
```

```
    {name: "Laferne",    gender: "F", age: 35, timeSeconds: 1572},
    {name: "Jerome",     gender: "M", age: 22, timeSeconds: 1384},
    {name: "Yipeng",     gender: "M", age: 29, timeSeconds: 1347},
    {name: "Jyothi",     gender: "F", age: 39, timeSeconds: 1462},
    {name: "Chetan",     gender: "M", age: 36, timeSeconds: 1597},
    {name: "Giuseppe",   gender: "M", age: 38, timeSeconds: 1570},
    {name: "Oksana",     gender: "F", age: 23, timeSeconds: 1617}
];
```

3. In the console, paste in the code for the **minsSecs()** helper function, also from the *Sample Data for Examples* section of this chapter:

```
const minsSecs = timeSeconds =>
        Math.floor(timeSeconds / 60) + ":" +
        Math.round(timeSeconds % 60).toString().padStart(2, '0');
```

4. Type the following code into the console:

```
const getPacesWithNames = runners => runners.map(runner =>
    ({name: runner.name, pace: runner.timeSeconds / 3.1}));


const pacesWithNames = getPacesWithNames(runners);
```

This code shows a simple way of adding context to the array elements: rather than returning just a single value from the mapping function, an object with multiple fields can be returned instead that includes as many fields as desired. In this case, the object has the **name** and **pace** fields for each array element.

5. We can see the output by using the following code:

```
// print each value
pacesWithNames.forEach(paceObj =>
    console.log(`name: ${paceObj.name}\tpace: ${minsSecs(paceObj.
pace)}`));
```

After running the preceding commands, your console log should look like the one shown in the following screenshot. Notice the list of names and paces at the bottom:

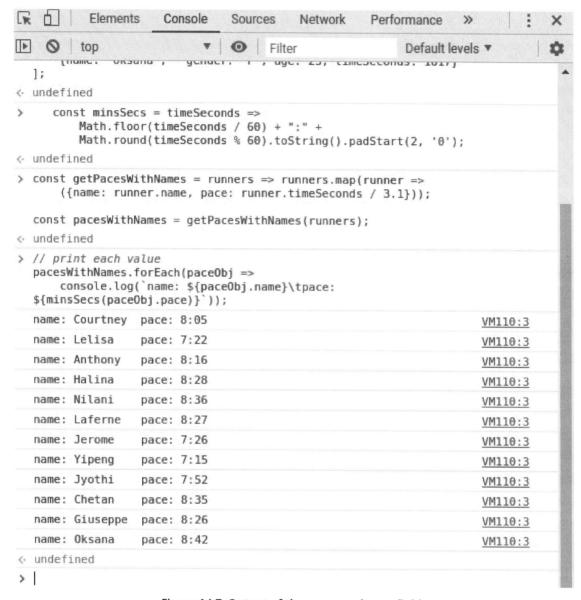

Figure 14.7: Output of the name and pace fields

You'll notice that we have all the same runners from the original data but without gender, age, or times in seconds. We've also added a new value called **pace**, which we created with the **getPacesWithNames** function.

What if you want your array to contain elements with all the original fields and append an additional **pace** field?

6. We could use the spread operator you learned about earlier. Type the following into the console:

```
const addPacesToRunners = runners => runners.map(runner =>
    ({...runner, pace: runner.timeSeconds / 3.1}));
```

7. The ...**runner** spread syntax effectively clones all the key-value pairs in the object, adds them to the new mapped value, and displays the output. Add and run the **addPacesToRunners** function to your console.

> **Note**
>
> Copies will be made of the fields. As before, we do not want to just modify the original object so that we can add the new field either, as this has the potential for side effects.

8. The following code runs the function and displays the results in the console:

```
const pacesWithAllFields = addPacesToRunners(runners);
pacesWithAllFields.forEach(paceObj => console.log(paceObj));
```

Once you run the **forEach()** function to iterate over the elements of the **pacesWithAllFields**, you should get a list of runners with all the original data, but in addition, there will be a new field for the average pace:

```
> const pacesWithAllFields = addPacesToRunners(runners);
  pacesWithAllFields.forEach(paceObj => console.log(paceObj));
  ▶ {name: "Courtney", gender: "F", age: 21, timeSeconds: 1505, pace: 485.4838709677419}    VM257:2
  ▶ {name: "Lelisa", gender: "M", age: 24, timeSeconds: 1370, pace: 441.93548387096774}     VM257:2
  ▶ {name: "Anthony", gender: "M", age: 32, timeSeconds: 1538, pace: 496.1290322580645}     VM257:2
  ▶ {name: "Halina", gender: "F", age: 33, timeSeconds: 1576, pace: 508.38709677419354}     VM257:2
  ▶ {name: "Milani ", gender: "F", age: 27, timeSeconds: 1601, pace: 516.4516129032257}     VM257:2
  ▶ {name: "Laferne", gender: "F", age: 35, timeSeconds: 1572, pace: 507.09677419354836}    VM257:2
  ▶ {name: "Jerome", gender: "M", age: 22, timeSeconds: 1384, pace: 446.4516129032258}      VM257:2
  ▶ {name: "Yipeng", gender: "M", age: 29, timeSeconds: 1347, pace: 434.51612903225865}     VM257:2
  ▶ {name: "Jyothi", gender: "F", age: 39, timeSeconds: 1462, pace: 471.61290322580646}     VM257:2
  ▶ {name: "Chetan", gender: "M", age: 36, timeSeconds: 1597, pace: 515.1612903225806}      VM257:2
  ▶ {name: "Giuseppe", gender: "M", age: 38, timeSeconds: 1570, pace: 506.4516129032258}    VM257:2
  ▶ {name: "Oksana", gender: "F", age: 23, timeSeconds: 1617, pace: 521.6129032258065}      VM257:2
  ← undefined
> |
```

Figure 14.8: Results of addPacesToRunners with the pace field appended

> **Note**
>
> Do not use the spread technique if you expect your code to run in older browsers. Use alternatives such as **Object.assign()** to clone your fields. Here's how **addPacesToRunners** could be coded for older environments:
>
> ```
> const addPacesToRunners = runners => runners.map(runner =>
>       Object.assign({}, runner, {pace: runner.timeSeconds /
> 3.1}));
> ```
>
> Alternatively, transpilers such as Babel support the spread syntax, even in older browsers.

In this exercise, we looked at using the **Array.prototype.map** method and how we can use functional programming design patterns to combine functions to create complex results. We used **addPacesToRunners** in combination with **minsSecs** and **pacesWithNames** to print the pace of each runner in addition to the data from the original set. Importantly, we added the additional data value of pace without modifying the original dataset. Using the techniques in this exercise thus allows you to retain context when mapping values.

In the next section, we will learn about another array method, **reduce**, which allows us to take a set of values from an array and compute them into a single value.

The Array.prototype.reduce method

Similar to **map()**, the array **reduce()** method operates on every element of an array. It is used when you need to compute a single value from them.

A simple example of this is if you need the sum of a collection of numbers:

```
const sum = [2, 4, 6, 8, 10].reduce((total, current) => total + current,
0);
console.log(sum);
```

The output of the preceding function will be as follows:

```
// output:
// → 10
```

Here, the **reduce()** method takes two parameters: a combining function and a start value (0, in this case). It causes the combining function to be called repeatedly with each array element in turn, as it does in a **for** loop. For each invocation, the present element is passed as the **current** value, along with the **total** value so far (sometimes referred to as the accumulator).

The first time the combining function is invoked, **total** is the start value (**0**) and **current** is the first number in the array (**2**). The addition, that is, **total + current**, results in the value of **2**.

The second time the combining function is invoked, **total** is the result of the previous invocation (**2**) and **current** is the second number in the array (**4**). The addition, that is, **total + current**, results in **6**.

This process is repeated for the remaining elements in the array until there are no elements remaining to process. Here is a simple table that shows the values at each invocation:

Invocation #	Total	Current	Result (total + current)
Call #1	0 (start value)	2	2
Call #2	2 (previous result)	4	6
Call #3	6 (previous result)	6	12
Call #4	12 (previous result)	8	20
Call #5	20 (previous result)	10	30

Figure 14.9: Invocation value and their result

Here is another visualization of this reduction process that may help you see it more clearly:

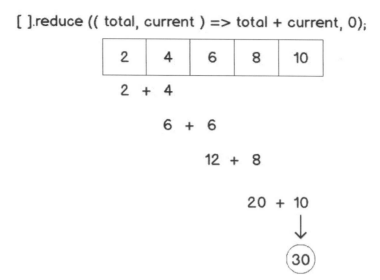

Figure 14.10: A depiction of the reduction process

Going back to using our **runners** dataset, here's how you can use **reduce()** to compute the average pace of all runners. But first, recall the code from the previous section that used **map()** to calculate the pace for each runner and returned the results in a new array:

```
const getPaces = runners => runners.map(runner => runner.timeSeconds /
3.1);
const paces = getPaces(runners);
```

We can use these paces to calculate the average with **reduce()**:

```
const getAvgPace = paces => paces.reduce(
    (total, currentPace) => total + currentPace, 0) / paces.length;
console.log(minsSecs(getAvgPace(paces)));
```

The output of the **reduce()** function will be as follows:

```
// output:
// → 8:08
```

First, in **reduce()**, we calculate the sum of all **pace** values using a similar technique as when we summed up the array of numbers. But there's one additional step. Rather than returning the sum, we divide it by the length of the array before returning the result.

Exercise 14.06: Grouping with Array.prototype.reduce

What if you wanted to calculate the average pace of all runners grouped by gender? We can do this with **reduce()**, but it is a bit more involved than the previous example. In this exercise, we'll implement one approach to grouping.

Unlike when we calculated the average of straight numbers, for group averages, we'll need to do this in two steps: first, gather the sum and count of each gender, and then calculate the averages in a second step.

The following outlines the approach for the summing and counting step:

- Use an empty object (**{}**) as our starting value.

- When cycling through the array elements, get the group **sum** and **count** stats calculated so far for the gender of the current element. (If there are no stats for gender yet, create an empty group with **sum** and **count** set to **0**.)

- Add the pace of the current element to the group sum.

- Increase the count of the group by **1**.

Here are the steps to do this:

1. In the Google Chrome browser, go to Developer Tools (go to the menu with the three dots at the upper-right of the screen | **More Tools** | **Developer Tools**, or just hit the F12 key).

2. In the console, paste in the sample runner data (beginning with **const runners =** **[...]**) from the *Sample Data for Examples* section of this chapter.

3. In the console, paste in the code for the **minsSecs()** helper function, which is also from the *Sample Data for Examples* section of this chapter.

4. We will make use of the **pacesWithAllFields** value from the example in the *Array.prototype.map()* section, which creates a new array with a calculated **pace** field added to each element. Type the following into the console:

```
const addPacesToRunners = runners => runners.map(runner =>
    ({...runner, pace: runner.timeSeconds / 3.1}));
const pacesWithAllFields = addPacesToRunners(runners);
```

5. The following is the code for this first summing and counting step, which we outlined previously:

```
const groupSumPaceByGender = runners => runners.reduce((groups,
runner) => {
    const gender = runner.gender;
    groups[gender] = groups[gender] || {pace: 0, count: 0};
    groups[gender].pace += runner.pace;
    groups[gender].count += 1;
    return groups;
}, {});
const sumPacesByGender = groupSumPaceByGender(pacesWithAllFields);
```

6. At this point, the object that results from **sumPacesByGender** will have two keys that represent the gender values, that is, "**M**" and "**F**". The value for each is also an object, in which there are **pace** and **count** fields that contain the calculated stats for gender corresponding to the key.

7. Displaying such objects in the JavaScript console is a bit clunky and unwieldy. A trick is in order: we'll convert the object into formatted JSON text and display that instead. Type the following code into the console:

```
console.log(JSON.stringify(sumPacesByGender,null,4));
```

This will output the JSON with a 4-space indentation:

```
// output:
// → {
// →        "F": {
// →            "pace": 3010.645161290322,
// →            "count": 6
// →        },
// →        "M": {
// →            "pace": 2840.6451612903224,
// →            "count": 6
// →        }
// → }
```

8. Now that we have the sums and counts for each group determined, we can proceed to the second step and calculate the average of each group. We can do this by using **Object.keys()** to get an array with the keys of the object (that have the values "**M**" and "**F**") and then call **Array.prototype.map()** with a function to calculate the average for each gender. Type the following into the console:

```
const calcAvgPaceByGender = sumPacesByGender =>
    Object.keys(sumPacesByGender).map(gender => {
        const group = sumPacesByGender[gender];
        return {gender: gender, avgPace: group.pace / group.count};
    }
);
const avgPaceByGender = calcAvgPaceByGender(sumPacesByGender);
```

9. Let's write the code to display the output:

```
console.log("Average pace by gender:");
avgPaceByGender.forEach(entry => console.log(
    `gender: ${entry.gender}  average pace: ${minsSecs(entry.
avgPace)}`));
```

10. The output should be displayed as follows:

```
> const avgPaceByGender = calcAvgPaceByGender(sumPacesByGender);
< undefined
> console.log("Average pace by gender:");
  avgPaceByGender.forEach(entry => console.log(
      `gender: ${entry.gender}  average pace: ${minsSecs(entry.avgPace)}`));
  Average pace by gender:
  gender: F  average pace: 8:22
  gender: M  average pace: 7:53
< undefined
> |
```

Figure 14.11: Grouping the result of gender pace with Array.prototype.reduce

This output allowed us to take a large number of data points and "reduce" them to a smaller amount of results in an efficient manner.

In this exercise, we looked at using the **Array.prototype.reduce** method for grouping. As in the previous exercise, we combined several functions to create a more complex result, without modifying the original dataset. First, we added the **pace** value for each entry in the set using **addPacesToRunners**, then we created a group sum for each gender with **groupSumPaceByGender**, and finally, we used **calcAvgPaceByGender** to get a value for the average pace for both males and females in the race.

In the next section, we'll talk about the concept of composition. We've used composition several times already in this chapter, that is, each time we combined smaller functions to create a larger process. However, we haven't looked at the concept specifically and spoken of its importance in the functional paradigm. We'll also look at the **pipe()** and **compose()** functions, which make combining functions in this way easier and more readable.

Composition with compose() and pipe()

In the previous exercise, we saw that starting from the runners array, we required three different functions to calculate the average pace for each gender:

- **addPacesToRunners**: This is used to calculate the pace per mile.

- **groupSumPaceByGender**: This is used to sum the pace of each gender.

- **calcAvgPaceByGender**: This is used to calculate the average pace for each gender.

Each function required the result of the one before it as input in order to do its job. Basically, it did the following, though it may not have been apparent up to this point:

```
const result1 = addPacesToRunners(runners);
const result2 = groupSumPaceByGender(result1);
const avg = calcAvgPaceByGender(result2);
```

This is equivalent to the following, that is, using nested functions and removing the intermediate variables:

```
const avg =
    calcAvgPaceByGender(groupSumPaceByGender(addPacesToRunners(runners)));
```

This is the idea of composition: that multiple simple functions are combined to build a more complex function. The result of each function is passed along to the next one.

We can create high-order functions called **compose** and **pipe** to achieve function composition in a more general manner, though. Putting aside the actual implementation for a moment, let's see how the functions would be used. With **compose**, the preceding nested functions would be written as follows:

```
const avgWithComposition =
    compose(calcAvgPaceByGender, groupSumPaceByGender, addPacesToRunners);
```

This function would be used as follows:

```
const avgResult = avgWithComposition(runners);
avgResult.forEach(entry => console.log(
    `gender: ${entry.gender}  average pace: ${minsSecs(entry.avgPace)}`));
```

The output of the function would be as follows:

```
// output:
// → gender: F average pace: 8:22
// → gender: M average pace: 7:53
```

Note that, perhaps counter-intuitively, the functions in **compose** are actually called in reverse order from how they are given in the parameter list, that is, right to left. So, the **addPacesToRunners** method is first invoked with the **runners** argument (even though it is the last function in the given list), then the results are passed to **groupSumPaceByGender**, and finally, those results are passed to **calcAvgPaceByGender**.

Many people find this function call order unnatural, though it is consistent with the order we called our nested functions above. The **pipe** function is similar to **compose**, but functions are composed in the opposite direction, left-to-right rather than the right-to-left. The **pipe** approach is more consistent with linear thinking: first, do A, then B, then C, and the functions to do A, B and C would be given in that order.

With **pipe**, the equivalent code would be:

```
const avgWithPipe =
    pipe(addPacesToRunners, groupSumPaceByGender, calcAvgPaceByGender);

const resultPipe = avgWithPipe(runners);
resultPipe.forEach(entry => console.log(
    `gender: ${entry.gender}  average pace: ${minsSecs(entry.avgPace)}`));

// output:
// → gender: F average pace: 8:22
// → gender: M average pace: 7:53
```

Implementation of compose() and pipe()

Now, let's look at one way we could actually implement these functions. The implementations are similar, but we'll start with **pipe** first as it is a bit easier to understand.

It turns out to be a pretty straightforward implementation when using **Array. prototype.reduce**:

```
function pipe(...fns) {
    return input => fns.reduce((prev, fn) => fn(prev), input);
}
```

The **pipe** function takes one or more functions passed in as parameters, which are converted into an array of functions with the spread operator, that is, **. . .fns**. Then, we apply **reduce** to the function array, starting by invoking the first function, **fn**, with the **input** argument passed in as **prev**. On the next invocation, the result of the first function is passed (as **prev**) and used as the parameter when calling the next function in the array. The rest of the functions in the array are processed in a similar fashion, with the result value of the final function returned.

Note that this function can be simplified a bit by using **full fat-arrow** notation:

```
const pipe = (...fns) => input => fns.reduce((prev, fn) => fn(prev),
input);
```

As far as **compose** is concerned, recall that it is almost the same as **pipe** except that the order of functions is processed from right to left rather than left to right. Consequently, the implementation of **compose** is also basically the same, but rather than using **Array. prototype.reduce**, the sister function, **Array.prototype.reduceRight**, is utilized instead. The **reduceRight** function processes the array in reverse order from **reduce** and operates on the last element of the array first, then operates on the second to last element, and so on.

Here's the implementation of **compose**:

```
const compose = (...fns) => input =>
    fns.reduceRight((prev, fn) => fn(prev), input);
```

Currying Functions

Currying is taking a function with multiple arguments and breaking it down into one or more additional functions that take just one argument and eventually resolve to a value. The initial function call does not take all the arguments but returns a function whose input is the remaining arguments and whose output is the intended result for all the arguments.

That was a mouthful, so let's look at an example. Say you have a simple **sum** function:

```
function sum(a, b) {
    return a + b;
}
```

Let's express this as a curried function in arrow notation:

```
const sum = a => b => a + b;
```

Notice that we have two levels of functions here, and each function takes one parameter. The first function takes one parameter, **a**, and returns another function, which takes the second parameter, **b**.

> **Note**
>
> If you are having trouble seeing the two function levels, here's an equivalent that may help:
>
> function sum(a) {
>
>   return function(b) {
>
>   return a + b;
>
>   };
>
> };
>
> You can also write it in arrow notation:

```
const sum = a => function(b) {
    return a + b;
};
```

To invoke this curried **sum** function with multiple arguments, you would need to use the following rather awkward syntax:

```
let result = sum(3)(5);     // 8
```

This indicates to first call **sum** with the parameter value **3**, then call the function that is returned with the parameter **5**.

But most often, you wouldn't invoke curried functions this way, and here's where the real utility of currying will become apparent. Typically, the functions will be called one at a time, which allows us to create intermediate functions that "remember" the parameter that's passed to it.

For example, we can create the following intermediate functions:

```
const incrementByOne = sum(1);
const addThree = sum(3);


let result1 = incrementByOne(3); // result1 = 4, equivalent to calling
sum(1)(3)
let result2 = addThree(5);       // result2 = 8, equivalent to calling
sum(3)(5)
```

Both the intermediate functions remember their parameter: **incrementByOne** holds onto the parameter value of **1** (as in **sum(1)**) and **addThree** remembers **3**. These functions are also referred to as **partially applied** since the **a** parameter was applied to them, but the actual result is not known until the returned function is invoked with the **b** parameter. (Note that partial application is not quite the same as a curried function, though, as partial applications can hold on to multiple parameters, whereas curried functions always take only one argument.)

These are essentially new functions that could be potentially reused multiple times. They are also good candidates for **compose** or **pipe**, as these functions have only one parameter.

Exercise 14.07: More Uses for Composition and Curried Functions

In this exercise, you will further explore currying and composition. Most notably, you will see how you can create curried versions of common functions such as **Array.prototype.map** and **Array.prototype.filter** to compose other functions. In functional programming, common functions often need to be restructured so that they can be used as a building block for processing data in a chain of functions.

The exercise will once again use the **runners** dataset. You will create a function to scan the data and return the age of the oldest female runner. The challenge is to do this using composition with **compose** or **pipe**, thereby feeding the results of one function into the next one in the pipeline.

The basic outline of what we need to do is as follows:

- Create a function to filter the data just for female runners

- Create a function to map that data to just get the age of each runner

- Create a function that uses **Math.max()** to get the highest age value

- Compose the functions we've created so far and call them in sequence to get the final result

The following steps show you how we do this in detail:

1. Open the Chrome menu at the top-right of your browser window, then select **Tools | Developer Tools**.

2. Go to the console and paste in the sample runner data (beginning with **const runners = [...]**) from the *Sample Data for Examples* section of this chapter.

3. First, create a curried version of **Array.prototype.filter**. Type the following into the console:

```
const filter = fx => arr => arr.filter(fx);
```

4. Here, **fx** is the filtering function and **arr** is the array that is to be filtered. Note the ordering of the parameters, where the filtering function will be passed in before the array. This allows us to process the data itself as the last step.

5. Similar to **filter**, you will need to create a curried version of **Array.prototype. map**. Type the following into the console:

```
const map = fx => arr => arr.map(fx);
```

Here, **fx** is the function to be called to map each array element, and **arr** is the array itself that is to be mapped to something else.

6. The next function we need to restructure is **Math.max()**, which returns the highest number of the parameters passed in. Type the following into the console:

```
const max = arr => Math.max(...arr);
```

Here, **arr** is the array of numbers on which to find the max value. By default, **Math. max()** does not take an array as a parameter. However, by making use of the spread operator, that is, **...arr**, the individual array elements will be passed in as a series of parameters to **Math.max()** rather than as an array.

7. Type in the implementation of the compose function:

```
const compose = (...fns) => input =>
    fns.reduceRight((prev, fn) => fn(prev), input);
```

8. You are ready for our first attempt at composing these functions together. Type the following into the console:

```
const oldestFemaleRunner1 = compose(
    max,
    map(runner => runner.age),
    filter(runner => runner.gender === "F")
);
```

Remember that, with **compose**, the order of operations is from bottom to top. First, we have a filter function that picks out the female runners with the **runner. gender === "F"** expression. Next, we have a **map** function that *plucks* the **age** property from the female runners we resolved in the previous **filter** function and creates a new array with just the age values. Finally, **max** is called to obtain the oldest age from these values.

9. We now have all the functions composed, but we still haven't actually run the array data through them to obtain the result. To do so, type the following into the console:

```
const result1 = oldestFemaleRunner1(runners);
```

Now print the result:

```
console.log("Result of oldestFemaleRunner1 is ", result1);
```

You will get an output stating that the oldest female runner is 39:

```
// → output: Result of oldestFemaleRunner1 is 39
```

10. This works, but there is a slight improvement that can be made for the **femaleFilter** portion. Why not make it into a reusable function? We can do this like so:

```
const femaleFilter = filter(runner => runner.gender === "F");
```

Recall that **filter** was a curried function with two layers of parameters (**fx** and **arr**). Here, we are calling **filter** with the first parameter, **fx**, which results in a partially applied function. This **femaleFilter** function can now be used in any context, not just here.

Test the function by applying **femaleFilter** to compose the following:

```
const oldestFemaleRunner2 = compose(
    max,
    map(runner => runner.age),
    femaleFilter
);

const result2 = oldestFemaleRunner2(runners);

console.log("Result of oldestFemaleRunner2 is ", result2);
```

You will get an output stating that the oldest female runner is 39 when using the **filter** function, which is as follows:

```
// → output: Result of oldestFemaleRunner2 is 39
```

11. Some people find the bottom-to-top order of processing confusing and unintuitive. Luckily, we have the **pipe** function, which functions the same as **compose** but in a top-to-bottom order. First, type in the implementation of the pipe function itself:

```
const pipe = (...fns) => input => fns.reduce((prev, fn) => fn(prev),
input);
```

12. Here is the equivalent using **pipe**:

```
const oldestFemaleRunner3 = pipe(
    femaleFilter,
    map(runner => runner.age),
    max
);

const result3 = oldestFemaleRunner3(runners);

console.log("Result of oldestFemaleRunner3 is ", result3);
```

13. You will get the same output, that is, stating that the oldest female runner is 39 when using the pipe function, as follows:

```
// → output: Result of oldestFemaleRunner3 is 39
```

In this exercise, we looked at composition and currying in more detail and how these can be used in tandem to complement each other. We used the curried version of **filter** to pass a filter for the runner's gender, passed the results to a **map** function to get only the **age** value, and finally used **Math.max** to find the highest value from the array of **age** values. While the previous exercise involved some aspects of combining simple functions into a more complex process, in this exercise, we actually used **compose** to create a new function that combined the subfunctions. This allows the new function, **oldestFemaleRunner1**, to be used by others without them having to consider the underlying subfunctions.

In the next section, we'll learn about recursive functions – another vital aspect of functional programming that is somewhat limited in the JavaScript programming language due to the lack of something called tail-call optimization, which is present in other functional programming languages.

Function Recursion

Another technique of functional programming involves functions calling themselves recursively. This generally means you start with a big problem and break it down into multiple instances of the same problem, but in smaller chunks each time the function is called.

One common example of recursion is a function to reverse the characters of a string, **reverse(str)**. Think about how you can state this problem in terms of itself. Let's say you have a string, **"abcd"**, and want to reverse it to **"dcba"**. Recognize that **"dcba"** can be restated as follows:

```
reverse("bcd") + "a"
```

In other words, you are taking the input string and breaking it down into a smaller problem by taking off the first character and making a recursive call with the remaining characters of the string. This may be easier to see in the following code:

```
function reverse(str) {
    if (str.length == 1) return str;
    return reverse(str.slice(1)) + str[0];
}

reverse("abcd");    // => output: "dcba"
```

Let's break this down:

- The **if** condition of **str.length == 1** is the base case. When the input has exactly one character, there is nothing left to reverse, so the solution is just the character itself.

- Otherwise, use **String.slice()** with an index of **1** to get a new string minus the first character of the input. Use this as the input to make the recursive call to **reverse()**.

- Return the result of the recursive call, plus the first character of the string (**str[0]**).

Here's the step-by-step progression of calls:

```
reverse("abcd")    =>   reverse("bcd") + "a"
reverse("bcd")     =>   reverse("cd") + "b"
reverse("cd")      =>   reverse("d") + "c"
reverse("d")       =>   "d"
```

It is important to realize that these function calls are nested on the internal execution stack. Once the base case of one character is reached, the recursion finally has an actual return value, which causes the stack to "unwind." When this happens, the innermost function returns a value, then the function before it, and so on in reverse order until execution propagates back to the first call. This results in the return values of **"d"** for the innermost function, followed by **"dc"**, **"dcb"**, and finally our expected result: **"dcba"**.

Recursion could be useful as another technique for avoiding code that requires the mutation of state and looping. As a matter of fact, it is possible to code recursive implementations of almost any loop, and some purely functional programming languages have a preference for recursion. However, current JavaScript engines are not optimized for recursion, which puts a damper on this and limits its usefulness. It is too easy to write code that would result in slow performance and excessive memory consumption. (Future enhancements that would mitigate these problems have been proposed, but until then, you need to be very careful if you are considering using recursion in your programs.)

Exercise 14.08: Creating a Deck of Cards Using reduce()

We've looked at the basic elements of functional programming in JavaScript and a few data processing examples with runner data. But dealing with data doesn't have to be all number crunching – it can actually be fun. Take, for instance, a deck of cards, which in a way is simply a set of data values ordered in some way. In this exercise, we're going to create a deck of cards by combining four functions: **suits**, **rankNames**, and **createOrderedDeck**.

1. Create a function called **suits** and another called **rankNames** to describe the suits and values of a deck of playing cards. Rather than being arrays, they are functions that return arrays:

```
const suits =
    () => [
        { suit: "hearts", symbol: '&#9829;' },      // symbol: '♥'
        { suit: 'diamonds', symbol: '&#9830;' },    // symbol: '♦'
        { suit: 'spades', symbol: '&#9824;' },      // symbol: '♠'
        { suit: 'clubs', symbol: '&#9827;' }        // symbol: '♣'
    ];

const rankNames =
    () => ['A', '2', '3', '4', '5', '6', '7', '8', '9', '10', 'J',
'Q','K'];
```

2. Create a function called ranks that takes the rankNames array as input and returns each rank mapped as a key-value pair.

```
const ranks =
    rankNames => rankNames.map(rankName => ({ rank: rankName }));
```

3. Create a function called **createOrderedDeck** that takes **suits** and **rank** as input and returns all the possible combinations (for example, every card in the deck):

```
const createOrderedDeck =
    (suits, ranks) => suits.reduce(
        (deck, suit) => {
            const cards = ranks.map(rank => ({ ...rank, ...suit }));
            return deck.concat(cards);
        }, []);
```

We use **Array.prototype.reduce** with an empty array **[]** as the initial value. We then "iterate" over the **suits**, and use **Array.prototype.map** over the **ranks** to combine the suits and ranks by using the spread operator (...). The **Array.prototype.concat()** method then adds the new cards to the resulting array. Once the "nested loop" is complete, we end up with 52 unique cards with all the combinations of suits and ranks.

4. Next, we'll create an instance of a deck of cards by creating a variable from the result of **createOrderedDeck** and our **suits** and **ranks** functions:

```
const orderedDeck = createOrderedDeck(suits(), ranks(rankNames()));
```

5. To demonstrate what has been done so far, open up the Google Chrome browser, go to **Developer** Tools, and then paste in the preceding steps. After you've done that, type in **orderedDeck**. You should get an array like the one shown in the following screenshot. Try clicking on some of the items to look at the contained cards:

```
>  const suits =
       () => [
           { suit: "hearts", symbol: '&#9829;' },    // symbol: '♥'
           { suit: 'diamonds', symbol: '&#9830;' },  // symbol: '♦'
           { suit: 'spades', symbol: '&#9824;' },    // symbol: '♠'
           { suit: 'clubs', symbol: '&#9827;' }      // symbol: '♣'
       ];

   const rankNames =
       () => ['A', '2', '3', '4', '5', '6', '7', '8', '9', '10', 'J', 'Q','K'];
<  undefined
>  const ranks =
       rankNames => rankNames.map(rankName => ({ rank: rankName }));
<  undefined
>  const createOrderedDeck =
       (suits, ranks) => suits.reduce(
           (deck, suit) => {
               const cards = ranks.map(rank => ({ ...rank, ...suit }));
               return deck.concat(cards);
           }, []);
<  undefined
>  const orderedDeck = createOrderedDeck(suits(), ranks(rankNames()));
<  undefined
>  orderedDeck
<  (52) [{…}, {…}, {…}, {…}, {…}, {…}, {…}, {…}, {…}, {…}, {…}, {…}, {…}, {…}, {…}, {…}, {…}, {…}, {…}, {…}, {…}, {…}, {…}, {…},
   ▼{…}, {…}, {…}, {…}, {…}, {…}, {…}, {…}, {…}, {…}, {…}, {…}, {…}, {…}, {…}, {…}, {…}, {…}, {…}, {…}, {…}, {…}, {…}, {…},
   {…}, {…}, {…}] 🖼
       ▶ 0: {rank: "A", suit: "hearts", symbol: "&#9829;"}
       ▶ 1: {rank: "2", suit: "hearts", symbol: "&#9829;"}
       ▶ 2: {rank: "3", suit: "hearts", symbol: "&#9829;"}
       ▶ 3: {rank: "4", suit: "hearts", symbol: "&#9829;"}
       ▶ 4: {rank: "5", suit: "hearts", symbol: "&#9829;"}
       ▶ 5: {rank: "6", suit: "hearts", symbol: "&#9829;"}
       ▶ 6: {rank: "7", suit: "hearts", symbol: "&#9829;"}
       ▶ 7: {rank: "8", suit: "hearts", symbol: "&#9829;"}
       ▶ 8: {rank: "9", suit: "hearts", symbol: "&#9829;"}
       ▶ 9: {rank: "10", suit: "hearts", symbol: "&#9829;"}
       ▶ 10: {rank: "J", suit: "hearts", symbol: "&#9829;"}
       ▶ 11: {rank: "Q", suit: "hearts", symbol: "&#9829;"}
       ▶ 12: {rank: "K", suit: "hearts", symbol: "&#9829;"}
       ▶ 13: {rank: "A", suit: "diamonds", symbol: "&#9830;"}
       ▶ 14: {rank: "2", suit: "diamonds", symbol: "&#9830;"}
       ▶ 15: {rank: "3", suit: "diamonds", symbol: "&#9830;"}
       ▶ 16: {rank: "4", suit: "diamonds", symbol: "&#9830;"}
       ▶ 17: {rank: "5", suit: "diamonds", symbol: "&#9830;"}
```

Figure 14.12: List of a deck of cards using the reduce function

In this exercise, we looked at the **reduce** function we learned about earlier in the chapter and applied it to the situation of creating a deck of cards. We'll build on this in the next exercise to create a function that shuffles a deck randomly, in a way that would make it useful for games.

Exercise 14.09: Using the pipe Method to Create a Card Shuffling Function

Now that we have an ordered deck of cards, we'll look at how we can shuffle it. Of course, as with all functional code, we'll do this without modifying any existing variables.

1. Continuing in the same console as the previous exercise, define the **pipe** and **map** functions we discussed earlier. We won't use **compose** here, but you should get into the habit of defining these three functions for each program when writing functional code as you'll be using them a lot:

```
const compose =
    (...fns) => input => fns.reduceRight((prev, fn) => fn(prev),
input);
const pipe =
    (...fns) => input => fns.reduce((prev, fn) => fn(prev), input);
const map = fx => arr => arr.map(fx);
```

The **addRandom** function adds a field called **random** to each element. Note how the random number itself is obtained from a separate **randomizer** method. This is to keep the **addRandom** function as pure as possible, and isolate the code that has side-effects.

2. Create a **randomizer** variable, followed by an **addRandom** curry function:

```
const randomizer =
    Math.random;

const addRandom =
    randomizer => deck => deck.map(card => ({
        random: randomizer(),
        card
    }));
```

3. Create a **sortByRandom** function that sorts an input deck randomly:

```
const sortByRandom =
    deck => [...deck].sort((a, b) => a.random - b.random);
```

This function sorts the cards by the added **random** field. The **spread** operator (...) is used to clone the array before sorting it, rather than sorting the original array.

4. Create a **shuffle** function that takes a deck and a randomizer value (the randomizer can be changed later if there is a need for a more random value, as would be the case in real casino games). We then use **pipe** to create a function that combines **addRandom** (*to specify our randomizer*), **sortByRandom**, and a **map** function. Finally, we'll execute the **doShuffle** function we just created and use our deck of cards as the input:

```
const shuffle =
    (deck, randomizer) => {
        const doShuffle = pipe(
            addRandom(randomizer),
            sortByRandom,
            map(card => card.card)
        );
        return doShuffle(deck);
    };
```

The purpose of the curried **map** function is to remove the **random** field that was added earlier and just preserve the original fields related to the card itself.

5. Open up the Google Chrome **Developer Tools** session from the previous exercise. If you don't have it saved, you'll need to input the code from the previous exercise. At that point, input the preceding four code snippets from this exercise. With that, execute the **shuffle** function with **shuffle(orderedDeck, randomizer)** and then explore the returned object by clicking it and observing that the cards are shuffled, as shown in the following screenshot:

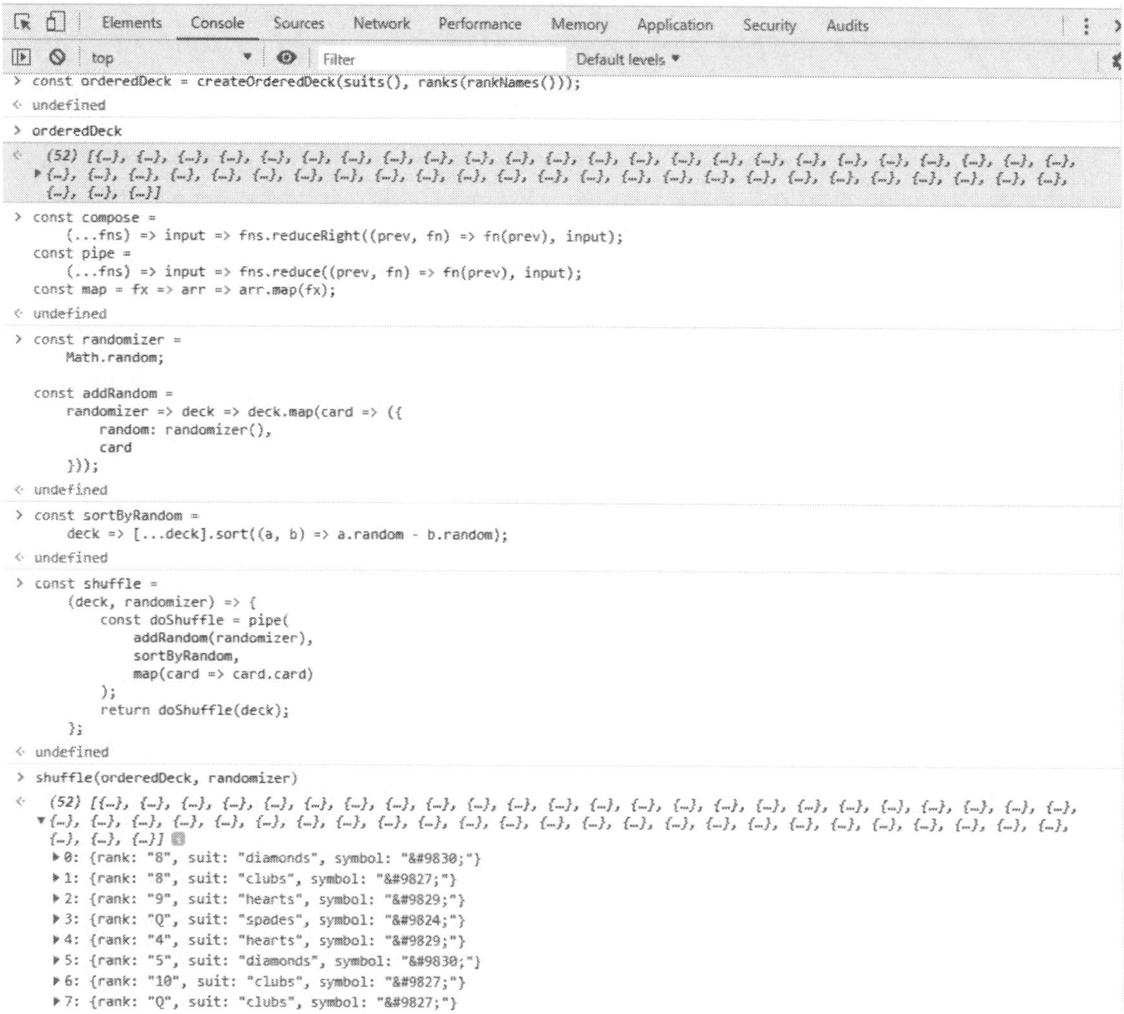

Figure 14.13: List of a deck of cards using the reduce function

We can see the shuffled lists of cards as using the **pipe and map** functions. We can now go ahead and use these functions to work on the Blackjack card game.

Blackjack

For the remainder of this chapter, we will be using what we've learned about functional programming to write an implementation of a simple variant of the card game Blackjack.

Unlike regular Blackjack, though, our game only has one player. The player can draw as many cards as they want (**hit**), as long as the total value does not exceed 21.

The total is the sum of the values of the cards in the player's hand. Cards have the following values:

- Numeric cards have their face value (for example, a 6 of hearts has a value of 6)

- A Jack, Queen, or King has a value of 10

- For simplicity, the Ace is worth 1 (unlike regular Blackjack, where it has a value of either 1 or 11)

If the total value exceeds 21, the hand has gone bust and the game is over.

Mapping Card Values to Cards

The two previous exercises will be very useful in the final assignment, where you'll be implementing a Blackjack game. Feel free to use those code snippets directly. Of course, it won't be sufficient to know just the cards' names – you'll also want to know the value of each card. The **map** function we previously explored will come in very handy for this. Enhance the **ranks** currying function from *Exercise 8: Creating a Deck of Cards Using reduce* to convert **rankNames** into both **rank** and **value** fields:

```
const ranks =
    rankNames => rankNames.map(
        (rank, index) => ({ rank, value: Math.min(10, index + 1) }));
```

This function takes advantage of the index passed in as the optional second parameter in the mapping function. The rank "**A**" is at index **0**, so the value resolves as **1** (since the formula is **index** + **1**). The rank "**2**" is at index **1**, so the value would resolve to **2** (since **index** + 1 = **2**). Same applies to the rest of the numbers, the value would resolve to the same as the number. Once we get to "**J**" and above, though, the value resolves to **10** due to **Math.min()**.

Now, enter **orderedDeck** and explore the object that is returned. You'll notice that all the items now have a value, and the value for the face suits (**J**, **Q**, **K**) are all 10:

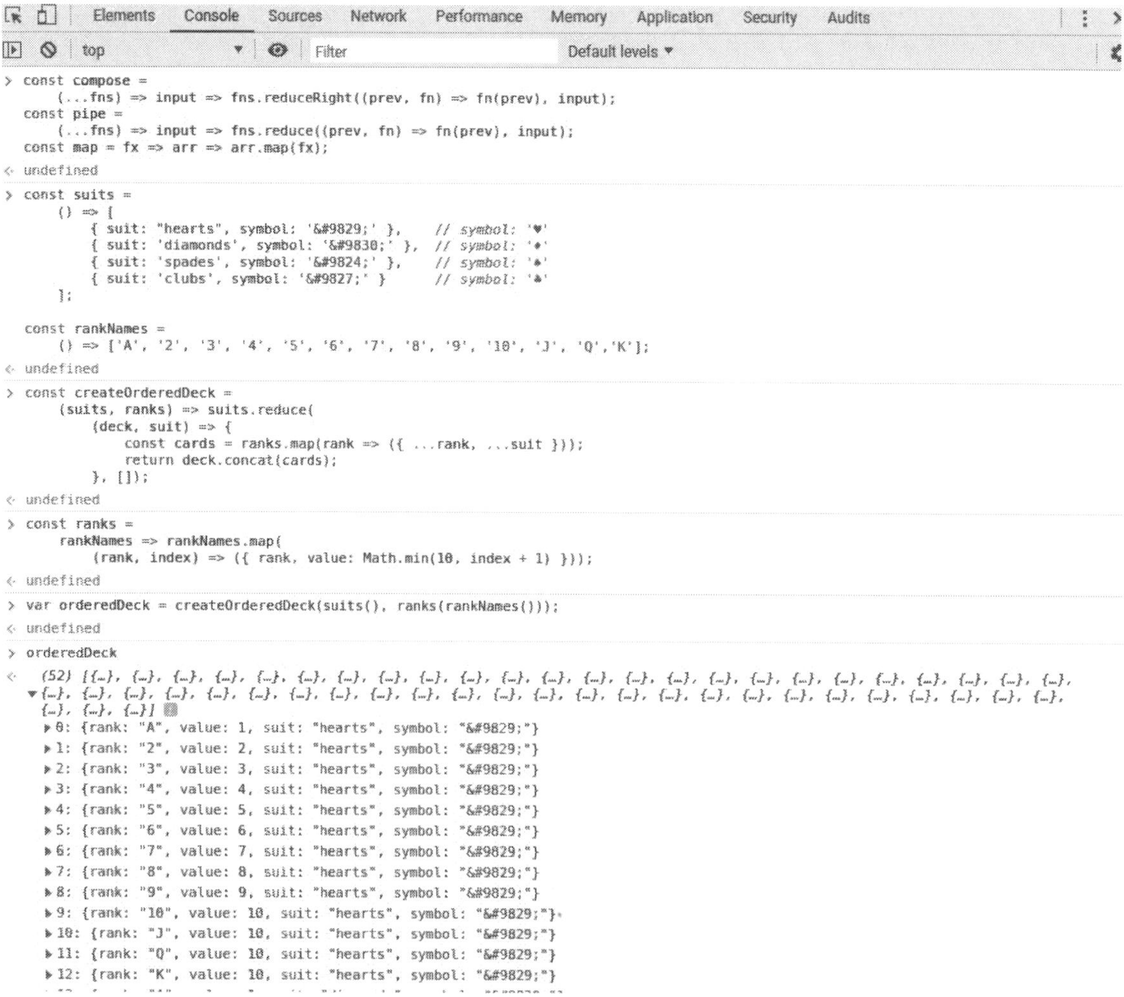

Figure 14.14: Ordered list of a deck of cards using the order function

With the functions we've now covered relating to cards using the basics of functional programming, that is, **map**, **reduce**, **compose**, and **pipe**, you will have a strong foundation for building your own card games.

Activity 14.01: Blackjack Card Functions

The aim of this activity is to get you to create some of the functions that are needed to code a Blackjack game with what you learned about functional programming. You will not be coding the whole game, just some of the core functions related to card logic.

In the GitHub project, you'll find a pre-built HTML file **start.html** with some CSS in it that you should use as a starting point.

The high-level steps for the activity are as follows:

1. Open the starting point HTML/CSS file called **blackjack/start.html**.

2. Add or implement the functions for creating a deck of cards using suits, rank names, and values.

3. Write implementations for the core functional programming methods, that is, **pipe**, **compose**, and **map**.

4. Add functions for drawing a card, getting the sum of a player's cards, checking whether a hand is over 21 points, and checking whether the game is over (the player stayed or went bust).

5. Add a function for updating the card display and card images.

6. Add a function for updating the status display, which tells the user the sum of their hand.

7. Add the **play**, **hit**, and **stay** handler functions for the different actions a user can take.

8. Finally, add any impure functions you may need, such as helpers for getting an element by ID or class.

9. Add a function for setting the state, as well as a function to trigger the game itself.

With these steps done, you should now be able to open the HTML file in a browser and have a running version of the game, as shown in the following screenshot:

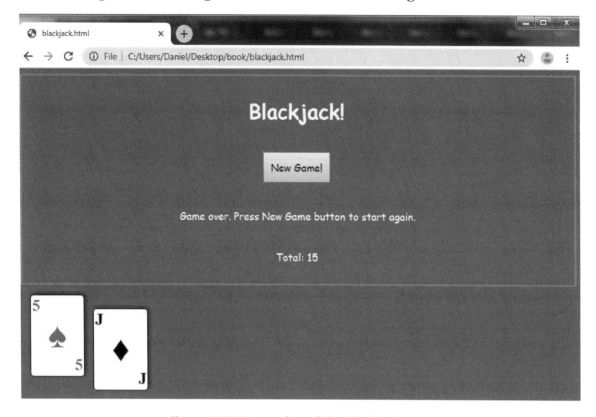

Figure 14.15: Screenshot of the Blackjack game

> **Note**
>
> The solution to this activity can be found on page 758.

Admittedly, this implementation of Blackjack is not very playable and won't win awards for visual design. However, it is a great demonstration of functional programming. See if you can use this code as a basis to implement your own full two-player version of the game.

Managing Blackjack Game State

This game only requires a small amount of state: namely, the player's hand, the game deck, and if the player has selected to stay (and not ask for another card). This state management is isolated to the following code:

```
const createState = (dom) => {
    let _state;
    const getState = () => [..._state];
    const setState =
        (hand, gameDeck, stay = false) => {
            _state = [hand, gameDeck];
            updateCardDisplay(dom, hand);
            updateStatusDisplay(dom, hand, stay);
        };
    return { getState, setState };
}
```

Notice the **return** statement at the end. Only the two methods **getState** and **setState** end up being exposed to the caller, but the **_state** variable remains safe in the closure and acts as the equivalent of a "private" field in object-oriented programming. In addition:

- To isolate the code that produces side-effects as much as possible, there is a separate parameter **dom** that has references to other functions that actually do DOM manipulation.

- The **getState** function returns a clone of the state fields (using the spread operator ...), not the actual values in the fields

- When **setState** is called, two other functions **updateCardDisplay** and **updateStatusDisplay** are called (presented soon) to update the respective portions of the display to correspond to the new state. These functions are designed to dynamically regenerate all the HTML related to the state values each time the state changes. his way there is no additional state needed in the display logic itself. (Popular web frameworks like Angular and React update displays in much the same way, though with some optimizations for the sake of performance).

The state is created at the start of the game:

```
startGame(createState(dom));
```

Blackjack Game Logic Flow

The **startGame** function itself registers three event handling functions to respond to the three buttons the user may click: **New Game**, **Hit** or **Stay**:

```
const startGame = (state) => {
    byId("playBtn").addEventListener("click", playHandler(randomizer,
state));
    byId("hitBtn").addEventListener("click", hitHandler(state));
    byId("stayBtn").addEventListener("click", stayHandler(state));
}
```

The **playHandler** function looks like this:

```
const playHandler = (randomizer, { getState, setState }) => () => {
    const orderedDeck = createOrderedDeck(suits(), ranks(rankNames()));
    let gameDeck = shuffle(orderedDeck, randomizer);
    [hand, gameDeck] = draw(gameDeck, 2);
    setState(hand, gameDeck);
};
```

First the deck is created and shuffled to create the full game deck. Two cards are then drawn from the game deck as the hand. The hand and remaining game deck (minus the two cards drawn) are saved by calling **setState** (which indirectly also triggers the screen to display the cards).

The **hitHandler** function follows a similar pattern:

```
const hitHandler = ({ getState, setState }) => () => {
    [hand, gameDeck] = getState();
    [card, gameDeck] = draw(gameDeck, 1);
    setState(hand.concat(card), gameDeck);
};
```

The current hand and game deck is retrieved by calling **getState**. Then one card is drawn from the game deck. This card is added to the hand and saved by calling **setState** (which once again indirectly also triggers the screen to display the cards).

The **stayHandler** is simpler. It doesn't make any state modifications besides calling **setState** with **true** in the last parameter, indicating the player has stayed:

```
const stayHandler = ({ getState, setState }) => () => {
    [hand, gameDeck] = getState();
    setState(hand, gameDeck, true);
};
```

Blackjack Game Display Functions

The **updateCardDisplay** function is the following:

```
const updateCardDisplay =
    ({ updateHTML }, hand) => {
        const cardHtml = hand.map((card, index) =>
            `<div class="card ${card.suit}"
                style="top: -${index * 120}px;
                        left: ${index * 100}px;">
                <div class="top rank">${card.rank}</div>
                <div class="bigsuit">${card.symbol}</div>
                <div class="bottom rank">${card.rank}</div>
            </div>`);
        updateHTML("cards", cardHtml.join(""));
    };
```

The HTML for each card in the hand is determined in this function using **Array.prototype.map** and joined together at the end to make one string. The calculations for the styles **top** and **left** take advantage of the optional **index** parameter of the mapping function to allow the cards to have a staggered effect. Different CSS classes **top**, **rank**, **bigsuit** and **bottom** position and size the different parts of the card. The suit name itself is also a CSS class to apply the correct color for the suit (black or red).

The other function related to display, **updateStatusDisplay**, is implemented as follows:

```
const updateStatusDisplay =
    ({ updateStyle, updateHTML }, hand, stay) => {
        const total = sumCards(hand);
        updateHTML("totalSpan", total);
        const bust = isBust(total);
        const gameover = isGameOver(bust, stay);
        showOrHide(updateStyle, "playBtn", !gameover);
        showOrHide(updateStyle, "hitBtn", gameover);
        showOrHide(updateStyle, "stayBtn", gameover);
        let statusMsg = gameover ?
            "Game over.  Press New Game button to start again." :
            "Select Hit or Stay";
        statusMsg = bust ? "You went bust!!! " + statusMsg : statusMsg;
        updateHTML("statusMsg", statusMsg);
    };
```

This function does several things:

- Calculates the total value of the cards and displays it

- Determines if the game is over by calling `isBust` and `isGameOver`. (If a hand is in play, the New Game button should not be visible. If the game is over or not active, the Hit and Stay buttons should not be visible. See Figure 14.16.)

- Shows or hides the different buttons depending on if the game is over or not

- Changes the status message depending on if the game is over or not

Figure 14.16: The Hit and Stay buttons are visible when the game is active

Effectively, this function actually drives much of the game flow, as the UI elements available to the user are set within it.

Blackjack Code Listing

The previous sections covered the most important parts of the code. The full code listing for the game is linked as follows:

https://packt.live/370zgaq

For simplicity, all the code is contained within one file, including all the CSS styles and JavaScript supporting functions. In a real-world application, though, you should consider splitting up the files.

Summary

In this chapter, you got a taste of functional programming. It is quite different from other programming paradigms such as imperative and object-oriented approaches, and it takes a while to get used to. But when properly applied, it is a very powerful way of structuring programs so that they're more declarative, correct, testable, and have fewer errors.

Even if you don't use pure functional programming in your projects, there are many useful techniques that can be used on their own. This is especially true for the `map`, `reduce`, and `filter` array methods, which can have many applications.

This chapter also only used functionality that's available in native JavaScript. But note that there are also a number of popular libraries available to assist with functional programming. These libraries facilitate practical functional programming concerns such as immutability, side-effect-free functions, composition, and automatic currying.

The topics we covered in this chapter will help you bolster the skills you need to pursue a programming project in the functional style.

In the next chapter, you will take a deeper look at asynchronous coding, including the history of asynchronous callbacks, generators, promises, and async/await. This will complete your journey through modern JavaScript development, priming you with all you need to create great-looking software.

15

Asynchronous Tasks

Overview

By the end of this chapter, you will be able to implement asynchronous programming and its different techniques; explore the pitfalls of callback hell and the pyramid of doom; illustrate the use of promises to execute code upon operation completion; use the new `async/await` syntax to make asynchronous code look and feel almost sequential; and apply the Fetch API to make remote service calls.

Introduction

Asynchronous tasks allow the execution of the main thread of a program to proceed even while waiting for data, an event, or the result of another process, and achieve snappier UIs as well as allowing some types of multitasking.

Unlike other languages that can have many concurrent threads executing, JavaScript typically runs in a single thread. So far, you have already learned in detail about how JavaScript's single-threaded model is enabled by the **event loop** and the associated **event queue**. Under the hood, the browser or the Node.js runtime has background threads that listen for events or issue service calls, and when a new event is captured or a service call responds, it is pushed into the event queue. JavaScript continually scans the event queue and triggers the handlers for those events when available. Event handlers are most commonly callback methods, but there are other types as well, such as *Promises*, which you will learn about in this chapter.

Some threads take longer than others. In a restaurant, preparing a steak takes more time than fulfilling an order for a glass of wine. However, since there is no dependency between these items, they can each be performed concurrently. But even if the wine was ordered minutes after the steak, there is a good chance the wine will be brought over before the steak, even by the same worker. This is essentially the idea of asynchronous processing. (To take the analogy a bit further, when each item is ready to be served to the customer, they will be placed in the worker's *queue* by the kitchen staff. The worker constantly checks their queue for more things to bring to the restaurant's patrons.)

The early versions of JavaScript mostly used callbacks to achieve asynchrony, but the negative consequences of creating callback hell soon became apparent, as you will see. Then, in ECMAScript 2015, an alternative was introduced, called Promises, which helped a lot but still left a bit to be desired. More recently, new keywords and syntax known as `async/await` were added in ECMAScript 2017, which simplified asynchronous code even further and made it resemble regular sequential code in many respects. You will explore each of these in the sections that follow.

In this chapter, you will also revisit *TheSportsAPI* that was introduced in *Chapter 10, Accessing External Resources*, which you used to query and retrieve sports-related data regarding teams, game scores, players, and upcoming events. It may be a good idea to reread that chapter to refresh your memory, as we will be expanding upon the material there.

Callbacks

As you explored in *Chapter 10, Accessing External Resources*, callbacks are the oldest and simplest means of executing asynchronous functionality in JavaScript. A callback is a specified function to be called once the result of an operation is ready. You saw this with the jQuery **$.ajax()** and **$.getJSON()** methods, where a function is called once a successful service call response is available; for example:

```
$.getJSON('https:/www.somesite.com/someservice',
    function(data) {

    // this function is a callback and is called once
        // the response to the service call is received

    }
);
```

Another area where callbacks are heavily used is for event handlers. Events can be considered asynchronous, as they can happen at unpredictable times and in any order. The callbacks to handle events are typically registered with the browser runtime and added to the event queue when calling **addEventListener()**.

setTimeout()

The **setTimeout()** function is the traditional way of scheduling code to run asynchronously at some point in the future. It is most commonly called with a parameter that specifies the number of milliseconds to wait before execution.

Exercise 15.01: Asynchronous Execution with setTimeout()

This exercise demonstrates how execution flows when using **setTimeout()** if that parameter is specified as **0** or just omitted:

1. In the Google Chrome browser, go into **Developer Tools** (the menu with three dots at the upper-right corner of the screen) | **More Tools** | **Developer Tools**, or just hit the F12 key).

2. In the **Console** tab, paste the code from the following file, but do not hit *Enter* yet. You can find the code in the file **exercise1.js**.

```
console.log("start");

setTimeout(function() {
```

```
        console.log("in setTimeout");
    }, 0);


console.log("at end of code");
```

Consider the code you pasted. You might think the function in the **setTimeout()** block would execute right away since it was specified to execute after zero milliseconds. But, in fact, this is not what happens. So, let's see the output.

3. Press the *Enter* key in the console to execute the code. The output will be the following:

```
start
at end of code
in setTimeout
```

Due to the way asynchronous processing works, the callback in **setTimeout()** is placed in the event queue to schedule it for later processing, while the execution of the main code proceeds. The callback will not get executed until the main code completes.

The overuse of **setTimeout()** can also lead to bad coding practices, as we will see in the next section.

Callback Hell and the Pyramid of Doom

Callbacks are perhaps the simplest and most straightforward approach to handling asynchronous requests, but if you are not careful, your code can get messy and unmanageable very quickly. This is especially true if you need to make a series of nested asynchronous service calls that depend on data returned from the previous call.

Recall *TheSportsDB* from *Chapter 10, Accessing External Resources*. Let's say you have a requirement to obtain a list of honors granted to the players of your favorite team.

In most cases, you would not know the identifiers for the player **id** parameter required by the API in advance. Consequently, you would need to first use an API service call to look at the team ID up, in order to obtain the player list. But there's a further caveat, it turns out that in order to do that, you now need to also know the identifier for the league of which the team is a part. Since you don't know the league ID, you need to find the league ID itself using yet another service.

For such requirements, you may end up with code that looks like the following code snippet (don't worry if you don't understand the code yet, as it will be covered in depth later). You will find the code of file **pyramid_of_doom_example.html** on GitHub in the following location:

```
// Pyramid of DOOM!!!
$.getJSON(ALL_LEAGUES_URL, function(leagueData) {
    const leagueId = findLeagueId(leagueData, LEAGUE_NAME);
    $.getJSON(ALL_TEAMS_URL, {id: leagueId}, function(teamData) {
        const teamId = findTeamId(teamData, TEAM_NAME);
        $.getJSON(ALL_PLAYERS_URL, {id: teamId}, function(playerData) {
            playerData.player.forEach(player => {
                $.getJSON(PLAYER_HONORS_URL, {id: player.idPlayer},
                    function(honorData) {
                        printHonors(honorData);
                    }
                );
            });
        });
    });
});
```

In other words, here is a case where, in order to get one piece of data in one call, there are dependencies on the results of other calls. Each callback uses the result of the previous call to invoke further calls.

Notice all the nested blocks that resulted from using callbacks. It starts with one function, which then includes another function, and then multiple levels of more functions within functions, and this results in a series of unruly end-bracket and end-parenthesis characters. The shape of this code resembles a pyramid rotated on its side, and therefore has the slang term of the *pyramid of doom*:

In this section, you revisited how asynchronous logic is traditionally implemented in JavaScript, and how using callbacks can get you into trouble and result in hard-to-manage spaghetti code. You also familiarized yourself with *TheSportsDB* API and implemented some new functionality that makes requests of it.

There are several alternatives to using callbacks for asynchronous processing that have been developed in recent years, including promises and the new **async/await** syntax. The next section will explore promises, which are a major improvement over callbacks, as you will see.

Promises and the Fetch API

In a nutshell, a promise is an object that wraps asynchronous logic and provides methods to access the results or errors once operation completes. It is a proxy for the result value until it is known, and allows you to associate handler functions rather than using callbacks. It is a *promise* to supply the value once it is known and available.

To get a good feel for how promises are used, you will first be introduced to the Fetch API, which uses promises heavily. Then, we will backtrack and dive into a detailed description of the promises themselves.

Fetch is another API that enables you to make network requests and REST service calls, similar to jQuery's AJAX methods or the native **XMLHttpRequest**. The main difference is that the Fetch API uses promises, which has a cleaner and more concise syntax that helps you avoid callback hell.

Typical Fetch API usage for a JSON request looks something like this:

```
fetch(someURL)
        .then(response =>response.json())
        .then(jsonData =>parseSomeDataFromResponse(jsonData))
        .then(someData =>doSomethingWithDataObtained(someData))
        .catch(error => console.log(error));
```

The **fetch()** call invokes the service call in the URL. Once a valid response is available, the function in the first **then()** block is executed. It receives the response as an argument, and, in this case, runs the **json()** method on it to convert the text into an object. The result of this method call is then made available to subsequent **then()** methods down the chain. Errors can also be handled by **catch()** methods.

Using the Fetch API to Get Player Honors

In this section, we will discard the jQuery callback methods used earlier to obtain player honor data and instead take an approach that utilizes promises (this gets us out of the callback Pyramid of Doom).

The Fetch API is relatively low-level and does not offer as many freebies as jQuery's **$.ajax()** and **$.getJSON()** functions, so we'll create a wrapper function called **myFetch()** to make the usage a bit nicer for our use case; specifically:

- Fetch only takes a full URL and does not encode parameters for you. The **myFetch()** function will include an optional second parameter for params as key-value pairs, which, if specified, will encode the parameter values and append the resulting query string to the URL.

- Fetch does not automatically parse the JSON response, so you'll include this in **myFetch()**.

- Fetch does not consider an HTTP status code as an error condition unless the code is 500 or above. But for our purposes, any response other than **200 (OK)** should be considered an error. You'll add a check for this.

> **Note**
>
> This wrapper is not appropriate for all use cases. You should tailor it to your particular needs.

Exercise 15.02: Refactoring the Honors List to Use the Fetch API

In this exercise, we will refactor the code to obtain a list of honors granted to the players of your favorite team. We will refactor it to use the Fetch API:

1. First, we will create a file that contains common pieces of code that will be used throughout this chapter. In a text editor or IDE, enter the following initial chunk of code. You can also find the code of file **players.js** on GitHub in the file location: https://packt.live/2KUdBY4

```
// hard coded data for purposes of illustration
const LEAGUE_NAME = "English Premier League";
const TEAM_NAME = "Arsenal";
const BASE_URL = "https://www.thesportsdb.com/api/v1/json/1/";
const ALL_LEAGUES_URL = BASE_URL + "all_leagues.php";
const ALL_TEAMS_URL = BASE_URL + "lookup_all_teams.php";
const ALL_PLAYERS_URL = BASE_URL + "lookup_all_players.php";
const PLAYER_HONORS_URL = BASE_URL + "lookuphonors.php";
```

This code has the URLs and data values for remote services we will be calling of *TheSportsDB* API.

2. Enter the following **myFetch()** method:

```
Function myFetch(url, params) {
    if (params) {
        url += "?" + encodeParams(params);
    }
    return fetch(url)
        .then(response => {
            if (!response.ok) {
                throw new Error(response.status);
            }
```

```
                    Return response.json()
            }
    );
}
```

This is the implementation of the wrapper function to **fetch()** that was mentioned earlier. First, if one or more or more parameter key-value pairs are specified, they are encoded into a query string and appended to the URL. After this, the **fetch()** function is called, and **then()** is executed when the response is available. If the HTTP status code is anything other than **200 (OK)**, an error is thrown. This causes it to be caught by the **catch()** function (if defined in the promise call chain). Finally, if all is okay, it calls **response.json()** to parse the JSON response into an object, which is returned as another promise to be passed along and resolved in the subsequent **then()** function.

3. Use the following helper function, which encodes the key-value pair parameters to be appended to the query string of the URL:

```
Function encodeParams(params) {
    return Object.keys(params)
        .map(k => encodeURIComponent(k) + '=' +
                encodeURIComponent(params[k]))
        .join('&');
}
```

4. Now, write the **findLeagueId()** function:

```
Function findLeagueId(leagueData, leagueName) {
    const league = leagueData.leagues.find(l => l.strLeague ===
leagueName);
    return league ? league.idLeague : null;
}
```

This code takes the result of the **ALL_LEAGUES_URL** service call and utilizes **find()** to locate the result that matches the desired league name. Once found, it returns the ID for that league (or **null** if there was no match found).

5. Write the **findTeamId()** function as follows:

```
Function findTeamId(teamData, teamName) {
    const team = teamData.teams.find(t => t.strTeam === teamName);
    return team ? team.idTeam : null;
}
```

Similar to the last function, this code takes the result of the **ALL_TEAMS_URL** service call and uses **find()** to locate the desired team.

6. Enter the **printHonors()** function:

```
Function printHonors(honorData) {
    if (honorData.honors != null) {
        var playerLI = document.createElement("li");
        document.getElementById("honorsList").append(playerLI);

        var playerName =
            document.createTextNode(honorData.honors[0].strPlayer);
        playerLI.appendChild(playerName);

        var honorsUL= document.createElement("ul");
        playerLI.appendChild(honorsUL);

        honorData.honors.forEach(honor => {
            var honorLI = document.createElement("li");
            honorsUL.appendChild(honorLI);

            var honorText = document.createTextNode(
                `${honor.strHonour} - ${honor.strSeason}`);
            honorLI.appendChild(honorText);
        });
    }
}
```

This function takes the result of the **PLAYER_HONORS_URL** service call and creates a list of player honors comprising the **<ul>** and **<li>** HTML tags.

7. We have now completed the common functions. Save this file with the filename **players.js**.

8. Create a new file in your editor or IDE. Enter the initial chunk of code from the following file. You can find the code on GitHub in the file location: https://packt. live/2XRGLMO

```
<html>
<head>
    <meta charset="utf-8"/>
    <script src="players.js"></script>
</head>
```

```
<body>

Arsenal Player Honors:
<ul id="honorsList"></ul>

<script>
```

9. Enter the following, which starts to replace the jQuery **$.getJSON** code with calls to the Fetch API:

```
myFetch(ALL_LEAGUES_URL)
    .then(leagueData => {
        const leagueId = findLeagueId(leagueData, LEAGUE_NAME);
        return myFetch(ALL_TEAMS_URL, {id: leagueId});
    })
```

Processing begins with calling the **myFetch()** wrapper function to invoke the service call that retrieves a list of all leagues. Once the response is available, the function specified in the **then()** method is invoked.

> **Note**
>
> There is no need to check for HTTP errors and you can assume the response was valid since error checking was already done in the implementation of the **myFetch()** function call outlined above. You also do not need to parse the JSON to an object.

The **findLeagueId()** function is then called to find the ID of the league you are interested in, which is needed for the next service call to get the teams in the league. Once found, **myFetch()** is then called again. The promise returned by the **myFetch()** function call is then returned, to be passed along for processing by the following **then()** block.

10. Enter the next **then()** clause to obtain the team ID:

```
    .then(teamData => {
        const teamId = findTeamId(teamData, TEAM_NAME);
        return myFetch(ALL_PLAYERS_URL, {id: teamId});
    })
```

In a similar fashion, once the response to the second service call is available, the function in the **then()** block is invoked. The response is searched to find the team ID needed for the next call, and **myFetch()** is called again to get all the players on the team.

11. Enter the next **then()** block to acquire the list of players on the team, which is needed to then query the honors of each player in turn:

```
.then(playerData => {
```

The browser (and JavaScript runtime) is more than capable of handling the invocation of multiple service calls simultaneously.

> **Note**
>
> A naive approach would be to invoke all the service calls in a serial or synchronous fashion one after another, but doing this would cause the browser (or JavaScript runtime) to lock up until all the service calls are done since JavaScript has a single-threaded model.

12. The **map()** function is called on the **playerData.player** list, which results in the list being iterated and a **myFetch()** call being invoked on each player on the list, and, hence, a number of new REST calls to *TheSportsDB* API. The resulting promises from each service call are collected in the **honorRequests** variable:

```
const honorReqests = playerData.player.map(player =>
        myFetch(PLAYER_HONORS_URL, {id: player.idPlayer}));
```

13. The **Promise.all()** method waits for all the service calls to complete before the associated promises are returned to be processed in the next **then()** block. Once available, the promises are returned as an array in the order the service calls were invoked. This array is iterated upon via **forEach()** to call **printHonors()** for each response:

```
    return Promise.all(honorReqests);
})
.then(honorResponses => honorResponses.forEach(printHonors))
```

14. Finally, there is a **catch()** method in case errors occur during the processing of the promise:

```
.catch(error => console.log(error));
```

This simply logs the error to the console (in a real application, you should consider somehow indicating to the user that an error occurred, such as by showing an error message in the UI).

15. Closeout the file with the following:

```
</script>

</body>

</html>
```

The code from the exercise has resulted in the browser such as the following:

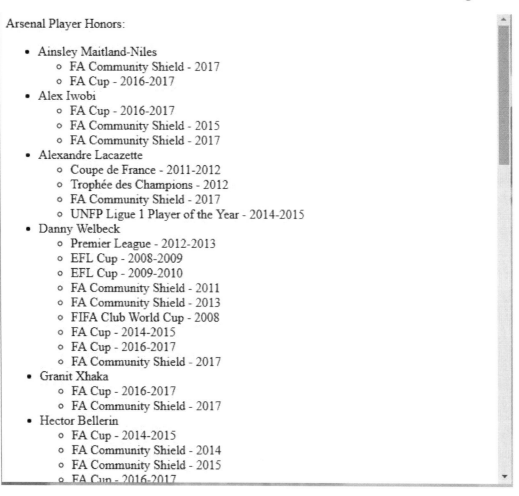

Figure 15.1: Sample output of player honors

In this exercise, we refactored the code to use the Fetch API. This was processed differently. *TheSportsDB* API only offers a service call to retrieve the honors for one player at a time. Consequently, to get the honors of all players on the team, you need to invoke many service calls, one for each player on the team. Here's where asynchrony comes in handy. Thus, the browser (and JavaScript runtime) is more than capable of handling the invocation of multiple service calls simultaneously. We will improve this in the next section.

An Improvement for Better Performance

The preceding code works, but there is still another improvement worth making. As a consequence of using **Promise.all()**, no results will display until all the requests to get player honors have returned. This produces a pause longer than necessary when loading the list.

You can improve perceived performance if you begin to display the list entries the moment the honor data of the first player is available, then the honors of the second player, and so on. You can do this even if the data for the rest of the players have not arrived yet, as long as you maintain the correct player order while displaying the list of entries.

To accomplish this, the basic approach is to create a promise to which a sequence of events are attached. You would take the promises returned by **myFetch()** for the respective players and attach them one by one to the sequence, as in the following pseudo-code:

```
promise
  .then(createPromiseForPlayer1())
  .then(printDataForPlayer1())        // print once data for player 1 is
loaded
  .then(createPromiseForPlayer2())  // etc
  .then(printDataForPlayer2())
  .then(createPromiseForPlayer3())
  .then(printDataForPlayer3())
  .then(createPromiseForPlayer4())
  .then(printDataForPlayer4())
```

Our actual implementation will use **forEach()** to loop over the players to add them to the sequence. The promise for the sequence itself is created with **Promise.resolve()**, which results in a promise that resolves right away with no return value. But that's fine since this promise just serves as a placeholder to chain other items with a series of **then()** calls.

The earlier code that looked like this:

```
.then(playerData => {
    const honorReqests = playerData.player.map(player =>
        myFetch(PLAYER_HONORS_URL, {id: player.idPlayer}));
    return Promise.all(honorReqests);
})
.then(honorResponses => honorResponses.forEach(printHonors))
.catch(error => console.log(error));
```

Is now replaced with the following. You can find the code on GitHub in the file **other/ fetch_example_improved.html**

```
.then(playerData => {
    const sequence = Promise.resolve();

    playerData.player.forEach(player =>
        sequence
            .then(() => myFetch(PLAYER_HONORS_URL, {id: player.idPlayer}))
            .then(printHonors));

    return sequence;
})
.catch(error => console.log(error));
```

The resulting sequence will end up with a chain of **then()** clauses to fetch and print the honor data for each player, in the manner explained in the preceding pseudo-code.

For those more inclined to functional-style code, here is an alternate implementation. I'll let you decide which one of the two is more straightforward and clear.

```
.then(playerData =>playerData.player.reduce((sequence, player) =>
        sequence
            .then(() =>myFetch(PLAYER_HONORS_URL, {id: player.idPlayer}))
            .then(printHonors)
    , Promise.resolve())
)
```

Tidying Up Fetch Code

The preceding code presented to process promises with the **then()** and **catch()** methods executes correctly but is admittedly rather verbose and unwieldy. Could we do better? Let's try to make each **then()** and **catch()** into one-liners by refactoring the processing of each block into its own method.

The following code replaces the promise code that starts with **myFetch()** contained above. You can find the code on GitHub in the file **other/fetch_tidied.html**

```
myFetch(ALL_LEAGUES_URL)
    .then(leagueData =>getTeamsInLeague(leagueData, LEAGUE_NAME))
    .then(teamData =>getPlayersOnTeam(teamData, TEAM_NAME))
    .then(playerData =>getPlayerHonors(playerData))
    .catch(console.log);
```

Note how much more clean the code now reads, and you can more clearly see the progression of what the code is doing just from how the functions are named (that is, first get all leagues, then the correct league, then the right team, and so on).

The supporting functions you need to add are as follows. These basically have the code that was formerly in each corresponding **then()** block, which is restructured into their own functions:

```
function getTeamsInLeague(leagueData, leagueName) {
    const leagueId = findLeagueId(leagueData, leagueName);
    return myFetch(ALL_TEAMS_URL, {id: leagueId});
}
Function getPlayersOnTeam(teamData, teamName) {
    const teamId = findTeamId(teamData, teamName);
    return myFetch(ALL_PLAYERS_URL, {id: teamId});
}
function getPlayerHonors(playerData) {
    const sequence = Promise.resolve();
    playerData.player.forEach(player =>
        sequence
            .then(() => myFetch(PLAYER_HONORS_URL, {id: player.
idPlayer}))
            .then(printHonors));
    return sequence;
}
```

> **Note**
>
> Stay tuned for the activity at the end of the chapter, where this code will be cleaned up and simplified even further using other advanced techniques such as currying.

Some Fetch API Usage Details

This section briefly summarizes some details of the Fetch API, which was introduced earlier.

> **Note**
>
> Some of the settings are noteworthy, but their full details are not within the scope of this chapter. These settings will be indicated since they might be important for you if your use case requires them.

The full method signature for the **fetch()** method is the following:

```
fetchResponsePromise = fetch(resource, init);
```

The **init** parameter allows you to assign certain custom settings to the request. Some of the available options include:

- **method**: The request method, for example, **GET** and **POST**.

- **headers**: Any headers that should be sent along with your request, contained within a **Headers** object (as shown in the following code snippet).

- **body**: Anything, such as a **string**, **Blob**, or **BufferSource**, that you want to add to your request. Typically used for **POST** requests.

- **credentials**: If the resource you are accessing requires credentials for authentication/authorization, you would specify this setting. Possible values are **omit**, **same-origin**, and **include** (the full details of **credentials** are not within the scope of this chapter).

- **cache**: The cache mode to be used for the request. Valid values are **default**, **no-cache**, **no-store**, **reload**, **force-cache**, and **only-if-cached** (the full details of caching are not within the scope of this chapter).

    An example usage for a **POST** request is as follows:

```
const url = "http://mysite.com/myservice";
const data = {param1: 1234};
let responsePromise = fetch(url, {
    method: 'POST',
    headers: {
        'Content-Type': 'application/json',
    },
```

```
      body: JSON.stringify(data)
})
.then(response => response.json());
```

The **fetch()** method returns a promise that resolves to a **response** object that represents details pertaining to the response returned from the request. The following are the most important properties of the **response** object; all the properties are read-only:

- **Response.headers**: Contains the headers associated with the response as an object with key-value pairs. The **headers** object contains methods to access them, such as using **Headers.get()** to retrieve the value for a given key, or **Headers.forEach()** to iterate over the key/value entries and call a function for each; for example:

```
var headerVal = response.get("Content-Type");
      // application/json


response.headers.forEach((val, key) => {
    console.log(key, val);
});
```

> **Note**
>
> For cross-domain requests, there are restrictions on what headers are visible.

- **Response.ok**: A **Boolean** indicating whether the response was successful. A response is considered successful if the status code is in the range of **200–299**.

- **Response.status**: The status code of the response, such as **404** to indicate a **Not Found** error.

- **Response.statusText**: The status message text that corresponds to the status code, such as **OK** for **200**.

In this section, you were introduced to promises and how they are used in the Fetch API. You saw how to retrieve remote data and how to handle errors.

Some developers feel that Fetch is a bit low-level and prefer other alternatives for remote requests. One popular library is the Axios library. As an example, where they feel Fetch is not ideal, Axios automatically transforms JSON responses to objects, whereas the transformation must be done explicitly in Fetch. There are also differences as to what statuses are considered errors to be handled in the **catch()** blocks (as Fetch only considers status codes of **500** or above to be errors, but for many use cases, any status code that is not **200** should be an error condition).

In most cases, there is no need to introduce another dependency into our code. The shortcomings mentioned can be overcome by creating simple wrappers around Fetch specific for your use cases, such as how you implemented the **myFetch()** wrapper function. Accessing the API though the wrapper offers most of the same functionality Axios would provide, however, you have more control.

In the next section, you will explore promises in detail.

Some Details Concerning Promises

You will now dig into the details of what promises are and how they are used in general, not necessarily in the context of service calls.

The constructor of a promise looks like this:

```
new Promise(function(resolve, reject) {
});
```

You would pass in an executor function that takes two arguments: **resolve** and (optionally) **reject**. When the promise is instantiated, this function is executed immediately. Your implementation of the executor function would typically initiate some asynchronous operation. Once the return value is available, it should then call the passed-in **resolve** function or **reject** if there is an error or other invalid condition. If an error is thrown in the executor function, it also causes the promise to be rejected (even if **reject** is not called explicitly).

Put into pseudo-code, this is similar to the following:

```
const promise = new Promise((resolve, reject) => {
    // do something asynchronous, which eventually calls either:
    //    resolve(someValue);   // fulfilled
    // or
  //    reject("failure reason");   // rejected
});
```

A promise can be in one of three possible states: **fulfilled**, **rejected**, or **pending** (not yet fulfilled or rejected). A promise is said to be settled once it is no longer in the pending state (either fulfilled or rejected).

As a simple example, consider a promise whose purpose is to introduce a deliberate 3-second delay to your processing. You could implement this using **setTimeout()** as follows:

```
const timeoutPromise = new Promise((resolve, reject) => {
    setTimeout(() => {
        // call resolve() to signal that async operation is complete
```

```
        resolve("Called after three seconds!");
    }, 3000);
});
timeoutPromise.then(console.log);
```

This would result in the message **Called after three seconds** printing to the console. Note that **reject()** is not explicitly called in this instance (and the **reject** parameter can actually even be omitted if you wish).

Now for some details concerning what happens depending on the return value of the executor function. If the function:

- **Returns a value**: The promise returned by **then** gets resolved with the returned value as its value.

- **Doesn't return anything**: The promise returned by **then** gets resolved with an **undefined** value.

- **Throws an error**: The promise returned by **then** gets rejected with the thrown error as its value.

Exercise 15.03: Creating a Utility Function to Delay Execution

In this exercise, you will produce a utility function for the creation of a promise to add a delay after another promise completes before the execution proceeds. This can be used if you want to do an async operation such as a service call, but do not want to process the result right away. This function will then be tested by making a service call and printing the result after a delay:

1. In the Google Chrome browser, go into **Developer Tools** (the menu with three dots at the upper-right corner of the screen) | **More Tools** | **Developer Tools**, or just hit the F12 key).

2. In the **Console** tab, paste in the following and hit *Enter*: You can find the code on GitHub in the file location: https://packt.live/2XM98vE

```
function addDelay(ms, promise) {
    return promise.then(returnVal =>
        new Promise(resolve =>
            setTimeout(() => resolve(returnVal), ms)
        )
    );
}
```

This is our first attempt at a solution for this simple case, and the implementation resembles the preceding **timeoutPromise** code.

3. You will test it by calling the service in *TheSportsDB* that gets the next event for a league and print the result to the console (the league ID is hardcoded in the URL for the purposes of this test). Paste the following code into the console and hit *Enter*.

```
const BASE_URL = "https://www.thesportsdb.com/api/v1/json/1/";
constnextEventUrl = BASE_URL + "eventsnextleague.php?id=4328";
addDelay(3000, fetch(nextEventUrl))
  .then(response =>response.json())
  .then(nextEvents => console.log(nextEvents.events[0].strEvent));
```

The preceding code results in the message **Bournemouth vs Norwich** in the console after 3 seconds, though your event will likely be different.

> **Note**
>
> You could have used the more robust **myFetch()** wrapper from the previous sections rather than **fetch()** as well.

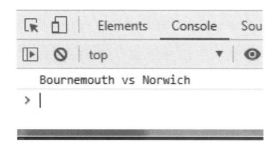

Figure 15.2: Screenshot of the result

In this exercise, we learned how to add a delay to processing using the **addDelay()** function. This can be used if you want to do an **async** operation such as a service call, but do not want to process the result right away. In the next section, we will refine this function further.

Further Refinements to addDelay()

Now, by way of a bonus, let's see if you can think of different use cases for the **addDelay()** utility function presented in the preceding exercise, and how you can specify different parameter options to support these use cases.

The code in the preceding exercise works fine, but what if you wanted to make it more seamless and simply introduce a delay instruction as one of the **then()** clauses? For example:

```
fetch(nextEventUrl)
    .then(addDelay(1000))
    .then(response =>response.json())
    .then(nextEvents => console.log(nextEvents.events[1].strEvent));
```

This form is a bit cleaner and easier to see the flow (that is, fetch the response, add a delay of 1 second, and then process).

In order to support this, you now have two ways in which the parameters can be specified:

- If two parameters are present, this is a simple case and a promise is returned that completes when the delay is over.

- If only one parameter is present, there was no promise passed in at all. Here, rather than returning a promise, you will return a function that takes the promise as a parameter, with the expectation that the **then()** invocation will supply the promise when invoking the function. This function then makes a recursive call to the same **addDelay()** function with two parameters.

Our code now becomes the following:

```
function addDelay(ms, promise) {
    if (promise === undefined) {
        // In this case, only one param was specified.  Since you don't have
        // the promise yet, return a function with the promise as a param and
        // call addDelay() recursively with two params
        return promise =>addDelay(ms, promise);
    }

    // if you reached this far, there were two parameters
    return promise.then(returnVal =>
        new Promise(resolve =>
setTimeout(() => resolve(returnVal), ms)
        )
    );
}
```

There is one other use case you should consider that would make the utility function even more versatile. Let's say you don't start out with a promise at all and just want to return a value after a delay.

You can support this by calling **Promise.resolve()** with the value to convert it to a promise, which essentially treats it as an immediately fulfilled promise for that value. In the case that the value is already a promise, this call would have no effect.

> **Note**
>
> Calling **Promise.resolve()** on promise parameters is mentioned as a best practice anyway in the promise specification guide.

In general, when an argument is expected to be a promise, you should also allow thenables and non-promise values by resolving the argument to a promise before using it. You should never do type detection on the incoming value, overload between promises and other values, or put promises in a union type.

The final code looks like the following. You can find the code on GitHub in the file **other/addDelay.js**

```
function addDelay(ms, promise) {

    if (promise === undefined) {
```

In this case, only one parameter was specified. Since you don't have the promise yet, return a function with the promise as a parameter and call **addDelay()** recursively with two parameters:

```
        return promise =>addDelay(ms, promise);
    }
```

If you reached this far, there were two parameters:

```
    return Promise.resolve(promise).then(returnVal =>
        new Promise(resolve =>
setTimeout(() => resolve(returnVal), ms)
        )
    );
}
```

And here's the code to test the three scenarios:

```
const BASE_URL = "https://www.thesportsdb.com/api/v1/json/1/";
const nextEventUrl = BASE_URL + "eventsnextleague.php?id=4328";
```

Use case one is where two parameters are specified, so it executes a promise after a delay:

```
let p1 = addDelay(3000, fetch(nextEventUrl))
  .then(response => response.json())
  .then(nextEvents => console.log("Use 1: " + nextEvents.events[0].
strEvent));
```

Use case two is where only one parameter is specified, so it returns a function that takes the promise as a parameter with the expectation that the **then()** invocation will supply the promise when invoking the function:

```
let p2 = fetch(nextEventUrl)
  .then(addDelay(1000))
  .then(response =>response.json())
  .then(nextEvents => console.log("Use 2: " + nextEvents.events[1].
strEvent));
```

Use case three is where we just want to return a value after a delay:

```
let p3 = addDelay(2000, "This is a passed in value")
  .then(result => console.log("Use 3: " + result));
```

The output **All done!** should be written as follows:

```
Promise.all([p1, p2, p3])
  .then(() => console.log("All done!"));
```

The order of the output from the preceding code would be as follows:

```
    Use 2       (after 1 second)
    Use 3       (after 2 seconds)
    Use 1       (after 3 seconds)
```

The expected output will be as follows:

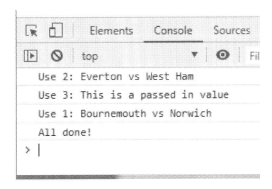

Figure 15.3: Screenshot of output

Remember, this is not a sequential code, even though it reads that way. It is important to wrap your head around this when working with asynchronous logic:

- When the code that sets up **Use 1** executes, it schedules the function to be called back after three seconds. But the main thread of execution continues immediately to set up **Use 2** and does not wait for 3 seconds to complete.

- **Use 2** is then scheduled for 1 second in the future and will end up being triggered way before **Use 1**, so it is output first. Before this even happens, though, once again, the main thread of execution continues immediately to **Use 3**.

- **Use 3** is then scheduled for 2 seconds in the future. This is the second one to trigger and produce output, as **Use 1** won't trigger until 3 seconds have passed.

- Finally, **Use 1** triggers and outputs when the third second is reached:

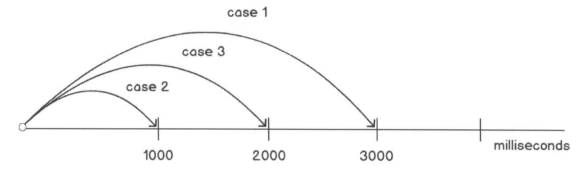

Figure 15.4: Use cases shown in a diagram

In this section, you learned the details of how promises are created and used. Promises have become an important part of JavaScript and many libraries and APIs use them. Promises have also become a basis for extending the language further and supporting them directly with new keywords, as you will soon see.

The next section will explore **async/await**, which expands the use of promises with a new syntax.

Async/Await

New additions to recent versions of JavaScript (since ES2017-ES8) make working with asynchronous logic easier, more transparent, and result in your code looking almost as if it were synchronous. This is the **async/await** syntax, which is one of the most exciting and useful additions to the language in recent years. We'll just dive right in and get a feel for how the **async** and **await** keywords are used by way of an example.

We will now present the changes you would make to refactor the promise code as you left it in the *Further Refinements to addDelay()* section to use **async/await** instead. Firstly, recall the main processing code that looked like this:

```
myFetch(ALL_LEAGUES_URL)
  .then(leagueData => getTeamsInLeague(leagueData, LEAGUE_NAME))
  .then(teamData => getPlayersOnTeam(teamData, TEAM_NAME))
  .then(playerData => getPlayerHonors(playerData))
  .catch(console.log)
```

When refactored to use the **await** syntax, it will look like the following. You can find the code on GitHub in the file **other/async_await.html**

```
    try {
        let leagueData = await myFetch(ALL_LEAGUES_URL);
        let teamData = await getTeamsInLeague(leagueData, LEAGUE_NAME);
        let playerData = await getPlayersOnTeam(teamData, TEAM_NAME);
        await getPlayerHonors(playerData);
    } catch (err) {
        console.log("caught error: " + err);
    }
```

The **await** keyword indicates that the function that follows returns a promise, and signals to the browser or JavaScript runtime to wait until the promise resolves and returns a result.

Using **await** is really just syntactic sugar as an alternative to calling **promise.then()**, and the result is the same as the value that would be passed as a parameter if **promise. then()** were called. But using **await** allows you to capture the result in a variable and looks as if you were writing synchronous code.

Also, notice how error handling is done using a typical **try...catch** block rather than a **catch()** function. This is another way in which **await** enables asynchronous code to be more seamless.

Another method we will refactor is **myFetch()**. Previously, it looked like this:

```
function myFetch(url, params) {
    if (params) {
        url += "?" + encodeParams(params);
    }
    return fetch(url)
        .then(response => {
            if (!response.ok) {
                throw new Error(response.status);
            }
```

```
                    return response.json()
            }
    );
}
```

Refactored, it will now look like this:

```
async function myFetch(url, params) {
    if (params) {
        url += "?" + encodeParams(params);
    }
    let response = await fetch(url);

    if (!response.ok) {
        throw new Error(response.status);
    }
    return response.json()
}
```

The **async** keyword before the function definition indicates that the function always returns a promise. Even if the actual value the function returns is not a promise, JavaScript will take care of wrapping that value in a promise automatically. In this case, the return value is the object resulting from the **response.json()** call, but what actually gets returned is a promise that wraps this. (The **await** keyword on the caller end would typically be used to unwrap the value again, but there are use cases where there is a need to work with the promise directly as well.)

Also notice how the **fetch()** function call now has an **await** keyword in front of it, rather than processing it utilizing the typical promise API with **then()**.

There is another function you can refactor as well from a previous section: **getPlayerHonors()**. This is what it looked like before:

```
function getPlayerHonors(playerData) {
    const sequence = Promise.resolve();

    playerData.player.forEach(player =>
        sequence
            .then(() => myFetch(PLAYER_HONORS_URL, {id: player.idPlayer}))
            .then(printHonors));
    return sequence;
}
```

Remember that the purpose of this code is to make a REST service call to get player honor data for multiple players. Refactoring the code to use **async/await**, you can simplify it a bit and remove the sequence. Here's the new code:

```
async function getPlayerHonors(playerData) {
    const playerPromises = playerData.player.map(async player =>
        myFetch(PLAYER_HONORS_URL, {id: player.idPlayer}));

    for (constplayerPromise of playerPromises) {
        printHonors(await playerPromise);
    }
}
```

The **array.map()** function affects an iteration of all the players and calls **myFetch()** for each to get the honor data, resulting in an array of promises. Notice that you used the **async** keyword on the left of the arrow function. This is perfectly valid and just signals to **array.map()** that the function returns a promise. During processing, the execution of **array.map()** will not wait for the first function to complete before calling the next one. This makes the technique of utilizing **array.map()** with **async** well suited for launching concurrent requests.

Afterward, there is a second iteration using a standard **for...loop**, this time, of the promises produced earlier. The **await** keyword when calling **printHonors** would result in the execution waiting until the promise resolves before printing the available result. Also, since you are in a loop, you ensure the output is printed in the correct order.

> **Note**
>
> There is another important caveat to be aware of when using the **await** keyword: it only works if it is used within a function that is marked with the **async** keyword in front of it. Attempting to use it in a regular function or in top-level code will result in a syntax error. (For this reason, in the code that follows, notice that you will place the main processing code in an anonymous **async** function.)

Asynchronous Generators and Iterators

There is another implementation technique for the preceding **getPlayerHonors()** function to consider using it. This makes use of generator functions, which were described in *Chapter 5, Beyond the Fundamentals*. Generators, in general, are a recent and rather complex addition to the JavaScript language, and iterators are even newer, so not all browsers and runtime environments support them yet. We will therefore not spend a lot of time explaining them. But we just want to touch on them and explain very briefly how generators and iterators could be used with **async**.

Here's the implementation. You can fnd the code on GitHub in the file **other/async_ generator_impl.html**

```
async function* getPlayerHonorsGenerator(playerData) {

    const playerPromises = playerData.player.map(async player =>
        myFetch(PLAYER_HONORS_URL, {id: player.idPlayer}));

    for (const playerPromise of playerPromises) {
        yield playerPromise;
    }
}


async function getPlayerHonors(playerData) {
    for await(const player of getPlayerHonorsGenerator(playerData)) {
        printHonors(player);
    }
}
```

The first **getPlayerHonorsGenerator()** function should look mostly familiar, as it is similar to the previous implementation, but with some important differences. The asterisk (*) that follows the **function** keyword indicates that it is a generator function, which means it returns multiple values via subsequent calls.

Notice the **yield** keyword in the loop. When **yield** is reached, execution passes back to the caller (which is actually the second function). When the generator function is called again, the execution picks up from where it left off in the middle of the loop and returns the next value. Once the loop ends, all the values have been returned, and the generator signals that it is done.

The second function calls the generator function using the **for-await...of** iterator syntax. The **await** keyword right after **for** makes it an **async** iterator. While performing the iteration, the execution will wait for each promise returned by the generator (via **yield**) to resolve in turn before executing the body of the loop.

Generators are a complex topic. However, by adopting this technique, you are able to access the results of multiple asynchronous calls in a clean looping syntax.

Activity 15.01: Refactoring Promise Code to await/async Syntax

Over the course of this chapter, you have explored how to take synchronous code and refactor it to use callbacks, promises, and **async/await** syntax. This activity will tie up some loose ends and challenge you to make some aspects of the code even better, partially by using the skills you learned in previous chapters.

The steps for completion are as follows:

1. Firstly, recall the following code from *Exercise 15.03, Creating a Utility Function to Delay Execution* of this chapter, which uses promises to test three different uses of our **addDelay** function.

2. Rewrite it to use the **async/await** syntax.

3. For the purposes of this activity, you are not permitted to use **Promise.all()** (even though, in normal programming, it would be a good way to wait for the completion of multiple promises).

> **Hint**
>
> Be careful where you place your **await** keywords, as the three cases do not resolve in order.

The expected output is:

Arsenal Player Honors:

- Ainsley Maitland-Niles
  - FA Community Shield - 2017
  - FA Cup - 2016-2017
- Alex Iwobi
  - FA Cup - 2016-2017
  - FA Community Shield - 2015
  - FA Community Shield - 2017
- Alexandre Lacazette
  - Coupe de France - 2011-2012
  - Trophée des Champions - 2012
  - FA Community Shield - 2017
  - UNFP Ligue 1 Player of the Year - 2014-2015
- Danny Welbeck
  - Premier League - 2012-2013
  - EFL Cup - 2008-2009
  - EFL Cup - 2009-2010
  - FA Community Shield - 2011
  - FA Community Shield - 2013
  - FIFA Club World Cup - 2008
  - FA Cup - 2014-2015
  - FA Cup - 2016-2017
  - FA Community Shield - 2017
- Granit Xhaka
  - FA Cup - 2016-2017
  - FA Community Shield - 2017
- Hector Bellerin
  - FA Cup - 2014-2015
  - FA Community Shield - 2014
  - FA Community Shield - 2015
  - FA Cup - 2016-2017

Figure 15.5: Sample output of player honors

Note

The solution to this activity can be found on page 763.

Before we move on to the next activity, we will review briefly what currying is. Currying is taking a function with multiple arguments and breaking it down into one or more additional functions that take just one argument and eventually resolve to a value. The initial function call does not take all the arguments but returns a function whose input is the remaining arguments and whose output is the intended result of all the arguments.

Activity 15.02: Further Simplifying Promise Code to Remove Function Parameters

Shifting back to promises, we concluded the **async/await** section by tidying up the promise code to make the **then()** clauses one-liners. Here's the code again to refresh your memory:

```
myFetch(ALL_LEAGUES_URL)
    .then(leagueData =>getTeamsInLeague(leagueData, LEAGUE_NAME))
    .then(teamData =>getPlayersOnTeam(teamData, TEAM_NAME))
    .then(playerData =>getPlayerHonors(playerData))
    .catch(console.log)
```

This is pretty good, but could you do even better?

Now, we need to think of a way to simplify the code and remove the function parameters entirely, so it would look like this:

```
myFetch(ALL_LEAGUES_URL)
    .then(getTeamsInLeague(LEAGUE_NAME))
    .then(getPlayersOnTeam(TEAM_NAME))
    .then(getPlayerHonors)
    .catch(console.log)
```

> **Hint**
>
> Think about how you might defer the processing of the first parameter of **getTeamsInLeague()** and **getPlayersOnTeam()**. Refactor those functions to return another function that finally processes this parameter instead using currying techniques, which you learned about in *Chapter 14, Understanding Functional Programming*.

The original code is repeated here for your convenience (the **getPlayerHonors()** function already takes only one parameter and, therefore, has no need to be further simplified for this purpose):

```
function getTeamsInLeague(leagueData, leagueName) {
constleagueId = findLeagueId(leagueData, leagueName);
    return myFetch(ALL_TEAMS_URL, {id: leagueId});
}


function getPlayersOnTeam(teamData, teamName) {
constteamId = findTeamId(teamData, teamName);
    return myFetch(ALL_PLAYERS_URL, {id: teamId});
}
```

The steps for completion are as follows:

1. In technique #1, refactor **getTeamsInLeague** so that it now only takes one parameter, **(leagueName)**, rather than two parameters that are actually needed to determine the full result **(leagueData, leagueName)**. The other parameter is deferred till later.

2. In technique #1, instead of returning the promise from **myFetch** directly, you return another curried function that takes **leagueData** as its parameter. It is only a partially applied function at this point.

3. Technique #2 is really the same idea but uses a function variable and multiple levels of arrow functions rather than a regular function.

4. Finally, when **getTeamsInLeague(LEAGUE_NAME)** is invoked in the **then()** clause, the function returned above would be fully applied, with the resolved value from the previous promise passed in as the implied **leagueData** parameter.

5. The process when calling **getTeamsInLeague(LEAGUE_NAME)** is incomplete at that point and returns another function to complete it. So, call a partially applied function.

    The expected output of the activity is the same as in *Exercise 15.02, Refactoring the Honors List to Use the Fetch API*, which gives a sample output of player honors.

    > **Note**
    >
    > The solution to this activity can be found on page 765.

Summary

Like promises, **async/await** has become very important in JavaScript. You saw how this syntax helps your code appear almost like a synchronous code and can make your code clearer with regard to your desired intent. It even enables error handling in a more standard way with **try/catch**.

But this is sometimes deceptive and can get you into trouble if you are not careful. It is important to understand how an asynchronous code differs from sequential code, in particular, how asynchronous code is triggered by event loops and does not block the main execution thread. The same is true with promises themselves, but with **async/await** looking so similar to synchronous code, it could be easy to forget this fact.

That said, **async/await** is still very powerful and worth using. We have reached the end of this book. By now, you have gained a comprehensive understanding of the foundations and basics of JavaScript. You have also fully understood JavaScript syntax and structures for the web and beyond. Now, you are ready to build out intellectually challenging development problems to apply in everyday work.

Appendix

About

This section is included to assist the students to perform the activities present in the book. It includes detailed steps that are to be performed by the students to complete and achieve the objectives of the book.

Chapter 1: Getting to Know JavaScript

Activity 1.01: Creating an Alert Box Popup in the Web Browser

Solution

1. Press F12 to open the developer tools that are integrated within it. If this doesn't work, a right-click may expose a prompt so that you can do this as well:

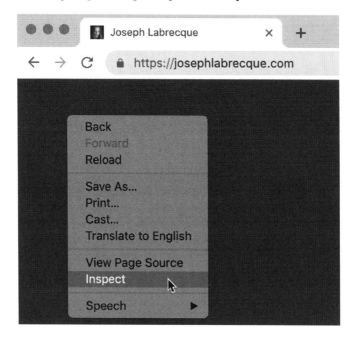

Figure 1.18: Choosing Inspect in Google Chrome

2. The developer tools may default to the console. If not, there is likely to be a **Console** tab you can click on to activate it. The console allows you to write JavaScript code directly within the web browser itself:

Figure 1.19: The Developer Tools Console tab in Google Chrome

3. Within the console, write the following command:

```
var greeting = 'Hello from JavaScript!';
alert(greeting);
```

4. Hit *Return/Enter* to execute the code. The code will execute within the browser environment.

    You should see an alert appear in the browser viewport displaying your message, as shown here:

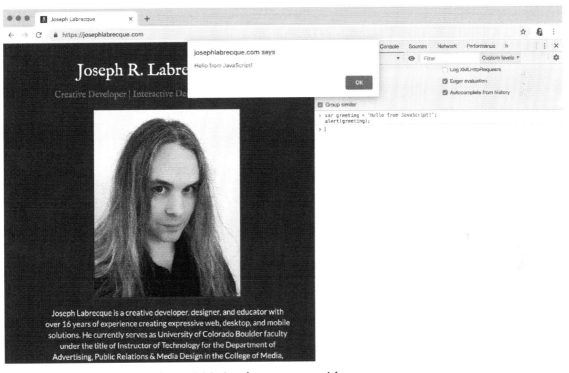

Figure 1.20: An alert appears with our message

What does that code do? It declares a variable, using the **var** keyword, with the **greeting** identifier on the first line. As part of this same line of code, we then use the = assignment operator to assign a **'Hello from JavaScript!'** text string value to our variable.

On the second line, we use the **alert()** function and pass in our **greeting** identifier as an argument. The result is that the web browser displays an alert overlay with the text value applied to the identifier we passed in.

Chapter 2: Working with JavaScript

Activity 2.01: Adding and Modifying an Item to/in the To-Do List

Solution

1. Create the HTML file yourself and paste in the HTML code to get started:

Figure 2.28: The initial to-do list's appearance

2. The first thing we need to do is assign an ID to our list in order to identify it via code. To do this, add an **id** attribute to the **ol** element and give it a value of **todo-list**. With that complete, we can then address this element directly with JavaScript:

```
<ol id="todo-list">
```

3. Using a bit of JavaScript code, we can now create a new variable named **parentContainer**. This will refer to the ordered list container element that holds all of our list items. We'll use the ID we assigned in the previous step to address this element directly via the use of the **getElementById()** method:

```
var parentContainer = document.getElementById('todo-list');
```

4. Create a new HTML **<li>** list item element via JavaScript. Right now, the element only exists in memory since we have to add it to a visual container. It also has no text content associated with it:

```
var newItem = document.createElement('li');
```

5. Now, let's populate the list item with a data value. Set the **innerText** of our **newItem** node to a string. The value of that string can be whatever you like, but it should fit within the concept of a to-do list:

```
newItem.innerText = "Research Wines";
```

6. Now that the new HTML element has been created and populated with text, we can add it to the visual document by appending it to a chosen parent container that already exists:

```
parentContainer.appendChild(newItem);
```

7. We then need to add an extra line of JavaScript below all the others that currently exist within our **<script>** tag to modify the element's appearance. We will reference the last child element within our ordered list and change the **style** attribute to add a CSS color rule. You can set the actual color of the text to whatever you like—I'm going to use **crimson**:

```
parentContainer.lastChild.style.color = "crimson";
```

8. Now, to verify the execution order through code, add the following line of JavaScript directly underneath the initial declaration of **parentContainer**:

```
console.log('Beginning List Count: ' + parentContainer.children.
length);
```

9. Then, add the following line right before the closing **<script>** tag:

```
console.log('End List Count: ' + parentContainer.children.length);
```

10. With that completed, refresh your browser view and a seventh item should appear on your list. Do keep an eye on the developer tools console to verify the execution order of our code! Not only will the new item be added to the existing ordered list, but it will also display with crimson text instead of the usual white:

Figure 2.29: A list item has been added to our to-do list and styled in crimson

The complete code will be as follows:

activity-complete.html

```
30    <ol id="todo-list">
31        <li>Wash Laundry</li>
32        <li>Clean Silver</li>
33        <li>Write Letters</li>
34        <li>Purchase Groceries</li>
35        <li>Retrieve Mail</li>
36        <li>Prepare Dinner</li>
37    </ol>
38    <script>
39        var parentContainer = document.getElementById('todo-list');
```

The full code is available at: https://packt.live/2q8CGY1

This is just a simple example of how JavaScript can have a direct influence over other aspects of the environment it is run with.

Chapter 3: Programming Fundamentals

Activity 3.01: The To-Do List Shuffle Program

Solution

1. All the coding is done in the **activity.js** file. Add the code after the comment shown in each step. Create the array of **todo** items:

```
// Declare and initialize the todo list array
let todoList = [
  "Wash Laundry",
  "Clean Silver",
  "Write Letters",
  "Purchase Groceries",
  "Retrieve Mail",
  "Prepare Dinner"
];
```

2. Examine the **ol** element in the HTML document file called **activity.html** and notice that it has an **id** attribute with the value of **todo-list**:

```
<ol id="todo-list">
</ol>
```

3. You can create an object variable, referencing the **ol** element using the **document. getElementById** method:

```
// The todo list element
let todoEle = document.getElementById('todo-list');
```

4. Next, write a function that accepts a list element object and an array of values. The function removes the **li** elements from the list element and then loops through the array, creating new **li** elements for each value in the array:

```
// Function to replace an HTML DOM list li elements with array items.
function replaceListElements(listEle, listItems){
  listEle.innerHTML = "";
  for (let i= 0; i<= listItems.length - 1; i++){
    let liEle = document.createElement("li");
    liEle.appendChild(document.createTextNode(listItems[i]));
    listEle.appendChild(liEle);
  }
}
```

The first line uses the **innerHTML** property to remove all the contents of the list element object. The **for** loop iterates through the array. The first line in the **for** loop creates an **li** element object named **liEle**. The next line uses the **liEle** object's **addChild** method to append a text node to the **liEle** object. The **document.createTextNode** method provides the item in the array as a proper node object. The last line appends the **liEle** object to the **listEle** object.

5. The final step is to call the function:

```
// Update the todo list view with initial list of items
replaceListElements(todoEle, todoList);
```

This function will execute when the **activity.js** file is loaded.

6. Save the **activity.js** file and reload the **activity.html** file in the web browser. It should appear as follows:

Figure 3.24: **activity.js** and **activity.html** file output

7. Examine the **button** element in the HTML document file called **activity.html** and notice that it has an **id** attribute with the value of **shuffle-button**:

```
<button id="shuffle-button">Shuffle</button>
```

You can create an object variable referencing the **button** element by using the **document.getElementById** method:

```
// The shuffle button element.
let shuffleButtonEle = document.getElementById('shuffle-button');
```

8. Next, you need to listen for click events and call a function that will handle the event. The **shuffleButtonEle** object's **addEventListener** method can do that for you. The first argument is the name of the event, and the second argument is the name of the function:

```
// Add event listener function for the shuffle button element.
shuffleButtonEle.addEventListener('click', shuffleButtonClicked);
```

9. Now, we need to write the **shuffleButtonClicked** function:

```
// Function to handle click events for the Shuffle button
function shuffleButtonClicked(e){
  replaceListElements(todoEle, getNewShuffledArray(todoList));
}
```

The only line of code is used to call the **replaceListElements** function. The first argument is the **todoEle** object for the **ol** element. The second argument is the **getNewShuffledArray** function, which is using the **todoList** array as an argument. The **getNewShuffledArray** function returns an array that's been shuffled.

10. Save the **activity.js** file and reload the **activity.html** file in the web browser. Then, click the Shuffle button to see the list change.

11. Take a moment to examine the comments in the **getNewShuffledArray** function to see how it works. It shuffles the array elements, and appears as follows:

```
function getNewShuffledArray(sourceArray){
```

12. Now, make a copy of **sourceArray** and set the index to make a swap, starting with the last:

```
var newArray = [].concat(sourceArray);
let swapIndex = newArray.length;
```

13. Create an index to make a swap with **swapIndex** and swap the value of **swapIndex**:

```
let swapWithIndex;
let swapIndexValue;
```

14. Create a **while** loop called **swapIndex** that's not equal to **0** and pick an index to swap with the current index from **0** to the current **swapIndex**:

```
while (0 !== swapIndex) {
  swapWithIndex = Math.floor(Math.random() * swapIndex);
```

15. Now, reduce **swapIndex** by **1** and make a copy of the **swapIndex** value. Then, replace the **swapIndex** value with the **swapWithIndex** value, and replace the **swapWithIndex** value with the **temporaryValue** value:

```
  swapIndex -= 1;
  swapIndexValue = newArray[swapIndex];
  newArray[swapIndex] = newArray[swapWithIndex];
  newArray[swapWithIndex] = swapIndexValue;
}
return newArray;
```

The shuffled To-Do list will look similar to something as follows:

Figure 3.25: Shuffled list 1

Another example of a shuffled To-Do list is as follows:

Figure 3.26: Shuffled list 2

Chapter 4: JavaScript Libraries and Frameworks

Activity 4.01: Adding an Animation to the Todo List Application

Solution:

1. Go to cdnjs.com and get the jQuery CDN URL.

2. Load the library into the head tag of your existing Todo-List-HTML using a script tag. This will allow you to use jQuery within your code:

```
<head>
    // ... links and meta tags from the previous activity
<script src="https://cdnjs.cloudflare.com/ajax/libs/jquery/3.4.1/
jquery.min.js"></script>
</head>
```

Inside **activity.js**, you need to change the **todoEle** variable. Change it to a jQuery element:

```
// The todo list element
// let todoEle = document.getElementById('todo-list'); // old
let todoEle = $('#todo-list'); // new
```

Inside the **replaceListElements** function, you can now use functions on the **todoEle** element that jQuery provides you with.

3. Hide and clear what's inside the element using the necessary jQuery functions:

```
function replaceListElements(listEle, listItems){
  // listEle.innerHTML = „"; // old
  listEle.hide();
  listEle.empty();
  for (let i= 0; i<= listItems.length - 1; i++){
    let liEle = document.createElement("li");
    liEle.appendChild(document.createTextNode(listItems[i]));
    listEle.appendChild(liEle);
  }
}
```

4. Inside the for loop, create the **liEle** list item element, set the text contest, and append it to the **listEle** list element:

```
function replaceListElements(listEle, listItems){
  listEle.hide();
  listEle.empty();
```

```
for (let i= 0; i<= listItems.length - 1; i++){
 // let liEle = document.createElement("li");
 // liEle.appendChild(document.createTextNode(listItems[i]));
 // listEle.appendChild(liEle);

 let liEle = $(document.createElement("li"));
 liEle.append(document.createTextNode(listItems[i]));
 liEle.appendTo(listEle);
 }
}
```

5. Finally, slowly fade in the new sorted todo list, that is, **listEle**:

```
function replaceListElements(listEle, listItems){
listEle.hide();
listEle.empty();

 for (let i= 0; i<= listItems.length - 1; i++){
 let liEle = $(document.createElement("li"));
 liEle.append(document.createTextNode(listItems[i]));
 liEle.appendTo(listEle)
 }

 listEle.fadeIn('slow');
}
```

6. Now, open the HTML in your browser and click the Shuffle button. The todo list should fade out, shuffle, and fade in again:

Figure 4.17: Output Image

Now, let's go over the **Velocity.js** method. Go to <u>cdnjs.com</u> and get the **velocity.js** CDN URL.

Load the library into the head tag of your existing Todo-List-HTML using a script tag. This will allow you to use velocity.js within your code:

```
<head>
    // ... previous links and meta tags
<script src="https://cdnjs.cloudflare.com/ajax/libs/velocity/2.0.5/
velocity.min.js"></script>
</head>
```

7. Inside the **replaceListElements** function, you can now use Velocity to hide (by setting opacity to 0) the list element, **listEle**, and then empty the elements inside of it:

```
function replaceListElements(listEle, listItems){
  Velocity(listEle, { opacity: 0 }, { duration: 0 })
  listEle.innerHTML = "";


  for (let i= 0; i<= listItems.length - 1; i++){
    let liEle = document.createElement("li");
    liEle.appendChild(document.createTextNode(listItems[i]));
    listEle.appendChild(liEle)
  }
}
```

8. To fade the list element back in, animate **listEle** using Velocity and set the opacity to **1**. Set the code after the for loop:

```
function replaceListElements(listEle, listItems){
  Velocity(listEle, { opacity: 0 }, { duration: 0 })
  listEle.innerHTML = "";


  for (let i= 0; i<= listItems.length - 1; i++){
    let liEle = document.createElement("li");
    liEle.appendChild(document.createTextNode(listItems[i]));
    listEle.appendChild(liEle)
  }

  Velocity(listEle, { opacity: 1 }, { duration: 500 })
}
```

9. Now, open the HTML in your browser and click the *Shuffle* button. The **todo** list should fade out, shuffle, and fade in again.

10. Finally, using the Anime method, go to <u>cdnjs.com</u> and get the **Anime.js** CDN URL. It will appear the same as the previous output.

11. Load the library into the head tag of your existing Todo-List-HTML using a script tag. This will allow you to use **Anime.js** within your code:

```
<head>
     // ... previous links and meta tags
<script src="https://cdnjs.cloudflare.com/ajax/libs/animejs/2.2.0/
anime.min.js"></script>
</head>
```

12. Inside the **replaceListElements** function, you can now use **Anime.js** to move (by using translateX = -1000) the list element, **listEle**, out of view and then empty the elements inside of it:

```
function replaceListElements(listEle, listItems){
  anime({
    targets: listEle,
    translateX: -1000
  });

  listEle.innerHTML = "";

  for (let i= 0; i<= listItems.length - 1; i++){
    let liEle = document.createElement("li");
    liEle.appendChild(document.createTextNode(listItems[i]));
    listEle.appendChild(liEle)
  }
}
```

13. To show the newly shuffled todo list, use **Anime.js** to animate the **listEle** list element back into view (by using translateX = 0). Do so inside a timeout to ensure that the shuffling has been done already:

activity.anime.js

```
21 function replaceListElements(listEle, listItems){
22   anime({
23     // ANIME SOLUTION
24     targets: listEle,
25     translateX: -1000
26   });
27   listEle.innerHTML = "";
28
29
30   for (let i= 0; i<= listItems.length - 1; i++){
31     let liEle = document.createElement("li");
32     liEle.appendChild(document.createTextNode(listItems[i]));
33     listEle.appendChild(liEle)
34   }
```

The full code is available at: https://packt.live/2Kd08dx

14. Now, open the HTML in your browser and click the *Shuffle* button. The **todo** list should fade out, shuffle, and fade in again. It will appear the same as the previous output.

Chapter 5: Beyond the Fundamentals

Activity 5.01: Simple Number Comparison

Solution

1. Create the function signature:

```
function average_grade() {
```

2. Copy the function arguments to a variable. This should be a new Array instance:

```
var args = Array.prototype.slice.call(arguments);
```

3. Sum all the values of the arguments and store them in a variable:

```
var sum = 0;
for (let i=0; i<args.length; i++) {
    sum += Number(args[i]);
}
```

Remember to convert the grade values into a Number instance so that they can be correctly added together.

4. Get the average of the sum and store it in a variable:

```
var average = sum / args.length;
```

5. Using the average, calculate the student's grade and return it. This can simply be a list of conditionals:

```
if (average < 35) {
  return "F";
}
if (average >= 35 && average < 45) {
  return "D";
}
if (average >= 45 && average < 60) {
  return "C";
}
if (average >= 60 && average < 75) {
  return "B";
```

```
        }
        return "A";
    }
```

The output will be visible as follows:

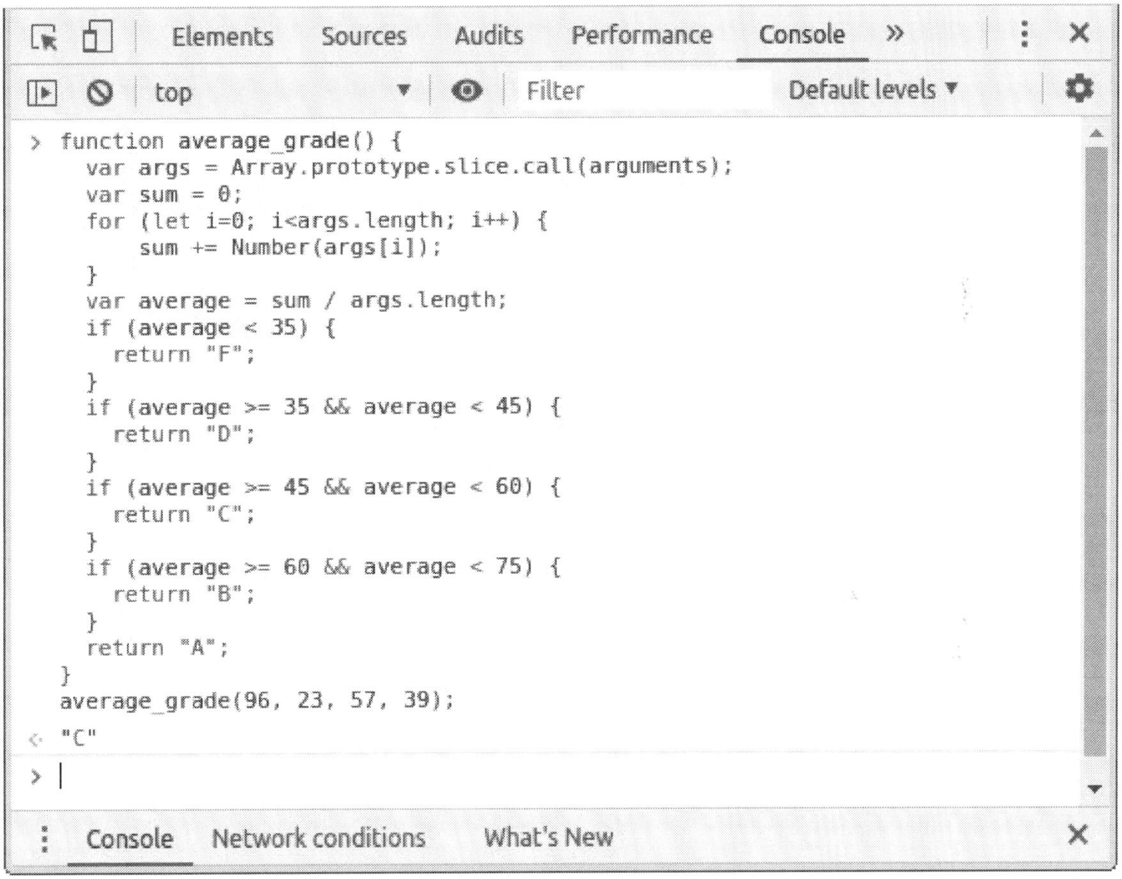

```
> function average_grade() {
    var args = Array.prototype.slice.call(arguments);
    var sum = 0;
    for (let i=0; i<args.length; i++) {
        sum += Number(args[i]);
    }
    var average = sum / args.length;
    if (average < 35) {
        return "F";
    }
    if (average >= 35 && average < 45) {
        return "D";
    }
    if (average >= 45 && average < 60) {
        return "C";
    }
    if (average >= 60 && average < 75) {
        return "B";
    }
    return "A";
  }
  average_grade(96, 23, 57, 39);
< "C"
> |
```

Figure 5.26: Activity 5.01 output

> **Note**
>
> The final condition will always be true if the others have failed, so the condition itself can be skipped. Each condition will not be evaluated if the previous condition has been returned from the function.

Activity 5.02: Creating a TODO Model

Solution

1. The first step is to declare the state. It must be declared outside of any function so that it exists between function calls:

```
let todos = [];
```

2. Next, create the helper function that will be used to find a TODO by **id** from the **state** array. To do this, simply look through the array and return the index once it's been found. If it isn't found and the end of the array is reached, then return **-1** to denote that no TODO with the specific **id** exists:

```
function modelFindIndex(state, id) {
  for (let i=0; i<state.length; i++) {
    if (state[i].id == id) {
      return i;
    }
  }
  return -1;
}
```

3. Now, create the function as described in the description of this activity:

```
function modelStateChange(state, action, data) {
```

4. The function will need to act differently, depending on the value of **action**. When modifying the data successfully, it should return the new state. First, handle adding a new TODO to the state for the **CREATE** action:

```
if (action == "CREATE") {
  console.log("created:", data);
  return state.concat(data);
}
```

Remember that the data needs to be written to the console with **console.log**.

5. Next, handle the **REMOVE** functionality. This will utilize the **modelFindIndex** function to locate the **TODO** to remove:

```
if (action == "REMOVE") {
  let data = modelFindIndex(todos, ev.detail);
   if (i > -1) {
     state = state.splice(i, 1);
     console.log("removed", data);
     return state
  }
 }
```

6. Finally, handle the **MODIFY** functionality. This step is a little more complex as the original data needs to be changed without changing the object reference:

```
if (action == "MODIFY") {
   let data = modelFindIndex(todos, ev.detail);
   if (i > -1) {
     state = state.splice(i, 1);
     console.log("removed", data);
     return state
  }
 }
}
```

Chapter 6: Understanding Core Concepts

Activity 6.01: Making Changes to the Model

Solution:

1. The page the form is in has an area to display messages. The form itself contains the title **textfield** and a description for the **textarea** field.

   The page loads in the model code from the previous chapter, but also a new script, which will be created shortly. The **body** tag has an in-page event handler assigned to its **onload** event, which will be included in the **create_todos.js** file.

   In order to use the model's module with events, you will need to extend it by providing an event handler for each action type. Add the following code to the bottom of the **model.js** file:

```
function modelInit() {
  document.addEventListener("CREATE", modelCreateHandler);
}
function modelCreateHandler(ev) {
  todos = modelStateChange(todos, "CREATE", ev.detail);
  document.dispatchEvent(new Event("CHANGED", {detail: {type:
"added", value: ev.detail}}));
}
```

2. In the **create_todos.js** file, add the **loadHandler** function:

```
function loadHandler() {
  model_init();
  let form = document.getElementById("todo_form");
  form.addEventListener("submit", createHandler);
  document.addEventListener("CHANGED", changedHandler);
}
```

   This function will initialize the model and set up any necessary event handlers. As you can see, it assigns the **CHANGED** event to the **changedHandler** function. Let's create that next.

3. **changedHandler** is a simple affair. It simply waits for the **CHANGED** event to be raised and then updates the notifications area when it does:

```
function changedHandler() {
   let msg = document.getElementById("notifications");
   msg.innerHTML = "The TODO model has been updated";
   setTimeout(() => {
      msg.innerHTML = "";
   }, 3000);
}
```

changedHandler clears the notifications area after three seconds to keep things clean.

4. Finally, you need to add the **createHandler** function, which handles the form's submission:

create_todos.js

```
16 function createHandler(ev) {
17    ev.preventDefault();
18    let title = document.getElementById("title").value,
19        description = document.getElementById("description").value,
20        msg = document.getElementById("notifications");
21    let errors = [];
22    if (title.trim() == "") {
23      errors = errors.concat(["Title is not valid"]);
24    }
25    if (description.trim() == "") {
26      errors = errors.concat(["Description is not valid"]);
27    }
28    if (errors.length > 0) {
29      msg.innerHTML = errors.join("/n");
30      setTimeout(() => {
```

The full code is available at: https://packt.live/2Xbd34R

The majority of this code simply ensures that values are supplied to the form before submission and will alert the user if this is not the case.

5. Now, give the application a spin. If all goes well, notifications should momentarily show when submitting the form, with different messages depending on whether the fields were populated. As an example, open the browser console and simply enter the following:

```
todos;
```

You should see the submitted **TODO** objects presented there, like so:

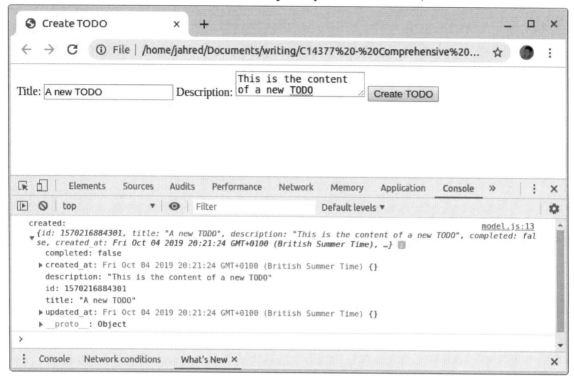

Figure 6.28: TODO submission form

Working with events provides a powerful means to keep your applications simple. What's more, it also empowers abstraction, allowing scripts to send data without them needing to know which other areas of your application are interested in those events. This promotes clean design and easier maintenance of your code.

Chapter 7: Popping the Hood

Activity 7.01: Finding out the Number of Stack Frames

Solution

- The function that establishes the call stack's limit is as follows:

  var frameCount = 0;

```
function stackOverflow() {
    frameCount++;
    stackOverflow();
}
```

  The solution starts out with the **frameCount** variable being initialized with the value **0**. The **stackOverflow()** function is declared, which will add 1 to the **frameCount** variable and then call itself, thus causing a stack overflow.

- Now, **setTimout()** function is initiated, which will log the value of **frameCount** to the console after a minimum of 500 milliseconds. Now, call the **stackOverflow()** function.

```
setTimeout(() => console.log(frameCount), 500);
stackOverflow();
```

  This takes the **console.log** function out of the main execution thread, allowing it to be called after the stack overflow error is thrown:

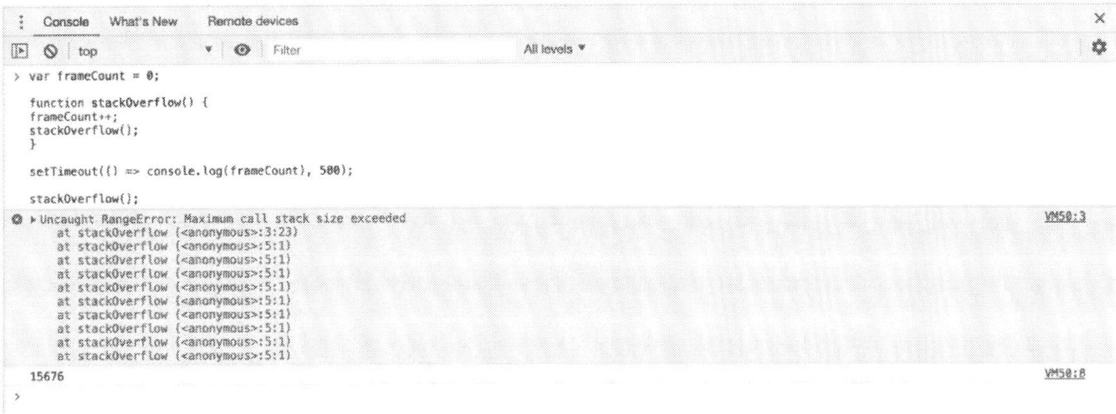

Figure 7.22: Showing the solution and number of stack frames being pushed before a stack overflow is triggered

Chapter 8: Browser APIs

Activity 8.01: Creating a Simple Fractal

Solution

1. We initialize the canvas and context as we did previously, but this time we add a point variable that we initialize with the coordinates of the center of the canvas:

```
let canvas = document.getElementById('canvas');
const width = window.innerWidth;
const height = window.innerHeight;
canvas.width = width;
canvas.height = height;
let context = canvas.getContext('2d');
// Set the starting point to the center of the canvas
let point = [width / 2, height / 2];
```

2. Then, we begin a new path and move the point to the coordinates that were assigned to the point variable:

```
context.beginPath();
context.moveTo(point[0], point[1]);
```

3. We declare i, which we will use as a multiplier to tell the function how long a line should be. We also declare two constants to hold the values for a margin between the fractal that we're drawing and the edge of the canvas, as well as a multiplier, which is used to increase the line length that is drawn. Then, we start a while loop, which will keep going while the point remains inside the canvas' bounds (plus the margin on each side):

```
let i = 1;
const OFFSET = 10;
const MARGIN = 5;
while (
  point[0] > MARGIN &&
  point[0] < width - MARGIN &&
  point[1] > MARGIN &&
  point[1] < height - MARGIN
) {
```

4. Inside the while loop, the values inside the point array are increased or decreased, depending on which direction the line is being drawn and depending on the value of i:

```
point[1] = point[1] - OFFSET * i;
```

5. Then, the lineTo function is called with the values in the point variable. Every other time a line is drawn, **i** is incremented. This means that the line's length doubles after each second drawing of a line. You could also increase **i** each time a line is drawn, and the result would be greater spacing between the lines:

```
context.lineTo(point[0], point[1]);
  point[0] = point[0] + OFFSET * i;
  i++;
  context.lineTo(point[0], point[1]);
  point[1] = point[1] + OFFSET * i;
  context.lineTo(point[0], point[1]);
  point[0] = point[0] - OFFSET * i;
  i++;
  context.lineTo(point[0], point[1]);
}
```

6. Finally, when the while loop's termination condition is met (when the point reaches within 5 pixels of one of the edges of the canvas), the stroke() method of the context is called to add a stroke to the lines we've described:

```
context.stroke();
```

There are many more methods available in the Canvas API, and many possibilities for their use. You can draw complicated patterns, pictures, and graphs, and animate anything you draw. You should explore the Canvas API in more depth to find out what it can do.

Activity 8.02: Playing Sound and Controlling Frequency Using Two Oscillators

Solution

1. Initialize an audio context and a volume node:

```
let context = new AudioContext();
let volume = context.createGain();
```

2. Create a gain node and connect it to the context's destination:

```
volume.connect(context.destination);
```

3. Initialize two oscillators (one for each coordinate of the cursor):

```
let osciA = context.createOscillator();
let osciB = context.createOscillator();
```

4. Set the oscillator types (feel free to use any types you like), connect them to the volume node, and call their start() methods:

```
osciA.type = 'sawtooth';
osciB.type = 'square';
osciA.connect(volume);
osciB.connect(volume);
osciA.start();
osciB.start();
```

5. Create an event listener that listens for the **mousemove** event on the **document** and set the oscillators' frequencies based on the cursor's position:

```
document.addEventListener('mousemove', event => {
  osciA.frequency.value = event.clientY;
  osciB.frequency.value = event.clientX;
});
```

The callback function that's passed to the event listener assigns the cursor's x and y values to the two oscillator nodes' frequency values every time the 'mousemove' event is fired. This is a simple solution: it inherently limits the upper-frequency values for each oscillator depending on the width and height of the browser window. This is fine as a demonstration, but a better implementation would assign the same arbitrary upper-frequency value at the right-most and bottom-most parts of the document, no matter its dimensions.

Activity 8.03: Audio Visualization

Solution

1. Create a simple HTML file with a link to a JavaScript file called scripts.js (or anything you want to call it), with a <canvas> element in the body and with an ID of canvas in the DevTools console:

```
<!-- index.html -->
<!DOCTYPE html>
<html>
  <head>
    <script src='scripts.js'></script>
  </head>
  <body>
    <canvas id='canvas'></canvas>
  </body>
</html>
```

2. In the scripts.js file, we will add an event listener on the document listening for a click event. As we saw in the *Audio* API section of this chapter, in many modern browsers, audio is disabled until the user has interacted with the page, so waiting for the click event is an easy way to make sure we don't get any errors in this regard:

```
// scripts.js
document.addEventListener('click', () => {
```

3. We then get hold of the canvas element, create a canvas context, set the canvas' width and height, and get its center x/y coordinates. We also instantiate a variable that will hold the Y value of the mouse's position:

```
// initialise canvas and related variables
let canvas = document.getElementById('canvas');
let canvasContext = canvas.getContext('2d');
let width = window.innerWidth;
let height = window.innerHeight;
canvas.width = width;
canvas.height = height;
let centerX = width / 2;
let centerY = height / 2;
let mouseY; // this will be set in the 'mousemove' event handler
```

4. Then, we will create an audio context, a gain node, an oscillator node, and an analyzer node. We connect the oscillator to the volume node and the analyzer node, and then connect the volume node to the audio context's destination:

```
// initialise Audio context, nodes and related variables
let audioContect = new AudioContext();
let volume = audioContect.createGain();
let osciA = audioContect.createOscillator();
let analyser = audioContect.createAnalyser();
let waveform = new Float32Array(analyser.frequencyBinCount);
osciA.type = 'sine';
osciA.connect(volume);
osciA.connect(analyser);
volume.connect(audioContect.destination);
volume.gain.value = 1;
osciA.start();
```

5. Next, we listen for mousemove events, and in the callback function for the event, we assign the cursor's X position to the oscillator's frequency value and the cursor's Y position to the mouseY variable. This means that the cursor's X position will control the frequency of the oscillation. We'll see what the mouseY variable is used for shortly:

```
// set oscillator frequency from mouse's x-position
document.addEventListener('mousemove', event => {
  osciA.frequency.value = event.clientX;
  mouseY = event.clientY;
});
```

6. Now, we come to the meat of the application. We call the draw() function. This function tells the browser that we want to draw a frame of an animation, and by proving the draw() function as the callback, it repeats this function once for each time the page is rendered:

```
// start drawing
draw();
```

7. Next, we get the waveform data from the analyzer, which is copied to the waveform array. Then, we clear the canvas from any previous stroke() methods and begin a new path:

```
// the draw function
function draw() {
  let drawing = window.requestAnimationFrame(draw); // Repeat the
drawing function on every animation frame
  analyser.getFloatTimeDomainData(waveform);
  canvasContext.clearRect(0,0,canvas.width,canvas.height); // empty
the canvas, so we don't get arcs drawn on top of each other
  canvasContext.beginPath();
```

8. Now, we come to looping through the waveform array. For each item in the array (which represents points of the waveform), we will plot a small section of a circle. The circle will be divided into as many sections as there are items in the array. Each section has a radius of half the width of the canvas, minus the mouse's Y position, plus the current chunk of the waveform's amplitude (multiplied by an arbitrary number, that is, 15). The result of this could be a negative number if the mouse is more than halfway across the screen, so we wrap the whole thing in Math.abs(), which returns the absolute value (no negatives!) of a number:

```
// plot a section of the circle for each part of the
waveform
    for(let i = 0; i<waveform.length; i++) {
        let radius = Math.abs(((width / 2) - mouseY) + (waveform[i] *
15));
```

9. Next, we need to set the start angle and end angle of the arc in radians. A whole circle is 2*π radians, but we're dividing the circle into as many arcs as there are items in the waveform array. Therefore, we can calculate the starting angle as ((2 / waveform.length) * i) *π, where waveforms.length is how many items there are and i is the current chunk of the waveform/our circle we're on. We just add 1 to i for the end angle as each chunk's end angle is the same as the next one's starting angle:

```
        let startAngle = ((2 / waveform.length) * i) * Math.PI;
        let endAngle = ((2 / waveform.length) * i) * Math.PI;
```

10. After all that is done, and we call the arc() method of the canvas context, we can call the stroke() method to add a stroke to all the arcs we just plotted:

```
        canvasContext.arc(centerX, centerY, radius, startAngle,
endAngle);
    }
```

11. Put that all together, run it, and click on the page: we should get a very nice oscillating circle, whose diameter increases with the cursor's y-position, and the oscillation of which matches the sound of the sine wave coming from the speakers. This, incidentally, can be controlled with the cursor's x-position. Big fun:

```
        canvasContext.stroke();
    };
})
```

Chapter 9: Working with Node.js

Activity 9.01: Create a Web Application to Upload, Store, and Save Image Details

Solution

1. Let's first go through the directory structure and define the folders to upload the images:

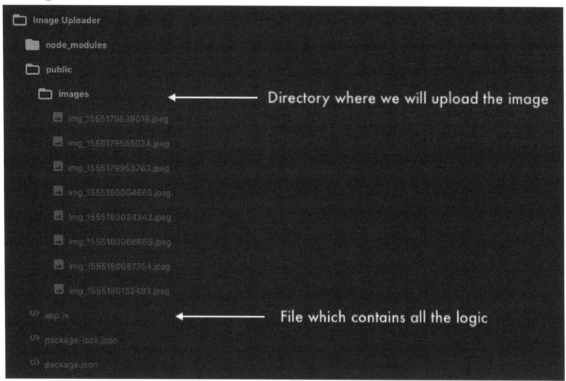

Figure 9.22: Directory structure for this activity

As you can see, in this project you will try to upload images in the **public/images** directory. This directory must be present at the root of the project and the current user should have read and write access to this directory. By default, you will get both the permissions to this directory.

> **Note**
>
> The source code will only contain two files (**app.js** and **package.json**). All the other files shown in the **images** directory in the preceding figure will not be present there. Once you start uploading files, you will see all the uploaded images there.

Before proceeding further, be sure to create a **public/images** directory in the root of this project that relates to **app.js** and **package.json**. The currently logged-in user of your machine must have the permissions to add files in this directory.

2. The first step is to import all the dependencies:

```
const express    = require('express');
const multer             = require('multer');
const MySQL              = require('MySQL');
const morgan     = require('morgan')
const app                = express();
const port               = 3000;
```

3. Then let's configure **morgan** to log each of our request details in the console. You can use **morgan** as a middleware:

```
// Middleware for logging requests
app.use(morgan(':method :status :url - :response-time ms'));
```

4. Now let's configure the database. In this project, you will use a **MySQL** database:

```
/*
 * Database
 */
// Creating MySQL Connection
let connection = MySQL.createConnection({
    host          : 'localhost',
    user          : 'root',
    password      : '12345678',
    database      : 'packt_JavaScript'
});

// Connection to db
connection.connect();
```

Make sure you pass the credentials of the user you created earlier while going through the *Setting Up Databases* section.

5. When your application has established a database connection, it's time to install **multer** by executing the following command through the terminal in the root of the project:

```
npm i multer --save
```

6. Now, let's configure **multer** by adding the code from the **app.js** file:

```
/*
 * File Upload Settings
 */
let storage = multer.diskStorage({
        destination: (req, file, cb) => {
                cb(null, 'public/images')
        },
        filename: (req, file, cb) => {
                let ext = file.originalname.split('.').pop();
                cb(null, 'img_' + Date.now() + '.' + ext);
        }
});
let upload = multer({storage: storage});
```

This code will set the destination where all files will be uploaded, which is **public/images**, and you are also changing the **filename** after upload to avoid issues with duplicate filenames.

7. Now let's configure some routes in your application:

app.js

```
39 /*
40 * Routing
41 */
42 // Landing route
43 app.get('/', (req, res) => res.send('Hello World!'))
44
45 // Upload image route
46 app.post('/upload/image', upload.single('image'), function (req, re s) {
47         // Column name: values
48         let payload = {
49                 filename: req.file.filename,
50                 type: req.file.mimetype,
51                 original_name: req.file.originalname,
52                 path: req.file.path,
53                 size: req.file.size
54 }
```

The full code is available at: https://packt.live/2NIE6RR

8. The last step is to start the server:

```
// Start listening to requests
app.listen(port, () => console.log(`App listening on port http://
localhost:${port}!`))
```

9. That's it. The server is now up and running. The final thing is to send a request to upload the image on the server. For this, we will use Postman (the Chrome extension) as our client:

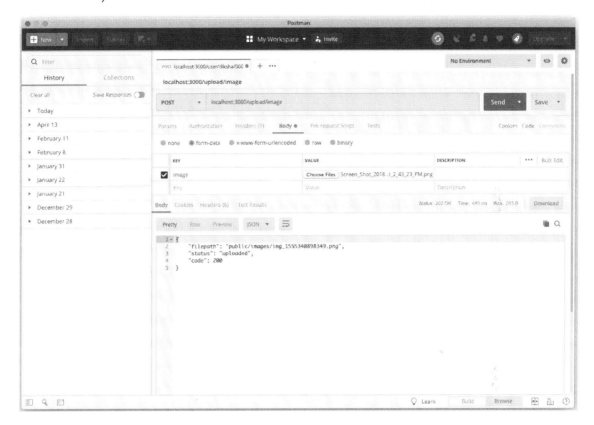

Figure 9.23: API response in Postman

Chapter 10: Accessing External Resources

Activity 10.01: Implement REST Service Calls Using Various Techniques

Solution:

1. Use **$.ajax()** with **method: 'post'** and **dataType: 'json'**:

`solution_using_jquery_ajax.html`

```
$.ajax({
    method: 'post',
    dataType: 'json',
    url: 'https://reqres.in/api/users',
```

2. Enclose your data fields in an object, **{}**:

```
data: {
    "name": "Beyonce Knowles",
    "occupation": "artist"
},
```

3. Create a **success** function to output the expected values:

```
success: function (data) {
    console.log("Returned id " + data.id +
                ", createdAt " + data.createdAt);
    console.log(data);
    }
});
```

The boilerplate HTML is omitted and left as an exercise for you. The preceding code would result in something like the following in the JavaScript Console in Google Chrome. (All the solutions presented have similar output):

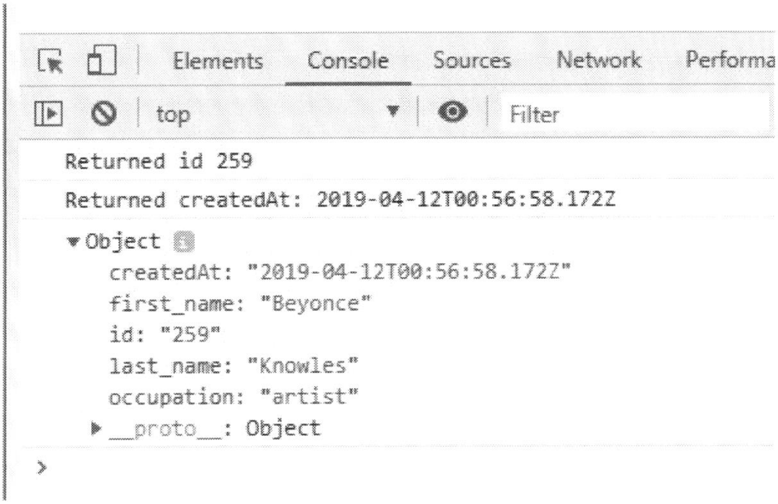

Figure 10.17: JavaScript Console output

4. Now, let's get the same output using the `$.post()` method and using the file `solution_using_jquery_post.html`:

```
$.post('https://reqres.in/api/users',
```

5. Enclose your data fields in an object, `{}`:

```
{
        "name": "Beyonce Knowles",
        "occupation": "artist"
    },
```

6. Create a **success** function to output the expected values:

```
function (data) {
        console.log("Returned id " + data.id +
                ", createdAt " + data.createdAt);
        console.log(data);
    },
```

7. As the last parameter to **$.post()**, use the **'json'** value to indicate the expected JSON return type:

```
'json'
    );
```

The output will be the same as is shown in *Figure* 10.17.

8. Finally, create a new **XMLHttpRequest** object:

```
const url = "https://reqres.in/api/users";
var xhttp = new XMLHttpRequest();
```

9. Call **open('POST')**:

```
xhttp.open('POST', url);
```

10. Set the **Content-type** and **Accept** request headers to the appropriate values:

```
xhttp.setRequestHeader("Content-type", "application/json");
xhttp.setRequestHeader('Accept', 'application/json');
```

11. Create a function for **onreadystatechange** that checks for a status code of **201 (Created)** and parses the JSON data with **JSON.parse()**:

```
xhttp.onreadystatechange = function() {
    if (this.readyState == 4 && this.status == 201) {
        const data = JSON.parse(this.response);
        console.log("Returned id " + data.id +
                    ", createdAt " + data.createdAt);
        console.log(data);
    }
}
```

12. Call **JSON.stringify()** on the input data to convert it to JSON format:

```
var data = JSON.stringify({
    "name": "Beyonce Knowles",
    "occupation": "artist"
});
```

13. Send the JSON data when calling **send()**:

```
xhttp.send(data);
```

The output will be the same as is shown in *Figure* 10.17.

Chapter 11: Creating Clean and Maintainable Code

Activity 11.01: Expanding Phone Number Matching Patterns to Accept Multiple Formats

Solution:

1. Observe that only the characters at the beginning of each pattern differ, but the last characters, **XXX–XXXX**, are the same in both patterns.

2. For the differing characters, for our regex to match either format correctly, you can specify the regex snippets that correspond to each format as alternate expressions of an alternation. Recall that alternations take the form of **(expression1|expression2)**:

```
([2-9]\d{2}-|\([2-9]\d{2}\) )
where Regex for XXX-\Regex for (XXX)
```

3. Combine it with the rest of the original regex to get the complete regex:

```
^([2-9]\d{2}-|\([2-9]\d{2}\) )\d{3}-\d{4}$
```

4. Remember that the original regex, **\d{3}-\d{4}**, matches **XXX–XXXX**, which is the same for both patterns. We only needed the alternation for the beginning parts of each pattern that differed. The **^** and **$** characters also enforce that there are no other characters before or after the acceptable ones.

Now, when you replace this correct regex into our tool, only the first two test strings match (as expected)

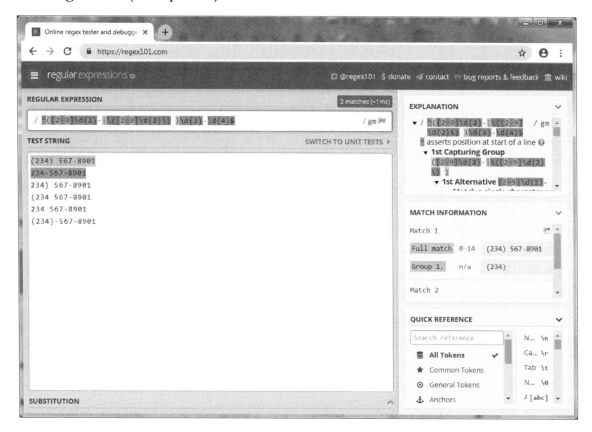

Figure 11.23: After using the correct regex, only the first two test strings match (as expected)

In *Exercise 11.01*, *The Effect of the g Flag*, and this activity, we created regex expressions to accept US number formats. We will now modify the regex to accept non-US number formats.

Activity 11.02: Expanding Phone Number Matching Patterns to Accept a Particular Format

Solution:

1. Construct the regex for the **+xxx** pattern (where between 1-3 digits are acceptable):

```
(\+\d{1,3} )?
```

We need two things here:

The first + needs to be escaped due to it being a special character.

Notice the parenthesis with ? after it. This specifies that whole expression within the parenthesis can occur 0 or 1 times. In other words, the characters in the expression are optional. The \d{1,3} expression is a range quantifier requiring between 1 and 3 digits.

2. By prepending this to the regex from the previous activity, the whole regex is now as follows:

```
^(\+\d{1,3} )?([2-9]\d{2}-|\([2-9]\d{2}\) )\d{3}-\d{4}$
```

> **Note**
>
> See the previous activity for a full description of the latter parts of the regex.

3. To kick it up one more notch, here are some of the changes we can make to the regex that allows us to use space or dot characters as digit separators rather than only dashes:

```
^(\+\d{1,3} )?([2-9]\d{2}|\([2-9]\d{2}\))[-. ]\d{3}[-. ]\d{4}$
```

The [-.] set allows a dash, dot, or space character to be used as the separator.

This modification now allows all the formats shown in the following screenshot to match:

> **Note**
>
> One flaw with this regex is that it allows you to mix and match what characters are used as separators. For example, you can use a dash and dot, like so: 234-567.8910. It is possible to make the regex stronger, but the result will end up being very long and convoluted.

Activity 11.03: Refactoring to Clean Code

Solution:

> **Note**
>
> There are many ways the code could be refactored. The following solution represents one way, along with explanatory comments.

1. Use the **activity_solution.html** file. The HTML code remains the same as the original code. Only the contents of the **<script>** section are replaced.

2. We start refactoring the code by creating a function called **processForm()**:

```
document.getElementById("calc_button").addEventListener("click
", processForm);

function processForm() {
    resetErrorsAndResults();
    const formFields = getFormFields();

    const validationError = formFields.validate();
    if (validationError) {
        displayError(validationError);
        return;
    }

    const result = doCalculation(formFields);
    displayResult(result);
}
```

The original code had one very long method that did all the form field processing, validations, and calculations. The new code creates new methods for different concerns. These methods are short and mostly focused on just one task.

The code reads like a narrative story with paragraphs and sentences in mostly plain English. It is easy to see the logic and flow just by reading it, and there's not much clutter: reset the errors and results, get the form fields, validate the fields and show errors (if any), do the calculation, and display the results. The gory details of each of these are contained within other methods.

3. We will also create a function called **resetErrorsAndResults()**. By the name and implementation, it is easy to tell what the purpose of this function is, and the function is limited to just that specific purpose:

```
function resetErrorsAndResults() {
    document.getElementById("error").innerHTML = "";
    document.getElementById("result").innerHTML = "";
}
```

4. For the next refactoring, we have decided to create a class that holds form field values and performs validations:

activity_solution.html

```
63  class FormFields {
64      constructor(numHours, payRate, workerType) {
65          this.numHours = numHours;
66          this.payRate = payRate;
67          this.workerType = workerType;
68      }
69
70      validate() {
71          let validationError = this.validateNumHours();
72          if (validationError) {
73              return validationError;
74          }
```

The full code is available at: https://packt.live/372KXxp

Validation methods are simple and only return a string with an error message if the regex test fails. Displaying error messages is a separate concern (unlike the original code, which combined the concerns). It contains a constructor where the form field values are passed in rather than us having to get the values directly from the form, thus allowing the class and validations to be tested independently of the form itself.

5. Next, we create a function called **getFormFields()**. This function is limited to getting the values from the form and creating an instance of the **FormFields** class:

```
function getFormFields() {
    const numHours = document.getElementById("numHours").value;
    const payRate = document.getElementById("payRate").value;
    const workerType =
        document.querySelector('input[name="workerType"]:checked').
value;

    return new FormFields(numHours, payRate, workerType);
}
```

These methods have no side effects as they facilitate testing. This is because the return values are always predicable for a given set of input parameters.

6. The **displayError()** and **displayResult()** functions are straightforward and do just one thing:

```
function displayError(error) {
    document.getElementById("error").innerHTML = error;
}
function displayResult(result) {
    document.getElementById("result").innerHTML =
        `Total pay check: ${result.toFixed(2)}`;
}
```

The **switch** statement in the original code was just screaming out "refactor me" to separate functions for each case! We will refactor this so that it uses an associative array called **calculateFunctions**. The key of each entry in the array is **workerType** and the user that's selected from the radio buttons, along with a reference to the function that contains the corresponding calculation logic for the value. These are minimal comments since the method, object, and variable names are self-documenting.

7. Also, the **calculateStandardWorkerPay()**,
   calculateNoOvertimeWorkerPay(), and
   calculateDoubleOvertimeWorkerPay() functions take the same two
   parameters and have the same return value definition, so they could be called
   abstractly in **doCalculation()**:

activity_solution.html

```
108 const calculateFunctions = {
109     "standard": calculateStandardWorkerPay,
110     "no_overtime": calculateNoOvertimeWorkerPay,
111     "double_overtime": calculateDoubleOvertimeWorkerPay
112 };
113
114 function doCalculation(formFields) {
115     // determine function to use for calculation based on worker type
116     const calculateFunction = calculateFunctions[formFields.workerType];
117     return calculateFunction(formFields.numHours, formFields.payRate);
118 }
119
120 function calculateStandardWorkerPay(numHours, payRate) {
121     if (numHours < 40) {
122         return numHours * payRate;
123     }
```

The full code is available at: https://packt.live/373ThN5

In a real application, you may consider using one of the many available validation
frameworks rather than rolling your own. For calculation purposes, this implementation
chose to use functions in an associative array. One alternative to consider is creating a
class hierarchy where subclasses implement or override a calculation method in a base
class.

Chapter 12: Using Next-Generation JavaScript

Activity 12.01: Creating a Project to Recognize and Compile TypeScript Files

Solution:

1. The first step is to create a new project directory, then **cd** into it, and initialize it for npm:

```
mkdir my_app
cd my_app
npm init
```

2. Next, install Parcel as a global library:

```
npm install -g parcel
```

3. Now, you will need to install TypeScript, which you can also save as a global library:

```
npm install -g typescript
```

4. To generate the configuration for TypeScript, you simply need to call the TypeScript CLI tool, **tsc**, and pass it the **--init** flag:

```
tsc --init
```

If all went well, you should be presented with a message such as the following:

```
message TS6071: Successfully created a tsconfig.json file.
```

You should also find a new **tsconfig.json** file in the root of your project folder.

5. Next, create a directory called **src** and place an **index.ts** file within it. Add the following code as the file's content:

```
const message:string = "Hello, World!";
console.log(message);
```

6. With everything in place, update the **package.json** file to include the following script:

```
"build": "parcel build src/index.ts"
```

7. Finally, run the script by invoking the **npm** executable:

```
npm run build
```

You should see a successful **Built** message output onscreen, as well as the expected **dist** folder containing transpiled **js** files in the project root.

Chapter 13: JavaScript Programming Paradigms

Activity 13.01: Creating a Calculator App

Solution

1. Create an empty file and call it **procedural.js**.

2. Initialize an array that will maintain the history of function calls:

```
lethistoryList = [];
```

3. Now, create simple addition, subtraction, multiplication, division, and power functions:

procedural.js

```
3 function add(m, n){
4 historyList.push(['ADD', m, n]);
5 return m+n;
6 }
7
8 function subtract(m, n){
9 historyList.push(['SUB', m, n]);
10 return m-n;
11 }
12
13 function multiply(m, n){
14 historyList.push(['MUL', m, n]);
15 return m*n;
16 }
```

The full code is available at: https://packt.live/2Xf6kHk

4. Create a **history** function, which will maintain the history of function calls:

```
function history(){
 historyList.map((command, index)=>{
  console.log(index+1+'.', command.join(' '));
 })
}
```

Call all the functions one by one with some random numbers as parameters:

```
console.log('ADD 2 3 :', add(2, 3));
console.log('SUB 2 3 :', subtract(2, 3));
console.log('MUL 2 3 :', multiply(2, 3));
console.log('DIV 2 3 :', divide(2, 3));
console.log('POW 2 3 :', pow(2, 3));
```

5. Now, print the **history**:

```
console.log('----------------HISTORY---------------');
history();
```

The output of this code will be as follows:

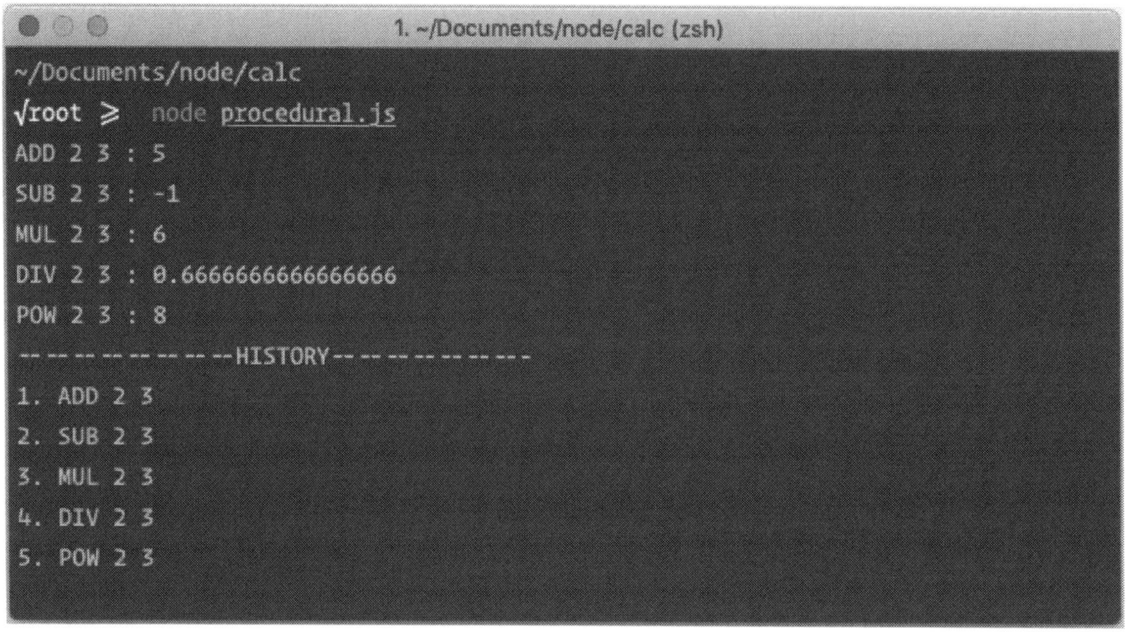

Figure 13.15: Output with the procedural approach

6. Now, create a class and call it **calculator**:

```
class Calculator {
}
```

7. Then, initialize a **historyList** array, which will maintain the history of all function calls:

```
constructor() {
  this.historyList = []
}
```

8. Now, create simple **add**, **subtract**, **multiply**, **divide**, and **pow** methods:

oop.js

```
6   add(m, n) {
7     this.historyList.push(['ADD', m, n]);
8     return m+n;
9   }
10
11  subtract(m, n) {
12    this.historyList.push(['SUB', m, n]);
13    return m-n;
14  }
15
16  multiply(m, n) {
17    this.historyList.push(['MUL', m, n]);
18    return m*n;
19  }
```

The full code is available at: https://packt.live/2O70oMi

9. Add one more method, which will show the history of the operations:

```
history() {
  this.historyList.map((command, index)=>{
    console.log(index+1+'.', command.join(' '));
  })
}
```

10. Lastly, create an instance of this class and call its method with simple numbers to perform mathematical operations:

```
let calc = new Calculator();
console.log('ADD 2 3 :', calc.add(2, 3));
console.log('SUB 2 3 :', calc.subtract(2, 3));
console.log('MUL 2 3 :', calc.multiply(2, 3));
console.log('DIV 2 3 :', calc.divide(2, 3));
console.log('POW 2 3 :', calc.pow(2, 3));
```

11. To check its history, call the **history** method of the **calculator** class:

```
calc.history();
```

The output of this code will be as follows:

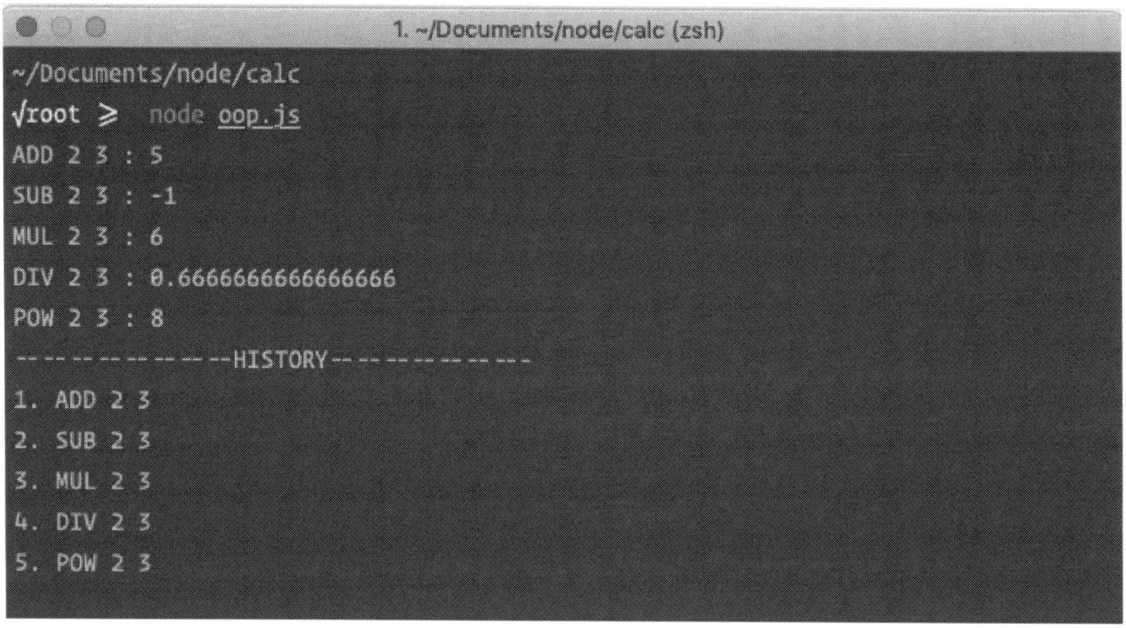

Figure 13.16: Output with the object-oriented approach

Chapter 14: Understanding Functional Programming

Activity 14.01: Blackjack Card Functions

Solution:

1. In the **blackjack/start.html** file, find the opening script tag and add some functions for defining the elements of a deck and creating an ordered deck:

solution.html

```
88 const suits =
89      () => [
90          { suit: "hearts", symbol: '&#9829;' },     // symbol: '♥'
91          { suit: 'diamonds', symbol: '&#9830;' },   // symbol: '♦'
92          { suit: 'spades', symbol: '&#9824;' },     // symbol: '♠'
93          { suit: 'clubs', symbol: '&#9827;' }       // symbol: '♣'
94      ];
95 const rankNames =
96      () => ['A', '2', '3', '4', '5', '6', '7', '8', '9', '10', 'J', 'Q', 'K'];
97
98 const ranks =
99      rankNames => rankNames.map(
100         (rank, index) => ({ rank, value: Math.min(10, index + 1) 101 }));
```

The full code is available at: https://packt.live/2QgJ0Y2

2. Below this code, define how to create a deck by adding the core functional programming methods:

```
const compose =
    (...fns) => input => fns.reduceRight((prev, fn) => fn(prev),
input);

const pipe = (...fns) => input => fns.reduce((prev, fn) => fn(prev),
input);

const map = fx => arr => arr.map(fx);
```

3. Next, add the functions for shuffling a deck, as we did in *Exercise 14.09: Using the pipe Method to Create a Card Shuffling Function*:

solution.html

```
117 const addRandom =
118     randomizer => deck => deck.map(card => ({
119         random: randomizer(),
120         card
121     }));
122
123 const sortByRandom =
124     deck => [...deck].sort((a, b) => a.random - b.random);
125
126 const shuffle =
127     (deck, randomizer) => {
128         const doShuffle = pipe(
129             addRandom(randomizer),
130             sortByRandom,
131             map(card => card.card)
132         );
```

The full code is available at: https://packt.live/2QlDGCZ

4. Now, we will add functions for drawing a card, getting the sum of a player's cards, checking whether a hand is over 21 points, and checking whether the game is over:

```
const draw =
    (deck, n = 1) => [deck.slice(0, n), deck.slice(n)];


const sumCards =
    cards => cards.reduce((total, card) => total + card.value, 0);


const isBust =
    total => total > 21;


const isGameOver =
    (bust, stay) => bust || stay;
```

5. Next, we need to add a way to update the visual display and the cards shown to the user. One way this can be done is as follows:

```
const updateCardDisplay =
    ({ updateHTML }, hand) => {
        const cardHtml = hand.map((card, index) =>
            `<div class="card ${card.suit}"
                style="top: -${index * 120}px;
                    left: ${index * 100}px;">
                <div class="top rank">${card.rank}</div>
                <div class="bigsuit">${card.symbol}</div>
                <div class="bottom rank">${card.rank}</div>
```

```
                  </div>`);
          updateHTML("cards", cardHtml.join(""));
      };
```

6. The next part of the visual display is the status display, which tells the user the sum of their hand and whether the game is over. The implementation that will be used in this solution consists of the two functions shown in the following code:

```
const showOrHide =
    (updateStyle, element, hide) =>
        updateStyle(element, "display", hide ? "none" : "");


const updateStatusDisplay =
    ({ updateStyle, updateHTML }, hand, stay) => {
        const total = sumCards(hand);
        updateHTML("totalSpan", total);
        const bust = isBust(total);
        const gameover = isGameOver(bust, stay);
        showOrHide(updateStyle, "playBtn", !gameover);
        showOrHide(updateStyle, "hitBtn", gameover);
        showOrHide(updateStyle, "stayBtn", gameover);
        let statusMsg = gameover ?
            "Game over.  Press New Game button to start again." :
            "Select Hit or Stay";
        statusMsg = bust ? "You went bust!!! " + statusMsg :
statusMsg;
        updateHTML("statusMsg", statusMsg);
    };
```

7. Now, we're going to add functions for each action a user can take, such as **play**, **stay**, and **hit**. We will call these handlers:

```
const playHandler = (randomizer, { getState, setState }) => () => {
    const orderedDeck = createOrderedDeck(suits(),
ranks(rankNames()));
    let gameDeck = shuffle(orderedDeck, randomizer);
    [hand, gameDeck] = draw(gameDeck, 2);
    setState(hand, gameDeck);
  };


const hitHandler = ({ getState, setState }) => () => {
    [hand, gameDeck] = getState();
    [card, gameDeck] = draw(gameDeck, 1);
    setState(hand.concat(card), gameDeck);
  };
```

```
const stayHandler = ({ getState, setState }) => () => {
    [hand, gameDeck] = getState();
setState(hand, gameDeck, true);
};
```

8. You may have noticed that, in the solution steps, there are some variables that haven't been defined. We've saved these for a section at the end that includes all non-purely functional code:

`Solution.html`

```
206 // impure functions
207
208 const byId =
209      elementId => document.getElementById(elementId);
210
211 const updateHTML =
212      (elementId, html) => byId(elementId).innerHTML = html;
213
214 const updateStyle =
215      (elementId, style, value) => byId(elementId).style[style] = value;
216
217 const randomizer =
218      Math.random;
```

The full code is available at: https://packt.live/2FnuFCH

9. We now have almost a completely working game. All we need to do is set the state and call that to tell the game to start:

```
const createState = (dom) => {
    let _state;
    const getState = () => [..._state];
    const setState =
        (hand, gameDeck, stay = false) => {
            _state = [hand, gameDeck];
            updateCardDisplay(dom, hand);
            updateStatusDisplay(dom, hand, stay);
        };
    return { getState, setState };
}


startGame(createState(dom));
```

With these steps done, you should now be able to open the HTML file in a browser and have a running version of the game, as shown in the following screenshot:

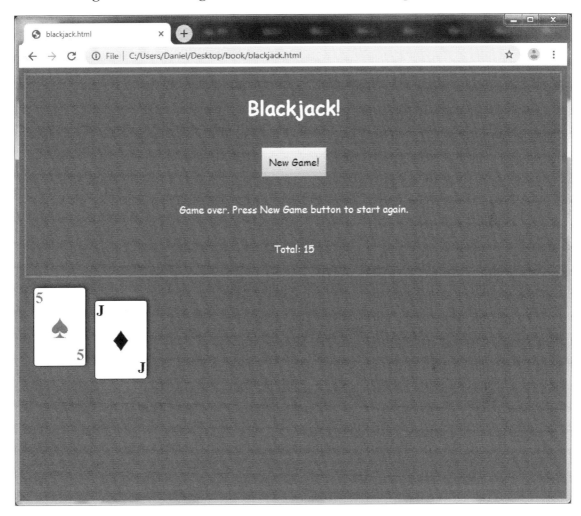

Figure 14.17: Screenshot of the Blackjack game

If you're unsure about whether you followed the solution steps correctly, feel free to take a look at the **blackjack/solution.html** file and compare it with your own implementation.

Chapter 15: Asynchronous Tasks

Activity 15.01: Refactoring Promise Code to await/async Syntax

Solution

Here's one implementation of equivalent code that uses **async/await**:

1. Define the promise variables as follows:

```
(async () => {
    let p1 = use1();
    let p2 = use2();
    let p3 = use3();
```

2. It would not have been correct to place the **await** keyword in the initial block when calling each function like this:

```
let p1 = await use1();
let p2 = await use2();
let p3 = await use3();
```

This is because each of the use cases has a different timeout defined. If you used **await** when calling **use1()**, it would have caused a delay of 3 seconds until it completed before **use2()** was even initiated, which is not what you want. Rather, our desire is for all three use cases to trigger one right after the other with no delay, so they execute concurrently.

3. You then have the three **await** keywords:

```
await p1;
await p2;
await p3;
```

4. It made sense to refactor each case into its own asynchronous functions: **use1()**, **use2()**, and **use3()**. The **async** keyword indicates that these functions are asynchronous ones (you could have used inline **async** functions, but this would have made for rather confusing and awkward syntax):

activity1_solution.js

```
31      console.log("All done!");
32 })();
33
34 async function use1() {
35      let response = await addDelay(3000, fetch(nextEventUrl));
36      let nextEvents = await response.json();
37      console.log("Use case 1: " + nextEvents.events[0].strEvent);
38 }
39
40 async function use2() {
41      let response = await fetch(nextEventUrl);
42      await addDelay(1000);
43      let nextEvents = await response.json();
44      console.log("Use case 2: " + nextEvents.events[1].strEvent);
```

The full code is available at: https://packt.live/32JulHw

In this activity, the order in which you wait for promises does not matter. Even though **await use1** will end up waiting 3 seconds, by the time **await use2** and **await use3** are called, both of those promises would have already been completed a second or two before, so they would just move on right away.

Activity 15.02: Further Simplifying Promise Code to Remove Function Parameters

Solution

Here's one possible implementation. The two functions are very similar and have been refactored using two different styles for demonstration purposes. However, it is perfectly acceptable to solve the challenge using one or the other technique for both of the functions:

1. In technique #1, refactor **getTeamsInLeague** so that it now only takes one parameter, **(leagueName)**, rather than two parameters that are actually needed to determine the full result **(leagueData, leagueName)**. The other parameter is deferred until later:

```
function getTeamsInLeague(leagueName) {
```

2. In technique #1, instead of returning the promise from **myFetch** directly, you return another curried function that takes **leagueData** as its parameter (the parameter you deferred in the last step). It is only a partially applied function at this point:

```
return leagueData => {
    const leagueId = findLeagueId(leagueData, leagueName);
        return myFetch(ALL_TEAMS_URL, {id: leagueId});
    }
}
```

3. Technique #2 is really the same idea, but uses a function variable and multiple levels of arrow functions rather than a regular function:

```
// technique #2 - use a function variable and multiple arrow functions
const getPlayersOnTeam = teamName => teamData => {
    const teamId = findTeamId(teamData, teamName);
    return myFetch(ALL_PLAYERS_URL, {id: teamId});
}
```

4. Finally, when **getTeamsInLeague(LEAGUE_NAME)** is invoked in the **then()** clause, the function returned above would be fully applied, with the resolved value from the previous promise passed in as the implied **leagueData** parameter:

```
myFetch(ALL_LEAGUES_URL)
    .then(getTeamsInLeague(LEAGUE_NAME))
    .then(getPlayersOnTeam(TEAM_NAME))
    .then(getPlayerHonors)
    .catch(console.log)
```

5. To perhaps make this plainer, let's consider this as if it were written with **async/await** syntax. Refer to the following code. On the second line, the process when calling **getTeamsInLeague(LEAGUE_NAME)** is incomplete at that point and returns another function to complete it. Only when calling this partially applied function on the third line would you finally have the desired result:

```
const allLeagueData = await myFetch(ALL_LEAGUES_URL);
const partiallyAppliedFunction = getTeamsInLeague(LEAGUE_NAME);
const league = await partiallyAppliedFunction(allLeagueData);
```

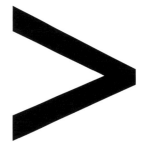

Index